Collective Choice and Social Welfare

AMARTYA SEN

Collective Choice and Social Welfare

An Expanded Edition

Harvard University Press

Cambridge, Massachusetts
2017

First published by Holden-Day, 1970
Revised edition published by North-Holland Publishing Company, 1979
First expanded edition published in the United Kingdom by Penguin Books, 2017

First Harvard University Press edition, 2017
First Printing

Set in 9.25 pt/12.5 pt Sabon LT Std
Typeset by Jouve (UK), Milton Keynes

*Library of Congress Cataloging-in-Publication Data is available from the
Library of Congress.*

ISBN 978-0-674-97160-8 (cloth: alk. paper)

Contents

Preface (1970)

The theory of collective choice belongs to several disciplines. Economics is one of them but not the only one. While this book is part of a series in 'mathematical economics texts', no attempt has been made to confine the treatment to economic problems exclusively. Indeed the approach of this book is based on the belief that the problem cannot be satisfactorily discussed within the confines of economics. While collective choice is a crucial aspect of economics (notably of welfare economics, planning theory and public economics), the subject relates closely to political science, in particular to the theory of the state and the theory of decision procedures. It also has important philosophical aspects, related to ethics and especially to the theory of justice.

The book is divided into starred chapters which contain formal analyses, and unstarred ones which are quite informal. They alternate. A non-technical reader can get an intuitive idea of the main arguments from the unstarred chapters. However, for precise statement of results as well as proofs, the starred chapters have to be read.

The partitioning of the book into formal and informal chapters is a stylistic experiment. Many problems of collective choice require a rigorous and formal treatment for definiteness, and informal arguments can indeed be treacherous, but, once the results are obtained, their meaning, significance and relevance can be discussed informally. In fact, a purely formal discussion of significance would be unnecessarily narrow. The book attempts to cater to two distinct groups of readers, viz., those who are primarily interested in the relevance of the results rather than in their formal statement and technical derivation, and those who are also concerned with the latter. Thus, the partitioning of the book into starred and unstarred chapters does have some rationale, aside from reflecting the author's incurable schizophrenia.

The mathematics used in the book mainly involves the logic of relations. The main results of mathematical logic employed in proving theorems on collective choice are stated, discussed and proved in Chapter 1*. The book is in this sense self-contained.

The field of collective choice is vast. It has not been possible to cover all the branches, and still less to discuss all of them equally thoroughly. While it is hoped that the book covers the major branches of the literature adequately, it must be recognized that the judgment of the relative importance of different branches represents the author's own bias.

For facilities of typing and duplication of two versions of this manuscript I am grateful to the Delhi School of Economics and to the Harvard Institute of Economic Research. The actual typing of the two versions was done very efficiently by Mr C. G. Devarajan and Mrs. Helen Bigelow, respectively.

I must express my indebtedness to people who have influenced this book. My interest in the problem was first aroused by some stimulating discussions with Maurice Dobb when I was an undergraduate at Trinity College, Cambridge, about a decade and a half ago, and I have had discussions with him intermittently ever since. My debt to Kenneth Arrow is immense, not merely because his pioneering work has opened up several avenues of research in the field of collective choice, but, more personally, because he has gone through the entire manuscript and has suggested many important improvements. John Rawls read entirely the first version of the manuscript, which was prepared during 1966–7, and has put me right on several questions, especially on the philosophical side of the problem. During 1967–8, Tapas Majumdar, James Mirrlees and Prasanta Pattanaik read the first draft of the manuscript and suggested numerous improvements both of substance and style, and the final version of the book reflects the impact of their comments. I have also benefited from the joint seminar on this subject that Arrow, Rawls and I conducted at Harvard University during 1968–9, in particular from the participation of Franklin Fisher, A. Gibbard, Stephen Marglin, Howard Raiffa, Jerome Rothenberg, Ross Starr, David Starrett and Richard Zechhauser. I have also had useful discussions with, or helpful comments from, Dipak Banerjee, Robert Cassen, Partha Dasgupta, Peter Diamond, Jan Graaff, Frank Hahn, Bengt Hansson, John Harsanyi, Hans Herzberger, Ken-Ichi Inada, Tjalling Koopmans, Abba Lerner, Paul Samuelson, Thomas Schelling, and Subramaniam Swamy. But I am, alas, reconciled to the fact that none of these gentlemen can be held responsible for the errors and shortcomings of this work.

New Preface (2017)

Social Choice and this Book

A society consists of a group of people with a variety of preferences and priorities. To make fitting social decisions on behalf of the group as a whole, the society must take serious note of the people's (possibly diverse) views and interests. Aggregate assessment is central to social choice theory, but to determine how such aggregate social decisions should be made is not an easy task. There can be, as Horace pointed out long ago, 'as many preferences as there are people'. That is the task that social choice theory has to address.

Problems of social choice arise in many different ways, from electing national governments and holding referendums on public policies to facilitating people's economic and social opportunities and safeguarding the rights and liberties of individuals and minorities. We also have to deal with global problems, including decisions about international trade and economic relations, cross-border peace and avoidance of terrorism, having reasonable arrangements for the movement of people, encouraging educational and cultural exchange, and, of course, preserving the world's climatic health, which is so challenging right now. Our lives are surrounded by social choices of various kinds.

In addition to the formidable problems of deciding on national and international policies and on social priorities, the subject of social choice also includes making difficult judgements on what is happening to a group such as a nation – or even to the world population as a whole. Is it better off or worse than it was earlier? Has social inequality in the group diminished or increased? Is there more poverty now than before? How extensive is it? Or, to go into institutional judgements, can the social decisions that emerge be seen as really democratic?

The early roots of social choice theory can be found in the work of French mathematicians of the eighteenth century, led by the Marquis de Condorcet. These contributions were made in a society sympathetic both to enlightenment and to democracy in which the need to treat people equally, and as reflective creatures, was gathering momentum. This would be most sharply articulated in the French Revolution, which erupted even as the early social choice theorists – Condorcet, Borda and others – were presenting their mathematical theorems that shared the general goal of treating people as equals. Kenneth Arrow, the founder of modern social choice theory in the twentieth century, is an heir to this egalitarian tradition.

Arrow's impossibility theorem presented a startling – and profound – formal result showing that some apparently undemanding conditions relating social decisions to individual preferences in a democratic way cannot be simultaneously satisfied through any procedure. (The challenges posed by this far-reaching theorem are discussed in the Introduction that follows, and in Chapters A1 to A2*.) The implications of Arrow's formulation of social choice, as well as of his impossibility theorem, are indeed momentous, as the development of the discipline of social choice theory has revealed. There have been challenges to Arrow's result, but also extensions of it, and there are, furthermore, a number of contributions on the ethical and political interpretations of Arrow's axioms and of the results he obtained. In fact, Arrow's subversive challenge has dialectically generated an extraordinarily large literature on social choice. This book, to a great extent, is a part of it.

1950, the year in which Arrow published his pioneering paper on social choice theory which made him (a young graduate student) a world leader of innovative social thought, also saw a number of geopolitical developments of interest to practical social choice. Communist China received widespread diplomatic recognition, the United Nations despatched troops to the Korean War, the Republic of India was established with its new democratic constitution, and

Senator Joseph McCarthy went on a political rampage in his campaign to find 'un-Americanism' among Americans. Social choice theory is relevant – in different ways – to all these highly practical matters. And so it is to academic intrigues related to group decisions, well portrayed, for example, in C. P. Snow's popular novel, *The Masters*, which was published in the same year – 1951 – in which Arrow's classic book was released, consolidating the lessons of his 1950 paper.

Despite the relevance of social choice theory, it would be quite eccentric to think of *formal* social choice theory as being immediately applicable to each of these social choice events. The development of mathematical social choice theory has, in fact, tended to concentrate on theoretical analyses at some distance from instant application, even though (as is discussed and illustrated in this book) they are ultimately relevant to practical concerns. The interrelations between formal analysis and informal discussions, and their respective roles, are important to understand. Apparent remoteness has its advantages, not least in allowing the development of sophisticated techniques of analysis that need formal reasoning and the use of mathematical methods, which would have been hard to sustain if every analytical departure had to be justified in terms of instant application to day-to-day matters.

The conceptual generality of axiomatic methods has also allowed applications of similar analytical results in widely different fields. For example, while Arrow's immediate concern was with welfare economics, and, in particular, with the attempts led by Abram Bergson (1938) and Paul Samuelson (1947) to reconstruct 'social welfare functions' on what were seen as the ruins of utilitarian welfare economics, his results were equally relevant to political issues of democracy and participatory governance. As Samuelson (1957, p. viii) rightly noted, Arrow's 'mathematical politics' does throw 'new light on age-old conundrums of democracy'.

There is also a close link between the approach of social choice theory and the devising of various economic and social measures, such as indicators of inequality, poverty, mobility and living standards. These connections, some of which are among the subjects investigated in this book (both in the original 1970 version and in the new chapters of this enlarged edition), show the relation between the pure theory of social choice and the variety of practical problems that are faced in a number of fields, such as applied welfare economics, the evaluation of social and economic achievements, the assessment of democratic procedures, the pursuit of liberty and human rights, and the appraisal of justice and injustice.[i]

INDIVIDUAL VALUES AND SOCIAL CHOICE

So how should we think about the modern social choice theory that Arrow initiated? Following Bergson and Samuelson, Arrow was concerned with an aggregate 'social welfare function' that represents the interests of the people involved. He proceeded to link that aggregate function to the *values* of the individuals in the society. It is the functional relation between individual values and social choice that became the definitive formulation of the social choice approach presented in Arrow's 1951 book, *Social Choice and Individual Values*, which further pursued the arguments presented in his 1950 essay.

My own work, presented in my 1970 book – and extended here – was directly inspired by Arrow's pioneering work. The focus of the book is on *normative* social choice theory, rather than the largely descriptive and predictive subject of voting theory. The investigation of the variety of voting procedures that have been – or can be – used is also an interesting subject, and I have written elsewhere on voting procedures, especially in 'How to Judge Voting Schemes' (Sen (1995b)).[ii] This book, however, is concerned mainly with the foundations of social choice theory and welfare economics and their connections with ethics and political philosophy. However, the principal voting methods, such as majority decision, have a strong relevance to normative social choice theory as well, and they will receive attention here in that context.

Arrow used the term 'social welfare function' to describe the *relation* between individual values and social welfare, and this is a part of his attempt to give social choice a democratic foundation. This was entirely in line with what the Marquis de Condorcet wanted to do in his theories about the future of France after the Revolution – a revolution that was only on the horizon as Condorcet was establishing his mathematical results in the early 1780s, and pursuing his less formal investigations in *Esquisse*. In that world of European Enlightenment, there were also other – less mathematical – explorations of systematic social assessment, presented by Adam Smith (1759), (1790), Tom Paine (1776), (1791), Immanuel Kant (1788), Jeremy Bentham (1789), Mary Wollstonecraft (1790), (1792), and others, and many of their ideas are also strongly relevant, as will be discussed, to the discipline of social choice.

GETTING INVOLVED

Arrow's *Social Choice and Individual Values* revolutionized the formal analysis of social decisions, and led to the birth of modern social choice theory. The year of its publication, 1951, was also the year I started my undergraduate education at Presidency College in Calcutta. I was fortunate to encounter this book as a first-year undergraduate only a few months after it appeared. My attention was drawn to it by my brilliant classmate Sukhamoy Chakravarty, who was, among his many other distinctions, a voracious reader and a remarkable scholar. He had borrowed Arrow's newly arrived book from a local bookshop with an indulgent owner. I remember him one morning excitedly showing me Arrow's monograph and telling me, 'This book will interest you very much!' He was right. In long sessions sitting in the Coffee House on College Street, across the road from our college, Sukhamoy and I discussed Arrow's formal results and informal insights, including the significance of the 'impossibility theorem'. That was the beginning of my life-long interest in the subject. The book fitted in very well with my already developing interest in democracy and justice. I took an immediate liking to social choice theory as a deeply engaging subject, even though I realized that using a mixture of mathematical and non-mathematical reasoning to address very basic social problems of the world appeared rather eccentric to most of my classmates and teachers. (Tapas Majumdar, a very young teacher then, was the hugely encouraging exception who talked with me extensively on what I was so excited about.)

After two years studying economics and mathematics in Calcutta, when I went to Cambridge University in 1953, my attempts to get my fellow students – and teachers – interested in social choice theory were a dismal failure. The few exceptions were all in my college, Trinity, and they included, among my fellow undergraduates, Michael Nicholson, a brilliant economist with very wide interests, and Maurice Dobb and Piero Sraffa – two great Marxist econo-mists – among my teachers. While she was very kind to me in general, I could not make one of my teachers, Joan Robinson, an outstanding economist, take any interest whatever in what was becoming my intellectual priority. She was very close – and very kind – to me, but clearly she considered my interest in social choice theory as some-thing of a weakness of will – *akrasia*, as the ancient Greeks would have called it. Since I lacked self-confidence, it was particularly important for me that Maurice Dobb encouraged me strongly to pur-sue my growing interest, and also that Amiya Dasgupta, a great Indian economist and a close family friend (who had a big influence on my education), told me that I should have the courage to work on whatever I wanted to be involved in, rather than on 'what Joan Rob-inson – or anyone else – advised'.

Later, when I became a lecturer at Cambridge, my renewed efforts to get some social choice into the curriculum were no more success-ful, but I was allowed to teach a devised course in 'welfare economics', which included some airing of social choice theory. I was told by the Economics Faculty Board that this was a very special concession to me, which they hoped I would appreciate. I did.

Even though I had the good fortune of having illuminating discus-sions on subjects related to social choice theory with Samuel Brittan, James Mirrlees and Christopher Bliss, who were themselves studying in Cambridge, it was only after I left Cambridge that I could get more than a few others around me – students and colleagues – to take systematic interest in social choice. This hap-pened wonderfully at the Delhi School of Economics (which the students called 'the D-School'), where I began teaching in 1963. I had begun working on social choice problems in my 'free time' at Cambridge when I was a young teacher, but also earlier while doing my Ph.D. thesis on a very different subject – how to choose between techniques of production – which my teachers had half-convinced me was a 'worthier' and more 'practical' subject. My quickly written doctoral thesis was published under the title *Choice of Techniques* (Sen 1960). I was not unhappy with it, since it did something to resolve an active debate then going on about the criteria for evaluating alternative techniques (happily, the book went into several reprints), but my interest in the subject did not last long.

Meanwhile, however, I became increasingly convinced that there was much work to be done on social choice, and, in particular, that Arrow's impossibility result was ultimately a constructive beginning of a systematic subject that needed further pursuit and development, rather than being the 'end' of an enquiry – an elegant demolition of the hope of reasoned democratic politics, as it was so often being interpreted. I was eager to devise a new and constructive course on social choice theory at the Delhi School of Economics. This fitted in well with other courses I was teaching in Delhi, consisting of the principles of micro-economics and elementary game theory at the D-School, and epistemology and mathematical logic in other parts of Delhi University. The original (1970) version of this book emerged from the notes for the lectures I gave on social choice theory at the D-School.

The inspiration for teaching that course, in an evolving form over the eight years I taught there, related closely to my interest in developing a more systematic basis for the evaluation of economic, social and political conditions of people around the world, including the miserable lives that most of my fellow Indians lived (a subject that deeply interested many of my students, some of whom would go on to become leading political economists of India, such as Prabhat Patnaik). It related also to my growing involvement with the mathematical results on the subject, going back to the pioneers such as Condorcet, Borda and, of course, Arrow. I got involved also with the sizeable literature the subject had generated over the centuries. (The mathematician Charles Dodgson, more widely known as Lewis Carroll, provided some much-needed amusement, along with some important – if unorganized – formal results on aggregate decisions.)

However, what really consolidated my commitment to teach – and to pursue further my research on – social choice theory was the response I received from my students, whose enthusiasm and encouragement made me feel vindicated in having initiated lectures and classes on the subject. We 'talked' social choice often enough, and new results in formal social choice theory kept being established by the more adventurous among my students. To take one extraordinarily distinguished example, the skill and originality of a student from Orissa, Prasanta Pattanaik, took my breath away as he showed his ability to solve new analytical problems – however difficult – as fast as I could formulate them. Pattanaik wrote his doctoral thesis with amazing rapidity (Pattanaik (1967a)), and then quickly published a number of far-reaching papers on social choice theory in the best economics journals (Pattanaik (1968a), (1968b), (1970)). Meanwhile, his doctoral dissertation, when published as a book (Pattanaik 1971), had a big impact on the literature on social choice.

During my years at the D-School, I also visited Berkeley, in 1964–5, and Harvard, in 1968–9. At both places I tried out the new things I was working on in social choice and inflicted them mercilessly on my colleagues and students. I benefited immensely from the fact that my students and colleagues in both Berkeley and Harvard took an interest in what I was trying to do. I was fortunate to receive valuable comments from Peter Diamond, John Harsanyi, John Searle, Dale Jorgenson, Daniel McFadden, Tibor Scitovsky, John Williamson, Benjamin Ward, Roy Radner, Bernie Saffran and Carl Riskin among others at Berkeley (and from Dipak Banerjee, who too was visiting Berkeley, like me, that year).

At Harvard in 1968–9 I taught a course on social choice and justice jointly with Kenneth Arrow and John Rawls. It generated interesting discussions among our students (they included Allan Gibbard, who would soon establish himself as a great social choice theorist, as well as emerging as a leading philosopher) and a galaxy of non-students who were sitting in (including Howard Raiffa, Robert

Dorfman, Thomas Schelling, Franklin Fisher, Stephen Marglin, Richard Zeckhauser, David Starrett, Ross Starr, Jerome Rothenberg and many others). Another course, which I taught jointly with Stephen Marglin and Prasanta Pattanaik (also visiting Harvard that year) on cost–benefit analysis, led to excellent discussions on the relation between the theory and practice of social choice.

My interest in social choice was intensified and sharpened by the evolving interpretations of free speech and social commitment that the student agitations were generating at Berkeley and Harvard while I was there, with the Free Speech Movement at Berkeley in 1964–5, and the anti-war demonstrations and occupations at Harvard in 1968–9. I spent a lot of well-rewarded time listening to students in the American campuses, just as I did at the D-School on a more regular basis through the 1960s.

WHAT DID THE 1970 BOOK
TRY TO DO?

The original 1970 book not only aimed at presenting social choice theory as it then stood, but it was also an ambitious attempt at substantially expanding Arrow's social choice framework, consolidating his insights, extending some of his results, questioning and relaxing some of the restrictions imposed by him, and proposing – with considerable nervousness – some modifications of how to think about social choice.

Even as I tried to cover the subject of social choice as a whole, I had to pay particular attention to the extensions and emendations to the Arrow framework that I was trying to pursue. The emendations included, among other changes, incorporating interpersonal comparisons of utilities within the social choice framework. Since Arrow believed – in line with the dominant thinking in economics around 1950 – that interpersonal comparisons of utility had 'no meaning', he made no special room for interpersonal comparisons of different individuals' well-being – or personal advantages – in his axiom structure. There had been, however, some imaginative attempts at incorporating interpersonal comparisons in specific contexts, pursued particularly by William Vickrey, John Harsanyi and Patrick Suppes. Even though a comprehensive framework for the incorporation of interpersonal comparisons demanded a fuller and more versatile overall structure (and also the accommodation of different kinds of interpersonal comparisons, for example of levels, units, ratios and other features), the brilliant insights presented in these early departures were extremely important.

The use of interpersonal comparisons turned out to be a significant move (discussed in Chapters 7 to 8*). Indeed, Arrow's impossibility result no longer holds once interpersonal comparisons – even just of the *levels* of utilities of different persons – are admitted for use in the social choice framework. The 1970 edition explored the use of interpersonal comparisons in several different ways. There are interpretational issues related both to epistemology (what does knowledge of interpersonal comparisons stand for? How can we get at it?) and to mathematics (how can we put different persons' utilities together through invariance conditions appropriate to the kind of comparison we are seeking?). By opening up various alternative possibilities of interpersonal evaluation (rather than none), the move had the effect of transforming the back-to-the-wall struggle to escape impossibility into a constructive engagement on choosing among different values and priorities, all of which become available with the use of interpersonal comparisons in different ways, in addressing problems in welfare economics and social measurement. It was also shown that interpersonal comparisons can be partial, rather than total, since some types of comparison are quite easy to make, but others very hard. The use of partial comparability, in a defined framework, led to the possibility of partial orderings, for example of utility sum-totals (the usability of such an approach and its usefulness are discussed in Chapters 7 and 7*).

This departure, on incorporating interpersonal comparisons of well-being (and personal advantage), was consolidated and radically expanded through a number of remarkably powerful contributions coming from a new generation of social choice theorists (including Peter Hammond, Louis Gevers, Claude d'Aspremont, Eric Maskin, Kotaro Suzumura, Charles Blackorby, David Donaldson, John

Weymark, Kevin Roberts, Philippe Mongin and Mamoru Kaneko, among others). Kenneth Arrow himself joined in this transformative exercise in social choice theory.

Another substantial departure the book tried to make was the recognition of the importance of personal liberties and the accommodation of the idea of rights within the axiomatic system of social choice (discussed in Chapters 5 to 6*). Even though the early pioneers of radical thinking in the Enlightenment period made considerable use of the moral – and political – force of the idea of rights and liberties (I think particularly of Condorcet, Thomas Paine, Mary Wollstonecraft and John Stuart Mill), social choice theory had tended to follow Jeremy Bentham in rejecting the idea of rights except in the institutionalized form of legislated rights. The Arrow framework gave no room to rights. I argued against this and proposed some radical changes: for example, Mill on the social importance of liberty (taking us beyond utility numbers) demands our attention no less than Bentham does on the putative relevance of his calculus of utilities. It turns out that the implications of bringing in such a change can be quite far-reaching. One of the results presented in the book – 'the impossibility of the Paretian liberal' – generated a large literature of its own, with applications, disputations and extensions, in the decades following 1970.

Another attempted departure in the first edition involved dropping Arrow's demand for the transitivity of social preference, and taking seriously the questions about the legitimacy of the very idea of 'social preference' that were being raised by James Buchanan and others. Buchanan (1954a) had argued, in an early, elegant critique of Arrow's work, that the impossibility result arose from the artificial use of a transitive 'social preference'. He claimed that such use made no sense whatever, since the society was not a person and it could not be seen as having a 'preference'. I was convinced that Buchanan must be largely right as far as institutional choices (such as voting rules) are concerned, but not for such exercises as making social welfare judgements. More immediately, I was not persuaded that removing that Arrovian requirement would really resolve the impossibility theorem, even though it was not until much later that I could complete the proof of the impossibility theorem without any demand of collective rationality at all (the proof was first presented in my Presidential Address to the Econometric Society in 1984, which was called 'Internal Consistency of Choice' and published later in *Econometrica*).

However, it became clear that weakening the Arrow demands of collective rationality, without correspondingly altering the social choice framework, would have a strong impact on the validity of the impossibility theorem. From the late 1960s, there were major advances made in extending social choice results through dropping social transitivity and weakening the internal consistency conditions in the work of a number of leading social choice theorists, including Allan Gibbard, Bengt Hansson, Prasanta Pattanaik, Andreu Mas-Colell, Hugo Sonnenschein, Kotaro Suzumura, Donald Brown, Thomas Schwartz, Peter Fishburn, Charles Plott, Rajat Deb, George Bordes, Douglas Blair, Robert Pollak, Peter Hammond, John Ferejohn, Ariel Rubinstein, Donald Campbell, Jerry Kelly, Kevin Roberts, David Kreps, Maurice Salles, David Kelsey and Yasumi Matsumoto, among others. This line of work, while technically concentrated, had relevance (ultimately) to the basic conceptual points made in Buchanan's far-reaching critique of the idea of social preference.

THIS EXPANDED EDITION

Since a huge amount of research went into social choice theory in the 1970s and 1980s, the 1970 edition of this book was fortunate to receive attention. By now, four and a half decades have passed since its publication, and there has been a huge volume of new work on the subject. The original book clearly needed substantial supplementation (though not, I believe, supplanting, since the old material remains relevant). It is this necessary supplementation that I have attempted to present in the new chapters of this enlarged edition.

Over the decades, I have been very fortunate in enjoying and benefiting from the company of some extraordinary philosophers, economists and mathematicians at various places (London, Oxford, Harvard) where I have taught and researched on social choice theory and on related subjects that bear on it. In addition to the profound influence on my work of Kenneth Arrow, John Rawls, Hilary Putnam and Bernard Williams, the contributions made on my thinking on social choice by Kotaro Suzumura, Tony Atkinson, James Mirrlees, Peter Hammond, Nicholas Stern, Edmund Phelps, Wulf Gaertner, Nicholas Baigent, Robert Nozick, Thomas Scanlon, Isaac Levi, Robert Pollak, Martha Nussbaum, Philip Pettit, Philippe Van Parijs, Sudhir Anand, Eric Maskin, Eric Nelson, Erin Kelly, Elizabeth Anderson, Barry Mazur, Jean Drèze and Cass Sunstein have been immeasurable.

Eric Maskin and I have regularly taught a course – often on social choice theory – at Harvard, with great gain for me. We were recently joined by Barry Mazur, a great mathematician, for a course on 'reasoning by mathematical models' offered jointly by the Philosophy and Mathematics Departments, and right now Maskin and I are preparing a course, jointly with Cass Sunstein, on 'democracy and human rights' offered in the Harvard Law School as well as the Philosophy Department. My joint course with Eric Nelson, a couple of years ago, on 'the foundations of justice' also yielded critical discussion on a subject closely related to social choice theory. I have also greatly benefited from joint courses on political philosophy with Thomas Scanlon, Robert Nozick, Joshua Cohen, Michael Sandel and Philippe Van Parijs.

My work on the philosophical underpinning of social choice has not only been greatly helped by my interactions with Rawls, Putnam, Williams and my fellow course teachers, but also with W. V. O. Quine, Howard Raiffa, Derek Parfit, Thomas Nagel, Isaac Levi, Ronald Dworkin, Patrick Suppes, Donald Davidson, Ian Hacking, Gerald (Jerry) Cohen, Onora O'Neill, Stig Kanger, Bengt Hansson, W. G. Runciman, Philip Pettit, Nancy Cartwright, John Broome, Jon Elster, Julian Blau, Quentin Skinner, Thomas Schwartz, Myles Burnyeat, John Dunn, Frederic Schick, Joseph Raz, E. F. (Ned) McClennen, Jonathan Glover, Ted Honderich, Michael McPherson, Daniel Hausman, Christian List, Frances Kamm, Erin Kelly, Debra Satz, Fabienne Peter, John Tasioulas and Elizabeth Anderson, among others.

Among economists and other social scientists who have contributed to my understanding of social choice in many distinct ways, I must of course first count Kenneth Arrow, but additionally I have also had the good fortune of interacting with John Hicks, Paul Samuelson, Leo Hurwicz, Robert Solow, Michio Morishima, Frank Hahn, W. M. (Terence) Gorman, John Harsanyi, Menahem Yaari, Tibor Scitovsky, Kotaro Suzumura, James Mirrlees, A. B. (Tony) Atkinson, Peter Hammond, Jean-Jacques Laffont, Nicholas Stern, Dale Jorgenson, Louis Gevers, Claude d'Aspremont, Franklin Fisher, Bezalel Peleg, Wulf Gaertner, Tapas Majumdar, Dipak Banerjee, Michael Nicholson, Charles Blackorby, Prasanta Pattanaik, John Ferejohn, John Chipman, Sudhir Anand, Angus Deaton, John Muellbauer, Stephen Marglin, Jerry Green, Charles Plott, Christopher Bliss, Robert Pollak, Alan Kirman, Michel Le Breton, John Weymark, David Kreps, Mukul Majumdar, Jorgen Weibull, Julius Margolis, Nicholas Tideman, George Akerlof, Joseph Stiglitz, Meghnad Desai, Kaushik Basu, Siddiqur Osmani, Rajat Deb, Ravi Kanbur, John Vickers, Richard Tuck, Pranab Bardhan, Amiya Bagchi, Christian Seidl, James Heckman, Partha Dasgupta, Geoffrey Heal, Graciella Chichilnisky, Maurice Salles, Philippe Mongin, Eric Maskin, John Roemer, Jean Drèze, Lars-Gunnar Svensson, Peter Svedberg, Peter Coughlin, Bhaskar Dutta, Bina Agarwal, Paul Anand, David Kelsey, Ariel Rubinstein, Kevin Roberts, Roger Myerson, Robert Sugden, Anthony Shorrocks, James Foster, Ben Fine, Mark Machina, Vincent Crawford, Ted Groves, Esfandiar Maasoumi, Arjun Sengupta, Sanjay Reddy, S. Subramaniam, Esther Duflo, Bertil Tungodden, Abhijit Banerjee, Martin Ravallion and Marc Fleurbaey, among others.

My use of the idea of capability has been radically advanced by the work of Martha Nussbaum and her philosophical insights. In my attempts to come to grips with ideas of well-being and capability, I have had the opportunity to work with Mahbub ul Haq, Lal Jayawardena, Lincoln Chen, James Heckman, Frances Stewart, Paul Streeten, Siddiqur Osmani, Nanak Kakwani, Jocelyn Kynch, Stephan Klasen, Sabina Alkire, Mozaffar Qizilbash, Enrica Chiappero-Martinetti, Ingrid Robeyns, Reiko Gotoh, Meghnad Desai, Sudhir Anand, Selim Jahan, Sakiko Fukuda-Parr, Barbara Harriss, Jane Humphries, Jennifer Prah Ruger, Erik Schokkaert, Polly Vizard, Tania Burchardt, Wiebke Kuklys and Flavio Comin, among others, and to this I must add my collaboration with Joseph Stiglitz and Jean-Paul Fitoussi in preparing a report for President Sarkozy of France on indicators of economic and social progress. These are long lists of people (and there must have been others) interacting with whom has brought me benefit in many different ways, in my thinking on social choice.

THE CHAPTERS

The first edition of this book involved a stylistic experiment, dividing the chapters into informal ones (unstarred) and those with formal and mathematical reasoning (starred). Unstarred and starred chapters alternated, with the mathematical reasoning confined to the starred chapters; the unstarred chapters used only ordinary language, in order to be accessible to all. The experiment seemed to work, helping me to reach a wider audience than I could have expected for a book with as much technical content, but the dichotomy of the chapters also fitted in well with my view of social choice as a subject that demands both mathematical analysis and informal assessment (more on this later). The new chapters included here – eleven in all – also follow the same dichotomy (with five starred and six unstarred chapters). I must note here that my resolve to soldier on with the division of starred and unstarred chapters has been much strengthened by the encouragement I have received from my colleague and teaching partner Eric Maskin, and by the generous observations on my 1970 book by Ariel Rubinstein (2012), related to his own work (which, incidentally, I greatly admire).

The expanded edition begins with a new Introduction to social choice theory, following which the book is arranged chronologically. The 1970 chapters come first, followed by the new chapters. There is much to be said for reading the chapters in that sequence, since the old ones spell out more fully the motivations underlying some of the departures, and also include an unhurried view of the subject of social choice. The new chapters try to present the current state of social choice theory, taking particular note of interesting and important analyses that have emerged in the recent decades. They are written in such a way that readers can follow them without having read the old chapters first, but, in choosing that course, they would then miss out on some of the motivational discussions, as well as on the historical emergence of clearly defined social choice problems. They would also have to look back at the old chapters if and when some results or analyses presented there are cited in the new chapters.

I must comment briefly on what may be new in the freshly written additional chapters, and how, in particular, the new chapters relate to the old. Some of the proofs have become shorter through new reasoning. This applies even to the establishing of the classic Impossibility Theorem of Arrow, which can now be proved very briefly and simply, without abandoning Arrow's commitment to rely only on elementary logic (see Chapters A1 and A1*). None of this streamlining would, of course, have happened without the basic insights that Arrow himself had brought to the subject.

Some generalizations of the old results have also emerged. The properties of social preference, such as transitivity, can be relaxed and made less demanding, but it turns out that elements of authoritarianism continue to linger in the Arrovian framework (in the absence of interpersonal comparisons). The last step of this relaxation is to drop the very idea of social preference *altogether*, along with dropping all conditions of internal consistency of social choice that tend to take us indirectly towards the idea of social preference. It emerges that if the Arrow conditions are appropriately redefined for a choice framework, then again the Arrow impossibility result firmly resurfaces (see Chapters A2 and A2*).

This result allows us to address James Buchanan's far-reaching doubts more fully. It must first be noted that in some contexts the idea of an as-if 'social preference' does make sense. For example, in welfare-economic exercises on whether a society is better off or not, there is no need to abandon (indeed, quite the opposite) the idea of such social relations as 'better than' or 'preferred to'. But when the context is different, for example in elections or referendums on political subjects, we may need no more than a fair process, without invoking any idea of something being 'socially better' or 'socially preferred' in any intrinsic sense (but simply consider whether a winner has been 'fairly chosen'). It turns out, reflecting the understanding emerging from the new extended theorem, that, even for the choice of a fair process, satisfying the motivations behind Arrow's conditions (such as the Pareto principle, non-dictatorship, independence of irrelevant alternatives), the impossibility result holds without making any use of the idea of social preference (see Chapter A2*). While Buchanan's critique of Arrow about the legitimacy of the idea of social preference has much interest on its own, his contention that the Arrow impossibility result would collapse if this critique is accepted does not, in fact, survive. This does not diminish the importance of the constructive part of Buchanan's intervention – bringing out the significance of fair processes, which can be really important – but the dismissive part of his contention about Arrow's Impossibility Theorem turns out to be not sustainable.

Allowing interpersonal comparisons by substantially extending the Arrow framework, pursued in the 1970 edition, is further consolidated and explored. In the first version of the book, it was demonstrated (see Chapter 8*) that Arrow's Impossibility Theorem will continue to hold, without any relief whatsoever, even when individual preferences are informationally enriched through 'cardinal utilities' (telling us about relative intensities of preference over different pairs of alternatives). So cardinality alone does not help us to escape Arrow's impossibility, but when used along with interpersonal comparisons, cardinality takes us much further (that is, further than comparisons of levels of utilities alone). In taking the informationally enriched route – with both interpersonal comparisons and cardinality of individual utilities – we can pursue welfare economics and normative measurement with good scope for making ethical judgements (such as the pursuit of equity in different forms), often using insights drawn from theories of justice (see Chapters A3 and A3*).

DEMOCRACY, MAJORITY AND RIGHTS

The demands of democracy were briefly discussed in the 1970 edition. This subject is more fully investigated in this expanded edition (see Chapters A4, A4* and A6). Since majority rule can be seen as a part of democracy, there was some interest in identifying the necessary and sufficient conditions for consistent majority decisions presented in the original edition (based on work I had done jointly with Prasanta Pattanaik: Sen and Pattanaik (1969)). A result of particular interest established by Eric Maskin (1995), and developed further by him and Partha Dasgupta, shows that if some restriction of permissible combinations of individual preferences generate consistent results in any voting procedure, then it would do so for majority rule as well. But the converse does not hold (majority decisions can work in some cases where the other voting rules do not). In this sense majority rule turns out to be something of a superior aggregation procedure.

Majority rule does, of course, have many merits well known to political theorists – and, indeed, to the public as a whole. It is, however, important to recognize that, when it comes to welfare economics, majority decision is not a particularly just, or even a plausible, way of judging alternatives. A majority of relatively prosperous people can, in search of their own gain, overwhelm a minority of the poorest and the most miserable. To follow the verdicts of the majority rule in such cases would be particularly unjust.

Also majority rule pays little attention to minority rights and individual liberties, and, depending on the nature of the social aggregation being considered, majority rule may or may not be an appropriate social choice procedure. The approach of rights, liberties and freedoms receives extensive examination in Chapters A5 and A5* of this extended edition.

If there are limitations that apply to majority decision's ethical status in many contexts, it is important to note that some sins which are often attributed to majority rule may, in fact, be the result of a misidentification. The unfortunate fact is that in public discussion the choice of the largest plurality – that is, the selection of the alternative with the largest first-preference support – is often confused with majority decision. Plurality rule chooses the alternative with the most first-preference votes when the electorate is restricted to voting only for their most preferred candidate. However, a plurality winner can, in fact, receive only a minority – even a small minority – of votes cast. The candidate with the most first preferences can also be the least preferred by most. A majority of voters can even place the plurality winner at the very bottom of the list (as will be discussed in Chapter A4*).

In the US Republican Primaries for the 2016 Presidential election, Donald Trump made his way to being chosen as the Republican Presidential candidate through a sequence of primary victories, in the first seventeen of which he failed to get a majority (in Arkansas he got only 33 per cent). A majority of voters rejected him in each of these elections. But he faced more than one opponent every time, so that the non-Trump vote was split. Although Mr Trump won pluralities in all these primaries, he could well have been defeated in many of them, if there were a majority vote, facing one opponent at a time.

A majority winner is one who defeats – or ties with – every other candidate in each pairwise head-to-head contest. Such a majority winner need not always exist (the conditions that guarantee the existence of a majority winner are discussed in Chapter A4*), but when one does exist that winner may well be quite different from a plurality winner. Mr Trump may well have been out of contention long before he ended up being adopted as the official Republican candidate had the system been one of looking for a majority winner through pairwise comparisons (easily identifiable if all candidates are ranked by the voters), rather than giving victory to the plurality winner.[1]

To consider another problem, when a plurality system generates a majority of seats in a parliament on the basis of a minority of votes, issues of popular approval have to be carefully analysed. For example, in the last Indian general elections (held in 2014), the plurality-winning party, the Bharatiya Janata Party (BJP), received only 31 per cent of the votes (the BJP is part of the so-called Hindutva movement, but a majority of Hindu voters did not vote for the BJP). However, the party won a significant majority of seats in the lower house of the Indian Parliament (thanks to the British-type

---

[1] See Eric Maskin and Amartya Sen, 'How to Let the Majority Rule', *New York Times*, Sunday, 1 May 2016. Also Maskin and Sen (2017).

constituency-based plurality elections in India). With its allies, the BJP-led alliance commanded a somewhat higher percentage of votes, 39 per cent, which still falls far short of a majority. There is, of course, nothing illegitimate in governing a country on the basis of a minority of votes if the ruling group has a majority of Parliamentary seats (though the electoral system may call for critical scrutiny). It is, however, important for a government far short of majority support not to pretend to speak (as has sometimes happened) as if it represents the majority of people – not to mention the entire nation. Even a majority of votes does not give a government license to be intolerant of dissenting views, and a government with only minority support has very strong reasons to be careful not to try to suppress individuals' freedom of expression on the ground that they are 'anti-national'.

PARTIAL ORDERINGS

One of the more important departures in this book (both in the original 1970 edition and in this expanded edition) is the use of *partial ordering* as the basic relation of social ranking (when such a ranking makes sense), rather than demanding, as the Arrovian framework does, the *completeness* of admissible social rankings. A complete ranking demands that every pair of alternatives can be ranked firmly against each other – either x is better than y, or worse than y, or exactly as good. A partial ranking, indeed even a partial ordering (satisfying the demands of transitivity), can leave some pairs unranked. The relevance of partial orderings received considerable attention in the original (1970) edition, but their role and use are more fully explored in this extended version.

The departure has big implications. The classical framework of optimization used in standard choice theory can be expressed as choosing, among the feasible options, an 'optimal' (or 'best') alternative – that is, an alternative that is at least as good as every other alternative. In contrast, a 'maximal' alternative – formally defined – is one which is not worse than (or, at least, not known to be worse than) any other alternative. If we cannot rank x and y against each other – for whatever reason – there is no optimal or best alternative in this pair (x, y), but both are, under these circumstances, definitely maximal.

The mathematical distinction between the 'optimal' and the 'maximal' is of critical importance in the theory of sets and relations (on which see the classic mathematical treatise of Bourbaki, *Éléments de mathématique*). The general discipline of maximization differs from the special case of optimization in taking an alternative to be a reasoned choice when it is not known to be worse than any other (whether or not it is also seen to be as good as all the others). For an element of a set to qualify as maximal, we have to make sure that it is *not worse* than any other available alternative; it is not necessary to show that it is *better than*, or *as good as*, all other alternatives. The basic contrast between maximization and optimization arises from the possibility that the preference ranking R may be incomplete, that is, there may be a pair of alternatives x and y such that x is not seen (at least, not *yet* seen) as being at least as good as y, and, further, y is not seen (at least, not yet seen) as at least as good as x.

In the famous philosophical story of Buridan's ass, the ass died of starvation because it could not choose between two stacks of hay, neither of which it could decide was better than (or even as good as) the other. It overlooked the existence of a maximal choice – either haystack would have been a reasoned *maximal* choice, and either would have been definitely better than starving to death. Buridan's ass may have died for the cause of optimal choice, but it is not hard to see that, when a maximal choice exists, to decide to do nothing because no optimal alternative has emerged is not very smart.

The admission of partial orderings vastly expands the applicability of social choice theory. This makes it possible, for example, to arrive at practical solutions despite some remaining disagreement, since the partial ranking of agreement may allow us to do many useful things. There may well be little hope of complete agreement, for example, on what to do in taking care of the global environment (or, more particularly, in trying to prevent global warming), or on what must be done urgently to try to curb global pandemics, or remove medical neglect across the world. And yet we can, with adequate public discussion and active advocacy, hope to get agreement on partial remedies that need not await a complete resolution of all our differences. This issue will be more fully discussed in the last chapter, Chapter A6.

REASONING AND INFORMATION

The importance of public reasoning was emphasized by the pioneers of Enlightenment thought, including Condorcet, Smith and Kant in the eighteenth century and Mill and Marx in the nineteenth, whose ideas contributed to the development of social choice theory. In the first phase of the revival of the theory in the twentieth century that focus took a somewhat subsidiary place in the burst of enthusiasm and interest in exploring the remarkable mathematical consequences of imposing plausible-looking axioms for the aggregation of individual preferences – often yielding an impossibility – led by Arrow's stunning theorem. However, the pessimistic results of these explorations themselves drew attention forcefully to the need to re-examine the acceptability of particular axioms and the plausibility of considering variations in individual priorities resulting from discussion and public reasoning. Both these concerns brought the literature firmly back to the kind of combination of formal aggregation procedures and interactive public discussion which particularly appealed to Condorcet. In the new emphasis on public reasoning, Arrow's theorem, and other results inspired by it, played a big part, but a leading role was also played by the constructive efforts of James Buchanan – following John Stuart Mill and Frank Knight – to advance the understanding of democracy as 'government by discussion'.

Open discussion with extensive public reach and scrutiny can have a powerfully positive role in making elections and votes better informed. However, in the absence of critical scrutiny, a wide public reach can also distort people's understanding of the issues and facts. Herd effects can be seen not only in the dissemination of truth through learning from signals, but also in the spread of false beliefs (on which see Abhijit Banerjee (1992)). Furthermore, misinformation is sometimes skilfully planted in political debates (with big electoral implications) through business advocacy, state propaganda, interest-group lobbying or media bias (sometimes related to the ownership and control of the media). For example, the political disarray related to the British vote on 23 June 2016 to leave the European Union (the 'Brexit' vote, as it has come to be called) is at least partly due to the factual distortions that were widely disseminated before the vote. Indeed, as I write this Preface in the summer following the vote, the 'Leave' campaign seems to be presenting clarifications – often involving corrections – of what the campaigners had said before the vote (for example, about how much Britain pays on a regular basis to the European Union which could, allegedly, be 'channelled into the National Health Service' after Brexit). Just as freedom of speech is important for democracy, so are well-organized and reliable facilities to 'fact check'.

The importance of the connection between opinion formation and widespread public communication and critical scrutiny was well discussed by Quintus Tullius Cicero in 64 BC, in his little pamphlet on 'how to win an election' (written to help his brother Marcus, the better-known Cicero, win the position of Consul, the highest office in the Roman Republic). That connection is, in fact, central to social choice in general, which deals, ultimately, with human lives in the company of others. It is, however, necessary for social choice theory to relate formal analyses (including mathematical results) to informal, transparent and easily shared discussions.

The role of social communication and public scrutiny has also been emphasized by political and social philosophers, from Adam Smith and David Hume to Frank Knight and James Buchanan, whose works have direct bearing on problems of social choice (as was discussed earlier in this Preface). Many of the ideas extensively explored in this book, such as developing an adequate framework for informational broadening, making systematic the use of interpersonal comparisons of well-being (including partial interpersonal comparability), recognizing the importance – and contingent adequacy – of partial orderings of social alternatives, and the weakening of consistency conditions demanded from social preference and social choice, call simultaneously for formal investigation and for critical and informed public scrutiny.

Our deeply felt real-world concerns have to be integrated with the analytical use of formal and mathematical reasoning. The need for this pluralism of types of reasoning also provides part of the rationale behind dividing the chapters of this book into unstarred and starred ones, with the former confined to entirely informal reasoning, easily accessible to all. The new chapters, like the older ones, have been written in such a way (as explained earlier) that a reader who shuns the starred chapters – and avoids going through the mathematical reasoning – can still follow the main arguments presented here. We need the formal analyses because the subject matter of social choice includes logical and mathematical complications that have to be sorted out. However, the important issues of social choice also demand, and cannot do without, 'ordinary language' scrutiny. Mathematical reasoning is sometimes necessary to vindicate parts of that scrutiny, but it cannot take its place.

Acknowledgements

'Happiness is beneficial for the body,' Marcel Proust said in *Remembrance of Things Past*, 'but it is grief that develops the powers of the mind.' It is safe to say that, among the utilities of grief, Proust could not have been thinking of the rewards of sadness in arriving at 'impossibility theorems' in the search for democratic mechanisms for rational social decisions. It is, however, certainly true that these initially disappointing searches – spread over two centuries – have also unleashed huge powers of the mind, and in particular have generated some spectacular analytical results on social evaluation and decision making – thus establishing the intellectually engaging discipline of social choice theory. The outstanding minds of great analytical theorists – from Condorcet in the eighteenth century to Kenneth Arrow in our own time – have turned a frustrating search into the exciting adventure of moving from individual assessments into reasoned social evaluation.

I have greatly benefited from the opportunity of joining this extraordinary adventure, and also of applying lessons from the discipline of social choice to other areas – economics, politics and philosophy – in which I have tried to work, including such varied subjects as hunger and famines, inequality and poverty, identity and violence, fairness and injustice, and knowledge and objectivity. So I should begin by acknowledging my debt to the pioneering thinkers for leading us to a subject that is intellectually challenging and socially important, and has far-reaching relevance.

In addition to the pioneers of social choice theory, I must acknowledge what I owe to the profound thinkers who worked in other areas of human understanding but whose ideas have powerful relevance to social choice – as became clear to me when I began my research, initially inspired by Kenneth Arrow. I think particularly here of Adam Smith, Immanuel Kant and Mary Wollstonecraft, some of the greatest figures of the European Enlightenment, and of John Stuart Mill and Karl Marx shortly thereafter, none of whom were social choice theorists in any formal sense, but whose ideas had profound implications for social choice reasoning, at least as I have been persuaded to see it. A similar sense of gratitude applies to the wonderfully innovative thinking of John Rawls, Bernard Williams and Hilary Putnam, among others, in our own time.

My long journey in social choice theory has now stretched well over fifty years. I cannot describe adequately how much I have benefited over the decades from the intellectual company of other social choice theorists, such as Prasanta Pattanaik, Peter Hammond, Kotaro Suzumura and Eric Maskin. Kotaro's arrival at the London School of Economics in the early 1970s changed my entire research programme, adding to my strong interactions, already in progress, with Peter Hammond. I should recollect here also Fuad Aleskerov, Paul Anand, Sudhir Anand, Nick Baigent, Kaushik Basu, Ken Binmore, Charles Blackorby, Walter Bossert, Donald Campbell, Claude d'Aspremont, Rajat Deb, Bhaskar Dutta, Marc Fleurbaey, James Foster, Wulf Gaertner, Louis Gevers, Jerry Kelly, Michel Le Breton, Isaac Levi, James Mirrlees, Philippe Mongin, Herve Moulin, Siddiq Osmani, Philip Pettit, Kevin Roberts, Maurice Salles, Arunava Sen, S. Subramaniam, Robert Sugden, John Weymark, among others, whose ideas and comments have often transformed my own social choice research. In addition to these influences of others working on social choice, I have also greatly benefited from ideas in related disciplines of a number of my long-standing friends, including, among others, Elizabeth Anderson, Tony Atkinson, Dipak Banerjee, Akeel Bilgrami, Christopher Bliss, François Bourguignon, Gerry Cohen, Joshua Cohen, Partha Dasgupta, Angus Deaton, Ronald Dworkin, Jean-Paul Fitoussi, Jerry Green, Terence (W. M.) Gorman, Frank Hahn, Daniel Hausman, Ravi Kanbur, Jean-Jacques Laffont, Richard Layard, Mukul Majumdar, Michael McPherson, Michio Morishima, Thomas

Nagel, Robert Nozick, Martha Nussbaum, Derek Parfit, Joseph Raz, Emma Rothschild, Thomas Scanlon, David Starrett, Nicholas Stern, Joseph Stiglitz, Cass Sunstein, Philippe Van Parijs, and of course my frequent co-author Jean Drèze.

In the two Prefaces, respectively of the old 1970 edition and this enlarged 2017 version, I have discussed extensively how a great many people have influenced – and helped – my work. I would like to express here my deep gratitude to all of them. Since they have been individually identified in the two Prefaces, I will not repeat all the names here. But I want to record that they include my teachers (particularly Tapas Majumdar, Maurice Dobb and Piero Sraffa), my students at different universities (including, chronologically, Prasanta Pattanaik, Kaushik Basu, Siddiq Osmani, Rajat Deb, Ben Fine, Ravi Kanbur, David Kelsey, Stephan Klasen, Felicia Knaul, Jennifer Prah Ruger, and more than a hundred others who taught me a great many things even as I tried to instruct them), and my co-teachers in different academic institutions (including Kenneth Arrow and John Rawls, but also – other than those already mentioned – Stephen Marglin, Christine Jolls and Eric Nelson, among others). My co-workers in the development of the capability approach to individual and social valuation have also been significantly influential on my social choice work (as I have discussed in the New Preface and to which I will return in Chapter A3).

In writing this enlarged edition, the 1970 version of the book had to be integrated with eleven new chapters added here, in addition to a substantive New Preface and New Introduction. This proved to be a bigger project than I had imagined it would be when the attempt at producing this enlarged edition began. Since the book uses some mathematical reasoning (separated out in the 'starred' chapters) as well as arguments in ordinary language, there was also a difficult job of integration. In undertaking these tasks I have been immensely helped by my Editor, Stuart Proffitt, who has also suggested numerous improvements in the presentation in all the chapters as they were drafted.

In seeing the book through the press, I have been much helped by the very efficient work of Richard Duguid, Charlotte Ridings,

Sandra Fuller and Ben Sinyor. I have also had the excellent help of my research assistants at Harvard, in particular Kaveh Danesh, Priyanka Menon and Kirsty Walker. To them all I am most grateful.

This enlarged edition would not have been possible without the frequent advice and guidance of Sudhir Anand. I have depended on his counsel both on substance and on presentation in critically important ways.

Finally, I should mention that my recent interests in social choice problems have been very closely linked with the regular courses on social choice theory that I teach at Harvard along with Eric Maskin, with whom I have also been privileged to do some joint work. Together with Kotaro Suzumura, Peter Hammond and Sudhir Anand, I want to acknowledge Eric Maskin as the strongest influence on this extended edition.

A.S.
November 2016

New Introduction (2017)

Challenges of group choice can be extensive and exacting, particularly because of the divergent interests and concerns of its members. Social thinkers have speculated, for a very long time, on how the concerns of the members of a society can be reflected in one way or another in the decisions taken in a responsive society (even if it is not fully democratic). For example, Aristotle in ancient Greece and Kautilya in ancient India, both of whom lived in the fourth century BC, explored various different possibilities in social choice in their classic books, called *Politics* and *Economics* respectively.[i]

Social choice theory is a very broad discipline, covering a variety of distinct questions, and it may be useful to note a few of them as illustrations of its subject matter. When would *majority rule* yield unambiguous and consistent decisions? How can we judge how well a *society as a whole* is doing in the light of the disparate interests of its different members? How can we accommodate *rights and liberties* of persons while giving due recognition to the preferences of all? How do we measure *aggregate poverty* in view of the varying predicaments and miseries of the diverse people who make up the society? How do we evaluate public goods such as the natural environment, or epidemiological security?

Further, some investigations, while not directly a part of social choice theory, have been helped by the understanding generated by the study of group decisions – such as the causation and prevention of famines and hunger, or the forms and consequences of gender inequality. Going much beyond that, a theory of justice can substantially draw on insights, as well as analytical results, from social choice theory (as I have discussed in my book, *The Idea of Justice*: Sen 2009a). The reach and relevance of social choice theory can be very extensive indeed.

EARLY ORIGINS

As was discussed in the Preface, social choice theory as a formal discipline first came into its own around the time of the French Revolution. The subject was pioneered by French mathematicians in the late eighteenth century, such as J. C. Borda (1781) and the Marquis de Condorcet (1785). They addressed social choice problems in rather mathematical terms and initiated the intellectual discipline of social choice theory in terms of voting and related procedures. The intellectual climate of the period was greatly influenced by the European Enlightenment, with its interest in reasoned construction of a social order.

Indeed, some of the early social choice theorists, most notably Condorcet, were also among the intellectual leaders of the French Revolution. Condorcet noted that Turgot, the pioneering French economist and a governor of the French province of Limoges, whom Condorcet greatly admired, was the first statesman who 'deigned to treat the people as a society of reasonable beings'. Condorcet admonished Jacques Necker, an opponent of Turgot, for 'exaggerating the stupidity of people', and he took great interest, especially in his later works, on the interactive decision-making in assemblies, including the 'assemblées d'administration', charged with making decisions about taxation, public works, militias, the use of public funds and the management of public goods.

The French Revolution, however, did not usher in a peaceful social order in France. Despite its momentous achievements in changing the political agenda across the whole world, in France itself it not only produced much strife and bloodshed, it also led to what is often called, not inaccurately, the 'Reign of Terror'. Indeed, many of the theorists of social co-ordination who had contributed to the ideas behind the Revolution, took their own lives (including Condorcet) when it became likely that others would do it for them. Problems of social choice did not, in this case, receive an intellectual resolution.

The motivations of the early social choice theorists included the avoidance of both instability and arbitrariness in arrangements for social choice. The ambitions of their work focused on the development of a framework for rational and democratic decisions for a given group, paying adequate attention to the preferences and interests of its members. However, even the theoretical investigations typically yielded rather pessimistic results. Condorcet noted, for example, that majority rule can be caught in an impasse when every alternative is defeated in a majority vote by some other alternative.

This possibility is worth illustrating here, as an example of difficulties of social choice – an issue that would be pursued in a much more general form in the twentieth century by Kenneth Arrow through his 'impossibility theorem'. Consider three persons (1, 2 and 3), ranking three alternatives (x, y and z) in a social choice menu:

- 1 prefers x to y and y to z,
- 2 prefers y to z and z to x, and
- 3 prefers z to x and x to y.

In a majority vote, x defeats y, while y defeats z, and z in turn defeats x. So every alternative is defeated by some other alternative. This is sometimes called a 'majority cycle', and there is clearly an inconsistency of social choice here. But the more immediate point, on which Condorcet concentrated, is that there is no clear winner (or, as the literature has come to call it, no 'Condorcet winner', defined as an alternative that can prevail, in pairwise contests, over every other alternative).[ii]

This particular impasse is sometimes called 'the paradox of voting' (though Condorcet himself did not call it that). Condorcet considered this case along with a number of other problems in majority voting. One example that he considered in the context of this 'paradox of voting' has an interesting contemporary ring, with the three alternatives being defined as: (1) 'any restriction placed on commerce is an injustice'; (2) 'only those restrictions placed through general laws can be just'; and (3) 'restrictions placed by particular orders can be just'.[iii] He showed that with some possible individual preferences, each of these three alternatives may be defeated by another alternative.

MODERN SOCIAL CHOICE THEORY

Even though there is no continuous line of work on social choice theory following this early lead of French mathematicians, the subject received sporadic attention in various later writings, some by very distinguished authors (such as Lewis Carroll, the author of *Alice in Wonderland*, who wrote some engaging and important papers on group decisions under his real name, Charles. L. Dodgson (Dodgson (1876), (1884))). But in its modern – and fully axiomatized – form, modern social choice theory received its first rigorous foundation in the works of Kenneth J. Arrow.

Arrow's Ph.D. dissertation, containing his famous 'impossibility theorem', was first reported in an article (Arrow (1950)) and then published as a monograph (Arrow (1951a)), which became an instant classic. Economists, political theorists, moral and political philosophers, sociologists and even the general public took rapid notice of what seemed like – and indeed was – a devastating exercise of logic. Within a comparatively short time, social choice theory in a modernized and systematically axiomatic form was firmly established as a discipline, with immediate and extensive implications for economics, philosophy, politics and the other social sciences.

Like Condorcet with his 'voting paradox', Arrow too was very concerned with the difficulties of group decisions and the inconsistencies to which they may lead. Arrow's 'impossibility theorem' (formally, the 'General Possibility Theorem') is a mathematical demonstration of breathtaking elegance and power, which showed that even some very mild conditions of reasonableness could not be simultaneously satisfied by any social choice procedure that identifies a social ordering for each cluster of individual preference orderings.

It is worth having a basic understanding of the nature of the Arrow impossibility theorem since it has played such a big part in the initiation of modern social choice theory. The fundamental challenge that Arrow considered is that of moving from individual preferences over different states of affairs to a social preference over those states, reflecting something like an 'aggregation' of the points of views of all the members of the society. He wanted the social preference to be an 'ordering' (sometimes called a 'complete ordering', which is a fuller description). A ranking is an ordering if (1) any two alternatives can be ranked – one preferred to the other, or the opposite, or they are indifferent to each other (this is called the 'completeness' of the ranking), and (2) the ranking has a requirement of coherence that goes by the name of 'transitivity' (a flash of grammatical language in the field of preferences), which demands that if an alternative x is taken to be at least as good as y, and y to be at least as good as z, then x must be judged to be at least as good as z. Arrow saw these demands on a social ranking as a requirement of 'collective rationality'.

Arrow took *individual* preferences to be complete orderings of the states of affairs, which is rather less problematic than the corresponding demand for social preference. To give some traction to the exercise of seeking consistency, Arrow also assumed that there are at least three different alternatives to choose from and only a finite number of voters.

A social choice procedure that takes us from a cluster of individual preference orderings (one ordering per person) – which is called a 'profile' of individual preferences – to a social preference ordering is a 'social welfare function', with the underlying idea that if a state of affairs x is socially ranked above another y, then it can be reasonably said that the state x yields more 'social welfare' than y. The impossibility theorem shows that a set of very mildly demanding conditions of reasonableness cannot be satisfied together by any social welfare function – that is, by any such procedure of social aggregation.

Consider the following four axioms characterizing a social welfare function, specifying a social ordering of alternative states of affairs for each profile of individual preference orderings over those states.[1]

- Unrestricted Domain (U) claims that a social welfare function must work for every profile of individual preferences (that is, generate a social ordering for every cluster of individual preferences – one per person).

[1] This is a somewhat simplified – and a little less demanding – version of the set of conditions that Arrow himself used (Arrow (1963)).

- Independence of Irrelevant Alternatives (I) requires that the social ranking of any pair of alternatives must depend on the individual rankings only over that – 'relevant' – pair.

- The Pareto Principle (P) instructs that if everyone strictly prefers some alternative x to another alternative y, then social ordering too must place x strictly above y.

- Non-dictatorship (D) demands that there should be no dictator, i.e. no person such that whenever that person strictly prefers any x to any y, then society must invariably place x strictly above y.

Arrow's impossibility theorem shows that these mild-looking axioms U, I, P and D cannot be simultaneously fulfilled by any social aggregation procedure (or social welfare function).

This is not only an astonishing analytical result, but also one that generated much despair in the search for rational social choice procedures based on individuals' own preferences. It also seemed like an anti-democratic result of profound reach (which, as will be discussed later on, is not a correct interpretation). One common interpretation of this result was that only a dictatorship would avoid social inconsistencies, but a dictatorial rule would, of course, involve both an extreme sacrifice of participatory decisions and a gross insensitivity to the heterogeneous interests of a diverse population.

Two centuries after the flowering of the ambitions of social rationality in Enlightenment thinking and the writings of the theorists of the French Revolution, the subject seemed to be inescapably doomed. Social appraisals, economic evaluations and normative statistics would have to be, it seemed, inevitably arbitrary or irremediably despotic. Arrow's 'impossibility theorem' aroused immediate and intense interest (and generated a massive literature in response, including many other impossibility results).[iv] It also led to the diagnosis of a deep vulnerability in the discipline of social choice theory.

Unfortunately, the pessimism generated by Arrow's impossibility result also tended to undermine his immensely important *constructive* programme of developing a systematic social choice theory that would succeed in characterizing particular ways of making participatory decisions that are possible for a society to have.[v] The original version of this book (Sen (1970a)), was partly concerned with discussing and explaining the tendency towards impasse in social choice theory (and presented a few new impossibility results as well), but it was mostly aimed at redirecting social choice theory in a constructive direction. It was an attempt to provide a solid basis for the motivating departure that moved Arrow to research in this area in the first place – before he hit the barrier of his impossibility result. In this extended edition the constructive programme is further extended (on which see the New Preface).

IMPOSSIBILITY RESULTS AND PROXIMATE POSSIBILITIES

Before proceeding further, a general methodological issue about the existence of impossibility theorems can be fruitfully sorted out. Starting with Arrow's impossibility theorem, modern social choice theory has had a fair collection of 'impossibility results' (as will be discussed in the chapters to follow). In that context, the general relationship between possibility and impossibility results demand attention, in order to understand the nature and role of impossibility theorems.

In an early paper, originally published in French in 1952, Arrow explained the problem with his characteristic clarity:

> Certain properties which every reasonable social choice function should possess are set forth. The possibility of fulfilling these conditions is then examined. If we are lucky, there will be exactly one social choice function that will satisfy them. If we are less fortunate, there can be several social choice functions satisfying the conditions or axioms. Finally, it will be the height of bad luck if there exists no function fulfilling the desired conditions.[vi]

His 'impossibility theorem', Arrow explained, reflects this 'height of bad luck'.

How far is the distance between good luck and bad? There is, in fact, a close connection in this area of analytical reasoning between being 'lucky' and having the 'height of bad luck', which is worth commenting on. When a set of axioms regarding social choice can all be simultaneously satisfied, there may be several possible procedures that work, among which we have to choose. In order to choose between the different possibilities through the use of discriminating axioms, we have to introduce *further* axioms, until only one possible procedure survives. When that sole survivor emerges, we get from the process a kind of axiomatic derivation of a particular and unique social choice rule, and that surely can be seen as being really 'lucky' in getting to a positive possibility result. But note that if we over-shoot a little and have no surviving procedure left, then we get immediately to the 'height of bad luck'. This is something of an exercise in brinkmanship. We have to go on making more and more axiomatic demands regarding good properties that a social choice procedure should satisfy, thereby cutting down alternative possibilities, which had survived earlier – and less exacting – demands. In the process we are moving – implicitly – *towards* an impossibility, but then we try to stop just before all possibilities are eliminated: when one and only one option remains. That great achievement of 'best possible luck' comes fleetingly as we move from 'being not very lucky' to having 'the height of bad luck', with the very best luck situated on a narrow cliff in between.

Thus, it should be clear that a full axiomatic determination of a particular method of making social choices must inescapably lie next door to an impossibility – indeed, just short of it. If it lies far from an impossibility (with various positive possibilities that all work), then it cannot give us an axiomatic derivation of any specific method of social choice, for the rivals are all there. It is therefore to be expected that constructive paths in social choice theory, derived from axiomatic reasoning, would tend to be paved on one side by impossibility results, and on the other by multiple possibilities. If constructive results in social choice theory are thought to be rather 'fragile' (as they are often described), that is exactly what we should expect for strictly analytical reasons. No conclusion about the fragility of social choice theory as a subject – or a *field* – emerges from this proximity.

In fact, the literature that has followed Arrow's work has established both a set of impossibility theorems and, especially from the

1970s onwards, a reasonable collection of positive possibility results.[vii] The two classes of results lie quite close to each other. The real issue is not, therefore, the ubiquity of impossibility (which will always lie close to the axiomatic derivation of any specific social choice rule), but the reach and reasonableness of the axioms to be used. We have to get on with the basic task of obtaining workable rules that satisfy reasonable requirements, rather than throwing up our arms in despair at encountering the 'height of bad luck' – lying just a step beyond the pinnacle of good luck.

CRISIS IN WELFARE ECONOMICS

Social choice difficulties apply *inter alia* to what is called 'welfare economics' – an old subject aimed at judging social states in terms of the well-being (and other concerns) of the people, on which A. C. Pigou's distinguished book, *The Economics of Welfare* (1920), is something of a classic account. The subject, however, had taken quite a hard hit in the 1930s, even before Arrow's impossibility result further darkened the prospects of systematic welfare economics. The crisis came because of economists' new-found conviction that there was something really unsound in making use of interpersonal comparison of individual utilities, which had been the basis of traditional welfare economics. It is important to understand the crisis that welfare economics faced, even before Arrow's impossibility result posed further challenges. Let me turn briefly to the nature of that crisis now, before examining how Arrow's new result in social choice theory affected welfare economics.

Traditional welfare economics, which had been developed by utilitarian economists (such as Francis Y. Edgeworth (1881); Alfred Marshall (1890); and Arthur C. Pigou (1920)), had taken a very different track from the vote-oriented social choice theory. It took inspiration not from Borda (1781) or Condorcet (1785), but from their contemporary Jeremy Bentham (1789). Bentham had pioneered the use of 'utilitarian' calculus to obtain judgements about the social interest by aggregating the personal interests of the different individuals in the form of their respective welfares, which Bentham saw simply as utilities, reflecting pleasures or happiness.

Bentham's concern – and that of utilitarianism in general – was with the *total utility* of a community. The focus was on the total sum of utilities, irrespective of the distribution of that total, and in this we can see some blindness of considerable ethical and political concern. For example, a person who is unlucky enough to have a uniformly lower capability to generate enjoyment and utility out of income (say, because of a physical or mental handicap) would also be given, in the ideal utilitarian world, a *lower* share of a given total income, because of his or her lower ability to generate utility out of that income. This is a consequence of utilitarianism's single-minded pursuit of maximizing the sum-total of utilities – no matter how unequally distributed.[viii] However, the utilitarian interest in taking comparative note of the gains and losses of different people is not in itself a negligible issue. And this concern makes utilitarian welfare economics deeply interested in using a class of information – the comparison of utility gains and losses of different persons – with which Condorcet and Borda had not been directly involved.

Utilitarianism has been very influential in shaping welfare economics, which was dominated for a long time by an almost unquestioning adherence to utilitarian calculus. But by the 1930s utilitarian welfare economics came under severe fire. It would have been quite natural to question (as Rawls 1971 would masterfully do later on, in formulating his theory of justice) the utilitarian neglect of distributional issues and its concentration only on utility sum-totals, in a distribution-blind way. But that was not the direction in which the anti-utilitarian critiques went in the 1930s and in the decades that followed. Rather, economists came to be persuaded by arguments presented by Lionel Robbins and others (who were themselves deeply influenced by logical positivism, as a school of philosophy) that interpersonal comparisons of utility had no scientific basis: 'Every mind is inscrutable to every other mind and no common denominator of feeling is possible' (Robbins (1938), p. 636). Thus, the epistemic foundations of utilitarian welfare economics were seen as incurably defective.

There followed attempts to do welfare economics on the basis of each person's respective ordering of social states, without any interpersonal comparisons of utility gains and losses of different persons. While utilitarianism and utilitarian welfare economics are quite indifferent to the *distribution* of utilities between different persons (concentrating, as they do, only on the *sum-total* of utilities), the new regime, without any interpersonal comparisons in any form, further reduced the informational base on which social choice could draw. The already-limited informational base of Benthamite calculus was made to shrink further to Borda's and Condorcet's voting space – the simple rankings of different individuals (I am referring here to Condorcet's work as a voting theorist, not as a general – and splendid – social philosopher, as he also was: see particularly Condorcet (1795), (1955)). The use of different persons' utility rankings without any interpersonal comparison is analytically quite similar to the use of voting information – each individual taken separately – in making social choice.

ATTEMPTED REPAIRS AND
FURTHER CRISES

Faced with this informational restriction, utilitarian welfare economics gave way, from the late 1930s, to what came to be called – hugely over-ambitiously – 'new welfare economics', which used only one basic criterion of social improvement, *viz*, the 'Pareto comparison'. The Pareto criterion only asserts that an alternative situation would be definitely better if the change would increase the utility of every one.[2] A good deal of subsequent welfare economics restricted attention to 'Pareto efficiency' (that is, only to making sure that no further Pareto improvements are possible). This criterion takes no interest whatever in *distributional* issues, which cannot be addressed without considering conflicts of interests and of preferences. So, if one person gains while everyone else loses (no matter

---

[2] In a somewhat more assertive version the Pareto criterion can declare a state to be better than another if it enhances the utility of at least one person and does not reduce that of anyone else.

how many – nor by how much), we were not allowed to declare this change to be a deterioration, if we stuck only to Pareto efficiency.

This reticence, it seems fair to guess, would have appealed to Emperor Nero, who evidently enjoyed playing his music while Rome burned and all other Romans were plunged into misery. In general, the Pareto efficiency of a state of affairs would not be disturbed even if many people are forced into terribly famished lives in that state, while some others lead lives of extreme luxury, *provided* the misery of the destitutes cannot be reduced without cutting into the lives of the super-rich. A state of affairs can have the glory of being Pareto efficient while being disgustingly unjust.

Some further criterion – beyond Pareto efficiency – is clearly needed for making social welfare judgements with a greater reach.[3] This necessity was insightfully explored by Abram Bergson (1938) and Paul A. Samuelson (1947). This search led directly to Arrow's (1950), (1951a) pioneering formulation of social choice theory, relating social preference (or decisions) to the set of individual preferences, that is (as discussed earlier) to the search for what Arrow called a 'social welfare function'. It was in the framework of social welfare functions that Arrow established his powerful impossibility theorem, showing the incompatibility of some very mild-looking conditions (discussed earlier, including Pareto efficiency, non-dictatorship, independence of irrelevant alternatives, and unrestricted domain). This generated further pessimism in an already gloomy assessment of the possibility of a reasoned and satisfactory welfare economics.[ix]

---

[3] To try to remedy this gap by taking a sideways leap, as was proposed by some leading economists (including Nicholas Kaldor (1939) and John Hicks (1939b)), into the so-called 'compensation tests', which favour any change in which the gainers have gained so much that they can compensate the losers (without having actually to pay any such compensation), would be oddly short of justification. ('Look here – you have lost a lot and I have gained even more, but I have gained so much that I can compensate you for your loss, and therefore this is a better social situation, even though I will not, of course, compensate you at all – OK?'). Compensation tests seem to be invoked these days only in some textbooks on law and on international trade, but rarely in welfare economics proper. See Chapter 2* of the original (1970) book for critical scrutiny of the illusory – and happily short-lived – promise of compensation tests.

In order to avoid this impossibility result, different ways of modifying Arrow's requirements were tried out in the literature that followed, but other difficulties continued to emerge.[x] The force and widespread presence of impossibility results consolidated the sense of pessimism, and this became a recurrent theme in welfare economics and social choice theory in general. By the mid-1960s, William Baumol (1965), a distinguished contributor to economics in general and welfare economics in particular, judiciously remarked that 'statements about the significance of welfare economics' had started having 'an ill-concealed resemblance to obituary notices'.[xi] This was certainly a correct reading of prevailing views. But, as Baumol also noted, we had to assess how sound these views were. We especially have to ask whether the pessimism associated with Arrovian structures in social choice theory is devastating for welfare economics as a discipline.

WELFARE ECONOMICS AND VOTING INFORMATION

It can be argued that the 'obiturial' climate of welfare economics in its post-utilitarian phase was largely the consequence of the epistemic penury of welfare economics based on confining informational inflow to voting-like inputs. Voting-based procedures are entirely natural for some kinds of social choice problems, such as elections, referendums, or committee decisions.[4][xii] They are, however, altogether unsuitable for many other problems of social choice. When, for example, we want to get some kind of an aggregative index of social

[4] There are, however, some serious problems arising from a possible lack of correspondence between votes and actual preferences, which could differ because of strategic voting – rather than honest expression of real preferences – aimed at the manipulation of voting results. On this see the remarkable impossibility theorem of Gibbard (1973) and Satterthwaite (1975), and Pattanaik (1973), (1978). See also Dutta and Pattanaik (1978), Peleg (1978a), (2002), Laffont (1979), Dutta (1980), Laffont and Maskin (1982), Maskin (1985) and Barberà (2011). For an excellent introduction to the important subject of implementation theory and mechanism design, not taken up in this book, see Maskin and Sjöström (2002).

welfare, we cannot rely on such procedures for at least two distinct reasons.

First, voting requires active participation, and if some groups tend not to exercise their voting rights (perhaps due to cultural conditioning, or because of procedural barriers that make voting difficult and expensive), the preferences of those groups tend to have quite inadequate representation in social decisions. For example, because of lower participation, the interests of substantial groups – for example of African Americans in the United States – had, until recently, found limited influence on national politics. And yet reasonable social welfare judgements cannot ignore the interests of those who are reluctant to vote (for one reason or another), or whose attempts at voting are frustrated by systematic barriers, often imposed by the exclusionary tactics of political activists. Even the voting results may be seriously distorted because of the gap between preferences and the actual casting of votes.

Second, even with the active involvement of everyone in voting exercises, we cannot but be short of important information needed for welfare economic evaluation. It is absurd to think that social welfare judgements can be made without some understanding of issues of disparities that characterize one society or another. Voting information, taken on its own, turns a blind eye to such comparisons. Ultimately, that limitation is related to the eschewing of interpersonal comparison of well-being, on the wisdom of which professional economists remained oddly convinced for several decades.

There was also the exclusion of what economists call 'cardinal utility', which takes us beyond merely the ranking of alternatives in terms of being better or worse (or indifferent) – the so-called 'ordinal utility' – to give us some idea of the relative gaps between the utility values of different alternatives (allowing statements like, 'not only does her utility ranking place x higher than y and y higher than z, but the utility gap between x and y is larger – in fact twice as large – as that between y and z'). Utilitarian welfare economics uses cardinality of utilities as well as interpersonal comparison of these utilities, and the new orthodoxy that emerged in the 1930s, disputed the scientific status of both cardinality and of the interpersonal comparison of utilities of different persons.

INFORMATIONAL PENURY AS A CAUSE OF SOCIAL CHOICE PROBLEMS

It is also worth recollecting that utilitarian philosophy, and – influenced by it – traditional welfare economics as well, had huge informational restrictions of its own. It was not allowed to make any basic use of *non-utility information*, since everything had to be judged ultimately by utility sum-totals in consequent states of affairs. To this informational exclusion was now added the further exclusion of interpersonal comparisons of utilities, along with cardinal utility, disabling the idea of utility sum-totals, without removing the exclusion of non-utility information. This barren informational landscape made it hard to arrive at any systematic judgement of social welfare, based on *informed reasoning*. Arrow's theorem can be interpreted, in this context, as a demonstration that even some very weak conditions – in this case Arrow's axioms – relating individual preferences to social welfare judgements cannot be simultaneously satisfied in a world of such informational privation (on this see Sen (1977c), (1979a)).

The problem is not just one of impossibility. As is shown in the new Chapter A1*, given Arrow's axioms U (Unrestricted Domain), I (Independence of Irrelevant Alternatives) and P (Pareto Principle), the relation between the profile of individual preferences and the social ranking emerging from it has to forgo taking any note of the nature of the alternatives (that is, the social states), and go simply by the individual preferences over the alternatives, no matter what they are. If person 1 is decisive in the choice over any pair (a, b) – for whatever reason – then that person would be decisive in the social preference over every other pair of alternatives (x, y) as well, even though the nature of the choice involved may radically differ because of the nature of the social alternatives under consideration.

This requirement is sometimes called 'neutrality' (a usage that had the support – I hope only half-hearted support – of Arrow (1963) himself), though it is a peculiarly kind term for what is, after all, a sanctification of informational blindness (other than the sight of utility information). Perhaps the alternative term used for it, namely 'welfarism' (on which see Sen (1977c), (1979a)), is more helpful, in that we cannot make any direct use of information about states of affairs other than through the individual welfares they respectively generate – and that again only in the form of utilities. Further, the utility information used must not involve any cardinality of interpersonal comparison. All this amounts to insisting that social choices satisfying the Arrow axioms must be made with very little information indeed.

The demand of so-called 'neutrality' tends to play havoc with the discipline of reasoned social choice. Consider, for example, a cake division problem in which everyone prefers to have a larger share of the cake. If, in this cake division problem, an equal division between two persons in the form of (50, 50) is socially preferred to person 1 having 99 per cent of it, with the other having only 1 per cent, in the form (99, 1), it is clearly being judged that person 2's preference should prevail over person 1's, *in this case*. But, if so-called neutrality is demanded, then, due to the insistence that the nature of the alternatives should not make any difference to whose preferences prevail, an opposite type of inequality, with person 2 having nearly all the cake in the form of (1, 99) should be socially preferred over a (50, 50) division, through the requirement that person 2, decisive over the earlier choice, should be decisive over all other choices as well.

It is hard to escape the thought that something has gone badly wrong in the underlying intellectual system – and that problem arises even before any impossibility result emerges. What we are doing here is insisting that welfare judgements must be based on something like voting data, taking note of who prefers what, but not of who is rich and who is poor, or who gains how much from a change compared with what the losers lose. There is no direct way of getting interpersonal comparisons of different persons' well-being (or, for that matter, cardinality of welfares or utilities) from voting data. We must go beyond the class of voting rules (explored by Borda and Condorcet as well as Arrow) to be able to address distributional issues.

Arrow had ruled out the use of interpersonal comparisons since he had followed the general consensus that had emerged in the 1940s that (as Arrow put it) 'interpersonal comparison of utilities has no meaning' (Arrow (1951a), p. 9). The totality of the axiom-combination used by Arrow had the effect of confining social choice mechanisms to rules that are, broadly speaking, of the voting type. His impossibility result relates, therefore, to this class of rules with its informational poverty, as was mentioned earlier.

It should be emphasized that, unlike ruling out the use of interpersonal comparison of utilities, which Arrow explicitly invoked, the insistence on restricting social choice procedures only to voting rules is not an assumption Arrow directly imposed. It is, in fact, a combined result of the different axioms that he uses, and can be seen as an analytical consequence of the set of apparently reasonable axioms postulated for social choice. Interpersonal comparison of utilities is, of course, explicitly excluded, but in the process of proving his impossibility theorem Arrow also shows that a set of seemingly plausible assumptions, taken together, logically entail other features of voting rules as well, in particular something close to so-called 'neutrality' or 'welfarism' (discussed earlier).[xiii] This entails that no effective note be taken of the *nature* of social states, and that social decisions must be based only on the votes that are respectively cast in favour of – and against – them.

Note how different kinds of information are excluded from being used through different means. The eschewal of interpersonal comparisons of utilities eliminates the possibility of taking note of inequality of utilities – and also of differences in gains and losses of utilities. On the other side, the component of so-called 'neutrality' – derived as a logical conclusion from other axioms (in particular, unrestricted domain, independence and the Pareto principle) – prevents attention being indirectly paid to distributional issues through taking explicit note of the nature of the respective social states (for example, of the income inequalities in the different states, such as who has a larger share of the cake in the cake-division example discussed earlier). The informational restrictions, taken together, make it very hard to discriminate between the alternatives in terms of standard principles, such as inequality aversion.

INCORPORATING MORE INFORMATION IN SOCIAL DECISIONS

To lay a broader foundation for a constructive social choice theory (broader than the framework Arrow chose), we have to make room for accommodating more information. There is a need in particular to resist the historical consensus against the use of interpersonal comparisons of individual welfares (or utilities) in social choice, which was dominant when Arrow initiated the subject. However, to proceed on that constructive route, we have to address two difficult, but important, questions. First, can we systematically incorporate and use something as complex as interpersonal comparisons of the well-being of many different people? Can this be a territory of disciplined analysis, rather than a riot of confusing (and possibly confused) ideas? Second, how can the analytical results be integrated with practical use? On what kind of information can we sensibly base actual interpersonal comparisons? And will the relevant information be actually available to be used?

The first set of questions concerns analytical system-building, and the second that of epistemology as well as practical reasoning. The second issue requires a re-examination of the informational basis of interpersonal comparisons, and I will presently argue that it calls for an inescapably qualified, but constructive, response.

The first question can be addressed more definitively through constructive analysis. Without going into the technicalities that have emerged in the literature, I would like to report that interpersonal comparisons of various types can be fully axiomatized and exactly incorporated in social choice procedures, and this can be done (as is shown in Chapter 7* in the 1970 book, and further extended here in Chapter A3*). Without going into technicalities here (which are reserved for the formal chapters), we can note that the extent of interpersonal comparability can be incorporated in the relational constraints we impose in being able to combine numbers reflecting the well-being (or utilities) of different persons (formally these constraints are called 'invariance conditions').

Consider a case of full comparability, by first beginning with well-being numbers 1, 2, 3 for person 1 from social alternatives x, y and z, respectively, with the corresponding numbers for person 2 being 2, 3, 1. Since there is no naturally fixed unit of well-being, we can easily enough take the well-being numbers of person 1 from x, y and z to be 2, 4, 6, instead of 1, 2, 3. Full interpersonal comparability of a very demanding kind would require that, if we re-scale person 1's well-being numbers by doubling them, we must do the same for person 2, and transform her well-being numbers from 2, 3, 1 to a corresponding set 4, 6, 2. With such tying up implied by this kind of full interpersonal comparability, it would not make any real difference whether we work with the original numbers (1, 2, 3 for person 1, and 2, 3, 1 for person 2), or deal instead with the symmetrically transformed numbers (2, 4, 6 for 1, and 4, 6, 2 for 2). As different types of interpersonal comparability (such as 'level comparability' or 'unit comparability') are considered, we shall have correspondingly different invariance conditions.

The formal statements capture them with exactness, as the starred chapters demonstrate. Through the use of 'invariance conditions' in a generalized framework that allows the use of well-being numbers going beyond simple rankings (as in the Arrow framework), we get what are called *social welfare functionals* (SWFL), which allow the use of much more information than Arrow's social welfare functions (SWF) permit.[xiv]

Indeed, interpersonal comparisons need not even be confined to 'all-or-none' dichotomies. We may be able to make interpersonal comparisons to some extent, but not in every comparison, nor of every type, nor with tremendous exactness. To illustrate, we may invoke the example of Nero and the burning of Rome discussed earlier. It seems reasonable to argue that there should be no great difficulty in accepting that Nero's utility gain from the burning of Rome on those eventful nights in July in AD 64 was smaller than the sum-total of the utility loss of all the other Romans taken together – perhaps hundreds of thousands of them who suffered from the fire (so movingly described by Cassius Dio). But this does not require us to presume that we can put everyone's utilities in an exact one-to-one correspondence with each other. There is no requirement here that we can make an exact comparison between the welfare gain of Nero and the welfare loss of any particular resident of Rome. The aggregative conclusion that the welfare loss of the suffering Romans put together exceeded the welfare gain of Nero can allow considerable variations in the exact correspondence between welfare measures of Nero and the other Romans. There may, thus, be room for demanding 'partial comparability', denying both the extremes – full comparability and no comparability at all.

The different extents of partial comparability can be given mathematically exact forms, precisely articulating the extent of the variations that may be permitted.[xv] It can also be shown that there may be no general need for terribly refined interpersonal comparisons for arriving at definite social decisions. Quite often, rather limited levels of partial comparability will be adequate for making social decisions. Thus the empirical exercise need not be as ambitious as is sometimes feared.

WHAT DIFFERENCE DOES IT MAKE?

Before proceeding to the informational basis of interpersonal comparisons, let me ask an important analytical question: how much of a change in the possibility of social choice is brought about by systematic use of interpersonal comparisons? Do Arrow's impossibility and related results go away with the use of interpersonal comparisons in social welfare judgements? The answer, briefly, is yes: the additional informational availability allows sufficient discrimination to escape impossibilities of this type. For example, we can introduce the Rawlsian distributive principle of *maximin*, which takes the form of giving priority to the interests of the worst-off person (or persons).[5]

---

[5] For compatibility with the Pareto principle (as well as for making reasonable sense), this would have to be done in a lexicographic form, so that in a case of the worst-off persons tying with each other in terms of their respective well-being in a comparison between two states of affairs, we go by the interests of the second worst-off (on this see Chapters 9 and 9* of the 1970 edition). Rawls used the rule of lexicographic maximin (which has been given the rather inelegant name of 'leximin') not in utility comparisons, but in the comparisons of 'primary goods' – the general-purpose resources (such as income, wealth, etc.) – people respectively have.

There is an interesting contrast here, which was touched on in the New Preface to this edition. It can be shown that admitting cardinality of utilities *without* interpersonal comparisons does not change Arrow's impossibility theorem at all, which can be readily extended to cardinal measurability of utilities (see Chapter 8* of the 1970 edition). In contrast, the possibility of only 'ordinal' interpersonal comparisons (so that the rankings of well-being between different persons remain invariant) is adequate to break the exact impossibility. We knew, of course, that with some types of interpersonal comparisons demanded in a full form (including cardinal interpersonal comparability), we can use the classical utilitarian approach. But it turns out that even weaker forms of comparability would still permit making consistent social welfare judgements, satisfying all of Arrow's requirements, in addition to being sensitive to distributional concerns (even though the possible rules will be confined to a relatively small class).[xvi]

The distributional issue is, in fact, intimately connected with the need to go beyond voting rules as the basis of social welfare judgements. As was discussed earlier, utilitarianism too is in an important sense distribution-indifferent: its programme is to maximize the *sum-total* of utilities, no matter how unequally that total may be distributed.[xvii] But the use of interpersonal comparisons can take other forms as well, allowing public decisions to be sensitive to *inequalities* in well-being and opportunities.

The broad approach of social welfare functionals opens up the possibility of using many different types of social welfare rules, which differ in the treatment of equity as well as efficiency and also in their informational requirements.[xviii] This analytical broadening has been actually used to bring in many different kinds of interpersonal comparisons and their use for social welfare judgements, as well as for the construction of normative indicators for actual use in policy analysis (see Chapters A3 and A3*).[xix]

INTERPERSONAL
COMPARISON OF WHAT?

Even though the analytical issues in incorporating interpersonal comparisons have been, on the whole, well sorted out, there still remains the important practical matter of finding an adequate approach to the empirical discipline of making interpersonal comparisons and then using them in practice. The foremost question to be addressed is this: interpersonal comparison of *what*? Even though the debates about interpersonal comparison of well-being have been, historically, concentrated on the comparison of 'utilities', in which utilitarian philosophers were particularly interested, the issue of interpersonal comparison in general is much broader than that.

Indeed, the formal structures of social welfare functions are not, in any sense, specific to utility comparisons only, and they can incorporate other types of interpersonal comparisons as well. The principal issue is that of accounting of individual advantage, which can take the form of comparisons of mental states of happiness or desires (which have been championed by utilitarian philosophers), but need not be so confined. Instead of anchoring on information on mental states, interpersonal comparisons can possibly focus on some other way of looking at individual well-being or individual advantage, for example in terms of freedoms or substantive opportunities (seen in the perspective of a corresponding evaluative discipline, which can go well beyond the narrow limits of utilitarianism).

The rejection of interpersonal comparisons of utilities in welfare economics, and in social choice theory that followed positivist criticism (such as that of Robbins (1938)), was firmly based on interpreting them entirely as comparisons of mental states. As it happens, even with such mental state comparisons, the case for unqualified rejection is hard to sustain. Indeed, as has been forcefully argued by the philosopher Donald Davidson (1986), it is difficult to see how people can understand anything much about other people's minds and feelings, without making some comparisons with their own minds and feelings. Such comparisons may not be extremely precise, but we know from analytical investigations that very precise interpersonal comparisons may not be needed to make systematic use of interpersonal comparisons in social choice.

If interpersonal comparisons are not seen as factual assessments, but taken to be entirely matters of opinion or of value judgements, then the question can also be raised as to how the divergent opinions or valuations of different persons may be *combined* together (this looks like a social choice exercise on its own). Kevin Roberts (1995) has investigated this particular formulation, taking interpersonal comparison to be an exercise of aggregation of opinions. In general, the task of social aggregation of judgements or opinions demands different kinds of axiomatic demands than the requirements that make sense in aggregating the self-interests of different persons (on the distinction, see Sen (1977b)). Le Breton and Trannoy (1987) have presented a powerful analysis of aggregating individual preferences about income distributions, and, recently, Christian List and Philip Pettit (2005), (2011) have clarified the particular challenges that have to be faced in judgement-aggregating exercises in social choice.

If, however, interpersonal comparisons are taken to be of different persons' well-being, and taken to have a firm factual basis (e.g. some people being objectively more miserable than others), then the need for an evidential search becomes important and urgent – an exercise that would be more of a part of epistemology than that of ethics.[xx] Even though pessimism about such 'factual comparisons' of utilities – and related mental metrics – has been quite dominant in the economic literature for more than half a century, there have been new methods, including experimental observations, that have given ground for optimism in the measurement and interpersonal comparison of utilities.[xxi]

CAPABILITIES AND PRIMARY GOODS

The main ground for scepticism for basing interpersonal comparisons of welfare on the comparative assessment of mental states may not, however, lie in epistemic difficulties in getting a reliable factual picture (contrary to what Lionel Robbins argued). There are important ethical grounds for not concentrating too much on mental-state comparisons or utilities – seen as pleasures or desires – in comparing how different persons are respectively doing.

Utilities may sometimes be very malleable in response to persistent deprivation. A hopeless, poverty-struck destitute, or a downtrodden labourer living under exploitative economic arrangements, or a subjugated housewife in a society with entrenched gender inequality, or a tyrannized citizen under brutal authoritarianism, may come to terms with her deprivation. She may take whatever pleasure she can from small achievements, and adjust her desires to take note of feasibility (thereby helping the fulfilment of her adjusted desires). But her success in such adjustment will not make her deprivation go away. The metric of pleasure or desire may sometimes be quite inadequate in reflecting the extent of a person's substantive deprivation.

There may indeed be a case for taking incomes, or commodity bundles, or resources more generally, to be of direct interest in judging a person's advantage.[xxii] The interest in incomes or resources can arise for many different reasons – not merely for the mental states that opulence may help to generate.[xxiii] In fact, the Difference Principle in Rawls's (1971) theory of 'justice as fairness' is based on judging individual advantage in terms of a person's command over what Rawls calls 'primary goods', which are general-purpose resources that are useful for anyone to have (no matter what his or her exact objectives are).

This procedure can be improved upon by taking note not only of the holdings of primary goods and resources, but also of interpersonal differences in converting them into the capability to live well. Indeed, it is possible to argue in favour of judging individual advantages in terms of the respective capabilities that the different persons have, giving them the freedom to live the way they have reason to value (on which see Sen (1980), (1985a), (1985b) and Nussbaum (1988), (1992), (2001), (2011)). This approach focuses on the substantive freedoms that people have, rather than only on the particular outcomes with which they end up. For responsible adults, the concentration on freedom rather than only achievement has some merit, and it can provide a general framework for analysing individual advantage and deprivation in a contemporary society (on this see Chapter A3).[xxiv]

The extent of interpersonal comparisons may only be partial – often based on the intersection of different points of view. But the use of such partial comparability can make a major difference to the informational basis of reasoned social judgements.

The capability approach runs parallel to attempts to see human well-being in terms of fulfilment of 'basic needs'.[xxv] The perspective of basic needs focuses on human beings as 'needy' creatures, whereas the capability approach concentrates on the 'freedom' that human beings can enjoy and have reason to value. There is a philosophical difference here that I shall not explore further in this work (see, however, Sen (1985a), (2009a)).

POVERTY AS CAPABILITY DEPRIVATION

The variety of information on which social welfare analysis can draw can be well illustrated by the study of poverty and the battle against it. The intellectual as well as the policy challenges involved in what Angus Deaton has called 'the great escape' are as important to the subject of social choice as they are central for the basic engagements of the social sciences in general.[6] The broadening of poverty studies makes many demands, some of which have clear connections with issues central to the social choice literature.

Poverty is typically seen in terms of the lowness of incomes, and it has been traditionally measured simply by counting the number of people below the poverty-line income; this is sometimes called the head-count measure. A scrutiny of this approach, which has been an important part of contemporary social choice literature, yields two different types of question. First, is poverty adequately seen as lowness of income? Second, even if poverty is seen as low income, is the

---

[6] Angus Deaton's book *The Great Escape* brings out the variety of social, political, economic and scientific, as well as organizational, issues involved in 'the story of mankind's escaping from deprivation and early death, of how people have managed to make their lives better, and led the way for others to follow' (Deaton (2013), p. ix).

aggregate poverty of a society best characterized by some index of the head-count measure of the number falling below the chosen cut-off 'poverty line' income?

I take up these questions in turn. Do we get enough of a diagnosis of individual poverty by comparing the individual's income with a socially given poverty-line income? What about the person with an income well above the poverty line who suffers from an expensive illness (requiring, say, kidney dialysis)? Is deprivation not ultimately a lack of opportunity to lead a minimally acceptable life, which can be influenced by a number of considerations, including, of course, personal income, but also physical and environmental characteristics, and other variables (such as the availability and costs of medical and other facilities)? The motivation behind such an exercise relates closely to seeing poverty as a serious deprivation of certain basic capabilities. This alternative approach leads to a rather different diagnosis of poverty from the ones that a purely income-based analysis can yield.[xxvi]

This is not to deny that lowness of income can be very important in many contexts, since the opportunities a person enjoys in a market economy can be severely constrained by her level of real income.[xxvii] However, various contingencies can lead to variations in the 'conversion' of income into the capability to live a minimally acceptable life, and if that is what we are concerned with, there may be good reason to look beyond income poverty (see Sen (1976b), (1984), (1992a), and Foster and Sen (1997)). There are at least four different sources of variation: (1) personal heterogeneities (for example, proneness to illness); (2) environmental diversities (for example, living in a storm-prone or flood-prone area); (3) variations in social climate (for example, the prevalence of crime or epidemiological disadvantages); and (4) differences in relative deprivation connected with customary patterns of consumption in particular societies (for example, being relatively impoverished in a rich society, which can lead to deprivation of the absolute capability to take part in the life of the community).

That a relative deprivation of income can lead to an absolute deprivation of a basic capability was first discussed by Adam Smith (1776). Smith argued that 'necessary goods' (and, correspondingly, minimum incomes needed to avoid basic deprivation) must be defined differently for different societies, and he also suggested a general approach of using a variable 'poverty-line' income for different societies, even if the cut-off levels of capabilities are much the same. As Smith discussed, not having money enough to buy a linen shirt or leather shoes may prevent a person in a rich society, where most people wear linen shirts and leather shoes, from 'appearing in public without shame' in a way that a person without such a shirt or shoes may not be prevented from doing the same in a poorer society, where dress-codes are less exacting.

There is, thus, an important need to go beyond income information in poverty analysis, and, instead, to see poverty as capability deprivation. However (as was discussed earlier), the choice of the informational base for poverty analysis cannot really be dissociated from pragmatic considerations, particularly informational availability. It is unlikely that the perspective of poverty as income deprivation can be dispensed with in the empirical literature on poverty, even when the limitations of that perspective are entirely clear. Indeed, in many contexts the rough-and-ready way of using income information may provide the most immediate approach to the study of severe deprivation.[7]

For example, the causation of famines is often best seen in terms of a radical decline in the real incomes of a section of the population, leading to starvation and death (on this see Sen (1981)).[xxviii] The dynamics of income earning and of purchasing power may indeed be the most important component of a famine investigation. This approach, in which the study of causal influences on the determination of the respective incomes of different groups plays a central part, contrasts with an exclusive focus on agricultural production and food supply, which is often found in the literature on this subject.

The shift in informational focus from food supply to entitlements (involving incomes as well as supply, and the resulting relative prices)

---

[7] These issues link with the political advocacy for a 'basic income guarantee' for all, even when the ultimate ethical focus is not on incomes but on the quality of human lives (and the capabilities that people enjoy). These interlinked issues have been illuminatingly discussed by Philippe Van Parijs (1995).

can make a radical difference, since famines can occur even without any major decline – possibly without *any* decline at all – of food production or supply.[xxix] If, for example, the incomes of rural wage labourers, or of service providers, or of craftsmen, collapse through unemployment, or through a fall in real wages, or through a decline in the demand for the relevant services or craft products, the affected groups may have to starve, even if the overall food supply in the economy is undiminished. Starvation occurs when some people cannot establish entitlement over an adequate amount of food, through purchase or through food production, and the overall supply of food is only one influence among many in the determination of the entitlements of the respective groups of people in the economy. Thus, an income-sensitive entitlement approach can provide a better explanation of famines than can be obtained through an exclusively production-oriented view. It can also yield a more effective approach to the remedying of starvation and hunger (on this see particularly Drèze and Sen, (1989)).

The nature of the problem tends to point to the particular 'space' on which the analysis has to concentrate. It remains true that, in explaining the exact patterns of famine deaths and sufferings, we can get additional understanding by supplementing the income-based analysis with information on the conversion of incomes into nourishment, which will depend on various other influences such as metabolic rates, proneness to illness, body size, etc. An important further issue is the distribution of food *within* the family, which may be influenced by several factors other than family income. Issues of gender inequality and the treatment of children and of old people can be important in this context. Entitlement analysis can be extended in these directions by going beyond the family income into the conventions and rules of intrafamily division, including the presence of gender bias against girls.[xxx] These issues are undoubtedly important for investigating the incidence of nutritional failures, morbidities and mortalities.

I turn now to the second question. The most common and most traditional measure of poverty has tended to concentrate on head counting – the number of people below the poverty line. But it must also make a difference as to *how far* below the poverty line the poor individually are, and, furthermore, how the deprivation is *shared and distributed* among the poor. The social data on the respective deprivations of the individuals who constitute the poor in a society need to be aggregated together to arrive at informative and usable measures of aggregate poverty. This is a social choice problem, and axioms can indeed be proposed that attempt to capture our distributional concerns in this constructive exercise (on this see Chapters A3 and A3*).[xxxi]

Several distribution-sensitive poverty measures have been derived axiomatically in the recent social choice literature, and various alternative proposals have been analysed. Among the new ones are the recent attempts to make use of multi-dimensional poverty measures, powerfully pursued – in different forms – by Atkinson and Bourguignon (1982), Maasoumi (1986) and Alkire and Foster (2011a), (2011b), among others.

I shall not go into a comparative assessment of these measures here, nor into axiomatic requirements that can be used to discriminate between them.[8] However, I must also emphasize the fact that we face here an embarrassment of riches (the opposite of an impasse or impossibility), once the informational basis of social judgements has been appropriately broadened.[xxxii] Many alternative poverty measures, each with some plausibility, and all within the informational boundaries in the broadened format, compete with each other for attention. To axiomatize exactly one particular poverty measure, and rejecting the others, we shall have to indulge in the 'brinkmanship' of which I spoke earlier, by adding other axiomatic demands until we are just short of an impossibility, with only one surviving poverty measure. We can debate the relative merits of alternative sets of axioms, but that exercise may not have an unambiguous identification of the 'best' axioms. The choice of axioms may also depend, to a considerable extent, on the context in which a measurement of poverty is being sought (for a social or a political critique, or for long-run economic planning, or for

---

[8] A fairly extensive account of the literature up to the 1990s can be found in my joint critical survey with James Foster (Foster and Sen (1997)).

immediate public policy, or for discussion of international actions, such as respective contributions to be made for a global climate policy). In fact, depending on the purpose of our exercise we may have good grounds for using different measures of poverty. Assessment of poverty is relevant in many different contexts with disparate motivations that make us seek poverty measurement. Motivational contingency is widely relevant for the entire discipline of normative measurement.

CAPABILITY DEPRIVATION AND GENDER INEQUALITY

Poverty cannot be dissociated from the misery caused by it, and, in this sense, the classical perspective of utility can also be invoked. However, the malleability of mental attitudes, on which I commented earlier, may in many cases tend to hide or muffle the extent of deprivation. The indigent peasant who manages to build some cheer in his life should not be taken as 'not poor' on grounds of that mental accomplishment.

This adaptation can be particularly important in dealing with gender inequality and deprivation of women in traditionally unequal societies. This is partly because perceptions have a decisive part to play in the cohesion of family life, and the culture of family living tends to put a premium on making allies out of the ill-treated. Women may – often enough – work much harder than men (thanks particularly to the rigours of household chores and the need to care for infants and the elderly, traditionally seen – quite unfairly – as women's responsibility), and also receive less attention in health care and nutrition. And yet the perception that there is an incorrigible inequality here may well be missing in a society in which asymmetric norms are quietly dominant.[xxxiii] Under these circumstances, this type of inequality and deprivation may not adequately surface in the scale of the mental metric of dissatisfaction and discontent.

A socially cultivated sense of contentment and serenity may even affect the perception of morbidity and illness. When, many years ago, I was working on a famine-related study of post-famine Bengal in 1944, I was quite struck by the remarkable fact that the widows surveyed had hardly reported any incidence of being in 'indifferent health', whereas wido*wers*, complained massively about its widespread prevalence (Sen (1985a), Appendix B). Similarly, it emerges in interstate comparisons in India that the states that are worst provided in education and health-care facilities typically report the *lowest* levels of perceived morbidity, whereas states with good health care and school education indicate *higher* self-perception of illness (with the highest morbidity reports coming from the best-provided states, such as Kerala, which has the highest longevity and literacy rates in India).[9] Mental reactions, the mainstay of classical utility, can be a very defective basis for the analysis of deprivation.

Thus, in understanding poverty and inequality, there is a strong case for looking at real deprivation and not merely at mental reactions to that deprivation. There have been many recent investigations of gender inequality and women's deprivation in terms of undernutrition, clinically diagnosed morbidity, observed illiteracy and even unexpectedly high mortality (compared with physiologically justified expectations).[xxxiv] Interpersonal comparisons of a variety of living conditions can easily be a significant basis of studies of deprivation of women and of inequality between the sexes. They can be accommodated within a broad framework of welfare economics and social choice, helped by the removal of debilitating informational constraints common in traditional welfare economics which

---

[9] The methodological issues underlying the contradictory rankings of good health services (and indeed of good health) and the *perception* of having good health can be analysed in terms of 'positional objectivity' (a concept I have investigated in Sen (1993b), (2009a)). The angst of the relatively better-provided for and better-educated people of Kerala against the remaining shortcomings of their health care is real and of relevance of its own. And yet it would be a mistake to guess the relative goodness of health and the adequacy of health care by comparing the extents of complaints and anguish from different positions, for example between badly provided health care in Uttar Pradesh and the much better facilities in Kerala (where the perception of ill health is much stronger). What is observationally objective from a given position may not be a guide to how the objective opportunities of health care can be compared and contrasted in interpositional comparisons.

would tend to rule out the use of many categories of relevant and telling information, important to the understanding of gender inequality.[xxxv]

VOTING AND MAJORITY DECISIONS

The inadequacy of voting information for welfare economics should be clear enough, for reasons that I have been discussing here. But that does not eliminate the relevance of voting processes for social choice theory. The importance of elections and referendums can hardly be denied in social choice procedures. Even though the voting process is quite insufficient as a way of making welfare economic judgements, there are political decisions that a society has to make for which the procedure of voting remains a major route to social choice.

The 'paradox of voting', explored by Condorcet, may not dispose of the possibility of reasoned welfare economics, but there are other exercises of social choice for which that impasse – and many similar problems – must continue to cast a gloomy shadow. How should we address those difficulties?

One of the possibilities much explored in this context has been the confinement of individual preference profiles to a 'restricted domain', which would avoid problems of contradiction in voting results, and can also prevent the non-existence of a satisfactory voting outcome (indeed, may guarantee a Condorcet winner that can defeat every other candidate in pairwise majority vote). In the discussion so far, I have made no attempt to confine attention to particular configurations – or 'profiles' – of individual preferences, ignoring others. Formally, this catholicity is required by Arrow's condition of 'unrestricted domain', which insists that the social choice procedure must work for every conceivable cluster of individual preferences. It must, however, be obvious that, for any decision procedure, some preference profiles will yield inconsistencies and incoherence of social decisions while other profiles will not produce these results.

Arrow (1951a) himself had initiated, along with Duncan Black (1948a), (1948b), (1958), the search for adequate restrictions that would guarantee consistent majority decisions. The sufficient conditions for this can be vastly expanded through using a process of reasoning not dissimilar to Arrow's own (Sen (1966a) and Chapter 10* in the 1970 book). The necessary and sufficient conditions of domain restriction for consistent majority decisions can indeed be precisely identified (see Sen and Pattanaik (1969)).[xxxvi] While much less restrictive than the earlier conditions that had been identified, they are still rather demanding (see Chapters 10* and A4*).

Choice problems for a society come in many shapes and sizes, and there may be less comfort in these results for some types of social choice problems than for others. When distributional issues dominate and when people seek to maximize their own 'shares' without concern for others (as, for example, in a 'cake division' problem, with each person preferring any division that increases his or her own share, no matter what happens to the others), majority rule will tend to be thoroughly inconsistent. But when there is a matter of national outrage (for example, in response to the inability of a democratic government to prevent a famine), the electorate may be reasonably univocal and thoroughly consistent. Also, when people cluster in parties, with complex agendas and dialogues, involving give and take as well as some general attitudes to values like equity or justice, the ubiquitous inconsistencies can yield ground to more congruous decisions.[xxxvii]

Even though voting impasse cannot be generally eliminated, it appears that majority rule is, in fact, far less vulnerable to contradictions than other procedures of voting. As discussed by Eric Maskin in a paper called 'Arrow Impossibility Theorem: Where Do We Go from Here?' (2014), it can be shown that if there is a domain restriction for which any voting rule other than the majority rule works well, then so would majority rule for that domain. This dominance relation in favour of majority rule was discussed in the new Preface to this edition. There is a well-defined sense in which majority rule is the least vulnerable among all the voting rules, which are all vulnerable in one way or another.

LIBERTY AND RIGHTS

The informational widening considered so far has been mainly concerned with the use of interpersonal comparisons. But this need not be the only form of broadening that can enhance the possibility of informed social choice. More than a century and a half ago, John Stuart Mill (1859) investigated how a good society should try to guarantee the liberty of each person.

Liberty has many different aspects, including two rather distinct features:

(1) *the opportunity aspect*: we should be able to achieve what we choose to achieve in our respective personal domains, for example, in our private life; and

(2) *the process aspect*: we can make our own choices in our personal domains (no matter whether we achieve what we want).

In social choice theory, the formulation of liberty has been primarily concerned with the former, that is, the opportunity aspect.

Seen in the perspective of the opportunity aspect, liberty demands that each person should be decisive in safeguarding certain things in his or her 'personal domain', without interference by others (even if a majority – or even all others – are keen on interfering). Mill considered various examples of such personal domains over which the person involved should be able to prevail, for example in the quiet practice of his or her own religion. Note that the 'opportunity aspect' cannot be safeguarded by leaving the person's own action to be self-chosen (as a 'process' guarantee), since others could interfere, for example through making hugely disturbing loud noises, or even by organizing intrusive demonstrations, making life difficult for the person trying to live a quietly religious life. It is the duty of a society, Mill argued, to make sure that a person's own choices over a personal domain prevail (in this case, guaranteeing that the person can perform his or her private religious actions, without being stopped by others, and also without being hindered by interferences by the actions of others).

It is the conflict of this opportunity aspect of liberty with the Pareto principle (given unrestricted domain) that is the subject of the impossibility theorem which is sometimes referred to as 'the liberal paradox', or 'the impossibility of the Paretian liberal' (see Sen (1970c), and in this book Chapters 6, 6*, A5 and A5*). Unlike the Arrow theorem, this impossibility theorem does not depend on the independence of irrelevant alternatives (condition I), which is not invoked. Instead, it is shown that unrestricted domain (U) and the Pareto principle (P) cannot be combined with 'minimal liberty', demanding only that at least two persons are each decisive over the choice over one pair – with their difference being 'personal' to the respective person. There is a huge literature on the subject, disputing the result, extending it, resolving the acknowledged problem, and questioning the interpretation of liberty.[xxxviii] The theorem shows the impossibility of satisfying even a very mild demand for 'minimal liberty' when combined with an insistence on Pareto efficiency (given unrestricted domain).

Turning now to the process aspect, seeing liberty as a guaranteed process of leaving people to be free to do certain things in their own personal sphere is a requirement that has been particularly pursued by a number of writers in this field (led by Robert Nozick 1974), and joined in many different ways by others).[xxxix] In this perspective, it does not really matter what the actual outcome is, in so far as liberty is concerned, as long as people remain free to do what they want in their personal domain.

It is hard to deny that liberty has both these aspects. If I do not want smoke to be blown in my face, my liberty to have that does not depend primarily on what I do, but mostly on what others do. Leaving me free with my own action cannot eliminate this violation of my personal liberty. Even though the formulation of process-based liberty has been much refined from the simple statements originally made by Nozick (1974), and has been set out in 'game-form' formulation (see Gaertner, Pattanaik and Suzumura (1992)), the limitations arising from the neglect of actual outcomes – often important for the realization of liberty – remains. I shall examine the question more fully in Chapters A5 and A5*.

The existence of an opportunity aspect of liberty is adequate to show a conflict between minimal liberty and the Pareto principle (given unrestricted domain) and the opportunity aspect of liberty – the impossibility of the Paretian liberal stands. However, for an appropriate understanding of the demands of liberty, the process aspect of liberty also deserves attention. An exclusive concentration on the opportunity aspect cannot be adequate (no matter how adequate it may be for proving the existence of the so-called liberal paradox). But it is also important to avoid the opposite narrowness of concentrating exclusively on the process aspect only, as some recent writers have preferred to do. Important as processes are, they cannot obliterate the relevance of the opportunity aspect which must also count. Indeed, the importance of *effectiveness* in the realization of liberty in one's personal life has been recognized as important for a long time – even by commentators deeply concerned with processes, from John Stuart Mill (1859) to Frank Knight (1947), Friedrich A. Hayek (1960) and Buchanan (1986). The difficulties of having to weigh process fairness along with effectiveness of liberty-respecting outcomes (such as, in Mill's example, a person's success in being able to practise his own religion) cannot be avoided simply by ignoring the opportunity aspect of liberty through an exclusive concentration on the process aspect.

How might the conflict of the Paretian liberal be resolved? Different ways of dealing with this friction have been explored in the literature (as will be discussed in Chapters A5 and A5*). However, it is important to see that, unlike Arrow's impossibility result, the liberal paradox cannot be satisfactorily resolved through the use of interpersonal comparisons. Indeed, neither the claims of liberty, nor that of Pareto efficiency, need be significantly contingent on interpersonal comparisons. The force of one's claims over one's private domain lies in the *personal* nature of that choice – not in the *relative intensities* of the preferences of different persons over a particular person's private life (being 'full of passionate intensity' does not give the intruder the right to intrude).

Rather, the resolution of this problem lies elsewhere, in particular in the need to see each of these claims as being qualified by the importance of the other – once it is recognized that they can be in possible conflict with each other. Indeed, the main point of the liberal paradox was precisely to identify that possible conflict. A satisfactory resolution of this impossibility must include taking an evaluative view of the acceptable priorities between personal liberty, on one side, and the pull of immediate pleasures and desires on the other. There is no escape from reasoned scrutiny in the pursuit of a satisfactory resolution of these diverse attractions.

CONCLUDING REMARKS

Impossibility results in social choice theory – led by the pioneering work of Kenneth Arrow (1951a) – have often been interpreted as being thoroughly destructive of the possibility of reasoned and democratic social choice, including welfare economics. This book argues against that view. In fact, all these impossibility results, including Arrow's classic theorem, invite engagement and social reflection rather than resignation. We do know, of course, that democratic decisions can sometimes lead to incongruities. To the extent that this is a feature of the real world, its existence and reach are matters for objective recognition. Inconsistencies arise more readily in some situations than in others, and it is possible to identify the situational differences and to characterize the processes through which consensual and compatible decisions can emerge.

Condorcet himself was very keen on public debates as a solution to social problems. In the literature of formal social choice theory, that dialogic aspect of Condorcet's priorities has not received as much attention as it has in the alternative approach – often called 'public choice theory' – led particularly by James Buchanan. While that broadening is to the credit of the 'public choice' tradition, that tradition has been limited through its tendency to presume that people always behave in a rather narrowly self-centred way – as *homo economicus* in particular – even though Buchanan ((1986), p. 26) himself noted some 'tension' on this issue (see also Geoffrey Brennan and Loren Lomasky (1993)). There is no shortage of self-seeking behaviour in the world, but is that the only motivation human beings have? It is hard to think that social institutions, such as the National Health Service, can work at all, if doctors and medical staff all acted constantly and exclusively for their own well-being and success (despite all the accountability that can be imposed by institutional features).

Adam Smith is sometimes described as the original proponent of the ubiquity and ethical adequacy of 'the economic man', but that is fairly sloppy history. In fact, Smith (1776), (1790) had examined the distinct disciplines of 'self-love', 'prudence', 'sympathy', 'generosity', and 'public spirit', among others, and had discussed not only their intrinsic importance, but also their instrumental roles in the success of a society, and their practical influence on actual behaviour. The demands of rationality need not be geared entirely to the use of only one of these motivations (such as self-love), and there is plenty of empirical evidence to indicate that the presumption of an uncompromising pursuit of narrowly defined self-interest is as mistaken today as it was in Smith's time.[xl] Just as it is necessary to avoid the high-minded sentimentalism of assuming that all human beings (and public servants in particular) try constantly to promote some selfless 'social good', it is also important to escape what may be called the 'low-minded sentimentalism' of assuming that everyone is constantly motivated only by simple self-interest – and nothing else.

Efforts to explain every socially consequential action as some kind of a cunning attempt at maximization of purely private gain are not uncommon in social analysis, and are frequently present in parts of modern economics – a tendency that Alexis de Tocqueville noticed when he visited America in the first half of the nineteenth century. It is an interesting question as to whether the presumption of exclusive self-interestedness is a more common general belief in America than in Europe, without its being a general characteristic of *actual* behaviour on either side of the Atlantic. Indeed, Tocqueville (1840) believed that this was indeed the case:

> The Americans . . . are fond of explaining almost all the actions of their lives by the principle of self-interest rightly understood; they show with complacency how an enlightened regard for themselves constantly prompts them to assist one another and inclines them willingly to sacrifice a portion of their time and property to the welfare of the state. In this respect, they frequently fail to do themselves

justice; for in the United States as well as elsewhere people are some-times seen to give way to those disinterested and spontaneous impulses that are natural to man; but the Americans seldom admit that they yield to emotions of this kind; they are more anxious to do honour to their philosophy than to themselves.[xli]

In this respect the 'public choice' tradition has been rather Ameri-can, in Tocqueville's sense, in assuming that everyone pursues only self-interest – and nothing else. In contrast, social choice theory has been more true to its European ancestry in making room for many different kinds of motivations that people may have. On the other hand, social choice theory has been more negligent than public choice theory in making room for the role of public discussion in the forma-tion of values. As the famous Chicago economist Frank Knight, who deeply influenced the public choice theorists, noted: 'Values are estab-lished or validated and recognized through *discussion*, an activity which is at once social, intellectual, and creative' (Knight (1947), p. 280). There is, in fact, much force in Buchanan's ((1954a), p. 120) assertion that this is a central component of democracy ('government by discussion') and that 'individual values can and do change in the process of decision-making'. That recognition would have received approval from Condorcet, judging from his own writings on society and politics in the *Esquisse*.

This issue has some real practical importance. To illustrate, in studying the fact that famines occur in some countries but not in others, I have tried to point to the phenomenon that no major famine has ever taken place in any country with a multiparty democracy with regular elections and with a reasonably free press (see Sen 1982c, 1983c and Drèze and Sen 1989). This applies as much to poorer democratic countries (such as India or Botswana) as to richer ones. This is largely because famines, while killing millions, do not much affect the direct well-being of ruling classes and dictators, who have little political incentive to prevent famines unless their rule is threat-ened by them. And yet famines are easily preventable. The economic analysis of famines across the world indicates that only a small pro-portion of the population tends to be stricken – rarely more than

5 per cent or so. Since the shares of income and food of these poor groups tend normally to be no more than 3 per cent of the total for the nation, it is not hard to rebuild their lost share of income and food, even in very poor countries, if a serious effort is made in that direction (see Sen (1981), Drèze and Sen (1989)). The need to face public criticism and to encounter the electorate provides the government with the political incentive to take preventive action with some urgency.

The question that remains is this. Since only a very small proportion of the population is struck by a famine (typically 5 per cent or less), how can it become such a potent force in elections and in public criticism? This indicates some tension with the assumption of universal self-centredness. It seems that we do have the capacity – and often the inclination – to understand and respond to the predicament of others. There is a particular need in this context to examine value formation that results from public discussion of miserable events, in generating sympathy and commitment on the part of citizens to do something to prevent their occurrence.

Even the idea of 'basic needs', fruitfully used in the development literature, has to be related to the fact that what is taken as a 'need' is not determined only by biological and uninfluencible factors. For example, in those parts of the so-called Third World in which there has been increased and extensive public discussion of the consequences of frequent childbearing on the well-being and freedom of mothers, the perception that a smaller family is a 'basic need' of women (and men too) has grown, and in this value formation a combination of democracy, free public media and basic education (especially female education) has been very potent. The implications of this finding are particularly important for rational consideration of the so-called 'world population problem'.

Similar issues arise in dealing with environmental problems. The threats that we face call for organized international action as well as changes in national policies, particularly for better reflecting social costs in prices and incentives. But they are also dependent on value formation, related to public discussions, both for their influence on individual behaviour and for bringing about policy changes through political processes. There are plenty of 'social choice problems' in all this, but in analysing them we have to look not only for an appropriate reflection of *given* individual preferences, or for the most acceptable procedures for choices based on those preferences, but also to go beyond both these aspects to allow the possibility of value formation. We need to depart both from the assumption of unresponsive individual preferences and from the presumption that people are purely self-interested specimens of *homo economicus*. Useful insights on social choice come from many different sources, and we have to recognize that important fact.

A NOTE ON THE TEXTS

1. I should warn the reader that there are, in a few cases, some slight differences in the mathematical notations used in the old (1970) edition and in the chapters added in the new (2017) edition. For example, the subset notation for weak set inclusion (set Y includes all the elements of X, but possibly – though not necessarily – other elements too) is shown as $X \subset Y$ in the starred 1970 chapters, and as $X \subseteq Y$ in the starred 2017 chapters.

2. The literature on social choice is quite vast by now, and I have not tried to comment on every publication that is worthy of note. I have, however, included in the bibliography a number of publications that I have not discussed in this book but which may, depending on the reader's interest, be very worth reading. I have also drawn attention to them in the name index.

Collective Choice and
Social Welfare (1970)

To Nabaneeta

Chapter 1
Introduction

I.I. PRELIMINARY REMARKS

There is something in common between singing romantic songs about an abstract motherland and doing optimization exercises with an arbitrary objective function for a society. While both the activities are worthy, and certainly both are frequently performed, this book, I fear, will not be concerned with either. The subject of our study is the relation between the objectives of social policy and the preferences and aspirations of members of a society.

It is, of course, possible to take the view that a society is an entity that is independent of the individuals in it, and that social preference need not be based on the preference of the members of the society. Or that there might be a dependence, but one could abstract from it, and simply 'assume' that society has a personality and a preference of its own.[1] Anyone who finds his fulfilment in this assumption is entirely welcome to it, and this book must bore him. This study is concerned precisely with investigating the dependence of judgments on social choice and of public policy on the preferences of the members of the society.

Judgments on collective choice, while related to the needs and desires of the members of the community, can, however, take widely different form. The calm economic technician who states that imposing a tax on commodity α will be inoptimal provides a

---

[1] While this position is taken in some of the socialist literature, it was sharply rejected by Marx: 'What is to be avoided above all is the re-establishing of "Society" as an abstraction *vis-a-vis* the individual.' (Marx (1844), p. 104.)

45

judgment on collective choice of one type. The angry crowd which, on 14 July 1789, responded to de Launay, the governor of Bastille, by shouting, 'Down with the second drawbridge!'[2] was involved in a collective choice of a somewhat different kind. The subject is wide enough to cover both, but the approach to these problems must, of course, differ substantially. This diversity is an essential aspect of the subject of collective choice, and indeed a great deal of the richness of the field is related to this.

A study of different relations between individual preferences and social choice is one of our chief concerns. Varieties here are enormous. For example, someone might take the view, implicitly or explicitly, that only his aspirations should count in social choice. Or only the homogeneous interests of a particular class, or a group. Or one might argue that everyone's preference 'should count equally', but that statement itself can be interpreted, as we shall presently see, in many different ways. And corresponding to each interpretation we get a different system of making collective choice. This book is much concerned with these systems – their nature, their operations, and their implications.

I.2. INGREDIENTS OF COLLECTIVE CHOICE

To assert that social choices should depend on individual preferences leaves the question open as to what should be the form in which individual preferences would be relevant. In his classic study, Arrow (1951) takes orderings of the individuals over the set of alternative social states to be the basic constituent of collective choice. He is concerned with rules of collective choice which make the preference ordering of the society a function of individual preference orderings, so that if the latter set is specified, the former must be fully determined.

An ordering is a ranking of all alternatives vis-a-vis each other.

[2] G. Lefebvre, *The Coming of the French Revolution*, trans. by R. R. Palmer, Vintage Books, New York, 1957, p. 101.

The formal properties of an ordering are discussed in Chapter 1*,[3] but we might briefly state here that the ranking relation must satisfy three characteristics to count as an ordering. Consider the relation 'at least as good as'. First, it must be 'transitive', i.e., if x is at least as good as y, and y is at least as good as z, then x should be at least as good as z. This condition of rationality is analysed in some detail in Chapter 1*. Second, the relation must be 'reflexive', i.e., every alternative x must be thought to be at least as good as itself. This requirement is so mild that it is best looked at as a condition, I imagine, of sanity rather than of rationality. Third, the relation must be 'complete',[4] i.e., for any pair of alternatives x and y, either x is at least as good as y, or y is at least as good as x (or possibly both). A man with a preference relation that is complete knows his mind in choices over every pair.

It is important to distinguish between indifference and lack of completeness. Our daily language is often loose enough to fail to distinguish between the two. If I 'don't know' which one to choose, this could possibly mean that I am indifferent, though a more natural meaning is that I cannot make up my mind. The logical difference between the two is simple enough. Consider the two statements:

(1) x is at least as good as y
(2) y is at least as good as x

In the case of 'indifference' both are being asserted, and, in the case of lack of 'completeness', neither.

Each individual is assumed to have an ordering over the alternative social states, and society is supposed to have an ordering based on the set of individual orderings, as the problem is posed by Arrow. We shall have to depart from this classic framework in some respects. First, for consistent choice it is not needed that the society should have an ordering. For example, if x is preferred to y, y is preferred to

---

[3] The reader can also consult Tarski (1965); Arrow (1951), Chapter 2; or Debreu (1959), Chapter 1.
[4] Logicians seem to prefer the expression 'connected' to 'complete', but there is then the danger of a confusion with the topological property of 'connectedness'.

z, and z is indifferent to x, then there is a best alternative in every choice situation, but transitivity is violated. If the choice is over the pair (x, y), x can be chosen; if over (y, z), y is to be preferred; if over (z, x), either can be chosen; and if it is a choice from the set of all three alternatives (x, y, z), then x is to be selected, for it is the only alternative which is at least as good as the two others. Is this a satisfactory basis of choice? It is difficult to decide, for while it is a sufficient basis, it does violate some rationality property. The precise property it violates (property β) is spelt out in Chapter 1*. We shall discuss this question in detail in terms of its implication in Chapter 4, but at this stage simply note that the problem can be considered without requiring that social preference be fully transitive. We shall indeed take the problem in this general form, introducing transitivity as a special assumption later on, e.g. in Chapter 3.

Second, for some choice problems we do not even need completeness. Suppose that x is preferred to y and also to z, but y and z cannot be compared, then the preference ordering will be incomplete, but still we can choose a best alternative, viz., x, given the choice between x, y, and z. However, should the choice be between y and z, then we are in trouble. Whether we can dispense with completeness depends on the nature of the choice. Obviously completeness is a desirable characteristic of social preference, but we shall not make a fetish of it. A preference relation that is reflexive and transitive but not necessarily complete is called a quasi-ordering, and its formal properties are studied in Chapter 1*. Exercises with incomplete social preferences will figure in Chapters 2, 8 and 9, and in the corresponding starred chapters.

Third, it is arguable that social choice should depend not merely on individual orderings, but on their intensities of preference. Cardinal welfare functions for individuals may be considered. As an example it may be said that if person 1 wants very strongly that society should choose x rather than y, while person 2 wants very marginally that y be chosen and not x, then in this two-person world there is a good case for choosing x. This argument is somewhat misleading, for in this exercise we are not merely specifying preference intensities of the individuals, we are making interpersonal comparisons between these. There may or may not be any harm in this, but the fact remains that the persuasive nature of the argument is based on the additional feature of interpersonal comparisons and not on the purely personal measures of preference intensity. The use of cardinality with interpersonal comparisons will be discussed in Chapter 7 and that without it in Chapter 8, and in the corresponding starred chapters.

Fourth, the question of interpersonal comparisons is itself an interesting one. It can be used even without cardinality (Chapters 7, 7*, 9 and 9*), and it can be applied in various doses (Chapters 7 and 7*). If collective choice depends not merely on individual orderings but also on interpersonal comparisons of levels of welfare or of marginal gains and losses of welfare of individuals, a new set of possibilities open up.

The use of interpersonal comparisons is widely thought to be arbitrary, and many people view these comparisons as 'meaningless' in not being related to acts of choice. One way of giving meaning to such comparisons is to consider choices between being person A in social state x or being person B in social state y. For example, we could ask: 'Would you prefer to be Mr A, an unemployed labourer, in state x, or Mr B, a well-paid employed engineer, in state y?' While the answer to the question does involve interpersonal comparisons, I should hazard the view that it is not entirely beyond our intellectual depth to be able to think systematically about this choice. It is possible to introduce preferences involving such alternatives into the mechanism of collective choice. This approach will be taken up in Chapters 9 and 9*.

We would, therefore, consider alternative frameworks for collective choice with alternative views on the necessary *ingredients* of such choice, varying from purely individual orderings, as in the system of Arrow, to individual welfare functions with or without cardinality and with or without interpersonal comparability of various types.

1.3. THE NATURE OF INDIVIDUAL PREFERENCES

It is possible to argue that a theory of collective choice should be concerned merely with the derivation of social preference from a set of individual preferences, and need not go into the formation of individual preferences themselves. This view has attractions, not the least of which is its convenience in limiting the exercise. However, it is a somewhat narrow position to take, and the genesis of individual preferences may indeed be relevant for postulating rules for collective choice. We shall find that the effectiveness of different rules of collective choice depends much on the precise configuration of individual preference orderings, and these configurations will, in general, reflect the forces that determine individual preferences in a society. Just as social choice may be based on individual preferences, the latter in their turn will depend on the nature of the society. Thus, the appropriateness of alternative rules of collective choice will depend partly on the precise structure of the society.

The content of individual preferences is also an important issue. In some studies of social choice a distinction is made between individual preferences as they actually are and what they would be if people tried to place themselves in the position of others. This is an important distinction and one that will be examined in some detail (see Chapters 9 and 9*), but it will be a mistake to assume that preferences as they actually are do not involve any concern for others. The society in which a person lives, the class to which he belongs, the relation that he has with the social and economic structure of the community, are relevant to a person's choice not merely because they affect the nature of his personal interests but also because they influence his value system including his notion of 'due' concern for other members of society.[5] The insular economic man pursuing his self-interest to the exclusion of all other considerations may represent an assumption that pervades

---

[5] This is, of course, an important issue for historical studies; see, for example, Hobsbawm (1955).

much of traditional economics,[6] but it is not a particularly useful model for understanding problems of social choice. No attempt will be made in this study to rule out interpersonal interdependences.

A useful preliminary exercise is a study of the logical properties of preference relations, and this is what is presented, with an eye to subsequent use, in Chapter 1*. Many of these results are well-known, though quite a few are not, mainly because the development of the study of preference relations in the standard literature has been largely motivated by consumption theory and demand analysis, which is not always helpful for problems of collective choice.

---

[6] Formally, this takes the form of ruling out externalities. See also Arrow's contrast between 'tastes' and 'values' (Arrow (1951), p. 18).

Chapter 1*
Preference Relations

1*1. BINARY RELATIONS

Let $x \, R \, y$ represent a binary relation between x and y, e.g., 'x is at least as good as y,' or 'x is greater than y.' If this relation does not hold, e.g., if 'x is not at least as good as y,' or if 'x is not greater than y,' we write $\sim(x \, R \, y)$.

One way of specifying such a binary relation over a set S is to specify a subset R of the square of S, denoted $S \times S$, defined as the set of all ordered pairs (x, y) such that x and y both belong to S. Instead of saying $x \, R \, y$ holds, we can then say that (x, y) belongs to R. The study of binary relations on S does not, therefore, differ essentially from the study of subsets of $S \times S$. While we shall not study preference relations in this manner, the reader is free to do the translation should it appear more convenient.

The notation given below will be used in what follows. For a discussion of the underlying concepts, the reader is referred to any standard introduction to mathematical logic, e.g., Carnap (1958), Church (1956), Hilbert and Ackermann (1960), Quine (1951), Suppes (1958) or Tarski (1965).

$\exists$	the existential quantifier ('for some')
$\forall$	the universal quantifier ('for all')
$\rightarrow$	conditional ('if, then')
$\leftrightarrow$	equivalence ('if and only if')
$\sim$	negation ('not')
$\lor$	alternation (the inclusive 'or')

    &   conjunction ('and')

    $=$ identity ('the same as')

    $\in$ element of ('belongs to')

    $\subset$ subset of ('is contained in')

    $\cap$ intersection of ('elements belonging to both sets')

    $\cup$ union of ('elements belonging to either set')

One can think of a variety of properties that a binary relation may or may not satisfy. The following have been found important in different contexts:

(1) *Reflexivity:* $\forall x \in S: x R x.$

(2) *Completeness:* $\forall x, y \in S: (x \neq y) \rightarrow (x R y \veebar y R x).$

(3) *Transitivity:* $\forall x, y, z \in S: (x R y \,\&\, y R z) \rightarrow x R z.$

(4) *Anti-symmetry:* $\forall x, y \in S: (x R y \,\&\, y R x) \rightarrow x = y.$

(5) *Asymmetry:* $\forall x, y \in S: x R y \rightarrow \sim(y R x).$

(6) *Symmetry:* $\forall x, y \in S: x R y \rightarrow y R x.$

Consider, as an illustration, the relation 'at least as tall as' applied to the set of all mountain peaks with measured heights. The relation is reflexive, since a peak is as tall as itself. It is complete, for if peak A is not at least as tall as peak B, then peak B will be at least as tall as (in fact, taller than) peak A. It is transitive, since peak A, being at least as tall as peak B which is itself at least as tall as peak C, must imply that peak A is at least as tall as peak C.[1] It is not anti-symmetric, since peaks A and B could be of the same height without being the same peaks. Nor is it asymmetric, since A being at least as tall as B does not preclude the possibility that B will be as tall as A.[2] Nor is it symmetric, since A being at least as tall as B does not at all impose any compulsion that B must be at least as tall as A.

---

[1] The relation 'being brother of' applied to men, while occasionally thought to be transitive, is not really so. Person A may be brother of B and B brother of A, so that by transitivity A should be brother of himself – a luxury that, alas, must be denied to A.

[2] Note that asymmetry implies anti-symmetry, but not vice versa. If $x R y \rightarrow \sim(y R x)$, then the antecedence $(x R y \,\&\, y R x)$ is always false, and hence the implication is logically correct in the case of anti-symmetry.

It may be easily checked that the relation 'taller than' would satisfy transitivity, anti-symmetry and asymmetry, but not reflexivity, completeness and symmetry.

Binary relations of certain standard types (i.e., with given properties) have been assigned specific names for convenience. Unfortunately the terminology varies from author to author, and there are some important inconsistencies which one must be aware of. For example, for Arrow (1951) an 'ordering' is reflexive, transitive and complete (irrespective of anti-symmetry), while for Debreu (1959) an 'ordering' is reflexive, transitive and anti-symmetric (irrespective of completeness).

We specify below the terminology to be used in this book and also note a few alternative names used in the literature.[3]

	Properties satisfied	Name to be used in this work	Other names used in the literature
1.	reflexivity and transitivity	quasi-ordering	pre-ordering
2.	reflexivity, transitivity and completeness	ordering	complete pre-ordering; complete quasi-ordering; weak ordering
3.	reflexivity, transitivity and anti-symmetry	partial ordering	ordering
4.	reflexivity, transitivity completeness and anti-symmetry	chain	linear ordering; complete ordering; simply ordering
5.	transitivity and asymmetry	strict partial ordering	
6.	transitivity, asymmetry and completeness	strong ordering	ordering; strict ordering; strict complete ordering

[3] See, for example, Birkhoff (1940), Bourbaki (1939), Tarski (1965) and Church (1956), and, in the economic literature, Arrow (1951) and Debreu (1959).

1*2 MAXIMAL ELEMENTS AND CHOICE SETS

Corresponding to the binary relation of 'weak preference' R ('at least as good as'), we can define relations of 'strict preference' P and of 'indifference' I.

DEFINITION 1*1. $x P y \leftrightarrow [x R y \ \& \ \sim(y R x)]$

DEFINITION 1*2. $x I y \leftrightarrow [x R y \ \& \ y R x]$

The elements of a set which are not dominated by any others in the set may be called the maximal elements of the set with respect to the binary relation in question.

DEFINITION 1*3.   *An element x in S is a maximal element of S with respect to a binary relation R if and only if*

$$\sim[\exists y: (y \in S \ \& \ y P x)]$$

The set of maximal elements in S is called its maximal set, and is denoted $M(S, R)$.

An element x can be called a 'best' ('greatest', in the context of size relations) element of S if it is at least as good (great) as every other element in S with respect to the relevant preference relation R.

DEFINITION 1*4.   *An element x in S is a best element of S with respect to a binary relation R if and only if*

$$\forall y: (y \in S \rightarrow x R y)$$

The set of best elements in S is called its choice set, and is denoted $C(S, R)$.

Two comments might be worth making for the purpose of clarification. First, a best element is also a maximal element but not vice versa. If $x R y$ for all y in S, then clearly there is no y in S such that $y P x$. On the other hand, if neither $x R y$ nor $y R x$, then x and y are both maximal elements of the set (x, y), but neither is a best element. Thus, $C(S, R) \subset M(S, R)$.

Second, $C(S, R)$ or $M(S, R)$ may well be empty. For example, if $x P y$, $y P z$ and $z P x$, there is neither a best element, nor any element not bettered by any other. If transitivity holds, $M(S, R)$ could be empty if the set is infinite, e.g., $x_2 P x_1, x_3 P x_2, \ldots, x_n P x_{n-1}, \ldots$. On the other hand, even with transitivity and finiteness, $C(S, R)$ may be empty, e.g., $\sim(x R y) \& \sim(y R x)$, which makes both x and y members of the maximal set of (x, y) but neither a member of the choice set of (x, y).

1^*3. A SET OF RESULTS FOR QUASI-ORDERINGS

We shall now derive certain elementary results for quasi-orderings. These will apply, naturally, to orderings, chains, and partial orderings as well, since these are special cases of quasi-orderings.

LEMMA 1^*a. *If R is a quasi-ordering, then for all $x, y, z \in S$*

   (1) $x I y \& y I z \to x I z$

   (2) $x P y \& y I z \to x P z$

   (3) $x I y \& y P z \to x P z$

   (4) $x P y \& y P z \to x P z$

Proof.

   (1) $x I y \& y I z \to (x R y \& y R z) \& (y R x \& z R y)$
                  $\to x R z \& z R x$
                  $\to x I z$

   (2) $x P y \& y I z \to x R y \& y R z$
                  $\to x R z$

So (2) can be false only if $z R x$, i.e., only if $x I z$. Suppose this is the case; then $x I y$, since $x I z \& y I z \to x I y$, by (1). But $x I y$ is false.

   (3) The proof is exactly similar to that of (2).

   (4) It can be seen that $x P y \& y P z \to x R y \& y R z \to x R z$. So (4) can be false only if $z R x$, i.e., only if $x I z$. However, if $x I z$, then $z P y$, given (3) and $x P y$. But $z P y$ is false.

We shall refer to the four properties (1)–(4) as II, PI, IP, and PP, respectively.

The following two results are elementary:

LEMMA 1*b. *Any finite quasi-ordered set has at least one maximal element.*[4]

Proof. Let the elements be $x_1, x_2, \ldots, x_n$. Let us put $a_1 = x_1$. We now follow the recursive rule that $a_{j+1} = x_{j+1}$ if $x_{j+1} \, P \, a_j$, and $a_{j+1} = a_j$ otherwise. By construction, a_n must be maximal.

LEMMA 1*c. *If R is reflexive, then $x \, P \, y \leftrightarrow [x] = C([x, y], R)$.*[5]

Proof.

$$x \, P \, y \to x \, R \, y \, \& \sim (y \, R \, x)$$
$$\to [x] = C([x, y], R)$$

since $x \, R \, x$ by reflexivity.

$$[x] = C([x, y], R) \to x \, R \, y \, \& \sim (y \, R \, x)$$

since $y \, R \, y$ by reflexivity,

$$\to x \, P \, y$$

Thus x is the only element of the choice set of $[x, y]$ if and only if x is preferred to y.

The relation between maximal sets and choice sets is important for some exercises. We have noted already that $C(S, R) \subset M(S, R)$. We may note further the following result:

LEMMA 1*d. *If for a quasi-ordering R, $C(S, R)$ is non-empty, then $C(S, R) = M(S, R)$.*

Proof. Suppose $x \in C(S, R)$. Then

$$z \in M \, (S, R) \to \sim (x \, P \, z)$$
$$\to x \, I \, z$$

[4] See Theorem 1.4 in Birkhoff (1940), p. 8. Birkhoff speaks of 'partially ordered systems', but the proof does not use the property of anti-symmetry.
[5] See Lemma 2 in Arrow (1951), p. 16.

since $x\,R\,z$,

$$\to \forall y\colon [y \in S \to z\,R\,y]$$

by Lemma 1*a and the fact of $x \in C(S, R)$,

$$\to z \in C(S, R)$$

Hence, $M(S,\ R) \subset C(S,\ R)$. It follows now from the fact that $C(S,R) \subset M(S,R)$, that $C(S,R) = M(S,R)$.

The following result is also convenient:

LEMMA 1*e. *For any quasi-ordering R over a finite set S,*

$$\forall x, y\colon [x, y \in M(S, R) \to x\,I\,y] \leftrightarrow [C(S, R) = M(S, R)]$$

Proof. Suppose to the contrary, $C(S,\ R) \neq M(S,\ R)$, but $\forall x,\ y\colon$ $[x, y \in M(S, R) \to x\,I\,y]$. Then by Lemma 1*d, $C(S, R)$ is empty. Let $x_0 \in M(S, R)$. Now, clearly, $\sim[x_0 \in C(S, R)] \to \exists x_1 \in S\colon \sim(x_0\,R\,x_1)$. Since x_1 cannot belong to $M(S,\ R)$, as that would have implied $x_0\,I\,x_1$, clearly x_1 belongs to its complement $C_M(S, R)$. But this implies that: $\exists x_2 \in S\colon x_2\,P\,x_1$. Yet x_2 cannot belong to $M(S, R)$, since that would have implied $x_0\,I\,x_2$ and thus $x_0\,P\,x_1$. So x_2 belongs to $C_M(S, R)$. By similar reasoning, $\exists x_3 \in S\colon [x_3\,P\,x_2\ \&\ x_3 \in C_M(S, R)]$.

Proceeding this way when there are n alternatives in $C_M(S, R)$, we obtain the last alternative x_n such that $x_n \in C_M(S, R)$ and $x_n\,P\,y$ for all y in $C_M(S, R)$. Furthermore, $\sim(x_0\,P\,x_n)$ since $x_0\,P\,x_n$ would lead, by transitivity of P, to $x_0\,P\,x_1$, which is false. Since all elements of S except x_0 belong, by our demonstration, to $C_M(S, R)$, it now follows that x_n is after all a maximal element. But x_n is supposed to belong to the complement set $C_M(S, R)$. This contradiction establishes one part of the lemma. (Note that the finiteness of S is not necessary for the proof, and only the finiteness of $C_M(S, R)$ is used. Lemma 1*e can, thus, be appropriately generalized.)

The converse is immediate. Let $C(S,\ R) = M(S,\ R)$. Hence $x, y \in M(S, R) \to x, y \in C(S, R)$, so that $x\,R\,y\ \&\ y\,R\,x$, which implies $x\,I\,y$.

1*4. SUBRELATIONS AND COMPATIBILITY

Consider two quasi-orderings Q_1 and Q_2. We now introduce the notion of being a 'subrelation'.

DEFINITION 1*5. *Let Q_1 be a subrelation of Q_2 if and only if for all $x, y \in X$,*

(1) $x \, Q_1 \, y \to x \, Q_2 \, y$
(2) $[x \, Q_1 \, y \ \& \ \sim(y \, Q_1 \, x)] \to \sim(y \, Q_2 \, x)$

That is, whenever x is 'at least as good as' (or, alternatively, 'better than') y according to Q_1, it is so according to Q_2 as well, but not necessarily vice versa.

It is important also to note the concept of compatibility of a quasi-ordering with an ordering.

DEFINITION 1*6. *If Q, a quasi-ordering, is a subrelation of an ordering R, then R is said to be compatible with Q.*

Next, we shall note two standard results without proving them here.

LEMMA 1*f. *For every quasi-ordering Q, there is an ordering R compatible with Q.*[6]

LEMMA 1*g. *If Q is a quasi-ordering such that $\forall x, y \in S \subset X$: $x \, Q \, y \leftrightarrow x = y$, and T is an ordering of elements of S, then there is an ordering R of all elements of X such that R is compatible with both Q and T.*[7]

For any particular application the two lemmas are trivial, but they are not so in their full generality. Lemma 1*g, it may be noted, subsumes Lemma 1*f, and asserts that any quasi-ordering can be completed consistently with an ordering of a subset over which the quasi-ordering in question is incomplete for every pair.

---

[6] See Szpilrajn (1930), pp. 386–9. Szpilrajn is concerned with partial orderings, but the proof for quasi-orderings is similar.
[7] Arrow (1951), pp. 64–8.

We can define the compatibility of two quasi-orderings as follows:

DEFINITION 1*7. *Two quasi-orderings Q_1 and Q_2 are compatible if and only if there is an ordering compatible with each.*

The following results are immediate:

LEMMA 1*h. *If a quasi-ordering Q_1 is a subrelation of a quasi-ordering Q_2, then Q_1 and Q_2 are compatible.*

LEMMA 1*i. *If Q is a quasi-ordering such that $\forall x, y \in S \subset X$: $x \, Q \, y \leftrightarrow x = y$, and T is a quasi-ordering of elements of S, then there is an ordering R of all elements of X such that R is compatible with both Q and T.*

Lemma 1*i is a slight extension of 1*g. By Lemma 1*f, an ordering T^* can be defined over S such that T^* is compatible with T, and by Lemma 1*g there is an ordering R defined over X such that R is compatible with Q and T^*. It is trivial to prove that if R is compatible with T^* over X, and T is a subrelation of T^*, then R is compatible with T. What it does mean, however, is that if we take two quasi-orderings such that each violates completeness for every pair of alternatives for which the other is complete, then they are compatible. In social choice this may be important in permitting the use of a number of independent principles of preference.

1*5. CHOICE FUNCTIONS AND QUASI-TRANSITIVITY

In Section 1*2 we defined a choice set. We can now define a choice function.

DEFINITION 1*8. *A choice function $C(S, R)$ defined over X is a functional relation such that the choice set $C(S, R)$ is non-empty for every non-empty subset S of X.*

To say that there exists a choice function $C(S, R)$ defined over X is thus equivalent to saying that there is a best element in every non-empty subset of X. The existence of a choice function is obviously important for rational choice.

If a preference relation violates completeness, clearly a choice function will not exist. There will be some pair x, y in X, for which neither $x R y$, nor $y R x$, so that the choice set of this pair (x, y) will be empty. Similarly, a violation of reflexivity will make a choice function impossible, since there will then be some alternative x, such that it would not be regarded as good as itself.

If on top of reflexivity and completeness we also assume transitivity, then we get an ordering. Before we consider the possibility of getting a choice function in spite of violating transitivity, an elementary result on orderings is noted.

LEMMA 1*j. *If R is an ordering defined over a finite set X, then a choice function C(S, R) is defined over X.*

The proof is similar to that for Lemma 1*b and is omitted here. When the set X is not finite, the existence of an ordering over X does not, of course, guarantee a choice function; for example, we might have $x_j P x_{j-1}$ for $j = 2, 3, \ldots, \infty$.

While, given reflexivity and completeness, transitivity is a sufficient condition for the existence of a choice function over a finite set, it is not a necessary condition. A weaker sufficiency condition is noted below.

DEFINITION 1*9. *If for all $x, y, z \in X$, $x P y$ & $y P z \rightarrow x P z$, then R is quasi-transitive.*

This condition was earlier referred to as PP, in the context of Lemma 1*a.

LEMMA 1*k. *If R is reflexive, complete and quasi-transitive over a finite set X, then a choice function C(S, R) is defined over X.*[8]

Proof. Let there be n alternatives in $S \subset X$, viz., $x_1, \ldots, x_n$. Consider first the pair (x_1, x_2). By reflexivity and completeness of R, there is a best element in this pair. The proof is now completed by induction

---

[8] See Sen (1969), Theorem II; also Pattanaik (1968a). For infinite sets it is necessary that P be 'founded', i.e., no infinitely long descending chains are permitted. This is one aspect of the concept of well-ordering of Whitehead and Russell (1913). On this and other questions concerning choice functions, see Herzberger (1968).

through showing that if $(x_1, \ldots, x_j)$ has a best element, then so does $(x_1, \ldots, x_j, x_{j+1})$. Let a_j be a best element of the former set, so that $a_j \, R \, x_k$, for $k = 1, \ldots, j$. Either $x_{j+1} \, P \, a_j$, or $a_j \, R \, x_{j+1}$. If the latter, then a_j is a best element of $(x_1, \ldots, x_{j+1})$ as well. If the former, then x_{j+1} can fail to be a best element of $(x_1, \ldots, x_{j+1})$ only if $x_k \, P \, x_{j+1}$ for some $k = 1, \ldots, j$. Then by quasi-transitivity of R, we must have $x_k \, P \, a_j$, which contradicts $a_j \, R \, x_k$. This completes the proof.

It is to be noted that while quasi-transitivity is sufficient, it is not necessary for a choice function to exist for a finite set. Indeed it can be shown that no condition defined over only triples can be necessary for the existence of choice functions. The property of *acyclicity* may now be introduced.

DEFINITION 1*10. *R is acyclical over X if and only if the following holds:*

$$\forall x_1, \ldots, x_j \in X: [\{x_1 \, P \, x_2 \; \& \; x_2 \, P \, x_3 \; \& \; \ldots \; \& \; x_{j-1} \, P \, x_j\} \to x_1 \, R \, x_j]$$

LEMMA 1*l. *If R is reflexive and complete, then a necessary and sufficient condition for C(S, R) to be defined over a finite X is that R be acyclical over X.*

Proof. First the proof of necessity. Suppose R is not acyclical. Then there is some subset of j alternatives in X such that $x_1 \, P \, x_2, \ldots,$ $x_{j-1} \, P \, x_j, x_j \, P \, x_1$. Clearly there is no best element in this subset, so that a choice function does not exist over X. The proof of sufficiency can begin with noting that if all the alternatives are indifferent to each other then they are all best, so that we need be concerned only with cases where there is at least one strictly ordered pair, say, $x_2 \, P \, x_1$. Now, x_2 can fail to be the best element of S only if there is some element, say x_3, in X such that $x_3 \, P \, x_2$. If $x_1 \, P \, x_3$, then by acyclicity $x_1 \, R \, x_2$, which is a contradiction. Thus, x_3 is a best element of (x_1, x_2, x_3). Proceeding this way we can exhaust all the elements of S without the choice set becoming empty. So acyclicity is necessary and sufficient.

It may be noted that acyclicity over triples only, i.e., $\forall x, y, z \in X: [x \, P \, y \; \& \; y \, P \, z \to x \, R \, z]$, is not a sufficient condition for the existence of a choice function, for acyclicity over triples does not imply acyclicity over the whole set. Consider, for example, the set of four alternatives x_1, x_2, x_3, x_4, such that $x_1 \, P \, x_2, \, x_2 \, P \, x_3, \, x_3 \, P \, x_4, \, x_4 \, P \, x_1$, $x_1 \, I \, x_3$ and $x_2 \, I \, x_4$. No triple violates acyclicity, but the whole set violates it, and there is no best element in the whole set.

Finally, it follows from Lemma 1*k and 1*l that quasi-transitivity, which is a condition on triples, does imply acyclicity. The converse, however, does not follow.

1*6. PREFERENCE AND RATIONAL CHOICE

The existence of a choice function is in some ways a condition of rational choice. A choice function has been defined here on the basis of a binary preference relation, so that the existence of a non-empty choice set is equivalent to the existence of some alternative which is regarded as at least as good as every other one in the set. This is itself a rationality property, noted in the context of majority rule by Condorcet as early as 1785.

We can, however, also define certain rationality conditions in terms of the properties of the choice function (see Arrow (1959)). For this purpose we take $C(S)$ as any choice function defined over some X, not necessarily derived with respect to some binary preference relation. It is, of course, easy to consider choice functions that cannot possibly be derived from any binary relation, e.g., $C([x, y, z]) = [x]$, and $C([x, y]) = [y]$. To guarantee that not only can we choose, but we can choose rationally, certain properties of the choice function may have to be specified. We consider (see Sen (1969)):

Property α: $x \in S_1 \subset S_2 \rightarrow [x \in C(S_2) \rightarrow x \in C(S_1)]$, for all x

Property β: $[x, y \in C(S_1) \, \& \, S_1 \subset S_2] \rightarrow [x \in C(S_2) \leftrightarrow y \in C(S_2)]$, for all x, y.

Property α states that if some element of subset S_1 of S_2 is best in S_2, then it is best in S_1. This is a very basic requirement of rational choice, and in a different context has been called the condition of 'the independence of irrelevant alternatives'.[9] Property β is also appealing, though it is perhaps somewhat less intuitive than property α. It requires that if x and y are both best in S_1, a subset of S_2, then one of them cannot be best in S_2 without the other being also best in S_2. To give an example, property α states that if the world champion in some game is a Pakistani, then he must also be the champion in Pakistan, while property β states that if some Pakistani champion is a world champion, then *all* champions of Pakistan must be champions of the world.

The remainder of this chapter leans heavily on Sen (1969).

LEMMA 1*m. *Every choice function $C(S, R)$ generated by a binary relation R satisfies property α but not necessarily property β.*

Proof. If x belongs to $C(S, R)$, clearly $x \, R \, y$ for all y in S and therefore $x \, R \, y$ for all y in any subset of S. Hence property α is satisfied.

Now consider a triple, x, y, z such that $x \, I \, y$, $x \, P \, z$, and $z \, P \, y$. It is clear that $[x, y] = C([x, y], R)$, and $[x] = C([x, y, z], R)$. This violates property β.

There seems to be a close relationship between a choice function fulfilling property β and the underlying preference relation satisfying condition PI, which was mentioned in the context of Lemma 1*a.

DEFINITION 1*11. *Relation R is PI-transitive over X if and only if for all x, y, z in X, $x \, P \, y$ & $y \, I \, z \rightarrow x \, P \, z$.*

LEMMA 1*n. *A choice function $C(S, R)$ generated by a binary relation R satisfies property β if and only if R is PI-transitive.*[10]

Proof. It has been noted earlier that a binary relation must be complete and reflexive to generate a choice function. New suppose that PI is violated. Then there is a triple x, y, z such that $x \, P \, y$, $y \, I \, z$ and $z \, R \, x$. Obviously $[y, z] = C([y, z]), R)$. Further, $z \in C([x, y, z], R)$, but $\sim[y \in C([x, y, z], R)]$. Thus property β is violated.

---

[9] See Nash (1950), Chernoff (1954), Radner and Marschak (1954), and Luce and Raiffa (1957). This condition should not, however, be confused with Arrow's (1951) condition of the same name, which is a condition on the functional relationship between social preference and individual preferences; see Chapter 3*.
[10] Sen (1969), Theorem III.

Conversely, suppose that property β is violated. Then we have a pair x, y such that x, $y \in C(S_1, R)$, $x \in C(S_2, R)$ and $\sim[\, y \in C(S_2, R)]$ when $S_1 \subset S_2$. Clearly, there exists some z in S_2 such that $z\,P\,y\ \&\ x\,R\,z$. We know that $x\,I\,y$, since x, $y \in C(S_1, R)$. Now, $z\,P\,y\ \&\ y\,I\,x \to z\,P\,x$, by PI-transitivity. But we know that $x\,R\,z$. Hence R cannot possibly satisfy PI. This completes the proof of the lemma.

What is the precise interrelationship between PP (quasi-transitivity), PI, and transitivity?

LEMMA 1*o.   (a) *In general, PP and PI are completely independent of each other.*

(b) *Together, PP and PI imply transitivity, given completeness of R.*

Proof.   Statement (a) is proved by considering two examples. Consider $x\,P\,y$, $y\,P\,z$ and $z\,P\,x$. This violates PP, but not PI. Next, consider $x\,P\,y$, $y\,I\,z$ and $x\,I\,z$. This violates PI, but not PP.

Statement (b) is proved by making the contrary supposition that PI and PP hold, but transitivity does not. Then for some triple x, y, z we must have $x\,R\,y$, $y\,R\,z$ and $\sim(x\,R\,z)$, i.e., $z\,P\,x$, by the completeness of R. Now, $x\,R\,y$ implies $x\,P\,y \lor x\,I\,y$. Suppose $x\,P\,y$. Then from $z\,P\,x$ and by virtue of PP we must have $z\,P\,y$. But this is false. Therefore $x\,I\,y$. Then from $z\,P\,x$ and by virtue of PI we must have $z\,P\,y$, which is the same false statement. This contradiction establishes the result, and this completes the proof of the lemma.

However, if R must generate a choice function, then there is a close relationship between PI and PP, viz., PI implies PP (though the converse does not hold). Thus, PI is then equivalent to full transitivity.

LEMMA 1*p.   *If a binary relation R generates a choice function, then PI-transitivity implies that R is an ordering.*[11]

Proof.   Reflexivity and completeness of R are trivial. By Lemma 1*o we need only show that PI implies PP.

Suppose PP is violated. Then there is a triple x, y, z such that $x\,P\,y$, $y\,P\,z$ and $z\,R\,x$. If $z\,P\,x$, then $C([x, y, z], R)$ will be empty. Hence $z\,I\,x$ holds. But $[y\,P\,z\ \&\ z\,I\,x] \to y\,P\,x$, by PI. We know,

---

[11] Sen (1969), Theorem IV.

however, that $x \, P \, y$. Thus PI must also be violated. Thus PI implies PP, so that PI also implies that R is an ordering (in view of Lemma 1*o), which completes the proof.

From Lemma 1*n and 1*p we immediately obtain the following result as a corollary:

LEMMA 1*q.   *A choice function $C(S, R)$ derived from a binary relation R satisfies property β if and only if R is an ordering.*[12]

To extend the picture on the different aspects of transitivity, we also note some further entailment relations which hold whether or not a choice function exists.

LEMMA 1*r.   *If R is complete, then (a) $PI \leftrightarrow IP$; (b) $PI \rightarrow II$; and (c) PP & $II \rightarrow PI$.*

The proofs are omitted here, but for (*a*) can be found in Sonnenschein (1965) and Lorimer (1967), and for (*b*) and (*c*) are given in Sen (1969). They are all straightforward.[13]

Finally, we show in the form of two diagrams the main relations between PP, PI, II, IP, and transitivity T of R, the existence of $C(S, R)$ over a finite S, and the fulfilment of the rationality conditions α and β. The direction of the arrow represents the direction of implication. In Diagram 1*2, the implications within the box hold if the choice function $C(S, R)$ exists.

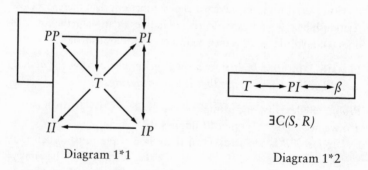

Diagram 1*1

Diagram 1*2

---

[12] Sen (1969). See also Arrow (1959).

[13] Some important results on preference and choice, which we do not go into here, will be found in Herzberger (1968) and Hansson (1969).

Chapter 2
Unanimity

2.1. THE PARETO CRITERION

A very simple criterion of comparison of social welfare is associated with the name of Pareto (Pareto (1897)). In this approach the two following rules are used: (a) if everyone in the society is indifferent between two alternative social situations x and y, then the society should be indifferent too; and (b) if at least one individual strictly prefers x to y, and every individual regards x to be at least as good as y, then the society should prefer x to y. This criterion has an obvious appeal. When (a) is satisfied, it does not matter for anyone which of the two alternatives is chosen by the society; hence it is safe to choose either. When (b) is satisfied, it is in no one's interest to be at y rather than at x, and it is in someone's interest to be at x rather than at y; hence it seems reasonable to say that the society, as an aggregate of the individuals, does prefer x to y.

To get our terminology unambiguous, when (a) is fulfilled we shall say that the society is Pareto-wise indifferent between x and y, and when (b) is fulfilled that x is Pareto-wise better than y. We can now consider the concept of *Pareto-optimality*. In a given choice situation, consider the set of alternatives X from which choice would have to be made. An alternative x belonging to that set will be described as Pareto-optimal if there is no other alternative in the set which is Pareto-wise better than x. That is, x is Pareto-optimal if we cannot choose an alternative that everyone will regard to be at least as good as x and which at least one person will regard to be strictly better than x.

A great deal of modern welfare economics has been based on this approach. The 'optimality' of a system or of a policy is often judged in terms of whether it achieves Pareto-optimality or not.[1] This may seem alright as far as it goes, but how far does it go? If one individual prefers x to y, and another prefers y to x, then we cannot compare them socially using the Pareto rule no matter how the rest of them evaluate x vis-a-vis y and no matter how many of them there are. It is clear that the social preference relation derived from the Pareto criterion, while reflexive and transitive (given that each individual has a quasi-ordering), may not have the property of completeness, even when all the individuals constituting the society have complete preference orderings. Precisely how incomplete the Pareto criterion will be depends on how unanimous the individuals are. On the one extreme lies the case in which everyone has the same preference ordering,[2] when the social ordering will in fact be, for this special case, complete. At the other end lies the case in which two individuals have strictly opposite preferences,[3] when no alternatives whatever could be compared with each other by using the Pareto rule. Neither extreme may be common, and in an intermediate case some comparisons can be made by using the Pareto rule, but not all. How many comparisons can be made will depend on the precise circumstances.

In the difficult field of welfare economics even small mercies count, so there is much to commend in the Pareto criterion, in spite of its incompleteness. But there is a danger in being exclusively concerned with Pareto-optimality. An economy can be optimal in this sense even when some people are rolling in luxury and others are near starvation as long as the starvers cannot be made better off without cutting into the pleasures of the rich. If preventing the

---

[1] See the literature on the optimality of competitive equilibrium, e.g., Arrow (1951a), Debreu (1959).

[2] It does not have to be strictly the same, as long as whenever x is preferred to y by some individual, all others regard x to be at least as good as y.

[3] More explicitly, of the two individuals each has a strong ordering over the entire range of alternatives, and whenever one prefers one alternative to an entire range of alternatives, and whenever one prefers one alternative to another, the other individuals prefer the latter to the former.

burning of Rome would have made Emperor Nero feel worse off, then letting him burn Rome would have been Pareto-optimal. In short, a society or an economy can be Pareto-optimal and still be perfectly disgusting.

2.2 PARETO-INCLUSIVE CHOICE RULES

We shall call methods of going from individual orderings to social preference 'collective choice rules' (CCR). For example, the 'method of majority decision' (MMD) is one such CCR whereby x is declared as socially at least as good as y if and only if at least as many people prefer x to y as prefer y to x. The MMD often yields intransitive social preference, but it is always 'decisive' over every pair in the sense that it yields complete preference orderings, i.e., either x is socially at least as good as y, or y is socially at least as good as x. The Pareto criterion, taken on its own, also generates a CCR, but it is not pair-wise decisive, because of the possible incompleteness of the Pareto relation. The Pareto-optimal elements are not ranked vis-a-vis each other.

A CCR that subsumes the Pareto relation, but possibly goes beyond it, will be called a Pareto-inclusive CCR. The MMD is a Pareto-inclusive CCR. If x is Pareto-superior to y, then x must strictly win over y in a majority vote, but x and y may be Pareto-wise incomparable and still one of the two will win over the other (or the two will tie, indicating social indifference) in a majority vote. If the Pareto criterion is found to be compelling, then our interest should focus on Pareto-inclusive CCRs.

One way of gelling a 'best' alternative specified from a Pareto-optimal set with more than one element is to order the Pareto-optimal alternatives. We may wish, for example, to take note of considerations of income distribution,[4] since the Pareto criterion is efficiency-oriented and neutral between income distributions. There are difficulties in this, some of which we shall discuss later on.

[4] See Fisher (1956) and Kenen and Fisher (1957).

A particularly simple way of extending the Pareto relation is to declare all Pareto-optimal points as indifferent. This will amount to a deliberate exclusion of distributional considerations. I cannot believe that this will appeal to many people, but I do not doubt that it might appeal to some, if the almost exclusive concern with the Pareto relation in modern welfare economics is any indication. We shall have the occasion to examine it more closely in Chapters 5 and 5*.

It is also possible to have CCRs that are not 'decisive', but which generate preference relations that are more extensive than the Pareto relation and subsume it. This can be seen in certain criteria of aggregate welfare (Chapters 7 and 7*), of bargaining solutions (Chapters 8 and 8*), and of justice (Chapters 9 and 9*). It is fair to say that most CCRs that are usually considered are Pareto-inclusive, at least in a weaker form.

In the weaker form of the Pareto principle, x may be declared as socially better than y, if *everyone* strictly prefers x to y. This criterion says less than the usual Pareto criterion since nothing is stated about a case where someone prefers x to y and everyone regards x to be at least as good as y.

If x is Pareto-superior to y in this more demanding sense, it will be difficult to argue that x should not be socially preferred to y. If everyone in the society wants x rather than y, in which sense can society prefer y to x, or even be indifferent or undecided?[5] This is a fairly compelling argument, but I would doubt that it is altogether unexceptionable. If the choice between a pair of alternatives must be based exclusively on individual preferences over that pair only, then the problem looks simple enough. But if one thinks of a CCR such that the social choice over x and y depends also on individual preferences over other pairs (e.g., x and z, and y and z), then the picture is not that clear. It is perhaps too complicated an argument to go into without some further study of collective choice rules, and we postpone a discussion on this until Chapter 6. For the moment we shall take the Pareto criterion as compelling. The fact

[5] Cf. Cassen (1967).

remains, however, that it is severely incomplete and something more is needed.

2.3. CONSENSUS AS A BASIS OF COLLECTIVE ACTION

In spite of this incompleteness of the Pareto quasi-ordering, arguments have been put forward in recent years in favour of exclusive reliance on general consensus or unanimity as a basis of social action. Buchanan and Tullock (1962), in particular, have produced a very painstaking analysis of the consequences of such an approach, which they have contrasted favorably with other approaches. Departures from the unanimity rule are tolerated by them only when it is too expensive to reach decisions unanimously.

> The individualistic theory of the constitution we have been able to develop assigns a central role to a single decision-making rule – that of general consensus or unanimity. The other possible rules for choice-making are introduced as variants from the unanimity rule. These variants will be rationally chosen, not because they will produce 'better' collective decisions (they will not), but rather because on balance, the sheer weight of the costs involved in reaching decisions unanimously dictates some departure from the 'ideal' rule. (Buchanan and Tullock (1962), p. 96)

When there is a unanimity of views on some issue, clearly this provides a very satisfactory basis for choice. Difficulties in social choice arise precisely because unanimity does not exist on many questions. What do we do then? One answer is to insist on unanimity for a *change*, and if there is no such unanimity for any proposed change, then to stick to the *status quo*. The rule for social choice then can be summed up thus: Given that some prefer an alternative x to the status quo y and no one regards x to be worse than y, x is socially preferred to y; and when this condition is not satisfied the status quo y is preferred to the other alternative x.

This method is one of supreme conservatism. Even a single person opposing a change can block it altogether no matter what everybody else wants.[6] Marie Antoinette's opposition to the First Republic would have saved the monarchy in France, and the world would have seen very little change. Clearly there is something grotesquely unsatisfactory about a social decision rule like this.

It has been argued by Buchanan and Tullock that 'modern political theorists have perhaps shrugged off the unanimity requirement too early in their thinking' (Buchanan and Tullock (1962), p. 250) and that 'the existence of conflicts of interest does not preclude the attainment of unanimity' (p. 255). It is certainly true that even when unanimity of views does not exist to start with, discussions and bargaining may eventually bring it about. It is also true that this process of compromises and 'trades' among themselves is essentially 'equivalent to the logrolling process'.[7] I can eschew my mild opposition to your proposal in return for your support for mine about which I feel more strongly. Indeed, unanimity can emerge when none existed to start with.

This is a valuable point, and a theory of collective choice must take into account such compromises. Two explanatory observations are, however, worth making in this context. First, a collective choice rule, as we have envisaged it, is based on individual orderings over complete descriptions of social states x, y, etc., which represent all possible combinations of decisions on separate issues, and this

---

[6] Buchanan and Tullock (1962) refers to the 'paradoxical result *that the rule of unanimity is the same as the minority rule of one*' (p. 259). But they point out the important logical distinction between the power of 'taking action' and that of 'blocking action', and it is for the latter that unanimity gives such power to each. What is, however, doubtful is Buchanan and Tullock's statement that this distinction 'represents the difference between the power *to impose external costs on others* and the power *to prevent external costs from* being imposed' (p. 259). It depends much on what kind of action is involved. Buchanan and Tullock discuss cases of compulsory contribution, e.g. for road repair. However, if an antipollution move is lost for lack of unanimous support, one individual (e.g., the owner of a smokey factory) will be exercising power to impose an *external* cost on others.

[7] Buchanan and Tullock (1962), p. 255. See Chapter 10 of their book for an illuminating discussion of this process. See also Wilson (1968a), (1968b), (1968c).

includes logrolling compromises. What the Buchanan-Tullock argument points out is that over some choices involving such compromises unanimity might exist even though there are conflicts of interests in separate issues. This does not, of course, mean that the individual orderings must be, in general, largely unanimous.[8]

Second, it could not be overemphasized that what compromises people are ready to accept depends much on their own assessment of their relative bargaining power. The fact that all members of a community come to accept a certain social situation does not necessarily mean that it is unanimously preferred to other social alternatives. A labourer in a monopsonistic labour market may accept certain terms of agreement feeling that he cannot hope to get anything better, but this does not mean that it is unanimously preferred to an alternative set of terms. This is a simple enough point but it does indicate that the general acceptance of a compromise solution should not be interpreted as universal endorsement. In Chapters 8 and 8* bargaining solutions will be examined in the light of the requirements of an ethical model.

It is, however, interesting to enquire into implications of taking Pareto-incompleteness as equivalent to social indifference. We shall do this in Chapter 5, and we shall present in Chapter 5* a set of axioms that are necessary and sufficient for this rather arbitrary rule.

---

[8] In the context of the 'impossibility theorem' of Arrow, to be discussed in the next chapter, Buchanan and Tullock have asserted that when 'votes are traded', 'the particular type of irrationality described by Arrow is impossible' (Buchanan and Tullock (1962), p. 332; also footnote 14, p. 359). This seems to be based on a misinterpretation of the nature of the alternatives over which the individual preferences are defined. On this question, see Arrow (1963), p. 109.

Chapter 2*
Collective Choice Rules and
Pareto Comparisons

2*1. CHOICE AND PARETO RELATION

Let X be the set of social states. The preference relation of the ith individual is R_i, and let there be n such person, $i = 1, \ldots, n$. Let R refer to the social preference relation. We assume that each individual has an ordering, i.e., for each i, R_i is reflexive, transitive, and complete. For the relation of social preference R, no such assumption is easy to make, and indeed it is part of our exercise to see whether R will have these characteristics or not. We do not, therefore, demand at this stage[1] that R must be an ordering.

DEFINITION 2*1. *A collective choice rule is a functional relation f such that for any set of n individual orderings $R_1, \ldots, R_n$ (one ordering for each individual), one and only one social preference relation R is determined, $R = f(R_1, \ldots, R_n)$.*

DEFINITION 2*2. *A collective choice rule is decisive if and only if its range is restricted to complete preference relations R.*

We now define Pareto preference $(\bar{P})$, indifference $(\bar{I})$, and preference or indifference $(\bar{R})$.

DEFINITION 2*3. *For all x, y in X*

(1) $x \bar{R} y \leftrightarrow [\forall i : x R_i y]$
(2) $x \bar{P} y \leftrightarrow [x \bar{R} y \& \sim(y \bar{R} x)]$

---

[1] In Chapter 3* we shall examine the particular case when R is required to be an ordering, which corresponds to Arrow's 'social welfare function'.

(3) $x \bar{I} y \leftrightarrow [x \bar{R} y \ \& \ y \bar{R} x]$

We can derive a collective choice rule from the Pareto relation by requiring that $x \bar{R} y \leftrightarrow x R y$. We can, alternatively, merely require that $x \bar{R} y \to x R y$, or that $x \bar{P} y \to x P y$, or that $x \bar{I} y \to x I y$, without the converse implication. This will be a *condition* on a collective choice rule, rather than a rule itself.

It is easy to check that $\bar{R}$ must be a quasi-ordering.

LEMMA 2*a.   *Relation $\bar{R}$ is a quasi-ordering for every logically possible combination of individual preferences.*

Proof.   Since $\forall x \in X: x R_i x$, $\bar{R}$ is reflexive. Further,

$$\forall x, y, z \in X: [x \bar{R} y \ \& \ y \bar{R} z] \to \forall i: [x R_i y \ \& \ y R_i z]$$
$$\to \forall i: x R_i z$$
$$\to x \bar{R} z$$

Relation $\bar{R}$ is not necessarily an ordering, for it may violate completeness. When will $\bar{R}$ be an ordering?

LEMMA 2*b.   *A necessary and sufficient condition for $\bar{R}$ to be an ordering and for $R = \bar{R}$ to be a decisive collective choice rule is that*

$$\forall x, y \in X: [(\exists i: x P_i y) \to (\forall j: \ x R_j y)]$$

Proof.   For any pair x, y, if $x I_i y$ for all i, then the condition is trivially fulfilled, and also $x \bar{I} y$. If, on the other hand, $\exists i: x P_i y$, then $\forall j: x R_j y$, and hence $x \bar{R} y$. On the other hand, if the condition is violated, then $\exists i: x P_i y \ \& \ \exists j: y P_j x$, and $\sim(x \bar{R} y) \ \& \ \sim(y \bar{R} x)$ and completeness is violated. Thus the condition is sufficient *and* necessary.

We can define a weaker version of the strict Pareto relation.

DEFINITION 2*4.   *For all x, y in X*

$$x \bar{\bar{P}} y \leftrightarrow \forall i: x P_i y$$

We note, without proofs, two results. The proofs are obvious.

LEMMA 2*c.   *Both $\bar{P}$ and $\bar{\bar{P}}$ are strict partial orderings (transitive and asymmetric) for every logically possible combination of individual preferences.*

LEMMA 2*d. $\forall x, y \in X: x \, \overline{\overline{P}} \, y \rightarrow x \, \overline{P} \, y$

To assume that $x \, P \, y \leftrightarrow x \, \overline{\overline{P}} \, y$ for all x, y, does not define a collective choice rule. This is because $\sim(x \, \overline{\overline{P}} \, y)$ leaves it undecided as to whether $y \, R \, x$. We know that $x \, P \, y \leftrightarrow [x \, R \, y \, \& \, \sim(y \, R \, x)]$, so that $\sim(x \, P \, y)$ can coexist with incompleteness, i.e., $\sim(x \, R \, y) \, \& \, \sim(y \, R \, x)$, or, with indifference, $x \, I \, y$. We can assume that $x \, R \, y \leftrightarrow x \, \overline{\overline{P}} \, y$, or $x \, R \, y \leftrightarrow \sim(x \, \overline{\overline{P}} \, y)$, or something in between. These are collective choice rules, and note that in the first case R may be incomplete, while in the second case it must be complete.

We can make similar observations about $\overline{P}$, and similarly consider $x \, R \, y \leftrightarrow x \, \overline{P} \, y$, or $x \, R \, y \leftrightarrow \sim(y \, \overline{P} \, x)$, or something else. Once again R under the first may violate completeness, while R under the second cannot.

Traditional welfare economics has been essentially 'Paretian' in the sense of taking $x \, R \, y$ whenever $x \, \overline{R} \, y$ and $x \, P \, y$ whenever $x \, \overline{P} \, y$. We can call the class of collective choice rules satisfying these conditions Pareto-inclusive choice rules.

DEFINITION 2*5.   *A collective choice rule is Pareto-inclusive if and only if its range is restricted to social preference relations R such that the Pareto relations $\overline{R}$ is a subrelation of R, i.e.,*

$$\forall x, y \in X: [(x \, \overline{R} \, y \rightarrow x \, R \, y) \, \& \, (x \, \overline{P} \, y \rightarrow x \, P \, y)]$$

Social states are Pareto-optimal if they are not Pareto-inferior to any other alternative in S.

DEFINITION 2*6.   *For any n-tuple of individual preferences $(R_1, \ldots, R_n)$, a state $x \in S$ is Pareto-optimal in S if and only if $\sim[\exists y \in S: y \, \overline{P} \, x]$. A Pareto-optimal state is also called economically efficient.*

LEMMA 2*e.   *For every set of individual preferences $(R_1, \ldots, R_n)$ over any finite set of social states S, there is at least one Pareto-optimal state.*

Proof.   By Lemma 2*a, the Pareto preference relation $\overline{R}$ is a quasi-ordering. And the Pareto-optimal subset is merely the maximal set of S with respect to $\overline{R}$, i.e., $M(S, \overline{R})$, as defined in Chapter 1*.

By Lemma 1*b, $M(S, R)$ must be non-empty when S is finite and R is a quasi-ordering.

2*2. COMPENSATION TESTS

We turn now to a set of attempts at extending the Pareto rule in the form of 'compensation tests'. Let $S(x)$ be all the social states that can be reached through redistribution starting from x. Of course, $x \in S(x)$. The compensation test as developed by Kaldor (1939) declares x to be superior to y if and only if we can reach a state z through redistribution from x such that $z\,P\,y$ according to the Pareto criterion, i.e., if there is a move from y to x the gainers can compensate the losers and still retain some gain.

DEFINITION 2*7. *According to the Kaldor compensation test for any $x, y \in X$:*

$$[x\,P\,y] \leftrightarrow \exists z: [z \in S(x)\ \&\ \forall i: z\,R_i\,y\ \&\ \exists i: z\,P_i\,y]$$

This subsumes the strict preference relation generated by the Pareto criterion in the sense that if $x\,\bar{P}\,y$, then x is better than y in terms of the Kaldor criterion. This is obvious since $x \in S(x)$. We may note, now, a sad result, first demonstrated by Scitovsky (1941).

LEMMA 2*f. *The Kaldor test is inconsistent with every possible CCR under some configuration of preferences.*

Proof. This follows from the fact that we may have $x\,P\,y$ and $y\,P\,x$ according to the Kaldor test. Take $x, y \in X$ such that $\exists z \in S(x): z\,\bar{P}\,y$, according to the Pareto criterion, and $\exists w \in S(y): w\,\bar{P}\,x$, according to the Pareto criterion.[2] The inconsistency is immediate.

This inconsistency is eliminated by the Scitovsky compensation test.

---

[2] For the factual plausibility of this inconsistency, see Scitovsky (1941) and Little (1950).

DEFINITION 2*8. *According to the Scitovsky compensation test, for any $x, y \in X$: $x \, P \, y$ if and only if $x \, P \, y$ & $\sim(y \, P \, x)$ according to the Kaldor compensation test.*

However, the preference relation generated by the Scitovsky compensation test may not be transitive, nor even quasi-transitive (see Gorman (1955)).

LEMMA 2*g. *The Scitovsky compensation test may yield an intransitive P.*

Proof. It is readily checked that there is no contradiction in assuming that for some $x, y, z \in X$:

(1) $[\exists x' \in S(x): x' \, \bar{P} \, y]$ & $\sim[\exists y' \in S(y): y' \, \bar{P} \, x]$
(2) $[\exists y' \in S(y): y' \, \bar{P} \, z]$ & $\sim[\exists z' \in S(z): z' \, \bar{P} \, y]$
(3) $\sim[\exists x' \in S(x): x' \, \bar{P} \, z]$

Clearly, $x \, P \, y$, $y \, P \, z$, but not $x \, P \, z$, according to the Scitovsky test.

A sufficient condition for the transitivity of P under the Scitovsky test is given below.[3]

LEMMA 2*h. *If for all x, y in X*

$$[\exists x' \in S(x): x' \, \bar{P} \, y] \to \forall y' \in S(y): [\exists x'' \in S(x): x'' \, \bar{R} \, y']$$

then P, under the Scitovsky test, is a strict partial ordering.

Proof. For any triple $x, y, z \in X$,

$$x \, P \, y \ \& \ y \, P \, z \to \exists x' \in S(x): x' \, \bar{P} \, y \ \& \ \exists y' \in S(y): y' \, \bar{P} \, z$$
$$\to \exists x'' \in S(x): x'' \, \bar{R} \, y' \ \& \ y' \, \bar{P} \, z$$

by assumption,

$$\to \exists x'' \in S(x): x'' \, \bar{P} \, z$$

Hence $x \, P \, z$, unless $\exists z' \in S(z): z' \, \bar{P} \, x$. But this assumption, if true, will imply that $\exists z'' \in S(z): z'' \, \bar{R} \, x' \ \& \ x' \, \bar{P} \, y$. But we know that

---

[3] Cf. Samuelson (1950b). Samuelson is not concerned with transitivity as such, but his condition of a complete outward movement of the 'utility possibility frontier' is, in fact, sufficient for transitivity of strict preference.

$\sim[\exists z'' \in S(z): z'' \, \overline{P} \, y]$, since $y \, P \, z$, according to the Scitovsky test. This contradiction establishes $x \, P \, z$, and hence the lemma.

In fact, with the quoted assumption, the Kaldor preference relation and the Scitovsky preference relation are identical, since $x \, P \, y \rightarrow \sim(y \, P \, x)$ in the Kaldor test. The Kaldor test is perfectly consistent in this particular case.

Chapter 3
Collective Rationality

3.1. THE BERGSON-SAMUELSON WELFARE FUNCTION

A rational and systematic way of thinking about social welfare is to try to define an ordering for the society over all possible alternative states. This fundamental idea, among others, was expressed in a seminal paper by Bergson (1938), though he put it somewhat differently. Social welfare can be thought to be a real-valued welfare function, W, 'the value of which is understood to depend on all the variables that might be considered as affecting welfare' (Bergson (1948), p. 417). Such a social welfare function W may subsume the Pareto relation, if Pareto catches our fancy, though there is no real compulsion to assume even this. It can be defined in many alternative ways using many alternative criteria. The approach is very general (see Samuelson (1947), Chap. 8).

As an example of the use of this approach, we can refer to the literature on 'social indifference curves'. Using the Pareto indifference rule, one way of defining social indifference is that everyone in the society be indifferent. Scitovsky was concerned with this problem in a classic paper (1942) and required two alternative bundles of commodities to belong to the same social indifference curve if and only if everyone were indifferent between the two bundles for some distribution of each over the individuals. This concept can be extended by using the Bergson social welfare function. While person 1 may be better off in x than in y, and person 2 may be better off in y than in x, society might still be indifferent if the overall social judgment is that the gain of one exactly compensates the loss of another. Samuelson (1956), Graaff (1957), and others have analysed the difference between keeping social walfare constant in the sense of Scitovsky and doing so in the sense of Bergson. If the Bergson social welfare function is Pareto-inclusive, as it is generally assumed to be, then social indifference in the sense of Scitovsky implies *that* in the sense of Bergson, but not vice versa. This corresponds to the statement that the Pareto quasi-ordering is subsumed by a Pareto-inclusive social ordering (see Chapter 2*).

The concept of a Bergson welfare function is simple, perhaps deceptively so, and some observations in clarification may be called for. First, the *form* of the welfare function is not yet specified, and only a framework of rational thought is suggested. If nothing more were to be said than the conception of a Bergson welfare function, we would not have gone much further.[1] 'Specific decisions on ends' (Bergson (1948), p. 417) have to be systematically introduced, thereby specifying the characteristics of the relation, and this is where difficulties are likely to be experienced.[2]

Second, nothing whatever is said in this analysis as to *who* provides the ends represented by the social welfare function. It may represent the views of an ethical observer, or the decisions of a consistent majority, or the dictates of an oligarchy, or the whims of a dictator, or the values of a class, or even be given simply by tradition. Nothing is specified about the genesis of the social ordering.

Finally, on a rather technical point, the particular method of representation chosen is unnecessarily restrictive. For the purpose of being able to choose between alternative social states, it is not really necessary that a real-valued W function must exist. What is needed is a complete social ordering R over all possible alternatives,[3] and

---

[1] See Samuelson (1947), p. 222:

> The subject could end with these banalities were it not for the fact that numerous individuals find it of interest to specify the form of W, the nature of the variables, z, and the nature of the constraints.

[2] See, for example, Graaff (1957) on the relevance of the convexity of 'Bergson frontiers' in the context of the theory of index numbers.

[3] What is really needed for choice is not even an ordering, but a preference relation that specifies a 'best' alternative in every choice situation. We discussed this in Chapter 1 and we shall go into it more deeply in Chapter 4.

this can exist without there being any real-valued welfare function corresponding to it.[4] For example, a complete 'lexicographic ordering' over a two-dimensional real space cannot be represented by any real welfare function.

A simple example of a lexicographic ordering is the following: Let the welfare levels of two persons be represented respectively by W_1 and W_2, and let it be decided that the social objective is: (a) maximize W_1, and (b) given the same value of W_1, maximize W_2. Suppose W_1 and W_2 can each take any value in the range 0 to 1, and the object is to represent social welfare W as a real-valued function of W_1 and W_2 representing the lexicographic ordering specified. No such representation is possible.[5] There is a perfectly fine social ordering R, but there is no social welfare function in this case as defined by Bergson. I do not believe, however, that we would do any injustice to Bergson's and Samuelson's ideas if we simply take R as a social welfare function rather than taking its real-valued representation W.[6]

3.2. ARROVIAN SOCIAL WELFARE FUNCTION

The concept of a social welfare function W as proposed by Bergson (1938) and developed by Samuelson (1947) cleared up several barriers to rational thought on social choice. It was an important step in the history of welfare economics ending a rather confused debate begun by Robbins' (1932) celebrated attack on utilitarianism. In extending this idea, Arrow (1951) asked the question: What should determine the particular Bergson social welfare function to be used? In particular, how

[4] If risk is present, the ordering referred to should be over all possible 'lotteries', and not merely over the certain alternatives.
[5] See Debreu (1959). See also Little (1949a), Chipman (1960), Banerjee (1964) and Richter (1966).
[6] Bergson and Samuelson were writing at a time when it was common to assume that all orderings were representable by a utility function. Compare Hicks' (1939b) concern with 'ordinal utility' rather than with orderings. Samuelson himself was a pioneer in bringing about the change of approach.

would the function W (or more generally the social ordering R) depend on individual preference orderings? Or, in other words, what should be the collective choice rule (as we defined it in the last chapter)?

Before we proceed further, two warning notes are due. First, Arrow's use of the expression social welfare function is different from that of Bergson and Samuelson.[7] A collective choice rule that specifies *orderings* for the society is called a social welfare function (hereafter, SWF) by Arrow. Any ordering for the society (more accurately, its real-valued representation) is a Bergson-Samuelson social welfare function (hereafter, swf). An Arrow SWF determines a Bergson swf (or the ordering R underlying it) on the basis of individual orderings. The relation between the two is simple enough, but the two are not the same, and the terminology has been responsible for some confusion. Since our chief concern is with exercises of the kind that Arrow considered, we shall use the unqualified term social welfare function in his sense, but it is merely a matter of convenience and we resist the temptation to go into the semantic suitability of one use vis-a-vis the other.

Second, Arrow's SWF is a particular type of collective choice rule such that each social preference that is determined is an ordering, i.e., reflexive, transitive and complete. While Arrow is exclusively concerned with SWFs, some of the problems with which Arrow is involved apply more generally to all CCRs. There are, however, others (including the famous 'impossibility theorem') which are specific to SWFs only.

While from the point of view of logic an SWF or a CCR can be defined in any consistent way we like, consistency is not the sole virtue that a collective choice mechanism has to satisfy. For example, it is logically perfectly alright to postulate the following SWF: If person A ('that well-known drunkard') prefers x to y, then society should prefer y to x, and if A is indifferent, then so should be society. As an SWF this can be best described by a non-technical term, viz. wild, and in serious discussions it may be useful to restrict the class of SWFs (and of CCRs, in general) by eliminating possibilities like this. One way of doing it is to require that the SWF (or CCR) must

---

[7] On this see Arrow (1951), pp. 23–4, and Samuelson (1967).

satisfy certain conditions of 'reasonableness'. Since reasonableness is a matter of opinion, it is useful to impose only very mild conditions, and one might wonder whether one could really restrict the class of SWFs very much by such a set of mild conditions. Well, surprisingly the problem comes from the other end. In his 'General Possibility Theorem' Arrow proved that a set of very mild looking conditions are altogether so restrictive that they rule out not some but *every possible* SWF. We now turn to this problem.[8]

3.3. THE GENERAL POSSIBILITY THEOREM

The four conditions that Arrow uses in his theorem are informally discussed here, with emphasis on their rationale, and later presented formally in Chapter 3*.

First, as a method of going from individual preferences to social preference, the SWF must be wide enough in scope to work from any logically possible set of individual orderings. Consider, for example, the Pareto principle as a choice rule. It gives a perfectly fine social ordering if the individual preferences are unanimous in the sense described in the last chapter. But it will not yield a social ordering in other situations, in which it will yield incomplete preference relations, and hence it fails to satisfy this requirement of Arrow. Similarly, the method of majority decision may yield intransitivities unless the individual preference orderings satisfy certain patterns (discussed in Chapters 10 and 10*), and hence the MMD also fails this test. This requirement that the rule must work for every logically possible configuration of individual preference orderings we shall call the *condition of unrestricted domain,* or condition *U,* for short.

Second, the SWF must satisfy the Pareto principle in the weak

---

[8] We follow here the second verson of Arrow's theorem, first put forward in Arrow (1952) and then in the second edition of his book, Arrow (1963), Chap. VIII. The original version presented in Arrow (1950), (1951), contained a small error in its formulation, which was corrected by Blau (1957). See also Inada (1955), (1964), and Murakami (1961) for other impossibility theorems related to Arrow's.

form, i.e., if everyone prefers x to y, then society must also prefer x to y. We have already discussed this condition in Chapter 2. We shall call it the *weak Pareto principle*, or condition P.

Third, Arrow requires that social choice over a set of alternatives must depend on the orderings of the individuals only over *those* alternatives, and not on anything else, e.g., on rankings of 'irrelevant' alternatives that are not involved in this choice. Suppose the choice is between x and y, and individual rankings of x and y remain the same, but the rankings of x vis-a-vis some other alternative z changes, or the rankings of z vis-a-vis another alternative w alters. What is required is that the social choice between x and y should still remain the same. To give an analogy, in an election involving Mr A and Mr B, the choice should depend on the voters' orderings of A vis-a-vis B, and not on how the voters rank Mr A vis-a-vis Lincoln, or Lincoln vis-a-vis Lenin.[9] This requirement is called the *condition of independence of irrelevant alternatives*, or condition I.

Finally, it is required that the SWF should not be dictatorial. That is, there should be no individual such that whenever he prefers x to y, society must prefer x to y, irrespective of the preference of everyone else. This is called the *condition of non-dictatorship*, or condition D.

The rather stunning theorem that Arrow proved is that there is no SWF that can simultaneously satisfy all these four conditions, mild as they look. Each looks innocuous enough, but together they seem to produce a monster that gobbles up all the little SWFs in the world.

The theorem is proved in Chapter 3*. We turn now to a discussion of the significance of the result.

---

[9] Views on Lincoln or Lenin could enter the picture (indeed *must* do so) if and only if the voters' orderings of A vis-a-vis B should themselves change as a consequence of a revision of opinion on Lenin or Lincoln.

3.4. A COMMENT ON THE SIGNIFICANCE OF ARROW'S RESULTS

It has been known for a long time that some methods of combining individual preferences into social preference lead to inconsistencies. Condorcet (1785) had noted intransitivities of majority decision almost two centuries ago. Analysis of inconsistencies of majority rule attracted such colourful thinkers as C. L. Dodgson (1876), better remembered as Lewis Carroll. The most discussed case of such inconsistency, the so-called 'paradox of voting', was presented by Nanson (1882). This example provides a very good introduction to the nature of the problem, and may be profitably stated here. Consider three individuals 1, 2 and 3, and three alternatives x, y and z. Let individual 1 prefer x to y, and y to z, and individual 2 prefer y to z, and z to x, and individual 3 prefer z to x and x to y. It is easily checked that x can defeat y by two votes to one, y can defeat z by the same margin, so that transitivity requires that x should defeat z in a vote too. But, in fact, z defeats x by two votes to one. Thus, the method of majority decisions leads to inconsistencies.

This is, in itself, a very interesting result, because the method of majority decision is a highly appealing CCR. In particular it can be easily checked that the MMD satisfies condition P, condition I, and condition D. But it fails to satisfy condition U, so that the MMD is not an acceptable SWF if these four tests are used. The importance of Arrow's theorem lies in the fact that it shows that this problem occurs not only for the method of majority decision, which is after all only one method of social choice, but for every method known or unknown that can be conceived of. There simply is no possibility of getting a SWF such that the four conditions stated can be simultaneously fulfilled.

It may be useful to illustrate this impossibility with some other well-known methods of social decision. A very old method is the so-called 'rank order' method of voting. A certain number of marks are given to each alternative for being first in anyone's preference ordering, a smaller number for being second in someone's ordering, and so on; then the total number of marks received by each alternative is added up, and the one with the highest score wins. For example, in a three alternative case, let 3 be assigned for being first, 2 for being second, and 1 for being third. It is easily seen that this SWF is not dictatorial, so that it passes condition D. It conforms to the Pareto rule, thereby passing condition P. It also yields a complete social ordering starting from any set of individual orderings, and thus satisfies condition U. For example, note that, in the case of Nanson's 'paradox of voting' quoted earlier, x, y and z each receive six marks, and the outcome is not an inconsistency but a tie.

However, it does not pass condition I. Consider the following simple example: Let individual 1 prefer x to y and that to z, whereas individuals 2 and 3 prefer z to x and that to y. With the method of marking outlined, x receives 7 marks and so does z, and the outcome is a tie between the two. Now, consider a second case when everyone's ranking of x vis-a-vis z remains the same, but individual 1 changes his mind about an irrelevant alternative, viz., y, and decides that it is worse than both x and z. This change keeps the total score of x unchanged, but z gets one more mark, scoring 8, and now defeats x with its score of 7. While everyone's ordering of x and z are still the same, the social choice between x and z is not the same, and this of course violates condition I. So this SWF also fails to pass the test of the four conditions.

Next consider a somewhat odd CCR. Let the social preference be determined by an entirely specified traditional code implying a given ordering R^* of the social states. This satisfies condition U (trivially, since individual preferences do not really have any role), condition I (also trivially), and condition D (since no individual is a dictator and only a traditional code dictates). But this curious SWF fails to pass the Pareto principle. Suppose the code requires that x be preferred to y. This remains so even if every person in the community prefers y to x, which violates condition P.

We can go on multiplying examples. The importance of the General Possibility Theorem lies in the fact that we can predict the result in each case, viz., that the specific example considered will not pass the four conditions, even without examining it. The theorem is completely general in its nihilism, and saves a long (and perhaps endless) search.

Chapter 3*
Social Welfare Functions

3*1. THE IMPOSSIBILITY THEOREM

A particular class of collective choice rules corresponds to Arrow's social welfare functions.

DEFINITION 3*1. *A social welfare function (henceforth, SWF) is a collective choice rule f, the range of which is restricted to the set of orderings over X. This restriction is to be called condition O on f.*

Arrow's general possibility theorem consists of imposing certain conditions on a social welfare function *f* and showing that these conditions are mutually incompatible. We state these conditions below.[1]

Condition U (unrestricted domain): The domain of the rule *f* must include all logically possible combinations of individual orderings.

Condition P (Pareto principle): For any pair, *x*, *y* in *X*, $[\forall i : x\,P_i\,y] \to x\,P\,y$.

Condition I (independence of irrelevant alternatives): Let *R* and

---

[1] We have used different labeling of the conditions from Arrow's own and used the first letter of the crucial word to facilitate recollection. We use the version in Arrow (1963).

	Arrow's		*Ours*	
Condition 1′	no name		condition *U*	unrestricted domain
Condition *P*	Pareto principle		condition *P*	Pareto principle
Condition 3	independence of irrelevant alternatives		condition *I*	independence of irrelevant alternatives
Condition 5	non-dictatorship		condition *D*	non-dictatorship

R' be the social binary relations determined by f corresponding respectively to two sets of individual preferences, $(R_1, \ldots, R_n)$ and $(R'_1, \ldots, R'_n)$. If for all pairs of alternatives x, y in a subset S of X, $x R_i y \leftrightarrow x R'_i y$, for all i, then $C(S, R)$ and $C(S, R')$ are the same.

Condition D (non-dictatorship): There is no individual i such that for every element in the domain of rule f, $\forall x, y \in X: x P_i y \rightarrow x P y$.

Note that we have defined these conditions generally for any collective choice rule f (and not necessarily for an SWF), so that we can use these conditions later for exercises on rules other than SWF. Note also that with condition D we have included the bound 'for every element in the domain of rule f'. In the absence of such a universal bound, there is the logical danger of regarding a totally indifferent man as a dictator, since for him the antecedence $x P_i y$ is false for all x, y in X. Arrow's somewhat rough definition is open to this ambiguous interpretation, which would be far from Arrow's intention.

We assume throughout this book that there are at least two persons in the society and at least three alternative social states. There are few problems of collective choice in a one-man society, and transitivity is trivial if there are only two alternative social states. Arrow's 'General Possibility Theorem' is the following. This is the later version of the theorem, to be found in Arrow (1963).

THEOREM 3*1.   *There is no SWF satisfying conditions U, P, I and D.*

We prove this theorem below via two definitions and a lemma.[2] The lemma may be recognized to be of importance in its own right quite aside from the importance of the General Possibility Theorem.

DEFINITION 3*2.   *A set of individuals V is almost decisive for x against y if x P y whenever x P_i y for every i in V, and y P_i x for every i not in V.*

---

[2] The proof of the theorem given here is logically equivalent to Arrow's own proof. Arrow's proof is somewhat opaque, particularly since the use of the crucial condition I (i.e., his Condition 3) is never clarified; in fact this condition is never even mentioned in the proof. What we have done is to reset Arrow's proof somewhat differently.

DEFINITION 3*3. *A set of individuals V is decisive for x against y if x P y when x P_i y for every i in V.*

Notationally, we separate out a certain individual J, and denote $D(x, y)$ to mean that J is almost decisive for x against y, and denote $\bar{D}(x, y)$ to mean that J is decisive for x against y.[3] Note that $\bar{D}(x, y) \rightarrow D(x, y)$.

LEMMA 3*a. *If there is some individual J who is almost decisive for any ordered pair of alternatives, then an SWF satisfying conditions U, P and I implies that J must be a dictator.*

Proof. Suppose that person J is almost decisive for some x against some y, i.e., $\exists x, y \in X: D(x, y)$. Let z be another alternative, and let i refer to all individuals other than J. Assume $x P_J y$ & $y P_J z$, and that $y P_i x$ & $y P_i z$. Notice that we have not specified the preferences of persons other than J between x and z.

Now, $[D(x, y)$ & $x P_J y$ & $y P_i x] \rightarrow x P y$. Further, $[y P_J z$ & $y P_i z] \rightarrow y P z$ from condition P. But, $[x P y$ & $y P z] \rightarrow x P z$ by the transitivity of the strict social ordering relation P.

This result, $x P z$, is arrived at without any assumption about the preferences of individuals other than J regarding x and z. It is, of course, true that we have assumed $y P_i z$ and $y P_i x$. Now, if these rankings of x vis-a-vis y, and of y vis-a-vis z, have any effect on the social choice between x and z, we violate condition I (independence of irrelevant alternatives). Hence, $x P z$ must be independent of these particular assumptions. Hence it must be the consequence of $x P_J z$ alone irrespective of the other orderings. But this means that J is decisive for x against z.

$$D(x, y) \rightarrow \bar{D}(x, z) \tag{1}$$

---

[3] Roughly, a person is 'almost decisive' if he wins if there is opposition, and he is 'decisive' proper if he wins whether he is opposed or not. Note that if 'positive association between individual and social values' (see Chapter 5) is assumed, then the two definitions will be equivalent. *Then* if a person is decisive in spite of opposition, he must be so when others do not oppose him. For Theorem 3*1, however, such a condition is not included. And, in the absence of it, to be decisive is somewhat stronger than being almost decisive, for the former implies the latter but not vice versa.

Now, suppose $z\, P_J\, x\ \&\ x\, P_J\, y$, while $z\, P_i\, x\ \&\ y\, P_i\, x$. By condition P, we must have $z\, P\, x$. And since $D(x, y)\ \&\ x\, P_J\, y\ \&\ y\, P_i\, x$, we conclude that $x\, P\, y$. By transitivity, $z\, P\, y$. And this with only $z\, P_J\, y$, without anything being specified about the preferences of the other individuals between y and z. Hence, J is decisive for z against y. The argument is exactly similar to that used in obtaining (1).

$$D(x, y) \to \bar{D}(z, y) \tag{2}$$

Interchanging y and z in (2), we can similarly show

$$D(x, z) \to \bar{D}(y, z) \tag{3}$$

By putting x in place of z, z in place of y, and y in place of x, we obtain from (1),

$$D(y, z) \to \bar{D}(y, x) \tag{4}$$

Now,
$$
\begin{aligned}
D(x, y) &\to \bar{D}(x, z), \quad \text{from (1)}\\
&\to D(x, z), \quad \text{from Definitions 3*2 and 3*3}\\
&\to \bar{D}(y, z), \quad \text{from (3)}\\
&\to D(y, z),\\
&\to \bar{D}(y, x), \quad \text{from (4)}
\end{aligned}
$$

Therefore,

$$D(x, y) \to \bar{D}(y, x) \tag{5}$$

By interchanging x and y in (1), (2) and (5), we get

$$D(y, x) \to [\bar{D}(y, z)\ \&\ \bar{D}(z, x)\ \&\ \bar{D}(x, y)] \tag{6}$$

Now,
$$
\begin{aligned}
D(x, y) &\to \bar{D}(y, x), \text{ from (5)}\\
&\to D(y, x)
\end{aligned}
$$

Hence from (6), we have

$$D(x, y) \to [\bar{D}(y, z)\ \&\ \bar{D}(z, x)\ \&\ \bar{D}(x, y)] \tag{7}$$

Combining (1), (2), (5) and (7), it is seen that $D(x, y)$ implies that individual J is decisive for every ordered pair of alternatives (six in all) from the set of three alternatives (x, y, z) given conditions U, P and I. Thus J is a dictator over any set of three alternatives containing x and y.

Now, consider a larger number of alternatives. Take any two alternatives u and v out of the entire set of alternatives. If u and v are so chosen that they are the same as x and y, then of course $\bar{D}(u, v)$ holds, as can be shown by taking a triple consisting of u, v and any other alternative z. If one of u and v is the same as one of x and y, say, u and x are the same but not v and y, then take the triple consisting of x (or u), y and v. Since $D(x, y)$ holds, it again follows that $\bar{D}(u, v)$, and also $\bar{D}(v, u)$.

Finally, let both u and v be different from x and y. Now, first take (x, y, u), and we get $\bar{D}(x, u)$, which implies of course $D(x, u)$. Now, take the triple (x, u, v). Since $D(x, u)$, it follows from previous reasoning that $\bar{D}(u, v)$, and also $\bar{D}(v, u)$. Thus $D(x, y)$ for some x and y, implies $\bar{D}(u, v)$ for all possible ordered pairs (u, v). Therefore, individual J is a dictator, and Lemma 3*a is proved.

Finally, Theorem 3*1 is proved by using Lemma 3*a.

Proof. We show that given conditions U, P and I, there must be an individual who is almost decisive over some ordered pair of alternatives. We make the contrary supposition and show that it leads to an inconsistency.

For any pair of alternatives, there is at least one decisive set, viz., the set of all individuals, thanks to condition P. Thus, for every pair of alternatives there is also at least one almost decisive set, since a decisive set is also almost decisive. Compare all the sets of individuals that are almost decisive for some pair-wise choice (not necessarily the same pair), and from them choose the smallest one (or one of the smallest ones). Let this set be called V, and let it be almost decisive for x against y.

If V contains only one individual, then we need not proceed further. If, however, it contains two or more individuals, we divide V into two parts, viz., V_1 containing a single individual, and V_2 containing the rest of V. All individuals not contained in V form the set V_3.

Due to condition U we can assume any logically possible combination of individual orderings. We pick the following:

(1) For all i in V_1, $x\, P_i\, y$ & $y\, P_i\, z$.
(2) For all j in V_2, $z\, P_j\, x$ & $x\, P_j\, y$.
(3) For all k in V_3, $y\, P_k\, z$ & $z\, P_k\, x$.

Since V is almost decisive for x against y, and since every individual in V prefers x to y, and every individual not in V does the opposite, we must have $x\, P\, y$. Between y and z, only V_2 members prefer z to y, and the rest prefer y to z, so that if $z\, P\, y$, then V_2 must be an almost decisive set. But V was chosen as the smallest almost decisive set, and V_2 is smaller than that (being a proper subset of it). Hence $\sim(z\, P\, y)$. Thus, for R to be complete as needed for condition U, $y\, R\, z$ must hold. But $x\, P\, y$ & $y\, R\, z \rightarrow x\, P\, z$. But only the individual in V_1 prefers x to z, the rest prefer z to x, so that a certain individual has turned out to be almost decisive. Hence there is a contradiction in the original supposition.

Note that this proof stands even if V_3 is empty, as will be the case if V contains all the individuals – a possibility that has not been ruled out.

The theorem now follows from Lemma 3*a, since an individual almost decisive over some pair must be a complete dictator.

Chapter 4
Choice Versus Orderings

4.I. TRANSITIVITY, QUASI-TRANSITIVITY AND ACYCLICITY

An SWF is a special type of collective choice rule; it requires that all social preferences be orderings, i.e., social preferences must be reflexive, complete and transitive. It was noted in Chapter 1 that if it is required that there be a best alternative in every subset (i.e., there be a 'choice function'), reflexivity and completeness are not dispensable, but transitivity is not really necessary. Given reflexivity and completeness of a preference relation, the necessary and sufficient condition for the existence of a choice function is a condition that we called 'acyclicity' in Chapter 1*. If x_1 is preferred to x_2, x_2 to x_3, and so on until x_n, then acyclicity requires that x_1 be regarded as at least as good as x_n. Obviously, this is a much weaker condition than transitivity, which would have required that x_1 be strictly preferred to x_n, and further would have required the transitivity of indifference.[1] Transitivity, incidentally, is essentially a condition on 'triples', i.e., on sets of three alternatives. If for all triples transitivity holds, then it must hold for the

---

[1] Acyclicity is a close cousin of Houthakker's (1950) 'semi-transitivity', defined in the context of revealed preference theory, viz., if x_1 is revealed preferred to x_2 and so on until x_n, then x_n must not be revealed preferred to x_1. Given completeness, acyclicity and semi-transitivity are equivalent except for the difference between being 'preferred' and being 'revealed preferred'. The latter is, in one respect, *less* demanding, since in the context of demand theory alternatives are offered in specific sets ('budget sets'), and is, in another respect, *more* demanding since indifference is ruled out in most presentations of revealed preference theory.

entire set, no matter how long a sequence we take. This is not true of acyclicity. A preference relation may be acyclical over all triples and yet may violate acyclicity for the entire set, as was demonstrated in the penultimate paragraph of Section 1*5 in Chapter 1* (pp. 62–3).

The 'impossibility' result of Arrow applies to SWFs. But if Arrow's objective is merely to ensure that 'from any environment, there will be a chosen alternative,'[2] then that can be guaranteed by merely requiring acyclicity of social preference without requiring transitivity. We shall call collective choice rules which generate preference relations that are sufficient for the existence of choice functions, social decision functions (SDF).

Is the distinction between SWF and SDF significant, or is it hair splitting? It appears that it is somewhat significant. For one thing, the 'impossibility' result of Arrow is valid for SWFs but not for SDFs, as shown in Sen (1969). There are collective choice rules which are sufficient for social choice and which satisfy all the four conditions of Arrow (Theorem 4*1). In fact, these conditions can be strengthened substantially (e.g., in ruling out local dictators as well as global dictators, in demanding the strong Pareto principle and not merely the weak Pareto principle as Arrow does), and still there is no inconsistency (Theorems 4*2 and 4*4). Arrow's impossibility theorem is precisely a result of demanding social orderings as opposed to choice functions.

An illustration would help. Consider a CCR which declares x to be socially better than y if it is Pareto-superior to y, and declares x to be socially at least as good as y if y is not Pareto-superior to x. Consider now the case of the 'paradox of voting', discussed earlier, where person 1 prefers x to y and y to z, person 2 prefers y to z and z to x, and person 3 prefers z to x and x to y. The CCR specified will declare x, y and z to be all indifferent to each other. There is no problem in

---

[2] Arrow (1963), p. 120. Arrow also emphasizes the importance of 'the independence of final choice from the path to it'. When the choice set includes more than one alternative, this is never exactly true, in a strict sense, even with full transitivity, since which of the best alternatives will be chosen may depend on the path. However, it is guaranteed that one of the best alternatives will be chosen independently of the path, given transitivity. The same holds with acyclicity, provided indifference is followed by trying out *both* the indifferent alternatives against the remaining alternatives.

this case, and both acyclicity and transitivity hold. Next consider only persons 1 and 2 and let there be no person 3. By our CCR we now have y socially preferred to z, x and y indifferent, and x and z also indifferent. Transitivity does not hold, but acyclicity does, and there is a best alternative in every subset. This can be shown to be true for every configuration of individual preferences, so that condition U holds. This SDF also satisfies the Pareto Principle, since it is based on it; satisfies the independence of irrelevant alternatives, since social preference between any x and any y depends only on individual preference between x and y; and also meets the non-dictatorship condition, since the CCR does not declare x to be socially better than y unless everyone regards x to be at least as good as y.

A weaker condition than transitivity but stronger than acyclicity is 'quasi-transitivity', which is a condition that can be fully stated in terms of triples. If x is preferred to y, and y to z, then x should be preferred to z. This is somewhat like transitivity, but this does not require that indifference be transitive. The CCR described in the last paragraph yields quasi-transitive social preference relations, and is, therefore, fairly easy to analyse in terms of triples only. The difference between transitivity and quasi-transitivity, though apparently mild, is in fact sufficient to take us away from Arrow's impossibility result concerning social ordering to a straightforward possibility result concerning social choice.

4.2. COLLECTIVE CHOICE AND ARROW'S CONDITIONS

Does this mean that the Arrow problem is not really serious for social choice? I am afraid it does not. What all this really shows is how *economic* Arrow's impossibility theorem is. Relax any of his restrictions and the result collapses; if it had not we would have been able to strengthen Arrow's theorem immediately. The conditions that Arrow showed to be inconsistent are not conditions that he regarded as *sufficient* for a satisfactory system of collective choice, but what appeared to him to be plausible *necessary* conditions. That these conditions are not likely to be regarded as sufficient should be clear from the example in terms of which we showed the consistency of these conditions. It made all Pareto-optimal points indifferent, and this is unlikely to appeal to anyone who is worried by distributional considerations. While that was only one example, it is not at all clear that other examples will be more appealing.

In fact, it may be noted that Lemma 3*a, which says that any person who is decisive over a pair must be a dictator, still holds, for the proof does not use anything more than quasi-transitivity. Using this result, it can be proved[3] that all SDFs that satisfy conditions U, I, P and D, and yield quasi-transitive social preference must represent an 'oligarchic' form of decision taking. There would be an identifiable and unique group of persons in the community such that if any one of them strictly prefers any x to any y, society must regard x to be at least as good as y; and if all members of the group strictly prefer x to y, then society must also prefer x to y. The example that we used corresponded to the case where the entire community belonged to this 'oligarchy'; the other cases would appear to be, *prima facie*, less attractive.

Of course, even quasi-transitivity is not necessary for an SDF, since acyclicity is sufficient for choice functions. And it is possible to consider more complex but also more appealing examples with acyclicity. But the fact remains that the Arrow conditions must be recognized to be too weak rather than too demanding, as is usual to assume in the context of his 'impossibility' result. An SDF can pass all the tests of Arrow and still look very unappetizing. In the next few chapters and notes, some other conditions on collective choice will be introduced and analysed.

4.3. RATIONALITY AND COLLECTIVE CHOICE

There is also a second reason for not jubilating at the formal absence of the Arrow impossibility for a social choice function. The fact that

---

[3] Proved by A. Gibbard in 1969 in an unpublished paper.

a best alternative exists in each subset is itself a sound basis for rational choice, but is it a completely satisfactory basis? Consider the case where x is preferred to y, y is preferred to z, and x and z are indifferent. A choice function exists, and in particular, for the choice over all the three alternatives x is the unique best alternative, being no worse than either of the other two. But consider the choice over x and z. There each is 'best', since each is as good as the other. Would it be right to describe a choice process as 'rational' if it can choose either x or z given the choice between the two, but must choose specifically x if the choice is over the triple x, y, z? This is a violation of property β (defined in Chapter 1*), which requires that if two alternatives are both best in a subset, then one of them should not be best in the whole set, without the other also being best in that set. The other rationality property, which we called property α, does not seem to cause much trouble. It requires that if x is best in a whole set, then it must be best in all its subsets also. This is satisfied by all CCRs with which we have been concerned so far. Is property α sufficient, or should we also require property β?

Various selection processes do not, in fact, satisfy property β. Two Australians may tie for the Australian championship in some game, neither being able to defeat the other, but it is perfectly possible for one of them to become the world champion alone, since he might be able to defeat all non-Australians, which the other Australian champion may not be able to do. Similarly, two poets or scientists could get the same national honours, with only one of them receiving some international honour such as the Nobel Prize, without this appearing as irrational in any significant sense.

Whether social choice functions should be required to satisfy property β, thus remains a somewhat problematic issue. Given everything else, it would of course appear to be better that β be satisfied rather than that it be violated. But there *is* a real conflict involved here, and other things are not necessarily the same. We know that a relation generating a choice function that satisfies property β must be an ordering (Lemma 1*q). Hence an SDF that generates preference relations yielding choice functions satisfying β must be an SWF. The Arrow impossibility theorem about SWFs will get readily transformed into an impossibility theorem about SDFs if property β is also imposed as a necessary condition of social choice (Theorem 4*5). Then at least one of the four conditions of Arrow must be suppressed for the sake of consistency. The real question is, therefore, not whether property β is a good thing, but whether it is a better thing than any of the other four conditions in the context of an SDF. Something has to give, and property β, while in itself attractive, may be thought to be more dispensable than the other possible candidates for elimination.

However, as was argued in the last section, the picture is really more complex than would appear from concentrating exclusively on the 'impossibility theorem'. There are other conditions that must be considered in the context of choosing a satisfactory mechanism of collective choice. In this field, there are many conflicts and many dilemmas, and since Arrow's is only one of them, it is not sufficient to try to solve only that particular problem. In the chapters that follow Chapter 4*, we go into some of these problems, which should help us to take a more comprehensive view of the problem of collective choice.

Chapter 4*
Social Decision Functions

4*1. POSSIBILITY THEOREMS

A collective choice rule f that invariably specifies a social *ordering R* is an SWF. But, as we noted in Chapter 1*, an ordering is neither a necessary nor a sufficient condition for the existence of a choice function. It is sufficient for finite sets but is not necessary even then. We may thus think about extending the range of the collective choice rule f to include those preference relations that are not orderings, but which nevertheless generate a choice function.

DEFINITION 4*1. *A social decision function (henceforth SDF) is a collective choice rule f, the range of which is restricted to those preference relations R, each of which generates a choice function C(S, R) over the whole set of alternatives X. This restriction is to be called condition O* on f.*

It may be noted that if we consider infinite sets X, an SWF may not be an SDF, but with finite sets X, an SWF is always an SDF, but not the converse.

Does this extension of the range of a collective rule in the case of finite sets affect the impossibility result of Arrow? It certainly does, as was noted in Chapter 4.[1]

THEOREM 4*1. *There is an SDF satisfying conditions U, P, I and D for any finite set X.*

---

[1] On this, see Sen (1969).

Proof. An example will be sufficient for the proof. Define

$$x \, R \, y \leftrightarrow \sim[(\forall i: y \, R_i \, x) \; \& \; (\exists i: y \, P_i \, x)]$$

Clearly R is reflexive and complete. Further, the SDF satisfies conditions P, I and D. We show now that R is quasi-transitive for every logically possible combination of individual orderings.

$$[x \, P \, y \; \& \; y \, P \, z] \rightarrow [\{\forall i: x \, R_i \, y \; \& \; \exists i: x \, P_i \, y\} \; \& \; \forall i: y \, R_i \, z]$$
$$\rightarrow [\forall i: x \, R_i \, z \; \& \; \exists i: x \, P_i \, z]$$
$$\rightarrow x \, P \, z$$

Thus, R is quasi-transitive, and by Lemma 1*k, no restriction need be put on the domain of the SDF defined, i.e., condition U is also satisfied. This completes the proof.

Note that the social preference relation R generated by the SDF defined above is merely quasi-transitive, and is not fully transitive. Suppose there are two individuals 1 and 2 and three alternatives x, y, z, such that $x \, P_1 \, y \; \& \; y \, P_1 \, z$ and $z \, P_2 \, x \; \& \; x \, P_2 \, y$. We then have $x \, P \, y$, $y \, I \, z$ and $x \, I \, z$. This is clearly intransitive.[2] All that is guaranteed is that a 'best' alternative will be present in every subset, i.e., a choice function will exist, no matter what the individual preferences are.

We can strengthen Theorem 4*1 by strengthening the Pareto rule and the non-dictatorship condition. Define

Condition P* (strong Pareto rule): For any pair, x, y in X,

$$[\forall i: x \, R_i \, y \; \& \; \exists i: x \, P_i \, y] \rightarrow x \, P \, y$$

and

$$[\forall i: x \, I_i \, y] \rightarrow x \, I \, y$$

Condition D*: For no individual i does there exist a pair x, y in X such that for all $(R_1, \ldots, R_n)$ in the domain of f either of the following conditions holds:

---

[2] Thus the SDF quoted is not an SWF with unrestricted domain, and this is not a counter-example to Arrow's General Possibility Theorem.

(1) $x P_i y \rightarrow x P y$

or

(2) $x R_i y \rightarrow x R y$

Condition P^* is defined corresponding to $\bar{P}$ in Chapter 2*, Definition 2*3, and it is obviously a more demanding condition than condition P. Condition D^* is strengthened in two ways. First, while condition D rules out a global dictator, D^* rules out even a local dictator. No individual should be decisive over even a single pair. Second, it also rules out dictatorships of the kind that a weak individual preference R_i could imply a weak social preference R over any pair of alternatives.

Clearly, condition P^* implies condition P, and condition D^* implies condition D, but not vice versa in either case. The following theorem does, however, hold:

THEOREM 4*2. *There is an SDF satisfying conditions U, P^*, I and D^* for any finite set X.*

The proof is provided by the same example as in the proof of Theorem 4*1. It would, thus, appear that the impossibility result of Arrow does not carry over to collective choice rules that are sufficient for choosing a best alternative in every subset, even though they may not be sufficient for generating an ordering.

This concerns the position with finite sets. With infinite sets such an SDF does not exist. Indeed the following result is then true:

THEOREM 4*3. *For an infinite set X, there is no SDF satisfying conditions U and P.*

Proof. Let every individual have the same ordering with antisymmetry, i.e., a chain, such that $x_2 P_i x_1, x_3 P_i x_2, \ldots$. By condition U such a set of individual preference orderings must be in the domain of f, and by condition P there can be no socially best element in the set X, which proves the theorem.

While superficially Theorem 4*3 looks like a disturbing theorem, in fact what it points out is that this way of posing the problem does not make much sense when the set of alternatives X is infinite. Since *individual* choice functions might not exist even if individual orderings exist over an infinite set, there is no point in invariably expecting the existence of a *social* choice function. Further, the following theorem holds:

THEOREM 4*4. *If at least one individual ordering R_i for each element in the domain of f generates a choice function over the set X, then there is an SDF satisfying conditions P, I and D^*, and condition U subject to the restriction noted.*

Proof. Choose the collective choice rule such that $x \ R \ y \leftrightarrow \sim[\forall i: y \ P_i \ x]$, for all x and y. It is clear that $[x \in C(S, R_i)] \rightarrow [x \in C(S, R)]$, for any x in any S, and any i. It follows that since at least one individual has a choice function, then so must society. Fulfilment of conditions P, I and D^* can be easily shown.[3]

The complications raised by infinite sets do not, thus, appear to be particularly profound in this case. The real difficulty in seeking a solution of the 'impossibility problem' in terms of the SDF (as opposed to SWF) resides in the relevance of property β as a rationality condition on choice. It was shown in Chapter 1* that while a choice function generated by a binary relation always satisfies property α, it satisfies property β if and only if R is an ordering. If property β is found to be an essential aspect of rational choice (we examined this question in Chapter 4), then the following theorem may be found to be disturbing:

THEOREM 4*5. *There is no SDF satisfying conditions U, P, I and D, such that each R in the range of the SDF must generate a choice function that satisfies property β.*

The proof follows directly from Lemma 1*q and Theorem 3*1.

---

[3] Note that condition P^* may be violated. It is not possible to strengthen Theorem 4*4 by replacing condition P by P^*, as the following counter-example shows. Let all individuals be indifferent between all alternatives, except one individual who has a chain with no best element. By condition P^*, society must then have the same chain with no best element.

Theorem 4*5 represents the 'impossibility problem' directly in terms of collective choice and its rationality, and clarifies one of the major issues involved. The question seems to turn on whether or not we impose the rationality condition β.[4]

---

[4] See also Chapters 5, 5*, 6, and 6*.

Chapter 5
Values and Choice

5.1. WELFARE ECONOMICS AND VALUE JUDGMENTS

Welfare economics is concerned with policy recommendations. It explores the ways of arriving at such conclusions as 'Given the choice between social states x and y, x should be chosen.' It is obvious that welfare economics cannot be 'value-free', for the recommendations it aims to arrive at are themselves value judgments. In view of this it must be regarded as somewhat of a mystery that so many notable economists have been involved in debating the prospects of finding value-free welfare economics.

The so-called 'New Welfare Economics' (1939–50) was much concerned with deriving policy judgments from purely factual premises.[1] To quote one of the most distinguished writers of the period:

> In fact, there is a simple way of overcoming this defeatism, a perfectly objective test which enables us to discriminate between those reorganizations which improve productive efficiency and those which do not. If A is made so much better off by the change that he could compensate B for his loss, and still have something left over, then the reorganization is an *unequivocal improvement*.[2]

---

[1] See the controversies involving Kaldor (1939), Hicks (1939a), (1941), Scitovsky (1941), Samuelson (1950b) and Little (1949b), (1950). See also Graaff (1957) and Mishan (1960).

[2] Hicks (1941), p. 108; italics added.

This would seem to run counter to the widely held philosophical view asserting 'the impossibility of deducing an "ought"-proposition from a series of "is"-propositions'.[3] Recently a set of doubts have been raised about the validity of this 'law'[4] and its logical compatibility with some other propositions in ethics.[5] But it would be a mistake to think that the search for value-free welfare economics that characterized the so-called New Welfare Economics had anything to do with these doubts. For reasons that are somewhat obscure, being 'value-free' or 'ethics-free' has often been identified as being free from interpersonal conflict. The implicit assumption seems to be that if everyone agrees on a value judgment, then it is not a value judgment at all, but is perfectly 'objective'.

It is for this reason that the Pareto principle has been often taken to be free from value judgments. On the negative side, Robbins' celebrated attack on the use of value judgments in economics concentrated exclusively on the difficulties of interpersonal comparisons (Robbins (1932)). The Hicksian comment on the 'objectivity' of the compensation test quoted above is also based on the idea that if compensations are paid, everyone is better off, and there is no interpersonal conflict.[6] It is remarkable that even Samuelson concluded his definitive article on New Welfare Economics by asserting that 'the only consistent and *ethics-free* definition of an increase in potential real income of a group is that based upon a uniform shift of the utility possibility function for the group.'[7] We have chosen to comment on the stalwarts; other illustrations of the same assumption are easy to find throughout the literature on welfare economics.

---

[3] Hare (1961), p. 29. This is sometimes called 'Hume's Law', after a statement made by him in the *Treatise*, III. I, i.

[4] See, for example, Black (1964) and Searle (1964), (1969).

[5] See, for example, Sen (1966b).

[6] Hicks (1941), p. 109. However, to argue that it is an 'unequivocal improvement' when compensations 'could' be paid whether they are actually paid or not reintroduces the interpersonal conflict.

[7] Samuelson (1950b), pp. 19–20; italics added. If real income comparisons are value judgments, then this is not an 'ethics-free' definition. If, on the other hand, such comparisons are not value judgments, then this is not the *only* 'ethics-free' consistent definition. See, however, Samuelson (1947), Chap. 8.

While the view under discussion is analytically objectionable, its commonsense rationale is quite clear. If everyone agrees on a certain value judgment, the fact that it cannot be verified may not cause any great commotion. There is a clear difference between value judgments that everyone accepts and those that some do and some do not. What is, however, odd in all this is the fact that people should be at all moved to look for 'value-free' or 'ethics-free' welfare criteria.[8] Unanimous value judgments may provide the basis of a great deal of welfare economics, but this is so not because these are not value judgments, but because these value judgments are acceptable to all. This banality would not be worth stating had the opposite not been asserted or implied in much of the literature.

5.2. CONTENT OF WELFARE ECONOMICS: A DILEMMA

Welfare economics is concerned with policy recommendations. A policy recommendation may be derived using (a) some factual premises, (b) some value judgments, and (c) some logic needed for the derivation. The first is the subject matter of 'positive' economics and not of welfare economics. The second cannot be a subject, it is alleged, of scientific discussion, for one cannot argue on value judgments (as Robbins put it, 'it is a case of thy blood or mine'[9]). The third, viz. logic, is a separate discipline altogether. What then can be the subject matter of welfare economics? Does it exist at all?

Though he does not quite hold it in this bald form, Graaff's (1957) masterly banishment of welfare economics is in a similar spirit. In fact, nihilism has been the dominant note in a number of studies on welfare economics bearing, as Baumol puts it, 'an ill-concealed resemblance to obituary notices'.[10] If the subject matter of welfare

---

[8] For a critique of the economists' handling of the meaning and relevance of value judgments, see Little (1957). See also Streeten (1950) and Dobb (1969).

[9] Robbins (1932), p. 132.

[10] Baumol (1966), p. 2.

economics is empty, as it might be thought to be on the reasoning outlined in the last paragraph, it is small wonder that nihilism should appeal. The trouble with that reasoning, however, is that it is grossly misleading, being based on very arbitrary definitions.

First of all, the logical exercises involved in deriving policy recommendations cannot be excluded from the body of welfare economics. In any discipline involving analytical reasoning, logic is involved, either as informal argumentation, or as formal logic, or as mathematical operations. Whether these exercises are classed as branches of logic, or of the discipline in question, is largely a matter of *convenience*. That it seems to be more convenient to permit economists to do the logical exercises needed for deriving policy recommendations in economics rather than leaving these for the logicians or mathematicians is, therefore, a fairly compelling reason for regarding these to be part of the discipline of welfare economics. Indeed a variety of studies that are taken to be part of traditional economics, e.g., those dealing with the existence, efficiency and stability, of competitive general equilibrium are almost exclusively logical exercises.

Secondly, value judgments are not always assumed to be simply 'given' in exercises of policy recommendations. In fact the problem of the existence of the social welfare function (SWF) in the sense of Arrow is concerned with the question of getting a set of value judgments for the society as a whole (reflected by the social ordering) based on the orderings of the individuals. Again the exercises here take mainly a logical form, but the contours of the problem are defined by the question of moving from the preferences of the individuals to social values on the basis of which public choices are to be made. Much of the recent discussion on economic welfare has, naturally enough, been concerned with this basket of problems.

Finally, the dichotomy between facts and values implicit in the reasoning in the nihilistic argument seems to be doubtful. It is based on a reading of the nature of value judgments that is extremely limited. It can in fact be argued that controversies in welfare economics have often tended to be futile because of an inadequate recognition of the nature of value judgments.[11] We turn to this question in the next section.

5.3. BASIC AND NON-BASIC JUDGMENTS

A partitioning of value judgments into two classes should be helpful for our purpose.[12] A value judgment can be called 'basic' to a person if the judgment is supposed to apply under all conceivable circumstances, and it is 'non-basic' otherwise.[13] For example, a person may express the judgment, 'A rise in national income measured both at base and final year prices indicates a better economic situation.' We may ask him whether he will stick to this judgment under all factual circumstances and go on, enquiring, 'Would you say the same if the circumstances were such and such (e.g., if the poor were much poorer)?'[14] If it turns out that he will revise the judgment under certain circumstances, then the judgment can be taken to be non-basic in his value system. If, on the other hand, there is no situation when a certain person will, say, regard killing a human being to be justifiable, then 'I should not kill a human being' is a basic value judgment in his system.

The distinction is a simple one and lies at the root of the relevance of factual considerations in ethical debates. Roughly, it can be argued that, in so far as a certain value judgment is basic to its author, one cannot really dispute it in the same way one disputes a factual or an analytical assertion, but if it non-basic, a dispute on it can take a factual or analytical form.

---

[11] For a fine study of theories of value judgments, see Nowell-Smith (1954). A particularly interesting approach can be found in Hare (1960), (1963).

[12] This and other methods of partitioning value judgments are presented in Sen (1967b).

[13] It is not asserted here that both the categories *must* be non-empty.

[14] An alternative line to take is to ask him what he would do if the criterion led to intransitivity of preference, as is indeed possible under some circumstances (see Gorman (1955), and also Chapter 2* above).

A few warnings may be worth recording to prevent a possible misunderstanding of the nature of the distinction. First, the factual circumstances that are admissible are not necessarily probable ones. Note the following interchange:

A: Men and women should be allowed to dress as they like.

B: Even if it turned out that mini-skirts caused cancer in the eyes of the beholder?

A: Not in that case, of course. But I don't think that situation very likely.

The judgment nevertheless is non-basic, and a dispute on it can take a factual form, even though I doubt that the dispute on this one would be very fruitful.

Second, a value judgment may be made conditional on certain circumstances. If the judgment is to be shown to be non-basic, this will have to be done not by considering cases that violate those conditions, but by considering others that do not. Suppose I express the judgment, 'On rainy days, I should carry an umbrella.' This is not shown to be non-basic by demonstrating that I recommend a different course of action for a sunny day, but by showing that I may recommend something else even for a rainy day, if, say, an umbrella costs half one's annual income.

Third, a set of judgments that an individual holds might turn out to be *logically* inconsistent, and, if so, all of them cannot be basic. A man who judges that 'consumption today should be maximized,' and 'consumption a year hence should also be maximized' is not involved in such a logical conflict, since the two judgments conflict only under specific (though plausible) factual circumstances. At least one of the two judgments must be non-basic, but not for analytical reasons. In contrast, the kindly man who wishes everyone an income higher than the national average seems to have an analytical problem of some magnitude.

5.4. FACTS AND VALUES

If a person puts forward a value judgment and another person denies it, what, we might ask, can they argue about? They differ on what should be chosen given a choice between some alternatives. Given that the persons understand the meaning of the value judgment in the same way, what remains to be disputed? They can, of course, discuss the 'reasons' for holding the value judgment or not holding it. But what, it might be asked, do we mean by 'reasons'? How can there be a 'reason' for accepting or denying a value judgment, as opposed to a factual or a logical statement?

The answer seems to be fairly clear. If the judgment is non-basic, one 'reason' for disputing it may be a doubt about its underlying factual or analytical assumption. Even when one accepts Hume's celebrated law that prescriptive conclusions cannot be derived from exclusively factual premises, there is no doubt that prescriptive conclusions can be drawn from factual premises *among others*. Therefore, someone disputing a value judgment put forward by another person can have a scientific discussion on the validity of the value judgment by examining the truth of the underlying factual premise or the logical derivation. Thus the 'reasons' for recommending the rejection of a value judgment may be purely scientific.

Now, if the judgment expressed happens to be a 'basic' one in the value system of the person expressing it, then and only then can it be claimed that there can be no factual or analytical method of disputing the judgment. That many of the value judgments we habitually express are not basic seems to be fairly easy to demonstrate.

From a non-basic judgment dependent on a particular factual assumption, it is of course possible to move to another judgment independent of that factual assumption. Consider, for example, the value judgment, 'The government should not raise the money supply more than in proportion to the real national output,' based, let us assume, on a factual theory relating money supply and output to inflation. If this theory of inflation is disputed, which would be a legitimate reason against the value judgment in question, the person may move on to a more fundamental value judgment. 'The government should not do anything that leads to inflation.' If that too is based on some factual assumption, making it non-basic, the process of moving backwards, as it were, may be repeated. From judgment J_0 based on factual assumptions F_1, one moves to a judgment (or a set of judgments) J_1 independent of F_1; if that is dependent on factual assumptions F_2, one moves to judgments J_2 independent of both F_1 and F_2. In this way one might hope to reach ultimately, in this person's value system, some basic value judgment J_n, though there is no guarantee that one would definitely get there.

Some generalizations about the futility of arguing on value judgments are based on considering the nature of *basic* value judgments, sometimes loosely called 'ends'. Indeed, this implicit concentration on basic value judgments has had a pronounced and fundamental effect on the development of economics. Economists have been, with few exceptions, shy of having any dispute on value judgments as such, and the classic statement of the position was that by Robbins in his famous treatise on the nature and significance of economics, '. . . it does not seem logically possible to associate the two studies [ethics and economics] in any form but mere juxtaposition. Economics deals with ascertainable facts; ethics with valuation and obligations.'[15] This contrast would hold if ethics dealt only with basic judgments. Robbins explains his position in the following manner:

> If we disagree about ends it is a case of thy blood or mine – or live or let live according to the importance of the difference, or the relative strength of our opponents. But, if we disagree about means, then scientific analysis can often help us to resolve our differences. If we disagree about the morality of the taking of interest (and we understand what we are talking about), then there is no room for argument.[16]

The crucial difficulty with this approach is that it is not quite clearly determinable whether a certain end, or the corresponding

[15] Robbins (1932), p. 132.
[16] Robbins (1932), p. 134.

value judgment stating the end, is basic or not. To take Robbins' own example, why must both parties' judgments on the morality of interests be necessarily basic?

Of course, we need not take such a simple view, and we may supplement the Robbinsian argument by some other test of basicness. We may *ask* the person concerned whether a certain judgment is basic in his value system. But since no one would have had occasion to consider all conceivable alternative factual circumstances and to decide whether in any of the cases he would change the judgment or not, his answer to the question may not be conclusive. Another method is to ask the person concerned to think of a series of suitable revisions of factual assumptions, and ask him whether in any of the cases considered he will change the judgment. This process never establishes basicness, though it can establish that the judgment is not non-basic in any obviously relevant way.

It is interesting to note that some value judgments are demonstrably non-basic, but no value judgment is demonstrably basic. Of course, it may be useful to *assume* that some value judgments, not shown to be obviously non-basic, *are* basic, until and unless a case crops up when the supposition is shown to be wrong. In this respect there is an obvious analogy with the practice in epistemology of accepting tentatively a factual hypothesis as true, until and unless some new observations refute that hypothesis.

It may, incidentally, be noted that a basic value judgment need not necessarily be an 'ultimate' principle such as J_n defined above. A suitable constraint might convert a non-basic value judgment into a basic judgment. An illustration may clarify this point. 'A rise in national income at every set of positive prices implies a better economic situation' may be non-basic, because the person expressing it may not hold this if he finds a 'worsening' of income distribution.[17] From this, in getting a basic judgment, we can move in either of two directions. Either we can enquire whether there is a more *fundamental* value

---

[17] Problems in distinguishing between the size of the national income and its distribution are of course well-known. See especially Samuelson (1950b), Little (1957) and Graaff (1957).

judgment (e.g., aggregate utility maximization) to which a rise in national income corresponds, when the income distribution is no worse. Or, we can ask whether the person concerned will always accept the judgment that 'a rise of national income indicates a better economic situation *if* the income distribution (measured, say, by the Gini-coefficient) is unchanged.' If not, we can constrain the judgment further. So that even if there exist no 'ultimate' value judgments that can be found out by the first method, there may be basic judgments that can be obtained by suitable constraining.

However, the difficulty of ascertaining basicness remains also with the second method, and even if we knew that some basic value judgments existed we might not be able to decide whether a certain judgment were one of those. The fundamental difficulty with the 'emotivist' thesis of the impossibility of rational arguments on value judgments beyond a point, is this difficulty of decidability. It may be true that 'in the end there must come a point where one gets no further answer, but only a repetition of the injunction: Value this because it is valuable,'[18] but there is no sure-fire test which tells us whether such an ultimate point has in fact arrived. From this we do not, unfortunately, get a rule to decide when rational disputation is potentially fruitful and when it is not. Non-basicness of a judgment in someone's value system can sometimes be conclusively established, but the opposite is not the case, and to take a given value judgment to be basic is to give it, at best, the benefit of the doubt. It seems impossible to rule out the possibility of fruitful scientific discussion on value judgments.

5.5. INDIVIDUAL ORDERINGS AND CHOICE RULES

Consider the following problem: An individual A firmly prefers social state x to state y. But he knows that everyone else in the community prefers y to x. And further, individual A is strongly anti-dictatorial in his approach to collective choice. What should he

[18] Ayer (1959), p. 244. See also Stevenson (1944), (1963).

do? If he recommends y, he will be running against his own preference. If he recommends x, he will be violating his anti-dictatorial values. There is clearly a conflict that he has to face.

In the models of collective choice, this conflict is an inescapable one. Individual values are relevant to the exercise in two ways: (a) they affect individual preferences R_i, and (b) they are concerned with the choice of collective choice rules CCR. Values reflected in (a) and (b) could easily conflict, and both sets of judgments cannot be 'basic'.

One way of resolving the problem is to treat the judgments underlying the CCR to be basic in a sense that individual orderings R_i are not. The model may be one where individuals express their preferences and the CCR tries to give appropriate representation to these preferences, but once the CCR selects a social ordering, individuals feel obliged to accept that ordering as the right one, no matter what individual ordering they expressed earlier. An example of such a model can be found in professorial selection processes in some universities, where there are two rounds of voting. In the first the candidates are voted on, and once a decision is reached everyone formally votes for the chosen man in the second round, thereby making his selection 'unanimous'.

However, this is not the only possible model. The opposite extreme will be a case where individuals are really completely committed to what they regard as the right preference R_i, and would reject a CCR that does not select that R_i for public policy. Individual attitudes to most actual collective choice mechanisms would tend to lie somewhere in between these extremes. One might not wish to raise a revolution every time one's preferences fail to get complete representation in collective choice, but then there are circumstances in which one would like to do precisely that and would try to change the mechanism of collective choice. Demands for liberty, equality and fraternity in the French Revolution were basically expressions of extreme dissatisfaction with the collective choice mechanism of the existing system. The prevalence of a CCR as an institutional feature in a society is no guarantee of its acceptance by all or even by many, since actually prevalent choice mechanisms reflect a balance of political and economic forces in the society and are not necessarily based on unanimous or even wide approval.

The real conflict arises when a person really approves of a CCR and also wants his own ordering of social states to be chosen for public policy. He cannot really do both except in the special circumstances in which the CCR he approves of chooses the social ordering he recommends. In general, one or the other set of judgments must be non-basic, possibly both.

Harsanyi (1955) has distinguished between an individual's 'subjective preferences' and his 'ethical preferences', and has given a specific interpretation to the distinction. Harsanyi takes a person's actual preferences R_i as his subjective preferences, while he defines ethical preferences as those preferences that he would have if he thought that he had an 'equal chance' of being in anyone's position.[19] Harsanyi takes a set of axioms which ensure that each person will maximize expected utility. This is a rather specific model, and while it is attractive it is also open to some simple objections (see Chapter 9).

The distinction can be given a broader meaning in the context of a CCR. A person may be required to choose between possible CCRs in terms of his moral values. A CCR thus chosen can be called his ethical CCR. A social preference relation yielded by such a person's ethical CCR, given an actual set of individual preferences, can be taken to be that person's ethical preferences. Harsanyi's definition corresponds to a particular procedure of aggregation and represents an important special case of this more general approach.[20]

I do not wish to enter into the suitability of the term 'ethical' in this context. Presumably the ethical values involved here are those relating to combining preferences, and one could have introduced other ethical values. But it is important to distinguish between a person's preferences as they actually are and what he thinks he would accept as a

---

[19] In placing oneself in the position of another, as Harsanyi defines it, one is assumed to take on that person's subjective features (including his preferences), and not merely his objective circumstances. Contrast Samuelson (1964) in extending a model of Lerner (1944) on 'equal ignorance'. See Pattanaik (1968b) on Harsanyi. See also Leibenstein (1965).

[20] This is not strictly right, since the Harsanyi procedure is based not on individual orderings but on individual utility functions. The Harsanyi example is really a special case of an ethical 'social welfare functional', to be defined in Chapter 8.

basis of public policy given the preferences of others and given his values on collective choice procedures. Thus interpreted, there is no conflict between the two sets of preferences that he may entertain, since they are concerned with two different types of problems. One might wish that others had the same ordering R_i as one had oneself (hence one's commitment to the R_i), but given the preferences of the others one might accept the social preference emerging from a particular CCR (hence one's commitment to the CCR). This distinction will be found useful in discussing specific problems of collective choice.

5.6. CONDITIONS ON CHOICE RULES

There could be conflicts also between values that one would like to see reflected in the CCR. One such example is provided by Arrow's impossibility theorem. Conditions U, P, I and D, when imposed on a CCR subject to condition O (i.e. on an SWF), will conflict. Clearly, not all these values could be basic.

Of these conditions, condition U, which demands an 'unrestricted domain', is in a somewhat different logical level from the rest. The other conditions specify or qualify what should be done given certain configurations of individual preferences. Condition U, on the other hand, asserts that the CCR must work for all possible configurations of individual preferences. It is, of course, certainly possible to maintain that certain configurations of individual preferences would never occur.[21] If a person believed that some configurations could, in practice, be ruled out, he may have no reason to demand condition U for the CCR or the SWF.

There could be a more subtle conflict if a person believed that a CCR was a good one for most circumstances that are plausible, but was objectionable for certain configurations of preferences that might

---

[21] The Marxist position that people's preferences depend on their class interests would immediately rule out certain logically possible configurations. In fact, any deterministic theory of individual preferences would tend to restrict the pattern of individual preferences somewhat, thereby reducing the need for the condition of unrestricted domain.

not be very plausible. The goodness of a CCR is not independent of the actual preference configurations, and in demanding that it works well in *all* circumstances one might be ruling out good rules that would have done nicely in most cases, but not in all. We shall go into this question further while discussing specific rules, e.g., the method of majority decision (Chapters 10 and 10*). In demanding condition U on top of others like conditions O, P or I, one is requiring that the transitivity of social preference, or the Pareto principle, or the independence of irrelevant alternatives, should not be violated by the CCR even for a single configuration of individual preferences, whether that configuration is plausible or not. This is what precipitates Arrow's impossibility result.

We can consider some other general conditions on CCRs. For CCRs that satisfy the independence of irrelevant alternatives, May (1952) has proposed a set of conditions. The condition of *anonymity* requires that if you have my preferences and I have yours, and so on, i.e., if a given set of preferences is permuted among the individuals, social preference should remain invariant. *Neutrality* requires that the rule of choice should not discriminate between alternatives, and whatever criterion permits us to say that x is socially as good as y should also be sufficient for declaring w to be as good as z, after replacing x and y by w and z, respectively, in the criterion.[22] *Positive responsiveness* requires that the relation between individual and social preferences must be positive, i.e., if x is considered as being socially as good as y in some situations and now x goes up in someone's preference vis-a-vis y and does not fall in anyone's preference, then x must now be regarded as socially strictly better than y.

These conditions look appealing, and May has proved that the only decisive CCR with an unrestricted domain, which is independent of irrelevant alternatives, and is also anonymous, neutral and positively responsive, is the method of majority decision (see Theorem 5*1). If someone approves of all those conditions but is

---

[22] In the formal statement of this condition in Chapter 5*, 'neutrality' is defined to incorporate 'independence of irrelevant alternatives'. This is true of May's formulation as well.

unwilling to accept the majority decision rule, then he has a problem, for at least one of these judgments must be rejected.

Further, for some configurations of individual preferences, majority decision yields social preferences that are intransitive and in fact even violate acyclicity (e.g., in the case of 'the paradox of voting'). Hence, if we demand the conditions noted in the last paragraph, then we must reject not merely transitivity of social preference but also acyclicity (Theorem 5*2). If we like acyclicity, then at least one of the other conditions must be rejected. This is an impossibility result similar to Arrow's and it poses another problem of difficult choice.[23]

If instead of demanding positive responsiveness we demand *non-negative responsiveness* (i.e., if x does not fall vis-a-vis y in anyone's ordering, then it must not fall in the social ordering vis-a-vis y), the picture changes somewhat. We now have some freedom and can satisfy acyclicity and even quasi-transitivity. Further, suppose we strengthen the Pareto principle by demanding that x be socially better than y if someone (not necessarily everyone) prefers x to y, and everyone regards x to be at least as good as y. Then it can be shown that the CCR must be the Pareto-extension rule which follows the Pareto rule and completes it arbitrarily by declaring all Pareto-incomparable pairs as socially indifferent (Theorem 5*3). We used such a CCR in proving Theorem 4*1, and earlier we discussed its relevance to theories of collective choice of Buchanan and Tullock (1962) and others (Chapter 2). Under this rule, if y is not Pareto-superior to x, then x is socially as good as y.

Many people will reject immediately the Pareto-extension rule with its complete avoidance of distributional judgments. But they may hesitate to reject any of the conditions such as quasi-transitivity, or anonymity, or independence of irrelevant alternatives, or unrestricted domain, or the Pareto principle, which together imply that the CCR chosen must be the Pareto-extension rule. This too is a

---

[23] Another interesting result due to Hansson (1969) shows that the independence of irrelevant alternatives, neutrality and anonymity when imposed on an SWF make all alternatives socially indifferent. The result does not, however, hold for SDFs as will be clear in Chapter 5*.

dilemma belonging to a wide class of which Arrow's impossibility result is another example.

It may also be noted that the difference between the majority rule and the Pareto-extension rule, which are rules in two very different traditions, appears to be rather small in terms of the underlying conditions. The method of majority decision, like the Pareto-extension rule, satisfies the conditions of independence, anonymity, neutrality, non-negative responsiveness, the strict Pareto principle, and unrestricted domain. The difference between the two is that the MMD satisfies positive responsiveness (and not merely non-negative responsiveness), which the Pareto-extension rule does not; and the Pareto-extension rule satisfies quasi-transitivity of social preference, which the MMD does not. If one were to look at these conditions without knowing the relevant theorems, one need not have guessed how crucial these little variations in conditions might be. Arrow christens a condition as that of 'positive association' which is even weaker than our condition of 'non-negative responsiveness',[24] but a shift from May's 'positive responsiveness' to Arrow's 'positive association' takes us almost all the way from the case of the majority rule to the very different case of the Pareto-extension rule.

The main moral is that these conditions are difficult to judge in isolation and must be viewed along with the other conditions with which they may be combined. Judgments of this kind on the nature of the CCR tend to be non-basic, and it is relevant for us to enquire into the precise circumstances in which these conditions might be used, before we put our signature on the dotted line. Some more conditions and some more conflicts are discussed in Chapters 6 and 6* to pursue further this line of reasoning.

---

[24] Arrow's 'positive association' requires that if x does not fall vis-a-vis y in anyone's judgment, then if x was previously preferred to y it must still be preferred. It does not say anything about the case where x was previously indifferent to y. Non-negative responsiveness would have required that in this case too, x should not fall vis-a-vis y, i.e., x must remain at least as good as y.

Chapter 5*
Anonymity, Neutrality and Responsiveness

5*1. CONDITIONS FOR MAJORITY RULE

A set of conditions on collective choice rules may be satisfied by no rule (as with Arrow's four conditions for all rules satisfying condition O), or by many rules (as with the imposition of only the Pareto principle and non-dictatorship on choice rules). In between lies the case in which the conditions can all be satisfied by one rule and one rule only. We shall illustrate this with a set of conditions that are necessary and sufficient for the method of majority decisions (see May (1952)), which we first define.

DEFINITION 5*1. *The method of majority decision holds if and only if*

$$\forall x, y \in X: x \ R \ y \leftrightarrow [N(x \ P \ y) \geqq N(y \ P \ x)]$$

where for all a, b in X, $N(a \ P \ b)$ is the number of people for whom $a \ P_i \ b$.

Note that since indifference will affect both sides, this is equivalent to defining $x \ R \ y \leftrightarrow [N(x \ R \ y) \geqq N(y \ R \ x)]$, where N is the number of individuals i such that $x \ R_i \ y$ (see Arrow (1951)).

The method of majority decision (MMD) belongs to a class of collective choice rules such that the social preferences between x and y depend only on individual preferences between x and y. This is implied by condition I.

LEMMA 5*a. *For any decisive collective choice rule satisfying condition I, the social preference relation R over each pair x, y in X must be a function of individual preferences R_i only over x, y.*

The proof is immediate.

We shall now define three conditions on collective choice rules satisfying condition I.

DEFINITION 5*2. *For all pairs* $(R_1, \ldots, R_n)$ *and* $(R'_1, \ldots, R'_n)$ *of n-tuples of individual orderings in the domain of a collective choice function f, which maps them respectively into R and R',*

(1) *If* $(R_1, \ldots, R_n)$ *being a reordering of the components of* $(R'_1, \ldots, R'_n)$ *implies that* $\forall x, y \in X: x\, R\, y \leftrightarrow x\, R'y$, *then and only then anonymity (condition A) holds.*

(2) *If* $\forall x, y, z, w \in X: [(\forall i: x\, R_i\, y \leftrightarrow z\, R'_i\, w)\, \& \, (\forall i: y\, R_i\, x \leftrightarrow w\, R'_i\, z)] \rightarrow [(x\, R\, y \leftrightarrow z\, R'w)\, \& \, (y\, R\, x \leftrightarrow w\, R'z)]$, *then and only then neutrality (condition N) holds.*

(3) *If* $\forall x, y \in X: [\forall i: \{(x\, P_i\, y \rightarrow x\, P'_i\, y)\, \& \, (x\, I_i\, y \rightarrow x\, R'_i\, y)\}\, \& \, \exists k: \{(x\, I_k\, y\, \& \, x\, P'_k\, y) \veebar (y\, P_k\, x\, \& \, x\, R'_k\, y)\}] \rightarrow (x\, R\, y \rightarrow x\, P'y)$, *then and only then positive responsiveness (condition S) holds.*

Anonymity requires that social preferences should be invariant with respect to permutations of individual preferences. Neutrality demands that if two alternatives x and y, respectively, have exactly the same relation to each other in each individual's preference in case 1 as z and w have in case 2, then the *social* preference between x and y in case 1 must be exactly the same as the social preference between z and w in case 2. Positive responsiveness requires that if some individual's preference shifts relatively in favour of x vis-a-vis y with everyone else's preference between x and y remaining the same, then social preference should shift positively in the direction of x, and if the society was previously indifferent, now it must strictly prefer x.

LEMMA 5*b. *For any collective choice rule neutrality (N) implies independence of irrelevant alternatives (I).*

The proof follows directly from Definition 5*2 (2) if we put $x = z$ and $y = w$.

THEOREM 5*1. *Conditions U, A, N and S are together necessary* *and sufficient for a decisive collective choice rule to be the method of majority decision.*[1]

Proof. It is clear from the definition of MMD that it satisfies all the four conditions mentioned, so we need concern ourselves only with the sufficiency part of the proof. By Lemma 5*b Condition I is satisfied and therefore we need look at R_i *only over* x and y for social preference over x and y. By anonymity (A), social preference must depend only on the numbers of individuals preferring x to y, y to x, and being indifferent, respectively. By neutrality (N), if $N(x\ P\ y) = N(y\ P\ x)$, then $x\ I\ y$, as can be checked by assuming the contrary and then permuting x and y in each individual's preference ordering. Given that for x, y in X, $[N(x\ P\ y) = N(y\ P\ x)] \to x\ I\ y$, then by positive responsiveness, $[N(x\ P\ y) > N(y\ P\ x)] \to x\ P\ y$. But then this *is* the method of majority decision.

The following corollary of Theorem 5*1 poses a slight problem for collective choice:

COROLLARY 5*1.1. *No SWF can satisfy conditions U, A, N and S.*

The proof follows directly from Theorem 5*1 by noting that some configuration of individual preferences does yield an intransitive majority preference relation so that this choice rule will not be an SWF.

Corollary 5*1.1, is, however, weaker than Theorem 3*1 (the General Possibility Theorem) proved earlier and is implied by it. This is readily proved with the help of the two following lemmas:

LEMMA 5*c. *A collective choice rule that is anonymous must be non-dictatorial.*

LEMMA 5*d. *A decisive collective choice rule that is neutral and positively responsive satisfies the strict Pareto principle.*

The proof of Lemma 5*c is immediate from the definitions. In proving Lemma 5*d, we note that by neutrality, $[\forall i: x\ I_i\ y] \to x\ I\ y$. Hence, by positive responsiveness, if $\exists i: x\ P_i\ y\ \&\ \forall i: x\ R_i\ y$, then $x\ P\ y$.

The strict Pareto principle (P^*) implies the weak Pareto principle

---

[1] This is a doctored version of May's (1952) theorem.

(P), so that Corollary $5^*1.1$ follows directly from Theorem 3^*1, and Lemmas 5^*c and 5^*d. The following is, however, a stronger result. The impossibility continues even if we impose the conditions on an SDF as opposed to an SWF.

THEOREM 5^*2. *There is no SDF satisfying conditions U, A, N and S.*

The proof, in view of Theorem 5^*1 and Lemmas 5^*c and 5^*d, consists of showing that for some configuration of individual preferences, the method of majority decision violates acyclicity, e.g., with three individuals 1, 2, 3, and three alternatives, x, y, z, let $x\,P_1\,y\,P_1\,z$, $y\,P_2\,z\,P_2\,x$, and $z\,P_3\,x\,P_3\,y$, so that $x\,P\,y$, $y\,P\,z$, $z\,P\,x$, by MMD.

Arrow's condition of 'positive association between individual and social preferences' is somewhat in the same spirit as, though weaker than, condition S (positive responsiveness). We can make Arrow's condition stronger, but keeping it still weaker than condition S, and observe the implication of replacing condition S by this condition.[2]

Condition R (non-negative responsiveness): For all pairs $(R_1, \ldots, R_n)$ and $(R'_1, \ldots, R'_n)$ of n-tuples of individual orderings in the domain of a collective choice function f, which maps them respectively into R and R', non-negative responsiveness holds if and only if

$$\forall x, y \in X: [\forall i: (x\,P_i\,y \rightarrow x\,P'_i\,y) \,\&\, (x\,I_i\,y \rightarrow x\,R'_i\,y)]$$
$$\rightarrow [(x\,P\,y \rightarrow x\,P'\,y) \,\&\, (x\,I\,y \rightarrow x\,R'\,y)]$$

As long as x does not go down in anyone's preference ordering, it must not do so in the social ordering. Would a weakening of condition S into the weaker condition R make any significant difference? It indeed would, as we show in the next section.

5^*2. PARETO-EXTENSION RULES

We define a pair of collective choice rules derived from converting Pareto incompleteness into Pareto indifference, as used in the proofs of Theorems 4^*1 and 4^*4, respectively,

---

[2] Cf. Murakami's (1968) 'monotonicity'.

DEFINITION 5*3.   (1) *The weak Pareto-extension rule (henceforth,* WPE), *is a collective choice rule such that*

$$\forall x, y \in X: x \, R \, y \leftrightarrow \sim(y \, \bar{\bar{P}} \, x)$$

(2) *The Pareto-extension rule (henceforth,* PE) *is a collective choice rule such that*

$$\forall x, y \in X: x \, R \, y \leftrightarrow \sim(y \, \bar{P} \, x)$$

Before proving a theorem on the necessary and sufficient conditions for a collective choice rule to be the Pareto-extension rule, two lemmas are noted.

LEMMA 5*e.   *If there is some individual J who is almost decisive for any ordered pair of alternatives, then a collective choice rule satisfying conditions U, P and I, and always yielding a quasi-transitive and complete social preference relation, implies that J must be a dictator.*

Though this is a generalization of Lemma 3*a, the proof of Lemma 3*a given is sufficient in proving Lemma 5*e, since only the quasi-transitivity property of R was used in the proof without requiring full transitivity (see pp. 90–92).

If $x \, P_i \, y$ by some i implies $x \, R \, y$ and not necessarily $x \, P \, y$, then individual i is decisive in a weaker sense.

DEFINITION 5*4.   *A person J is semi-decisive for x against y if $x \, R \, y$ whenever $x \, P_J \, y$. He is almost semi-decisive for x against y if $x \, R \, y$ whenever $x \, P_J y$, and $y \, P_i \, x$ for all $i \neq J$.*

Notationally, $\bar{S}(x, y)$ and $S(x, y)$ will stand, respectively, for person J being semi-decisive and almost semi-decisive.

LEMMA 5*f.   *If there is some individual J who is almost semi-decisive for any ordered pair of alternatives, then a collective choice rule satisfying conditions U, P and I, and always yielding a quasi-transitive and complete social preference relation, implies that J is semi-decisive over every ordered pair of alternatives.*

Proof.   The proof is very similar to that of Lemma 3*a. Let person J be almost semi-decisive over some x against some y, i.e. $S(x, y)$. In the triple

(x, y, z) let person J have the preference, $x P_J y$ & $y P_J z$, and all other individuals $i (\neq J)$ hold: $y P_i z$ & $y P_i x$. By condition P, $y P z$. Since $S(x, y)$, clearly $x R y$. If $z P x$, then $y P x$ (by quasi-transitivity), which is impossible. Hence, by the completeness of R, $x R z$. But the preferences of all $i \neq J$ are unspecified between x and z, and only J definitely prefers x to z. Hence, J is semi-decisive for x against z. Hence, $S(x, y) \rightarrow \bar{S}(x, z)$.

By taking $z P_J x$ & $x P_J y$, and for all $i \neq J$, $z P_i x$ & $y P_i x$, we can show similarly that $S(x, y) \rightarrow \bar{S}(z, y)$. By interchanging y and z in this we obtain $S(x, z) \rightarrow \bar{S}(y, z)$. And by considering a case where in the proof of $S(x, y) \rightarrow \bar{S}(x, z)$, x is replaced by y, y by z, and z by x, we obtain $S(y, z) \rightarrow \bar{S}(y, x)$. Hence, $S(x, y) \rightarrow \bar{S}(x, z) \rightarrow \bar{S}(y, z) \rightarrow \bar{S}(y, x)$. Hence, $S(x, y)$ alone implies all the following three results: $\bar{S}(x, z)$, $\bar{S}(z, y)$ and $\bar{S}(y, x)$.

Now interchanging x and y, we would find that $S(y, x)$ implies $\bar{S}(y, z)$, $\bar{S}(z, x)$ and $\bar{S}(x, y)$. But $S(x, y) \rightarrow \bar{S}(y, x)$. Hence $S(x, y)$ implies $\bar{S}(x, y)$, $\bar{S}(y, x)$, $\bar{S}(y, z)$, $\bar{S}(z, y)$, $\bar{S}(x, z)$, $\bar{S}(z, x)$, and J is semi-decisive for every pair in the triple (x, y, z).

The extension to any number of alternatives is exactly as in Lemma 3^*a, and this, when spelt out, completes the proof of Lemma 5^*f.

Finally, the determination of the Pareto-extension rule in terms of conditions on a CCR is given.

THEOREM 5^*3. *For a CCR that always yields a quasi-transitive and complete social preference relation, conditions U, I, P* and A, are together necessary and sufficient for the CCR to be the Pareto-extension rule.*

Proof. As in the proof of Theorem 3^*1, compare all the sets of individuals who are almost decisive for some pair-wise choice (not necessarily the same pair), and from these choose the smallest one (or any one of the smallest, if there is more than one smallest set). Let this set be called V, and let it be almost decisive for x against y. If V contains only one individual, then by anonymity every individual must be almost decisive for x against y, and by Lemma 5^*e every individual must be a dictator, which is impossible. Hence V must have more than one individual.

Partition all the individuals in V into two groups with V_1 consisting of any one particular individual (say J) and V_2 consisting of all individuals who are not in V_1 but are in V, V_3 consists of all the others. Consider now the following configuration of individual preferences, exactly as in the proof of Theorem 3*1, over x, y and some z.

(1) For all i in V_1, $x\, P_i\, y$ & $y\, P_i\, z$.
(2) For all j in V_2, $z\, P_j\, x$ & $x\, P_j\, y$.
(3) For all k in V_3, $y\, P_k\, z$ & $z\, P_k\, x$.

Since V is almost decisive for x against y, and everyone in V does prefer x to y, and everyone not in V prefers y to x, we have $x\, P\, y$. Since only those in V_2 prefer z to y, and all others prefer y to z, if we take $z\, P\, y$, then V_2 will turn out to be an almost decisive set, but this is impossible since V, of which V_2 is a proper subset, is the smallest almost decisive set. Hence, $y\, R\, z$. If we now take $z\, P\, x$, then by quasi-transitivity and by $x\, P\, y$, we must have $z\, P\, y$. But in fact $y\, R\, z$, so that we must conclude that $x\, R\, z$, by the completeness of R. But the single individual in V_1 is the only one who prefers x to z, and all others prefer z to x. Hence J is almost semi-decisive for x against z. Hence, by Lemma 5*f, J is semi-decisive for every ordered pair of alternatives.

By anonymity, every individual must be semi-decisive for every ordered pair of alternatives. Hence,

$$\forall i: [\forall x, y: (x\, P_i\, y \rightarrow x\, R\, y)]$$

This means that $\forall x, y: x\, P\, y \rightarrow \forall i: x\, R_i\, y$. But by the Pareto principle P^*, we know that

$$\forall x, y: [(\forall i: x\, R_i\, y\ \&\ \exists i: x\, P_i\, y) \rightarrow x\, P\, y]$$

and

$$\forall x, y: [\forall i: x\, I_i\, y \rightarrow x\, I\, y]$$

Hence, $\forall x, y: [(\forall i: x\, R_i\, y\ \&\ \exists i: x\, P_i\, y) \leftrightarrow x\, P\, y]$. Further, by the completeness of R,

$$\forall x, y: [x\, R\, y \leftrightarrow \sim(\forall i: y\, R_i\, x\ \&\ \exists i: y\, P_i\, x)]$$

But this *is* the Pareto-extension rule, and the proof of Theorem 5*3 is now complete.

It is easy to check that the Pareto-extension rule also satisfies neutrality (condition N) and non-negative responsiveness (condition R). While the MMD satisfies conditions U, I, A, N, P^* and S, the Pareto-extension rule satisfies conditions U, I, A, N, P^* and R, and quasi-transitivity of social preference (see Theorems 5^*1 and 5^*3, and Lemma 5^*d). A relaxation of responsiveness (from S to R) and a strengthening of properties of social preference (imposing quasi-transitivity) seem to transform the majority rule into the Pareto-extension rule.

Chapter 6
Conflicts and Dilemmas

6.1. CRITIQUE OF ANONYMITY
AND NEUTRALITY

The assumptions of anonymity and neutrality are quite powerful conditions when imposed on a social decision function, as we saw in Chapter 5*. How appealing are these conditions? It may first be noted that many actual collective decision procedures violate these conditions. Procedural matters may be decided by a simple majority vote in the United Nations' General Assembly, whereas matters of substance require a two-thirds majority. Hence collective choice, in this case, is not neutral. It is, however, anonymous, but things change if we move from the General Assembly to the Security Council, for only five particular countries have the right of the veto.

The free market allocation procedures, whether under capitalism or under market socialism (e.g., the Lange-Lerner system) are definitely non-neutral and non-anonymous. I choose my consumption basket and you choose yours, and a permutation of our preferences can result in a different social outcome even if the available social alternatives remain the same. This violates anonymity. Neutrality is violated too. Suppose that in one case I prefer having my walls blue rather than white with the rest of the social state being Ω, whereas you have the opposite preference. The market mechanism may guarantee that my walls will be blue. In another case I might prefer having your walls blue rather than white (the rest of the social state being $\hat{\Omega}$), while you have the opposite preference. This is simply a substitution of alternatives, but the market mechanism may make your walls white and not blue. This violates neutrality.

That the market mechanism may violate anonymity or neutrality is not a compelling argument against these principles. One could adhere to them and argue: 'so much the worse for the market mechanism.' Indeed the failure of the market mechanism to take note of 'externalities' is one of the well-known deficiencies of the market system. However, values of individual freedom of choice are much deeper than the expression they find in the market mechanism; and they require a closer scrutiny.

6.2. LIBERAL VALUES AND AN IMPOSSIBILITY RESULT

It can be argued that certain social choices are purely personal, e.g., everything else in the society being Ω, Mr A lies on his back when he sleeps (x), and everything else being Ω, Mr A lies on his belly when he sleeps (y). Suppose Mr A prefers y to x, whereas many others may want the opposite. It is possible to argue that the social choice between x and y is a purely personal matter since Mr A is the only one 'really' involved, and the rest are just 'nosey'. It is also possible to choose a CCR such that in this purely 'personal' choice Mr A's preference should be precisely reflected by social preference.

A very weak form of asserting this condition of liberalism (condition L) is that each individual is entirely decisive in the social choice over at least one pair of alternatives, e.g., Mr A being decisive between x and y. In general there could be more than one such pair, partly because (a) there are other examples of such personal choices, e.g., Mr A doing a spot of yoga exercise before retiring (however revolting others might find the idea), and (b) even with the back-or-belly-sleep case there would be more than one such pair, since Ω could be different, e.g., if it is alright for Mr A to sleep on his belly rather than on his back when Mr B's kitchen walls are pink, it should be alright to do the same when Mr B's kitchen walls are crimson. Thus condition L is really rather weak; while a liberal should accept condition L he must want something more.

A still weaker requirement than condition L is given by condition

L^*, which demands that at least *two* individuals should have their personal preferences reflected in social preference over one pair of alternatives each. This condition is extremely mild and may be called the condition of 'minimal liberalism', since cutting down any further the number of individuals with such freedom (i.e., cutting it down to one individual) would permit even a complete dictatorship, which is not very liberal.

Now the unfortunate fact is that this most mild condition L^* is inconsistent with conditions U (unrestricted domain) and P (weak Pareto principle) when imposed on an SDF, as shown in Sen (1970c), and reproduced below in Theorem 6*1. This impossibility result can be contrasted with Arrow's impossibility theorem.

Condition L^* (minimal liberalism) is somewhat stronger than Arrow's condition D (non-dictatorship), even though it seems to be much weaker than what 'liberalism' requires. Conditions U and P are shared by Arrow's theorem and Theorem 6*1. Condition I (independence of irrelevant alternatives) is required in Arrow's theorem but not in Theorem 6*1. Further, the Arrow conditions apply to SWFs (i.e., condition O is imposed), whereas in this other theorem merely an SDF (i.e., condition O^*) is required, which does not require transitivity but only acyclicity of social preference. Acyclicity is, of course, strictly weaker than transitivity. Still the impossibility holds, and is, thus, rather disturbing.

An illustration could clarify the nature of the problem. Let the social choice be between three alternatives involving Mr A reading a copy of *Lady Chatterley's Lover*, Mr B reading it, or no one reading it. We name these alternatives a, b, and c, respectively. Mr A, the prude, prefers most that no one reads it, next that he reads it, and last that 'impressionable' Mr B be exposed to it, i.e., he prefers c to a, and a to b. Mr B, the lascivious, prefers that either of them should read it rather than neither, but further prefers that Mr A should read it rather than he himself, for he wants Mr A to be exposed to Lawrence's prose. Hence he prefers a to b, and b to c. A liberal argument can be made for the case that given the choice between Mr A reading it and no one reading it, his own preference should be reflected by social preference. So that society should prefer that no one reads it, rather than having

Mr A read what he plainly regards as a dreadful book. Hence c is socially preferred to a. Similarly, a liberal argument exists in favour of reflecting Mr B's preference in the social choice between Mr B reading it and no one reading it. Thus b is preferred to c. Hence society should prefer Mr B reading it to no one reading it, and the latter to Mr A reading it. However, Mr B reading it is Pareto-worse than Mr A reading it, even in terms of the weak Pareto criterion, and if social preference honours that ranking, then a is preferred to b. Hence every alternative can be seen to be worse than some other. And there is thus no best alternative in this set and there is no optimal choice.

6.3. CRITIQUE OF ACYCLICITY

It may be noted that there is no conflict between the Pareto principle and the condition of minimal liberalism over any particular pair of alternatives, even with unrestricted domain. The conflict arises when we put together more than one pair. One way out may be to reject pair-wise choice and not to generate a choice function out of a social preference relation. It is certainly possible to argue that a be chosen in the choice between a and b, b be chosen given the choice between b and c, c be chosen in the choice between c and a, and, say, a be chosen in the choice between a, b and c. This will not be a collective choice rule, as we have defined it, since no social preference relation can represent this. In particular it will violate property α, since a is best in (a, b, c), but not so in (a, c).

An argument for dropping acyclicity is difficult to construct, but one possible line is precisely to refer to Theorem 6*1 and similar results. If neither condition P nor condition L^* may be relaxed, and if the choice mechanism should work for configurations of individual preference orderings noted in Theorem 6*1 (or in Section 6.2 above), then acyclicity must go. If P and L^* are 'irresistible' forces, then acyclicity must be a moveable object.

But this is not really an attractive way out. First, a rejection of acyclicity in this case will mean that the choice function will not be based on a relation of pair-wise preference, and furthermore, even the rationality property α will be violated. Why select a in a choice between a, b and c, and reject it in a choice between a and c? Property α is a most appealing condition.

Second, avoiding the paradox by rejecting acyclicity is really cheating; it works only because conditions P and L^* are imposed here as conditions on pair-wise choice, whereas acyclicity makes social choice essentially non-pair-wise. Given acyclicity of social preference, it would be necessary to redefine conditions P and L^*. We might require (condition $\hat{P}$) that x should not be in the choice set $C(S)$ of the society if the set S contains some alternative y which is preferred by everyone to x. We also require (condition $\hat{L}^*$) that there are two pairs of alternatives (x and y, and z and w) and two individuals 1 and 2 such that if individual 1 (respectively 2) prefer x to y (respectively z to w), then y (respectively w) should not be in the social choice set $C(S)$ if x (respectively z) is in the set S, and if individual 1 (respectively 2) prefers y to x (respectively w to z), then x (respectively z) should not be in the choice set $C(S)$ if y (respectively w) is in the set S. Conditions $\hat{P}$ and $\hat{L}^*$ merely restate the Pareto principle and the principle of minimal liberalism for a choice function that is not necessarily generated by a preference relation. It is easy to show that conditions $\hat{P}$, $\hat{L}^*$ and U are inconsistent when imposed on a collective choice mechanism (strictly not a CCR) that specifies a social choice function, given the set of individual preference orderings. In fact the previous example with a, b and c, will suffice and it can be shown that by condition $\hat{P}$, the choice set for (a, b, c) must not include b, and by condition $\hat{L}^*$, that choice set must not include a or c. Hence the choice set must be empty. If we relax acyclicity, then the motivation of the conditions requires that the conditions be restated, and this brings back the impossibility. Relaxing acyclicity is, thus, not a very promising way out.

6.4. CRITIQUE OF LIBERAL VALUES

It is, of course, possible to argue for the rejection of condition L^*. One argument may be the following: The idea that certain things are a person's 'personal' affair is insupportable. If the colour of Mr A's walls disturbs Mr B, then it is Mr B's business as well. If it makes Mr A unhappy that Mr B should lie on his belly while asleep, or that he should read *Lady Chatterley's Lover* while awake, then Mr A *is* a relevant party to the choice.

This is, undoubtedly, a possible point of view, and the popularity of rules such as a ban on smoking marijuana, or suppression of homosexual practices or of pornography, reflect, at least partly, such a point of view. Public policy is often aimed at imposing on individuals the will of others even on matters that may directly concern only those individuals. However, condition L^* is really extremely weak and a rejection of it is to deny such liberal considerations *altogether*. Only one pair of alternatives per person is involved in condition L^* and that for only two persons. My guess is that condition L^*, in that very weak form, and even the somewhat stronger condition L, will find many champions.[1] To deny condition L^* is not merely to violate liberalism, as usually understood, but to deny even the most limited expressions of individual freedom. And also to deny privacy, since the choice between x and y may be that between being forced to confess on one's personal affairs (x) and not being so forced (y). Thus support for L or L^* may come even from people who are not 'liberals' in the usual sense.

6.5. CRITIQUE OF THE PARETO PRINCIPLE

An alternative is to reject the Pareto principle. It was pointed out in Chapter 2 that this principle, particularly in its 'weak' form, is something of a sacred cow in the literature on social welfare. But one can construct an argument against it based on examples of the type considered in Section 6.2 and Theorem 6*1. It may be argued that it is

---

[1] The appeal of L or L^* would depend on the nature of the alternatives that are offered for choice. If the choices are all non-personal, e.g., to outlaw untouchability or not, to declare war against another country or not, conditions L or L^* should not have much appeal. However, in choices involving personal variations L or L^* would be appealing. It is not being suggested that the conflict in question will be disturbing in every collective choice situation, but that there are many real choices where this conflict may raise serious difficulties.

not merely important to know who prefers what, but also *why* he has this preference. Mr *A* does not wish to read the book himself if the choice is between his reading it and no one reading it, but he wants to deny Mr *B* the advantage of reading it (an advantage that *B* values vis-a-vis not reading it). This particular nature of *A*'s preference ordering, it could be argued, distracts from the value of *A*'s preference for his reading the book vis-a-vis *B* reading the book. Preferences based on excessive nosiness about what is good for others, should be, it could be argued, ignored.

This line of reasoning, appealing or not, raises doubts also about things other than the Pareto principle. First, if social choice were to depend not merely on individual preferences but also on other things, e.g., the causation of those preferences, then the concept of a collective choice rule (and therefore also of an SWF or an SDF) is itself in doubt. Social preference would then no longer be a function of individual preferences only.

Second, it may, however, be argued that the collective choice mechanism cannot really work on information of such a complicated nature as causation of (or reasoning behind) an individual ordering, and the only way it can take this consideration into account is by using preferences over other pairs of alternatives, as in the case noted above. Mr *A*'s preference for his reading the book rather than Mr *B* reading it could be thought to be rendered unimportant if it is noted that given the choice Mr *A* would rather not read it at all. If this approach is accepted, then we are confined to a CCR (and possibly an SWF or an SDF), but condition *I* (the independence of irrelevant alternatives) is violated.

In Theorems 6*1 and 6*2, condition *I* is not used as such, but the social decisions generated by the Pareto principle satisfy condition *I* and even this implicit use of the condition may be objectionable.[2] If social preference between *x* and *y* should depend on individual preferences only between *x* and *y*, then the weak Pareto principle seems to be altogether compelling. If, however, such an independence is not assumed, then it can be argued that the set of individual preferences

---

[2] The use of condition *I* in the proof of Arrow's General Possibility Theorem (Theorem 3*1) is, of course, much more direct and pervasive (see proof of Lemma 3*a).

between x and y is inadequate information for a social choice between x and y. In this respect it seems slightly misleading to call the Pareto quasi-ordering 'the unanimity quasi-ordering',[3] since the unanimity in question is only over the particular pair.

If the Pareto principle is rejected, the consequence of that for collective choice in general and for welfare economics in particular must be immense. Most of the usual political choice mechanisms are Pareto-inclusive. While free market allocation does not necessarily achieve Pareto-optimality when externalities are present, Pareto-optimality is taken to be a goal that is regrettably missed. What seems to follow from the problem under discussion is that Pareto-optimality may not even be a desirable objective in the presence of externalities in the shape of 'nosiness'.[4] The consequences of all this are far-reaching.

Once again, the rejection of the Pareto principle cannot be a source of great joy. It is a highly appealing criterion and many would hesitate a lot to let it go. Bringing in 'irrelevant' alternatives, as was done in the reasoning, is somewhat worrying, especially since the evidence of 'nosiness', which may or may not be regarded as deplorable, is only indirect. Mr A's reason for preferring to read the book himself rather than giving it to Mr B may be based on A's expectation of B's social behaviour after he reads that 'dangerous' book. Merely by looking at A's preference ordering, no conclusive evidence for *genuine* nosiness can be found. While the Pareto principle seems to be open to doubt, a violation of it seems to require some caution.

6.6. CRITIQUE OF UNRESTRICTED DOMAIN

The use of condition U in practically all impossibility theorems in collective choice tends to be important. For many configurations of

---

[3] Arrow (1951) p. 36.
[4] Incidentally, in the example, the 'liberal' solution, viz., b in (a, b, c), is not merely not Pareto-optimal, it is also a point of disequilibrium. So the market will not achieve the Pareto-inoptimal 'liberal' solution either.

individual preferences no conflict between conditions P and L^* (or L) will arise. If in reality actual preferences were all of such a benign type, then the problem under discussion may be shrugged off. We did, however, find examples that seemed plausible and which led to a conflict.

While the problem cannot be dismissed this way, it can certainly be argued that the eventual guarantee for individual freedom cannot be found in mechanisms of collective choice, but in developing values and preferences that respect each other's privacy and personal choices.

In the dilemmas and conflicts discussed in this chapter, a few lessons seem obvious. The Pareto principle does, of course, conflict with minimal liberalism unless individual preferences fall into certain specific patterns. This choice may cause no great confusion for a determined liberal.[5] The type of reasoning that justifies L^* seems to debunk a complete adherence to the Pareto principle P. There is no great tragedy even for the no-nonsense man who denies the notion of 'nosiness' and takes A's interest in B's 'personal' affairs as justification for regarding that to be A's affair also. He would very likely accept condition P and reject L^*. The real dilemma is only for an intermediate observer, who finds the concept of nosiness meaningful and relevant, but does not want the Pareto principle to be rejected even when individual preferences are nosey. This position is slightly schizophrenic, but that is no great consolation since a great many people *are* schizophrenic in this sense.

It is also possible to argue that whether a certain condition on a CCR such as the Pareto principle, or minimal liberalism, is a good condition or not might depend much on what patterns of individual preferences would actually hold, and not on what patterns are logically conceivable. A condition may be fine for a CCR with a certain restricted domain and another may be alright for a CCR with a different restricted domain, and, given a possible conflict between the

---

[5] The term liberal is used in many senses. not all of which are consistent. Here, it is used to refer to a person who is deeply concerned with preserving individual freedom from interference by others.

two, we might choose with an eye to the likely sets of individual preferences. It is possible to argue for a CCR that satisfies condition P over a domain Δ^1 and satisfies condition L^* over a domain Δ^2, with Δ^1 and Δ^2 having some, but not all, common elements. This prospect may not make the air electric with expectations, but it is formally a possible way out of the disturbing dilemma.

Chapter 6*
The Liberal Paradox

6*1. LIBERALISM VERSUS THE PARETO PRINCIPLE

Liberal values seem to require that there are choices that are personal and the relevant person should be free to do what he likes. It would be socially better, in these cases, to permit him to do what he wants, everything else remaining the same. We define the condition of liberalism in a very weak form.

Condition L (liberalism): For each person i there is at least one pair of distinct alternatives (x, y) such that he is decisive in the social choice between them in either order, i.e., $x\, P_i\, y \to x\, P\, y$, and $y\, P_i\, x \to y\, P\, x$.

This condition can be weakened by requiring such limited decisiveness not for all persons, but for at least some. If we demand it for only one, then of course it is not a case of liberalism, since it will be consistent with dictatorship as well. So we must require it for at least two individuals.

Condition L* (minimal liberalism): There are at least two persons k and j and two pairs of distinct alternatives (x, y) and (z, w) such that k and j are decisive over (x, y) and (z, w), respectively, each pair taken in either order.

Obviously, $L \to L^*$, but not vice versa.

THEOREM 6*1. *There is no SDF satisfying conditions U, P and L*.*

Proof. If (x, y) and (z, w) are the same pair, then obviously condition L^* cannot hold. If the pairs have one of the elements in common, say $x = z$, then let $x\,P_k\,y$, $w\,P_j\,x$, and $\forall i: y\,P_i\,w$. By condition L^*, $x\,P\,y$ and $w\,P\,x$, and by condition P, $y\,P\,w$. This violates acyclicity and there is no best alternative.

Next, let all four of the alternatives be distinct. Assume now that $x\,P_k\,y$, $z\,P_j\,w$ and $\forall i: (w\,P_i\,x\ \&\ y\,P_i\,z)$.[1] By condition L^*, $x\,P\,y\ \&\ z\,P\,w$. By condition P, $w\,P\,x\ \&\ y\,P\,z$. But this too violates acyclicity. Hence there is no SDF that will satisfy condition L^* and P, given condition U, which completes the proof.

Note that the condition of the independence of irrelevant alternatives is not imposed. Nor do we require social preference to be transitive, or even quasi-transitive, and all that is ruled out is acyclicity. Then theorem is disturbing, and even the corollary given below, which is much weaker, is disturbing.

COROLLARY 6*1.1. *There is no SDF satisfying condition U, P and L.*

6*2. EXTENSIONS

A dilemma close to the one in Theorem 6*1 can be posed by relaxing the conditions that the two persons be decisive in either order, and requiring instead that they be decisive over two *ordered* pairs that are distinct in each element.

Condition L^{**}: There are at least two persons k and j and two ordered pairs of alternatives (x, y) and (z, w), all four alternatives being distant, such that $x\,P_k\,y \to x\,P\,y$, and $z\,P_j\,w \to z\,P\,w$.

THEOREM 6*2. *There is no SDF satisfying conditions U, P and L^{**}.*

The proof is the same as in the second paragraph of the proof of Theorem 6*1. Note, however, that neither does L^* imply L^{**}, nor does L^{**} imply L^*, so that the two theorems are independent.

---

[1] Note that there are orderings *compatible* with each of the individual preference relations specified.

Finally, we propose another condition L^{***}.

Condition L^{***}:   There are at least two persons k and j and two ordered pairs of alternatives (x, y) and (z, w), with $x \neq z$ and $y \neq w$, and such that $x P_k y \rightarrow x P y$, and $z P_j w \rightarrow z P w$.

THEOREM 6*3.   *There is no SDF satisfying conditions U, P and L^{***}.*

The proof, which is omitted here, is in the same line as that of Theorem 6*1. Note that $L^{**} \rightarrow L^{***}$, and $L \rightarrow L^* \rightarrow L^{***}$, so the Theorem 6*3 subsumes Theorems 6*1 and 6*2, and Corollary 6*1.1, without being subsumed. The logical gain is, however, not matched by a significant gain in relevance, so that in discussing the liberal dilemma, we could very well concentrate on Theorem 6*1, which is what we did in Chapter 6.

Chapter 7
Interpersonal Aggregation and Comparability

7.1. INDEPENDENCE OF IRRELEVANT ALTERNATIVES

It was noted in Chapter 3 that the rank-order method of voting is an SWF which satisfies condition U, P and D, but not condition I. In Chapter 6 some arguments against the imposition of condition I were put forward in the specific context of the liberal paradox. Other reasons have also been noted in the literature (see Rothenberg (1961); also Wilson (1968c)). It should, however, be observed that relaxing condition I opens up a number of possibilities, of which the rank-order method is only one. In fact, the classic approach of utilitarianism is ruled out by condition I, and if the condition of the independence of irrelevant alternatives is relaxed, that avenue may also be explored. However, it is not merely condition I that rules out aggregating individual utilities. The very definition of a collective choice rule outlaws it, since a CCR makes the social ordering a function of the set of individual orderings. Any change in utility measures without a change of the individual orderings R_i must leave the social ordering R generated by any CCR completely unchanged. This applies, naturally, also to such special cases of a CCR as an SWF and an SDF. But even if a CCR is redefined, so that the utility measures are admitted as arguments, the problem of condition I could remain.

It may not be obvious how condition I prevents the use of utilitarianism. The name 'independence of irrelevant alternatives' is somewhat misleading. Two aspects of it must be distinguished. First, condition I is violated when, in the social choice involving x and y, the individual rankings of a third alternative, say z, vis-a-vis either x or y or any other alternative, become a relevant factor, with an influence. This we can call the 'irrelevance' aspect of the condition. Second, the condition, as stated, is violated if in the social choice involving x and y anything other than the individual *orderings* over x and y get a place, e. g., preference intensities. This may or may not include the placing of irrelevant alternatives in individual orderings. This we can call the 'ordering' aspect of the condition. The 'irrelevance' aspect is only a part of the 'ordering' aspect, though in the naming of the condition, concentration seems to be only on the 'irrelevance' aspect (see Rothenberg (1961) and Sen (1966c)).

An example will perhaps clarify the logical difference. Suppose each individual had a unique cardinal scale of utility and this for every one had been but together in a gigantic book, published in heaven. Suppose we wanted to use these cardinal utility indicators in a social choice involving two alternatives social states, x and y. We would not have to look at any irrelevant alternatives for the purpose of constructing a scale, since each individual's utility scale could be looked up on any weekday in any public library that has this precious book. Let us imagine that after adding up the difference in the utilities between x and y for the individuals, the sum came out positive, and using utilitarianism we declared x to be socially preferred to y. Meanwhile people started feeling a change in their utility scales. Shortly afterwards, let us further imagine, it was announced in heaven that people's utility scales had changed, and a new edition of the book was being made available presently. It turned out on inspection that everyone's ordering of x and y, and indeed of all other certain alternatives, had remained the same, but the cardinal gaps between them had changed. After adding up the differences in the utilities between x and y for all individuals, this time it turned out that the sum was negative, and so y was declared socially preferred to x. This involved a violation of Arrow's condition of the independence of irrelevant alternatives. But no irrelevant alternative had ever entered the picture. This is a case of violation of the 'ordering' aspect of the condition without involving the 'irrelevance' aspect of it.

In practice, however, this may not make much actual difference, in spite of the analytical differences involved. Individual utilities are not found in natural cardinal units, and cardinalization follows experimental observations, yielding a set of numbers that are unique *but for* an increasing linear transformation. Since the utility scale has to be fixed by specifying the utility value of two points on it, implicitly or explicitly, the other alternatives come into this valuation.[1] In trying to achieve an interpersonal correspondence, for the sake of social aggregation, this has to be done, and then any use of preference intensity violates not only the 'ordering' aspect of the condition, but also its 'irrelevance' aspect.

An illustration might help might to clarify the point. Let us imagine that there are only three alternatives relevant for our consideration, viz., x, y and z. Let individual 1 rank them in the order stated. Some experiment also reveals the following utility numbers for the three: 200, 110, and 100, respectively, but the numbers are unique *up to* a linear transformation. There is, thus, no natural correspondence between the utility numbers of the different individuals. A common convention is to attach the value 0 to the worst alternative, and the value 1 to the best. A linear transformation of the original set of numbers, therefore, yields 1 for x, 0.1 for y, and 0 for z. By a similar method of normalization let the utility numbers of two other individuals turn out to be exactly the same, in particular, 1 for y, 0.6 for x, and 0 for z. If the community consists of these three, x wins over y, for the aggregate utility from x is 2.2, and that from y is 2.1. Next imagine that individuals 2 and 3 revise their opinion of z, an irrelevant alternative in the choice between x and y. They now regard z to be just as good as x. While everyone's attitude to x and y has remained the same, nevertheless the utility numbers of x and y will change for persons 2 and 3. For them, x will now have value 0, while y will continue to get 1. Now y will win over x, y having an aggregate utility of 2.1 as opposed to x's 1. The social ordering between x and y is reversed by a change in the position of an irrelevant alternative, z.[2]

---

[1] This will be so even if the utility numbers were unique up to a proportional transformation, for the 'units' will still be arbitrary.

[2] The particular example discussed here is a slight variation of the one discussed by Arrow (1963), p. 32.

Note that the result is not due to the particular method of normalization used. For example, if we follow the rule of taking the worst alternatives as 0, and the aggregate of utilities from all the social states[3] as 1, the same problem can occur. It does occur, as it happens, in the numerical example discussed above. In the initial situation, which this method of numbering, individual 1 gets (10/11) unit of utility from x, (1/11) from y, and 0 from z, while individuals 2 and 3 get (5/8) from y, (3/8) from x, and 0 from z. Here, x yields more aggregate utility than y. Now if z moves up to be indifferent to x for individuals 2 and 3, the numbers become (0, 1, 0) for (x, y, z), respectively, for individuals 2 and 3. Now, y yields more aggregate utility than x, reversing the social choice between x and y, as a consequence of a change in the ordering involving an irrelevant alternative. The problem is indeed perfectly general, and arises entirely because of the fact that the utility scales have arbitrary 'units'.[4]

7.2. COMPARABILITY, CARDINALITY AND DISCRIMINATION

The question of arbitrariness of individual utility units is largely a reflection of the problem of interpersonal comparability. If utility scales of different persons are calculated separately, as in experimental methods involving, say, the von Neumann-Morgenstern approach, then interpersonal correspondences are left completely undefined. It is possible to, say, double the units of one individual, leaving it the same for others, and this will immediately alter the interpersonal trade-offs.

In our fancy example in the last section, involving the big book, this problem was avoided because the utility measures came for

---

[3] The numbers of social states considered must be the same for all individuals.

[4] Being unique only up to a linear transformation, they also have arbitrary 'origins', but that is not crucial for utilitarianism, since it makes use only of utility differences between x and y.

everyone in a one-to-one correspondence. Behaviouristic measures of utility in terms of people's expressions include an interpersonally comparable element. It may be possible to say that person A is happier than person B by looking at delighted Mr A and morose Mr B. It may also be possible to make marginal comparisons. This approach to objective interpersonal comparability has been most elegantly put forward by Little (1950).[5]

In Chapter 7* an approach will be developed which permits interpersonal variability of any degree, from infinite variability to none. Meanwhile, however, we must be clear about the distinction between (a) getting a cardinal measure of individual welfare, and (b) getting some rules for interpersonal comparisons, and review the main theories in the light of these two questions.

One attempt at cardinalization of individual utility has been based on the assumption that the individuals cannot really make very fine comparisons, so that each person only has a finite number of 'levels of discrimination'. The difference between one discrimination level and the next is the minimum utility difference that is noticeable to the individual. The individual is 'indifferent' between all alternatives that belong to the same discrimination level and we can get a cardinal measure of the utility difference between any two alternatives by checking how many discrimination levels separate them. The cardinal scale thus obtained is, of course, unique up to positive linear transformation, and subject to the choice of an origin and a unit, a unique cardinal utility function is obtained. Based on this approach originally touched on by Borda (1781) and Edgeworth (1881), the problem of cardinalization has been explored by Armstrong (1951), Goodman and Markowitz (1952), and Rothenberg (1961), among others.

Regarding interpersonal comparability, Goodman and Markowitz make the normative assumption that the ethical significance of a movement from one discrimination level to the next is the same for each individual, and it is independent of the level from which this

---

[5] Little points out that, even though interpersonal comparisons may be, in this approach, perfectly objective, the goal of maximizing aggregate utility for the society is based on a value judgment, and one that may not be easy to accept.

change is made. The calculation becomes very simple with this assumption. If alternative x is to be compared with alternative y, check by now many discrimination levels does x exceed (or fall short of) y in each individual's scale; and then simply add the differences in levels, with appropriate sings.

The difficulties with this approach are reasonably clear. The practical problems in the use of this method in real life need not be emphasized here (they are, in any case, clear enough), but three are analytical difficulties also. First, as Goodman and Markowitz themselves point out, it is not possible to observe all the discrimination levels of an individual, given a fixed set of alternatives. Thus the numbering system depends on the actual availability of the alternatives. Suppose a new commodity becomes available, and this expands the set of feasible alternatives for the individual; it is now perfectly possible for new discrimination levels to emerge, which lie in between the old discrimination levels. This will alter the utility numbering system used for the individual. Thus the social evaluation between two alternatives x and y will not be independent of what other alternatives are available.

A second difficulty lies in the ethical assumption that the significance for social welfare of a change from one discrimination level to the next is the same for all individuals. Not only is this an arbitrary assumption, it is eminently objectionable when dealing with individuals who appear to differ in the sensitivity of their perception. Someone may have a small number of discrimination levels but feel very strongly about the difference between one level and another, and another may have a large number of discrimination levels but regard the difference between the one and the next to be not worth worrying about. In this case the Goodman-Markowitz system will be very partial.[6] Indeed, there are individuals who tend to be extremists and find things either 'magnificent' or 'horrible', while others finely

---

[6] In fact Arrow (1963) shows (pp. 117–18) that with the Goodman-Markowitz system a slight difference in the sensitivity of the two persons can make complete inequality (with no income going to the less sensitive individual and all to the other) the socially 'optimum' outcome in a problem of distribution.

differentiate between such things as 'excellent', 'good', 'mediocre', 'poor' and 'awful'. It seems manifestly unfair to make the ethical assumption that the welfare significance of moving the first individual from what he regards as 'horrible' to what he finds as 'magnificent' is no more than moving the second individual from what he finds 'poor' and what strikes him as 'mediocre'. What is particularly objectionable about this particular mechanism is not that it violates condition *I,* which of course it does, but that it implies an ethical assumption that will appear to be arbitrary and objectionable.

7.3. USES OF VON NEUMANN-MORGENSTERN CARDINALIZATION

The behaviour of a rational individual in a market involving no risks can be, in general, explained entirely in terms of ordinal utility.[7] If we try to derive a utility scale for an individual in terms of his behaviour under perfect certainty, without making some very special assumptions of 'independence' of commodity groups (or more generally, of action sets),[8] the utility numbers will be unique only up to a monotonic transformation. However, the situation changes radically when we consider rational behaviour in risky situations. As demonstrated by von Neumann and Morgenstern (1947), provided a person's behaviour satisfies a set of clearly definable postulates, we can find a set of utility numbers for him corresponding to the set of alternatives, such that his behaviour can be taken to be an attempt at the maximization of the mathematical expectation of these utility numbers.[9] These numbers can be shown to be unique up to a positive linear transformation.

---

[7] In fact, even the assumption of the existence of an ordinal utility is too demanding. With a lexicographic ordering, the alternatives may be completely ordered without there being a utility scale (even ordinal) that can be fitted to it. See Chapter 3.

[8] See Samuelson (1947), Leontief (1947a), (1947b), Debreu (1960), Koopmans (1966), Gorman (1968).

[9] The mathematical expectation of utility is the same thing as the 'moral expectation' of Bernoulli (1730). The utility from each alternative is weighted by its probability. See also Ramsey (1931).

A set of postulates sufficient for this was put forward by von Neumann and Morgenstern (1947), and other sets have been presented by Marschak (1950), and others. They have much in common, but the Marschak postulates are simpler to follow.

There are four postulates in the Marschak system: (a) the postulate of *complete ordering*, i.e., the relation of preference establishes a weak ordering among all prospects; (b) the postulate of *continuity*, i.e., if prospect x is preferred to prospect y and y in its turn is preferred to prospect z, then there is a probability mixture of x and z (a 'lottery' involving the two) that makes the individual indifferent between that mixture and the certainty of y; (c) the postulate of the number of non-indifferent prospects being *sufficient*, viz., there must be at least four mutually non-indifferent prospects; and (d) the postulate of the *equivalence of the mixture of equivalent prospects*, i.e., if prospect x and prospect x^* are indifferent, then for any prospect y, a given probability mixture of x and y must be indifferent to a similar mixture of x^* and y.[10]

We cannot possibly go into a detailed evaluation of this approach here. We should, however, note a few of the simpler problems of using this approach. First, it is clear that the postulates imply the following 'monotonicity' property: 'If one alternative is better than another increase the probability of the former at the expense of the latter. If opportunities are unlimited, choose the prospect that promises the best history with 100% probability.'[11] But, as Marschak points out, a mountain climber with the 'love of danger' (or of gambling) may prefer a survival chance of 95% to that of, say, 80%, but also to one of 100%. For him monotonicity will not do.

A second reservation concerns the postulate of continuity. A person who regards gambling or taking chances as 'sinful' may prefer a

[10] There are three different versions of postulate (c) discussed by Marschak. We have chosen the one which is easiest to comprehend. Samuelson (1952) calls postulate (d) 'the strong independence assumption'. It is also called 'the sure-thing principle' especially in the literature of game theory.

[11] Marschak (1950), p. 138. (The result follows from Theorem 6 of Marschak.) The word 'history' is used in a somewhat special sense here, meaning the prospects over 'future time Intervals, up to a certain time point called horizon', defined by Marschak as 'future history' (p. 113).

very poor life with taking no chances (x) to gambling with a good prospect to win a fortune (y), and that to gambling with no prospect to win (z). But there may not be any mixture of x and z that will make him indifferent to y, for once he takes a chance on x, i.e., a chance on 'a very poor life with taking no chances', he is in the sinful quota anyway, and then might sensibly prefer gambling with a good prospect to win (y) to all combinations of x and z. For him the preference for x against y lies in its purity, which is destroyed with a gamble involving x and z. This is a violation of postulate (b).

Postulate (d) is also open to doubt. It does not, of course, rule out people enjoying 'taking a chance' or hating it, as von Neumann and Morgenstern correctly point out.[12] But a person may get his thrill from the *number* of lotteries that he takes part in, and not only on the overall probabilities. It is a fair bet that a gambler may prefer to have several goes at the wheel to having one simple turn representing the probabilities of the whole series for the evening compounded into one.

What is, however, certainly true is that the postulates do not rule out people having simple attitudes towards gambling as such, viz., liking it or not liking it, as long as this is related only to the overall probability distribution, simple or compound. The utility numbers take the attitude to risk into account, and this is indeed one of the sources of objection to the use of these utilities for social choice. Arrow has pointed out that the von Neumann-Morgenstern utility indicators may not be the appropriate scale to use for social choice, i.e., 'if we are interested primarily in making a social choice among alternative policies in which no random elements enter. To say otherwise would be to assert that the distribution of the social income is to be governed by the tastes of the individuals for gambling.'[13]

This objection, in spite of its faintly priggish air, is a strong one, and relates to the general problem of arbitrariness of *any* cardinal

---

[12] See von Neumann and Morgenstern (1947), p. 28, in the context of their postulate C. See also Marschak (1950), p. 139.

[13] Arrow (1951), p. 10.

scale in choices over certain alternatives. This arbitrariness applies to other methods of cardinalization, such as the approach of assuming the independence of action sets.[14] For example, a person may happen to satisfy independence in choosing between social states on earth given hypothetical states in heaven and vice versa, and this could help the cardinalization of his utilities on earth. Should this cardinal element be relevant for social choices here and now? This is not at all obvious. Further, the independence assumption needed in this case is stronger than that required for von Neumann-Morgenstern cardinalization (viz., postulate (d) of Marschak discussed above), since the latter does not deny complementarity in the usual sense, as the former does.[15]

All this is somewhat discouraging, but not decisively so. First, any particular cardinal scale is 'arbitrary' only in the sense that, in choices over the set of certain alternatives (or over a relevant subset of it), individual behaviour is consistent with other methods of scaling as well. But in an ethical argument one may wish to choose some particular scaling in spite of this 'arbitrariness', on some *other* grounds that may be additionally specified. Second, as Harsanyi (1953), (1955), has argued, we may be interested in individual preferences over social states with an as-if element of uncertainty deliberately built into it, as was noted in Chapter 5. People's 'ethical judgments' may be defined as judgments they would subscribe to if they had an equal chance of being in anyone's shoes. With this interpretation, individual preferences will be choices over risky alternatives, and people's 'attitude to gambling' may indeed be an appropriate element in social choice. Thus there are frameworks of collective choice for which the von Neumann-Morgenstern cardinalization *is* the relevant one.

Third, all is not lost if more than one method of cardinalization are found to be relevant. Procedures of aggregation can still be used

---

[14] See Samuelson (1947), Leontief (1947a), (1947b), Debreu (1960), Koopmans (1966) and Gorman (1968). See also Luce and Tukey (1964) and Luce (1966).

[15] See Samuelson (1952), Manne (1952), Malinvaud (1952) and others in the same number of *Econometrica*, 20, 1952.

to obtain quasi-orderings that rank some social states vis-a-vis each other, though not necessarily all of them (see Chapter 7*, especially Section 7*4). We can use each measure and take the common rankings, which will thus be non-controversial. This problem will be discussed in Sections 7.5 and 7*4.

Cardinal measurability is only a part of the problem of using utilitarianism;[16] another is interpersonal aggregation. With von Neumann-Morgenstern cardinalization, this difficulty is as serious as in any other system, since the measures are entirely personal. Any method of interpersonal normalization is open to criticisms. It may be argued that some systems, e.g., assigning in each person's scale the value 0 to the worst alternative and the value 1 to his best alternative, are interpersonally 'fair', but such an argument is dubious. First, there are other systems with comparable symmetry, e.g., the system we discussed earlier of assigning 0 to the worst alternative and the value 1 to the *sum* of utilities from all alternatives. Neither system is noticeably less fair than the other (one assumes equal maximal utility for all and the other assumes equal average utility for all), but they will yield different bases of social choice.[17] Second, in comparing the utility measures of different persons, one may wish deliberately to take account of interpersonal variability of capacity for satisfaction, e.g., one may wish to give special consideration to handicapped people whose enjoyment measure may be thought to be uniformly lower.[18]

---

[16] This expression 'utilitarianism' is being used very broadly here as the approach of maximizing aggregate individual welfares. In fact, 'utilitarianism' corresponds to that special case where individual welfare is identified with individual 'utility' defined as the person's psychological feeling of satisfaction. It has now become conventional in economics and in some other social sciences to define utility as any measure of individual welfare, not necessarily a measure of 'pleasure' in the sense of Bentham. We follow this practice, even though it is a somewhat doubtful procedure. Contrast Little (1950).

[17] In an important contribution, Hildreth (1953) considers two specially defined social states X and Y such that everyone prefers X to Y, and assigns two fixed real values a and b to them, respectively, in everyone's utility scale (p. 87). This too, given the assumption, is a possible method of interpersonal normalization.

[18] This is not easy to do in the utilitalian framework, but is important in other approaches, e.g., in Rawls' theory of justice (Chapter 9).

Again, the situation is not really quite hopeless, though the problems are serious. One way of facing the problem is to use a number of alternative schemes of interpersonal normalization and select those pair-wise rankings which are invariant with respect to the choice of any of these schemes. We discuss this approach of 'partial comparability' in the next section, or more formally in Chapter 7*.

7.4. PARTIAL COMPARABILITY

Suppose we are debating the consequence on the aggregate welfare of Romans of the act of Rome being burnt while Nero played his fiddle. We recognize that Nero was delighted while the other Romans suffered, but suppose we still say that the sum total of welfare went down as a consequence. What type of interpersonal comparability are we assuming? If there is no comparability at all, we can change the utility units of different individuals differently, and by multiplying Nero's utility measures by a suitably large number it should be possible to make Nero's gain larger in size than the loss of others. Hence we are not assuming non-comparability. But are we assuming that every Roman's welfare units can be put into one-to-one correspondence with the welfare units of every other Roman? Not necessarily. We might not be sure what precise correspondence to take, and we might admit some possible variability, but we could still be able to assert that no matter which of the various possible combinations we take, the sum total went down in any case. This is a case intermediate between non-comparability and full comparability of units.

To take another example, suppose we denounce the existing inequality in the distribution of money income, and assert that this amounts to a lower aggregate of individual welfare. Are we assuming that we can put everyone's welfare units into one-to-one correspondence? We do not have to. We may be somewhat uncertain about the precise welfare functions of the different individuals and the precise correspondence between the respective welfare units, but we could quite reasonably still assert that in every possible case within the permitted variations the sum-total is less than what could happen with a more equal distribution. The attack of Robbins (1932) and others on interpersonal comparability does not distinguish between *some* comparability and *total* comparability of units, and the consequence has been the virtual elimination of distributional questions from the formal literature on welfare economics. (Among the exceptions are Lerner (1944), Dobb (1955), (1969), Fisher (1956), Mishan (1960), and a few others.)

What we may wish to do is to introduce some limited variability in the relative welfare units of different individuals, and deal not with one-to-one correspondences but with many-to-many correspondences. The general framework is developed in Chapter 7* but here we can illustrate the approach in terms of a simple example.

Consider the following case: There are three individuals *A*, *B* and *C*, and three alternatives *x*, *y* and *z*. As arbitrators we are trying to figure out which alternative is socially most desirable in terms of aggregate welfare. We first obtain the cardinal welfare functions of the three; each of these is of course unique only up to an increasing linear transformation. We reflect on the correspondences between the welfare units of the three individuals, but cannot decide completely. We may be inclined to use, say, the familiar normalization procedure of setting the welfare from the worst alternative as 0 and that from the best alternative as 1 for each individual, even though we may not be really convinced that this is exactly right. Suppose that this yields Table 7.1.

Table 7.1. Tentative Welfare Indicators

Individuals	Alternatives		
	x	*y*	*z*
A	1	0.90	0
B	1	0.88	0
C	0	0.95	1

In terms of welfare sum the tentative ordering is *y*, *x*, *z*, in decreasing order. What other criterion can we use? Note that no alternative in this collection is Pareto-superior to any other. In terms of majority decision, we get a consistent social ordering, with *x* being socially preferred to y and that being preferred to z, but it raises some doubts. It would appear that C's preference for y over x is very sharp, while the preference of A or B for x over y is rather mild. But this comparison of 'sharpness' or 'mildness' depends on our assumptions about interpersonal comparisons. If, for example, we blow up the welfare levels of A ten times, by choosing correspondingly smaller units for A, then A's welfare from x, y and z will respectively be equal to 10, 9 and 0. Then A's preference for x over y (measured by 1) will look even sharper than C's preference for y over x (measured by 0.95).

Is a ten-fold blow-up for A legitimate? Our value judgments may be imprecise and we may be agreeable to accept some variability, but we might nevertheless feel that a ten-fold blow-up is too large a variation. We may set the limit as raising or lowering the welfare units of any person by a factor of, say, 2 either way. If any alternative has at least as large a welfare sum as any other unit for every possible combination within these limits the former can be said to have at least as large an aggregate welfare as the latter. To check this we obtain the welfare differences in our first estimate (Table 7.2).

Table 7.2. Tentative Welfare Differences

Individuals	Between		
	x and y	y and z	z and x
A	0.10	0.90	−1.00
B	0.12	0.88	−1.00
C	−0.95	−0.05	1.00

We first take x and y for comparison. Under the first estimate the sum of the welfare difference of the three individuals between x and y is −0.73, so that y seems to be favored. We can, however, change these welfare difference measures. The most favorable combination for x against y is to double A's and B's measures and to halve C's measures. This yields a net gap of −0.035, so that y still has a larger welfare sum than x. Hence y can be declared to be better than x, according to the aggregation criterion with the specified degree of variability

Coming to y and z, the most favorable combination for z is to halve the welfare measures of A and B and to double it for C, but still the welfare sum for y is larger than that for z by 0.79. Hence y is better than z.

However, the comparison of z and x is inconclusive. As they stand in Tables 7.1 and 7.2, x has a larger welfare sum, but if we halve A's and B's welfare measures and double C's, we get a difference in favor of z and not x. Hence the aggregation relation must be declared to be incomplete over this pair. But, as it happens, this does not affect the choice between x, y and z, since y is noted to be better than both x and z. There is a unique best element.

This is a very simple example; the general framework is analysed in Chapter 7*. The example considered here is a special case of what is called 'strong symmetry' in that chapter. 'Strong symmetry' is a special case of 'weak symmetry', which is itself a special case of 'regularity'. There will be no attempt here to summarize the results of Chapter 7* besides noting that (a) under every assumption of comparability, however partial, the aggregation relation R^a is always reflexive and transitive; (b) R^a always subsumes the Pareto quasi-ordering and coincides with it under non-comparability; (c) under 'regularity', if the extent of partial comparability is made more strict, then the aggregation relation gets extended monotonically; (d) under 'weak symmetry' we can find a measure of the degree d of partial comparability between 0 and 1, such that $d = 0$ implies non-comparability, $d = 1$ implies complete comparability of units, and $d^1 > d^2$ implies that the aggregation quasi-ordering under the latter will be a subrelation of that under the former. Thus, under some relatively mild assumptions, we would find a very well-behaved sequence of quasi-orderings, each a subrelation of the next, starting with the Pareto quasi-ordering under non-comparability and ending up with a complete ordering under full comparability of units ('unit comparability'). A complete ordering can, of course, be reached for degrees of comparability less than 1, and it is possible that a 'best' element may emerge for even lower degrees partial comparability. Incidentally, in the example quoted, we had $d = 0.25$, and even with such a low degree of comparability a best alternative was seen to emerge. With a degree of comparability of 0.71 or more, a complete ordering would have been reached in that example. Complete comparability is not merely a doubtful assumption, it is also quite unnecessary.

7.5. ADDING ORDINAL-TYPE WELFARE

Just as haziness of values may exist about interpersonal comparisons, there might be some haziness even in measuring individual utility. As was noted before, more than one system of cardinalization is possible, and ethically it may be difficult to establish the superiority of one system over the others. If all these systems are admitted, then each individual will be associated with a set of utility functions, not all linear transformations of each other, unlike the case of cardinality. They will, of course, all be positive monotonic transformations of each other. But, unlike the case of strict ordinality, not every monotonic transformation will be necessarily included. We shall call this case that of 'ordinal-type' welfare. One extreme case of this is strict ordinality, when the set includes all positive monotonic transformations, while the other extreme is strict cardinality when only positive *linear* transformations are included.

With ordinal-type utility and partial comparability, it is possible to obtain a quasi-ordering of aggregation using the rule that if x has at least as large a welfare sum as y under every measure of individual utilities (given by the measurability assumptions) and under every interpersonal correspondence (given by the comparability assumptions), then and only then is x at least as good as y. Irrespective of the particular measurability and comparability assumptions chosen, an aggregation relation thus defined will be a quasi-ordering (i.e., will be transitive and reflexive), and will incorporate at least the Pareto quasi-ordering. The stricter the measurability and comparability assumptions, the more extensive will be the quasi-ordering. It is of course, possible to obtain a complete ordering even with less than strict cardinality and less than full comparability.

The formal analysis is presented in Section 7*4. The important point to note here is that cardinality and full interpersonal comparability of individual welfare units are *sufficient but not necessary* assumptions for rational choice under aggregate welfare maximization. Hence the rejection of these assumptions does not render the approach impotent, in contrast with what seems to be frequently held. The wide appeal of aggregate welfare maximization as an approach to the analysis of collective choice, of which classic utilitarianism is a special case, is based on an implicit use of a framework wider than that permitted by complete comparability and cardinality. Such a general framework, which is defined and analysed in Chapter 7*, does lack the sure-fire effectiveness of classical utilitarianism, which is one of its very special cases, but it avoids the cocksure character of utilitarianism as well as its unrestrained arbitrariness.

Chapter 7*
Aggregation Quasi-Orderings[1]

7*1. COMPARABILITY AND AGGREGATION

Let X be the set of alternative social states, x. Every individual i has a set L_i of real-valued welfare functions, W_i, each defined over X. If individual welfare is 'ordinally measurable', then every element of L_i is a positive monotonic transformation of every other element and furthermore every positive monotonic transformation of any element of L_i belongs to L_i. If, on the other hand, individual welfare is 'cardinally measurable', then every element of L_i is a positive linear transformation of every other element, and every positive linear transformation of any element of L_i belongs to L_i.[2] In this section and in the two following, cardinal measurability of individual welfare will be assumed. In Section 7*4, aggregation with non-cardinal utility will be studied.

To sum the levels of individual welfare, we have to choose one element from every L_i. We shall call any such n-tuple of individual welfare functions a functional combination.

DEFINITION 7*1. *A functional combination, W, is any element of the Cartesian product $\prod_{i=1}^{n} L_i$, denoted L.*

---

[1] This chapter is closely related to Sen (1970b).

[2] By a positive linear transformation, mappings of the following kind are meant: $U^1 = a + bU^2$, where a and b are constants, and $b > 0$. Strictly speaking, these are 'affine transformations', and not linear transformations, a term that algebraists would reserve for homogeneous transformations of the type $U^1 = bU^2$.

For the purpose of comparison of aggregate welfare of alternative social states in X, we define a subset $\bar{L}$ of L, and sum the individual welfare differences between any pair x, y in X for every element of $\bar{L}$. The specification of $\bar{L}$ reflects our assumptions of interpersonal comparability. We denote $x\, R^a\, y$ for x having at least as much aggregate welfare as y.

DEFINITION 7*2.　*A comparison set $\bar{L}$ is any specified subset of L, such that we declare that x has at least as much aggregate welfare as y, for any pair x, y, if and only if the sum of the individual welfare differences between x and y is non-negative for every element W of $\bar{L}$, i.e.,*

$$\forall x, y \in X: [x\, R^a\, y \leftrightarrow \forall\, W \in \bar{L}: \sum_i \{W_i(x) - W_i(y)\} \geqq 0]$$

We define $x\, P^a\, y$ as $x\, R^a\, y$ and $\sim(y\, R^a\, x)$, and $x\, I^a\, y$ as $x\, R^a\, y$ and $y\, R^a\, x$.

Certain distinguished cases of interpersonal comparability deserve special mention, and should help to illustrate the relation between interpersonal comparability and the comparison set. (We refer to the ith element of any W as W_i; it is the welfare level of person i.)

DEFINITION 7*3.　(1) *Non-comparability holds if and only if $L = \bar{L}$.*

(2) *Full comparability holds if and only if $\overline{W}$ being any element of $\bar{L}$ implies that $\bar{L}$ includes only and all functional combinations W such that for all i,*

$$W_i = a + b\, \overline{W}_i$$

where a, and $b > 0$, are constants, invariant with i.

(3) *Unit comparability holds if and only if $\overline{W}$ being any element of $\bar{L}$ implies that $\bar{L}$ includes only and all functional combinations W such that for all i,*

$$W_i = a_i + b\, \overline{W}_i$$

where a_i can vary with i but $b > 0$ must be invariant with respect to i.

In the case of non-comparability the set L of functional combinations is not restricted in any way to arrive at the comparison set $\bar{L}$. In the case of full comparability a particular one-to-one correspondence is established between the welfare functions of different individuals. In the case of unit comparability if the welfare function of one individual is specified, it specifies a one-parameter family of welfare functions for every other individual, each member of the family differing from any other by a constant (positive or negative). It may be noted that with unit comparability the absolute levels of individual welfare are not comparable (e.g., it makes no sense to say that person A is better off than person B), but welfare differences *are* comparable (e.g., it does make sense to say that person A gains more than B in the choice of social state x rather than y). In this case, welfare units are comparable (there is a one-to-one correspondence of welfare units), though the origins are arbitrary.

The following results concerning the binary relation of aggregation R^a are important. $\bar{R}$ and $\bar{P}$ are the Pareto preference relations as defined in Definition 2*2.

THEOREM 7*1.   *With cardinally measurable individual welfares*

(1) *For any* $\bar{L}$, *i.e., for every possible assumption of interpersonal comparability,* R^a *is a quasi-ordering.*

(2) *For any* $\bar{L}$, *i.e., for every possible assumption of interpersonal comparability,* $\bar{R}$ *is a subrelation of* R^a, *i.e.,* $\forall x, y \in X: [x \bar{R} y \rightarrow x R^a y]$ *and* $[x \bar{P} y \rightarrow x P^a y]$.

(3) *With non-comparability,* $R^a = \bar{R}$.

(4) *With unit comparability, or with full comparability,* R^a *is a complete ordering.*

Proof.   (1) Reflexivity of R^a follows directly from each W_i being an order-preserving transformation of R_i for every element of L. Transitivity of R^a is also immediate:

$$[x R^a \ y \ \& \ y R^a \ z] \rightarrow \sum_i [W_i(x) - W_i(y)] \geq 0 \qquad \text{and}$$

$$\sum_i [W_i(y) - W_i(z)] \geq 0 \qquad \text{for all } W \in \bar{L}$$

$$\rightarrow \sum_i [W_i(x) - W_i(z)] \geq 0 \qquad \text{for all } W \in \bar{L}$$

$$\rightarrow x R^a z$$

(2) For any $x, y \in X$:

$$x \bar{R} y \rightarrow \forall i: [W_i(x) - W_i(y)] \geq 0 \qquad \text{for every } W \in L$$
$$\rightarrow x R^a y$$

since $\bar{L} \subset L$. Further,

$$x \, \bar{P} \, y \rightarrow [\exists i : x \, P_i \, y \; \& \; \forall i : \; x \, R_i \, y]$$
$$\rightarrow \exists i : [W_i(x) - W_i(y)] > 0 \; \&$$
$$\forall i : [W_i(x) - W_i(y)] \geq 0 \qquad \text{for every } W \in L$$
$$\rightarrow x \, P^a \, y$$

since $\bar{L} \subset L$.

(3) In view of (2) all we need show is $x \, R^a \, y \rightarrow x \, \bar{R} \, y$. For any x, y in X, $\sim(x \, \bar{R} \, y) \rightarrow \exists j : y \, P_j \, x \rightarrow \exists j : [W_j(y) - W_j(x)] > 0$, for every $W \in L$. For each W, define $\alpha_1(W) = W_j(y) - W_j(x)$, and $\alpha_2(W) = \sum_{i, i \neq j} [W_i(x) - W_i(y)]$. Take any arbitrary $W^* \in \bar{L}$. If $\alpha_1(W^*) > \alpha_2(W^*)$, then clearly $\sim(x \, R^a \, y)$. Suppose, however, that $\alpha_1(W^*) \leq \alpha_2(W^*)$. Consider now $W^{**} \in L$ such that $W_i^{**} = W_i^*$ for all $i \neq j$, and $W_j^{**} = nW_j^*$, where n is any real number greater than $\alpha_2(W^*)/\alpha_1(W^*)$. Clearly, $\alpha_1(W^{**}) > \alpha_2(W^{**})$, and $W^{**} \in L$. Since $\bar{L} = L$, given non-comparability, we have $\sim(x \, R^a \, y)$, which completes the proof.

(4) In view of (1) all we need show is the completeness of R^a. First assume unit comparability. Take any $W^* \in \bar{L}$, and any $x, y \in X$. Obviously, $\sum_i [W_i^*(x) - W_i^*(y)] \geq 0$, or ≤ 0. Since for every $W \in \bar{L}$, for each i, $W_i = a_i + b \, W_i^*$, for some $b > 0$, we must have $\sum_i [W_i(x) - W_i(y)]$ either non-negative for each $W \in \bar{L}$, or non-positive for each $W \in \bar{L}$. Hence, R^a must be complete. Since full comparability implies that $\bar{L}$ is even more restricted, clearly R^a must also be complete in this case.

7*2. PARTIAL COMPARABILITY

Partial comparability is the term used for all cases of interpersonal comparability lying in between unit comparability and non-comparability. Let $\bar{L}(0)$ and $\bar{L}(1)$ stand respectively for $\bar{L}$ under non-comparability and unit comparability.

DEFINITION 7*4. *If $\bar{L}$ is a subset of $\bar{L}(0)$ and a superset of $\bar{L}(1)$, then partial comparability holds. We shall refer to $\bar{L}$ under partial comparability as $\bar{L}(p)$.*

We know from Theorem 7*1 that the aggregation relation R^a is a quasi-ordering under every case of partial comparability. Since for the purpose of aggregation we are really interested in the welfare *units* and not in the respective *origins*, it is convenient to specify the set of vectors b of coefficients of individual welfare measures with respect to any comparison set $\bar{L}(p)$. The set of b must obviously be defined with respect to some particular $W^* \in L$ chosen for normalization, which we may call the reference element. Since the choice of W^* is quite arbitrary, the properties of the set of b that we would be concerned with should be independent of the particular W^* chosen. We denote the ith element of b as b_i.

DEFINITION 7*5. *The set of all vectors b such that some $W \in \bar{L}(p)$ can be expressed for some vector a as $(W_1, \ldots, W_n)$, where*

$$W_i = a_i + b_i W_i^*$$

is called the coefficient set of $\bar{L}$ with respect to W^*, and will be denoted $B(W^*, \bar{L})$. When there is no possibility of ambiguity we shall refer to $B(W^*, \bar{L})$ as B.

A representation of B may be helpful. Consider the n-dimensional Euclidean Space E^n, n being the number of individuals. With unit comparability, B is an open half-line with origin 0, but excluding 0.[3] If some element b of the coefficient set B is revealed, the rest can be obtained simply by scalar multiplication by $t > 0$. The precise specification of the half-line from origin 0 will depend on the element W^* chosen for the representation; the important point is that in this case B will simply be one ray from the origin. Incidentally, if W^* is chosen from $\bar{L}$, then for all i, j, we must have $b_i = b_j$ for all b.

On the other hand, with non-comparability, B will equal the positive orthant of E^n, i.e., the entire non-negative orthant except the boundary.[4] Any strictly positive vector can be chosen as b.

Given the set of social states X and the set of individual utility

---

[3] It is necessary to exclude 0 since only *positive* linear transformations are permitted.

[4] The boundary is excluded since only *positive* linear transformations are allowed.

functions defined over X, we might wonder what the relation would be between the size of B and the aggregation quasi-ordering generated in each case. We first obtain the following elementary result with R^1 and R^2 being two aggregation quasi-orderings with respect to B^1 and B^2, respectively.

LEMMA 7*a.   If $B^2 \subset B^1$, then for all $x, y \in X$: $x\,R^1\,y \to x\,R^2\,y$.

The proof is obvious. It may be remarked that it does not follow that $x\,P^1\,y \to x\,P^2\,y$, so that R^1 need not be a subrelation of R^2 whenever $B^2 \subset B^1$. An illustration will suffice. In a two-person world, take $W^* \in \overline{L}$ as the reference element. Compare a case of unit (or full) comparability requiring $b_1 = b_2$ for each W in $\overline{L}$, with a case of strictly partial comparability, where we can choose b_1/b_2 from the closed interval $(1, 2)$. Assume further that

$$[W_1^*(x) - W_1^*(y)] = [W_2^*(y) - W_2^*(x)] > 0$$

Clearly, $x\,I^1\,y$ in the first case and $x\,P^2\,y$ in the second. Hence R^1 is not a subrelation of R^2.

We have defined partial comparability so generally that any B from a half-line to the entire positive orthant falls in this category. It would be reasonable to expect, however, that B under partial comparability will satisfy certain regularity conditions. First, the coefficients should be scale-independent. If $b \in B$, then for all $\lambda > 0$, $(\lambda b) \in B$, i.e., B should include all points on the half-line $0, b$, except 0 itself. For example, if $(1, 2, 3)$ is a possible b, then so should be, say, $(2, 4, 6)$, for nothing essential depends on the scale of representation. This implies that B will be a cone with vertex 0 but excluding 0 itself, i.e., it is the complement of 0 in a cone with vertex 0.

Second, it seems reasonable to assume the convexity of B. For example, given a coefficient of 1 for individual 1, if we are ready to apply both the coefficients 1 and 2 to individual 2's welfare units, then we should be ready to apply 1.5 as well. More generally, if b^1 and b^2 are two elements of B, then so is $tb^1 + (1 - t)b^2$ for any $t: 0 < t < 1$. Since with the exception of 0, B is a cone, this is equivalent to the convexity of the cone.

AXIOM 7*1.   *Scale-independence and convexity: If $b^1, b^2 \in B$, then* *for all t^1, $t^2 \geq 0$, except for $t^1 = t^2 = 0$, it can be concluded that $(t^1 b^1 + t^2 b^2) \in B$.*

This axiom is more or less unexceptionable. In the next section we introduce a series of increasingly stronger requirements.

7*3. REGULARITY AND SYMMETRY

We introduce now an axiom of regularity.

AXIOM 7*2. *Regularity: For every possible partition of the set of individuals into two subsets (V^1 and V^2), if B^2 is a proper subset of B^1, then*

$$\exists(b^1 \in B^1 \& b^2 \in B^2): [\{\forall i \in V^1 : b_i^2 < b_i^1\} \& \{\forall i \in V^2 : b_i^2 > b_i^1\}]$$

THEOREM 7*2. *With cardinal individual welfares, given Axiom 7*2, $B^2 \subset B^1$ implies that R^1 is a subrelation of R^2.*

Proof. If $B^1 = B^2$, then clearly $R^1 = R^2$, so that we can concentrate on the case when B^2 is a proper subset of B^1. In view of Lemma 7*a all that need be proved is that $x P^1 y \to x P^2 y$, for all $x, y \in X$. Suppose, to the contrary, that for some $x, y \in X$, we have $x P^1 y \& \sim(x P^2 y)$. In view of Lemma 7*a this implies that $x P^1 y$, $x R^2 y$ and $y R^2 x$. Since $x I^2 y$, we must have $\forall b^2 \in B^2: \sum_i [W_i^*(x) - W_i^*(y)] b_i^2 = 0$. Partition the individuals into two groups J and K such that $i \in J$ if and only if $x P_i y$, and $i \in K$ otherwise. By Axiom 7*2, we can assert that $\exists b^1 \in B^1: \sum_i [W_i^*(x) - W_i^*(y)] b_i^1 < 0$, or $\forall i : x I_i y$. But neither of the alternatives could be true, since $x P^1 y$, and this contradiction establishes the theorem.

It may be noted that Axiom 7*1 is not necessary for Theorem 7*2. However, this fact may not be very important from a practical point of view, since convexity and scale-independence appear to make Axiom 7*2 less objectionable.

How demanding a condition is the regularity axiom? Consider B^1 and B^2 as two convex cones (excluding the vertex). What the regularity axiom asserts is that if B^2 is a proper subset of B^1, then there is at least one half-line in B^2 that is an interior *ray*[5] of B^1. All that this excludes is the possibility that the relaxation of comparability is so biased that all permitted cases in the smaller set are simply boundary positions in the larger set. This is, in any case, impossible if the linear dimension of the cone representing B^2 is n, when n is the number of individuals. Further, even if the linear dimension of B^2 is less than n, the regularity axiom will hold unless the move from B^2 to B^1 is severely biased.

A somewhat stronger requirement than regularity is the requirement of what we call 'weak symmetry'.

AXIOM 7*3. *Weak symmetry: For every pair of coefficient sets B^1 and B^2, we have*

$$\left[\exists i, j : \sup_{b^1 \in B^1}\left(\frac{b_i^1}{b_j^1}\right) > \sup_{b^2 \in B^2}\left(\frac{b_i^2}{b_j^2}\right)\right] \rightarrow \left[\forall i, j : \sup_{b^1 \in B^1}\left(\frac{b_i^1}{b_j^1}\right) > \sup_{b^2 \in B^2}\left(\frac{b_i^2}{b_j^2}\right)\right]$$

This is a much stronger requirement than the regularity axiom. With the latter it is sufficient that one ray in $B^2 \subset B^1$ be an interior ray of B^1, whereas with weak symmetry every ray in B^2 has to be interior in B^1, if B^2 is a proper subset of B^1. When the extent of comparability is relaxed between any pair of individuals, it has to be relaxed for every pair of individuals in the case of weak symmetry. However, the precise extent of the relaxation may vary from pair to pair (hence it is 'weak', to be contrasted with 'strong symmetry' later). It also imposes a directional symmetry between each individual in a pair. If the least upper bound on the ratio of coefficients goes up between i and j, then the greatest lower bound of the ratio must go down (i.e., the least upper bound of the ratio between j and i must go up). The motivation of Axiom 7*3 is to rule out directional bias in alternative cases of partial comparability. This yields the following important result:

---

[5] An interior ray of a cone C is a ray (r) such that C contains an ε neighbourhood of (r) for some $\varepsilon > 0$. For this we have to define a metric on rays related to the usual topology of E^n. This can be done in many ways that are essentially similar. See Dunford and Schwartz (1958), Vol. I, or Fenchel (1953).

LEMMA 7*b. *With cardinal individual welfares, given Axioms 7*1 and 7*3, the binary relation of set inclusion defines an ordering over the class of all coefficient sets.*

Proof. Since $B \subset B$ for all B, and $B^3 \subset B^2$ & $B^2 \subset B^1 \rightarrow B^3 \subset B^1$, for all B^1, B^2 and B^3, we know that $\subset$ must be reflexive and transitive. If $B^1 \neq B^2$, then, given convexity, for some i, j, $\sup_{b1 \in B^1}(b_i^1/b_j^1)$ is either strictly greater or strictly less than $\sup_{b2 \in B^2}(b_i^2/b_j^2)$. Without loss of generality, let it be strictly greater. Then by the weak symmetry axiom, we have for all i, j, $\sup_{b1 \in B^1}(b_i^1/b_j^1) > \sup_{b2 \in B^2}(b_i^2/b_j^2)$. Since B^1 and B^2 are convex cones (excluding the vertex), this implies that $B^2 \subset B^1$.

In view of Theorem 7*2 and Lemma 7*b, we obtain immediately the following result, noting the fact that Axiom 7*3 implies Axiom 7*2:

THEOREM 7*3. *For cardinal individual welfares, if R^1 and R^2 are two aggregation quasi-orderings generated by two cases of partial comparability, then, given Axioms 7*1 and 7*3, either R^1 is a subrelation of R^2, or R^2 is a subrelation of R^1, and the binary relation between quasi-orderings of 'being a subrelation of' defines a complete ordering over all possible aggregation quasi-orderings under partial comparability.*

We have thus a sequence of aggregation quasi-orderings, each a subrelation of the next, starting from the Pareto quasi-ordering, which is yielded by non-comparability, and ending up with a complete ordering, which is yielded by unit comparability. In between lie all cases of partial comparability, and as the extent of partial comparability is raised, i.e., as B is shrunk, the aggregation quasi-ordering gets extended (if it changes at all), without ever contradicting an earlier quasi-ordering obtained for a lower extent of partial comparability.

A measure of the degree of partial comparability may be useful in this case. Define for every ordered pair of individuals i, j, the following ratio, which we shall call the comparability ratio:

$$C_{ij} = \inf_{b \in B}(b_i/b_j) / \sup_{b \in B}(b_i/b_j)$$

We can define the degree of partial comparability as the arithmetic mean of the comparability ratios for every ordered pair of individuals.

DEFINITION 7*6. *Given Axioms 7*1 and 7*3, the degree of partial comparability $d(B)$ will be measured by the arithmetic mean of c_{ij} for all ordered pairs i, j.*

Since each c_{ij} must lie within the closed interval $[0, 1]$, the degree of partial comparability is also defined over this interval. Further, the following theorem holds:

THEOREM 7*4. *For cardinal individual welfares, given Axioms 7*1 and 7*3, $d(B) = 0$ implies that the aggregation quasi-ordering will be the same as the Pareto quasi-ordering R, and $d(B) = 1$ implies that it will be an ordering. Further, if $d(B^2) > d(B^1)$, the aggregation quasi-ordering R^1 will be a subrelation of the aggregation quasi-ordering R^2.*

Proof. If $d(B) = 1$, clearly $c_{ij} = 1$ for each ordered pair i, j. In this case B will consist of only one ray through the origin, and unit comparability will hold. We know from Theorem 7*1 that in this case R^a will be a complete ordering. If, on the other hand, $d(b) = 0$, each c_{ij} must equal zero, so that the ratio b_i/b_j can be varied without bound (except those already implied in each b_i being a positive number) for every i, j. This implies that non-comparability holds, and from Theorem 7*1 we know that $R = \bar{R}$.

If $d(B^2) > d(B^1)$, then for some i, j, $c_{ij}^1 < c_{ij}^2$. This implies that for some pair i, j, either sup $(b_i^1/b_j^1) >$ sup (b_i^2/b_j^2), or inf $(b_i^1/b_j^1) <$ inf (b_i^2/b_j^2). If the former, then it follows from Axiom 7*3 that B^2 is a proper subset of B^1. If the latter, then sup $(b_j^1/b_i^1) >$ sup (b_j^2/b_i^2), and once again B^2 must be a proper subset of B^1. Now, since weak symmetry implies regularity, it follows from Theorem 7*2 that R^1 must be a subrelation of R^2.

It is clear from Theorem 7*4 that if weak symmetry holds in addition to the relatively harmless assumptions of convexity and scale-independence, then all cases of partial comparability can be measured by a precise degree, $d(B) = q$, of partial comparability, with interesting properties. It is a real number q lying in the closed interval $[0, 1]$, and the corresponding quasi-ordering R^q is a subrelation of all quasi-orderings obtained with all higher degrees of partial comparability $(d > q)$, while all quasi-orderings with lower degrees of partial comparability $(d < q)$ are subrelations of R^q. This monotonicity property in the relation between the continuum of degrees of comparability in the interval [0, 1] and the sequence of aggregation quasi-orderings from the Pareto quasi-ordering to a complete ordering is a phenomenon of some importance.

It should also be noted that it is not *necessary* to assume $d(B) = 1$ for a complete ordering to be generated, though it is sufficient. Even with $d(B) < 1$, completeness may be achieved. The necessary degree will depend on the precise configuration of individual welfare functions.

A more restrictive case than weak symmetry is that of 'strong symmetry', which is defined below.

AXIOM 7*4. *Strong symmetry: There exists some functional combination* $W^* \in \overline{L}(p)$ *such that for each* $B(W^*, \overline{L})$, $\sup_{b \in B} (b_i/b_j)$ *is exactly the same for all ordered pairs* i, j.

Obviously, strong symmetry implies weak symmetry, but not vice versa. Further, under strong symmetry c_{ij} is the same for all i, j. We can express the degree of partial comparability simply as any c_{ij}. It is to be noted that the property of having the same upper bound is one that depends on which W^* we choose as the reference point; W^* is thus no longer inconsequential. The strong symmetry axiom asserts that for *some* W^* this set of equalities holds, but not, of course, for every arbitrary choice of W^*.

An example of strong symmetry, related to a case discussed in Chapter 7 is the following: Consider the restriction that for some real number p, $0 < p < 1$, for all i, j we must have $p < (b_i/b_j) < 1/p$. The degree of partial comparability according to Definition 7*6 will be given by p^2, which will itself lie in the closed interval [0, 1], and as p would be raised from 0 to 1 we would move monotonically from non-comparability to unit comparability.

With strong symmetry, a sufficient degree of partial comparability that will guarantee the completeness of the aggregation quasi-ordering is easy to specify. For any pair of alternatives x, y in X, partition the individuals into two classes, viz., J consisting of all those who prefer

x to y, and K consisting of all those who regard y to be at least as good as x.

Define

$$m(x,\ y) = \sum_{i \in J} [W_i^*(x) - W_i^*(y)]$$

and

$$m(y,\ x) = \sum_{i \in K} [W_i^*(y) - W_i^*(x)]$$

Now define $a(x,y)$ as the following:

$$a(x,\ y) = \frac{\min[m(x,\ y),\ m(y,\ x)]}{\max[m(x,\ y),\ m(y,\ x)]}$$

THEOREM 7*5. *For cardinal individual welfares, with convexity, scale-independence and strong symmetry, the aggregation quasi-ordering will be complete if the degree of partial comparability is greater than or equal to a^*, where $a^* = \sup_{x,y \in X} a(x,y)$.*

Proof. For any pair x, y, completeness can fail to be fulfilled if and only if $\sum_i [W_i(x) - W_i(y)] > 0$ for some $W \in \bar{L}$, and < 0 for some other $W \in \bar{L}$. First consider W^*. Without loss of generality, let $\sum_i [W_i^*(x) - W_i^*(y)] > 0$, i.e., $m(x,y) > m(y,x)$. We have to show that the sum of welfare differences between x and y is non-negative for all $W \in \bar{L}$. Assume the degree of partial comparability to be d, so that the welfare units of each individual can be raised at most by a ratio $p = d^{1/2}$, and can be reduced at most by a ratio $1/p$. If, contrary to the theorem, the sum of welfare differences between x and y is negative for any $W \in \bar{L}$, then, $[pm(x,y) - (1/p)\, m(y,x)] < 0$. Hence, $p < [m(y,x)/m(x,y)]^{1/2}$. But this is impossible, since $p^2 = \sup_{x,y \in X} a(x,y)$. This contradiction proves that the aggregation quasi-ordering must be complete.

It is clear that unit comparability is an unnecessarily demanding assumption, and some degree of strict partial comparability, i.e., $d < 1$, may yield a complete ordering – precisely the same ordering as one would get under unit comparability (or full comparability).

7*4. ADDITION OF
NON-CARDINAL WELFARE

It has been assumed so far that each element of L_i is a positive linear transformation of every other element, i.e., individual welfare is cardinally measurable. This is an unnecessarily strong assumption for exercises in partial comparability. In what follows this restriction is relaxed, and L_i can include elements which are not linear transformations of each other, though each must be a positive monotonic transformation. However, not every positive monotonic transformation need be included. We can, thus, have cases that are more restricted than cardinal measurability and less so than ordinal measurability.

DEFINITION 7*7.   *If, for each i, each element of L_i is a positive monotonic transformation of every other element of L_i, and every positive linear transformation of any element of L_i is in L_i, then individual welfare is ordinal-type.*

It may be remarked that the welfare measure being strictly ordinal (including *all* positive monotonic transformations) and being strictly cardinal (including *only* positive linear transformations) are both special cases of welfare being of the ordinal-type. Ordinal-type is, in fact, a very general class of measurability.

We define L as before, viz., as the Cartesian product of L_i for all i, and $\overline{L}$ as any subset of it, as before, in the context of the aggregation relation R^a, as in Definition 7*2. The definition of non-comparability remains unchanged, viz., $L = \overline{L}$. The following theorem is a generalization of three of the four statements in Theorem 7*1:

THEOREM 7*6.   *With ordinal-type individual welfares*

(1) *For any $\overline{L}$, R^a is a quasi-ordering.*
(2) *For any $\overline{L}$, R^a is a subrelation of $\overline{R}$, i.e.,*

$$\forall x, y \in X : [\{x \,\overline{R}\, y \to x \,R^a\, y\} \ \& \ \{x \,\overline{P}\, y \to x \,P^a\, y\}].$$

(3) *With non-comparability, $R^a = \overline{R}$.*

The proofs are exactly as in Theorem 7*1, for the property of cardinality is not used in the proofs.

Next, consider a choice over precisely one pair $x, y \in X$. Take any element W^* in $\bar{L}$. Denote g_i^* as

$$g_i^* = [W_i^*(x) - W_i^*(y)]$$

Suppose first that g_i^* is not zero. For any element W in $\bar{L}$, let $\hat{b}_i$ be a real number such that

$$g_i^* \hat{b}_i = [W_i(x) - W_i(y)] = g_i$$

Consider now the n-tuple $(\hat{b}_1, \ldots, \hat{b}_n)$ denoted $\hat{b}$.

DEFINITION 7*8. *For any specified pair* $x, y \in X$, *the set of all* $\hat{b}_i$ *such that* $g_i = g_i^* \hat{b}_i$, *for all i for some W in* $\bar{L}$, *is called the coefficient set of* $\bar{L}$ *with respect to* W^*, *and is denoted* $\hat{B}(W^*, \bar{L})$.

It is easily checked that, if cardinality holds, then the coefficient set $\hat{B}$ will be the same no matter which pair x, y we take, and further it will be the same as the coefficient set B as defined in Definition 7*5. It is now easily checked that Lemmas 7*a and 7*b, and Theorems 7*2, 7*3 and 7*4, are all valid with ordinal-type welfare, if we consider only one pair of alternatives x, y, after replacing B with $\hat{B}$ in all the axioms. Each of the axioms is now defined for each pair x, y.

Further, we know from Theorem 7*6 that R^a under ordinal-type individual welfare must be a quasi-ordering irrespective of the number of alternatives involved. This permits us to establish the following theorems immediately:

THEOREM 7*7. *For ordinal-type individual welfares, if Axiom 7*2 holds for each pair* $x, y \in X$, *then* $\bar{L}^2 \subset \bar{L}^1$ *implies that* R^1 *is a subrelation of* R^2.

THEOREM 7*8. *For ordinal-type individual welfares, given Axioms 7*1 and 7*3 holding for each pair* $x, y \in X$, *if* R^1 *and* R^2 *are two aggregation quasi-orderings, then either* R^1 *is a subrelation of* R^2, *or* R^2 *is a subrelation of* R^1.

THEOREM 7*9. *For ordinal-type individual welfares, given Axioms 7*1 and 7*3 holding for each pair* $x, y \in X$,

$$\left[\forall x, y: d(\hat{B}) = 0 \right] \to R^a = \bar{R}$$

$$\left[\forall x, y: d(\hat{B}) = 1 \right] \to R^a \qquad \text{is an ordering}$$

and

$$\left[\forall x, y: d(\hat{B}^2) > d(\hat{B}^1) \right] \to R^1 \qquad \text{is a subrelation of } R^2.[6]$$

The theorems are easily established by using Theorem 7*6, and Theorems 7*2, 7*3 and 7*4.

---

[6] Note that $d(\hat{B})$ is now defined separately for each pair $x, y \in X$.

Chapter 8
Cardinality With or Without
Comparability

8.1. BARGAINING ADVANTAGES AND
COLLECTIVE CHOICE

In using individual welfares functions for collective choice, there are at least three separate (but interdependent) problems, viz., (a) measurability of individual welfare, (b) interpersonal comparability of individual welfare, and (c) the form of a function which will specify a social preference relation given individual welfare functions and the comparability assumptions. In Chapters 7 and 7*, while a number of alternative assumptions about (a) and (b) were considered, the operation on individual welfare measures was simply one of addition. It is, of course, possible to combine them in other ways.

In his solution to the 'bargaining problem', Nash (1950) takes the *product* (and not the *sum*) of individual welfares after a suitable choice of origins. The model is one of two persons, though it is possible to generalize it. There is a certain social state $\tilde{x}$ (the 'status quo') which will be the outcome if the two persons fail to strike a bargain. If $\tilde{x}$ is regarded by both as being at least as good as every alternative that can be achieved through bargaining, then the problem will be trivial, since the absence of a bargaining contract cannot possibly possibly hurt anyone. If, on the other hand, there are cooperative outcomes that both prefer to $\tilde{x}$, then the problem may be interesting. It will, however, once again be rendered trivial if both parties have exactly the same choice set for the cooperative outcomes, for they can then choose an outcome which it best for both. The problem is given its bite by a conflict of interest of the two persons. Both gain from cooperation, but one gains more with some contracts than others, while the other gains less with those. This is what the bargain is about.

Nash specifies assumptions about individual behaviour under uncertainty that permit a cardinal representation of individual preferences. He proposes a solution that is given by maximizing the product of the differences between the utility from a cooperative outcome x (Pareto-superior to $\tilde{x}$) and the status quo outcome $\tilde{x}$ for the two, i.e., maximizing $[U_1(x) - U_1(\tilde{x})][U_2(x) - U_2(\tilde{x})]$. This amounts to maximizing the product of utilities after a suitable choice of origin.[1]

It is readily apparent that the Nash solution has the property of being invariant with respect to the changes of origins and units of individual utility functions. The origins get subtracted out, and the units simply change the scale of product without changing the *ordering* of the outcomes by the value of the product. This is where the absence of interpersonal comparability is absorbed, since any individual's utility units and origin can be shifted without any regard to the origin and the units of other person's utility.

While this invariance with respect to the choice of origin and unit of individual utility function can be preserved by other functional forms as well,[2] the simple product formulation satisfies also the requirement, which Nash imposes, of 'symmetry' in the treatment of the two individuals.[3] The exact axioms and the proof that the Nash solution is the only one to satisfy them are presented in Chapter 8*.

---

[1] It may be tempting to think of this operation as *addition* in disguise, since maximizing the product is equivalent to maximizing the sum of the logarithms of the numbers. All that is needed, it might be thought, is the interpretation of the logarithmic transformation of a utility function as a utility function itself. However, this is illegitimate, since cardinality, as used by Nash (and indeed others), permits only linear transformations, which rule out a logarithmic transformation. Further, what would be needed is a mixture, viz., first some transformation to get $U_i(\tilde{x}) = 0$, and *then* a logarithmic shift. It is not at all obvious what precise properties of preference will be preserved by such hybrid changes.

[2] For example, we can take $[U_1(x) - U_1(\tilde{x})]^\alpha [U_2(x) - U_2(\tilde{x})]^\beta$ with α and β as two positive real numbers.

[3] We can, of course, get this in the example given in footnote 2 by taking $\alpha = \beta$, but then the social *ordering* generated will be exactly the same as in the Nash system of comparing simple products.

Whether we add individual utilities, or multiply them, or play with them in some other way, the variability of units or origins of individual utilities poses a problem. It is instructive to contrast the way this problem is tackled in the two approaches we have considered so far. In the aggregation approach of Chapters 7 and 7*, origins are irrelevant since only *differences* in utility between x and y are added for all individuals to generate a social ordering. The units are crucial, but if variations in units for one individual are systematically related to variations in units of others, then the ranking of social states may not be very sensitive to these variations. The systematic relation may vary from a one-to-one correspondence (in the case of complete unit comparability) yielding a complete ordering, to none at all (non-comparability) when only Pareto preferences and indifferences are reflected in social choice. In between lies a variety of possibilities with quasi-ordering of varying extent of completeness. In contrast, in the Nash approach no such comparability is introduced, but the origins are knocked out through the use of the status quo and the units are rendered irrelevant through the multiplicative form. This makes the collective solution crucially dependent on the status quo point. Given everything else, a different status quo point will usually generate a different Nash solution.

Is this dependence on a precisely defined non-cooperative outcome justifiable? The answer to this question seems to depend a great deal on the objective of the exercise. In *predicting* the actual outcome of a bargaining battle, the status quo is clearly relevant, for it defines what will happen in the absence of the parties agreeing to a cooperative solution. There is always the threat that this outcome, which is inferior for both, will emerge as the actual outcome.[4] In splitting the gains

---

[4] The analysis can be extended by admitting specific 'threats' that the players may put forward as what they would do should there be no cooperative agreement. By threatening the other party with policies that will yield dire consequences to that party, a player may try to strengthen his own bargaining power. The Nash model can be extended to include such 'threats'; on this, see Nash (1953), and Luce and Raiffa (1957). It may, incidentally, be noted that theories of threat involve a particular problem that is not easy to dispose of, viz., should the bargaining fail, it may not really be in the interest of the threatening players to carry out their threats. Threatening to do something which

from an agreement, state is clearly relevant. Indeed, as Harsanyi has noted, there is a process of making and accepting concessions that was originally put forward by Zeuthen (1930) and which is not implausible, which will indeed yield precisely the Nash outcome.

This does not, however, mean that the Nash solution is an ethically attractive outcome and that we should recommend a collective choice mechanism that incorporates it. A best prediction is not necessarily a fair, or a just, outcome. In a labour market with unemployment, workers may agree to accept sub-human wages and poor terms of employment, since in the absence of a contract they may starve $(\tilde{x})$, but this does not make that solution a desirable outcome in any sense. Indeed, compared with $\tilde{x}$, while a particular solution may be symmetric in distributing utility gains from the bargain between workers and capitalists, we could still maintain that the workers were exploited because their bargaining power was poor.

It may be useful to clarify the contrast by taking Harsanyi's (1955) model of 'ethical judgments', even though it is only one possible model. What someone would *recommend* as a solution if he thought that he had an equal chance of being in either party's position, will yield, in that model, an 'ethical' recommendation. On the other hand, what he will *predict* as the likely outcome, taking the parties as they are, is a different thing altogether. The Nash 'bargaining solution' seems to be rather uninteresting from the former point of view, and might represent the latter if it represents anything at all. Whether or not the Nash solution is predictive (for doubts on this see Luce and Raiffa (1957)), its ethical relevance does seem to be very little.

This contrast is a very general one and can be brought out with ethical models different from Harsanyi's, e.g., with models of aggregate welfare maximization with partial comparability, or with models of fairness and justice of Rawls (1958), (1967), or with

---

harms the other player at the cost of harming oneself may be effective only if the other player believes that this player will in fact do such a thing should the bargaining fail; but clearly it is not in the rational interest of this one to do anything of the sort once the bargaining is dead. The theory of threats has to cope with this problem.

Suppes' (1966) 'grading principles', or with such collective choice mechanisms as the method of majority decision.

It is worth noting that many supposedly ethical solutions are similar in spirit to Nash's solution. For example, Braithwaite's (1955) interesting use of game theory as 'a tool for the moral philosopher' seems to be based on an identification of these two questions. In Braithwaite's example a certain Luke likes playing the piano in his room, and a certain Matthew likes improvising jazz on the trumpet in the adjacent room, with imperfect soundproofing between the rooms. They disturb each other if they play together, but, as might be expected, the trumpeter makes a bigger mess for the pianist than the pianist can for the trumpeter. The final solution that Braithwaite recommends divides up the time, giving substantially more time to the trumpeter than to the pianist. As Braithwaite ((1955), p. 37) puts it, 'Matthew's advantage arises purely from the fact that Matthew, the trumpeter, prefers both of them playing at once to neither of them playing, whereas Luke, the pianist, prefers silence to cacophony.' Matthew has the threat advantage in the absence of a contract, and it is indeed possible that Braithwaite's solution may well emerge should Luke and Matthew actually bargain.[5] But in what sense does this solution 'obtain maximum production of satisfaction compatible with fair distribution'?[6] An unbiased judge may well decide that the fact that Matthew can threaten Luke more effectively (and more noisily) than Luke can threaten Matthew does not entitle him to a bigger share of playing time. Matthew himself might concede that if he did not know whether he was going to be Luke or Matthew before deciding on a system of distribution of time he might well have ignored the threat advantage and recommended a more equal sharing of time. A solution based on the threat advantages of the two parties may indeed be manifestly unfair.

We should, however, note that it is possible to take the stand of a

[5] See, however, Luce and Raiffa (1957), pp. 145–50. See also Raiffa (1953), for an alternative approach, and Luce and Raiffa (1958), pp. 143–5.
[6] Braithwaite (1955), p. 9. See also Lucas (1959).

'hard-headed realist' that all ethical discussions are pointless and what is really interesting is the prediction of an outcome. What is the point of discussing what *should* happen if it will not? This point of view, which is of respectable antiquity, is not a very useful one to take for a theory of collective choice. First, part of the object of the study of collective choice is social criticism. In making use of certain widely held value judgments, particular collective choice mechanisms may be meaningfully criticized, which might in the long run help the development of a more appropriate choice mechanism. Second, bargaining power of different groups is itself a function of the appreciation of the nature of the society and its choice mechanisms. The feeling of injustice to a certain group (e.g., the workers) may itself contribute to bringing about institutions (e.g., trade unions) that alter the relative bargaining power of different groups. Rousseau's analysis of 'injustice' and Marx's theory of 'exploitation', to take two obvious examples, have had a bigger impact on the shape of the world than would have been predicted by the 'hard-headed realist'.[7] Third, there is often a conflict between the general principles that people swear by and the courses of action they choose. These principles may take the form of conditions on collective choice, and the analysis of their logical implications is an interesting and useful basis for discussion and argumentation on social decisions. It is useful also to examine the existing mechanisms of collective choice in the light of the general principles widely accepted in the society to check the consistency of theory and practice.

To conclude this section, the solutions put forward by Nash, Braithwaite, and others in similar models, might be relevant for predicting certain outcomes of bargains and negotiations, but they seem to be very unattractive solutions in terms of widely held value judgments about principles of collective choice. The special importance attached to the status quo point and to threat advantages, and the complete avoidance of interpersonal comparisons, seem to rule

---

[7] Lenin could finish writing only six chapters of his *The State and Revolution* because the October Revolution intervened.

out a whole class of ethical judgments that are relevant to collective choice.

8.2. CARDINALITY AND IMPOSSIBILITY

It may be noted that the dependence of social choice on attitudes to the status quo point ($\tilde{x}$) is a violation of the 'independence of irrelevant alternatives' when it has been redefined to apply to social preference being a function of individual welfare functions (as opposed to being a function of individual orderings). In fact, if on top of the Nash conditions we also demand that social choice between any two cooperative outcomes x and y must depend only on the welfare numbers for x and y of the two individuals, then an impossibility theorem would readily result.

This problem applies not merely to the Nash approach but to all uses of cardinality in the absence of any interpersonal comparability (i.e., assuming invariance of social choice with respect to positive linear transformations of individual utility functions). Indeed the Arrow impossibility result can be readily extended to the use of individual cardinal utility functions (rather than individual orderings) as the arguments of collective choice rules. A social welfare functional (SWFL) is a mechanism that specifies one and only one social ordering given a set of individual welfare functions, one function for each individual. Non-comparability requires that any transformation (permitted by the measurability assumption) of any individual's welfare function leaves the social ordering unchanged. Cardinality requires that all positive linear transformations of any utility function attributed to any individual are permitted. Given these, we may require the Arrow conditions, suitably modified to apply to an SWFL, viz., unrestricted domain, weak Pareto principle, non-dictatorship, and the independence of irrelevant alternatives. The first three are straightforward to redefine, while the last is redefined by making the social preference between x and y invariant as long as each individual's utility measure for x and y remain invariant. When these conditions are put together, what we get is another impossibility (Theorem 8*2), in the line of Arrow's general possibility theorem, but now applying to SWFLs with cardinal individual utility functions.[8]

It may be instructive to compare this impossibility result with the aggregation quasi-orderings that were obtained in Chapters 7 and 7*. That relation was based on invariance not with respect to every possible linear transformation of individual utility functions, but only with respect to some (those in L, a specified subset of L), reflecting our assumptions about interpersonal comparability. With unit comparability and cardinality, the aggregation rule is an SWFL with an unrestricted domain, satisfying the Pareto principle, non-dictatorship, and independence of irrelevant alternatives. The crucial difference lies in introducing comparability. It was noted before that if non-comparability is assumed, the aggregation quasi-ordering will coincide with the Pareto quasi-ordering (Theorem 7*1). What Theorem 8*2 shows is that not merely aggregation, but all Pareto-inclusive, non-dictatorial, irrelevant-alternative-independent rules of going from individual welfare functions to a social ordering will fail to generate a social ordering if cardinality is combined with non-comparability.

This is, of course, not surprising. Given non-comparability, the relative preference intensities of individuals over any pair can be varied in any way we like except for reversing the sign, i.e., without reversing the ordering, so that cardinality is not much of an advance over individual orderings when combined with non-comparability. To give some bite to cardinality we have to relax one of the other conditions. The Nash procedure violates the condition of the independence of irrelevant alternatives by making the choice set dependent on the status quo $\tilde{x}$, whereas the aggregation procedure does it through permitting interpersonal comparability fully or partly. Cardinality alone seems to kill no dragons, and our little St. George must be sought elsewhere.

---

[8] This confirms Samuelson's (1967) conjecture on this. Samuelson does not mention the requirement of non-comparability, but it is implied by his earlier discussion of invariance with respect to transformations of units and origin. Incidentally, in Sen (1966c), which Samuelson refers to in this context, the proposal was not to introduce cardinality alone, but in conjunction with comparability.

Chapter 8*
Bargains and Social Welfare Functions

8*1. THE BARGAINING
PROBLEM OF NASH

It is instructive to consider Nash's model of bargaining as an exercise in going from individual welfare functions to a social ordering assuming cardinality of individual welfare but no interpersonal comparability.[1] The solution depends on a distinguished social state $\tilde{x}$, which we may call the status quo point and which represents what would happen if there is no cooperation between bargainers. Here, X represents all social states that are available if the two parties cooperate. It is assumed that there are points in X that both prefer to the status quo $\tilde{x}$. Further, Nash's bargaining problem is concerned with a two-person society. While a natural extension of this to n-person cases exists, we shall let follow Nash's own formulation.

Each point x in X maps into a pair of utility numbers representing the welfare of the two individuals respectively, for any given W. The set of such pairs of utility numbers corresponding to the set of all elements in X for any W will be called $U(X, W)$, or U for short. It can be viewed as a subset of the two-dimensional Euclidean space. We shall, following Nash, assume U to be compact and convex.

Our presentation will, however, differ somewhat from Nash's own, but our five axioms will be essentially equivalent to Nash's eight-axiom presentation. We use Definition 7*1 of a functional

---

[1] See Nash (1950). For an excellent exposition and a critical evaluation see Luce and Raiffa (1957). See also Nash (1953), and Harsanyi (1956), (1966).

combination W, as any element of the Cartesian product $\prod_{i=1}^{n} L_i$ of individual sets of welfare functions.

DEFINITION 8*1. *A bargaining solution function (hereafter, BSF) is a functional relation that chooses one and only one social state $\bar{x} \in X$ for any specified functional combination $W \in L$, given the distinguished social state $\tilde{x} \in X$ representing the status quo.*

We shall use the following set of axioms:

AXIOM 8*1. *Well-behaved cardinal utility: For each i, every element of L_i is a positive linear transformation of every other element, and every positive linear transformation of any element of L_i belongs to L_i. Further, each W_i is continuous on X, and for any $W \in L$, U is compact and convex.*

AXIOM 8*2. *Non-comparability: The value of the BSF is invariant with respect to the choice of W in L.*

AXIOM 8*3. *Weak Pareto optimality: The range of the BSF is confined to only those elements $x \in X$ such that $\sim[\exists y \in X: y \stackrel{=}{P} x]$*

AXIOM 8*4. *Property α: If $\bar{x}$ is the solution given by the BSF when X is the set of social states and $\bar{x} \in S \subset X$, then $\bar{x}$ is the solution given by the BSF for S.[2]*

AXIOM 8*5. *Symmetry: If for some $W^* \in L$, $W_1^*(\tilde{x}) = W_2^*(\tilde{x})$, and for that $W^* \in L$, U is symmetric,[3] then $W_1^*(\bar{x}) = W_2^*(\bar{x})$.*

THEOREM 8*1. *For any X, a BSF satisfying Axioms 8*1–8*5 must yield that $x^0 \in X$ such that $x^0 \in X$, $x^0 \stackrel{=}{P} \tilde{x}$, and for any $W \in L$*

$$x^0 = x \left| \begin{array}{l} \max \left[W_1(x) - W_1(\tilde{x})\right] \left[W_2(x) - W_2(\tilde{x})\right] \\ x \in X \\ x \stackrel{=}{P} \tilde{x} \end{array} \right.$$

---

[2] This is called the independence of irrelevant alternatives by Luce and Raiffa (1957). It is, however, not to be confused with Arrow's condition of the same name. We discuss the condition corresponding to that of Arrow later; see Axiom 8*6. See Chapter 1* on property α.

[3] That is, if $(a, b) \in U$, then $(b, a) \in U$.

Proof. Obviously, point x^0 as described exists and is unique by the compactness and convexity of U. Further, it is obviously invariant with respect to the choice of $W \in L$ thanks to cardinality. Consider now that $W^* \in L$ such that $W_1^* (\tilde{x}) = W_2^* (\tilde{x}) = 0$, and $W_1^* (x^0) = W_2^* (x^0) = 1$; such a $W^* \in L$ exists by cardinality. By the choice of x^0, there is no $x \in X$: $W_1^* (x) \cdot W_2^* (x) > 1$. Hence, there is no $x \in X$: $[W_1^* (x) + W_2^* (x) > 2$, for if such an x existed, then a convex combination (W_1^*, W_2^*) of $(W_1^* (x), W_2^* (x))$ and $(1, 1)$ will yield $W_1^* W_2^* > 1$, and further, by convexity, (W_1^*, W_2^*) will belong to U. It is now easy to construct a symmetric set U^* on the utility space corresponding to X^*, which includes all $(W_1^* (x), W_2^* (x))$ for all $x \in X$, i.e., $X \subset X^*$, and no x such that $W_1^* (x) \geqq 1$, and $W_2^* (x) \geqq 1$, except $x = x^0$. By Axioms 8*3 (weak Pareto optimality) and 8*5 (symmetry), x^0 is yielded by the BSF for X^*, given $W^* \in L$. By Axiom 8*4 (property α), x^0 is yielded by the BSF for $X \subset X^*$, given $W^* \in L$. By Axiom 8*2 (non-comparability), x^0 is yielded by the BSF for X, given any $W \in L$. The proof is completed by checking that x^0 always satisfies Axioms 8*1–8*5.

While Nash's solution satisfies property α, which has been described as a condition of independence of irrelevant alternatives by Radner and Marschack (1954), Luce and Raiffa (1958), and others, it violates the cardinal equivalent of Arrow's independence of irrelevant alternatives. Here we define Arrow's condition in a very weak form appropriately for a BSF as opposed to a collective choice rule. Consider that x^0 is chosen and x^1 is rejected by the BSF from x, given some status quo $\tilde{x}$, so that x^0 is socially preferred to x^1. Assume now that $\tilde{x}$ changes, but everything else remains the same, including $W_i(x^0)$ and $W_i(x^1)$ for each i. If the choice between x^0 and x^1 should be independent of irrelevant alternatives, then clearly the BSF should not now choose x^1 and reject x^0.

AXIOM 8*6. *Independence: For some $W \in L$ and $\hat{W} \in \hat{L}$, each defined over X, if for all x, $\forall i$: $W_i(x) = \hat{W}_i(x)$, then the BSF must yield the same solution for $W \in L$ as for $\hat{W} \in \hat{L}$.*

It is obvious that the following result is true:

COROLLARY 8*1.1. *There is no BSF satisfying Axioms 8*1–8*6.*

The proof is immediate since the Nash solution is sensitive to $\tilde{x}$.[4] This property of the Nash solution is not necessarily objectionable in the context of a positive model of bargaining solutions, but its ethical limitations are important and were discussed in Chapter 8.

8*2. SOCIAL WELFARE FUNCTIONAL

We can now turn to a more general formulation of the problem of using cardinality with non-comparability. In line with an SWF we define a social welfare functional.

DEFINITION 8*2. *A social welfare functional (SWFL) is a functional relation that specifies one and only one social ordering R over X, for any W, i.e., for any n-tuple of individual welfare functions, $W_1, \ldots, W_n$, each defined over X.*

Note that an SWF is a special case of an SWFL, in which only the individual ordering properties are used. It may also be remarked that while the aggregation relation for any $W \in L$ is an SWFL, in Chapter 7* the aggregation relation was made a function of $\overline{L} \subset L$ and not necessarily of an individual element $W \in L$.

Corresponding to Arrow's conditions on an SWF, similar conditions are imposed on an SWFL.

Condition $\overline{U}$ (unrestricted domain): The domain of the SWFL includes all logically possible W, viz., all possible n-tuples of individual welfare functions defined over X.

Condition $\overline{I}$ (independence of irrelevant alternatives): If for all i, $W_i(x) = \hat{W}_i(x)$ and $W_i(y) = \hat{W}_i(y)$, for some pair $x, y \in X$, for some pair of welfare combinations W and $\hat{W}$, then $x \, R \, y \leftrightarrow x \, \hat{R} \, y$, where R and $\hat{R}$ are the social orderings corresponding to W and $\hat{W}$.

Condition $\overline{D}$ (non-dictatorship): There is no i such that for all elements in the domain of the SWFL, $x \, P_i \, y \leftrightarrow x \, P \, y$.

---

[4] There is, in fact, some redundancy in this, as will be clear from Section 8*2.

Condition $\bar{P}$ (weak Pareto principle): If for all i, $x\,P_i\,y$, then for all elements in the domain of the SWFL, consistent with this, we have $x\,P\,y$.

Condition $\bar{C}$ (cardinality):[5] For each i, every positive linear transformation of any element of L_i belongs to L_i.

Condition $\bar{M}$ (non-comparability): For any L, the social ordering R yielded by the SWFL for each $W \in L$ must be the same.

THEOREM 8*2. *There is no SWFL satisfying conditions $\bar{U}$, $\bar{I}$, $\bar{D}$, $\bar{P}$, $\bar{C}$ and $\bar{M}$.*

Proof. Consider a pair $x, y \in X$. For $W \in L$, we have $W_i(x)$ and $W_i(y)$ for all i. Consider now a change in the individual welfare functions, keeping the individual orderings the same, let L get transformed to $\hat{L}$. Clearly, by condition $\bar{C}$, which gives us two degrees of freedom for the welfare measure for each person, we can find $\hat{W} \in \hat{L}$, such that $W_i(x) = \hat{W}_i(x)$ and $W_i(y) = \hat{W}_i(y)$. By condition $\bar{I}$, $x\,R\,y \leftrightarrow x\,\hat{R}\,y$, where R and $\hat{R}$ are social orderings corresponding to W and $\hat{W}$. Hence, by $\bar{M}$, the social ordering must be the same for the elements of L as for those of $\hat{L}$. Thus, the only possible SWFLs satisfying conditions $\bar{I}$ and $\bar{C}$ are all SWFs, with R a function merely of the n-tuples of individual orderings $(R_1, \ldots, R_n)$.[6] But we know from Theorem 3*1 that no SWF satisfies conditions U, I, D and P, which conditions are implied by conditions $\bar{U}$, $\bar{I}$, $\bar{D}$ and $\bar{P}$, for SWFL. The proof is, thus, complete.

This problem did not arise for aggregation in Chapter 7*, since the collective choice criterion was defined there in terms of invariance for each W in a specified $\bar{L} \subset L$, without demanding invariance with respect to the choice of all W from L. The choice of $\bar{L}$ reflected our assumption about interpersonal comparability. Theorem 8*2 confirms the suspicion that mere cardinality without any comparability may not be helpful.

---

[5] We do not require that *all* elements of L_i are linear transformations of each. We can, however, add this without affecting the result. Incidentally, Condition $\bar{C}$ binds an SWFL only in conjunction with Condition $\bar{M}$.

[6] In fact, R over each pair of social states is a function of the n-tuple of R_i over *that* pair only.

Chapter 9
Equity and Justice

9.1. UNIVERSALIZATION AND EQUITY

One method of making interpersonal comparisons is to try to put oneself in the position of another. The approach, not surprisingly, has cropped up in various forms in different cultures almost throughout recorded history, though the use to which the approach has been put has varied a great deal from society to society.

The so-called Golden Rule of the gospel is an expression – a rather narrow one – of this approach: 'Do unto others as ye would that others should do unto you.' Kant's study of the 'moral law' is closely related to this approach of placing oneself in the position of others, as is his general rule: 'Act always on such a maxim as thou canst at the same time will to be a universal law.'[1] Sidgwick's principle of 'equity' or 'fairness' is a particularly useful expression of this approach:[2]

... Whatever action any of us judges to be right for himself, he implicitly judges to be right for all similar persons in similar circumstances. Or, as we may otherwise put it, 'if a kind of conduct that is right (or wrong) for me is not right (or wrong) for some one else, it

[1] See Kant (1785). In Abbott's translation, Kant (1907), p. 66.
[2] Sidgwick (1907), Book III, Chap. XIII, p. 379. Sidgwick attributed this to Kant: 'That whatever is right for me must be right for all persons in similar circumstances – which was the form in which I accepted the Kantian maxim – seemed to me certainly fundamental, certainly true, and not without practical importance' (p. xvii). For a survey of the generalization argument, see Singer (1961).

must be on the ground of some difference between the two cases, other than the fact that I and he are different persons.' A corresponding position may be stated with equal truth in respect of what ought to be done *to* – and not *by* – different individuals.[3]

A relatively recent extension of this approach is to be found in Hare (1952), (1963). Hare relates the question of 'equity', in the sense of Sidgwick, to the property of 'universalizability' of value judgments in general (viz., in exactly similar circumstances exactly similar judgments would have to be made), and makes this a matter of *meaning* rather than a moral principle that we might wish value judgments should satisfy. A quotation from Hare ((1961), pp. 176–7) might help to exemplify his interpretation.

> Suppose that I say to someone 'You ought not to smoke in this compartment,' and there are children in the compartment. The person addressed is likely, if he wonders why I have said that he ought not to smoke, to look around, notice the children, and so understand the reason. But suppose that, having ascertained about the compartment, he then says 'All right; I'll go next door: there's another compartment there just as good; in fact it is exactly like this one, and there are children in it too.' I should think if he said this that he did not understand the function of the word 'ought', for 'ought' always refers to some general principle; and if the next compartment is really exactly like this one, every principle that is applicable to this one must be applicable to the other. I might therefore reply: 'But look here, if you ought not to smoke in this compartment, and the other compartment is just like this one, has the same sort of

---

[3] The celebrated epitaph of Martin Engelbrodde has been quoted by Arrow (1963) as an example of this approach of 'extended sympathy'.

> Here lies Martin Engelbrodde,
> Ha'e mercy on my soul, Lord God,
> As I would do were I Lord God,
> And Thou wert Martin Engelbrodde.

The interesting question as to whether Lord God should be obliged to have mercy on Engelbrodde's soul under Sidgwick's principle of equity is left as an exercise to the reader. (Hint: Contrast 'as I would do' with 'as Thou wouldst want'!)

occupants, the same notices on the windows, &c., then obviously you oughtn't to smoke in that one either.'

Similarity of circumstances is interpreted by Hare (like Sidgwick) to include *as if* interpersonal permutations everything else remaining the same. If a white South African claims that apartheid is good, but concedes that his judgment would have been different if he were himself black, then in Hare's system he would reveal an ignorance of 'the way in which the word "good" functions'. In contrast, if the criterion was taken as a moral principle and not as a matter of meaning, then the white South African in question could be called, in some sense, *immoral*, but not, in any sense, *ignorant* (of the language of morals).

In all this, two different questions must be clearly distinguished: (a) the question of universalizability of value judgments, and (b) the question whether *as if* interpersonal permutations given other things should be taken as 'exactly similar' circumstances. We take up question (a) first.

Universalizability is indeed a widely accepted criterion, and as Arrow has argued in another context, 'value judgments may equate empirically distinguishable phenomena, but they cannot differentiate empirically indistinguishable states.'[4] The use of universalizability does, however, raise at least two difficult problems. First, taking universalizability as a logical necessity rather than as a moral principle implies a violation of the so-called 'Hume's Law', which asserts that no value judgment can be deduced from exclusively factual premises. Normative value, in this view, must be a function defined over factual states, and while there is no compulsion to accept any particular form for the function on factual grounds (as there may be in the classic 'naturalist' position), two identical factual states must be required to have the same normative value. If this is taken as a logical necessity, two states being factually exactly the same (a fact) seems to imply that they are equally good (a value judgment).[5] This need not

---

[4] Arrow (1963), p. 112.
[5] See Sen (1966b). In terms of the theory of identity, if $x = y$, then $f(x) = f(y)$, for all f. This is so even if f is a moral function. The former statement is factual and the latter is moral.

disturb anyone, except those committed totally to Hume's Law, which, however, does include Hare himself.[6]

A more important difficulty for universalizability than fidelity towards Hume's doctrine concerns the *scope* of the principle irrespective of whether it is interpreted as a logical necessity or as a normative rule. *Can* two situations really be exactly alike? If not, then universalizability is empty of content. If two situations are not exactly similar, they could, of course, be claimed to be 'relevantly similar', e.g. buying a car with a certain number on it and buying another car physically identical to it except for the number. The concept of relevant similarity, which itself involves a value judgment, is not easy to define, but one possible line is the following: If x and y are exactly similar except in some respects, and if a person's judgments in question involving x and y are independent of those respects, then x and y are relevantly similar in that person's system. In this extended form, universalizability will require that a person's judgments be exactly similar for x and y when the two alternatives are relevantly similar. There are problems with this extension, but they would seem to be less serious than the possibly vacuous nature of universalizability in its un-adulterated form.

We now turn to the second question. Do interpersonal permutations, everything else unchanged, preserve 'similarity'? If it is so taken, as Hare does, then Sidgwick's principle of equity is a direct consequence of universalizability. If not, then the question of relevant similarity arises, and we have to face the problem of the white South African referred to earlier who might claim that whether he is white or black *is* a relevant difference in his system. Hare would rule this out, but it seems to be possible to take the view that such a judgment, while 'wicked', is not impossible by virtue of the discipline of the language of morals.

There is a further difficulty with Hare's use of interpersonal permutations to develop a criterion for moral judgments. It is, in fact,

---

[6] 'I have been in the past, and still am, a stout defender of Hume's doctrine that one cannot deduce moral judgments from non-moral statements of fact' (Hare (1963), p. 186). See also Hare (1961), pp. 29–31, 79–93.

possible that no judgment might pass such a test, and questions might be asked about a case when an individual cannot honestly say that he will hold on to exactly the same judgments under every conceivable interpersonal permutation. Insofar as Hare is right in believing that the discipline of the moral language already in operation does require universalizability in this demanding sense, and insofar as this language is meaningfully used by people, it can be claimed that the criterion does not, by and large, define an empty set of value judgments. There is no doubt, however, that this is a hard requirement, especially since it is supposed to apply to every kind of moral judgment.[7]

A somewhat less demanding set of rules have been put forward by a number of writers in the specific context of judgments about 'fairness', 'justice' and 'ethical (as opposed to subjective) preferences'. These requirements are less stringent for two reasons. First, they are intended to apply to some limited categories of moral virtues (like fairness or justice). Second, and perhaps more important, the condition of making the same judgment under every conceivable permutation of personal positions is replaced by the requirement that the judgment be made in a situation where the individual is unaware of the exact position that he is to hold in any of the social states considered. Some of these approaches will now be examined.

9.2. FAIRNESS AND MAXIMIN JUSTICE

Rawls' analysis of the concept of fairness makes use of a hypothetical situation (the 'original position') where individuals choose 'principles' in a state of primordial equality without knowing their own placing in social states resulting from it, being ignorant even of their personal features in addition to social positions. In such a

---

[7] There has been considerable discussion among philosophers on the validity and usefulness of Hare's approach, touching on several issues. See, for example, Madell (1965), Montague (1965), Gauthier (1968), to quote just a few of these contributions. Hare himself outlines some problems, including that of the 'weakness of will', and the problem of the 'fanatic'; see Hare (1960), (1963).

situation the principles that would be generally accepted would satisfy the criterion of 'fairness', being the result of a fair agreement with no vested interests. (See Rawls (1958), (1963a), (1963b), (1967), (1968)).

Rawls derives his principles of 'justice' from his criterion of fairness. His concept of 'justice as fairness' expresses the idea that the principles of justice are those that would be chosen in an initial situation that is fair. Unlike in the model of Hare, it is not required that a moral judgment be held from *every* position that a person can occupy through interpersonal permutations. Instead, the principles of justice are those which would be accepted in a fair situation in the 'original position'.

A certain similarity of this view of justice with Rousseau's analysis of the 'general will' and of a hypothetical 'social contract' has been noted.[8] Principles of justice can be viewed as solutions of cooperative games in the 'original position'. However, Rawls' approach differs essentially from those of Nash (1950), (1953), Raiffa (1953) and Braithwaite (1955) in that the notions of 'fairness' and 'justice' are not related to cooperative solutions of bargaining problems in *actual* situations with given interpersonal inequalities (e.g. of economic wealth, political power, and similar contingencies), but with cooperative solutions in a state of primordial equality. Our reservations (see Chapters 8 and 8*) about the former as interpretations of fairness and justice do not, therefore, apply to Rawls.

Having thus established a framework for fairness, Rawls argues that the two following principles of justice would have been chosen in the 'original position': (a) 'each person participating in a practice, or affected by it, has an equal right to the most extensive liberty compatible with a like liberty for all'; and (b) 'inequalities are arbitrary unless it is reasonable to expect that they will work out for everyone's advantage, and provided that the positions and offices to which they attach, or from which they may be gained, are open to all' (Rawls (1958)).

---

[8] Runciman and Sen (1965) provide a game-theoretic interpretation of Rousseau's 'general will' and of Rawls' 'original position'.

The meaning of these principles is not altogether obvious, but on Rawls' analysis it turns out that the proper maximand is the welfare of the worst-off individual (Rawls (1963a)). The first principle recommends the extension of liberty of each as long as similar liberty is extended to all. Interpersonal conflicts is the subject matter of the second principle, which is interpreted to require that 'social inequalities be arranged to make the worst-off best-off', i.e. the welfare level of the worst-off individual be made as high as possible.

This last is a well-defined criterion when ordinal interpersonal comparisons can be made to discover who is the worst-off person. It is essentially a 'maximin' criterion, and the minimal element in the set of individual welfares is maximized.[9] Rawls' main focus is on the type of institutions to be chosen, but the maximin principle can be used also to order social states based on individual orderings. For any social state, we order the individuals in terms of their welfare and pick on the worst-off individual. His welfare level is noted for comparison with the welfare of the worst-off individual in another social state. As long as each individual has a complete ordering and some method exists to order the well-being of different individuals, i.e., to make interpersonal comparisons of levels of welfare, we can obtain a complete social ordering.

Is this maximin procedure an SWF in the sense of Arrow? It is not, for the Arrow SWF is a function that specifies one and only one social ordering for any given collection of individual orderings. Suppose every individual's ordering remains the same but the welfare level of individual i, who was previously the worst-off person in social state x, goes up for every alternative, making him no longer the worst-off man in situation x. Now the social ordering involving x, being based on a different individual's welfare, can be different. This would not be permitted by an SWF.

There is another way of looking at the contrast. An SWF, or more

---

[9] For the use of the Rawls criterion of justice, measurability of individual welfare is not really necessary, not even in the ordinal sense. The criterion can be presented in terms of orderings (Chapter 9*), and discussions on it can take place perfectly well without bringing in welfare measures at all.

generally a CCR, specifies a social preference relation based on the set of individual orderings of actual social states. For the Rawls type of comparison, what is needed is not an ordering merely of social states viewed from one's own position, but a ranking of social states with interpersonal permutations. The statement that individual i has a higher welfare level in state x than individual j has in state y can be translated as: it is better to be person i in state x than to be person j in state y. If there are m states and n individuals, what is involved is an ordering $\tilde{R}$ of mn alternatives. Given such an ordering, the Rawlsian maximin ordering of the m social states is immediately obtained.[10] A CCR (or an SWF) would have, on the other hand, made the social ordering dependent on n orderings, each defined over m social states. A CCR is thus based on n orderings of m elements, whereas a Rawlsian maximin choice mechanism is based on one ordering of mn elements.

This extended ordering over mn positions may reflect one individual's assessment, or may even represent the unanimous views of all. Unanimity is not absurd to assume here since everyone orders the positions, bearing in mind that being person i in state x means not merely to have the social position of i but also his precise subjective features.[11] However, differences in judgment between persons can still arise, and, if they do, a problem similar to that faced with a CCR, or an SWF, will be faced here as well. For the moment we assume unanimity in ordering 'positions', or assume that all the exercise is done by some consistent observer.

But how appealing is the maximin criterion as a social decision rule? It certainly does involve a number of problems when viewed as a formal criterion, of which the following may be important:

(1) While it satisfies the weaker version of the Pareto rule (condition P), it may violate its stronger version. Consider two situations x and y with the following welfare levels of two individuals A and B:

---

[10] Strictly, an ordering is not needed, since the non-worst-off positions can be ranked in any manner and may not even be ranked vis-a-vis each other.

[11] This identity of orderings of positions should not be confused with the identity of judgments about social states required in Hare's model. A person with a given ordering of positions could, nevertheless, recommend different choices, depending on which position he himself holds.

	Welfare of A	Welfare of B
state x	10	1
state y	20	1

The maximin rule will make x and y indifferent, while y is Pareto-wise superior to x. Since the accentuation of inequality is not to 'everyone's advantage', and the worst-off individual is no better off under y than under x, y is not socially judged better than x.[12]

(2) Our values about inequality cannot be adequately reflected in the maximin rule, because an exclusive concern with the well-being of the worst-off individual, or the worst-off group of individuals, hides various other issues related to equality. Consider the following alternative states:

	Welfare of A	Welfare of B	Welfare of C
state x	100	80	60
state y	100	61	61

The maximin rule will indicate that y is preferred to x. However, while the gap between B and C is reduced, that between A and B is accentuated. There are no simple measures of inequality for a group and our values also tend to be too complicated to be caught by a simple rule like 'make the worst-off best-off'.

---

[12] We can avoid this problem by defining a lexicographic ordering in the following form, without losing the essence of the maximin rule, for a community of n individuals:

(1) Maximize the welfare of the worst-off individual.

(2) For the equal welfare of the worst-off individuals, maximize the welfare of the second worst-off individual.

.
.
.

(n) For equal welfare of the worst-off individuals, the second worst-off individuals, ... , the $(n-1)$th worst-off individuals, maximize the welfare of the best-off individual.

In the example in the text, y is obviously preferred to x under this rule, which we can call the lexicographic maximin rule.

While this criticism is valid, its importance is not quite obvious. If the institutional features are such that a reduction of the gap between the average and the minimum can be achieved only through a reduction of inequality as measured by other indices, it will be somewhat pointless to lose much sleep on this question. Judgments of this kind tend to be non-basic and the factual background is important. Rawls' argumentation is based on a certain institutional framework, and to assess the effectiveness of his criterion we have to bear this in mind. However, it is likely that the difficulty will be more serious in the choice between social states in general, which is our problem, than in the choice between certain institutions, which is Rawls' focus of attention.

(3)   Because of the purely ordinal nature of it, the maximin criterion is not sensitive to magnitudes of gains and losses. There is no such thing here as a slight gain of the worst-off person being wiped out from a social point of view by big gains (as big as we dare to postulate) of the others. There is *no* trade-off.

(4)   For Rawls, the justification of the maximin rule lies in its relationship with the principle of 'fairness', and the above arguments may be irrelevant in that context. There is little doubt that the requirement of 'fairness' is highly appealing. If people choose a system while totally ignorant of their personal attributes, it certainly does satisfy an important value in our moral system. The link between the concept of 'fairness' and the two principles of 'justice' that identify the maximin rule lies in the belief that in a 'fair' agreement these two principles will be chosen. Is this argument acceptable?

The theory of decision-taking under uncertainty does not yield very definite conclusions on problems of this kind. Certainly with a predominantly pessimistic outlook the maximin rule will be the only one to choose. There are other arguments also, which Rawls (1967), (1968) specifies. The rule is clear and is relatively easy to handle. Unlike the approach of utilitarianism it is not blind to distributions of utility over the individuals. In its application to institutional choices it will militate against persecution, religious or otherwise, since the sufferings of the man under an inquisition will never be washed out by the gain, however large, of the inquisitor. In several institutional questions the appeal of the maximin approach is well demonstrated by Rawls. Nevertheless, the fact remains that Rawls' maximin solution is a very special one and the assertion that it *must* be chosen in the original position is not altogether convincing. Even if one rejects the criterion of maximizing expected utility, which we discuss in the next section, there are other criteria that must be considered.[13] The pessimism-optimism index of Hurwicz (1951), of which the maximin rule is an extreme case (corresponding to a degree of pessimism equal to 1), is a possibility that can be explored, after suitable generalization. To choose one particular decision rule, viz., maximin, out of many may be appropriate some time, but to claim that it must be chosen by rational individuals in the 'original position' seems to be a rather severe assumption.

It is not our purpose here to evaluate Rawls' highly original and valuable contribution to the notions of fairness and justice. His main interest is not so much in the ordering of social states, which is our concern, but with finding just institutions as opposed to unjust ones, which is a somewhat different problem. Rawls' approach to the latter problem is relevant to the former question also, but it is not a complete picture in that context.

Finally, it is worth noting that Rawls' principle of fairness is more fundamental than his principles of justice, which he derives from the former. And it is possible to accept Rawls' criteria of fairness without committing oneself fully to his identification of justice.[14] Indeed the idea of morally recommending a collective choice mechanism can be

---

[13] For a lucid introduction to various decision criteria, see Luce and Raiffa (1957), Chapter 13, and Raiffa (1968).

[14] A half-jocular, half-serious objection to the criteria of fairness of Rawls and others runs like this: Why confine placing oneself in the position of other human beings only, why not other animals also? Is the biological line so sharply drawn? What this line of attack misses is the fact that Rawls is crystallizing an idea of fairness that our value system does seem to have, rather than constructing a rule of fairness in vacuum based on some notions of biological symmetry. Revolutions do take place demanding equitable treatment of human beings in a manner they do not demanding equality for animals. 'If I were in his shoes' is relevant to a moral argument in a manner that 'if I were in its paws' is not. Our ethical systems may have had, as is sometimes claimed, a biological origin, but what is involved here is the *use* of these systems and not a *manufacture* of it on some kind of a biological logic. The jest half of the objection is, thus, more interesting than the serious half.

given considerable content in terms of the notion of an *as if* uncertainty as outlined by Rawls.

9.3. IMPERSONALITY AND EXPECTED UTILITY MAXIMIZATION

Harsanyi (1955) considers two sets of preferences for each individual. Their 'subjective preferences' are their preferences as 'they actually are'.[15] Their 'ethical preferences' must satisfy the characteristic of being 'impersonal'.

> An individual's preferences satisfy this requirement of impersonality if they indicate what social situation he would choose if he did not know what his personal position would be in the new situation ation chosen (and in any of its alternatives) but rather had an equal *chance* of obtaining any of the social positions existing in this situation, from the highest down to the lowest.[16]

This concept of 'impersonality' is very closely related to notions of 'universalizability' and 'fairness' discussed in the last two sections. Hare's 'universalizability' is the most demanding of the three conditions. To satisfy it a person's judgment must remain the same no matter whose shoes one is in. Rawls' 'fairness' required acceptance in the 'original position' without knowing in whose shoes one would be. Harsanyi's 'impersonality' requires acceptance under the assumption of equiprobability. Similarities between Rawls' and Harsanyi's concepts are striking, and would be even more so if the 'principle of insufficient reason' could be used to convert Rawls' 'ignorance' into Harsanyi's 'equiprobability'. Rawls rejects this and chooses the non-probabilistic maximin criterion. Harsanyi, however, defines his 'impersonality' directly in terms of *as if* equiprobability,

[15] These personal utility functions, of course, do not rule out interdependence between the individuals' utilities, and correspond to what Arrow calls 'values' rather than 'tastes' (Arrow (1963), p. 18; Harsanyi (1955), p. 315).

[16] Harsanyi (1955), p. 316. See also Vickrey (1945), p. 329. Also Harsanyi (1953), Leibenstein (1965) and Pattanaik (1968b).

and assumes further that individuals will satisfy the von Neumann-Morgenstern (or Marschak) postulates of rational behaviour under risk. (See Chapter 7 for a statement of the postulates.) Ethical preferences are, therefore, determined by expected utility maximization, and under the equiprobability assumption this boils down simply to maximizing the sum of utilities of all. Utilitarianism is, thus, vindicated on grounds of 'impersonality', and the relevant utilities are of the von Neumann-Morgenstern type, thereby easing the problem of cardinalization which we discussed in Chapter 7.

Aside from this direct approach to ethical preferences, Harsanyi also explores a more general approach to social choice. He proves the following theorem: If social preferences as well as all individual preferences satisfy the Marschak (or von Neumann-Morgenstern) postulates, and if everyone being indifferent implies social indifference, then social welfare must be a weighted sum of individual utilities.[17] There are various ways of using this theorem (see Pattanaik (1968b)). Harsanyi takes social preferences to be the 'social welfare function of a given individual',[18] and this provides a background to his notion of 'ethical preferences' which are a type of 'social preferences' in this sense. Under the equiprobability assumption, the ethical preferences are those social preferences which use the unweighted (i.e., equiweighted) sum of utilities.

How satisfactory is the test of impersonality? The following difficulties seem to be relatively serious.

(1) Consider a slave society with 99 free men and 1 slave. The latter serves the former to their convenience and to his great discomfort. Given an equal chance of being in anyone's position it is possible that someone might be ready to take a 1% chance of being a slave, since the 99% chance of being a free man served by a slave might tickle his fancy. Would a slave society be then morally supportable? Many people will not accept this test.

It might incidentally be noted that in this case the Rawlsian model of 'justice' will tend to give different judgments from that derived

---

[17] Theorem V in Harsanyi (1955), p. 314. See also Fleming (1952).
[18] Harsanyi (1955), p. 315.

from 'impersonality'. Since the maximin notion fixes on the welfare of the worst-off individual, problems of this kind cannot appear in the use of that criterion. Similarly, to claim that slavery or apartheid was 'just' with Hare's requirement of 'universalizability' would demand much more than the test used here. The author of the judgment will have to maintain this not merely under the equiprobability assumption of impersonality, but when imaging himself occupying (with certainty) every relevant position in that social situation.

(2) Consider now a somewhat different problem. Let there be two alternative social states represented by x and y with a two-person welfare situation as given below:

	Welfare of 1	Welfare of 2
state x	1	0
state y	$\frac{1}{2}$	$\frac{1}{2}$

In terms of expected utility, the assumption of impersonality will make each of them indifferent between x and y, since both have an expected value of $\frac{1}{2}$. Are they equally appealing? If someone values equality as such (and not for such derived reasons that equality maximizes the aggregate of individual welfares[19]), he may categorically prefer state y to x. It would appear that in social choices we are interested not only in the mathematical expectation of welfare with impersonality, but also with the exact distribution of that welfare over the individuals.

In an interesting and important note, Diamond (1967) has argued that the 'strong independence assumption' (or the 'sure thing principle'; see Section 7.3, p. 149) is the guilty party in the Harsanyi framework of social preference.[20] This assumption is included in the set of Marschak postulates accepted by Harsanyi.

[19] Note that the units in the above table are of individual welfare and not of income or output.
[20] See also Strotz (1958), (1961), and Fisher and Rothenberg (1961), (1962).

	0.5 probability		0.5 probability	
lottery I	$U_A = 1,$	$U_B = 0$	$U_A = 0,$	$U_B = 1$
lottery II	$U_A = 1,$	$U_B = 0$	$U_A = 1,$	$U_B = 0$

Diamond considers a case of two individuals (say, A and B) and two alternative 'lotteries' (say, I and II). If II is chosen, it is certain that individual A will have a unit of utility while B will have none. With I there is a probability of 0.5 that A will have one unit of utility and B none, while there is also a probability of 0.5 that B will have one unit of utility and A none.

In terms of aggregate expected utility maximization, I and II are equally good, having an expected aggregate value of 1. It seems reasonable to be indifferent between the second prize of I and that of II because they seem very much the same except for the substitution of name tags A and B. But the first prize of both the lotteries is the same, so that 'the sure thing principle' (or 'the strong independence assumption') would make us indifferent between I and II. But lottery II seems so unfair to individual B, while lottery I 'gives B a fair shake.' Hence Diamond's rejection of 'the sure thing principle' as applied to social choice.

It should, however, be noted that the Diamond argument depends crucially on the individual welfare levels (and thus also 'origins') being comparable – an assumption that is not needed for Harsanyi's model of aggregate welfare or, for that matter, in any model of aggregate welfare. Suppose we add 1 to individual B's welfare function, keeping A's welfare function unchanged. In the utility space the two lotteries get transformed to the following:

	0.5 probability		0.5 probability	
lottery I	$U_A = 1,$	$U_B = 1$	$U_A = 0,$	$U_B = 2$
lottery II	$U_A = 1,$	$U_B = 1$	$U_A = 1,$	$U_B = 1$

It will now be easy to build an argument in favor of II against I on much the same grounds ('a fair shake') as Diamond's reason for preferring I to II. And this is brought about by a mere change in the origin of one individual's welfare function, which leaves the ordering

COLLECTIVE CHOICE AND SOCIAL WELFARE (1970)

of aggregate welfare completely unchanged. Clearly the type of comparability that Harsanyi needs is in this respect less demanding than what Diamond needs for criticizing Harsanyi. Since neither Harsanyi nor Diamond states his assumptions of interpersonal comparability explicitly, the debate is not easy to evaluate. In our terminology (Chapters 7 and 7*), Harsanyi needs 'unit comparability' for the aggregation exercise, whereas Diamond needs 'full comparability' to be able to make his point.

It can also be asked whether the strong independence assumption is really guilty *even if* full comparability is assumed. Someone could argue that *after* the lottery takes place the end result will be that one person will have one unit of utility and the other none in the case of each lottery. So in terms of *actual* utility distribution rather than *anticipated* utility distribution, lottery I is no more egalitarian (and thus may really be no more attractive) than lottery II. Why should the process of lottery matter since the ultimate result is a 1–0 distribution anyway? This is a possible position to take, though there are people who would find much fairness in having the intermediate phase of randomization.[21]

Whether we accept strong independence or not, the attractiveness of expected utility maximization is in doubt. The example given in the table on p. 200 applies to expected utility maximization in general. And the argument for choosing $(\frac{1}{2}, \frac{1}{2})$ rather than $(1, 0)$ would appear to be rather strong, if full comparability is assumed. While utilitarianism in general and Harsanyi's criterion in particular would be indifferent between the two, the maximin rule would have favored the egalitarian distribution.[22] The crucial question is that of comparability, since unit comparability will rule out any possible consideration of equality in utility distributions without affecting utilitarianism and Harsanyi's criterion.

---

[21] In a seminar run jointly by Arrow, Rawls and myself, at Harvard in the fall of 1968, the participants (about thirty in all) were found to be roughly equally divided on this.

[22] This being a two-person case, some of the difficulties with Rawls' rather extreme criterion which we discussed in the last section could not possibly arise here.

It should also be added that just as we introduced 'partial comparability' of *units* in Chapters 7 and 7*, we can use partial comparability of utility *origins* (and more generally of *absolute levels* of welfare, cardinal or not) of different persons. The formal framework will be on the same lines as the framework of partial comparability of units, and we resist the temptation here to charge full steam into this area. The interested reader can try it out.

It is interesting to contrast the formal requirements of the maximin criterion with the utilitarian principle. The former requires comparability of levels of welfare, which the latter does not. On the other hand, the latter can be taken to be a sure-fire principle of social ordering in every possible case only if cardinality and unit comparability are assumed, while the maximin criterion works perfectly well with ordinality and even with ordering with no possible numerical representation. These technical considerations are not, of course, ethically decisive, but they certainly are relevant. Utilitarianism may be accepted with enthusiasm if we can compare differences of welfare for different persons, but not levels. On the other hand, if we cannot compare units, or if we can compare levels, the enthusiasm may be limited. In evaluating these principles for our own social judgments we can do worse than considering the types of interpersonal comparisons we tend to make.

9.4. GRADING PRINCIPLES OF JUSTICE

While both the maximin criterion and the utility principle yield complete social orderings given their respective measurability and comparability assumptions, Suppes' (1966) model of 'grading principles' yields only partial orderings. On the basis of these grading principles, Suppes devises simple ethical rules of behaviour in two-person games. Given the state of nature and the decisions or acts chosen by the two persons, the set of consequences on each can be found out. With S being the set of states of nature, D_1 and D_2 the respective sets of decisions or acts available to the two persons, and C_1 and C_2 the respective sets of consequences for the two persons.

Suppes' 'social decision function'[23] specifies values of C_1 and C_2 for each combination of S, D_1 and D_2. The object is to find a partial ordering of the pairs of consequences on the two.

Let $(x, 1)$ and $(x, 2)$ be the consequences on the two individuals 1 and 2, respectively, in some two-person decision situation that has to be compared with another when the consequences on the two, respectively, are $(y, 1)$ and $(y, 2)$. The point is to compare x with y in terms of 'extended sympathy'. We know that x will be Pareto-superior to y, if individual 1 regards $(x, 1)$ to be at least as good as $(y, 1)$, individual 2 regards $(x, 2)$ to be at least as good as $(y, 2)$, and at least one of them strictly prefers the respective component of x to that of y. The ranking *more just than* is, however, done for each individual separately in terms of his own tastes. The essence of the approach is to use the individual's ordering over the set of individual consequences, i.e., over $(x, 1)$, $(x, 2)$, $(y, 1)$, $(y, 2)$, etc., to obtain the required justice relation over the set of social states, i.e, over x, y, etc. If individual 1 finds that he prefers $(x, 1)$ to $(y, 1)$ and regards $(x, 2)$ to be at least as good as $(y, 2)$, then he judges x to be more just than y. He makes the same judgment if he prefers $(x, 2)$ to $(y, 2)$ and finds $(x, 1)$ at least as good as $(y, 1)$.

So far this is simply a Pareto-like judgment, done in terms of the individual's own preferences. But now he might reverse the actual interpersonal distribution of consequences. Suppose he finds that the above requirements are not satisfied, but the following set is. He strictly prefers $(x, 1)$ to $(y, 2)$ and regards $(x, 2)$ to be at least as good as $(y, 1)$. This is, he prefers to be himself in situation x than be in individual 2's shoes in situation y, and he likes being in individual 2's shoes in situation x at least as much as being himself in situation y. He might once again decide that x is more just than y. Exactly similarly, if he strictly prefers $(x, 2)$ to $(y, 1)$, and regards $(x, 1)$ to be at least as good as $(y, 2)$, he may again regard x to be more just than y.

The conditions outlined in the last two paragraphs indicate the basis of Suppes' 'grading principle of justice' for each individual, defining a partial strict ordering over the pairs of consequences. Since

[23] Not to be confused with the SDF defined in this work (see Definition 4*1)

the principle of comparison may appear to be slightly difficult, being unfamiliar and novel (a tribute to the originality of Suppes), the condition may be stated slightly differently (making it somewhat weaker), requiring strict preference for both the comparisons. The Suppes rule says that x is more just than y according to individual i, if either (a) he prefers to be himself at x rather than at y, and also prefers to be the other individual at x rather than at y, *or* (b) he prefers to be himself at x rather than the other individual at y, and prefers to be the other individual at x rather than himself at y. In either case, there is something superior at x vis-a-vis y in terms of his own preference ordering, either retaining the respecting positions or reversing them

Suppes demonstrates that the ordering relation 'more just than' does define a partial strict ordering over the set of pairs of consequences, i.e., the relation is 'asymmetric' and 'transitive'. Suppes then proceeds to use three definitions based on the grading principle of justice to outline two rules of ethical behaviour. A *justice-admissible element*[24] for an individual i is a pair of consequences which is not less just than any feasible pair of consequences, according to that individual's preference ordering. A *point of justice* is a set of strategies, one for each player, that leads to a justice-admissible element. A *justice-saturated strategy* for a player is a strategy such that, no matter which strategy the other player picks in the two-person game, the result is a point of justice.

Based on these definitions, Suppes suggests two rules of justice-oriented behaviour:

I If grading principles of justice of the two individuals yield the same partial strict ordering, and if there is a unique point of justice, then the strategy belonging to each point ought to be chosen.

II If for any player the set of justice-saturated strategies is non-empty, he ought to choose one.

These rules of behaviour will make sense only insofar as the *grading principle* of justice defined by Suppes makes sense, though the

[24] Suppes calls it '(J_i) admissible element'.

converse is not necessarily correct, since the rules of behaviour are to some extent arbitrary.[25] In what follows, we shall concentrate on the merits of the grading principle itself, which is closer to our concern with collective choice rules.

A merit of Suppes's grading principle of justice is that it seems to satisfy the requirement of 'universalizability' as outlined by Hare (1952), (1963), on one interpretation,[26] even in the context of interpersonal interchangeability. Since the rule of comparison is symmetrical between the positions of the individuals, the person can honestly claim that if he maintains that x is more just than y, he does so *irrespective* of being in his own position or that of the other person. Whether the first situation is $[(x, 1), (x, 2)]$ or $[(x, 2), (x, 1)]$ and the second situation is $[(y, 1), (y, 2)]$ or $[(y, 2), (y, 1)]$, makes no difference whatever to the ranking of justice between the two situations. It seems to pass, therefore, a demanding test.

A second advantage is that the approach of Suppes, unlike those of Harsanyi and of Rawls, does not require interpersonal comparisons of welfare. We do not have to compare the welfare levels of different persons, and all comparisons are made in terms of the ordering of a given individual with his own tastes and preferences. Furthermore, unlike in the Harsanyi approach, cardinalization of welfare indices of the individuals is not needed.

The avoidance of cardinalization and interpersonal comparisons is, however, achieved at some price. Unlike the orderings generated by Rawls' criterion, or that of Harsanyi, the rankings yielded by the grading principle of Suppes is *incomplete*. This need not be a very serious criticism, since the ordering, while incomplete, may nevertheless help to solve a set of important problems involving considerations of justice.

It is possible, however, to have a very serious reservation about the grading principle itself. As a consequence of doing all the

[25] See the example given by Suppes (1966) himself on pp. 304–5 to illustrate a case where a justice-saturated strategy yields what looks like a *less* 'equitable and just' solution than the equilibrium point analysis.

[26] There is, however, a different and more appropriate interpretation of Hare for which this is not true. See footnote 28 below.

comparisons in terms of the same individual's tastes, personal differences in preferences find little reflection in the principle. Consider the following example, where the two pairs of consequences are expressed in terms of commodities enjoyed by two individuals without any externalities: To give the sense of the difference in tastes, we take individual 1 to be a devout Muslim and individual 2 to be a devout Hindu, with the commodities in question being pork and beef. It is assumed that the Muslim likes beef and is disgusted by pork, while the Hindu enjoys pork but cannot bear the thought of eating beef. Assuming free disposal, the Muslim is indifferent between different amounts of pork, and the Hindu between different amounts of beef. The two alternative outcomes are given by x and and y.

	The Muslim	The Hindu
state x	2 pork, 0 beef	0 pork, 2 beef
state y	0 pork, 1 beef	1 pork, 0 beef

It is clear that y is Pareto-wise better than x, since the Muslim prefers 1 unit of beef to 2 units of pork, while the Hindu prefers 1 unit of pork to 2 units of beef. What about the grading principle of justice developed by Suppes? Alas, both individuals find x to be more just than y. The Muslim prefers $(x, 2)$ rather than $(y, 1)$, i.e. prefers to have 2 units of beef rather than having one unit of it. Also he is indifferent between $(x, 1)$ and $(y, 2)$, i.e., between having 2 units of pork and having 1 unit of it. Similarly, the Hindu prefers $(x, 1)$ to $(y, 2)$, and is indifferent between $(x, 2)$ and $(y, 1)$. So both find x to be preferable to y by the grading principle of justice. But y is Pareto-wise superior to x.

When the choice is between x and y, x is justice-admissible while y is not. It is easy to construct a game where x will correspond to the unique point of justice, and to get ethical endorsement in terms of the Suppes model for choosing strategies such that x becomes the outcome. The result seems extremely perverse. The source of the problem lies in the procedure whereby each individual can make comparisons in terms of his own tastes on behalf of himself as well as that of the others.[27] Unlike in the models of Harsanyi and Rawls there is no requirement in the Suppes model that one must take on the subjective features (in particular, tastes) of the other when one places oneself in his position. This is the source of the trouble.[28]

The problem, however, is easily removed. Placing oneself in the position of the other should involve not merely having the latter's objective circumstances but also identifying oneself with the other in terms of his subjective features. We call this the identity axiom in Chapter 9*, and it rules out the difficulty altogether, but at some price. On this interpretation a comparison of $(x, 1)$ with $(y, 2)$ or of $(x, 2)$ with $(y, 2)$ *is* an interpersonal comparison. This is not really a major loss, however. It should be fairly obvious from out earlier discussion that nothing of much interest can be said on justice without bringing in some interpersonal comparability. The required reformulation of the grading principles of Suppes merely brings this point home.

9.5. GRADING PRINCIPLE, MAXIMIN AND UTILITARIANISM

The grading principles of Suppes can be extended from his two person world to n-person societies, which is presented in Chapter 9*. Thus extended (and combined with the identity axiom), the Suppes relation can be seen to be a crucial building block of both the maximin relation and utilitarianism. If x is more just than y in the sense of Suppes (with the identity axiom imposed), then x must have a larger welfare aggregate than y (utilitarian relation) and also the worst-off individual at x must be at least as well off as any individual at y (maximin relation) (see Theorems 9*5 and 9*7).

[27] Cf. 'Do not do unto others as you would that they should do unto you. Their tastes may not be the same.' 'The Golden Rule' in 'Maxims for Revolutionists', in George Bernard Shaw, *Man and Superman*, London, 1903.

[28] Since placing oneself in the position of the other in Hare's model is supposed in include *subjective features* of the other, the Suppes criterion does not, in fact, pass the test of 'universalizability'.

This is an extremely important property. As we noted earlier, the conflicting claims of the maximin criterion and of utilitarianism are difficult to resolve. Each has some attractive features and some unattractive ones. The grading principle, when suitably constrained, seems to catch the most appealing common elements of the two.

However, since it yields only a strict partial ordering it is an incomplete criterion. What it does, essentially, is to separate out the relatively non-controversial part of interpersonal choice. It takes us substantially beyond the Pareto criterion. This is especially so in the n-person extension of the Suppes relation; the number of possible interpersonal permutations is given by $n!$, i.e., by $n(n-1)(n-2)\ldots 1$. There are only two permutations in a two-person world, but as many as 3,628,800 different interpersonal permutations in a ten-man world. The Pareto relation is concerned with only one particular one-to-one correspondence. In contrast, there are 3,628,800 *different* ways in which x can be more just than y in a ten-person society, using the extended grading principle.

The extended version of the grading principle is, thus, rich. While it does not yield a complete social ordering, it does squeeze out as much juice as possible out of the use of 'dominance' (or vector inequality), which is the common element in the maximin criterion, utilitarianism, and a number of other collective choice procedures involving interpersonal comparability.

Chapter 9*
Impersonality and Collective
Quasi-Orderings

9*1. GRADING PRINCIPLES
OF JUSTICE

The notion of justice, as we saw in Chapter 9, is closely connected with 'extended sympathy' in the form of placing oneself in the position of another.

DEFINITION 9*1. *Let (x, i) stand for being in the position of individual i in social state x.*

In the discussion so far we have always considered R_i over such alternatives as (x, i), (y, i), etc. Now, R_i will be defined also over such alternatives as (x, i), (y, j), etc., when $i \neq j$. Such an R_i, denoted $\widetilde{R}_i$, will be called an *extended* individual ordering.

DEFINITION 9*2. $\widetilde{R}_i$ *is the ordering of the i-th individual defined over the Cartesian product of X and H, where X is the set of social states, and H is the set of individuals.*

LEMMA 9*a. *A subrelation of $\widetilde{R}_i$ for each i is defined by R_i.*

The proof is obvious from the fact that $x\, R_i\, y$ is now defined as $(x, i)\, \widetilde{R}_i\, (y, i)$. We define $\widetilde{P}_i$ and $\widetilde{I}_i$ corresponding to $\widetilde{R}_i$.

It may be noted that x is Pareto-superior to y, i.e., $x\, \bar{P}\, y$, if and only if $\forall i: [(x, i)\, \widetilde{R}_i\, (y, i)]$ & $\exists i: [(x, i)\, \widetilde{P}_i\, (y, i)]$.

Suppes (1966) has defined an important criteria of justice by making use of extended sympathy in a two-person case. We present here an *n*-person extension of the Suppes model. It involves one-to-one correspondences from the set of individuals H to H itself, such that

210

$k = \rho(j)$, where person j is mapped onto person k. Let the set of all such one-to-one correspondences between H and H be called T. Now, $x \, J_i \, y$ is defined to be read as 'x is more just than y according to person i.'

DEFINITION 9*3. *For all pairs x, y in X,*

$$x \, J_i \, y \leftrightarrow \exists \rho \in T:$$
$$[\{\forall j: (x, j) \, \widetilde{R}_i \, (y, \rho(j))\} \& \{\exists j: (x, j) \, \widetilde{P}_i \, (y \, \rho(j))\}]$$

According to person i, x is more just than y if there is a one-to-one transformation from the set of individuals to itself such that he would prefer to be in the position of someone in x rather than in the position of the corresponding person in y, and also would prefer to be, or would be indifferent to being, in the position of *each* person in x than to be in the position of the corresponding person in y.

Suppes has shown (his Theorem 2) that, for the two-person case that he considers, J_i will be a strict partial ordering over possible social states. The result is generalized below for the n-person case.[1]

THEOREM 9*1. *Each J_i is a strict partial ordering over X, i.e., J_i is asymmetric and transitive, for every logically possible set of extended individual orderings $(\widetilde{R}_i)$.*

Proof. For any $x, y, z \in X$, and for any $i \in H$,

$$x \, J_i \, y \, \& \, y \, J_i \, z$$
$$\rightarrow \exists \rho, \mu \in T: [\{\forall j: (x, j) \, \widetilde{R}_i \, (y, \rho(j))\}$$
$$\& \{\exists j: (x, j) \, \widetilde{P}_i \, (y, \rho(j))\} \& \{\forall k: (y, k) \, \widetilde{R}_i \, (z, \mu(k))\}]$$
$$\rightarrow [\{\forall j: (x, j) \, \widetilde{R}_i \, (z, \pi(j))\} \& \{\exists j: (x, j) \, \widetilde{P}_i \, (z, \pi(j))\}]$$

where $\pi(j) = \mu(\rho(j))$. Since π is also a one-to-one correspondence between H and H, i.e., $\pi \in T$, we can conclude that $x \, J_i \, z$, which proves transitivity.

Asymmetry is now proved by contradiction. Suppose $x \, J_i \, y \, \& \, y \, J_i \, x$ for some $x, y \in X$. Then there are ρ and μ in T such that

---

[1] However, we cannot use Suppes' method of proof since he shows the result by a complete study of all possible cases – a method that works well for his two-person situation, but not well at all for general n-person situations.

$$\forall j: (x, j) \; \widetilde{R}_i \, (y, \rho(j)) \tag{1}$$

$$\& \; \forall k: (y, k) \, \widetilde{R}_i \, (x, \mu(k)) \tag{2}$$

$$\& \; \exists j: (y, j) \, \widetilde{P}_i \, (y, \rho(j)) \tag{3}$$

Without loss of generality, let a particular person j for whom (3) holds be called 1. From (2) and (3), we have for $\pi(j) = \mu(\rho(j))$,

$$(x, 1) \, \widetilde{P}_i \, (x, \pi(1)) \tag{4}$$

Clearly it is impossible that $\pi(1) = 1$. Without loss of generality, let $\pi(1)$ be called person 2.

From (1) and (2), we obtain

$$(x, 2) \, \widetilde{R}_i \, (x, \pi(2)) \tag{5}$$

Obviously, it is impossible that $\pi(2) = 2$, since $\pi(1) = 2$, and π is a one-to-one correspondence. It is also impossible that $\pi(2) = 1$, since (4) and (5) will then be contradictory. Let $\pi(2) = 3$.

Proceeding this way for distinct persons 3, 4, 5, ..., n, we obtain

$$
\begin{aligned}
(x, 3) \, \widetilde{R}_i \, (x, 4) \\
\vdots \\
(x, n - 1) \, \widetilde{R}_i \, (x, n)
\end{aligned}
\tag{6}
$$

From (4), (5) and (6), we conclude that

$$(x, 1) \, \widetilde{P}_i \, (x, n) \tag{7}$$

From (1) and (2), we know that

$$(x, n) \, \widetilde{R}_i \, (x, \pi(n)) \tag{8}$$

But since π is a one-to-one correspondence, and $\pi(n)$ cannot be 2, 3, ..., n, we must have $\pi(n) = 1$. Since (7) and (8) contradict, our initial supposition must be untenable, and hence J_i is asymmetric, which completes the proof.

The Suppes relation of justice J_i is, thus, a strict partial ordering, i.e., 'a grading principle' as Suppes defined such a principle (asymmetric and transitive). It is not, however, a collective choice rule as defined in Chapter 2*, since J_i depends not merely on the set of R_i but on $\widetilde{R}_i$, with each R_i being merely a subrelation of $\widetilde{R}_i$. We redefine a collective choice rule more generally in the next section.

9*2. SUPPES AND PARETO

DEFINITION 9*4. *A general collective choice rule (hereafter, GCCR) is a functional relation that specifies one and only one social preference relation R over the set of social states X, for any n-tuple of individual orderings* $(\widetilde{R}_1, \ldots, \widetilde{R}_n)$, *where each $\widetilde{R}_i$ is an ordering over the product of X and H.*

The grading principles of Suppes, as generalized here for the n-person case, are a set of GCCRs. It takes, in fact, the special form of determining $R = J_i$, on the basis of one and only one $\widetilde{R}_i$, and thus there are n such alternative principles when there are n individuals.

However, the following result seems disturbing:

THEOREM 9*2. *When the number of individuals is 2 or more, the weak Pareto strict relation $\overset{=}{P}$ is incompatible with each J_i, for $i = 1, \ldots, n$, for some logically possible set of individual preferences,* $\widetilde{R}_1, \ldots, \widetilde{R}_n$.

Proof. Let the individuals be numbered $1, \ldots, n$. Consider $\mu \in T$, such that $\mu(j) = j + 1$, for $j < n$, and $\mu(n) = 1$.

Consider the following preference rankings of each person i for some pair $x, y \in X$, for all j:

$$(x, \mu(j)) \, \widetilde{P}_i \, (y, j) \tag{9}$$

$$(y, i) \, \widetilde{P}_i \, (x, i) \tag{10}$$

Representing the inverse function of μ as μ^{-1}, we obtain the following from (9) and (10) for all i:

$$[(x, \mu(i)) \, \widetilde{P}_i \, (y, i)] \, \& \, [(y, i) \, \widetilde{P}_i \, (x, i)] \, \& \, [(x, i) \, \widetilde{P}_i \, (y, \mu^{-1}(i))] \tag{11}$$

For more than one individual being in the community, i.e., $n > 1$, $\mu(i)$ as defined is not the same as i, nor is i the same as $\mu^{-1}(i)$. Hence there is no contradiction in (9) and (10). For each $\widetilde{R}_i$, (9) defines n

ordered pairs with no elements in common, and together with (10) we get one strict order of four elements, viz., that given in (11).

We take any set of $(\widetilde{R}_i)$ that is compatible with (9) and (10). It is immediately clear that for each i, $x\,J_i\,y$, from (9). Also, it is obvious from (10) that $y\,\bar{\bar{P}}\,x$. This proves the theorem.[2]

A corollary is immediate.

COROLLARY 9*2.1.   *When the number of individuals is 2 or more, the Pareto strict relation $\bar{P}$ is incompatible with each J_i for $i = 1, \ldots, n$, for some logically possible set of individual preferences, $\widetilde{R}_1, \ldots, \widetilde{R}_n$.* This follows from: $\forall x, y \in X: x\,\bar{\bar{P}}\,y \rightarrow x\,\bar{P}\,y$. Since the grading principle may contradict the weak Pareto principle, it certainly can contradict the strong Pareto principle.

9*3. IDENTITY AXIOMS AND THE GRADING PRINCIPLES

The problem of incompatibility of the Pareto quasi-ordering with the strict partial orderings of justice can be eliminated by imposing certain restrictions on the individuals' extended preferences, $\widetilde{R}_i$. The identity axiom discussed in Chapter 9, and which can be justified on ethical grounds as an important part of the exercise of extended sympathy, serves this purpose as well.

AXIOM 9*1.   *Identity*: $\forall x, y \in X$:

$$[\forall i: \{(x, i)\,\widetilde{R}_i\,(y, i) \leftrightarrow \forall j: (x, i)\,\widetilde{R}_i\,(y, i)\}]$$

Each individual j in placing himself in the position of person i takes on the tastes and preferences of i.

THEOREM 9*3.   *Under the axiom of identity, for each person i, $\bar{P}$ is compatible with J_i, and further $\forall x, y \in X: [x\,\bar{P}\,y \rightarrow x\,J_i\,y]$.*

---

[2] A simple example for the two-person case is given by $[\{(x, 2)\,P_1(y, 1)\} \ \& \ \{(y,1)\,P_1(x, 1)\} \ \& \ \{(x, 1)\,P_1(y, 2)\}]$, and $[\{(x, 1)\,P_2\,(y, 2)\} \ \& \ \{(y, 2)\,P_2(x, 2)\} \ \& \ \{(x, 2)\,P_2(y, 1)\}]$, where $x\,J_i\,y$ for $i = 1, 2$, but $y\,\bar{\bar{P}}\,x$.

Proof.   For any $x, y \in X$:

$$x \, \bar{P} \, y \rightarrow [\{\forall i: (x, i) \, \widetilde{R}_i \, (y, i)\} \, \& \, \{\exists i: (x, i) \, \widetilde{P}_i \, (y, i)\}]$$
$$\rightarrow \forall i: [\{\forall j: (x, j) \, \widetilde{R}_i \, (y, j)\} \, \& \, \{\exists j: (x, j) \, \widetilde{P}_i \, (y, j)\}]$$
$$\rightarrow \forall i: x \, J_i \, y$$

A more demanding assumption is that given by the axiom of complete identity.

AXIOM 9*2.   *Complete identity:* $\forall i, j: \widetilde{R}_i = \widetilde{R}_j$.

It is trivial that under the axiom of complete identity, $J_i = J_j$ for all persons i, j. We can refer to R and J without subscripts under the axiom of complete identity, for the subscript will make no difference.

9*4. THE MAXIMIN RELATION OF JUSTICE

The criteria of justice put forward by Rawls (1958), (1963a), (1967), can now be formalized. While Rawls speaks about welfare measures, and finds out the maximin value (see Chapter 9), his criteria are general enough to be expressable in terms of orderings only. We shall refer to $\widetilde{R}$, which can be either interpreted as the extended ordering of a certain person i, $\widetilde{R}_i$, with the subscript dropped, or alternatively as $\widetilde{R}$, for all i under the axiom of complete identity. Under the former interpretation, the Rawls relation will reflect judgments on justice by a particular individual, while under the latter it will reflect everyone's judgments on justice. The maximin relation of justice will be denoted as M.

DEFINITION 9*5.   *For all pairs x, y in X:*

$$x \, M \, y \leftrightarrow [\exists k: \{\forall i: (x, i) \, \widetilde{R} \, (y, k)\}]$$

If it is no worse to be anyone in social state x than to be individual k in state y, then x is at least as just as y.

THEOREM 9*4.   *The maximin relation of justice M defines an ordering over the set of social states X, if $\widetilde{R}$ is defined over the entire product of X and H.*

Proof. It is obvious that M is reflexive. It is transitive, since

$$\forall x, y, z \in X: x \, M \, y \, \& \, y \, M \, z$$
$$\to ([\exists k: \{\forall i: (x, i) \, \widetilde{R} \, (y, k)\}] \, \& \, [\exists j: \{\forall i: (y, i) \, \widetilde{R} \, (z, j)\}]$$
$$\to [\exists j: \{\forall i: (x, i) \, \widetilde{R} \, (z, j)\}]$$
$$\to x \, M \, z$$

Finally, the completeness of M is proved by contradiction. Suppose $\sim(x \, M \, y) \, \& \, \sim(y \, M \, x)$ for some $x, y \in X$. Clearly

$$\sim[\exists k: \{\forall i: (x, i) \, \widetilde{R} \, (y, k)\}] \, \& \, \sim[\exists j: \{\forall i: (y, i) \, \widetilde{R} \, (x, j)\}]$$

This means that the set $[(x, i) \cup (y, j)]$ with $i = 1, \ldots, n$, and $j = 1, \ldots, n$, has no least ('worst') element with respect to $\widetilde{R}$. But this is impossible, since the set is finite and $\widetilde{R}$ is an ordering.[3]

For any given $\widetilde{R}$, Suppes' relation of justice J implies Rawls' relation of justice M, but not vice versa.

THEOREM 9*5. *For any given $\widetilde{R}$, for all x, y in $X: x \, J \, y \to x \, M \, y$, but the converse does not hold.*

Proof.

$$x \, J \, y \to \exists \rho \in T: [\forall j: (x, j) \, \widetilde{R} \, (y, \rho \, (j))]$$
$$\to \exists k: [\forall j: (x, j) \, \widetilde{R} \, (y, (k)]$$
$$\to x \, M \, y$$

To check the converse, consider the following ordering $\widetilde{R}$ in a two-person two-state world: $(y, 1) \, \widetilde{P} \, (x, 1), (x, 1) \, \widetilde{P} \, (x, 2)$ and $(x, 2) \, \widetilde{P} \, (y, 2)$. Clearly, $x \, M \, y$, but $\sim(x \, J \, y)$.

Notice, however, that even under the axiom of complete identity, the Pareto relation $\bar{P}$ (and the Suppes relation J) will not imply the strict preference relation of Rawls.[4]

LEMMA 9*b. *Even under the axiom of complete identity, $\exists \widetilde{R}: [x \, \bar{P} \, y \, \& \, y \, M \, x]$.*

---

[3] See Lemma 1˙j. The existence of a least element is proved in precisely the same way as the existence of a best element.

[4] However, it will imply strict preference under the lexicographic maximin rule, defined in footnote 12 in Chapter 9, p. 195.

Proof. Consider a pair x, y in X and two individuals 1 and 2 such that $(x, 1) \, \widetilde{P} \, (y, 1)$, $(y, 1) \, \widetilde{R} \, (x, 2)$ and $(x, 2) \, \widetilde{I} \, (y, 2)$. Since $(y, i) \, \widetilde{R} \, (x, 2)$ for $i = 1, 2$, we have $y \, M \, x$; but $x \, \bar{P} \, y$. It is trivial to extend the example to any number of individuals.

However, the strict version of Pareto preference $\bar{\bar{P}}$ does imply the strict Rawls relation. And, of course, the weak Pareto preference does imply the weak Rawls relation.

THEOREM 9*6. *Under the axiom of complete identity, for all x, y in X:*

(1) $x \, \bar{R} \, y \rightarrow x \, M \, y$; and
(2) $x \, \bar{\bar{P}} \, y \rightarrow [x \, M \, y \, \& \sim (y \, M \, x)]$.

Proof. For all x, y in X:

$$x \, \bar{R} \, y \rightarrow \forall i : (x, i) \, \widetilde{R}_i \, (y, i)$$
$$\rightarrow \exists k : [\forall i : (x, i) \, \widetilde{R} \, (y, k)]$$
$$\rightarrow x \, M \, y$$

Hence (1) holds.

$$(y \, M \, x) \rightarrow \exists k : [\forall i : (y, i) \, \widetilde{R} \, (x, k)]$$
$$\rightarrow \exists k : (y, k) \, \widetilde{R}_k \, (x, k)$$
$$\rightarrow \sim (x \, \bar{\bar{P}} \, y)$$

Hence (2) holds, since $x \, \bar{\bar{P}} \, y \rightarrow x \, \bar{R} \, y$, and $x \, \bar{R} \, y \rightarrow x \, M \, y$, by (1).

9*5. JUSTICE AND AGGREGATION

It is interesting to compare the relations of justice with the aggregation relation discussed in Chapter 7*. For this it is convenient to consider a weaker version of the Suppes relation J.

DEFINITION 9*6. *For all pairs x, y in X:*

$$x \, O_i \, y \leftrightarrow \exists \, \rho \in T : [\forall j : (x, j) \, \widetilde{R}_i \, (y, \rho(j))]$$

It can be checked that $x \, J_i \, y$ is equivalent to $x \, O_i \, y \, \& \sim (y \, O_i \, x)$.

Theorem 9*5 can be strengthened by noting that $x\,O\,y$ is sufficient for $x\,M\,y$, and $x\,J\,y$ is not needed.

COROLLARY 9*5.1. *For any given $\widetilde{R}$, for all x, y in X: $x\,O\,y \to x\,M\,y$, but the converse does not hold.*

The same proof holds as in Theorem 9*5.

We note, without proof, the following result:

LEMMA 9*c. *Each O_i is a quasi-ordering over X, i.e., O_i is reflexive and transitive, for every logically possible set of extended individual orderings $(\widetilde{R}_i)$.*

Consider any real-valued welfare function $U(x, i)$ defined for all i and all x in X.

DEFINITION 9*7. *For all x, y in X, $x\,A\,y$, i.e., x has at least as great a welfare aggregate as y, if and only if*

$$\sum_i \big[U(x, i) - U(y, i) \big] \geqq 0$$

For any U, A is obviously an ordering.

We turn next to the relation between A and O for any particular $\widetilde{R}$.

THEOREM 9*7. *If U is a real-valued representation of $\widetilde{R}$, then O is a subrelation of A.*

Proof. Suppose $x\,O\,y$, and for some ρ, $(x, j)\,\widetilde{R}\,(y, \rho(j))$, for all j. Then $\sum_i \big[U(x, i) - U(y, i) \big] = \sum_j \big[U(x, j) - U(y, \rho(j)) \big] \geqq 0$. Hence, $x\,A\,y$. Further, if $x\,J\,y$, then for some j, $(x, j)\,\widetilde{P}\,(y, \rho(j))$, and hence $x\,A\,y$ & $\sim(y\,A\,x)$.

Now, in terms of the model of Chapter 7*, any U corresponds to a particular $W \in L$, so that $W_i(x) = U(x, i)$.

COROLLARY 9*7.1. *For any assumption of measurability and interpersonal comparability of individual welfare, if each $W \in \overline{L}$ is a real-valued representation of $\widetilde{R}$, then O is a subrelation of R^a.*

The proof is immediate from Theorem 9*7.

It is to be noted that the assumption of cardinality is not needed (see Section 7*4). Given strict ordinality, a given $\widetilde{R}$ represents a complete interpersonal comparison of ordinal individual welfare levels. Given strict cardinality, however, a particular $\tilde{R}$ can coexist with $\bar{L}$ representing less than full comparability, since those interpersonal variations in origins and units are permitted which do not alter the ordering underlying U.

Chapter 10
Majority Choice and Related Systems

10.1. THE METHOD OF MAJORITY DECISION

Of all the collective choice rules, the method of majority decision has perhaps been more studied than any other. As early as 1770, Borda was providing sophisticated studies of voting procedures, and by 1785 Condorcet had sized up many of the analytical problems of majority rule. In the nineteenth century, interest in majority decision widened, and studies of it attracted as diverse scholars as Laplace (1814) and Lewis Carroll (i.e., C. L. Dodgson (1876).[1]

As a system, majority rule is used in various type of collective choices. It is easy to appreciate its wide appeal. As a CCR, it satisfies the Pareto principles (conditions P and P^*), unrestricted domain (condition U), non-dictatorship (condition D), independence of irrelevant alternatives (condition I), neutrality (condition N), anonymity (condition A), positive responsiveness (condition S), and several other appealing conditions. Indeed, the MMD is the only decisive CCR satisfying these conditions (in fact, the only one satisfying conditions U, N, A and S), as was shown in Theorem 5*1.

The deficiencies of the MMD are also important. First, as was pointed out in Chapters 3 and 4, the MMD can lead to intransitivity and, furthermore, to a violation of acyclicity. The famous case of 'paradox of voting' discussed in Chapter 3 is a simple example of

---

[1] On the history of studies of majority decision see Black (1958) and Riker (1961).

this. As an SWF, or even as an SDF, it does not work for some configurations of individual preferences.

Second, it violates conditions L and L^*, and gives little scope for personal freedom. If a majority wants me to stand on my head for two hours each morning, the MMD will make this a socially preferred state no matter how I view this exacting prospect. There are presumably areas of choice where even the most ardent supporter of majority rule will hesitate to recommend the MMD as the proper social decision procedure. But, if MMD is to be applied for some choices and not for others, problems of inconsistency can arise in much the same way it arose in Chapter 6.[2] The use of one decision procedure of some choices and another for others raises serious problems of consistency. Of course, MMD itself may, on its own, lead to intransitivity and to violations of acyclicity, but its combination with other rules seems to add a new dimension to the problem. Nevertheless, such a hybrid procedure may be preferred by many to an uncompromising use of MMD in every sphere of social choice.

Third, the MMD takes no account of intensities of preference, and it is certainly arguable that what matters is not merely the *number* who prefer x to y and the *number* who prefer y to x, but also *by how much* each prefers one alternative to the other. As was noted in Chapter 8, bringing in cardinality without interpersonal comparability may not help much, but with some comparability (not necessarily much) a lot can be achieved. In Chapter 7, the procedure of aggregation, of which utilitarianism is a special case, was studied with very weak assumptions, and the aggregation procedure may be thought to be a serious rival to the MMD.

Finally, aside from ignoring relative intensities of preference, the MMD also ignores any possible comparison between absolute levels of welfare of different persons. It takes account of such judgments as 'I would prefer to be in state x rather than in state y,' but not of such judgments as 'I would prefer to be Mr A in state x rather than Mr B in state y.' This is an advantage from some points of view, especially

---

[2] In fact, this is clear from Theorems 6*1–6*3, since the MMD subsumes the Pareto principle.

since the latter kind of preferences are rather difficult to collect and work on for practical exercises in collective choice. On the other hand, this characteristic of MMD (and indeed of all CCR, being based on individual orderings R_i rather than on $\tilde{R}_i$) does distract from its attractiveness. The criteria that were discussed in Chapter 9 which incorporate notions of fairness and justice would run counter to the MMD.

As an institutional procedure the MMD has the virtue of making effective use of individual orderings in a world of imperfect communication. Intensities of preference and relative measures of well-being are difficult to handle in an interpersonal context, and while our value judgments may make use of these concepts, they are not easy to put together and operate on. There are also practical difficulties in deciding which choices are really private and which are the concern of others. The MMD is a no-nonsense procedure and ignores all these complications. Making a virtue out of independence of irrelevant alternatives, neutrality, and anonymity, it takes the form of an uncomplicated institution. While its grossness jars somewhat, its simplicity, symmetry and primitive logic would seem to appeal to many.

10.2. PROBABILITY OF CYCLICAL MAJORITIES

How serious is the problem of inconsistency of majority decision? What is the probability of there being no 'majority winner', i.e., there being no alternative that has a majority over every other alternative in the set? These are difficult questions to answer, but there have been some attempts to tackle them.[3] Guilbaud (1952), Riker (1961), Campbell and Tullock (1965), (1966), Klahr (1966), Williamson and Sargent (1967), Garman and Kamien (1968), Niemi and Weisberg (1968) and De Meyer and Plott (1969), among others, have provided extensive studies of this problem.

---

[3] See Riker (1961) for a very fine review of problems of inconsistency under majority rule.

In all these calculations some assumptions must be made about the probability distribution of different individual orderings for each person. One assumption is particularly simple and has attracted many scholars, viz., that all orderings are equally likely for every individual.[4] Confining the analysis to strong orderings only, Guilbaud (1952) calculated that the probability of cyclical majorities was only 8.77%. Garman and Kamien (1968) and Niemi and Weisberg (1968) have obtained an exact pattern of probability of there being no majority winner as the number of voters is varied, as shown in Table 10.1. The table is based on there being three alternatives only, strict preferences of individuals and equiprobability.

Table 10.1. Probability of No Majority Winner
for Three Alternatives

Number of persons	Probability	Number of persons	Probability
1	0.0000	17	0.0827
3	0.0556	19	0.0832
5	0.0694	21	0.0836
7	0.0750	23	0.0840
9	0.0780	25	0.0843
11	0.0798	. . .	. . .
13	0.0811	∞	0.0877
15	0.0820		

It would be noted that the probability of an impasse, while never remarkably high, increases with the number of individuals involved. It increases rapidly to start with, but soon gets very insensitive; an increase in the number of voters from 9 to any figure must increase the probability of failure by less than 1%. Altogether, as Guilbaud

[4] Garman and Kamien (1968) call this an 'impartial culture', which seems a somewhat inappropriate name for a dubious factual assumption. In this 'impartial culture', given a two-alternative choice between my being beheaded at dawn and my living on, the probability of my preferring either to the other will be exactly one-half. I protest.

had noted, there is less chance than 1 in 11 that no majority winner will emerge.

The probability of failure is, however, very sensitive to the number of alternatives. In Table 10.2 the probabilities of the absence of a majority winner are presented for different numbers of alternatives when the number of individuals is very large. The source is Niemi and Weisberg (1968).

Table 10.2. Limiting Value of Probabilities of No Majority Winner

Number of alternatives	Probability	Number of alternatives	Probability
1	0.0000	20	0.6811
2	0.0000	25	0.7297
3	0.0877	30	0.7648
4	0.1755	35	0.7914
5	0.2513	40	0.8123
10	0.4887	45	0.8292
15	0.6087		

It appears that as the number of alternatives goes up, the probability of cyclical majorities will rise towards 1.

This would appear to be a somewhat depressing fact. But it really is not, for the equiprobability assumption *is* a very special one, and seems to involve a denial of society, in a significant sense. Depending on peoples' values and their personal and group interests there would be a fair amount of link-up between individual preferences. Individual preferences are determined not by turning a roulette wheel over all possible alternatives, but by certain specific social, economic, political and cultural forces. This may easily produce some patterns in the set of individual preferences. The patterns need not, incidentally, be one of agreement. Sharp disagreements may produce consistent and transitive majority decisions. For example, in a two-class society where 'class war' takes the form that all members of one class (e.g., capitalists) have exactly the opposite preference to each member of the other class (e.g., workers), majority decision must be transitive, irrespective of the number of people in each class.[5] Even in the absence of such a sharp contrast, there are patterns of individual preference which will avoid inconsistency of choice.[6]

Taking any probability distribution over possible orderings (not necessarily assuming equiprobability), Garman and Kamien (1968) and Niemi and Weisberg (1968) have obtained general expressions for the probability of there being no majority winner.[7] The results are, however, difficult to interpret. The probability distributions are supposed to apply to all individuals without difference, but depending on the nature of the social alternatives and variations of such things as tastes, class backgrounds, etc., of different individuals, the individuals' probability distributions may really differ substantially. These and other questions of appropriate choice of assumptions are not easy to answer for these probabilistic models.[8]

There is also a fundamental question of motivation and interpretation. It is not altogether clear what a probability distribution of individual orderings stands for. Are these *subjective probabilities* of some outside observer who knows the social states and the individuals,

---

[5] Cultures where the probability of cyclical majorities is greater than under equiprobability ('impartial culture') are called 'antagonistic' by Garman and Kamien (1968), p. 314. This is misleading, since antagonism between two classes can make majority rule vigorously consistent.

[6] We discuss these in the next section. On the probability line, an important approach is that of Williamson and Sargent (1967), whereby a slight link-up between the preferences of the different individuals is shown to produce a high probability of transitivity. The definition of slightness remains, however, problematic.

[7] If s_t is the probability that a person will select ordering t, r_t a random variable representing the number of individuals choosing ordering t, in a society of m individuals and n alternatives, the probability p of no majority winner is given by

$$P = \sum_{r \in R} \binom{m}{r_1, r_2, \ldots, r_{n!}} \prod_{t=1}^{n!} S_t^{r_t}$$

[8] See footnote 6 in Niemi and Weisberg (1968), p. 318. Also Klahr (1966), pp. 385–6.

but not their orderings? Or are these *frequencies* of different types of orderings turning up in different periods in the same society or in different societies? If we take the latter interpretation, in what sense does the set of alternatives remain the same while orderings on them vary, since the set of available choices will change over time and from society to society? If we take the former interpretation, presumably much will depend on the observer's sources of information and indeed on his attitude towards ignorance and uncertainty (e.g., his acceptance or rejection of the principle of 'insufficient reason').

A more well-defined and precisely relevant question is to ask: Given the variations over time (between now and period T) of the set of a available alternatives X, of the set of individuals H, and of the set of individual orderings (R_i) defined over X by each i in H, for each time period, in what proportion of the cases will the MMD fail to yield a majority winner and in what proportion of the cases will it succeed, between now and period T? It is reasonable to be interested in getting an answer to this question before recommending (or rejecting) the MMD for such a society, but it is not a question that can be answered in terms of the probability formulations over a given set of alternatives for a given set of individuals. However, an extension of these studies to include changes over time (or between societies) of individuals, alternatives, and ordering patterns, is not easy to make, and will require a great deal more empirical study than one can foresee in the subject in the near future.

The probability calculations reported earlier are, however, relevant to the more limited problem of getting an observer's subjective probability of cyclical majorities. This is not to be lightly dismissed, for it certainly may facilitate rational thinking about CCRs, but the relatively limited nature of the exercise should be kept in view.

10.3. RESTRICTED PREFERENCES

An alternative approach to the problem of cyclical majorities was initiated by Black (1948a) and Arrow (1951). They demonstrated that if the set of individual preferences satisfy a certain uni-modal pattern, which they called 'single-peaked preference', then majority decisions must be transitive irrespective of the number of individuals holding any of the possible orderings, provided the total number of persons is odd. The approach makes use of the qualitative pattern of preferences, rather than of a distribution of numbers (unlike the probability approach).

Single-peakedness is a characteristic with a certain amount of political rationality. If individuals classify alternatives in terms of some one dimension (e.g., how 'left-wing' is the alternative), and, in any pair-wise choice, vote for that alternative which is closer to one's own position, then the individual preference pattern is single-peaked. For example, consider a choice between EL (extreme left). ML (moderate left), JL (just left of centre), DC (dead centre), JR (just right of centre), MR (moderate right), and ER (extreme right). An extreme leftist will order them (in decreasing order) as: EL, ML, JL, DC, JR, MR, ER. An extreme rightist will have the ordering: ER, MR, JR, DC, JL, ML, EL. A dead-centrist will have an ordering which will incorporate two chains, viz., DC, JR, MR, ER, and DC, JL, ML, EL. Similarly, a just-leftist will subscribe to two chains, viz., JL, DC, JR, MR, ER, and JL, ML, EL. And so on. If the number of voters is odd, then irrespective of the total number involved and irrespective of the distribution of that total over the spectrum, majority decisions will be transitive.

The graphic aspect of the expression single-peaked can be understood by arranging the alternatives on a left–right horizontal line and having peoples' welfare levels, or utilities, represented on the vertical axis. All the utility curves will then look single-peaked.

While this bit of pictography may be helpful, some warnings are due. First, even if no utility representation of individual preferences are possible, they can still be single-peaked, because single-peakedness is a property of a set of orderings and not of utility functions. Second, it should be obvious that single-peakedness does not require that any arbitrarily chosen way of arranging the alternatives on the horizontal axis will make the utility curves of each uni-modal, but that there *exists* at least one method of sequencing them such that the utility curves will be uni-modal.[9] Third, strictly speaking it is not necessary that all alternatives be arrangeable in a single-peaked manner, but that every set of three alternatives ('triples') be so arrangeable. The latter is a weaker condition and is sufficient for the result. Finally, single-peakedness as defined by Arrow (1951) permits one flat portion in the utility curve under certain circumstances. So the nature of the graph is really somewhat more complex than one might be tempted to think.

The real condition is that if x, y, z is a right way of arranging three alternatives, then anyone who finds x at least as good as y must find y strictly better than z. Similarly, anyone who finds z at least as good as y must prefer y to x. This is, of course, equivalent to y being not worst according to any, i.e., everyone prefers y to either of the other two alternatives. Depending on other arrangements, viz. (y, z, x) and (z, x, y), single-peakedness will amount to z being not worst and x being not worst, respectively.[10] Thus, single-peakedness is equivalent to the characteristic of a partial agreement, viz., everyone agrees that some particular alternative is not worst in the triple.

This immediately raises the question: What about some alternative not being best, or some alternative not being medium, in anyone's preference ordering? These do equally well, and the generalized condition of 'value restriction'[11] requires that all agree that some alternative is not best, or all agree that some alternative is not worst, or all agree that some alternative is not medium in anyone's ranking in the triple. If value restriction (hereafter, VR) holds for every triple, then majority rule will be transitive if the number of voters is odd. It is not necessary that the same subclass of VR holds for each triple. In some triple some alternative may be 'not best', in another some alternative may be 'not

[9] There will, in fact, be two possible arrangements whenever there is one since uni-modality is direction-independent, and an exact reversing of the arrangement will do as well. For an analysis of single-peakedness in terms of 'unfolding theory', see Coombs (1964), Chaps. 9 and 19.

[10] This exhausts all possibilities, since uni-modality with (z, y, x), (x, z, y) and (y, x, z) are exactly equivalent, respectively, to uni-modality with the three arrangements mentioned.

[11] Sen (1966a). See also Vickrey (1960), Inada (1964b), Ward (1965) and Majumdar (1969b).

worst', in a third triple some alternative may be 'not medium', and so on, and transitivity will still hold. In fact a further weakening of the condition is possible. While persons indifferent over all three alternatives in a triple violate value restriction, they really cause no serious problem for transitivity. So indifferences over entire triples (i.e., 'unconcerned' individuals) are permitted and all that is needed is that the number of 'concerned' individuals be odd.

This requirement of oddness is, however, disturbing and unattractive. One might think that it would not matter too much if one of the voters could be elevated to an impotent chairmanship should the number of voters be even; but this is no good since the social preference will depend on precisely *who* is chosen for powerless glory. The restriction of oddness *is* serious, and is not easy to dismiss.

Fortunately it can be shown that the oddness restriction is unnecessary if we are interested in generating a social choice function and not a social ordering, i.e., if the MMD is to be an SDF and not an SWF.[12] As long as every triple satisfies VR, majority decisions will be quasi-transitive, irrespective of the number of individuals involved, and hence there will be a best alternative in every subset of alternatives. In fact it can also be shown that if individual orderings are strict (i.e., anti-symmetric), value restriction being satisfied for each triple is the necessary and sufficient condition for the MMD to be an SDF (Theorem 10*8; on the concept of 'necessity' see Definition 10*9).

When, however, individual orderings are not necessarily strict, then there are conditions other than value restriction that may work. One such condition is 'limited agreement',[13] which requires that everyone agrees that some alternative (say x) is at least as good as some alternative (say y) in each triple. A third condition is 'extremal restriction' (Sen and Pattanaik) (1969)), which demands that if someone prefers x to y and y to z, then z is uniquely best in someone's ordering if and only if x is uniquely worst in his ordering.

---

[12] Theorem VIII in Sen (1969). This result also occurs in the proof of Theorem I in Pattanaik (1968a). Fishburn (1970) has generalized this result for individual preference that are themselves quasi-transitive.

[13] This is a weakened version of Inada's (1969) 'taboo preferences'; see Sen and Pattanaik (1969).

Limited agreement (or LA) is easy to follow, but some explanatory remarks on extremal restriction (or ER) are in order. Extremal restriction subsumes various interesting cases. First, it covers what Inada (1969) calls 'echoic preferences', viz., that if anyone strictly prefers x to y and y to z, then no one strictly prefers z to x. It also covers Inada's 'antagonistic preferences', whereby if someone prefers x to y and y to z, then everyone else either has this particular ordering, or holds to its opposite (viz., preferring z to y and y to x), or finds x and z to be equally good. Finally, it covers Inada's 'dichotomous preferences', viz., every individual is indifferent between at least one pair of alternatives (not necessarily the same pair for each individual) in each triple.

It can be shown that if any triple satisfies ER, then the social preference generated by MMD must be fully transitive over it. If a triple satisfies LA, then the majority preference relation will be quasi-transitive. In fact, it can also be demonstrated that satisfying either VR, LA or ER in each triple is the necessary and sufficient condition for majority decision to be an SDF (Theorem 10*6; also Sen and Pattanaik (1969)). And as far as an SWF is concerned, i.e., generating a social ordering rather than a social choice function, the necessary and sufficient condition is that each triple must satisfy ER (Theorem 10*7; also Inada (1969) and Sen and Pattanaik (1969)).

These results clear up the extent to which qualitative patterns (as opposed to numerical distributions) of individual preferences can guarantee transitivity of the majority relation and the existence of a majority winner in each subset.[14] If these conditions are satisfied, then irrespective of the number distribution of individual preferences, rational social choice through majority rule will be possible. If by rational choice we mean the existence of a best alternative in each set (satisfying property α), then any one of ER, VR and LA will do.

[14] This is a somewhat more demanding requirement than the existence of a majority winner for the entire set only, as in the exercise by Garman and Kamien (1968), and Niemi and Weisberg (1968). Pattanaik (1968a) has shown that if all triples consisting of only *Pareto-optimal alternatives* are value restricted, then there is a majority winner. Extending this result, it is shown in Sen and Pattanaik (1969) that if all triples consisting of Pareto-optimal alternatives satisfy *either* VR *or* ER, then a majority winner must exist.

However, if we also want property β to be satisfied, then we must want a social ordering, so that we must demand ER. The question of the necessity of property β, which we found in Chapter 4 to be important for Arrow's general possibility theorem, is crucial also for rational choice through the MMD.

It is worth emphasizing that the patterns of individual preferences that are sufficient to avoid intransitivity or acyclicity do not require uniformity in any strict sense. Antagonism of various types are tolerated and, in fact, of certain types will lead gloriously to the fulfilment of VR or ER. Limited agreement requires some uniformity, but only over one pair in each triple. Value restriction requires agreement about some alternative's relative position, but in a very weak sense. People may disagree as to whether x is best or is worst, but as long as they agree that it is not medium, it will do. Similarly, they may agree that some alternative is not best (or not worst), but no more. Extremal restriction permits a wide variety of relations, viz., 'echoic' (partly similar), 'antagonistic' (sharply opposite), or 'dichotomonus' (just requiring one indifference for all in each triple, but not necessarily indifference between the *same* two alternatives).

Nevertheless, these conditions must be recognized to be fairly restrictive. and these restrictions may or may not be satisfied by specific societies. This is a question for empirical investigation. It would appear that in many economic problems of distribution and allocation none of the conditions will work in the absence of externalities.[15] For example, the division of a homogeneous cake between three persons with each person concerned only about his own share of the cake will beat all the conditions and produce cyclical majorities. One of the objectives in obtaining the necessary and sufficient conditions for rational choice under majority decision is to motivate purposive research on actual patterns of preferences.

---

[15] This is, however, not a great tragedy since the MMD is, in any case, an unsatisfactory basis for distributional decisions as it ignores preference intensities and avoids interpersonal comparisons (cf. Chapters 7 and 7*). The main appeal of the MMD is for political choices over a few fixed packages (e.g., party programmes) with distributional questions thoroughly mixed up with other issues.

10.4. CONDITIONS ON COLLECTIVE CHOICE RULES AND RESTRICTED PREFERENCES

It was noted in Chapter 5 that the MMD is the only decisive CCR with an unrestricted domain satisfying conditions I, N, A and S. It is interesting to ask whether the conditions on individual preferences, e.g., VR, ER or LA, that are sufficient for rational choice under the MMD, are also sufficient for collective choice rules that satisfy some but not all of these five conditions. This way the results can be generalized for wider classes of CCRs.

It is shown in Chapter 10* that any decisive CCR that is independent of irrelevant alternatives and neutral (N), and non-negatively responsive (R), must yield a quasi-transitive social preference relation if individual preferences are value restricted for each triple. Thus, VR works for a wide class of collective choice rules, e.g., two-thirds majority rule,[16] many-staged majority decisions,[17] strict majority rule,[18] semi-strict majority rule.[19] Similarly, LA works for any decisive CCR that is independent of irrelevant alternatives and neutral (N), non-negatively responsive (R), and Pareto-inclusive (P^*). This too will apply to many CCRs, though not to all for which VR will work.

On the other hand, ER is not easily extendable to other collective choice rules. A CCR may be neutral (N), anonymous (A), non-negatively responsive (R), and Pareto-inclusive (P^*), but still violate quasi-transitivity for individual preferences satisfying ER. If we strengthen non-negative responsiveness (R) to make it positive responsiveness (S), then we shall simply be back to the MMD.

---

[16] This CCR is widely used. To generate a complete ordering we may define that x is at least as good as y if and only if y is not preferred to x by a two-thirds majority.

[17] This includes representative democracy if the elected representative will represent the majority views of his constituents. See Murakami (1966), (1968) and Pattanaika (1968c).

[18] This is defined to mean that x is preferred to y if and only if it is not the case that at least 50% of all persons (and not merely of the non-indifferent ones) prefer y to x.

[19] This is a mixture of majority rule and strict and majority rule. See Definition 10*7.

We can, in some sense, get intermediate positions and in fact semi-strict majority rule permits us to get indefinitely close to the MMD, but as long as the CCR is not exactly the MMD, extremal restriction does not even guarantee quasi-transitivity (Theorem 10*5). But once we take the MMD, ER is sufficient for full transitivity. Extremal restriction seems to be cut out precisely for majority decisions. In this it differs sharply from value restriction and limited agreement.

Chapter 10*
Restricted Preferences and Rational Choice

10*1. RESTRICTED DOMAIN

Black (1948a) and Arrow (1951) have noted that if individual preferences have a certain pattern of 'similarity', then the MMD will yield transitive results. This amounts to a relaxation of condition U as applied to CCRs. The consequences of relaxing the condition of unrestricted domain by considering restrictions on the patterns of individual orderings are investigated in this chapter. The problem is interpreted more broadly than by Black (1948a) and Arrow (1951) in three respects.[1] First, we are interested not merely in the transitivity of social preference, but also in generating a social choice function, i.e., we are interested in the MMD as an SDF and not merely in it as an SWF. Second, MMD has certain properties, e.g., neutrality, as was noted in Chapter 5*. Some of the sufficiency conditions for majority decision are, in fact, sufficiency conditions for a wider class of collective choice rules satisfying a few but not all of the properties of the MMD. We study the sufficiency conditions in this more general setting. Third, for a certain class of restrictions, we identify the necessary and sufficient conditions for rational choice under the MMD.

Before some restrictions are specified, it will be covenient to separate out those persons who are indifferent between all the alternatives, for they introduce peculiar logical problems.

DEFINITION 10*1. *A concerned individual for a set of alternatives is one who is not indifferent between every pair of elements in the set.*

---

[1] This chapter relies heavily on Sen (1966a), (1969), and Sen and Pattanaik (1969).

We now define three specific restrictions.

DEFINITION 10*2. *Value restriction* (VR):[2] *In a triple* (x, y, z) *there is some alternative, say x, such that all the concerned individuals agree that it is not worst, or agree that it is not best, or agree that it is not medium, i.e., for all concerned i:*

$$[\forall i: x\, P_i\, y \vee x\, P_i\, z] \vee [\forall i: y\, P_i\, x \vee z\, P_i\, x]$$
$$\vee\, [\forall i: (x\, P_i\, y\, \&\, x\, P_i\, z) \vee (y\, P_i\, x\, \&\, z\, P_i\, x]$$

DEFINITION 10*3. *Extremal restriction* (ER):[3] *If for an ordered triple* (x, y, z) *there is someone who prefers x to y and y to z, then anyone regards z to be uniquely best if and only if he regards x to be uniquely worst, i.e.,*

$$(\exists i: x\, P_i\, y\, \&\, y\, P_i\, z) \rightarrow (\forall j: z\, P_j\, x \rightarrow z\, P_j\, y\, \&\, y\, P_j\, x)$$

A triple satisfies ER if and only if the above condition holds for every ordered triple obtainable from that triple.

DEFINITION 10*4. *Limited agreement* (LA):[4] *In a triple there is an ordered pair* (x, y) *such that everyone regards x to be at least as good as y, i.e.,* $\forall i: x\, R_i\, y.$

We shall refer to the number of individuals for whom $x\, P_i\, y$ as $N(x\, P\, y)$, the number for whom $x\, R_i\, y$ as $N(x\, R\, y)$, the number for whom $x\, P_i\, y\, \&\, y\, R_i\, z$ as $N(x\, P\, y\, R\, z)$, and so on.

Certain preliminary results are recorded next.

LEMMA 10*a. *ER, VR and LA are completely independent of each other, i.e., any pair of these three could be satisfied without the third, and any one of these could be satisfied without the remaining pair.*

---

[2] In Sen (1966a) value restriction was defined as a condition on the preferences of *all* individuals, concerned or unconcerned, but in the 'possibility theorem on value-restricted preferences' it was shown that it was sufficient to apply the restriction only to the concerned individuals. Here value restriction is defined in such a manner that only concerned individuals are involved.

[3] See Sen and Pattanaik (1969). See also Inada (1969).

[4] This is a weaker version of 'taboo preference' of Inada (1969). See Sen and Pattanaik (1969).

Proof. The proof follows from the following six examples:

(1) $x\,P_1\,y\,P_1\,z$
$z\,P_2\,y\,P_2\,x$
$y\,P_3\,x\,I_3\,z$
$x\,I_4\,z\,P_4\,y$

ER is satisfied, but VR and LA are violated by this set of individual preference patterns.

(2) $x\,P_1\,y\,P_1\,z$
$z\,P_2\,x\,P_2\,y$

ER is violated, but VR and LA are both satisfied.

(3) $x\,P_1\,y\,P_1\,z$
$z\,P_2\,y\,P_2\,x$
$y\,P_3\,z\,P_3\,x$

VR is satisfied, but ER and LA are violated.

(4) $x\,P_1\,y\,P_1\,z$
$y\,P_2\,z\,I_2\,x$
$z\,I_3\,x\,P_3\,y$

VR is violated, but ER and LA are both satisfied.

(5) $x\,P_1\,y\,P_1\,z$
$y\,P_2\,z\,P_2\,x$
$x\,P_3\,y\,I_3\,z$
$x\,I_4\,y\,P_4\,z$
$y\,I_5\,z\,P_5\,x$

LA is satisfied, but ER and VR are violated.

(6) $x\,P_1\,y\,P_1\,z$
$z\,P_2\,y\,P_2\,x$

LA is violated, but ER and VR are both satisfied.

The next result concerns the joint denial of VR, ER and LA.

LEMMA 10*b. *If a set of orderings over a triple violates VR, ER and LA, then there is a subset of three orderings in that set which itself violates VR, ER and LA.*

Proof. Over a triple, x, y, z, there are there are thirteen logically possible orderings, and there are 8192 ($= 2^{13}$) different subsets of the set of these thirteen orderings, of which one is empty. We label these orderings in a special manner for convenience, and drop subscript i in the preference relation, e.g., P is written for P_i, on grounds of aesthetics and convenience.

(1.1) $x\,P\,y\,P\,z$	(1.2) $x\,P\,y\,I\,z$	(1.3) $x\,I\,y\,P\,z$
(2.1) $y\,P\,z\,P\,x$	(2.2) $y\,P\,z\,I\,x$	(2.3) $y\,I\,z\,p\,x$
(3.1) $z\,P\,x\,P\,y$	(3.2) $z\,P\,x\,I\,y$	(3.3) $z\,I\,x\,P\,y$
(4) $\ \ x\,P\,z\,P\,y$	(5) $\ \ z\,P\,y\,P\,x$	(6) $\ \ y\,P\,x\,P\,z$
(7) $\ \ x\,I\,y\,I\,z$		

If ER is to be violated, at least one of these orderings must be a chain, i.e., satisfy anti-symmetry. Without loss of generality, ordering 1.1 is chosen, i.e., $x\,P\,y\,P\,z$. It may first be noted that there is no other ordering which, when combined with 1.1, will form a pair that violates VR and LA. Hence, the smallest set of orderings that violate VR, ER and LA, must have at least three elements.

It is easy to check that the only three-ordering sets inclusive of 1.1 that violate VR are given by [1.1, 2.1 *or* 2.2 *or* 2.3, 3.1 *or* 3.2 *or* 3.3]. There are nine such sets. Each of these violates ER, and only one satisfies LA, viz., [1.1, 2.2, 3.3], where $x\,R_i\,z$ for all i. There are, thus, eight three-ordering sets that violate VR, ER and LA, and this class of eight sets we call Ω.

Next, consider sets inclusive of 1.1, but having more than three orderings that violate VR, ER and LA. If these sets include any member of Ω, then the result follows immediately. It is easily checked that, in order to violate VR without including any member of Ω, a set of orderings inclusive of 1.1 must include at least one of the following four-ordering sets:[5]

(I) 1.1, 1.2, 1.3, 2.3 (III) 1.1, 1.2, 2.2, 2.3

(II) 1.1, 1.2, 1.3, 3.2 (IV) 1.1, 1.3, 3.2, 3.3

[5] This might appear to be not so if we include ordering 4 or 5 or 6, e.g., [1.1, 4, 5 *or* 3.2 *or* 2.3, 6 *or* 2.2 *or* 1.3]. But the last three elements of each of these possibilities do form a member of Ω except for the substitution of x and y, or y and z, or z and x.

None of these four-ordering sets, it may be noted, violates LA. For example, $y R z$ holds in every ordering in I. To include an ordering with $z P y$, either (a) we must include 3.1, 3.2 or 3.3, in which case the set will then include some member of Ω, or (b) we must include ordering 4 or 5, in which case again the set can be seen to include some member of Ω except for formal interchange of y and z, and of x and z, respectively. Similarly, II lacks $y P x$, III lacks $z P y$, and IV lacks $y P x$, and in each case the inclusion of any ordering filling this gap brings in some member of Ω. This establishes the lemma.

10^*2. VALUE RESTRICTION AND LIMITED AGREEMENT

First, we present a mundane but useful lemma involving value restriction.

LEMMA 10^*c.   *If a set of individual preferences is value restricted over a triple (x, y, z), at least one of equations (1), (2) and (3), and at least one of equations (4), (5) and (6) hold:*

(1) $N(x I y I z) = N(x R y R z)$ (4) $N(x I y I z) = N(y R x R z)$

(2) $N(x I y I z) = N(y R z R x)$ (5) $N(x I y I z) = N(x R z R y)$

(3) $N(x I y I z) = N(z R x R y)$ (6) $N(x I y I z) = N(z R y R x)$

Proof.   Suppose x is not best. Then those who had hold $(x R_i y \ \& \ y R_i z)$, or $(x R_i z \ \& \ z R_i y)$ must be unconcerned. Hence, (1) and (5) hold. Similarly, (2) and (4) hold if y is not best, and (3) and (6) hold if z is not best. Similarly, it is checked that if one of the alternatives is not worst, or not medium, at least two of conditions (1)–(6) must hold, one from (1)–(3), and one from (4)–(6).

THEOREM 10^*1.   *If a decisive collective choice rule is independent of irrelevant alternatives and neutral (N), and non-negatively responsive (R), and if individual preferences are value-restricted over a triple, then the rule must yield social preference relations that are all quasi-transitive over that triple.*

Proof. If quasi-transitivity is violated over a triple (x, y, z), then for some one-to-one correspondence between (x, y, z) and (u, v, w) we must have $u \, P \, v$, $v \, P \, w$ and $w \, R \, u$. It is now shown that if one of the equations (1)–(3) and one of (4)–(6) of Lemma 10*3 hold, then this configuration is impossible.

First consider (1). We can check that

$$(1) \rightarrow \forall i: \{\sim(x \, I_i \, y \, I_i \, z) \rightarrow \sim(x \, R_i \, y \, \& \, y \, R_i \, z)\}$$
$$\rightarrow \forall i: \{\sim(x \, I_i \, y \, I_i \, z)$$
$$\rightarrow [(x \, R_i \, y \rightarrow z \, P_i \, y) \, \& \, (y \, R_i \, z \rightarrow y \, P_i \, x)]\}$$
$$\rightarrow \forall i: \{[(x \, P_i \, y \rightarrow z \, P_i \, y) \, \& \, (x \, I_i \, y \rightarrow z \, R_i \, y)]$$
$$\& \, [(y \, P_i \, z \rightarrow y \, P_i \, x) \, \& \, (y \, I_i \, z \rightarrow y \, R_i \, x)]\}$$
$$\rightarrow [(x \, R \, y \rightarrow z \, R \, y) \, \& \, (y \, R \, z \rightarrow y \, R \, x)]$$

by neutrality and non-negative responsiveness,[6]

$$\rightarrow [(x \, R \, y \, \& \, y \, R \, z \, \& \, z \, R \, x \rightarrow (x \, I \, y \, \& \, y \, I \, z))]$$

Similarly,

$$(2) \rightarrow [(x \, R \, y \, \& \, y \, R \, z \, \& \, z \, R \, x)] \rightarrow (y \, I \, z \, \& \, z \, I \, x)]$$
$$(3) \rightarrow [(x \, R \, y \, \& \, y \, R \, z \, \& \, z \, R \, x)] \rightarrow (z \, I \, x \, \& \, x \, I \, y)]$$

Thus, if at least one of the three implications (1), (2) or (3) holds, then it is impossible to have $u \, P \, v$, $v \, P \, w$ and $w \, R \, u$, assigning (u, v, w) as (x, y, z), or as (y, z, x), or as (z, x, y). Similarly, if one of (4), (5) or (6) holds, then $u \, P \, v$, $v \, P \, w$ and $w \, R \, u$ is impossible for the assignments of (u, v, w) as (y, x, z), or as (x, z, y), or as (z, y, x). But there is no other possible assignment. Hence, if value restriction is satisfied by individual preferences over every triple, then the social preference relation must be quasi-transitive for every triple.

THEOREM 10*2. *If a decisive collective choice rule is independent of irrelevant alternatives and neutral (N), non-negatively responsive (R),*

---

[6] This is easily checked. If $(x \, P_i \, y \leftrightarrow z \, P_i \, y) \, \& \, (x \, I_i \, y \leftrightarrow z \, I_i \, y)$, then by neutrality, $(x \, P \, y \rightarrow z \, P \, y) \, \& \, (x \, I \, y \rightarrow z \, I \, y)$. Therefore, if $(x \, P_i \, y \rightarrow z \, P_i \, y) \, \& \, (x \, I_i \, y \rightarrow z \, R_i \, y)$, then by non-negative responsiveness, $(x \, P \, y \rightarrow z \, P \, y) \, \& \, (x \, I \, y \rightarrow z \, R \, y)$, so that $x \, R \, y \rightarrow z \, R \, y$. Similarly, $y \, R \, z \rightarrow y \, R \, x$.

and satisfies the strong Pareto criterion (P*), then it must yield a quasitransitive preference relation over a triple if individual preferences satisfy limited agreement over that triple.

Proof. Let x, y, z be any triple. Without loss of generality, let $\forall i: x \, R_i \, y$. Hence, $\forall i: (y \, P_i \, z \to x \, P_i \, z) \, \& \, (y \, I_i \, z \to x \, R_i \, z)$, so that, by neutrality and non-negative responsiveness,[7] we have $y \, R \, z \to x \, R \, z$. Similarly, $z \, R \, x \to z \, R \, y$. Thus, $(x \, R \, y \, \& \, y \, R \, z \, \& \, z \, R \, x) \to (x \, R \, y \, \& \, y \, I \, z \, \& \, x \, I \, z)$. Consider now the hypothesis $y \, R \, x$. Since $\forall i: x \, R_i \, y$, clearly the strong Pareto criterion implies that $\forall i: x \, I_i \, y$. Hence,

$$y \, R \, x \to \forall i: \{[(x \, P_i \, z \to y \, P_i \, z) \, \& \, (x \, I_i \, z \to y \, I_i \, z)]\}$$
$$\& \, \forall i: \{[(z \, P_i \, y \to z \, P_i \, x) \, \& \, (z \, I_i \, y \to z \, I_i \, x)]\}$$
$$\to [(x \, R \, z \to y \, R \, z) \, \& \, (z \, R \, y \to z \, R \, x)]$$

Thus,

$$(y \, R \, x \, \& \, x \, R \, z \, \& \, z \, R \, y) \to (y \, R \, x \, \& \, x \, I \, z \, \& \, z \, I \, y)$$

Relation R cannot violate quasi-transitivity without at least one of the two 'circles' $(x \, R \, y \, \& \, y \, R \, z \, \& \, z \, R \, x)$ or $(y \, R \, x \, \& \, x \, R \, z \, \& \, z \, R \, y)$ holding, and if either of them holds then at least two indifferences must rule in this set of three relations. This means that violation of quasi-transitivity is impossible, which establishes the theorem.

We do not, of course, need a special proof of the sufficiency of VR and LA for the method majority decision.

THEOREM 10*3. *If individual preferences satisfy either VR or LA over each triple, then the method of majority decision is an SDF over a finite set of alternatives for every possible configuration of individual preferences.*

Proof. By Theorem 5*1, the MMD is a pair-wise-decisive collective choice rule which satisfies neutrality and positive responsiveness and, by Lemma 5*d, this means that it also satisfies the strong Pareto principle and non-negative responsiveness. Hence, by Theorems 10*1 and 10*2, social preferences generated by the MMD must be

---

[7] The reasoning is given in footnote 6 on p. 239.

quasi-transitive when individual preferences satisfy VR or LA over each triple. But then, by Lemma 1.k, each of the social preference relations generated by the MMD will yield a choice function. Hence the MMD is a social decision function over all possible sets of individual preferences.

10*3. EXTREMAL RESTRICTION

Extremal restriction is now shown to be sufficient for the transitivity of the majority preference relation R.

THEOREM 10*4. *All logically possible sets of individual preferences satisfying extremal restriction for any triple are in the domain of the majority-decision SWF over that triple.*

Proof. If every individual is indifferent between at least two alternatives in a triple, then ER will be fulfilled for that triple trivially. Transitivity is easily proved in this case. Of the thirteen possible orderings over a triple (x, y, z) recorded in the proof of Lemma 10*b, only seven include at least one indifference, viz., (1.2), (1.3), (2.2), (2.3), (3.2), (3.3), and (7). Referring to the number of individuals holding any of the respective preference orderings as $N(1.2)$, $N(1.3)$, etc., it is clear that

$$
\begin{aligned}
(x \; R \; y \; &\& \; y \; R \; z) \\
&\to [\{N(1.2) + N(3.3) - N(2.2) - N(2.3)\} \geq 0 \\
&\qquad \& \; \{N(1.3) + N(2.2) - N(3.2) - N(3.3)\} \geq 0] \\
&\to \{N(1.2) + N(1.3) - N(2.3) - N(3.2)\} \geq 0 \\
&\to x \; R \; z
\end{aligned}
$$

Similarly, $u \; R \; v \; \& \; v \; R \; w \to u \; R \; w$, for any one-to-one correspondence between (x, y, z) and (u, v, w).

We now consider non-trivial fulfilment of ER; let someone hold (1.1). Suppose that contrary to the theorem, ER holds over this triple, but majority decisions are still intransitive. We know then that exactly one of the following must be true: $[x \; R \; y, \; y \; R \; z, \; z \; R \; x]$, 'the forward circle', and $[y \; R \; x, \; x \; R \; z, \; z \; R \; y]$, 'the backward circle'.

Suppose the former holds. Since there is an individual such that $x \, P_i \, y \, P_i \, z$, we have:

$$z \, R \, x \rightarrow [N(z \, P \, x) \geq N(x \, P \, z)]$$
$$\rightarrow [N(z \, P \, x) \geq 1]$$
$$\rightarrow [\exists i: z \, P_i \, y \, \& \, y \, P_i \, x], \qquad \text{by ER}$$

The last is a strict ordering over this triple, and applying ER once again we are left only with a set of four orderings that satisfy ER, which are (1) $x \, P_i \, y \, P_i \, z$; (2) $z \, P_i \, y \, P_i \, x$; (3) $y \, P_i \, z \, I_i \, x$; and (4) $x \, I_i \, z \, P_i \, y$. Referring to the number of persons holding each of these orderings as N_1, N_2, N_3 and N_4, respectively, we obtain

$$(x \, R \, y \, \& \, y \, R \, z \, \& \, z \, R \, x) \rightarrow [\{N_1 + N_4 \geq N_2 + N_3\}$$
$$\& \, \{N_1 + N_3 \geq N_2 + N_4\} \, \& \, \{N_2 \geq N_1\}]$$
$$\rightarrow [\{N_1 = N_2\} \, \& \, \{N_3 = N_4\}]$$
$$\rightarrow (y \, R \, x \, \& \, x \, R \, z \, \& \, z \, R \, y)$$

Thus, the forward circle implies the backward circle, and intransitivity is impossible.

The only remaining possibility is that the backward circle holds alone.

$$(z \, R \, y \, \& \, y \, R \, x) \rightarrow [N(z \, P \, y) - N(x \, P \, y)] + [N(y \, P \, x) - N(y \, P \, z)] \geq 0$$
$$\rightarrow [N \, (z \, P \, y \, R \, x) - N(x \, P \, y \, R \, z)$$
$$+ N(z \, R \, y \, P \, x) - N(x \, R \, y \, P \, z)] \geq 0$$
$$\rightarrow N(z \, P \, y \, R \, x) + N(z \, R \, y \, P \, x) > 0$$

since $N(x \, P \, y \, R \, z) > 0$, as someone holds $x \, P_i \, y \, P_i \, z$ by assumption.

Further, due to ER we must have

$$N(z \, P \, y \, I \, x) = N(z \, I \, y \, P \, x) = 0$$

Obviously, therefore, $N(z \, P \, y \, P \, x) > 0$.

Since we now know that someone holds $z \, P_i \, y \, P_i \, x$, in addition to someone holding $x \, P_i \, y \, P_i \, z$, the only permissible individual preference orderings are those numbered (1), (2), (3) and (4) above. The rest of the proof consists of showing that, under these circumstances, the backward circle implies the forward circle, and it is omitted here since it is exactly similar to the proof of the converse given above. Thus, intransitivity is impossible if ER is fulfilled.

While ER is sufficient for transitivity of majority decision, it is not so for rules that lie indefinitely close to the MMD. Consider a decisive collective choice rule that satisfies conditions U, N, A and R. It falls short of being the MMD by virtue of the difference between R (non-negative responsiveness) and S (positive responsiveness), as we know from Theorem 5*1. We may even go some of the way towards the MMD by imposing condition $P*$ as well. Can we get still closer to the MMD without going all the way?

An example of a decision rule that is neutral, anonymous and non-negatively responsive is the following:

DEFINITION 10*5. *The strict majority rule:*

$$\forall x, y \in X : [N(x \; P \; y)/N] > \tfrac{1}{2} \leftrightarrow x \; P \; y$$

where N is the total number of individuals. Further, $x \; R \; y \leftrightarrow {\sim}(y \; P \; x)$.

The following lemma is immediate:

LEMMA 10*d. *If* $x \; P \; y$ *according to the strict majority rule, then* $x \; P \; y$ *according to the method of majority decision.*

In fact, it may be noted that $x \; P \; y$ under majority decision requires that $N(x \; P \; y)$ be larger than $\tfrac{1}{2}N*$, where $N*$ is the number of non-indifferent individuals in the relation between x and y. Lemma 10*d thus follows simply from the fact that $N* \leq N$.

We know that the strong Pareto criterion will be implied by positive responsiveness in the presence of neutrality by Lemma 5*d, but the converse does not hold. Since positive responsiveness will also usher in majority decision, given the other conditions, one way of moving towards majority decision without getting there is to incorporate the strong Pareto criterion as well. Consider a Pareto-inclusive version of the strict majority rule.

DEFINITION 10*6. *The Pareto-inclusive strict majority rule:* $\forall x, y \in X : x \; P \; y$ *if and only if* $[\{N(x \; P \; y)/N\} > \tfrac{1}{2}] \; \underline{\vee} \; [\forall i : x \; R_i \; y \; \& \; \exists i : x \; P_i \; y]$. *Further,* $x \; R \; y \leftrightarrow {\sim}(y \; P \; x)$.

A continuum of group decision rules can now be defined, which will lie intermediate between the strict majority rule (in either the Pareto-inclusive form or not) and the method of majority decision. We can require $N(x\,P\,y)$ to be greater than some convex combination of N and N^*.

DEFINITION 10*7. *Semi-strict majority rule:*

$$\forall x, y \in X : N(x\,P\,y)/[pN + (1-p)N^*] > \tfrac{1}{2} \leftrightarrow x\,P\,y$$

for some given p chosen from the open interval $]0, 1[$. *Further, $x\,R\,y \leftrightarrow \sim(y\,P\,x)$.*

Clearly, if $p = 0$, then this is the majority rule, and if $p = 1$, then this is the strict majority rule. However, since we confine p to the *open* interval $]0, 1[$, these possibilities are ruled out, though we can come indefinitely near either the majority rule, or the strict majority rule.

Since within the class of semi-strict majority rule we can come indefinitely close to the method of majority decision, the question arises as to whether extremal restriction may be sufficient for some cases of semi-strict majority rule. It is now shown that ER is not sufficient for semi-strict majority rule no matter how close we are to the method of majority decision.

THEOREM 10*5. *Extremal restriction is not a sufficient condition for the quasi-transitivity of the semi-strict majority rule over any triple no matter which p we select.*

Proof. Since we are interested in the strong Pareto criterion also, we prove this theorem with a line of reasoning that will not be disturbed if we were to impose additionally Pareto-inclusiveness. Consider a triple x, y, z, and the following four individual preference orderings, which is a set that satisfies ER:

(1) $x\,P_i\,y\,P_i\,z$ (3) $y\,P_i\,z\,I_i\,x$

(2) $z\,P_i\,y\,P_i\,x$ (4) $x\,I_i\,z\,P_i\,y$

Let N_j be the number of individuals holding ordering j, for $j = 1, 2, 3, 4$. Take $N_1 = 2$, $N_2 = 1$, and $N_3 = N_4 = q$, where q is a positive integer such that $0 < 1/q < p$. It is easy to check that such a q always exists no matter how small $p > 0$ is. By construction, $x\,P\,y$, $y\,P\,z$, and $x\,I\,z$, which violates quasi-transitivity. This completes the proof.

We can, thus, get as close as we like to the majority rule, by taking p indefinitely close to 0, but ER remains insufficient. It is also clear that the Pareto criterion (weak or strict) will make no difference, since both are satisfied (trivially) by the group decisions specified above.

However, as soon as p instead of being close to 0 becomes 0, i.e., as soon as we have the method of majority decision, ER becomes a sufficient condition for not merely quasi-transitivity, but even for full transitivity, as shown in Theorem 10*4.

10*4 NECESSARY AND SUFFICIENT CONDITIONS FOR RATIONAL CHOICE

The necessary and sufficient conditions for deriving a social choice function or a social ordering through the method of majority decision for a finite set of alternatives are now derived. The definitions of sufficiency and necessity are first stated. Since these definitions will be applied to both SWF and SDF we shall refer to the domain of f, which will be interpreted appropriately in the respective cases.

DEFINITION 10*8. *A condition on the set of individual preferences is sufficient if every set of individual preferences satisfying this condition must be in the domain of f.*

DEFINITION 10*9. *A condition on the set of individual preferences is necessary if every violation of the condition yields a list of individual orderings such that some assignment of these orderings over some number of individuals[8] will make the individual preference pattern lie outside the domain of f.*

The definition of sufficiency was used by Arrow (1951), and that of necessity was first proposed by Inada (1969). These are not the

---

[8] Each individual must have one and only one ordering, but any given ordering can, of course, be assigned to as many individuals as we like, or to none at all.

only possible definitions of necessary and sufficient conditions, but they do make sense if restrictions have to be about the list of permissible orderings for individuals and not about the distribution of the number of individuals over possible orderings. If more than 50% of the concerned electors share the same chain, then no matter what orderings the others hold, majority decision will yield a social ordering. However, the restrictions that we consider are those that apply only to types of permissible preference orderings and not numbers holding them.

THEOREM 10*6. *The necessary and sufficient condition for a set of individual orderings over a finite set of alternatives to be in the domain of the majority-decision SDF is that every triple of alternatives must satisfy at least one of the conditions VR, ER and LA.*

Proof. Sufficiency of VR, LA and ER follows immediately from Theorem 10*1, 10*2 and 10*4. We need concern ourselves only with necessity.

We know from Lemma 10*b that if a set of individual orderings violates VR, ER and LA, then that set must include a three-ordering subset, which also violates those three restrictions. Further, from the proof we know that there are essentially eight three-ordering subsets[9] that violate VR, ER and LA, viz., [1.1, 2.1 *or* 2.2 *or* 2.3, 3.1 *or* 3.2 *or* 3.3], excluding [1.1, 2.2, 3.3], where

> (1.1) $x\,P\,y\,P\,z$
>
> (2.1) $y\,P\,z\,P\,x$ (2.2) $y\,P\,z\,I\,x$ (2.3) $y\,I\,z\,P\,x$
>
> (3.1) $z\,P\,x\,P\,y$ (3.2) $z\,P\,x\,I\,y$ (3.3) $z\,I\,x\,P\,y$

We have to show that in each of these eight cases some assignment of these orderings over some number of individuals will produce a majority preference relation that does not yield a choice function.

First consider the cases represented by [1.1, 2.1 *or* 2.3, 3.1 *or* 3.2].

---

[9] There are, in fact, forty-eight such subsets if we treat x, y and z as constants. But the remaining ones are all exactly like the one described below, but for the substitution of x for y and y for z. Exactly the same analysis in each case.

Let N_1 be the number of persons holding 1.1, N_2 the number holding 2.1 or 2.3, and N_3 the number holding 3.1 or 3.2. If we assume $N_1 > N_2$, $N_1 > N_3$ and $(N_2 + N_3) > N_1$, then we must have $x\,P\,y$, $y\,P\,z$ and $z\,P\,x$. A simple example is $N_1 = 3$, $N_2 = N_3 = 2$.

This leaves four cases. Consider next the following two sets, viz., [1.1, 2.1 *or* 2.3, 3.3]. With the same convention on numbering, if we take $N_2 > N_1 > N_3$, and $N_1 + N_3 > N_2$, we have again $x\,P\,y$, $y\,P\,z$ and $z\,P\,x$. A simple example is $N_1 = 3$, $N_2 = 4$ and $N_3 = 2$. Finally, we take the cases given by [1.1, 2.2, 3.1 *or* 3.2]. Taking $N_3 > N_1 > N_2$ and $N_1 + N_2 > N_3$, we get $x\,P\,y$, $y\,P\,z$ and $z\,P\,x$, as for example with $N_1 = 3$, $N_2 = 2$ and $N_3 = 4$. This completes the proof of necessity, which establishes the theorem.

Next the necessary and sufficient conditions for full transitivity of majority decisions are obtained.

THEOREM 10*7. *The necessary and sufficient condition for a set of individual orderings to be in the domain of the majority-decision SWF is that every triple of alternatives must satisfy extermal restriction.*

Proof. Consider the necessity of ER. Suppose ER is violated. This means that there is (say) some individual i such that $x\,P_i\,y\,P_i\,z$, while there is another whose preference satisfies *either* of the following patterns: (1) $z\,P_j\,x$, $z\,P_j\,y$ and $x\,R_j\,y$, or (2) $z\,P_j\,x$, $y\,P_j\,x$ and $y\,R_j\,z$. Let there be one individual i and one individual j. If j holds (1), then majority decision will yield $x\,P\,y$, $y\,I\,z$ and $x\,I\,z$, which implies a choice function but is not an ordering. Similarly, if j holds (2), then $x\,I\,y$, $y\,P\,z$ and $x\,I\,z$, which is also not an ordering. Hence the necessity of ER is proved. The sufficiency of ER has already been proved in Theorem 10*4 and the proof is now complete.

10*5 THE SPECIAL CASE OF ANTI-SYMMETRIC PREFERENCES

We may now consider a special case, viz., when individual preferences are chains, i.e., the orderings are anti-symmetric.

LEMMA 10*e. *If individual orderings are anti-symmetric, then* $ER \rightarrow VR$ *and* $LA \rightarrow VR$.

Proof. Suppose ER is satisfied over some triple. Since indifference is impossible, the case of trivial fulfilment of ER does not arise. Let us assume $x \, P_i \, y \, P_i \, z$ for some i. We know from ER that $\forall i: z \, P_i \, x \rightarrow z \, P_i \, y \, \& \, y \, P_i \, x$. If there is no individual such that $z \, P_i \, x$, then z is not best in anyone's ordering, since $\sim(z \, P_i \, x) \rightarrow x \, P_i \, z$, in the case of anti-symmetric ordering. In this case, VR holds. If, on the other hand, there is someone who holds $z \, P_i \, x$, and therefore $z \, P_i \, y \, P_i \, x$, then anyone holding $x \, P_i \, z$ must hold $x \, P_i \, y \, P_i \, z$ by ER. Since $\forall i: x \, P_i \, z \veebar z \, P_i \, x$, it follows that in this case $\forall i: \{x \, P_i \, y \, P_i \, z\} \veebar \{z \, P_i \, y \, P_i \, x\}$. Once again, VR is satisfied since y is not best (nor indeed worst) in anyone's ordering. Hence, $ER \rightarrow VR$.

Suppose LA is satisfied over some triple. Without loss of generality, let $x \, R_i \, y$ hold for all i, which in this case means $\forall i: x \, P_i \, y$. Hence, x is not worst (nor indeed is y best) in anyone's ordering. Thus VR holds, which completes the proof.

It may be noted that the converse does not hold. VR does not imply either ER or LA. This is readily checked by looking at the following configuration: $x \, P_1 \, y \, P_1 \, z$, $z \, P_2 \, y \, P_2 \, x$, and $y \, P_3 \, z \, P_3 \, x$. Both ER and LA are violated, but y is not worst in anyone's ordering, and hence VR holds.

The relevant theorems about the MMD as SDF and SWF, respectively, can now be derived for this special case.

THEOREM 10*8. *The necessary and sufficient conditions for a set of individual chains over a finite set of alternatives to be in the domain of the majority-decision SDF is that every triple must satisfy value restriction.*[10]

Proof. Since ER, VR and LA are sufficient for all individual orderings, strict or not, VR is clearly sufficient in the case of strict orderings. By Theorem 10*6, VR or ER or LA must hold for every

---

[10] This theorem holds even with the original definition of value restriction in Sen (1966a), and not merely for the modified Definition 10*2 given above.

triple as a necessary condition for the existence of a social choice function, and by Lemma 10*e if ER or LA holds, then so must VR, in the case of chains. Hence, VR is both sufficient *and* necessary.

THEOREM 10*9. *A necessary condition for a set of individual chains to be in the domain of a majority-decision SWF is that every triple of alternatives must satisfy value restriction, but it is not a sufficient condition.*

The proof of necessity is obvious from Theorem 10*7 and Lemma 10*e. The following example shows the insufficiency of VR: Let there be two individuals such that $x \, P_1 \, y \, P_1 \, z$ and $z \, P_2 \, x \, P_2 \, y$, which yields $x \, P \, y$, $y \, I \, z$ and $x \, I \, z$. Value restriction is satisfied, but there is an intransitivity.[11] Incidentally, the necessary and sufficient condition is still given by Theorem 10*7.

---

[11] It becomes also sufficient if the number of individuals is odd; see Sen (1966a).

Chapter 11
Theory and Practice

II.I. SYSTEMS OF COLLECTIVE CHOICE

It is clear that there are a number of radically different ways of basing social preference on the preferences of the members of the society. They differ from each other not merely in their exact procedures, but also in their general approach.

One particular approach has been formalized in the literature more than the others, and this is the case of a 'social welfare function' in the sense of Arrow (1951), where a social ordering R is specified for every set of individual orderings (R_i). A somewhat more choice-oriented category is what we called a 'social decision function', where a choice function is generated by a social preference relation R that is determined by the set of individual orderings (R_i). In general, an SWF is a special category of SDF, but there are exceptions.[1] In any case, if choice is our object, an SDF seems the appropriate starting point.

The demands of consistency of an SDF may be less than that of an SWF, and this affects various results, including the famous 'impossibility' theorem of Arrow (Chapters 3 and 4). However, there are similar problems in combining different principles of choice even for an SDF (Chapters 4, 5, and 6). While social preferences need not be transitive and may satisfy merely quasi-transitivity, or acyclicity, SDFs still have difficulty in incorporating a set of reasonable looking

---

[1] See Chapter 4. In this and subsequent references, the mention of an un-starred chapter should be taken to include a reference also to the corresponding starred chapter. The converse is, however, not intended.

conditions on collective choice. As it happens, some of these conditions are not really very reasonable, and the underlying conflicts can be clarified by taking different types of SDFs that bring out the precise properties of these conditions (Chapters 5 and 6).

Another approach is to demand less than an SDF, i.e., not to require that the social preference relation must generate a choice function. A quasi-ordering, which violates completeness but does give guidance to collective choice in many situations, is often helpful, since it may incorporate weaker (and more universally accepted) principles of collective choice, free from some of the maddening dilemmas. The alternatives are not all or none, and there are lots of reasonable intermediate possibilities (Chapters 7 and 9).

Individual preferences may also take different forms. Various collective choice systems are indeed based on more complete information on individual attitudes to social alternatives than will be conveyed by orderings only. Instead of orderings, utility functions may be used in an ordinal, or cardinal, form, or in some intermediate form which we categorized as ordinal-type (Chapter 7); and these utility, or welfare, measures can be used without interpersonal comparability (Chapter 8), or with it (Chapters 7 and 9). Further, comparability can be of various types, and under some assumptions a continuum of partial comparability of welfare units can be defined varying from non-comparability to complete comparability of units (Chapter 7).

Also, the concentration may not be on comparability of *units* of welfare, but of welfare *levels*. Instead of taking individual orderings R_i defined over social states ('I would prefer state x to state y'), collective choice may make use of individual orderings defined over the position of being any individual in any social state ('I would prefer to be Mr A in state x rather than Mr B in state y'). This permits the use of various criteria of fairness and justice (Chapter 9).

Diagram 11.1 gives a pictorial representation of different formulations of collective choice based on different types of information on individual preferences.[2] An arrow with a double head points to a special

---

[2] The notation is as defined before, viz., R and R_i as in Chapter 2*, L and $\overline{L}$ as in Chapter 7*, and $\tilde{R}$ and $\tilde{R}_i$ as Chapter 9*.

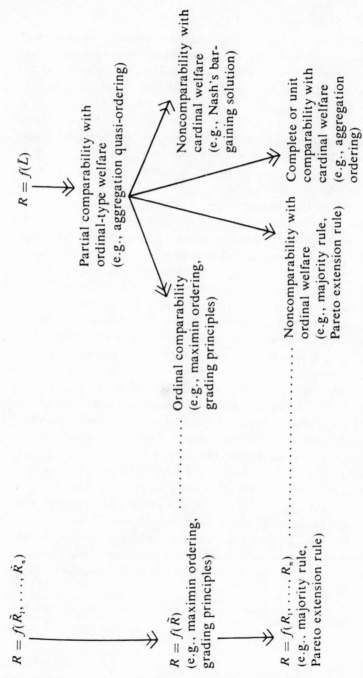

Diagram 11.1. Ingredients of Collective Choice Systems

case, and a dotted line represents near equivalence in the sense that all collective choice systems that have been considered which belong to one category also belong to the other.[3] Examples of each approach in terms of some well-known collective choice systems are noted in parentheses.

The diagram should be clear from our preceding analysis. Two explanatory remarks may, however, be useful. First, it may not be obvious that making social preference R a function of the set of individual orderings $(R_1, \ldots, R_n)$ is a special case of basing it on an extended ordering $\tilde{R}$, but it is so. It is clear that in $(R_1, \ldots, R_n)$ we have n separate orderings of m elements, each defined over $(x_1, i), \ldots, (x_m, i)$ for each individual i, whereas an R is an ordering over all these mn elements (Chapter 9*). Hence, an $\tilde{R}$ contains *inter alia* such n orderings $(R_1, \ldots, R_n)$. Thus, basing social preference on $(R_1, \ldots, R_n)$ is a special case of basing it on $\tilde{R}$, since the former type of information is contained in the latter.[4]

Second, basing social preference on the set of individual orderings is not precisely the same thing as basing it on the set of individual ordinal utility functions with non-comparability, since not all orderings are representable even by an ordinal utility. However, they are more or less equivalent for our purpose, since we did not consider any collective choice system that makes essential use of non-comparable ordinal representations of individual preference. The same applies to the near-equivalence of basing social preference on $\tilde{R}$ and basing it on ordinally comparable individual utility functions.[5]

---

[3] This is, however, not necessarily so far all *conceivable* collective choice systems.

[4] Further, if the identity axiom is assumed, then *every* individual $\tilde{R}_i$ will incorporate the entire set $R_1, \ldots, R_n$ (Chapter 9*).

[5] This is not strictly right, since ordinal interpersonal comparability may go with personal cardinal measurement, and we can then make some use of cardinality (e.g., in using Nash's (1950) bargaining solution, or solutions of Raiffa (1953) or Braithwaite (1955)).

II.2. INSTITUTIONS AND FRAMEWORK

While there are such wide varieties of approaches to collective choice, part of the variation simply reflects the different fields or contexts in which problems of collective choice arise. The problem may be one of choosing an institutional mechanism of decision taking, e.g., elections based on the majority rule or the rank-order method. Or it may be a problem faced by an individual, or a group, or a party, in making its own recommendations for social choice based on individual preferences. While calculations of the type involved in $\tilde{R}_i$ may be difficult to use in purely institutional mechanisms, for which it is easier to concentrate on the set of R_j, it may be quite appropriate to bring in $\tilde{R}_i$ in making recommendations.

Similarly, it may be difficult to find a means of reflecting cardinal welfare measures of individuals in a purely institutionalized choice system, but it may be quite possible for a planner to base his policy recommendations on his evaluation of *aggregate* gains and losses for the nation as a whole. This is especially so with systems that permit a considerable latitude in aggregation, e.g., with 'partial comparability' (Chapter 7). A planner may find it convenient in making up his mind to specify a subset $\overline{L}$ in L, whereas it may be impossible to devise a satisfactory mechanical procedure for specifying $\overline{L}$ for a purely institutionalized choice.

The existence of great varieties of collective choice procedures is, therefore, somewhat illusory. They may be relevant to different types of collective choice exercises. Since the field is so vast, it may indeed be useful to list a few different types of exercises that all come under the broad hat of the theory of collective choice, but which differ essentially from each other.

(1) *Institutional mechanisms* of social choice are based on some theory of collective choice. For example, the use majority rule will imply some implicit attachment to principles of anonymity, neutrality

and positive responsiveness (Chapter 5).[6] Similarly, a complete adherence to a free market system in the absence of externalities may be justified on grounds of Pareto optimality and to require no more than that it may involve the implicit use of the Pareto extension rule, with its implied principles (Chapter 5). Similarly, social institutions may include provisions for individual freedom for certain choices in the lines of condition L (Chapter 6).

(2) *Planning decisions,* typically taken by a committee responsible to some political body (e.g., a parliament), require some theories of relating goals of planning to individual preferences. Criteria like the aggregation rule (Chapter 7), or the maximin rule (Chapter 9), may be used implicitly or explicitly. Concern for 'aggregate welfare', or for 'welfare of the worst-off group', is quite common in public policy, even though the exercise may not usually be carried out very systematically.

(3) In making *social criticism,* or in *arguing on social policy,* one has to evaluate systems of collective choice. *Conditions* on collective choice systems are especially relevant here (e.g. those discussed in Chapters 3–9). This is a wide basket of problems varying from advising the existing government to arguing for its revolutionary overthrow. Many of the major advances on collective choice theories seem to have come from such eminently practical pursuits, especially the latter.[7] Social criticism and protest typically take the form of postulating principles of collective choice which the existing mechanisms do not satisfy.

(4) Problems of *committee decisions* are special cases of collective choice. Committees may be large or small, formal or informal, and institutions have to vary. With smaller groups, various institutional procedures are possible that may not be open to large groups, e.g., having informal systems of taking account of the intensities of preference (typical of many committees), or using an informal system

---

[6] There is also the question of transitivity and that of generating a choice function (Chapter 10)

[7] Cf. Gramsci (1957), pp. 140–42.

of vote trading (typical of legislative bodies). The question of transitivity is especially transparent for committee decisions (Chapter 10).

(5) Problems of *public cooperation* are dependent on collective choice procedures and their evaluation by the people. For many problems it is important not merely that justice should be done but also that it must be seen to be done. Planning for economic development may require imposing sacrifice on the population, and the division of the burden (e.g., of taxation) may involve considerations of fairness, justice, and measurements of relative gains and losses (Chapter 7 and 9). What is relevant here is not merely the problem of *achieving* fairness, justice, etc., but also of *making clear* that the choices made have these characteristics when seen from the point of view of the population at large. The difference between success and failure in planning is often closely related to public enthusiasm and cooperation, and while the so-called 'realists' not infrequently seem to pooh-pooh 'vague normative considerations' like fairness or justice, these considerations seem eminently relevant to success or failure even in terms of most crude indices.

11.3. EXPRESSION OF INDIVIDUAL PREFERENCES

There are several difficulties with devising systems of expression of individual preferences for the purpose of collective choice. First, there are game considerations which could distort preferences in the process of expression. 'Honest voting' is often not in a person's best interest.[8]

This is a perfectly general difficulty, but its relevance will vary greatly with the system of collective choice. As Murakami has argued, with those collective choice systems that are non-negatively responsive to individual preferences the scope of what voters can achieve by distorting their preferences is very limited.[9] This applies

---

[8] See Arrow (1951), pp. 80–81, Majumdar (1956) and Luce and Raiffa (1957), Section 14.8.

[9] Murakami (1968), Chapter 4, Section 10.

in particular to the MMD. By distorting his preferences a person cannot increase the weight on his most preferred alternative, for the greatest weight he can put on it is to vote sincerely.

An example in terms of the MMD may help to bring out this problem. Consider three individuals, viz., 1, 2 and 3, with person 1 preferring x to y and y to z, person 2 preferring y to x and x to z, and person 3 preferring z to x and x to y. Majority ordering will yield x socially preferred to y and z, and y socially preferred to z. Person 2 can disrupt the ordering by pretending to prefer y to z and z to x, which will create cyclical majorities of x over y, y over z, and z over x. But he cannot bring y into the choice set this way, since the most he can do to help y into the choice set is to vote honestly. He can knock x out of the choice set by dishonest voting, but he cannot put y into it.

From this, however, it should not be presumed that strategic distortion can never help an individual or a group to improve the social outcome under a mechanism that is non-negatively responsive. Even under the MMD insincere voting can help the selection of a preferred alternative. The following illustration brings this out.[10] Let there be three alternatives and four persons. Person 1 prefers x to both y and z between which he is indifferent; person 2 is indifferent between x and y and prefers each of these to z; person 3 prefers z to x and x to y; and person 4 ranks y above z and z above x. The MMD will yield under sincere voting: x preferred to y, y preferred to z, and x and z indifferent. Thus x is the sole element in the social choice set. Both 3 and 4 prefer z to x, even though for person 4 the most preferred alternative is not z. If 3 and 4 now pretend that they both prefer z to y and y to x, then the MMD will yield: z preferred to y, y preferred to x, and x and z indifferent. Now z is the sole member of the social choice set so that both 3 and 4 are better off through their sharp practice.[11]

---

[10] Suggested by Bengt Hansson. This case requires that two persons join hands. A case in which the insincerity of one is sufficient is the following. 1 and 2 prefer x to y and y to z; 3 prefers z to x and x to y, and 4 prefers y to z and z to x. With sincere voting the MMD yields x as the unique best element. If instead 4 pretends to prefer z to y and y to x, then z will be a majority winner also, and for him this is better.

[11] When, however, the social preference relation has to be an *ordering* this possibility is less open; see Murakami (1968). Murakami, therefore, recommends voting

Thus non-negative responsiveness or even positive responsiveness is no guarantee against insincere voting being an efficient strategy.

Incidentally, under some circumstances game considerations and vote trading may help to bring in some measures of intensities of individual preferences, and a vote-trading equilibrium does reflect a compromise of conflicting interests.[12] While there are problems in accepting these solutions as ethically optimal and fair (as discussed in Chapters 2 and 8), these models have much to commend as plausible representations of social choice, and they also help to clarify the ethical bases of these choices.

There have also been some attempts to get measures of cardinal intensities of preference of the individuals by examining their voting behaviour. It is certainly correct, as Coleman (1966b) has pointed out, that a voter may view his act of voting in terms of its probable effects, and given his preferences over the set of social alternatives his action will depend on his estimation of the probability distribution of the voting behaviour of the others, and also on the probability distribution of the consequences of the chance mechanisms that may be employed by the choice system, e.g., in breaking deadlocks. Thus, individual acts of voting can be viewed as a choice between lotteries, and will involve revelation of individual intensities of preference. However, the lotteries will, in fact, be severely limited in variety, so that any hope of constructing a utility function on this basis is not easy to entertain. We also have to know the subjective probability distributions of each individual concerning the others' voting behaviour to be able to calculate the utility measures. Thus it may not be possible to construct cardinal measures for practical social choices on the basis of merely observing actual voting behaviour. The approach is, however, enlightening.[13]

---

being done in a 'round-robin' manner, i.e., putting every alternative against every other alternative in pairwise voting, which would reveal intransitivities if there were any.

[12] See Buchanan and Tullock (1962), Coleman (1966a), (1966b) and Wilson (1968a), (1968c).

[13] For maximizing aggregate utility, we need, in addition to measures of individual cardinal utility, some system of interpersonal comparability. Coleman notes this as an arbitrary element. For descriptive models, one can treat this as a set of

There is, of course, a more primitive question as to whether individuals actually do behave in the manner postulated, i.e., maximizing the expected utility from voting by considering the probabilistic impact on actual social choices. This question needs further empirical investigation, but a preliminary doubt may be worth expressing at this stage. When a large number of voters are involved (e.g., in national elections), the probability that any individual's vote will affect the outcome is very small indeed, and even a tiny cost of voting (e.g., transport cost) may easily over-compensate that. Nevertheless, the turn-out in voting in such elections may be quite high.[14] This might indicate that the individuals are guided not so much by maximization of expected utility, but by something much simpler, viz., just a desire to record one's true preferences.[15]

It may, of course, be that people just enjoy voting. This could explain why people vote in large elections, but once this type of consideration is brought in, even the ordinal correspondence between votes and preferences is damaged. A person may be indifferent and still vote for one or the other alternative if he gets delight in voting. If, on the other hand, there is some cost from voting, he may abstain even through he may prefer one alternative to another, but not sufficiently strongly. In fact, the problem is present even when voting is a source neither of cost nor of delight. A person who is indifferent may then just as easily vote for either candidate as abstain. Thus whether the cost of voting is negative, positive, or zero, there will not be a one-to-one correspondence between (a) voting for x, (b) voting for y, and (c) abstaining, vis-a-vis (a) preferring x, (b) preferring y,

---

parameters, as in Coleman (1966a), (1966b). For normative models, however, systematic judgments on this have to be performed. (See Chapters 7, 8 and 9.)

[14] It is also possible that people are interested in the outcomes not merely in terms of who (or which) wins, but by what margin, which always changes with one's vote. This will tend to complicate models of utility revelation very considerably. Further, since the impact of one more vote on the winning (or losing) margin is small, the incentive of the voter to exercise his vote would still seem to require some explaining, if we must confine ourselves to the expected utility framework.

[15] Cf. Robinson (1964), p. 10.

and (c) being indifferent.[16] While analytically valid, this is not a terribly serious problem. If cost of voting is zero, then, for *large* groups of voters, the overall result may be very close to what would happen under the one-to-one correspondence. The real problem arises if there are costs or delight from voting, and if these magnitudes are relatively large. Even in this form this is just one of many problems that infest this problem-ridden branch of choice theory.

II.4. EFFICIENCY AND PARETO OPTIMALITY

The problems of communication (and use) of cardinal measures are more serious than those of orderings. This has been partly responsible for the usual concentration on only orderings in dealing with collective choice.[17] The most widely used approach, at least in economics, is that of Pareto optimality and of 'economic efficiency' (Chapter 2).

On the basis of the analyses in Chapters 5 and 6, the underlying

---

[16] In Sen (1964) this lack of one-to-one correspondence is shown to hold generally for all cases of continuous utility maximization. Honest expression of one's preference conflicts with maximizing a continuous utility function, which seems a little sad.

[17] Of course, in doing aggregation for such purposes as planning one can introduce certain variations in possible utility functions of an individual, and still get a quasi-ordering, in the same line as the approach developed in Chapter 7. An alternative, which is more demanding, is to supplement the planner's ignorance by a probability distribution, e.g., as proposed by Lerner (1944) in the context of the pure problem of distribution. Lerner assumes that the planner works on the basis of the same probability distribution for each individual over the possible utility functions (concave), and, given the problem of division of a given total of homogeneous income, must therefore recommend an equal division on grounds of maximizing expected utility. The equiprobability assumption needed is, however, quite strong (see Friedman (1947), and Samuelson (1964)), but one can generalize Lerner's approach through using any combination of probability distributions. One can also use decision criteria that do not use probability, e.g., the maximin strategy, and the Lerner conclusion about equality holds in this case as well under very general assumptions, as shown in Sen (1966c). However, problems of interpretation of ignorance and uncertainty remain, as do the problems of choice of one decision criteria among many possible ones.

assumptions of concentrating on Pareto optimality are clear. If one takes the view that Pareto optimality is the only goal, and as long as that is achieved we need not worry further (an approach that is implicitly taken in much of modern welfare economics, but rarely explicitly), then one is demanding precisely a CCR generating quasi-transitive social preference and satisfying condition U (unrestricted domain), I (independence of irrelevant alternatives), P^* (strong Pareto principle), and A (anonymity). These conditions together imply that we must declare all Pareto-optimal points as indifferent, as shown in Theorem 5^*3. This result gives an axiomatization of an approach that is implicit in a substantial part of modern welfare economics.

In some respects Theorem 5^*3 is quite disturbing. All the imposed conditions are superficially appealing, but the conclusion that all Pareto-optimal points are indifferent, irrespective of distributional considerations, is very unattractive. In fact, it is this aspect of modern welfare economics that is most often separated out for special attack.

What this result possibly reveals (as do other results in the book) is an important difficulty in postulating general conditions on collective choice rules, viz., these conditions are essentially opaque. It is easier to secure acceptance of these conditions than the acceptance of all of their implications. Arrow's (1951) general possibility theorem may also be interpreted in that light.[18]

We found difficulties with even a very limited use of Pareto optimality, viz., treating it as necessary but not a sufficient condition of overall optimality. In this case, Pareto optimality is usually thought to have compelling appeal.[19] But it turns out that even the weak version of the Pareto relation conflicts (Theorem 6^*3) with a very weak

[18] Similar difficulties would seem to arise in axiomatic attempts at establishing specific decision rules, e.g., Koopmans' (1960) elegant demonstration of the necessity of 'impatience' for rational accumulation programmes given certain axioms of decision making. See also Koopmans, Diamond and Williamson (1964). The axioms used are apparently appealing, but the approach is subject to the difficulty discussed above.

[19] Arguments for rejecting Pareto optimality over the choice of *actions* have been constructed by Zeckhauser (1968) and Raiffa (1968), making use of interpersonal differences of probabilistic expectations about the *consequences* of action. These are, however, not arguments for rejecting the Pareto relation over the set of

condition of individual liberty, which gives individuals the freedom to do certain personal things (e.g., choosing what one should read). Even if only two individuals are given such freedom and over one pair each, the Pareto relation may still have to be violated to ensure acyclicity, which is weaker than transitivity. The conflict between individual freedom and the weak Pareto relation cannot, of course, arise in a choice over a pair, but it can arise whenever more than two alternatives are involved. Hence, Pareto optimality even as a necessary but not sufficient condition is open to some question. That Pareto optimality is not easily achievable in the presence of externalities is widely known (see Koopmans (1957)), but what emerges from the analysis of Chapter 6 is a serious doubt about its *merit* as a goal in the presence of some types of externalities.

11.5. CONCLUDING OBSERVATIONS

Of the conditions on collective choice, the Pareto principle is thought to be the mildest of the mild. The difficulties that we encounter in making universal use of even the Pareto rule outlines the severeness of the problem of postulating absolute principles of collective choice that are supposed to hold in every situation. The simple principles that are normally put forward tend to be essentially 'non-basic' (Chapter 5). By a suitable choice of facts (e.g., by choosing specific configurations of individual preferences, or by selecting specific motivations behind individual orderings) it seems possible to play havoc with practically all the general principles that are usually recommended for universal application.

This position might appear to be at variance with the need for 'generalization' and 'universalization' that is emphasized in ethical theories from Kant onwards,[20] and which we discussed in Chapter 9.

---

consequences, or the set of social states completely specified. We are concerned with this latter question.

[20] 'Act always on such a maxim as thou canst at the same time will to be a universal law' (Kant (1785)). In Abbott's translation, Kant (1907), p. 66.

However, this contradiction is only superficial. It is not being argued here that no general principles exist that would secure total adherence of a person, but that the simple principles usually recommended are not of that type. Conditions of the type of 'anonymity' and 'neutrality' are based on very limited views of 'relevant similarity', leaving out, among other things, information on the relation between individuals and the nature of the alternatives (Chapters 5 and 6) and information on preference intensities (Chapter 7). 'Independence of irrelevant alternatives', while less restrictive, also concentrates on similarity in a narrow sense, viz., of individual rankings over the relevant pair. Preference intensities do not count (Chapter 7), nor does any indirect information that we get from observing rankings of other (but related) alternatives, which might indicate something about a person's motivation (Chapter 6). This last, rather than any consideration of preference intensities, seems crucial in our reservation about the Pareto principle (Section 6.5). What is in dispute is not the approach that in 'similar situations similar judgments must be made', but the criteria to decide which situations *are* similar. To make a completely general statement of 'relevant similarity' we may have to go into an enormously complicated criterion. Simple principles may be devised which will catch the essentials in many cases but not in all, and while these principles (e.g., conditions I, N, A, P and others) may superficially have the form of universal principles, they are in fact non-basic in most value systems.

Even non-basic principles, if sufficiently widely applicable, are helpful in understanding and evaluating collective choice procedures. Only a masochist can enjoy having to deal with the full array of details in every choice situation. Simple principles provide convenient shortcuts, and as long as we recognize these principles as useful guidelines rather than as masters to be obeyed to the bitter end, there is no problem. Arrow's general possibility theorem (Theorem 3*1), and other impossibility theorems (Theorems 4*3, 4*5, 5*1.1, 5*2, 6*1–6*3, 8*1.1, 8*2, 9*2, 9*2.1, 10*5) presented in this book, are to be viewed not as arguments for nihilism, but as positive contributions aimed at clarifying the role of principles in collective choice systems. The same is true of theorems that assert positive results about choice mechanisms (Theorems 4*1, 4*2, 4*4, 5*1, 5*3, 7*1–7*9, 8*1, 9*1, 9*3–9*7, 9*5.1, 9*7.1, 10*1–10*4, 10*6–10*9).

Once the non-basic nature of the usual principles of collective choice are recognized, some of the rigid distinctions must go. For example, in traditional welfare economics it is conventional to distinguish between Paretian judgments, which are treated as compelling, and non-Paretian judgments, which are treated as 'arbitrary'. This clear-cut dichotomy seems to be inopportune both because the Pareto principle is also partly arbitrary (Chapter 6) as well as because some of the other principles are also compelling in many situations (Chapters 5–7 and 9). An almost exclusive concentration on Paretian considerations has, on the one hand, confined traditional welfare economics into a very narrow box, and has, on the other hand, given it a sense of ethical invulnerability which does not seem to survive a close scrutiny.

A closely related point concerns the relative acceptability of different collective choice systems. Since the simple principles that the different systems satisfy seem to be essentially non-basic, it is quite clear that an evaluation of the relative desirability of different systems will depend on the nature of the society. One way of interpreting the various 'impossibility' results is to say that there is no 'ideal' system of collective choice that works well in every society and for every configuration of individual preferences (as proposed by the use of the condition of 'unrestricted domain' employed in virtually all the impossibility theorems). Some choice procedures work very well for some types of choice and some sets of individual preferences but not for others (see Chapters 5–7, 9, and 10), and naturally our evaluation of these procedures must depend on the type of society for which they may be considered. There is nothing outstandingly defeatist in this modest recognition.

Finally, it is worth emphasizing that while 'pure' systems of collective choice tend to be more appealing for theoretical studies of social decisions, they are often not the most useful systems to study. With this in view, this book has been much concerned with 'impurities' of one kind or another, e.g., *partial* interpersonal comparability (Chapters 7 and 9), *partial* cardinality (Chapter 7), *restricted* domains (Chapters 6 and 10), *intransitive* social indifference (Chapters 4 and 10), *incomplete* social preference (Chapters 7 and 9), and so on. The pure procedures, which are more well-known, seem to be the limiting cases of these systems with impurities.

Both from the point of view of institutions as well as that of frameworks of thought, the impure systems would appear to be relevant. The relative allocation of space in this book reflects a belief, which we have tried to defend, that, while purity is an uncomplicated virtue for olive oil, sea air and heroines of folk tales, it is not so for systems of collective choice.

Collective Choice and Social
Welfare (2017)

Chapter A1
Enlightenment and Impossibility

Even though democracy has a long history in various forms, the emergence of modern democratic systems relates closely to the ideas and events that surrounded the European Enlightenment. The development of democratic social arrangements drew on earlier sources and inspirations across the world, but it received a definitive delineation and emphatic support in Europe, in the second half of the eighteenth century, with the French Revolution and with the declaration of independence of Britain's American colonies. The basic strategy of social choice in drawing on individual preferences (taking note of the preferences of everyone) over the set of alternative social states to arrive at social decisions, which is central to modern social choice theory, is part of that shared democratic commitment.

In contemporary social choice theory, pioneered by Kenneth Arrow, democratic values are absolutely central, and the discipline has continued to be loyal to this basic presumption. For example, when an axiomatic structure, with reasonable-looking axioms, yields the existence of a dictator as an implication of jointly chosen – individually plausible – axioms, this is readily understood as a major embarrassment for that set of propositions, rather than taking the conclusion in favour of dictatorship to be acceptable on the ground that dictatorial rule is a logical corollary of axioms that have already been accepted and endorsed. We cannot begin to understand the intellectual challenge involved in Arrow's impossibility theorem without coming to grips with the need to include all the people in the process of social decision-making, which goes with a democratic commitment – an implicit pledge that would be deeply offended by accepting a dictatorial outcome, even when it is entailed by axiomatic requirements that individually seem reasonable enough. In this sense, any axiom system remains tentatively accepted, awaiting our examination of its actual consequences, for not only can we try to evaluate the chosen axioms individually, but we can also try to assess the joint use of a number of different axioms as a combined system. Facing an authoritarian conclusion, we have to think about what proposition might be dropped or modified to make the outcome less authoritarian.

What can be called 'preferences' of persons can, of course, be variously interpreted in different democratic exercises, and the differences are well illustrated by the contrasts between (1) focusing on votes or ballots (explored in the classic works of Borda and Condorcet), (2) concentrating on the interests of individuals (explored, in different ways, in the pioneering writings of David Hume, Jeremy Bentham and John Stuart Mill), and (3) drawing on the diverse judgements and moral sentiments of individuals about societies and collectivities (explored by Adam Smith and Immanuel Kant, among many others). The contrasts between alternative interpretations of preferences can be very important for some purposes. However, for the purpose of this book I shall follow the standard practice in social choice theory of using the generic term 'preference' to cover all these different interpretations of individual concerns which could be invoked, with clear identification, to serve as alternative informational bases of public decisions and of social judgements.

There is a possibility of confusion here about which we have to be particularly careful. Implicit attempts to see distinct objects as the same have been fairly widespread in parts of contemporary economics, and it is particularly important to understand that the use of the same term 'preference' with clearly delineated *alternative* interpretations does not involve any such presumption. What we have to avoid is to make the same term 'preference' stand *simultaneously* for several different things, such as personal interest, personal views on what should happen, personal priorities on what would be best for the society, and so on, thereby taking distinct objects to be definitionally the same.[1] For example, to presume that my understanding of my own interests must be identical to my reading of what would be best for the society would involve a serious epistemic bewilderment. The fact that the term 'preference' has alternative uses is difficult to escape, but we must not follow the lazy temptation to take these distinct uses to be much the same thing.

THE CHALLENGE

Before Arrow started working in this field, there were discussions, led by Abram Bergson and Paul Samuelson, of the need for a 'social welfare function' which would allow us to rank alternative social states in terms of their goodness from a social point of view – or in terms of 'social welfare' as Bergson (1938) and Samuelson (1947) called the sought-after object. In 1948, when Arrow was a graduate student, Olaf Helmer, a philosopher at the RAND Corporation (whom Arrow had met through Alfred Tarski, the great logician), wondered about the legitimacy of applying game theory to international relations ('the "players" were countries, not individuals', he worried). Helmer asked young Arrow, a Ph.D. student, 'In what sense could collectivities be said to have utility functions?' Arrow replied (I suspect with some disciplinary pride) that:

> economists had thought about the problem in connection with the choice of economic policies and that the appropriate formalism had been developed by Abram Bergson in a paper in 1938; it was a function, called by him the social welfare function, which mapped the vector of utilities of individuals into a [collective] utility.[i]

---

[1] The implicit identification of very different concepts of individual preference belongs to the territory of 'the rational fool', discussed in Sen (1976a), which we must be careful to avoid.

COLLECTIVE CHOICE AND SOCIAL WELFARE (2017)

As Arrow settled down to writing an exposition for Helmer on a combination of social choice axioms, he soon became convinced that no satisfactory method of aggregating a set of orderings – the preferences of the people – into one coherent ordering existed.

The impossibility theorem and related results and their proofs came within 'about three weeks'. There was huge interest in academic circles about this newly identified result. Arrow himself became fascinated by the challenge his result posed to reasoned social decisions, and he changed his dissertation topic – abandoning his already advanced research on mathematical statistics – to present and discuss the new finding. He also sent off a brief exposition of the result ('A Difficulty in the Concept of Social Welfare') to the *Journal of Political Economy*, at the request of the editor, which was promptly published (Arrow (1950)).

Arrow's impossibility result is often seen as a generalization of the old paradox of voting. Arrow himself encourages this view, and motivates the presentation of his impossibility result by referring to the voting paradox (as I did too in the Introduction). Person 1 prefers x to y and y to z; person 2 prefers y to z and z to x; person 3 prefers z to x and x to y. The result is that, in majority voting, x defeats y, y defeats z, and z defeats x. This is certainly a convincing demonstration that majority voting may not yield a consistent ordering, and also that there may be no majority winner at all. There is no doubt also that this voting paradox played a part in making Arrow think along the lines that he did. In describing his response to Olaf Helmer's request for a note on the social welfare function, Arrow mentions that he 'already knew that majority voting, a plausible way of aggregating preferences, was unsatisfactory; a little experimentation suggested that no other method would work in the sense of defining an ordering'.[ii]

How important is the demand, for Arrow's impossibility theorem, that social judgements take the form of a transitive ordering? It is easily shown (see Sen (1969)) that even a slight relaxation of that requirement, for example by demanding transitivity only of strict preference – formally called 'quasi-transitivity' – invalidates Arrow's result. I had noted this result more as a curiosity, rather than as (as I explained) a grand resolution of Arrow's deep problem, which it could not possibly be.[2] As it happens, Allan Gibbard, then a graduate student at Harvard, demonstrated immediately that new problems arise with the weakening of the transitivity condition, because quasi-transitivity yields an oligarchy (making a group of people jointly decisive, with veto power for each member of that privileged group – on this see Chapter A1*). There followed a huge collection of articles in the decade to follow, showing that weakenings tended to produce new problems, which could all be converted into impossibility theorems by axiomatically demanding the removal of those infelicities (such as ruling out oligarchy, or the existence of any person's veto power, and so on). I shall not go further into this large and rather formal literature in this chapter, but will return to it in Chapter A1*.

IS ARROVIAN IMPOSSIBILITY A GENERALIZATION OF THE CONDORCET PARADOX?

Is it really correct to think that the Arrow impossibility theorem is best seen as a generalization of the 'paradox of voting'? There is merit in that analogy for introductory purposes, but there is also a huge gulf between the two. Even though the basic axioms for the Arrow theorem concentrate on individual preferences over the set of alternative social states, it is not directly assumed by any of the axioms that we are not allowed to take note of the nature of the alternatives (the actual characteristics of 'states of affairs' of the society – what we may call 'social states'), and must assess them all only in terms of the preferences of individuals over those undescribed

---

[2] Kotaro Suzumura (2016) has explored an alternative weakening of the demand for full transitivity through allowing a little incompleteness in the social ranking, and this too can disestablish Arrow's impossibility result. This weaker consistency requirement – named 'Suzumura consistency' (following a suggestion by Walter Bossert (2008)) – shows how finely cut Arrow's consistency demand has to be for his impossibility conclusion to hold (see also Bossert and Suzumura (2010)). I will discuss the exact technical conditions in Chapter A1*.

states. In voting theory we cannot be predisposed to favour some social state (for example, because it involves, say, lower economic inequality) and are required to judge the states only through who prefers what (in fact only counting the number of votes in each direction). This is where a voting system may start, but it is hardly a plausible starting point for assessing the comparative merits of the different states in welfare economics.

Arrow did not begin with the social states being taken as undescribed boxes: it is the combination of axioms that takes him into that territory. So what are these axioms? I shall discuss them fully and formally in Chapter A1*, but we can for the moment state them informally and approximately. The Arrow social welfare function takes us from the combination of individual preferences to a social ordering (the social ranking is taken to be complete and transitive, as is assumed to be the case with individual preferences also).

The axiom called Universal Domain (U) demands that the social welfare function, taking us from the combination of individual preferences to the social ordering, works for every possible combination of individual preferences. The Pareto Principle (P) demands that if everyone in the society prefers one social state x to another y, then x will be ranked higher than y in the social ordering also. The axiom of Non-dictatorship (D) demands that there be no person with dictatorial power over the social ordering, that is, no person such that whenever he or she prefers any x to any y, then society must place that x above that y, no matter how other persons in the society place x in relation to y. The condition of Independence of Irrelevant Alternatives (I) insists that in socially ranking any pair of social states (x, y) only the preferences of the persons over x and y will count (it would not matter how, for example, they place an 'irrelevant' alternative z or w).

The ruling out of the use of all information about the nature of the alternatives (other than people's preferences over them) is a consequence of the combination of three of these axioms, Unrestricted Domain (U), Independence of Irrelevant Alternatives (I) and the Pareto Principle (P). Together they entail something very like the 'black-boxing' of the social states. In fact, a result ('Spread of Decisiveness', which is proved and discussed in Chapter A1*) shows the following: if a group of persons (or, for that matter, an individual) turns out to be decisive in getting their way in the choice over one pair of alternative social states (x, y), then – the Spread result shows – the group or individual will also be decisive over every pair of alternatives (a, b) in the set of social states. This rules out the relevance of the nature of the alternative social states involved in the choice, and also of the comparative predicaments of different individuals in different states of affairs. It does not matter how much inequality or poverty there is in one state or another, or how much violation of people's rights (such as habeas corpus) takes place in one case but not in another. All that state-related descriptive information will be drowned by the sole effectiveness of the individuals' preferences over them (no matter for what reason, and no matter how strong).

It is through this intermediate result that Arrow shows that his social welfare function, satisfying U, P and I, must work just like a voting rule. So, in this sense, it is wrong to think of the Arrow result as merely extending the Condorcet paradox to all voting rules. He first establishes – and the bulk of the proof of the impossibility theorem is concerned with exactly this – that the permitted social welfare functions must be voting rules. This is the big intermediate result, and *then* – and indeed *only* then – we come into the territory of voting and the realm to which the Condorcet paradox belongs. By then Arrow's proof is more than half completed.

WELFARE ECONOMICS AND POLITICAL RULES

There is also a second – more motivational – reason for not taking the Arrow impossibility theorem to be just a generalization of the voting paradox of Condorcet. Arrow was looking for a route to evaluating 'social welfare' – and that particularly in the context of welfare economics (led by Bergson and Samuelson) – and it is sensible to ask whether the method of majority decision would have been a possible route to that, even if it had no intransitivity or inconsistency whatever. It is, indeed, not unnatural to appeal to majority voting in settling political differences in a country, or in the context of international relations, which was the frame of reference for the question Helmer addressed to Arrow.[3]

However, no matter how satisfactory a vote-based resolution may be for political differences, it makes relatively little sense to look for voting rules for aggregation in welfare economics. Even if there were no Arrow impossibility and the method of majority vote were transitive (and this can be the case in a great many circumstances, to be discussed in Chapters A4 and A4*), it would be hard to argue that majority rule would really be 'a plausible way of aggregating preferences' in welfare economics. Arrow seems to have some sympathy for the pro-voting view when he says, 'In a collective context, voting provides the most obvious way by which individual preferences are aggregated into a social choice' (Arrow (1983), p. 125), and again: 'Majority voting is then a satisfactory social choice mechanism when there are two alternatives,' but 'it is not necessarily transitive' (Arrow (1983), pp. 168–9). But is the failure of transitivity really the most serious problem with majority voting in the 'welfare economic' context? Was Arrow taking too big a leap by answering Helmer's political question with Bergson's welfare-economic answer?

It is hard to believe that welfare-economic problems are crying out for a solution through voting. Even Arrow's own analysis in a different context makes it difficult to accept majority rule for welfare-economic decisions. In discussing a problem in which 'a number of individuals with completely egoistic preferences use the method of majority decision to divide up a fixed total of a single commodity', Arrow (1983, p. 87) makes the following observation

[3] There may be something unsatisfactory even in political problems in the possibility of going for a vote-based resolution instead of having further discussion, thereby neglecting the need for any required clarification and understanding of the issues involved. Voting on under-described – and sometimes misdescribed – alternatives, for a quick resolution, can go against a better informed – and wiser – social choice. There may be good reason for restraint before calling for a vote. There are many committees for professional decisions in which discussion-based consensus is understandably much preferred to a quick decision based on the counting of votes. I shall return to this question in Chapter A6 ('Reasoning and Social Decisions').

(in the course of his demonstration that there will be no majority winner): 'For any allocation which gives some individual, say 1, a positive amount, there is another, which gives 1 nothing and divides up his share in the first allocation among all the others; the second is preferred to the first by all but one individual.' Is this conceivably a good welfare-economic assessment of the cake-division problem?

Suppose, now, we forget about the problem of intransitivity and the absence of a majority winner, and let the feasible set of options consist exactly of the two alternatives (referred to in the quoted sentence of Arrow, but more completely specified):

x, when the cake is equally shared by persons 1, 2 and 3, and
y, when 1 gets nothing and the whole cake is divided up between 2 and 3.

There is no problem of intransitivity here (because there are only two distinct states), and no absence of majority winner (y wins over x by a two-to-one majority). But in what sense is y a 'satisfactory' welfare-economic outcome in this choice problem? Person 1 has been driven completely to the wall and 2 and 3 have been fattened up more. It is very hard to maintain that the majority rule is 'a plausible way of aggregating preferences' for these welfare-economic judgements. The problem is present even with just two alternatives before the question of transitivity even arises.

The majority method does have a good deal of plausibility for some types of problem, but making choices over differences in income distribution is not one of them. This would undermine its claim to be a possible route to 'social welfare', or, for that matter, towards 'social justice'. Arrow (1983, p. 87) has suggested that 'perhaps the deepest motivation for study of the theory of social choice, at least for the economist, is the hope of saying something useful about the evaluation of income distributions'. If this is indeed so, then the promise of majority rule as a social choice procedure is clearly hopeless, even if problems of intransitivity – or voting cycles – were never to arise.

I postpone until Chapters A3 and A3* further consideration of welfare economics and income distribution, and of the relevance of interpersonal comparisons of well-being of different individuals.

However, it is easy to note that as far as political decision-making is concerned, majority rule has considerable plausibility (I shall return to these issues in Chapters A4 and A4*). And to the extent that Arrow's impossibility theorem demonstrates the impossibility of having reasonable social-decision rules (in the absence of interpersonal comparisons), there is a really serious difficulty here for political decision-making. This is where generalizing the Condorcet paradox has immediate relevance (happily the picture is not as dire, particularly for majority rule, as it may first look – on which see Chapter A4*).

Voting is indeed a natural way of resolving social differences between people – through holding elections, organizing referendums, or seeking political mandates. The massive use of voting systems of different kinds across the world is not a mystery, since resolving differences on political matters through counting the number of supporters against that of detractors is an idea that has a huge, obvious and immediate appeal. If majority voting did not exist as a practice, it would have to be invented – for political resolutions (though not for welfare economics).

REASONING ABOUT SOCIAL CHOICE

People live together in societies, and when they disagree on something, and those disagreements survive despite extensive discussions, some method of arriving at a social agreement has to be found. In fact, even issues of inequality and poverty can be, at least to some considerable extent, addressed through social choice mechanisms of the voting kind, by asking people to judge what 'should' happen, rather than merely what alternative would serve their own interests best. The role of people's values, going beyond only their personal interests, is critically important here.

How are we to view the demands of reasoning in social decisions? How much guidance do we get from Aristotle's general recommendation that choice should be governed by 'desire and reasoning directed to some end'? There are several deep-seated difficulties here.

The first problem relates to the question: whose desires, whose ends? Different persons have disparate objects and interests. This is where Arrow's impossibility theorem comes into its own.[4] In trying to obtain an integrated social preference from diverse individual preferences, it is not in general possible to satisfy even some mild-looking conditions that would seem to reflect elementary demands of reasonableness (see Chapter 3 of the 1970 edition). Other impossibility results have also emerged, even without using some of Arrow's conditions, but involving other elementary criteria, such as the priority of individual liberty (see Chapter 6). We have to discuss why these difficulties arise, and how we can deal with them. Are the pessimistic conclusions that some have drawn from them justified? And, eventually, we also have to go into the postponed question of whether we can sensibly make aggregative social-welfare judgements in dealing with problems of economic and social inequality? Do procedures for social decision-making exist that reasonably respect individual values and preferences?

Second, another set of problems relates to questions raised by James Buchanan (1954a), (1954b), which were partly a response to Arrow's results but which are momentous in their own right. Pointing to 'the fundamental philosophical issues' involved in 'the idea of social rationality', Buchanan argued that 'rationality or irrationality as an attribute of the social group implies the imputation to that group of an organic existence apart from that of its individual components'.[iii]

---

[4] Arrow called his impossibility theorem 'General Possibility Theorem' – an oddly optimistic name for an impossibility result. In my Arrow Lecture at Columbia University, I took the liberty of suggesting that Arrow 'managed to find, in line with his sunny temperament, a rather cheerful name' for his impossibility theorem (Maskin and Sen (2014)). In his response, while commenting on my lecture (with his usual kindness), Arrow protested that he absolutely did not have a 'sunny disposition', and had always regarded himself 'rather as a gloomy realist'. The secret behind the name, Arrow went on to reveal, was that Tjalling Koopmans (another great economist, and evidently influential on the young Arrow) 'was upset by the term *impossibility*'. He 'disliked the feeling that things could not happen or change', and insisted 'on using the word *possibility*' (Arrow (2014), p. 58). I do share Koopmans' hopes and optimism – as does, I venture to guess (having known him for over half a century), Ken Arrow himself. However, this particular theorem is a genuine impossibility result, a fact that cannot be eradicated by re-naming it. Koopmans was perhaps thinking dialectically. Since the main approach of the present book is one of construction, I am encouraged by Koopmans' optimism, and I will not quibble on the difference between naming a theorem and naming a subject.

Buchanan was perhaps 'the first commentator to interpret Arrow's impossibility theorem as the result of a mistaken attempt to impose the logic of welfare maximization on the procedures of collective choice' (as has been rightly noted by Robert Sugden).[iv]

However, in addition, Buchanan was arguing that there was a deep 'confusion surrounding the Arrow analysis' – not just the impossibility theorem, but the entire framework used by Arrow and his followers – which ensued from the mistaken idea of 'social or collective rationality in terms of producing results indicated by a social ordering'.[v] We certainly have to examine whether Buchanan's critique negates Arrow's impossibility result (it will be shown in Chapter A2* why that is not the case), but we must also investigate the more general social issues raised by Buchanan, which are indeed important – in fact profound. This issue will be further discussed in Chapters A2 and A2*.

Third, Buchanan's reasoned questioning of the idea of 'social preference' suggests, at the very least, a need for caution in imposing strong 'consistency properties' in social choice, but his emphasis on procedural judgements suggests, much more ambitiously, that we should abandon altogether consequence-based evaluation of social happenings, opting instead for a procedural approach. In its pure form, such an approach would look for 'right' institutions, rather than 'good' outcomes, and would demand the priority of appropriate procedures, including the acceptance of what follows from these procedures. This approach, which is the polar opposite of the welfare-economic tradition based on classical utilitarianism of founding every decision on an ordering of different states of affairs (treating procedures just as instruments to generate good states), has not been fully endorsed by Buchanan himself, but significant work in that direction has occurred in public choice theory and in other writings influenced by his ideas.[5]

This contrast is particularly important in characterizing rights in general and liberties in particular. In the social choice literature, these characterizations have typically been in terms of states of affairs, concentrating on what happens in a society in relation to what the person whose liberty is being discussed wanted to happen.

---

[5] See, for example, the important contributions of Robert Sugden (1981), (1986).

In contrast, in the libertarian literature, inspired by the pioneering work of Robert Nozick (1974), and in related contributions using 'game-form' formulations (most notably, by Gaertner, Pattanaik and Suzumura (1992)), rights have been characterized in procedural terms, without referring to outcomes and social states that emerge. We have to examine how deep the differences between the disparate formulations are, and we must also scrutinize their respective adequacies. We also have to see how it is both possible and necessary to take note of procedures, as well as actual outcomes, simultaneously. These questions will be taken up in Chapters A5 and A5*.

Fourth, the prospects of rationality in social decisions must be fundamentally conditional on the nature of *individual* rationality. There are many different conceptions of rational behaviour of the individual. There is, for example, the view of rationality as the canny maximization of self-interest (the presumption of human beings as examples of '*homo economicus*', much used in public choice theory, fits into this framework). Arrow's (1951a) formulation is more permissive; it allows social considerations to influence the choices people make. Individual preferences, in this interpretation, reflect 'values' in general (taking note of social concerns), rather than being based only on more self-centred 'tastes', as Arrow calls them (p. 23). How adequate are the respective characterizations of individual rationality, and, through the presumption of a restricted understanding of rational behaviour (shared by many economic models), the depiction of actual conduct and choices?

Another issue, related to individual behaviour and rationality, concerns the role of social interactions in the development of values, and also the connection between value formation and the decision-making processes. Social choice theory has tended to avoid this issue, following Arrow's own abstinence: 'we will also assume in the present study that individual values are taken as data and are not capable of being altered by the nature of the decision process itself' (Arrow (1951a), p. 7). On this subject, Buchanan has taken a more permissive position – indeed emphatically so: 'The definition of democracy as "government by discussion" implies that individual values can and do change in the process of decision-making' (Buchanan (1954a), p. 120). We have to scrutinize the importance of this difference as well.

Chapter A1*
Social Preference

The proof of the Arrow theorem that is being presented here is agreeably short and is also quite easy to follow. It is, of course, inspired and influenced by Arrow's own proof, but some emendations in the strategy of the proof make it strikingly concise.[1] It is also a completely elementary proof, using nothing other than basic logic, like Arrow's own demonstration.[2]

The basic engagement of social choice with which Arrow was concerned involved evaluating and choosing from the set of available social states, with each social state x describing what is happening to the individuals and the society in the respective states of affairs. Arrow was concerned with arriving at an aggregate 'social ranking' R defined over the set of potentially available social states x, y, etc. With his democratic commitment, the basis of the social ranking R is taken to be the collection of individual rankings $\{R_i\}$, with each R_i standing for the respective person i's preference ranking over the set of alternative social states, available for social choice. It is this functional relation that Arrow calls the 'social welfare function'. Given any set of individual preferences, the social welfare function determines a particular aggregate social ordering R.

---

[1] An earlier version of this proof was presented in Sen (1995c), my Presidential Address to the American Economic Association, as footnotes 9 and 10. In my Arrow Lecture at Columbia University, this proof is examined and scrutinized (and included in Maskin and Sen (2014)).

[2] Providing short proofs of Arrow's theorem is something of a recurrent exercise in social choice theory. One has to be careful, however, not to make them artificially short by drawing on other mathematical results.

As was mentioned earlier, the fact that there can be problems of consistency in majority vote was demonstrated by the Marquis de Condorcet in the eighteenth century. It is useful to recollect how the so-called Condorcet paradox comes about.

Take three persons 1, 2 and 3 with the following preferences over three alternatives x, y and z.

1	2	3
x	y	z
y	z	x
z	x	y

In majority decisions, x defeats y, which defeats z, which in turn defeats x. The R generated by majority rule clearly violates transitivity. But, going beyond that, it violates even weaker conditions of consistency, such as 'acyclicity', which only demands the absence of any strict preference cycle, such as xPy, yPz, zPx, as we see here.[3] If, for example, we have xPy, yPz and xIz, then transitivity would certainly be violated, but not acyclicity. With an acyclic and complete social ranking, a majority winner does exist (namely x in the case of xPy, yPz and xIz), even though transitivity is violated. In contrast, Condorcet's example of a strict preference cycle not only violates social transitivity, but allows no majority winner either.

ARROW'S AXIOMS AND THE IMPOSSIBILITY RESULT

Arrow (1951a) defined a social welfare function – henceforth SWF – as a functional relation specifying one social ordering R for any given n-tuple of individual orderings $\{R_i\}$, one ordering for each person,

$$R = f(\{R_i\})$$

---

[3] On alternative demands of regularity that are weaker than transitivity, see Chapter 1* (from the 1970 edition).

Note that if a Bergson–Samuelson SWF is defined as a social ordering R, then an Arrow SWF is a function the *value* of which would be a Bergson–Samuelson SWF, interpreting R as the binary relation of 'social welfare'. Arrow's exercise, in this sense, is concerned with ways of arriving at a Bergson–Samuelson SWF.

Arrow proceeded to impose a variety of conditions that a reasonable SWF could be expected to satisfy. One of them deals with the multiple-profile characteristics of an SWF: the independence of irrelevant alternatives. For stating this condition, Arrow used the notion of a choice function for the society, $C(S)$, standing for what would be chosen (or can be chosen) from a set S (a parametric variable).

Condition I^A (Arrow's independence of irrelevant alternatives)

For any two n-tuples $\{R_i\}$ and $\{R'_i\}$ in the domain of f, and for any $S \subseteq X$, with the choice functions $C(\cdot)$, and $C'(\cdot)$ corresponding to $\{R_i\}$ and $\{R'_i\}$, respectively:

$$[\forall i: (\forall x, y \in S: xR_iy \Leftrightarrow xR'_iy)] \Rightarrow C(S) = C'(S)$$

This condition requires that, as long as individual preferences remain the same over a subset S of social states, the social choice from that particular subset should also remain the same.

Note that this condition – being choice functional – differs from the purely relational independence condition which we used in Chapter A1. Written more formally, and defining the restriction of a binary relation R over a subset S as $R|^S$, we reinterpret the pairwise relational independence condition we have been calling Condition I as the following demand:

Condition I (Relational independence):

The restriction of the social preference relation over any pair $\{x, y\}$ is a function of the n-tuple of restrictions of individual preferences over that pair,

$$R|^{(x,y)} = f^{(x,y)}(\{R_i|^{(x,y)}\}).$$

How do the two independence conditions relate to each other? Arrow articulates his axioms in a hybrid form – some relational, some choice functional. However, that irregularity can be removed by recollecting the fact that Arrow defined a choice function in purely relational terms. The choice set $C(S)$ is just those elements that are *best* according to the relevant binary relation of preference (in this case social preference) R. That is, he defined that for all subsets S of X:

$$C(S) = [x \mid x \in S \ \& \ \forall y \in S: xRy].$$

Given the binary specification of the choice function for society, as enunciated by Arrow, it is easily checked that the relational independence condition I is exactly equivalent to Arrow's choice-functional independence condition I^A. In the proofs that will be presented here, the relational Condition I will be used, because it simplifies matters and makes Arrow's theorem entirely relation-theoretic, without losing anything of its essential contents.

However, it must be remembered that Conditions I and I^A are not *generally* equivalent. When the choice function for the society cannot be represented by a binary relation (unlike in Arrow's own case), Condition I can be used without implying Condition I^A, and vice versa. Indeed, in a purely relation-theoretic framework with the use of Condition I, it need not even be assumed that a choice function for the society exists. In this sense, the result presented here is a generalization of Arrow's mixed framework of relation-cum-choice-functional articulation.

Consider now the following set of axioms, which are motivated by Arrow's original axioms but are, in fact, somewhat simpler – and also somewhat less demanding – which, taken together, are nevertheless perfectly adequate for the impossibility theorem.

U (Unrestricted Domain): For any logically possible set of individual preferences, there is a social ordering R.[4]

I^2 (Independence of Irrelevant Alternatives): The social ranking of any pair $\{x, y\}$ will depend only on the individual rankings of x and y.

---

[4] An ordering is a ranking that is reflexive, transitive and complete. For discussion on this, see the old (1970) Chapter 1*.

P (Pareto Principle): If everyone prefers any x to any y, then x is socially preferred to y.

D (Non-dictatorship): There is no person i such that whenever this person prefers any x to any y, then socially x is preferred to y, no matter what the others prefer.

It should be noted that the independence condition I^2 is not essentially different from relational independence I.

For what follows, we make the assumption that there are at least three distinct social states and a finite number of two or more individuals.

(T.A1*.1) Arrow's Impossibility Theorem: No social welfare function can simultaneously satisfy U, I^2, D and P.

One common way of putting this result is that a social welfare function that satisfies the conditions of unrestricted domain, independence and Pareto principle has to be dictatorial. This is a repugnant conclusion – antithetical to the democratic commitment – emanating from a collection of reasonable-looking axioms.

A dictator is decisive over any social choice, including choices over every pair of alternatives. That is, for any $\{x, y\}$, if the dictator prefers x to y, then society ranks x above y in the social ordering R. We can similarly define the concept of a 'decisive set' of individuals G – a subset (possibly also the whole) of the set of all individuals (assumed to be finite). This could be pairwise 'local' in the sense of applying over some particular pair of alternatives $\{x, y\}$, when x must be invariably socially preferred to y, whenever all individuals in G prefer x to y (no matter what the other individuals prefer). G is 'decisive' (or globally decisive) if it is locally decisive over every pair.

PROOF OF ARROW'S THEOREM

In proving Arrow's theorem, we first establish two intermediate results – or 'lemmas'.

(T.A1*.2) Spread of Decisiveness: If G is decisive over any pair $\{x, y\}$, then G is [globally] decisive.

Proof: Take any other pair $\{a, b\}$, different from $\{x, y\}$, and assume that everyone in G prefers a to x, that to y, and that to b. Let all others (not in G) prefer a to x, and y to b (we do not impose any condition on the rest of their preferences). By the Pareto principle, a is socially preferred to x, and y is socially preferred to b. By the decisiveness of G over $\{x, y\}$, x is socially preferred to y. Putting them together (that is, a preferred to x, that to y, and that to b), we have, by transitivity of strict preference, the result that a is socially preferred to b. By the Independence of irrelevant alternatives I, this must be related to individual preferences only over $\{a, b\}$. But only the preferences of individuals in the subset G have been specified, and others can rank a and b in any way, without restriction. So G is decisive over $\{a, b\}$. Similarly for all other pairs. So G is indeed [globally] decisive.[5] Note that this theorem – the Spread of Decisiveness – is in fact a result that takes us in the direction of what is called 'neutrality', so that the descriptive differences between x, y, a and b turn out to matter little as far as the decisiveness of any group (or individual) is concerned.

Along with showing the spread of decisiveness over the social states, we can show the reducibility of any decisive set of individuals, if there are two or more individuals in the decisive set.

(T.A1*.3) Contraction of Decisive Sets: If a set G of individuals is decisive (and if it has more than one individual), then a 'proper subset' of G is decisive as well.

Proof: Partition G into two subsets G^1 and G^2. Let everyone in G^1 prefer x to y, and x to z, with the ranking of y and z unspecified, and let everyone in G^2 prefer x to y, and z to y, with the ranking of x and z unspecified. Others not in G can have any preferences whatever. By the decisiveness of G, we must have x socially preferred to y. If, now, z is

---

[5] We are cutting a small corner here by assuming that a, b, x and y are all distinct social states. The reasoning is exactly similar when two of them are the same alternative.

taken to be socially at least as good as x for some configuration of individual preferences over $\{z, x\}$, then we must have z socially preferred to y (by transitivity, since x is socially preferred to y, for that configuration of preferences). Since no one's preference over $\{z, y\}$ other than those in G^2 has been specified,[6] and those in G^2 prefer z to y, G^2 is decisive over $\{z, y\}$, and thus, by the Spread of Decisiveness, G^2 must be [globally] decisive. Since that would make some reduced part of G decisive, we would have got what we wanted to show. To avoid this possibility, we must assume that our initial supposition, that z is at least as good as x, must be eschewed. But then x must be preferred to z. However, since no one's preference over $\{x, z\}$ has been specified, other than those in G^1 who prefer x to z, clearly G^1 is decisive over $\{x, z\}$. Thus by the Spread of Decisiveness, G^1 is [globally] decisive. So either G^1 or G^2 must be decisive, which establishes the Contraction of Decisive Sets.[7]

The proof of Arrow's impossibility result follows immediately.

Proof of (T.A1*.1)

By the Pareto principle, the set of all individuals is decisive. By the Contraction of Decisive Sets, some proper subset of all individuals must also be decisive. Take that smaller decisive set: some proper subset of that smaller set must also be decisive. And so on. Since the set of individuals is finite, we shall arrive, sooner or later, at one individual who is decisive, that is, who is a dictator, thereby violating the Non-dictatorship condition. This establishes Arrow's impossibility theorem.

The proof also brings out the difference that would be made if the set of persons (or voters) were infinite. We can go on making the decisive set of people smaller and smaller, and still not get to an individual who would be a dictator. In an important paper, Kirman and Sondermann (1972) build on this possibility to explore the concept of

---

[6] Note that this lack of specification of individual preferences over $\{z, y\}$ is consistent with what has been assumed about individual preferences over $\{z, x\}$.

[7] Note that the proof establishes a stronger result than what is formally stated in the lemma (T.A1*.3). When a decisive set is partitioned into any two subsets, then one of those subsets must be decisive. In topological terms, the class of decisive sets is, thus, an 'ultra-filter', on which a bit more will be said presently.

'invisible dictators', since the decisive set can be indefinitely reduced. We can debate whether this possibility should be enormously disturbing since the decisive set of people – however reduced – always has infinitely many persons, though containing a smaller and smaller proportion of the total society (so no one can dictate without having the support of infinitely many people, but most people are – and this may be seen as disturbing – effectively disenfranchised).[i]

QUASI-TRANSITIVITY AND SUZUMURA CONSISTENCY

After the Arrow theorem came to be discussed widely, there was speculation for some time as to whether the impossibility results of the type pioneered by Arrow could be avoided by weakening the requirement of collective rationality. There have been broadly two approaches to this question. One retains the Arrovian focus on a social preference relation, but weakens the consistency requirement from the full dose of transitivity to weaker demands. The other dispenses with the notion of social preference itself, and formulates the problem in choice functional terms. In this chapter, aimed at 'relational impossibilities', the use of the first approach is examined, leaving the second approach for the next technical chapter (Chapter A2*).

We begin with the case of *quasi-transitivity*, which demands only that strict preference be transitive, that is, for all x, y, z: $(xPy \ \& \ yPz)$ entails xPz. But other cases covered by full transitivity need not hold, that is, indifference may not be transitive, and mixed cases may not entail a resulting strict preference: for example xPy and yIz together do not entail xPz.

In establishing Arrow's theorem, two lemmas were used in the last section. It is easily checked that the Spread of Decisiveness requires no more than quasi-transitivity of social preference (only the transitivity of strict preference was used in the proof), while Contraction of Decisive Sets cannot be derived from quasi-transitivity alone, and was, in fact, established by using full transitivity of social preference. The latter result is crucial to deriving dictatorship from Arrow's

Conditions U, P and I (or I^A), and if that result is nullified by relaxing the requirement of consistency of social preference to quasi-transitivity only, the Arrow impossibility result will fail to hold.

Kotaro Suzumura (2016) has extensively discussed an alternative weakening of the condition of full transitivity through allowing a little incompleteness of ranking. Permitting incompleteness – and thus allowing us to distinguish between maximality and optimality – is a very important direction in which to proceed (as was discussed in the new Preface, and will be further analysed in the final chapter of this book, Chapter A6). 'Suzumura consistency' takes us towards maximality, rather than full optimality. It is a weaker demand than having a transitive ordering, but the difference disappears when the ranking is complete (the rather trivial requirement of reflexivity – that each x is taken to be as good as itself – is of course presumed in all the cases). Consider a sequence of weak preferences: $x_1 R x_2, x_2 R x_3, \ldots, x_{t-1} R x_t$. Given all this, Suzumura consistency insists that we must not have $x_t P x_1$.

This demand can be met if (x_1, x_t) are not ranked, which makes the ranking incomplete. If, however, the ranking is complete, then the demand of not having $x_t P x_1$ amounts to having $x_1 R x_t$, so that the gap between Suzumura consistency and transitivity of the ranking (or an ordering) vanishes.[ii] But this small variation does yield a number of important differences between the implications of Suzumura consistent social preference and a social ordering. There are various social choice possibilities that Suzumura-consistent rankings, even with other Arrow-like demands, allow, which complete social orderings do not. Among other things, this points to another way of escaping Arrow's impossibility theorem.

THE PARETO-EXTENSION RULE

Returning to quasi-transitivity, note that it is more than sufficient for generating a complete choice function from a reflexive and complete social preference relation over a finite set. Thus, the Arrow impossibility result can be shown to collapse if we relax the demand for full transitivity of the social preference relation to quasi-transitivity only (see Sen (1969); see also Pollak (1979) and Suzumura (1983), (2016)). A simple example of such a procedure is a social decision function that yields what has been called the 'Pareto-extension rule', with x being accepted to be socially preferred to y if and only if everyone prefers x to y. However, x and y are socially indifferent if they are either Pareto-indifferent, or – and here is the rub – Pareto-incomparable. The unattractiveness of the Pareto-extension rule (despite it providing a formal route to escape the Arrow impossibility) led to the question whether or not the Arrow conditions were in an important sense too weak, rather than too strong.

The Pareto-extension rule gives everyone a veto, in the sense that if anyone strictly prefers x to y, that will eliminate the possibility of y being preferred to x, and indeed will make sure that x is socially at least as good as y. In what was originally a term paper for a class jointly taught by Arrow, Rawls and myself in the spring semester at Harvard in 1969, Allan Gibbard (1969) showed that replacing full transitivity by quasi-transitivity of social preference leads to the existence of 'veto power' enjoyed by some people (the Pareto-extension rule is, in fact, the most 'democratic' of the permissible class, giving everyone veto power).[iii] The existence of a veto is a necessary result of resolving the Arrow problem through weakening transitivity of social preference to quasi-transitivity.

Define a person i as semi-decisive over some ordered pair $\{x, y\}$ if xP_iy implies xRy. A person has a veto if and only if he or she is semi-decisive over every ordered pair. To invoke the language used in Chapters 4 and 4* of the 1970 edition, a 'social decision function' (SDF) is obtained from an Arrovian social welfare function by removing the insistence that the social preference R must be an ordering, but demanding the weaker condition that R should be a reflexive and complete preference relation that generates a choice function, in the sense that it yields a non-empty choice set $C(S, R)$ for every non-empty set of social states S. For this result, quasi-transitivity of social preference is more than sufficient. An SDF is called 'oligarchic' (as defined by Gibbard (1969)) if and only if there is a unique group G of persons such that G as a whole group is fully decisive, and every member of G has a veto.

(T.A1*.4) Quasi-transitive Oligarchy Theorem:
  If H is finite and $\#X \geq 3$, then any SDF generating quasi-transitive social preference relations, satisfying Conditions U, P and I^2, must be oligarchic.

Just like the lemma on the Spread of Decisiveness, which continues to hold, it is possible to establish another neutrality-inclined result, a Veto-Spread lemma, asserting that any person who is semi-decisive over some ordered pair must be semi-decisive over all ordered pairs, i.e. must have a veto. The proof is completed by noting that no group other than a superset of G can be decisive since every member of G has a veto.[iv]

Adding an axiom that rules out any oligarchy would generate a new impossibility result instantly. Replacing transitivity by quasi-transitivity has translated the possibility of dictatorship into an oligarchy (with all its members having veto power), and while the existence of vetoers may be less unattractive than that of a dictator, it is unappetizing enough in failing to provide what can reasonably be seen as a grand resolution of the Arrow problem.

ACYCLICITY AND VETO POWER

Quasi-transitivity may also be thought to be too demanding a condition, especially since acyclicity, which is a weaker requirement than quasi-transitivity (see Chapter 1* from the 1970 edition), is sufficient for generating a finitely complete choice function based on the binary relation of social preference, i.e. for generating a social decision function SDF (to use the 1970 term). In a major follow-up, Mas-Colell and Sonnenschein (1972) presented a veto-result with acyclicity, without demanding quasi-transitivity, and the result can be readily extended (see Blair et al. (1976)), to the case of demanding a weaker condition of triple acyclicity (i.e. no cycles over triples, rather than no cycles over any subset of alternatives).[8]

[8] Each of these results, using the weaker condition of what is called 'collective

As an illustration of the class of results with weaker conditions of 'collective rationality', consider an elegant result established by Julian Blau and Rajat Deb (1977). This involves an alternative way of generating the vetoer result with only acyclicity through invoking a condition that may be called NIM (a combination of neutrality, independence and monotonicity), presented in a relation-theoretic form. The demand of neutrality – that of paying no attention to the description of a state of affairs (only to its placing in the preference orderings of individuals) – was discussed in the Introduction (and referred to earlier on in this chapter). Monotonicity, in the present context, relates social preference to individual preferences consistently in the same direction (that is, if an alternative x climbs up in any person's ordering (other things given), then it must not climb down in the social ranking). Condition NIM incorporates the force of neutrality and monotonicity in social choice, within the framework of relational independence.

For a formal statement, take any two profiles of individual preferences $\{R_i\}$ and $\{R'\}$.

Condition NIM (neutrality, independence with monotonicity):
  For any $x, y, a, b \in X$, if for all i, $xP_iy \Rightarrow aP'_ib$, and $xI_iy \Rightarrow aR'_ib$, then $xPy \Rightarrow aP'b$.

The theorem presented by Blau and Deb (1977) is:

(T.A1*.5) Acyclic neutral monotonicity vetoer theorem
  If $\#X \geq \#H$, with a finite H, then any SDF satisfying Conditions U and NIM must yield someone with a veto.[v]

To establish this, suppose – to the contrary – there is no vetoer. So there is no one who is semi-decisive over all pairs. By the neutrality and monotonicity properties of NIM, there is thus no one who is 'almost semi-decisive' over any pair (that is, winning if all others

---

rationality' (of which a transitive social ordering is a very strong demand), requires some supplementary assumption (such as 'positive responsiveness' or some other demand). The literature grew vastly in the 1970s and 1980s, and it is reviewed and scrutinized in my chapter on 'Social Choice Theory' in the *Handbook of Mathematical Economics* (edited by Kenneth Arrow and Michael Intriligator): Sen (1986b).

oppose her – she can't lose, thanks to the spirit of monotonicity, if some of her opponents stop opposing her). If someone were almost semi-decisive, then by monotonicity she would be actually semi-decisive over that pair, and by neutrality semi-decisive over every pair of alternatives, i.e. have veto power. So everyone loses over any pair if unanimously opposed by others. With this in mind, consider the following n-tuple of preference orderings (in descending order) over a subset $\{x_1, x_2, \ldots, x_n\}$ of X for the n individuals $1, \ldots, n$.

$$
\begin{aligned}
&1: \quad x_1, x_2, \ldots, x_{n-1}, x_n, \\
&2: \quad x_2, x_3, \ldots, x_n, x_1, \\
&\quad \cdot \\
&\quad \cdot \\
&n: \quad x_n, x_1, \ldots, x_{n-2}, x_{n-1}.
\end{aligned}
$$

Clearly, thanks to NIM, we must have: $x_1 P x_2$, $x_2 P x_3$, $\ldots$, $x_{n-1} P x_n$ and $x_n P x_1$. This violation of acyclicity shows the falsity of the contrary hypothesis of there being no one with veto power.

Thus, even acyclicity does not help very much in delivering us from the Arrow problem. In general, weaker consistency conditions combined with other properties leads to a weakening – rather than elimination – of the dictatorship result, in the form of the existence of vetoers. And acyclicity *is* necessary for binary choice using the Condorcet condition.[vi]

Following the initial cluster of results in the 1970s, Blair and Pollak (1982), (1983), Kelsey (1982), (1983a), (1983b) and Matsumoto (1985) established various extensions of impossibility results with conditions much weaker than transitivity of social preference. Blair and Pollak have shown in particular that even without neutrality, some of the sting of the veto power remains in the form of an individual being semi-decisive over $(m - n + 1)(m - 1)$ pairs of states, where m and n are, respectively, the numbers of states and individuals. Given the individuals, when larger and larger sets of states – without bounds – are considered, the proportion of pairs over which the individual is semi-decisive approaches unity (see Blair and Pollak (1982)). Kelsey (1982), (1983a), (1983b) has established similar results, without invoking neutrality and even without the use of the Pareto principle, about the arbitrariness of the resulting power distribution; someone being semi-decisive (or anti-semi-decisive) over a large proportion of pairs of states – approaching $\frac{1}{2}$ as more and more states are considered.

GETTING ARROW-TYPE IMPOSSIBILITY WITH SEMI-ORDERS

Among the weakenings of Arrow's collective rationality condition, the case of semi-orders is of particular interest, since the case for having semi-transitive preferences – for the individual as well as for society – has been discussed for a long time, going all the way back to J. C. Borda in the eighteenth century. Among other observations, Borda showed that an apparent indifference can really be a weak preference in one direction or another, when the intensity of preference is below what is 'noticeable'. Semi-orders lie in between assuming only quasi-transitivity (and nothing else) and full transitivity. We are tempted to ask: would the Arrow impossibility result hold with full force in such an intermediate ground (with 'quasi-transitivity plus', as it were)? The answer is yes, provided the number of distinct social states is large enough.

A semi-order is defined to satisfy the following two properties (in addition to quasi-transitivity, which is *inter alia* implied by each of these conditions)[vii]:

Semi-transitivity
   For any $x, y, z, a \in X$, if xPy and yPz, then xPa or aPz.

Interval order property
   For any $x, y, a, b \in X$, if xPy and aPb, then xPb or aPy.

Each of these properties implies quasi-transitivity for a complete R. Arrow's impossibility result can be established, as shown by Blau, Schwartz, Brown and others, with either of these less demanding properties, and still weaker structures.[viii]

(T.A1*.6) Arrow Impossibility for semi-transitivity
   If H is finite and $\#X \geq 4$, then there is no SDF satisfying

Conditions U, I, P and D, and yielding semi-transitive social preference.

In establishing this theorem, it may be first noted that since semi-transitivity implies quasi-transitivity, the lemma of 'Spread of Decisiveness' (T.A1*.2) holds here too. The rest of the proof follows the strategy of the elementary and short proof used earlier in this chapter to prove Arrow's impossibility theorem, and goes like this: The lemma about the 'Contraction of Decisive Sets' (T.A1*.3) can be re-established for semi-transitivity (demanding less than full transitivity). Let G be a decisive group, which is partitioned into two non-empty subsets G_1 and G_2. The following preference orderings are postulated, shown through a Hasse diagram, with everyone in G_1 and G_2 (that is all the people in G) preferring x to y, and y to z. But the members of G_1 prefer x to a (which members of G_2 may or may not), and people in G_2 prefer a to z, which G_1-members may or may not. Those who do not belong to G (that is neither to G_1 nor to G_2), can have any preference over these alternatives.

G_1 $\qquad\qquad\qquad\qquad\qquad\qquad$ G_2

Note that nothing has been said about the preferences of members of G_1 about their ranking over the pair (a, z), nor about the preferences of those who belong to G_2 over (x, a), nor about the preferences of others $(H - G)$ over any of these alternatives. By the decisiveness of G, xPy and yPz. By the condition of semi-transitivity of R, either xPa or aPz. In the first case (that is, if xPa), G_1 is decisive over $\{x, a\}$, and thus by the spread of decisiveness, G_1 is fully decisive. In the second case (that is, if aPz), G_2 is decisive over $\{a, z\}$, and thus by the spread of decisiveness, G_2 is generally decisive. Thus, either G_1 or G_2 is decisive, which is more than adequate to establish that if G is decisive, then so is some proper subset of G.

Given the re-establishment of the result (T.A1*.3) about the 'Contraction of Decisive Sets', the rest of the proof of Arrow's impossibility theorem remains the same.

(T.A1*.7) Arrow impossibility for interval order property

If H is finite and $\#X \geq 4$, then there is no SDF satisfying Conditions U, I, P and D, and yielding interval-ordered social preference.

In this case the following preference orderings are considered:

Note that the rankings of members of G_1 over the pair (a, y) are not specified, and nor are the rankings of the members of G_2 over (x, b). The others in $(H - G)$ can rank the alternatives in any possible way.

By the decisiveness of G, xPy and aPb. By the interval order property, either xPb or aPy. In the first case, G_1 is decisive; in the second case, G_2. The rest of the proof is unaltered.

Since a semi-order is both semi-transitive and an interval order, clearly it is, *a fortiori*, adequate to fully sustain the Arrow impossibility result. While for an ordering even one strict preference filters through one indifference and $PI \Rightarrow P$ and $IP \Rightarrow P$, i.e. $(xPy \ \& \ yIz) \Rightarrow xPz$ and $(xIy \ \& \ yPz) \Rightarrow xPz$, for a semi-order it is only the combined force of *two* strict preferences that is guaranteed to work through one indifference, i.e. $P^2I \Rightarrow P$, $IP^2 \Rightarrow P$, and $PIP \Rightarrow P$. Generalizing, let s-and-t-order only guarantee $P^sIP^t \Rightarrow P$, with s strict preferences preceding the indifference I, and t strict preferences following the indifference I. The Arrow impossibility result translates intact to this case in general, provided there are enough social states to allow the use of an s-and-t order, that is provided $\#X \geq s + t + 2$. Since an s-and-t-order need not be quasi-transitive, it is first established that an SDF satisfying Conditions U, I and P, and yielding an s-and-t-order, must lead to quasi-transitivity of social preference. Then the proof can follow a variant of the lemmas on the Contraction of Decisive Sets for

s-and-t-order (in the same way as the proofs for semi-transitivity and interval orders), and then the final result is an Arrow-type impossibility, with the additional demand for there being an adequate number of different social states to make the required preference profiles possible.

In the case of orderings, the original 'Arrow case', $s + t$ is 1, as a result of the social ranking being a fully transitive ordering, and it works for $\#X \geq 3$. In the case of semi-orders, $s + t$ is 2, and it works for $\#X \geq 4$. In the general finite case, s and t can be any positive integer or zero, and it works if $\#X \geq s + t + 2$. For an infinite X, the range of the SDF may be confined to the doubly infinite *union* of sets of all s-and-t-orders.

ON THE TOPOLOGY
OF DECISIVE SETS

Just as it is possible to speak prose without noticing that fact (as Monsieur Jourdain was surprised to find in Molière's *Le Bourgeois Gentilhomme*), it is possible also to be talking topology without sensing any topology around us. The Contraction of Decisive Sets was a precise remark on the topology of decisive sets. Having got this far, there is a case for explicitly thinking about the topology of decisive sets, and indeed it allows us to see some of the results we have been talking about in the light of topological results, and benefit from the insights of Monjardet (1967), (1983), Hansson (1972), (1976) and Brown (1973), (1974), (1975a), among others, who have commented in a precise way on the connections and the possibility of using – and systematizing – the analytical links between social choice theory and the topology of decisive sets.

Let Ω be the class of decisive sets of individuals – a subset of the power set of H. Decisiveness is considered globally over all pairs of social states, rather than in terms of local decisiveness over a particular pair (this is where the property of the 'Spread of Decisiveness' comes in, derived in Arrow's case from the combined effect of his axioms U, P and I). Consider the following properties:[ix]

(1) $H \in \Omega$,

(2) $[G \in \Omega \& G \subseteq J] \Rightarrow J \in \Omega$,

(3) $[G_1, G_2, ..., G_k \in \Omega$ for a finite $k] \Rightarrow$ the intersection of these G_i is non-empty

(4) $[G, J \in \Omega] \Rightarrow G \cap J \in \Omega$,

(5) $[G \notin \Omega] \Rightarrow H - G \in \Omega$.

Ω is a *pre-filter* if and only if it satisfies (1), (2) and (3). It is a *filter* if and only if it, additionally, also satisfies (4).[9] It is an *ultra-filter* if and only if it satisfies all these conditions, i.e. (1) to (5).

There have been a number of interesting and important studies of the properties of the class of decisive groups as a function of a number of determining variables, including the regularity properties of individual and social preferences.[x] Consider the transformation function $f: \{R_i\} \rightarrow R$. Each R_i and each R are taken to be reflexive and complete and, in addition, they are required to satisfy some regularity condition of consistency (the same for R_i as for R). It has been shown that for $f(\cdot)$ satisfying Conditions U, P and I:

1. acyclicity implies that Ω is a pre-filter;
2. quasi-transitivity implies that Ω is a filter;
3. semi-order properties imply that Ω is an ultra-filter; and
4. transitivity implies that Ω is an ultra-filter.

These results can be used to derive the various dictatorship and veto results studied in the earlier sections. In particular, in Arrow's case of full transitivity, Ω is an ultra-filter, so that if a subset of a decisive set is not itself decisive, then its complement will be (this, of course, yields, *inter alia*, the property of Contraction of Decisive Sets). If non-dictatorship were to hold, then each set of one person alone must be non-decisive, and thus by (5), in a community with n people, all sets with $n - 1$ people would be decisive. But this class of decisive sets has an empty intersection, thereby contradicting (3), and also (4). Hence the impossibility. The proof extends readily to semi-orders.

---

[9] In fact, given the other conditions, (3) will now be automatically fulfilled.

In the case of acyclicity, Ω is a pre-filter, and, by virtue of (3), there is a group of persons – Brown calls it a 'collegium' – such that every member of it belongs to every decisive set of persons.[10] With quasi-transitivity Ω is a filter, and by (4) the collegium would be decisive and thus define the oligarchy.

A huge number of other results of interest have also been obtained in social choice theory with varying conditions imposed on the notion of social preference. While I shall not try to accommodate them here, I hope that readers would have, by now, got some taste of what is going on. Consistency conditions imposed on choice functions for the society – without presupposing any idea of social preference – will be taken up in the next two chapters.

[10] Ferejohn (1977) has pointed out that this does not in itself imply that every member of the collegium has a veto, since the social decisions induced by the pre-filter may have to be supplemented by other procedures when some members of the collegium are indifferent.

Chapter A2
Rationality and Consistency

In mainstream economic theory, rationality of choice has been interpreted in several different ways, three of which have been most prominent:

(1) internal consistency of choice;
(2) self-interest maximization; and
(3) maximization in general.

These distinct notions have some connection with each other. Self-interest maximization is clearly a special case of maximization in general, and the point of specifically invoking the latter must be to allow the possibility of rationality taking the form of maximization other than that of self-interest. Similarly, certain conditions of internal consistency of choice behaviour would allow the entire picture of choice to be seen as the maximization of getting as much as possible in terms of some comparative relation defined over all the alternatives. Whether that binary relation can be seen as a preference relation or the relation of self-interest is a further question. Even though these different concepts of rationality of behaviour are not entirely disparate, they can yield very different understandings of what rationality of behaviour demands, since they approach the idea of rationality from different directions.

The approach of 'internal consistency of choice' assesses the correspondence between choices in different situations, comparing what options are chosen from different 'menus' (i.e. from different sets of available alternatives from which to choose). The internal consistency approach interprets the demands of rationality purely in terms of choices themselves, without anything else being invoked (i.e. choice is compared with choice, and *not* with objectives, values, preferences, or any other non-choice variable). What is examined is whether choices from different menus are consistent with each other (if such a concept of consistency makes sense, on which more later).

Even though seeing rationality as internal consistency may have some superficial appeal, it does not, in fact, take us very far. For example, a person can be consistently moronic in his or her choices. To illustrate, someone who always chooses the things he or she values least and hates most would have great consistency of behaviour, but can scarcely count as a model of rationality. Thus internal consistency fails altogether as a *sufficient* condition of rationality. But can it, nevertheless, make sense as a *necessary* condition?

This proposition has not much plausibility either. Indeed, the standard axiomatic conditions for alleged internal consistency proposed in the literature can be sensibly violated for very plausible reasons (see Chapter A2*). In fact, going further, the approach is foundationally misconceived. What counts as 'consistency' is basically undecidable without taking some note of the motivation of the chooser – what the person is trying to do, or achieve. But to invoke such motivational links would amount to an external reference (external to the acts of choice themselves), and then the consistency condition could not be one of pure *internal* consistency of choice. I shall come back to this issue presently (including the conceptual question of whether such a thing as pure internal consistency is a bizarre idea), and then discuss the question and its implications more formally in Chapter A2*.

In contrast with the pursuit of internal consistency, the second approach, rationality seen as cogent maximization of self-interest, obviously employs an external reference – that of promoting the person's own interest. So does the third approach, maximization in general, since whatever is to be maximized must invoke something external to the acts of choice (such as goals or objectives or values).

Even though in the formal discipline of social choice theory, conditions of internal consistency have been extensively used, the favourite approach in mainstream economics has been the self-interest view of rationality. The approach has been an integral component of what goes by the name of 'rational choice theory', which makes the self-interest approach rational *by definition* – a kind of conquest by nomenclature. By giving the name 'rational choice' to some specific kind of behaviour there is an implicit attempt to avoid any disputation on whether that kind of behaviour can actually be seen as rational. It rides roughshod over the fact that the long-used term 'rationality' has antecedent meanings – or at least established associations – which cannot be erased merely by a new definition.

The origins of the self-interest approach are often traced to Adam Smith's writings, and it is frequently asserted that 'the father of modern economics' saw each human being as tirelessly promoting his own particular interest, and nothing else. As history of thought, this diagnosis is, to say the least, extremely dubious (on this see Werhane (1991), Rothschild (2001) and Sen (1987a), (2009a)). Adam Smith did talk about the adequacy of self-interest as a motivation in some spheres of activity, for example in trading and exchange. He talked in a much-quoted passage about the sufficiency of self-interest in giving trading incentive to the butcher, the baker and the brewer, as well as buying incentive to the purchasers of these goods. However, he discussed the relevance of many other kinds of motivations for human behaviour in other economic activities. Indeed, Smith's writings on moral sentiments and on prudential concerns (particularly in his first book, *The Theory of Moral Sentiments*, first published in 1759) had a significant influence on related investigations undertaken by other 'Enlightenment thinkers', including Immanuel Kant and Condorcet. Smith has suffered not a little in the hands of some of his alleged followers, through the smallness that has been thrust upon him.

The view of rationality as self-interest maximization is not only arbitrary, it can also lead to serious descriptive and predictive problems in economics (as the new literature on 'behavioural economics' has contributed to bringing out). In many of our actions we evidently do pay attention to the demands of other values, such as altruism and social commitment, and to the need for co-operation. There are on-going challenges in explaining why people often work together in situations of mutual interdependence, why public-spirited behaviour is often observed (from not littering the streets to showing kindness and consideration to others), and why rule-based conduct standardly constrains narrowly self-seeking actions in a great many contexts. The observation of such dissonance between the theory and the actuality of behaviour has led to a remarkably large literature on skilfully elongating the self-interest model to deal with these challenges: for example, through considerations related to the future usefulness of a good reputation, or the influence of anticipated response by others (including presumptions that others enjoy co-operating and would respond accordingly).

Interesting and ingenious models have been constructed with added structure, without denying the relevance of self-interest pursuit. These hybrid models are frequently of great interest in themselves, and not just for extending the reach of self-interest maximization (see Richard Tuck 2008). Evolutionary game theory has given us good reasons to see the relevance of concerns such as reputation and behavioural norms as important constituents of the analysis of human choices (on this see Weibull (1995), Alger and Weibull (2016a), (2016b)). What is important to recognize here is that evolutionary reasoning – important as it certainly is – does not preclude the fact that people may also have real concerns, going beyond the cunning pursuit of self-interest and instrumental benefit (for example, behaving well may be influenced both by moral concerns and by a desire to cultivate a useful reputation). The power of indirect and consequential reasoning does not re-establish the adequacy of the self-interest approach to explain behaviour in all the different kinds of cases that actually arise, in economics and elsewhere.

In contrast with the hold of the self-interest theory of rationality in mainstream economics, that highly limiting assumption has not been widely used as a restrictive condition in social choice theory. However, the third approach to rationality, seeing it as reasoned choices aimed at the maximization of whatever it is that a person wishes to maximize – subject to relevant constraints – has had much appeal among many social choice theorists, including Kenneth Arrow. The individual values on which social choice is based in an Arrovian social welfare function are orderings of whatever the persons respectively want to pursue, and there is no imposed additional requirement that these values must reflect only the self-interests of the people involved. Arrow's (1951a) focus on 'values' (contrasted with 'tastes') in considering individual preferences tends to militate against such an imposition.

THE ROLE OF SOCIAL PREFERENCE

The need for orderly, overall judgements of social welfare (or the general goodness of states of affairs) was clarified by Abram Bergson (1938), (1966) and extensively explored by Paul Samuelson (1947). Following that departure, Arrow (1951a) defined a 'social welfare function' as a functional relation that specifies a social ordering R over all the social states for every set of individual preference orderings. Arrow's theorem shows the impossibility of arriving at a social welfare ordering based on individual preferences or values, given some apparently plausible axioms, making rather mild-looking demands.

As was mentioned in Chapter A1, in an important paper that was published shortly after Arrow's theorem was presented, James Buchanan (1954a) questioned whether it makes sense to talk about the preference of a society, since a society is not a person and cannot have a reflected preference. It must be asked whether Arrow's use of the idea of social preference should be viewed with scepticism, and, if so, what would remain of Arrow's big result.

In addressing these questions, we have to distinguish between two quite different uses of the notion of 'social preference', related respectively to the operation of *decision mechanisms*, and the making of *social welfare judgements*. The first notion of social preference is an imagined 'as if' preference, on the basis of which the choices actually made can be explained. This derivative view of social preference would be, formally, a relational representation of the choices emerging from decision mechanisms.

The second idea of social preference – as social welfare judgements – reflects a view of the social good: some ranking of what would be better or worse for the society. Such judgements can, of course, be made by a person or an agency. Here too an aggregation is involved, since an individual who is making judgements about social welfare, or about the relative goodness of distinct social states, must somehow combine the diverse interests and preferences of different people.

Buchanan's basic objection is certainly persuasive for the first interpretation (involving decision mechanisms), especially since there is no *a priori* presumption that the mechanisms used *must* – or even *should* – necessarily lead to choices that satisfy the requirements of binary representation – a precondition for yielding a social relation that could be seen as an 'as if' social preference. On the other hand, the second interpretation does not involve this problem. Indeed, any one commenting on social welfare would need, in one way or another, a concept of this kind, involving some variant of what can be called social preference. When applied to the making of social welfare judgements by an individual or an agency, Arrow's impossibility theorem thus cannot be disputed on the gratuitous ground that some imagined organic existence is being imputed to the society. Even though Buchanan's critique of Arrow's theorem would continue to apply to *mechanisms* of social decision (such as voting procedures), it would have no particular relevance to social welfare judgements – central to welfare economics.

So Buchanan's critique is not directly relevant to the discipline of welfare economics. However, it must be asked whether it disposes of Arrow-type impossibility theorems for social decision mechanisms. Buchanan's pointer that Arrow demands a binary preference relation (in fact more than that – an ordering relation) for the society would surely make the theorem not immediately applicable to social choice mechanisms. Can the Arrow result resurface in some form even when the idea of social preference relation is dropped, and even after the demands of internal consistency of social choice that can have a binary representation are eschewed?

ARROW'S IMPOSSIBILITY WITHOUT INTERNAL CONSISTENCY

It is indeed important to ask whether the dropping of the requirement that social choices be based on a binary relation (thereby confining our attention only to decision mechanisms without any implicit idea of an underlying social relation – or any condition of internal consistency) negate the impossibility problems identified by Arrow. A large literature, discussed in Chapter A1*, has already established that the arbitrariness of power, of which Arrow's case of dictatorship is an extreme example, lingers on in weaker – but disturbing – forms even when transitivity is dropped, so long as *some* regularity is demanded (such as the absence of strict cycles of ranking). There is, however, cause for going further, precisely for the reasons identified by Buchanan, and to drop not just the transitivity of social preference, but the idea of social preference itself. All that is needed from the point of view of choice, as Buchanan rightly noted, is that the decision mechanisms determine a 'choice function' for the society – that is, identify what is to be selected from each alternative 'menu' (or each opportunity set).

It has been demonstrated in the literature of social choice theory (to be taken up in Chapter A2*) that, if some conditions of internal consistency of the choice function are imposed (relating decisions over one menu in a consistent way to decisions over other – linked – menus), it can be shown that some arbitrariness of power would still survive. But the methodological critique of James Buchanan would still apply forcefully, reformulated in the following way: why should *any restriction whatever* be placed *a priori* on the choice function for the society? Why should not the decisions emerging from agreed social mechanisms be acceptable without having to check them against some preconceived idea of how choices made in different situations – from different menus – should relate to each other?

What happens, then, to Arrow's impossibility problem if *no restrictions whatever* are placed on the so-called internal consistency of the choice function for the society? Would the conditions relating individual preferences to social choice (i.e. the Pareto principle, non-dictatorship and independence) then be consistent with each other? The answer, in fact, is no, not so. If all these conditions are reformulated in ways that a choice-based, rather than relation-based, approach would demand, then the impossibility result would *re-emerge* (this was demonstrated in Sen (1993a)). If the

Pareto principle and the conditions of non-dictatorship and independence are redefined to take full note of the fact that they must relate to *social choices*, not to any prior notion of *social preference*, then a very similar impossibility emerges again. This is shown in Chapter A2*.

How does this 'general choice-functional impossibility theorem' work? The underlying intuition is this. Each of the conditions relating individual preferences to social decisions eliminates – either on its own or in the presence of the other conditions – the possibility of choosing *some* alternatives. And the conjunction of these conditions can lead to an empty choice set, making it 'impossible' to choose anything. The consequent absence of anything that can be chosen (with an empty choice set for a non-empty menu), given these conditions of external correspondence – between individual preferences and social choice – nullifies the existence of any choice function before any requirement of *internal consistency* of social choice can even be considered.

For example, the Pareto principle is just such a condition, and the object of this condition in a choice context, surely, is to avoid the selection of a Pareto-inferior alternative. Therefore, this condition can be sensibly redefined to demand that if everyone prefers x to y, then the social decision mechanism should be such that y should not get chosen if x is available. Indeed, to eliminate any possibility that we are implicitly or indirectly using any inter-menu consistency condition for social choice, we can define all the conditions for only *one given menu* (or opportunity set) S; that is, we can consider the choice problem exclusively over a given set of alternative states. The Pareto principle for that set S then only demands that if everyone prefers some x to some y in that set, then y must not be chosen from that set.

Similarly, non-dictatorship would demand that there be no person such that whenever she prefers any x to any y in that set S, then y cannot be chosen from that set. What about independence? We have to modify the idea of decisiveness of a group in this choice context, related to choices over this given set S. A group would be decisive for x against y if and only if, whenever all members of this group prefer any x to any y in this set S, then y is not to be chosen from S.

The choice-function-motivated independence condition would demand that any group's power of decisiveness over a pair (x, y) must be completely independent of individual preferences over pairs other than (x, y). If a group is able to ensure that an alternative x is socially rejected in the presence of y, then that 'rejection decisiveness' would continue to hold even if individual preferences over irrelevant alternatives alter.

Armed with these conditions of external correspondence between individual preferences and social choice, it can be shown that there is no way of going from individual preferences to social choice while satisfying conditions of independence, the Pareto principle, non-dictatorship and unrestricted domain, even without invoking any social preference, and without imposing any demand of collective rationality, or any inter-menu consistency condition on social choice.

The lessons to be drawn from all this for Buchanan's questioning of social preference would appear to be the following. The impossibility result identified in a particular form by Arrow can be extended and shown to hold even when the idea of social preference is totally dropped and even when no conditions are imposed on internal consistency of social choice (thereby eschewing what Arrow had called 'collective rationality'). So the impossibility problem identified by Arrow cannot be escaped by this move. This does not, however, annul the importance of Buchanan's criticism of the idea of social preference itself (in the context of choices emerging from *decision mechanisms* for the society, rather than from the concept of social welfare), since it is a valid observation in its own right.

THE IDEA OF INTERNAL CONSISTENCY OF CHOICE

The fact that we do not need to assume any internal consistency of choice to establish Arrow's impossibility theorem is analytically interesting and important, but it does not tell us much about whether the idea of internal consistency is actually a plausible way of thinking about reasoned individual behaviour, or about reasonable social choice. That proposed approach to reasoned choice deserves a serious examination on its own.

The idea of internal consistencies of choice was powerfully introduced by Paul Samuelson (1938) in the context of demand theory in economics in a justly famous foundational contribution, initiating a major field of enquiry called 'revealed preference theory'. The approach can be interpreted in several different ways. One interpretation that has received much attention in the subsequent literature (and has had a profound impact on the direction of mainstream economic research) is the programme of developing a theory of behaviour 'freed from any vestigial traces of the utility concept' (Samuelson (1938), p. 71). While this was not in line with the works of the most powerful demand theorists preceding Samuelson, its stalwarts soon became convinced that he was basically right. Even John Hicks, the author of the classic book on micro-economic theory, *Value and Capital* (Hicks (1939b)), who had earlier argued for the priority of the concept of preference or utility, became persuaded by the alleged superiority of the new approach, and warmly endorsed the study of human beings 'only as entities having certain patterns of market behaviour; it makes no claim, no pretence, to be able to see inside their heads'.[i]

In the same spirit, Ian Little (1949a) gave his stamp of methodological approval to this approach: 'the new [Samuelson's revealed preference] formulation is scientifically more respectable [since] if an individual's behaviour is consistent, then it must be possible to explain that behaviour without reference to anything other than behaviour'.[ii] *Really?* But why? A behaviour can result from many different kinds of alternative motivations, and it is not in the least clear how the need for thinking about the motivation behind any behaviour can be avoided if we try to understand the nature of a choice.

The problems with the idea and use of conditions of internal consistency of choice can be seen at two rather different levels: *foundational* and *practical*. At the foundational level, the basic difficulty arises from the implicit presumption underlying that approach: that *acts* of choice are, on their own, like *statements* which can contradict, or be consistent with, each other. That diagnosis is deeply problematic.

Statements *A* and *not-A* are contradictory in a way that choosing

x alone from $\{x, y\}$ and y alone from $\{x, y, z\}$ cannot be. If the pair of choice acts were to entail, respectively, the statements (1) x is a better alternative than y, and (2) y is a better alternative than x, then of course there would be a contradiction here (since 'being better than' is an anti-symmetric relation). But those choices do not *in themselves* entail any such statements (until some motivational presumptions are made). Given some ideas as to what the person is trying to do (this is an external correspondence), we might be able to interpret these actions as implied statements. But we cannot do that without invoking such an external reference. It is hard to think that there can be such a thing as *purely* internal consistency of choice.

Note also that even the apparently contradictory actions of 'saying A' and 'saying not-A' may not be really inconsistent in the way that the two statements themselves surely are. Indeed, depending on circumstances, the dual choice of 'saying A' and 'saying not-A' may well fit into canny behaviour patterns. For example, the person making the statements may want to be taken as mentally unsound, for example to establish diminished responsibility in a criminal case, or to be taken as unfit to stand trial. Or the person may simply want to confound the observer (there might be fun to be obtained there). Or want to satisfy his or her curiosity about how people react to apparently contradictory statements. The statements A and *not-A* do make a contradictory pair; the *speech acts* of saying them need not. Indeed, being consistent or not consistent is not the kind of thing that can happen to choice functions *without* interpretation – without a presumption about the context that takes us beyond the choices themselves.

At the practical level, how can we judge the cogency and even the coherence of a person's choices without some idea of what he or she is trying to do? A person choosing x and rejecting y on one occasion and going for y over x on another may well be inconsistent, as some axioms of choice theory would declare. But the person could instead have reason to choose a variety of experiences (having salmon for lunch and duck for dinner is not necessarily being inconsistent), and can have many different reasons for going home from work on a bus one day and by car on another. Trying to explain behaviour without reference to anything other than behaviour may not be a very smart epistemic or analytical approach to understanding the world. Different reasons may emerge that give individual choices quite distinct patterns and regularities.

However, Buchanan was right to argue that social choices made through decisional procedures for the society need not be checked for straightforward internal consistency, nor for the underlying 'social preference'. Procedure-based choices, even when very systematic, need not yield any 'underlying' specification of 'social preference'. We can also go further and question the wisdom of trying to impose some pre-conceived 'conditions of internal consistency' of people's behaviour in general – not just social preference. Since any choice act can be based on different kinds of reasons, depending on the motivations involved, we cannot invoke the idea of consistency without some presumptions – or understanding – of the motivations involved, and this need can make the consistency conditions – involving motivational reference – very different from demands of purely *internal* consistency of choice functions.

Chapter A2*
Problems of Social Choice

The possibility of eschewing the idea of social preference has received considerable attention in the literature of social choice theory in recent years. We need not bring in the binary relation of social ranking in specifying what may be chosen from different menus. A 'non-binary' formulation of social choice can work directly with a choice function for the society, which specifies the choosable alternatives $C(S)$ of which any one can be chosen for each particular menu S. The functional relation between the set of alternative menus S and the corresponding 'choice sets' $C(S)$ can be called the social choice function, and this need not invoke, at least explicitly, any binary relation of social preference. A 'functional collective choice rule' (FCCR) maps n-tuples of individual preference relations to a social choice function:

$$C(\cdot) = f(\{R_i\}).$$

How does this reformulation alter Arrow's impossibility result? In an obvious – and fairly trivial – sense, the impossibility theorem disappears with the use of a social choice function rather than social preferences, since the Arrow conditions, with the exception of independence of irrelevant alternatives, are relational demands. But along with the change of the social choice formulation, we must surely change Arrow's axioms into their 'corresponding' choice functional forms. What then?

A long series of contributions have explored this kind of reformulation, and regenerated the impossibility results (Arrow's and those inspired by his theorem) by adding some further conditions of consistency conditions for choices from different menus. Are these additional demands of internal consistency of choice really necessary for choice-functional translations of Arrow-type impossibilities?

In this chapter, we have to take up the following questions (among others):

(1) Can we characterize social choice functions that have some rationale of their own, and that are not dominated, if only implicitly, by the binary framework of choosing the 'most preferred' alternatives from the available menu?

(2) How can we translate Arrow's axioms into choice-functional forms appropriate for FCCRs, and possibly get to Arrow-type impossibility results through invoking additional conditions of inter-menu consistency (which can be seen as conditions of 'internal consistency' of choice functions)? Do these conditions of internal consistency take us back, if only implicitly, to preference-maximizing choice?

(3) Must the conditions of internal consistency be seen as demands of rationality, or of reasoned choice? More radically, does it make any sense at all to have 'internal consistency' of choice functions (without any external reference)?

(4) Can Arrow-type impossibilities be generated without invoking any condition of internal consistency, relying instead only on full translations of Arrow's axioms into appropriate non-binary choice functional formulations? In particular, can we get to the impossibility result without making any use of what Arrow called 'collective rationality'?

CLOSURES AND MAXIMALITY

I start by invoking the common mathematical idea of the 'transitive closure' of a binary relation, and then go on to examine the 'maximal' sets with respect to transitive closures. Consider a binary relation B. For intuitive understanding, we can think of B as a preference relation, even though the idea of a transitive closure applies to other interpretations as well. The transitive closure of B involves all binary relations we can get to through stringing together a sequence of that binary relation. The transitive closure B^* is obtained from the primitive binary relation B in the following way: xB^*y if and only if there is a sequence $z_1Bz_2, z_2Bz_3, \ldots, z_{k-1}Bz_k$, with $z_1 = x$, and $z_k = y$. For any binary relation B, the maximal subset $M(S, B)$ of a set S is the undominated subset of S with respect to the asymmetric factor B^A of B (xB^Ay being defined as xBy and *not* yBx).[1]

$$M(S,B) = [x \mid x \in S \,\&\, \text{not } \exists\, y \in S: yB^Ax].$$

We can generate two classes of maximal sets from the weak preference relation R, by looking respectively for (1) the maximal set with respect to the transitive closure R^* of the weak relation R, and (2) the maximal set with respect to the transitive closure P^* of the asymmetric factor P of R. They are respectively called 'weak closure maximality' and 'strong closure maximality'. It is easily checked that, in the particular case of the paradox of voting, both methods would generate a maximal set of all the three alternatives. However, in other cases, the two methods could yield possibly different results.[i]

ARROW AXIOMS FOR FCCR AND ESCAPE FROM IMPOSSIBILITY

These closure methods have been directly used or indirectly entailed in several contributions for the resolution of the Arrow dilemma through non-binary choice procedures.[ii] In what sense do these solutions resolve the Arrow paradox? Instead of demanding a social welfare function, they demand a social choice function,[iii] $g(S, \{R_i\})$, which specifies a non-empty subset $g(S, \{R_i\}) \subseteq S$, for every non-empty, finite $S \subseteq X$. This is essentially equivalent to making the value of the function $f(\{R_i\})$ a finitely complete choice function $C(\cdot)$ for the

---

[1] B^* is often called the ancestral of B (see Quine (1940) and Herzberger (1973)). The term 'ancestral' goes back to A. N. Whitehead and Bertrand Russell, and the concept back at least to Gottlob Frege in the nineteenth century.

society, and not – as with social welfare functions or social decision functions – a social preference relation R.

For such an FCCR $f(\cdot)$, the Arrow conditions can be readily translated in several distinct ways. The translation that has often been used (the limitations of which will be discussed later), takes the form of restricting choices over pairs only.

Condition $\hat{U}$ (unrestricted domain):

The domain of $f(\cdot)$ includes all logically possible n-tuples of individual orderings of X.

Condition $\hat{P}$ (pair-choice Pareto principle):

For all $x, y, \in X$, $(\forall i : \& \, xP_iy) \Rightarrow \{x\} = C(\{x, y\})$

Condition $\hat{D}$ (pair-choice non-dictatorship):

There is no individual i such that for all n-tuples in the domain of $f(\cdot)$ and for all preference profiles $\{R_i\}$, for each ordered pair $x, y \in X$, $xP_iy \Rightarrow \{x\} = C(\{x, y\})$.

The non-dictatorship condition can, in fact, be strengthened to a non-vetoer condition, and further extended to a condition of full anonymity.

Condition $\hat{A}$ (anonymity):

If $\{R_i\}$ is a permutation of $\{R'_i\}$, then $f(\{R_i\}) = f(\{R'_i\})$.

These conditions can now be combined with Arrow's independence of irrelevant alternatives (Condition I), which was already defined in choice-functional terms by Arrow (as was discussed in Chapter A1*).

(T.A2*.1) Choice-functional positive possibility theorem

For $\#H \geq 2$, there is an FCCR satisfying Conditions $\hat{U}$, I^A, $\hat{P}$, $\hat{D}$, and $\hat{A}$.

The reasoning behind the theorem can be seen by considering a particular example, e.g. the procedure generated by weak closure maximality or by strong closure maximality, applied to the majority rule relation R. The same operations can also be applied to other Pareto-inclusive, non-dictatorial, non-acyclic relations, of which there are plenty.

Consider the famous paradox of voting, with person 1 preferring

x to y and that to z, person 2 preferring y to z and that to x, and person 3 ranking the three alternatives in the order z, x, y. There is a strict preference cycle here, and each alternative is defeated in a majority vote by another alternative. However, moving away from preference maximization, consider maximality in terms of the transitive closures of preference relation. The procedure of weak as well as strong closure maximality identifies the following choices:

$$C(\{x, y\}) = \{x\}, C(\{y, z\}) = \{y\}, C(\{z, x\}) = \{z\}, \text{ and } C(\{x, y, z\}) = \{x, y, z\}.$$

This choice function is, of course, defiantly non-binary, but it meets all the choice-functional Arrow axioms, as defined above.

CONSISTENCY, BINARINESS AND ORDERINGS

Before we proceed further we should consider the relationship between a choice function and the binary relation it may be seen as generating through choice behaviour. Consider a choice function over a finite set X. To be able to choose from any non-empty finite subset S of X, $C(S)$ is taken to be non-empty. This is a basic requirement of the existence of a choice function. In addition we would have reason to consider what can be sensibly chosen from any subset. In the standard formulation of choice based on the maximization of some objective function, subject to constraints, the choice would be governed by the nature of the objective function. The relation of what is chosen from different subsets with the objective function can be called an 'external correspondence', since the objective function is not part of the data from the choice function itself – it is 'external' to choice. In contrast, an internal consistency condition of choice – discussed in Chapter A2 – relates choice from one menu to the choice from another, and such a consistency condition is clearly 'internal' to choice behaviour, or – more formally – 'internal' to the choice function.[iv]

Conditions of consistency of choice demand that the choices from different menus should be 'consistently' related to each other – and the rub lies in the idea of consistency. In most exercises, the consistency requirements fall into two essentially different categories (though they are sometimes combined), viz. *contraction* consistency and *expansion* consistency. The former deals with requirements of the kind that demand that something chosen from a set must – under certain conditions to be specified – continue to be chosen when the menu offered is *contracted*. The latter, on the other hand, insists that something chosen from a set must – under circumstances to be specified – continue to be chosen when the menu offered is *expanded*.

The most-used contraction consistency condition is called Property α (also called the Chernoff condition), while the natural complement of that condition is a requirement of expansion consistency which is called Property γ.[2] The set of definitions that follows are specified for all $x, y \in x$ and all $S, T \subseteq X$.

Property α (basic contraction consistency):

$$[x \in C(S) \ \& \ x \in T \subseteq S] \Rightarrow x \in C(T)$$

Property γ (basic expansion consistency):

$$[x \in C(S_j) \text{ for all } S_j \text{ in any class of subsets of } X] \Rightarrow x \in C(\cup_j S_j)$$

These two properties together make the choice function essentially binary in the sense that its informational content can be exactly captured by a binary relation R defined on X. Note that a choice function can be built up *from* a binary relation – we may find it convenient to think of it as a preference relation. On the other hand, a choice function can also be used – going in the 'converse' direction (from choice to relation) – to identify an underlying binary relation. This generated relation is sometimes called 'revealed preference'.

Consider the two-way correspondence between choice and binary relations. First we go from a binary relation R to a generated choice function $\hat{C}(S, R)$:

$$\hat{C}(S, R) = [x \mid x \in S \ \& \ \forall y \in S: xRy]$$

---

[2] Property α (basic contraction consistency) was defined in Chapter 1* in the 1970 edition of this book.

Consider now the opposite problem of constructing a binary relation of preference from a choice function. There are at least two distinct natural claimants to this role, viz. the revealed preference relation R_C given by choices over all subsets of X containing the pair that is being ranked, and the base relation $\bar{R}_C$ given by the choice exactly over that pair, i.e. what is chosen from the pair $\{x, y\}$.

Revealed preference relation

$$x R_C y \text{ if and only if } \exists S: [x \in C(S) \ \& \ y \in S].$$

Base relation

$$x \bar{R}_C y \text{ if and only if } x \in C(\{x, y\}).$$

It is obvious that $x\bar{R}_C y \Rightarrow xR_C y$, but in general not the converse.

Now, consider the elementary condition of internal consistency specified earlier, called Property α. That simple condition does imply the converse, i.e. guarantees that $xR_C y \Rightarrow x\bar{R}_C y$, since the pair $\{x, y\}$ is a subset of any set containing x, y and other alternatives, thereby mobilizing Property α. So, given α, we must have $R_C = \bar{R}_C$.

A choice function $C(S)$ will be defined as 'binary' (sometimes also called 'rationalizable') if and only if the revealed preference relation R_C generated by $C(S)$ generates back the same choice function $C(S)$ itself. It is called 'basic binary' if and only if the base relation $\bar{R}_C$ generated by it can generate back $C(S)$.

Binariness of choice function
$$C(S) = \hat{C}(S, R_C) \text{ for all } S \subseteq X.$$

Basic binariness of choice function
$$C(S) = \hat{C}(S, \bar{R}_C) \text{ for all } S \subseteq X.$$

Binariness lemma

A finitely complete choice function is binary if and only if it is basic binary, and also, if and only if it satisfies Properties α and γ.[3]

---

[3] See Sen (1971), Herzberger (1973) and Suzumura (1983). As Stig Kanger (1975) has pointed out, binariness in this sense is a very limited interpretation of 'choice based on preference'. More generally the chosen elements from a set A can be made

There are some alternative conditions of expansion consistency. A few are considered here, of which *Property β* was discussed earlier in Chapter 1* (in the original 1970 version of this book, included here).

Property β

$$[x, y \in C(T) \ \& \ T \subseteq S] \Rightarrow [y \in C(S) \Leftrightarrow x \in C(S)].$$

If both x and y are chosen in T, a subset of S, then one of them (say, y) cannot be chosen in S without the other (i.e. x) being also chosen from that larger set.

Property β can be *weakened* through replacing the consequent by demanding only that y be not chosen *exclusively* in S, whether or not x is among the chosen elements of T.

Property δ

$$[x, y \in C(T) \ \& \ T \subseteq S] \Rightarrow \{y\} \neq C(S).$$

We can quickly note two results without pausing for proofs (but they can be found in Sen 1971).

Transitivity lemma: A finitely complete choice function is binary with a transitive binary relational representation if and only if it satisfies Properties α and β.

Since completeness and reflexivity are not in doubt here, given the assumptions, this implies that Properties α and β are necessary and sufficient for being able to represent the choice function by an ordering relation (reflexive, transitive and complete).

Quasi-transitivity lemma: A finitely complete choice function is binary with a quasi-transitive binary relational representation if it satisfies Properties α, γ and δ.

The *Transitivity lemma* immediately helps us to extend the

---

to depend on a binary relation P_v that depends on the specification of a background set V. Binariness, as defined here, corresponds to taking $V = A$. Kanger (1975) provides a rich analysis of the more general case of choice based on preference.

Arrow impossibility theorem to social choice functions through imposing internal consistency conditions in the form of Properties α and β.

(T.A2*.2) Choice-functional impossibility theorem with consistency conditions α and β.

If H is finite and $\#X \geq 3$, then there is no FCCR satisfying Conditions $\hat{U}$, $\hat{P}$, I^A and $\hat{D}$, and generating choice functions satisfying conditions α and β.

The imposition of the conditions α and β will make the choice function binary with respect to a transitive ranking, in fact an ordering, and it is easily checked that Arrovian axioms, translated into FCCRs, will demand the Pareto principle and the non-dictatorship condition applied to the base relation $\bar{R}_C$. Further, the Arrovian Independence condition I^A must apply *inter alia* to sets of all pairs as well. The rest is a simple translation of Arrow's Impossibility Theorem, relational as it is, into this choice functional form, focusing on choices over pairs.

Similarly, all the other relational impossibilities, discussed in Chapter A1* (and in the literature cited there), have choice functional translations, including Allan Gibbard's oligarchy theorem.

(T.A2*.3) Choice-functional oligarchy theorem with consistency conditions α and δ.

If H is finite and $\#X \geq 3$, then any FCCR satisfying Conditions $\hat{U}$, $\hat{P}$, I^A and generating choice functions satisfying α and δ must be oligarchic.[v]

I end this discussion with four remarks. First, even though the combinations of conditions used here generate binariness of the choice function, it is not necessary to go that far in translating the relational impossibility results presented in Chapter A1* into corresponding choice functional forms. In fact, in the proofs needed for the respective theorems, the binariness property need not be invoked at all, and the whole discussion can take place in terms of choices over pairs, allowing us to interpret the relational conditions as demands on base relations $\bar{R}_C$. What are important for the proofs are, respectively, the transitivity and quasi-transitivity of the base relation of the choice function $\bar{R}_C$, whether or not that relation is embedded in a binary choice function.[4]

Second, even though I have presented here the choice functional translations of only a couple of relational impossibility results, these results all have choice functional translations through the use of appropriate conditions of internal consistency of social choice (Sen (1986a)).

Third, each of the weakening of the full transitivity conditions of the revealed preference has been considered here for complete rankings, without allowing weakenings that can come from relaxing the completeness requirement. As was discussed in Chapter A1*, a different class of weakening has been considered and explored by Suzumura, Bossert and others through dropping completeness. In particular, what has come to be called 'Suzumura consistency' differs substantially from transitivity, but coincides with it for complete (and reflexive) rankings. Suzumura consistency can be defined in choice functional terms (paralleling what was discussed in binary relational terms in Chapter A1*). It opens up an important avenue of social choice explorations in line with Suzumura's (2016) foundational work on rational choice.

Fourth, all the choice functional extensions of Arrow-type impossibility results rely critically on imposing internal consistency conditions on social choice functions. All these choice functional extensions are, therefore, subject to Buchanan's (1954a) reasoned scepticism about the rationale of having such conditions *at all* in the case of choices generated by social decision mechanisms.

And we can extend the scrutiny further, in the way already outlined in Chapter A2, examining whether the entire approach of internal consistency is not itself fragile because of the lack of an adequate intellectual rationale. In the rest of this chapter, I shall pursue the general sceptical scrutiny further, and end with the big question: would there be anything left of the Arrow impossibility

---

[4] There is a fairly extensive discussion of this question in my survey article in the *Handbook of Mathematical Economics* (Sen (1986b)), particularly in section 4.2 ('The Unimportance of Binariness in Arrow's Impossibility'), pp. 1094–7.

theorem if we withhold all internal consistency conditions altogether? The positive answer to that question – to be established presently – is of some importance, if only to recognize that the cogency of Buchanan's critique does not eliminate the basic issue of impossibility brought out by Arrow's foundational theorem.

CRITIQUE OF INTERNAL CONSISTENCY OF CHOICE

We can begin by questioning the idea of 'internal consistency' conditions of choice, and ask whether we can think of circumstances where the violation of those conditions would be the reasonable thing to do. In Chapter A2 we considered a case in which perhaps the most elementary condition of internal consistency, Property α, is violated. In particular, take the same example, now written more formally:

$$\{x\} = C(\{x, y\}),$$
$$\{y\} = C(\{x, y, z\}).$$

This pair of choices violates many of the standard conditions of internal consistency – not only Property α, but also (related to the violation of Property α) the axioms of revealed preference and the requirements of binariness of choice. And it might indeed appear odd – and 'contrary to reason' – that a person who chooses x (rejecting y) given the choice over x and y, can sensibly choose y (rejecting x) when z is added to the menu.

Is this innocuous-looking intuition really reasonable? In some cases it might be cogent enough, but in many cases the presumption of inconsistency can be easily disputed, depending on the context – if we know a bit more about what the person is trying to do (see Sen 1997a). Suppose the person faces a choice at a dinner table between having the last remaining apple in the fruit basket (y) and having nothing instead (x), foregoing the nice-looking apple. She decides to behave decently and picks nothing (x), leaving the one apple (y) for another person to enjoy. If, instead, the basket had contained two apples, and she had encountered the choice between having nothing (x), having one nice apple (y) and having another nice one (z), she could reasonably enough choose the apple (y), without violating any rule of good behaviour. The presence of another apple (z) makes one of the two apples decently choosable in good social behaviour, but this combination of choices would violate the standard consistency conditions, including Property α, even though there is nothing particularly 'inconsistent' in this pair of choices (given the person's values and scruples).

To take another example in the same general line (see Sen (1997a)), suppose the person is choosing between slices of cake offered to him, and he chooses x from $\{x, y\}$, and y from $\{x, y, z\}$, as described in this case. If he is simply trying to get the largest possible slice (an external correspondence), *then* – given that the sizes are all linearly ordered and easily assessed – he is indeed making some mistake. But suppose, instead, that he is trying to choose as large a slice as possible, subject to not picking the very largest, because he does not want to be taken as greedy, or because he would like to follow a social convention or a principle learned at his mother's knee: 'never pick the largest slice'. If the three slices in decreasing order were z, y, x, then he is behaving exactly correctly according to that principle – always choosing the second largest. We cannot determine whether the person is failing in any way without knowing what he is trying to do, that is, without knowing something external to the choice itself.[vi]

Notice, also, that the person who chooses an apple when another one is around (but not if it is the *last* one), or the person who tries to get as large a cake slice as possible (subject to its being *not the very largest*), is, in some basic sense, a *maximizer*. The ordering of the alternatives on the basis of which he or she is maximizing varies with the menu, but this does not deny that for *each menu* there is a clear and cogent ordering – the basis of the maximizing decisions. The principle is that of choosing the best rather than the largest – and the best depends critically on the contents of the menu (not on a menu-independent ranking of the size of the cake slices, or the presence of an apple). So the conditions he or she is violating, which are standardly presumed to be necessary conditions for maximization, need not be taken to be so for a broader interpretation of maximization.

Violations of Property α, and other common conditions of 'internal consistency', can be related to various different types of reason – easily understandable when the external context is spelled out.

(1) *Positional choice*: This was illustrated with the case of not wishing to take the last apple, or the largest slice of cake. Similarly, there may be a preference for not being the first to quit a job, cross a picket line, or break an implicit contract, while wanting to do so if the qualification is met.

(2) *Epistemic value of the menu*: What is offered for choice can give us information about the underlying situation, and can thus influence our preference over the alternatives, *as we see them*. For example, the chooser may learn something about the person offering the choice on the basis of what he or she is offering. To illustrate, given the choice between having tea at a distant acquaintance's home (x), and not going there (y), a person who chooses to have tea (x), may nevertheless choose to stay away (y), if offered – by that acquaintance – a choice over having tea (x) and having some cocaine (z). The menu offered may provide information about the situation – in this case say something about the distant acquaintance – and this can quite reasonably affect the ranking of the alternatives x and y, and yield the pair of choices being scrutinized here. It is, of course, true that the chooser has different information even about x (i.e. having tea with the acquaintance) when the acquaintance gives him the choice of having cocaine with him, and it can certainly be argued that in the 'intentional' (as opposed to 'extensional') sense, the alternative x is no longer the same. But an 'intentional' definition of alternatives would be, in general, quite hopeless in invoking inter-menu consistency, especially when (as in this case) the intentional characterization changes precisely with the alternatives available for choice, that is, with the menu offered.

(3) *Freedom to reject*: Some choices are geared to rejecting – in a free way – particular actions or outcomes in favour of a prominent

alternative. For example, fasting is not just starving, but deliberately starving when the freedom to eat well does exist. The point of fasting in the form of not eating (y), given the possibility of eating well (z), may become less clear when the only alternative is to be partly famished anyway (x). This too can yield the choices in the form being discussed here.

In general, this type of consideration (and other issues that invoke freedom) suggest that we see a chosen alternative x not as just x, but as x/S, that is, x chosen from the set S (possibly specifying which alternatives are rejected). Obviously, inter-menu consistency conditions are hard to invoke here (except with vacuous fulfilment), since with a change of the menu S the alternative available for choice x/S also changes.

There can be other interpretations that make sense of the choice configurations being examined. Even a desire to violate, deliberately, standard conditions of consistent behaviour could play a part, with odd motivations such as confusing the observer ('his jaw dropped!'), or to perplex an experimental economist. Fun comes to people in all kinds of unsuspected ways. These frivolous-looking examples are not always that frivolous – Sherlock Holmes had some insights to offer in dodging Professor Moriarty.

As Donald Davidson has noted, in a different context, the 'pro attitude' towards an action may include 'desires, wantings, urges, promptings, and a great variety of moral views, aesthetic principles, economic prejudices, social conventions, and public and private goals and values' (Davidson 1980, pp. 3–4). Once the external correspondences are seen as relevant, the plurality of such correspondences and the variety of forms they can take must be accommodated in investigating the implied conditions of internal correspondences. And, given this plurality, the possibility of getting one set of 'internal consistency' conditions that would invariably 'work' is extremely limited. The methodological problems in making sense of 'internal consistency' of choice are reinforced by the practical difficulty in getting some 'standard' conditions of 'internal correspondence' that might be unvaryingly justified by 'pro attitudes'.

INDIVIDUAL AND SOCIAL PREFERENCES

I return now to the subject of social choice theory, which involves the notion of individual preference as well as that of social choice. Consistency conditions are typically applied to each, but there is some asymmetry between the two. For one thing, it is possible to talk about an 'individual's preference' in simple descriptive terms in a way that is not so easy for 'the society's preference'. When individuals have clear preference orderings, the internal correspondences for the individual choice functions can be obtained as entailment relations without too much problem. On the other hand, ambiguities regarding what the society can be seen as preferring make it rather more difficult to deduce internal correspondences for choice functions for the society.

Indeed, the case for having a fuller reflection of this asymmetry between individual and social preference (and choice) was forcefully presented, as was mentioned earlier, in a penetrating critique by James Buchanan (1954a), who pointed to 'the fundamental philosophical issues' involved in 'the idea of social rationality'.[vii] This is a big topic which cannot be adequately discussed here (see, however, Sen 2002a), but it is important to examine whether results such as Arrow's impossibility theorem can be established without relying on 'the idea of social rationality'.

In fact, in dealing with the establishment of impossibility theorems (like that of Arrow), there is also a more immediate (though less profound) reason for having such an asymmetry. An impossibility theorem about the existence of social choice procedures will be standardly more general (and also harder to establish) over (1) a *narrower domain* (i.e. with a more limited class of admissible n-tuples of individual preferences over which the procedure has to work), and (2) a *wider range* (i.e. a larger class of permitted choice functions for the society which the procedure can use). In what follows, I shall take individual preferences to be all complete orderings (as Arrow did), making the domain narrow, but drop not only the idea of social preference but also all requirements of internal consistency of choice functions for the society, thereby making the range wide. If we were to allow instead the possibility that individual preferences themselves need not be orderings, then the same impossibility result would *a fortiori* hold, since a *broader* domain – allowing other combinations of individual preferences – cannot nullify the impossibility result established over a more limited domain.

RE-EXAMINING ARROW'S AXIOMS IN A CHOICE-BASED FRAMEWORK

Arrow's (1951a), (1952), (1963) 'General Possibility Theorem' was stated in the relational form for a *social welfare function*, except that the social ranking R that is generated must be an ordering (fully transitive as well as complete and reflexive). Since the social choices, in this framework, are determined by binary comparison through an ordering, they satisfy all kinds of conditions of 'internal consistency'. But these are *entailed* conditions (derived from the maximization based on the ordering relation); there is no *imposed* internal consistency here.

Arrow (1951a) did, however, link up the exercise of social valuation with that of social choice, and tied the binary relation of 'social preference' (satisfying 'collective rationality') to the corresponding choice functions, noting that 'one of the consequences of the assumption of rationality is that the choice to be made from any set of alternatives can be determined by the choices made between pairs of alternatives' (pp. 19–20). The exacting nature of choice based on fully transitive social orderings has attracted a good deal of attention in social choice theory, and in Chapter A1* we scrutinized the consequences – in terms of generating a class of impossibility results – of imposing various properties of the social preference relation: transitivity, quasi-transitivity, acyclicity, and so on.

The interrelations between these internal conditions of choice imposed on choice functions and the generated binary relations were investigated in the previous sections of this chapter. These imposed consistency conditions connect the choice functional properties to the 'collective rationality' of *as if* social preferences. The question to be examined now is whether the imposed internal consistency conditions can be dropped altogether without negating Arrow-type impossibility results.

How can this be done without adding something to the demands made on social choice? The answer lies in characterizing the external correspondence between individual preferences and social choice, making full use of the motivation behind the Arrow axioms. In particular, the Pareto principle simply links individual preferences over pairs to social choice over the pairs, and so does the condition of non-dictatorship. To recollect definitions earlier given:

Condition $\hat{P}$ (pair-choice Pareto principle):

For all $x, y, \in X, (\forall i: xP_iy) \Rightarrow \{x\} = C(\{x, y\})$

Condition $\hat{D}$ (pair-choice non-dictatorship):
There is no individual i such that for all n-tuples in the domain of $f(\cdot)$, for each ordered pair $x, y \in X, xP_iy \Rightarrow \{x\} = C(\{x, y\})$.

The condition of unrestricted domain is stated in much the same way as in Arrow's formulation.

In the variant of Arrow's impossibility theorem to be proved here, the idea behind the Arrovian revealed preference relation P^C will be particularly used. However, note that P^C, even though interpretable as strong revealed preference (x chosen and y rejected from some set), need not really be asymmetric in the absence of 'internal consistency' conditions. In the absence of inter-menu consistency, we cannot rule out that x may be chosen and y rejected from one set S, and y chosen and x rejected from another set T. This problem will not arise if we consider choices over one *given* set, relating the permissible social choices over that set to the different individual preference n-tuples that may occur. That is the way we shall proceed here, and will consider only one set of alternatives over which social choice is being characterized.

We need, therefore, a concept of Arrovian revealed preference P^C in terms of the rejection of a non-preferred alternative over a particular set S.

Set-specific Arrovian revealed preference: If for a specified set S containing both x and y, x is chosen and y rejected, then x is revealed preferred to y for set S, denoted $x\,P_S^C\,y$.

The modified version of Arrow's impossibility result will be proved here for any *fixed set S of social states*, without even raising the question of inter-menu consistency. But it must be recognized that the result will apply to *all* such sets (containing three or more distinct states) taken on their own – and there is no limitation of domain over sets of alternatives that is being devised or contemplated here.

ARROW IMPOSSIBILITY WITHOUT COLLECTIVE RATIONALITY

Consider the format of functional collective choice rules (FCCR), defined as: $C(S) = F(\{R_i\})$. Along with Arrow, we assume that there is a finite set H of individuals (n of them) and that the set S of alternative social states has at least three distinct elements.

In the relational framework, a set of individuals is decisive over a pair $\{x, y\}$ if and only if whenever everyone in that set strictly prefers x to y, we have xPy for the society as a whole. In translating this into choice functional terms we can concentrate on the power of a group to *reject* a non-preferred alternative.

Rejection decisiveness: A subset G of individuals is decisive over an ordered pair $\{x, y\}$ for a set S containing both, denoted $D_S^G(x, y)$, if and only if for every possible n-tuple of individual orderings: ($xP_i\,y$ for all i in G) entails that y must not be chosen from S. If G is rejection decisive over every ordered pair in S, then G is called rejection decisive over S, denoted D_S^G.

Of the four conditions in the binary version of the Arrow theorem, we have no problem with translating the demand of unrestricted domain (in this context, let us call it Condition U*). Nor is there any problem in seeing the Pareto principle in terms of rejection decisiveness – the set H of all individuals taken together is rejection decisive, that is, D^H_S. This only states that a strictly Pareto inferior alternative must not be chosen.

Further, Condition D^* of non-dictatorship can be re-characterized, through the notion of rejection decisiveness, in terms of the power to reject, again for a specified set S. It is done for each such set, even though for our proof here we can manage with the weaker demand by focusing on a particular set S.

Condition D^* (Rejection Non-dictatorship): *For any set S of social states, there exists no individual i who is rejection decisive over it.*

The remaining condition is that of independence of irrelevant alternatives. Arrow had defined it directly in choice functional terms, which we called condition I^A in Chapters A1 and A1*. This requires that if individual preferences over a set S of states remain the same, then the choice set $C(S)$ of S must also remain the same (Arrow (1951a); (1963, p. 27)). Changes in individual preferences over irrelevant alternatives must not affect the choice over S. For our present purpose, we do not need the full force of this exacting independence condition, but there is a need in particular to make sure that the rejection decisiveness of sets of individuals should not be compromised by changes in preferences over irrelevant alternatives. This requires strengthening the condition in this specific respect (along with a general weakening due to reducing the domain of the independence condition's applicability).

Take a subset G of individuals, and let them all prefer x to y. If for *every possible* ranking of this particular pair $\{x, y\}$ by *all* the other individuals (those not in G), there is an n-tuple of individual complete orderings (including rankings of the irrelevant alternatives) such that x must be chosen and y rejected from S, then G should be decisive over the pair $\{x, y\}$ for the set S. That is, the result that y be rejected from the set S should not be compromised by the influence of changes in the individual rankings of irrelevant alternatives (i.e. alternatives other than x and y). If, in an alternative scenario of individual preferences, some irrelevant alternative, say z, ends up being ranked high enough by the individuals compared with x, then there would, of course, be a case for not insisting on the selection of x from

S for that profile. But that would not alter the case for continuing to reject y from S which does contain x (whether or not vanquished for another individual preference profile by z). This demand (viz. that the power of rejection be independent of the preferences over irrelevant alternatives) forms the modified independence Condition I* to be used here.

Condition I* (Independent Decisiveness): *For any set S of social states, a set G of individuals is decisive over an ordered pair $\{x, y\}$, that is $D^G_S (x, y)$ provided the following condition holds: whenever $[xP_i y$ for all i in $G]$, for every possible combination of rankings of x and y by the individuals not in G, there is an n-tuple $\{R_i\}$ of complete orderings (extending those respective rankings of x and y) of all individuals such that $xP^C_S y$.*

To explain the requirement in another way, if the ability of members of group G, all of whom prefer x to y, to secure the rejection of y in the presence of x in S were to change with alterations in the individual rankings of alternatives *other than* x and y, then the power of rejection decisiveness would fail to be independent of irrelevant alternatives. Independent Decisiveness (I*) would not allow that to happen.

(T.A2*.4) (Choice-functional Arrow Impossibility Theorem): There is no F satisfying conditions U*, P*, D* and I*.

This is proved via two lemmas. In writing up the intermediate steps, we do not repeat that Conditions U*, P* and I* are being assumed (Condition D* is not needed at this stage).

Spread of Decisiveness Lemma: For all G, if $D^G_S (x, y)$ for some pair of states $\{x, y\}$ in S, then D^G_S, that is G is decisive over S.

Proof: We have to show that $D^G_S (x, y) \Rightarrow D^G_S (a, b)$, for all $\{a, b\}$. Take first the case in which $x = a$, so that it has to be demonstrated that $D^G_S (x, b)$. Let all members of G have $xP_i y$ and $yP_i b$. Individuals not in G share $yP_i b$, but can have any preference whatever between x and b. Also let everyone (whether or not in G) prefer x to all the other alternative states in S (other than x, y and b).

Given Condition P* (the rejection of Pareto inferior states), no alternative other than x, y, and b can be chosen from S. Nor, for the same reason, can b be chosen. By the decisiveness of G over $\{x, y\}$, y cannot be chosen either. Hence x must be chosen from S, as the only alternative that can be chosen. So we have $x\, P_S^c b$. Since the individuals not in G can have any ranking whatever between x and b, we conclude by Condition I* (independent decisiveness) that G is decisive over $\{x, b\}$ for the set S. Hence $D_S^G(x, y) \Rightarrow D_S^G(x, b)$.

By exactly similar reasoning, it is established that we must have $D_S^G(x, y) \Rightarrow D_S^G(a, y)$.

These two cases combined together permit deduction in all the other cases. If x, y, a, b are all distinct, then $D_S^G(x, y) \Rightarrow D_S^G(a, y) \Rightarrow D_S^G(a, b)$. For the case in which $x = b$ and $y = a$, we get, for some distinct z, $D_S^G(x, y) \Rightarrow D_S^G(x, z) \Rightarrow D_S^G(y, z) \Rightarrow D_S^G(y, x)$, which is the same as $D_S^G(a, b)$. The remaining cases, $D_S^G(a, x)$ and $D_S^G(y, b)$, are covered in exactly the same way, completing the proof of the lemma.

Thus if we know that a set G of persons is rejection decisive over any ordered pair in a set S, then it is rejection decisive over all the ordered pairs in that entire set S.

The next lemma turns to the contraction of decisive sets of people.

Contraction of Decisive Set: If some set G containing more than one individual is decisive over a set S of social states, then so is some proper subset of G.

Proof: Suppose not. Partition G into two proper subsets G^1 and G^2. It is adequate to show that either G^1 or G^2 must be decisive for any set S. Take states x, y and z in S. Let all persons in G^1 prefer x to y, and x to z (with y and z ranked in any way whatever), whereas all in G^2 prefer x to y, and z to y (with x and z ranked in any way whatever). Those not in G can have any preference ordering whatever, except that everyone (both in G and outside G) prefers x to all alternatives other than x, y and z (if any). By the Pareto rejection principle P*, no state other than x, y or z could be chosen from the set S.

Since all individuals in G rank x above y, we have (by D_S^G) that y must not be chosen from S. Note that all persons in G^2 prefer z to

y, and others (including those not in G^2) can rank that pair in any way whatever. If for *each* possible individual ranking of $\{z, y\}$, z must be chosen (and therefore $z P_S^C y$) for *some* n-tuple of individual preference orderings compatible with those rankings, then by independent decisiveness I*, G^2 is decisive over $\{z, y\}$ for set S. This, by the Spread of Decisiveness Lemma, would make G^2 decisive in general – and G^2 is, of course, a proper subset of G. This possibility, by hypothesis, is ruled out. Hence z is not chosen for *some* combination of individual rankings of $\{z, y\}$, for *all* preference n-tuples consistent with those rankings.

If z is not chosen, then x must be, since none of the other alternatives can be chosen, and hence $x P_S^C z$ in that case. By the preceding argument, this has to be the case for *all* possible n-tuples of complete individual orderings consistent with *some* combination of individual rankings of $\{z, y\}$. Since the rankings over $\{x, z\}$ were not restricted for anyone *not* in G^1 in any way whatever, this entails that for all such rankings of $\{x, z\}$, there is an n-tuple of individual preferences for which $x P_S^C z$ holds. Therefore, by independent decisiveness I*, we must conclude that G^1 is decisive over $\{x, z\}$ for S, and by the Spread of Decisiveness Lemma, G^1 is generally decisive over S. Thus either of the two proper subsets G^1 and G^2 of G must be decisive. This contradiction establishes the lemma.

Now the choice-functional Arrow impossibility theorem:

Proof of (T.A2*.4):   By the Pareto rejection principle P*, the set of all individuals is rejection decisive for any set S. By the lemma on the Contraction of Decisive Sets, some proper subset of this set will be rejection decisive also. Applying that contraction lemma again, there will be a proper subset of *that* which too will be decisive. By proceeding this way some individual will be shown to be decisive, since the set of all individuals is finite. That individual is, thus, a dictator, thereby violating the rejection of non-dictatorship condition D*, and this completes the proof.

ON ARROW'S IMPOSSIBILITY WITHOUT INTERNAL CONSISTENCY OF CHOICE

I make now four quick observations on this result. First, this proof really establishes a rather stronger result, of which (T.A2*.4) is an implication. What is shown is that, in any two-fold partition of a decisive set, either one part or its complement must be decisive.[5]

Second, the proof invokes only one set S of social states, and does not consider inter-menu consistency. This was adequate for our purpose, but it must be noted that the non-dictatorship condition D* is, as a result, stronger than Arrow's, in one important respect. It asks for the absence of an individual who could dictate the rejection of every state in a given set S, no matter what the other individuals prefer. This can be for any state S, but no concept of an inter-menu dictator has been used here.

Third, since only one set S of social states is used in the proof, the Pareto principle can be made correspondingly weaker, by restricting its applicability only to a *given* set S of three or more alternatives. It does not really matter whether we formally impose P^* or P^*_S; we apply it in either case to a *given* set S only.[6]

Fourth, this extension of Arrow's impossibility theorem not only does away with any imposed condition of 'internal consistency' of social choice, it also avoids altogether any requirement of 'collective rationality' in the form of a structured social preference relation (such as a transitive social preference ordering, as in Arrow's formulation).

---

[5] This is the 'ultra-filter' property of the topology of decisive sets which was discussed in Chapter A1*.

[6] Note that even if the Pareto principle or the independence condition is not restricted to a given set, this would not compromise the programme of eschewing *imposed* 'internal consistency' of social choice. Whatever inter-menu correspondences would be entailed by these conditions would be *implications* of external relations and not conditions of 'internal consistency' of social choice. But none of those *implied* inter-menu correspondences are, in fact, *used* in any way whatever in the proof. On related matters, see also Sen (1984), Matsumoto (1985), Denicolo (1985), (1987) and Baigent (1991a), (1991b).

CONCLUDING REMARKS

I have discussed in this chapter the approach of choice functional presentation of social choice in general and Arrow's impossibility theorem in particular. Reasons for avoiding the imposition of axioms of so-called 'internal consistency' of choice were discussed, and it was shown how this might be done. The alleged requirements of 'internal consistency' are conditions that demand that particular internal correspondences hold between different parts of a choice function, that is, between choices over different menus chosen from the set of alternatives.

The foundational difficulty with such conditions relates to the fact that choices are not, by themselves, statements that can or cannot be consistent with each other. Even speech acts are not equivalent to the contents of statements included in a speech. The cogency of so-called 'internal consistency' conditions cannot be assessed without seeing them in the context of some 'external correspondence', that is, some kind of demand originating outside the choice function itself (e.g. optimization according to an objective function).

Had the choice functional extension of the Arrow impossibility theorem been dependent on the invoking of conditions of internal consistency of choice, then some implicit use of collective rationality would have been involved. Theorem (T.A2*.4) shows that there is no such dependence. It turns out that neither internal consistency of social choice, nor any implicit idea of 'social preference' entailed by alleged 'collective rationality', is, in fact, the basic source of the impossibility problem identified by Arrow.

Chapter A3
Justice and Equity

In considering Arrow's (1951a) social welfare functions as a basis for judging social welfare, and for welfare economics in general, two questions immediately arise. First, why do the axioms presented by Arrow take no note of inequality or disparity or poverty, which – as we know from Arrow's other writings – have been among his major concerns as an economist? Why did he explore welfare economics with what would appear to be his hands tied behind his back? Second, why do we get into the impasse of Arrow's impossibility theorem so easily – a deadlock that has huge sticking power even when many of Arrow's axiomatic demands are relaxed (as the results presented in Chapters A1* and A2* demonstrate)? Is there a case for reformulating the social choice exercise in some radical way?

The first question is easy to answer by referring to the second. Once Arrow found – on his way to investigate the properties of social welfare based on individual preferences – that even the mild demands of regularity in the conditions of unrestricted domain, independence, Pareto principle and non-dictatorship were impossible to satisfy together, he could hardly have required that further demands – including those of equity or poverty-aversion – be also fulfilled, in addition to deadlocked conditions of regularity. Adding more demands when the ones already introduced – mild requirements of regularity – cannot be satisfied together would not have been a clever move.

Can it be said that one of the things we have learned from Arrow's impossibility theorem and related results, and the discussion and scrutiny that followed this mathematical development, is the need to alter the formulation of social choice problems, perhaps through broadening its informational base? I would argue that the short answer to the question is: yes. As was discussed in the Introduction, the informational inputs that the Arrovian formulation of social welfare functions allows us to use are extremely limited. While individual preferences – in an ordinal form – are used, no interpersonal comparisons of people's well-being, or any other comparative data about different people's respective advantages, are available for use in moving to social choice from individual preferences (though the individuals themselves remain, of course, free to use interpersonal comparisons of any kind they want in forming their own valuations).

Arrow had ruled out social use of interpersonal comparisons since he had followed the general consensus that had emerged in the 1940s that (as he put it) 'interpersonal comparison of utilities has no meaning' (Arrow (1951a), p. 9). The totality of the axiom combination used by Arrow had the effect of confining social choice procedures to rules that are, broadly speaking, of the voting type. And this is an awfully scanty informational basis for making social welfare judgements.

What happens if interpersonal comparisons of well-being are allowed into the informational basis of making social welfare judgements? If we can make comparisons between social states on the basis of interpersonally comparable information about different persons, many possibilities of making systematic social welfare judgements open up. Even 'ordinal' interpersonal comparisons, allowing only comparisons of levels but not of different persons' gains and losses, allow us to forge ahead. For example, from the priority of the worst-off that Rawls (1971) argues for in his 'Difference Principle', we certainly get a simple way of making social welfare judgements by ranking social states in terms of what would be better for those who are worst-off. And when we allow fuller, or more articulate, interpersonal comparisons, we can use many other types of social welfare assessment, including the classical approach of utilitarianism.[1] In this chapter, we shall have the opportunity to consider broadening the

---

[1] Use of interpersonal comparisons of well-being or advantages of different persons in making social judgements, to avoid Arrow's impossibility theorem, was one of the main proposals in the original 1970 version of this book.

informational framework further, allowing comparisons not merely of well-being, but also of other relevant interpersonal comparisons, such as human capabilities, or the extent of personal freedoms.

As was discussed in the Introduction, in between the general bad luck of there being a multiplicity of feasibilities (no identified 'right' solution) and what Arrow called 'the height of bad luck' with no feasible solution at all (the impossibility result), there lies the excellent possibility of having exactly one feasible solution – thereby identifying what we should go for. Once interpersonal comparisons are allowed into the informational basis of social welfare judgements, we typically have several possibilities that all satisfy Arrow's regularity requirements – and more. We have to choose between the different feasible solutions according to values that take us well beyond Arrow's regularity properties. This is exactly where our ethical concerns such as equity, or removal of deprivation, or enhancement of people's freedoms can enter into the discussion, and find a place in our critical scrutiny. Valuational decisions call for conscious – and discussable – reasoning about what we should value most.

INFORMATIONAL BASIS OF NORMATIVE JUDGEMENTS

It is useful to examine normative systems, including theories of justice, in terms of their respective informational bases. Each approach emphasizes some information about the states, achievements and opportunities of the people involved as being *central* to assessing justice and injustice in that society. Also, each theory *rules out* substantial use – or indeed any use – of information of many other types. For example, the utilitarian theory of justice attaches intrinsic importance to – and only to – the utilities of the individuals involved, and has no direct interest in the information about subjects such as the fulfilment or violation of rights or liberties, or about levels of incomes or affluence that people enjoy (even though there may be an *indirect* – and instrumental – utilitarian interest in rights or liberties and incomes because of their effects on individual utilities). Most forms of libertarianism, in contrast, concentrate on – indeed often only on – the fulfilment or violation of different kinds of rights and liberties, and of the right procedures, and attach no direct importance to levels of utilities or of incomes, or indeed of actual opportunities that people have.

It is particularly relevant in this context to examine two different but interrelated aspects of the informational basis of these theories, which I shall call *basal space* and *aggregation system*, respectively. The basal space of a theory of justice refers to the general class of variables to which the assessment of justice is sensitive under that theory, and (no less importantly) excludes other variables, even though these variables can be indirectly important through their causal influences on the basal space, or as informational proxies for unobserved basal variables. For example, the basal space for utilitarian theories of justice consists of the combinations of utilities of different individuals, and nothing else – rights, freedoms, opportunities, equal treatments – is valued except for instrumental reasons, or as proxies.[2]

The second aspect relates to the way discriminating use is made of the basal information in the respective theories of justice. For example, in the utilitarian theory, the utilities of the different individuals are simply added together to arrive at a utility sum-total, which serves as the basis of the relevant overall assessment of the social state. Exclusive reliance on the sum-total is called 'sum-ranking'. The system of aggregation through sum-ranking contrasts with, say, taking note of some measure of dispersion or inequality in addition to paying attention to the sum-total of the utilities of the different people.[i]

UTILITARIANISM AND WELFARIST JUSTICE

For well over a century welfare economics has been dominated by one particular approach: utilitarianism. It was initiated, in its modern

---

[2] The concept of utility is not uniform over different utilitarian theories, but all such theories deny the direct relevance of any variable that does not count as being part of its *particular* interpretation of utility.

form, by Jeremy Bentham (1789), and championed by such economists as Mill (1861), Sidgwick (1874), Edgeworth (1881), Marshall (1890) and Pigou (1920). Utilitarianism has been, in many ways, the 'official' theory of traditional welfare economics, and it tends to serve as the 'default programme' in mainstream welfare economic analysis: the theory that is implicitly summoned when no others are explicitly invoked.

Utilitarianism combines what we have been calling 'consequentialism', 'welfarism' and 'sum-ranking'. It is a result-oriented (and in that sense, consequentialist) theory that concentrates only on utility consequences (which is the informational base identified by welfarism), and, in particular, focuses on the sum-total of utilities (which is the demand that sum-ranking makes). The basal space of utilitarian evaluation consists of individual utilities. Utility is, in fact, a generic term, since the exact content of the space can differ depending on how 'utility' is defined (for example, whether as pleasure, or as fulfilled desires, or as representation of choice).

How acceptable is welfarism as a general basis of judgements of justice? One of the major limitations of this approach lies in the fact that the same collection of individual welfares may be associated with very different social arrangements, opportunities, freedoms and consequences. In one case, it may, for example, involve significant violations of accepted individual rights, but not in another case. The metric of utilities, particularly in its Benthamite form, cannot differentiate between the pain of torture and the pain of being taxed, but that identification goes against widely held values as well as mainstream ethical reasoning (even though some with a strong 'conservative' persuasion might be tempted by the view that taxation *is* indeed torture). So long as the utilities generated end up being the same (no matter through what process), utilitarianism demands that the two alternatives are treated as equivalent (and that no intrinsic importance be given to the radical differences between the distinct scenarios). This is an informational neglect for all welfarist approaches (whether we add the all-important utilities, or combine them in some other way). Utilitarianism is a special case of welfarism where the utility magnitudes are simply added up.

The informational neglect of non-utility information applies both to the disregard of overall freedoms (including what are sometimes called 'positive' freedoms), which may entail claims on others or on the state (e.g. the right to free elementary education, to unemployment insurance, or to basic health care), and to 'negative' freedoms, which demand non-interference by others (e.g. the requirements of personal liberty and autonomy).[ii] Welfarism's neglect of negative freedom (such as libertarian immunities) is obvious enough, but the positive – or over-all – freedoms are also neglected since they can be quite different from individual welfare achievements.

The informational limitation is made even stronger by the particular utilitarian interpretation of individual welfare, seeing it simply in terms of pleasures or desires, or as representations of choice. The last – utility as the real-valued representation of choice – does not, on its own, yield any obvious way of making interpersonal comparisons, since people do not get to choose between being one person or another. There have been fine attempts to close this gap through consideration of *hypothetical* choices – an approach pioneered by Vickrey (1945), (1960) and Harsanyi (1953), (1955). However, the resulting structure is not easy to apply in practice, even though it is quite useful as a conceptual device. In practice, the force of interpersonal comparison, which is necessary for using the utilitarian and other standard welfarist approaches, is sought – often implicitly – in the more classical understandings of utility as pleasure or as fulfilled desires.

Both the approaches rely ultimately on mental metrics – indicators of the extent of pleasure or of the strength of desire. The kind of scepticism that Lionel Robbins (1938) and others have expressed on this raises one type of problem. But this need not be an insuperable objection, since there are many practical ways in which we do make these comparisons, which need not take an all-or-nothing form.[iii] Furthermore, in recent years Kahneman (1990), (2000) and others have devised methods of making interpersonal comparison of mental metrics that have much epistemic plausibility within their own terms.

The difficulty with relying only, or primarily, on utility comparisons in the context of a theory of justice and in the assessment of inequality is not so much the problem of obtaining and disciplining this type of information, but the reliability of such mental statistics as fair reflections of what can be plausibly called the well-being of the persons involved. One very big problem arises from the mental adaptation that makes the extent of pleasure or the strength of desire a very unreliable guide to real deprivation. Our desires and expectations adjust to circumstances, particularly to make life bearable in adverse situations. The hopeless underdog does not lead a life of constantly desiring what he or she thinks is unfeasible, nor one of seeking pleasures that are unobtainable. Rather, the focus is on cutting desires to size and on taking joy from smaller successes. In so far as people in chronically deprived situations succeed in getting some attainable pleasures and in fulfilling their restrained desires, their deprivation may look less intense in the mental metrics of pleasures and desires, even when their lack of real opportunities continues unremedied.

The utilitarian calculus can, thus, be insensitive and unfair to those who are persistently deprived: oppressed minorities, social outcasts, exploited labourers, subjugated housewives, the severely disabled or the persistently unemployed. Indeed, aside from its effect on the utilitarian calculus, the utility-based notion of interpersonal comparisons is itself deeply problematic as the informational basis of social justice.

In addition to these general difficulties relating to various interpretations of 'welfarism' – and the reliance on utility comparisons – there are other problems for utilitarian theory that arise from the special limitations of 'sum-ranking', i.e. the procedure of aggregating collections of utilities simply by *addition*. A full-blooded utilitarian cannot differentiate two distributions of the same total utility. For example, it makes no difference in utilitarian evaluation whether one person has ten units of utility and another has two, or both have six units of utility each. This lack of concern with the distribution of welfares can indeed be seen as one of the various limitations of utilitarianism.

To be sure, sum-ranking does not eliminate a tendency towards seeking less unequal distributions of *incomes* (as opposed to utilities). When everyone is attributed the same utility function, with diminishing marginal utility from income (technically a utility function that is 'concave' on income), there would be a general case for more equal distributions of income when the total income to be distributed remains the same. However, even within this framework, it can be argued that, of the two reasons for abjuring income inequality, only one receives recognition in the utilitarian approach. Income inequality is *inefficient* in generating high utility sums given a shared utility function of this type – with diminishing marginal utility with increasing income. Of this utilitarianism takes good note. But income inequality can also be seen as *iniquitous* in generating disparities in the basal space of utilities. And in this utilitarianism, with sum-ranking, has no particular interest. This problem can be very big in the case of people with severe handicaps, or other strong disadvantages. In this perspective, equitable treatment calls for a framework that demands a rejection of sum-ranking as well as of welfarism, both of which are constitutive features of utilitarianism.

PROCEDURAL APPROACHES AND LIBERTARIAN THEORIES OF JUSTICE

The informational basis of utilitarian theory can be disputed for different reasons related to its axiomatic foundations, *viz.* consequentialism, welfarism and sum-ranking. The class of procedural theories of justice concentrate in particular on disputing consequentialism. For example, a theory that would see the requirements of justice only in terms of the operation of some rules (no matter what the consequences of these rules are) would be an example of a procedural theory. When very general rules are chosen, such as equal treatment in law and in the allocation of political rights, such a procedural theory of justice may go with widely different states of affairs, but the claim made by such a theory is that the variations in the actual state of affairs are not matters of justice. A good illustration would be Robert Nozick's famous argument that any 'patterning' of the outcome is not really a task of justice.

It is this indifference to consequent states of affairs, and in particular to the pleasures and pains that people end up having, which Jeremy Bentham (1789) argued was totally unacceptable. And this concern gave him the motivational justification for working towards his consequentialist theory of justice – choosing utilitarianism in particular – by adding welfarism and sum-ranking to consequentialism in a pure form. As a counterpoint, exclusively procedural theories of justice, in absolutely pure form – with total neglect of consequences – are relatively uncommon today (Nozick's libertarian theory is something of an exception). However, within a broadly procedural structure, the relevant rules can be made more or less sensitive to consequential concerns.

For example, 'equality of opportunity' can have both procedural and consequentialist demands, but much would depend on how 'opportunity' is defined. If, for instance, it is only required that no one be excluded from buying something which he or she can pay for (e.g. no one be excluded from the use of markets on grounds of race, gender or colour), there is a clear procedural demand here which can be very appealing – and also very important in many contexts. However, it may not be of great practical interest to a very poor person who cannot afford to buy that commodity anyway. Similarly, the requirement that jobs be open to all via open competition on the basis of qualifications does guarantee an important type of non-discrimination, but it does not do much for someone who did not have the opportunity to get the right kind of schooling which would allow him or her to acquire the necessary qualifications.

This kind of asymmetry can be removed by including within the demands of equality of opportunity something that makes sure that opportunities of schooling are similar or symmetrical. While this will eliminate another source of bad luck, even this will not help a person who does not have the economic means to make good use of the schooling opportunities – or the use of the acquired skill – because of economic pressures on his or her life. These issues will demand further broadening of the requirements of equality of opportunity (on which see Fleurbaey (1995a), (1995b), (2008), Fleurbaey and Maniquet (2011a), (2011b), (2012), and also Fleurbaey and Peragine (2013) – a powerful line of research that has broadened the reach of welfare economics very substantially).

Perhaps the most sharply defined class of procedural theories of justice consist of libertarian theories. While various libertarian arguments against utilitarianism and egalitarianism have been presented for a long time (some of the finest arguments were propounded by John Stuart Mill in 1859), it is only recently that fully worked out libertarian theories have been offered in the professional literature, particularly by Robert Nozick (1973), (1974). They have drawn on earlier – more general – concerns (for example, those analysed by Hayek (1960)), but they have gone on to make liberty and rights the constitutive components of an exclusive basal space.

The basal space of rights in the formulation chosen by Nozick (1974) consists of the fulfilment or violation of different rights. Since these judgements, as formulated in the theory, are not of the 'more or less' kind, but of the 'zero-one' type (either a right is violated, or it is not), the metric of the space is quite compressed. The aggregation system seeks the fulfilment of all the specified rights, and if there is violation of any such rights, there is a failure of justice. No trade-offs are accommodated within this approach.

Once this basic system is honoured and the extended demands of liberty, as interpreted, met, libertarianism permits the introduction of other concerns, even those of utilities, at a lower level of decisional status, 'if there are any choices left to make' (as Nozick famously put it).[iv] There can thus be a hierarchy of spaces, but the most powerful basal space, in this approach, is that of liberties and rights of various kinds. What is at issue in this theory of justice, therefore, is an extreme *priority of rights and liberties*.

In the purely libertarian theory, an extensive class of rights are treated as non-relaxable constraints that must be fulfilled and which, accordingly, bind political action.[v] They cannot be overridden by other goals, including that of better satisfying other objectives, or, for that matter, other rights.[3] People's entitlements related to their libertarian rights cannot be outweighed by the nature of their results – even when those results are clearly rather nasty. This version of libertarianism is thus quite insensitive to the actual social consequences of these

---

[3] These stark requirements are somewhat qualified by Nozick (1974) in the case of 'catastrophic moral horrors', and more qualifications have been introduced since then in Nozick (1989).

constraints and requirements. This insensitivity can be particularly problematic since the actual consequences of libertarian entitlements include the possibility of results that must be seen as quite terrible. For example, as I have discussed elsewhere (Sen (1981)), even large famines can occur without anyone's libertarian rights being violated: those who are destitute and unemployed may starve precisely because their entitlements do not give them enough food to eat (on this see Sen (1981) and Drèze and Sen (1989)).

It is hard to argue that a libertarian theory, with its extremely narrow informational focus and its neglect of human welfare and misery, can provide an adequate theory of justice in general, and, in particular, a sufficient theory for analysing inequality and inequity. There is, of course, a kind of 'egalitarianism' implicit in Nozick's libertarianism, to wit, everyone's liberties count – and count the same. But this basic equality has a very special coverage, given the nature of its basal space, and the demand for equality does not go beyond everyone having the same right to liberty in the form of constraints on the actions of others. The theory builds on a reasoned intuition which many people have: that liberty is rather special and must not be substitutable by other kinds of individual advantages. When, for example, we hear of a person being killed by a religious extremist, or by a racist mob, or by an oppressive state, we have reason to be more upset than we might be when we hear of a death caused by an accident or a natural event, even though the principal end-result, in a limited sense, is much the same (i.e. the death of the respective victim).

However, it can be argued that the acknowledgement of this asymmetry is not ground enough to give liberty irresistible force over all other concerns (such as the removal of abject poverty). Nor does it give us reason to demand the same priority for a whole class of other putative rights, which relate importantly to the functioning of economic instruments (like the role of property rights, including exchange and bequeathal, for the working of the market mechanism). But giving property rights the same status as personal liberty, as many versions of libertarianism seem inclined to do, can be seen as extending, well beyond its natural habitat, the traditional demands of personal liberty of the kind that John Stuart Mill argued for in his *On Liberty* (1859).

RAWLSIAN JUSTICE AS FAIRNESS

John Rawls's idea of grounding the requirements of justice on the need for fairness – he called his theory 'justice as fairness' – is a very important aspect of the Rawlsian analysis of justice (as was discussed in Chapter 9 of the 1970 version of this book). One form that the requirement of fairness can take is to demand that the social arrangements should reflect decisions that would be arrived at in a hypothetical state of primordial equality (Rawls calls it 'the original position'), where the nature of the basic structure of the society can be agreed upon without each person knowing exactly who is, in fact, going to be in that society.

In spelling out a just structure that would be arrived at, Rawls invokes two principles. The first demands the most extensive liberty for each, consistent with similar liberty for others. This has priority over the second principle, which insists on, first, keeping offices and opportunities open to all, and second (under the Difference Principle – a component of the second principle), that inequalities are regarded as unjust except to the extent that they work out to be in the interest of the worst off.

The basal space in Rawls' theory of 'justice as fairness' is rather complicated. There is a hierarchy in which liberty gets priority (as under 'libertarianism'). But the place of liberties is powerful but narrow (it does not include property rights or rights of exchange or bequeathal), and is essentially concerned with basic personal and political liberties. Beyond this first round of concern, and also beyond procedural fairness for all, there is a part of the basal space concerned with people's economic and social advantages. Rawls saw the personal advantages in terms of the respective person's holding of 'primary goods'. These are general-purpose *resources* that are useful for the pursuit of different objectives that the individual may have, and are 'things that citizens need as free and equal persons, and claims to these goods are counted as appropriate claims' (Rawls (1988), p. 257).[4] Primary goods are 'things that every rational man is presumed to want', and include 'income and wealth', 'the basic liberties', 'freedom of movement and choice of occupation', 'powers and prerogatives of offices and positions of responsibility', and 'the social bases of self-respect'.[vi]

In the basal space of primary goods, the Rawlsian Difference Principle demands that the least well-off groups are made as well-off as possible, in terms of an overall index of the holding of primary goods. A lexicographic form can be given to this priority (as proposed in Sen (1970a), and accepted in Rawls (1971), so that whenever the worst-off groups are equally well-off in a pairwise comparison, attention is shifted to the next worst-off group, and so on. This aggregation system has clearly egalitarian features, though the concentration is specifically on inequalities that affect the lives of the least advantaged people.

The 'priority of liberty' in the Rawlsian system is much less extensive and less restraining than in libertarian theory. The rights that are given priority by Rawls are far fewer and less demanding than those in the libertarian proposals (and in particular do not include property rights in general). However, these circumscribed rights (concerning personal and basic political liberties) have complete precedence over other social concerns, including the fulfilment of our most elementary needs and reasoned desires.

The case for this complete priority, even though applied to rather a limited class of rights, can be disputed through the recognition of the force of other considerations including that of needs, which occupy lower lexical priority, no matter how vital – and intense – these needs may be. Herbert Hart (1973) raised this question forcefully in an early critique of Rawls (1971), and Rawls (1993) himself recognized the force of the objection, making what look like some concessions.

---

[4] The coverage of 'resources' can be extended to include other *means*, and Ronald Dworkin (1981a), (1981b) took his system of ethical accounting in that direction, with the possibility of taking hypothetical insurance against possible handicaps.

It is, in fact, possible to distinguish between Rawls's strict proposal that liberty should receive overwhelming priority in the case of a conflict, and his general procedure of separating out personal liberty from other types of advantage for special emphasis. Acknowledging the pre-eminence of these rights need not take the sharp and extreme form that the claim of 'priority of liberty' seems to demand – overriding everything with which it might conflict. The critical issue is whether a person's liberty should be judged to have exactly the same kind of importance (no more) that other types of personal advantages (incomes, utilities, etc.) have – in particular, whether the significance of liberty for a society is adequately reflected by the weight that the person herself would tend to give to it in judging her *overall* advantage. The claim of pre-eminence of liberty and political rights can be seen as a denial of that symmetry.

The underlying issue, therefore, is whether the social importance of liberty and basic political rights can far exceed the value that would be attached to them by individuals in judging their overall personal advantage. In order to prevent a misunderstanding, I should explain that the social importance of liberty is here being contrasted with the personal advantage that people get from liberty, not with the value that citizens attach to liberty and rights in their *political* judgements. Quite the contrary, since the safeguarding of liberty rests ultimately on the general *political* acceptance of their importance. The contrast is, rather, with the extent to which having more liberty or rights increases an individual's own personal advantage. The citizens' judgement on the importance of liberty and other rights need not be based only on the extent to which they themselves expect to profit from these rights. So the claim is that the political significance of rights can far exceed the extent to which the personal advantage of the holders of these rights is enhanced by having these rights. There is, thus, an asymmetry with other sources of individual advantage, for example incomes, which would be valued largely on the basis of how much they contribute to the respective personal advantages. The safeguarding of basic political rights would have the policy priority that follows from this asymmetric prominence. While I shall not further pursue this issue here, it is a distinction to which importance can be, I believe, sensibly attached.[5]

What about the Difference Principle? Much of the early discussion of the Rawlsian framework (particularly among economists – see the excellent collection of essays edited by Edmund Phelps (1973a)) concerned his formula for aggregation given by the Difference Principle system. The maximin form (even when modified by its lexicographic extension) can be 'extremist' in giving complete priority to the worst-off's gain (no matter how small) over the better-off's loss (no matter how great), and there may be some neglect here of considerations of aggregative efficiency. But this is open to qualification and modification, without eliminating the concentration on the worst-off citizens – a focus in favour of which Rawls has provided strong arguments.[6]

A different type of criticism relates to the choice of basal space in Rawlsian theory. But before coming to that, it is important to see the merits of the space of primary goods, which does not suffer from the narrowness of focus that libertarianism has. While it does include liberties and rights among the primary goods (in addition to the role given to liberty under the first principle), it also includes other general-purpose means that give people the opportunity to pursue their respective objectives. Nor does the accounting of primary goods have the built-in bias against the persistently deprived – thanks to the phenomenon of adaptive attitudes – that the mental metric of utilities has.

However, primary goods are the *means*, not the *ends* that people seek. Nor do they reflect the *freedoms* that people actually have

---

[5] This question is more fully discussed in my Arrow Lectures, given at Stanford University (published in Sen (2002a), essays 21–23).

[6] Various compromises are possible, including using distribution-sensitive aggregation procedures that take us, in an equity-conscious way, from individual fortunes to social assessment. This seems to have been one of the basic ideas behind Atkinson's (1970), (1983), (2015) powerful departures in evaluative economics. See also Kolm (1969), (1972).

to pursue their own ends. The concentration, rather, is on the means – and only some of the means – that are relevant in generating these freedoms. We can ask: if we are interested in freedom, is it adequate to concentrate only on the means to freedom, rather than on the *extent* of the freedom that a person actually has? Since the conversion of these primary goods and resources into freedom of choice over alternative lives and achievements may vary from person to person, equality of holdings of primary goods or of resources can go hand in hand with serious inequalities in actual freedoms enjoyed by different persons. For example, a disabled person with a given basket of primary goods will enjoy less freedom in many significant respects than would an able-bodied person with an identical basket. An elderly person with special difficulties would have a similar problem. So would a person born into an adverse epidemiological environment, and there will be other handicaps for a person born with a greater genetic proneness to some disease.

Thus, despite the great advance that has been made in the theory of justice by Rawls's path-breaking work (recent theories mostly follow the routes explored by Rawls in one way or another, even when they choose to vary their ultimate destination), there remain difficulties in seeing justice entirely in terms of the Rawlsian principles and their implications for the basal space and aggregation system. In the context of assessing income distribution, the important lessons from Rawlsian analysis relate to the broadening of the context of judgement. The relevance of liberty and rights has already been commented on, but there is also the need to see that income is only one of the means – one of the primary goods – that help people to pursue their objectives and to live in freedom. This broadening remains deeply insightful, even though we may want to go further (as the present writer certainly does).

FAIRNESS AND
PREFERENCE-BASED EVALUATION

While the exercises outlined so far deal with the problem of social choice in rather comprehensive terms, there are some approaches that aim to do no more than separate out a subset of the set of all feasible social states for special commendation. The specified subset is seen as 'good', but there is no claim that they represent the 'best' alternatives. There is no attempt to give an answer to the overall problem of social choice, and the exercise is quite different from the specification of a social preference over the set of social states (as with social welfare functions or social decision functions). This general approach, which we may call the 'good quality approach', has been extensively used in the context of such concepts as Pareto efficiency, the core, equitability and fairness.

Is this, in any sense, a superior approach? In presenting his analysis of fairness based on equity and efficiency, Hal Varian makes the following critical comment on standard social choice theory:

> Social decision theory views the specification of the social welfare function as a problem in aggregating individual preferences. Its chief results are of the form. There are no reasonable ways to aggregate individual preferences ... Social decision theory asks for too much out of the process in that it asks for an entire *ordering* of the various social states (allocations in this case). The original question asked only for a 'good' allocation; there was no requirement to rank all allocations. The fairness criterion in fact limits itself to answering the original question. It is limited in that it gives no indication of the merits of two nonfair allocations, but by restricting itself in this way it allows for a reasonable solution to the original problem.[vii]

While technical efficiency is a common concept in the resource-allocation literature, in welfare economics the more common notion of efficiency is that of so-called 'Pareto optimality', which is sometimes referred to – more sensibly – as 'Pareto efficiency' or 'economic efficiency'.[7]

In a much-discussed concept of fairness (illuminatingly pioneered by Duncan Foley (1967)), the idea of 'envying' another person's better position has been used as a criterion of manifest inequality that counts towards the unacceptability of some social states.[8] This interesting concept of fairness has been extensively explored recently.[viii] If no individual prefers the bundle of goods that any other person has, compared with his own bundle, then that allocation is called *equitable*. If an allocation is both Pareto optimal and equitable, then it is called *fair*.

There is little doubt that the 'fairness' approaches have provided a worthwhile field for investigation. The ambitiousness of the traditional social choice formulations in seeking a social ordering, or a finitely complete choice function (specifying the optimal subsets for each exercise of choice over a finite set of alternatives), causes not a little problem (as Arrow's impossibility theorem and related results bring out), and here the fairness-related approaches have some potential advantage. On the other hand, it is difficult to agree on a particular quality as being overwhelmingly good (irrespective of other qualities), and partitioning the set of possibilities into good and bad subsets based on only one of these qualities. While Varian (1974) may be right to criticize traditional social choice approaches by arguing that there is no requirement to rank all allocations, an approach that gives no indication of the comparative merits of two non-fair allocations may not take us a great distance when fair allocations do not exist, or require conditions so exacting that they are unlikely to be practically achievable in the near future. The traditional social choice approach, in contrast, can offer more, since it discriminates more – even between the *bad* and the *worse*.

---

[7] It has sometimes also been called, very ambiguously (and mercilessly to the reader), simply 'optimality' or 'efficiency' (see, for example, Debreu (1959)). There is a good case for more clarity here.

[8] Note that the concept of envy used in these models is one of preferring the position of another, and not – as in another interpretation of envy – *suffering* from the superior position of another. It is only in the former sense that envy can be present *without* manifest externality of its own.

The chief contribution of the fairness literature may have been elsewhere. First, it has shown the relevance of informational parameters that traditional social choice approaches have tended to ignore in their single-minded concern with individual orderings of complete social states. Comparisons of different persons' positions within a state have been brought into the calculation, enlarging the informational basis of social judgements.[ix]

Second, in raising concrete questions regarding different aspects of states of affairs, the fairness literature has pushed social choice theory in the direction of more structure. Criteria such as unrestricted domain, or independence, or non-dictatorship, are very general requirements of good social choice procedures, while requirements of fairness or equity make the demands more specific. There is some obvious gain in this extension.

In a recent extension of the fairness approach, Fleurbaey and Maniquet (2011b) have outlined an approach that uses the idea of fairness that pays special attention to problems of equity as well as efficiency, attaching particular importance, in any comparison, to the preferences of the worse off. Adding an equity aspect to the traditional fairness literature is a major advance, and so is the analysis of using preferences of different persons to make these social judgements, which gives social choice theory a much-needed constructive edge. However, the alternatives over which preferences are considered are the resources that different persons respectively have. In this respect, the approach may be subject to the limitations – shared by the Rawlsian concentration on primary goods – of focusing on means, rather than the freedom to pursue ends (a problem discussed earlier in the context of assessing the Rawlsian theory of justice), though Fleurbaey and Maniquet consider ways and means of broadening their informational focus to deal with this issue.[9]

---

[9] Fleurbaey and Maniquet have discussed how their approach can be extended from working on individual resources to dealing with individual combinations of functionings that human beings achieve (see Fleurbaey and Maniquet (2011b), Chapter 7). There is much to learn from such an approach.

FUNCTIONINGS AND CAPABILITIES

In recent years there has been considerable discussion on an approach to justice that concentrates on people's capability to lead the kind of life they have reason to value – the things that they can do, or be. The roots of the approach can be traced to the ideas of Aristotle, and, to some extent, Adam Smith; it concentrates on the opportunities that people have to lead valuable and valued lives (see Sen 1980, 1985a, 1985b and Nussbaum 1988, 2006, 2011). Aristotle saw this achievement in terms of 'human flourishing'. Among other things, he pointed out, in *Nicomachean Ethics*, that wealth 'is evidently not the good we are seeking' – 'for it is merely useful and for something else'.[10]

This approach can help to systematize the investigation of quality of life – a subject of much interest in recent years. The widespread interest in an informationally rich evaluative framework, especially in the literature on economic development, provides excellent motivation for going in this direction. A theory of justice can use the ingredients of quality of life as the basal space.[x]

Concepts of quality of life are frequently used in an informal way, sometimes with an arbitrary choice of indicators. This is to some extent inevitable, in practice, given the gaps in the relevant data and the vagueness of the underlying concepts. But it is important to be sure how in principle the formal analysis would proceed had the relevant data been available, and had there been an opportunity to separate out the inescapable ambiguities in the nature of the subject matter from unnecessary obscurities resulting from inadequate analysis. Informational lacuna or

---

[10] The capability approach has also been much influenced by modern theories of justice, led by Rawls (1958), (1971), (1993), and by contemporary debates on social policy. For points of departure, see Sen (1980), (1985a), (1985b), (2009a), Nussbaum (1988), (1992), (2006), (2011), Nussbaum and Sen (1993), Nussbaum and Glover (1995), Chiappero-Martinetti (1996), (2000), Gotoh (2001), (2009b), Alkire (2002), (2005), Robeyns (2003), (2005), (2006), Qizilbash (2006), (2007), Ruger (2006), (2010), Anderson (2010a), (2010b), Alkire and Foster (2011b) and Basu and Lopez-Calva (2011), among other contributions.

complexity of concepts need not serve as an excuse for tolerating avoidable conceptual murkiness. Difficulties in observing utilities have not prevented the development of utility theory at the conceptual level (eventually having more practical use as well, for example in the works of Kahneman (1999)), and the search for clarity is important here too, even when practical applicability may be contingently limited.

A person's achieved life can be seen as a combination of 'functionings' (i.e. doings and beings), and, taken together, can be the basis for assessing that person's quality of life.[11] The functionings on which human flourishing depends include such elementary things as being alive, being well-nourished and in good health, moving about freely, and so on. It can also include more complex functionings, such as having self-respect and respect of others, and taking part in the life of the community (including 'appearing in public without shame'), on which Adam Smith in particular presented an extraordinarily insightful analysis in his *Wealth of Nations*.[xi]

The combination of different types of functionings presents the focal features of a person's life, with each of its components reflecting the extent of the achievement of a particular functioning. A person's 'capability' is represented by the set of combinations of functionings from which the person can choose any one combination. Thus, the 'capability set' stands for the actual freedom of choice a person has over the alternative lives that he or she can lead. There are many technical issues in the specification and analysis of functionings and capabilities, but the central idea is to see the basal space in terms of what people are able to be or able to do, rather than in terms of the means or resources they possess. In this view, individual claims are to be assessed not just by the incomes, resources or primary goods people respectively have, nor only with reference to the pleasures or utilities they enjoy, but in terms of the freedom they have to choose between different ways of living they can have reason to value.

---

[11] On different aspects of the capability approach, see the collections of essays in Nussbaum and Sen (1993), Comin, Qizilbash and Alkire (2008), Kakwani and Silber (2008), Anand, Pattanaik and Puppe (2009), Basu and Kanbur (2009), Gotoh and Dumouchel (2009a), Brighouse and Robeyns (2010) and Comin and Nussbaum (2014), in a fast-growing literature.

There is a huge – and rapidly growing – literature on this subject, and I shall not go into the complex evaluational problems that have been explored.[xii] It is also important to link the capability perspective with other approaches that have elements in common, without being quite the same. In fact, it would be misleading to see the capability approach as standing on its own as a guide to justice, since it focuses only on some specific aspects of well-being and freedom, and there are other concerns – for example the importance of processes and agencies – that need to be brought in to get a fuller understanding of justice than can be obtained within an exclusively 'capability approach'. I have tried to discuss the need for a broader approach in *The Idea of Justice* (Sen (2009a)).[xiii]

There are also important approaches to capability-related work (for example, James Heckman's (2007), (2012) pioneering research on the development of children – see also Cunha and Heckman (2009)) that lie at the periphery of – or even just outside – a narrow definition of 'the capability approach', and the usefulness of the idea of capability is much more extensive than what purism allows. For example, the kind of preference-based analysis used by Fleurbaey and Maniquet (2011b) applied to heterogeneous resources – and then extended to functionings – also provides a hugely promising basis for normative evaluation that makes good use of the capability perspective in a society with diverse fortunes as well as heterogeneous preferences. There is a lot more work to be done on these broader lines, without limiting the capability approach to an exclusive territory.

THE NEED FOR VALUATION AND WEIGHTING

The heterogeneity of the components in the basal space, such as different functionings, points inevitably to the need to weigh them against one another. This applies to all approaches that respect plurality in one form or another, including the Rawlsian focus on primary goods, or the Aristotelian focus on functionings and capabilities (which is present also in other theories that take note of different aspects of the quality of life).

This weighting requirement is often seen as a 'difficulty' with these approaches. But the heterogeneity in our value system – the plurality of concerns that we have reason to accept – makes it necessary for us either to face this plurality, with its consequent problems, or to ignore it in some arbitrary way, which is an evasion rather than a solution of a manifest issue. While we can decide to close our eyes to this issue by simply *assuming* that there is something homogeneous called 'the income' in terms of which everyone's overall advantage can be judged and interpersonally compared (and that variations of needs, personal circumstances, etc., can be, correspondingly, assumed away), this does not resolve the problem, only evades it.

Real income comparison involves aggregation over different commodities, and in judging comparative individual advantages there is the further problem of interpersonal comparisons, taking note of variations of individual conditions and circumstances. It is, of course, possible to reflect these variations in values of 'adjusted income' that can be appropriately defined, but that is only another way of stating the same problem, requiring that attention be paid to the valuation of heterogeneous factors, though expressed in the 'indirect' space of equivalent incomes. Measurements in the direct space (e.g. quality of life, or capability indicators) and those in the indirect space (e.g. equivalent incomes) would have a tight correspondence with each other, related to the underlying values on which both the normative exercises are based.[12] One way or another, the issue of valuation and weighting has to be faced.

It is crucial to ask, in any evaluative exercise of this kind, how the weights are to be selected. This is a judgemental exercise, and it can be resolved only through reasoned evaluation. In making *personal* judgements, the selection of the weights will be done by a person in the way he or she thinks is reasonable. But in arriving at an agreed

---

[12] For an insightful analysis of working on the dual space, see particularly Deaton and Muellbauer (1980b) and Deaton (1995).

range for *social evaluation* (for example, in social studies of poverty), there has to be some kind of a reasoned consensus on weights (even if it is of an informal kind).[xiv] While the possibility of arriving at a unique set of weights is rather unlikely, uniqueness is not really necessary to make agreed judgements in many situations, and may not indeed be required to construct a useful partial ordering – and sometimes not even for arriving at a fully complete ordering.[13]

In the democratic context, values are given a foundation through their correspondence with informed judgements by the people involved. The discipline of social evaluation has been extensively explored in the contemporary literatures on social choice theory as well as public choice theory. There is, in fact, much complementarity between them, and a more complete characterization of basing social judgements on public acceptance can be obtained by combining the two disciplines. I have tried to argue elsewhere (Sen (1995c), (2009a)) why and how this combination is needed. Public choice theory has provided more exploration of the role of discussion and negotiation in arriving at a consensus, whereas social choice theory has made a more extensive contribution on acceptable compromises in areas in which disagreements remain. This type of combination is needed not only for the informational basis and aggregation systems underlying theories of justice, but also in other areas of public policy and social action. Indeed, similar combinations (involving agreed norms and consensus, on the one hand, and acceptable compromises on the other) are needed even for setting a 'poverty line', or for the evaluation of an 'environmentally adjusted national income', or for the use of an 'inequality index' in national statistics (like Atkinson's 1970 measure for a chosen extent of inequality aversion, through the specification of parameter ε, possibly with public discussion of the pros and cons of various proposals). [xv]

---

[13] On some methodological issues of ranking with 'partial comparability', see Chapters 7 and 7*. See also Sen (1993a), (1997a), (2016).

INCOMES AND VALUES

The point has sometimes been made that it may be a mistake to move from the sure ground of real income statistics to the murky territory of other values and concerns. Is this a good argument for sticking to the commodity space and market valuation in making comparative judgements on personal advantages, rather than using information on functionings and other features of quality of life?[xvi] It is certainly true that market prices exist for commodities, and do not for functionings. But how can evaluatively significant weights – whether of commodities or of functionings – be simply 'read off' from some *other* exercise (in this case, of commodity exchange), without addressing the question of values in *this* exercise (the comparison of individual advantages)? There are two distinct issues here of practical importance. The first is the problem arising from the existence of externalities, inequalities and other concerns that suggest that market prices are not good indicators of social valuation, and must be adjusted for social use. We have to decide whether such adjustments should be made, and, if so, how this should be done. In doing this, an evaluative exercise cannot really be avoided.

The second – and the more fundamental – problem is that the market prices, even if seen as a cluster of useful 'exchange values', cannot give us guidance about *interpersonal comparisons* of welfare or advantage. Some confounding has occurred on this subject because of misreading the sensible tradition – sensible within its context – of taking utility to be simply the numerical representation of a person's choice. That is a useful way of defining utility for the analysis of the consumption behaviour of each person taken separately, but it does not offer any procedure whatever for substantive interpersonal comparison. Samuelson's (1947) elementary point that 'it was not necessary to make interpersonal comparisons of utility in describing exchange'[xvii] is the other side of the same coin: nothing about interpersonal comparison of utility is learned from observing exchange or 'the metric of exchange value'.

This is not just a theoretical difficulty of little practical interest; it can make a very big difference in practice as well.[14] For example, even if a person who is disabled or ill or depressed happens to have the same demand function as another who is not disadvantaged in this way, it would be quite absurd to assume that he or she can enjoy similar well-being and freedom with the help of a given commodity bundle as the other can get from it. At the practical level, perhaps the biggest difficulty in basing interpersonal comparisons of advantage on real-income comparisons lies in the diversity of human beings and the variability of the circumstances that influence their lives and opportunities. Differences in age, gender, talents, levels of disability, proneness to illness, epidemiological surroundings and other influences on people's lives can make two different people have quite divergent substantive opportunities even when they have the very same commodity bundle. When we have to go beyond simply observing market choices, which tell us little about interpersonal comparisons, we have to use *additional* information, rather than simply the good old 'metric of exchange value'.

The market mechanism does not pre-select, for evaluative use, some metric of social valuation. We have to do that ourselves. For informed scrutiny by the public, the implicit values have to be made more explicit, rather than being shielded from scrutiny on the false ground that they are part of an 'already available' evaluative metric. There is a real need for an openness to critical discussion of evaluative weights, and there is no escape from this necessity through an arbitrary re-interpretation of some pre-existing indicator that had been constructed for some other purpose. The making of collective decisions calls for social evaluation as well as public discussion, and reasoned scrutiny of such evaluation.

A REMARK ON THEORIES OF JUSTICE

Even though ideas of justice have been discussed over many centuries across the world, the discipline received a powerful boost during the

---

[14] For a lucid and illuminating discussion of the misleading consequences of the confounding of financial and social evaluation, see David Marquand (2014).

European Enlightenment in the eighteenth and nineteenth centuries. The stalwarts of the Enlightenment did not, however, speak in one voice, and it is useful to consider a divergence between two different lines of reasoning about justice among leading philosophers associated with the radical thought of that period.

One approach, which can be called the 'social contract' tradition, pioneered by Thomas Hobbes in the seventeenth century, concentrated on identifying perfectly just social arrangements that people could be unanimously expected to endorse if they reasoned without personal biases about what kind of a society they would ideally like to have. This approach has two distinct and separable features. First, it concentrates on the nature of the perfectly just society, rather than on making comparisons between justice in different societies, in terms of comparative justice and injustice. This perfection-focused approach concentrates only on the 'just' society that cannot be 'transcended' in terms of justice, and it is concerned with the partition between 'the just' and 'the unjust', rather than with comparative judgements of being 'more just' or 'less just'.

Secondly, the social contract approach has been institution-focused in the sense that it concentrates on getting the institutions right, rather than focusing on what results from these institutions and arrangements which are influenced also by other features of the society, such as actual behaviours and social interactions. The overall attention is thus focused on the excellence of the institutions and on rules of behaviour, not on the comparative merits of the different societies that actually emerge.

The social contract approach was powerfully explored, in different ways, by a number of Enlightenment philosophers, including Jean-Jacques Rousseau, John Locke and, to some extent, Immanuel Kant (though his analysis extended far beyond contractarian concerns). In contrast, a number of other Enlightenment theorists took a variety of approaches that aimed directly at actual social realizations in a comparative perspective. Many of their arguments were particularly aimed at removing cases of manifest injustice in the world. Different versions of such comparative thinking can be found, for example in the works of the Marquis de Condorcet, Adam Smith, Jeremy Bentham, Mary

Wollstonecraft, John Stuart Mill and Karl Marx, among a number of other leaders of innovative thought in the eighteenth and nineteenth centuries. Even though they proposed very different ways of making social comparisons, they were all involved, in one way or another, in making social comparisons that can identify how a society could be improved through removing some manifest injustices. It is the latter approach that can be seen as the foundation of what can be called the 'social choice' approach to justice.

In this book in general, and in this chapter in particular, I have discussed alternative normative approaches to equity and justice from the social choice perspective. I have had the opportunity elsewhere (particularly in Sen (2009a)) to discuss why I believe that the social choice approach, with its focus on 'social realizations' – including the outcomes as well as the processes through which those outcomes come about – has something to offer in the assessment of social justice that the social contract approach cannot match. Something similar can be said about welfare economics as well. The social choice approach can offer an understanding there, with its focus on comparative (rather than transcendental) judgements, and with its involvement with comprehensive outcomes (rather than institutional perfection). In the next chapter these connections and their extensive implications are further pursued.

Chapter A3*
Social Welfare Evaluation

It is often said that many of the important things in life are not measurable or quantifiable. Some go from there to warn that social reasoning should stay away, as far as possible, from any attempted incorporation of mathematical reasoning. These classicists, if I may call them that with due respect, are confronted by modernists – to use another devised term – who distrust the use of what they see as vague and foggy ideas, and propose, explicitly or by implication, keeping unmeasurable objects firmly out of serious social analysis.

Modernists have, in fact, been quite influential in the discipline of welfare economics, and also in the practice of economic and social assessment carried out by many national and global institutions. Indeed, the alleged lack of measurability of objects we value can play quite a big part in stifling critical discussion, advocating withdrawal from many important exercises that we have good reason to consider – and pursue. Sometimes it can also induce people to advocate concentrating on far less interesting, but allegedly more measurable, variables, such as GDP (Gross Domestic Product) or the value of material wealth.

Is it possible that the classicists and the modernists both misunderstand the analytical demands of measurement and evaluation? What kind of a quality is measurability? In evaluating alternatives, we can scarcely be uninterested in ranking them against each other, at least ranking those we can rank. The question to ask here is this: how close is measurability to ranking? I would argue that the connection is extremely close; indeed measurement and quantification can be seen as extensions of ranking relations.

WHAT IS MEASURABILITY?

Consider a ranking with certain regularity properties but which is not necessarily complete. A *quasi-ordering*, as we tend to call it in social choice theory (and French mathematicians such as Bourbaki call a 'pre-ordering'), is a transitive ranking relation that may or may not be complete. It may be useful to think of this as a 'partial ordering', with many alternatives ranked against each other, but with some pairs possibly remaining unranked.

It is hard to escape a partial ranking if we indulge at all in evaluation – however informal it may be. If we have an opinion on a subject, for example that someone is clearly more deprived – or more miserable (as we understand that concept) – than another person, it is hard to escape some use, even if only implicit, of a partial ordering. And a partial order is already some kind of measurement. If we are slaves to real numbers, you can even think of a numerical system in which a better alternative is given a higher number (though not necessarily the converse, for then it would have to be a complete order since real numbers are all fully ranked). This one-way quantification can have many very useful qualities (see Majumdar and Sen (1976), on the problem of 'representing partial orderings').

From that minimal base of measurement, we can climb up further and further, and consider stricter and stricter requirements with more and more features of measurability:

- from partial orderings to complete orderings;
- from complete orderings to numerically representable complete orderings;
- from representable complete orderings to orderings that are representable by numbers that are invariant up to a positive affine transformation ('cardinally measurable' in the economist's vocabulary);

- from affine invariance to invariance only up to positive multiplicative transformations (this is known as 'ratio-scale measurability').

And so on. On the other side, to go below what I called the minimum, we can also have so-called 'fuzzy' measures (Barrett and Salles (2011) is a good introduction to this promising, but still under-explored, area of 'fuzzy regularity').

These variations are all about the *extent* of measurability, rather than whether some concern is 'measurable or not', which is a clumsy and under-specified question. When someone says, 'Culture is really important for society, but it is not measurable', there is a bit of a problem already there. In saying something like this, if the person wants to present the view that not taking culture into account tends to produce worse societies, well, there is a partial ranking right there. It may be difficult to produce an overall assessment of societies taking culture into account, along with other considerations, but the difficulty there lies not in any intrinsic non-rankability (and, in that basic sense, non-measurability) of social states inclusive of cultural aspects, but in the practical difficulty in forming multifaceted judgements inclusive of culture, attaching relative weights on distinct concerns, which – along with culture – may be important.

It is hard to see these distinctions as differences in kind, rather than one of degree.[1] It is important to understand how measurability can take many different forms, without losing the analytical rigour of reasoning. The fear of being 'unmeasurable' can be a rather raw worry (more polemical than illuminating), and such a diagnosis can serve as a reactionary diversion from reasoning (reasoning that we can sensibly use, without demanding a higher degree of measurability than the object under discussion can actually have). It also explains why set theory (and, based on that, topological ideas) can be very useful in practical economic and social evaluation, without seeking measurability of a kind that physicists tend to seek in the natural sciences.

---

[1] Though I take seriously the complexity of that distinction. As John Littlewood (1967), the famous mathematician, asked: 'Is the difference between a difference of degree and a difference of kind a difference of degree or a difference of kind?'

WELL-BEING, CAPABILITY
AND UTILITY

In Chapter A3, a number of different ways of thinking about people's well-being have been considered. Different kinds of informational challenges are involved in having indicators of utility and capability (to consider two competing informational bases in analysing human well-being and opportunity). Utility can be defined in different ways, though most of the standard interpretations tend to be mental magnitudes, such as pleasures and desires. Mental magnitudes have well-known measurement problems of their own, which can, however, be plausibly addressed, as Daniel Kahneman and Alan Krueger, for example, have successfully done.[i] Capabilities are concerned with different aspects of people's freedom to do things that they have reason to value. Many capabilities – or the functionings to which they relate – are easy to pin down, while others may be difficult to assess. And different functionings, and the capability to secure them, may demand critical discussion on their relative importance.[ii] These complexities have to be faced, and yet it is possible to make sensible use of a plausible measurement of capabilities without cutting corners.[2]

Sometimes the point is made that since the functionings to which capabilities relate are diverse, the capability approach is not practically useable because of the weighting problem. In fact, however, diversity of ingredients is only an invitation to address the issue of relative values and weights, not an admonition to resign and go home. Indeed, when the valuation of inescapably diverse concerns is done implicitly, as in the measurement of GDP through the use of market prices for distinct commodities, we simply withhold our responsibility to evaluate, going instead for the mechanical use of some relative values that may have been fixed without any relevance to normative assessment

---

[2] Illuminating and elegant use of the capability perspective in dealing with children's well-being and development can be found in a series of powerful studies by James Heckman (2007), (2012), (2015).

(market prices can be hugely inappropriate for ethical evaluation when there are externalities, asymmetric information and big inequalities in income distribution).

The connection between public reasoning and the choice and weighting of capabilities in social assessment is important to emphasize. It also points to the absurdity of the argument which is sometimes presented, that claims that the capability approach would be usable – and 'operational' – only if it comes with a set of 'given' weights on different functionings in some fixed list of relevant capabilities. The search for given, pre-determined weights is not only conceptually ungrounded, it also overlooks the fact that the valuations and weights to be used may reasonably be influenced by people's continued scrutiny and by public discussion. It would be hard to accommodate this understanding with inflexible use of some pre-determined weights in a non-contingent form.

It can, of course, be the case that the agreement that emerges on the weights to be used may be far from complete, and we shall then have good reason to use ranges of weights on which we may find some agreement. A ranking of capabilities may well have to be a partial ordering. This need not, however, derail evaluation of public policy, or disable welfare-economic evaluations. The capability approach is entirely consistent with reliance on partial rankings and limited agreements. The main task is to get the weights – or ranges of weights – appropriate for the comparative judgements that can be reached through reasoning, and if the result is a partial ranking, then we can make precisely those judgements that a partial ranking allows. There is no obligation to feel compelled to opine on every comparative assessment that can be proposed.

INTERPERSONAL COMPARISONS AND NORMATIVE MEASUREMENT

It is hard to do serious welfare economics, as has already been discussed, without interpersonal comparisons of well-being, or of individual advantages assessed in some other way, such as through some indicators of freedoms or opportunities. The understanding that many welfare-economic assessments can be made with only partial comparability – and possibly also with partial cardinality – is discussed in Chapters 7 and 7* of the 1970 version of this book. The possibility of using utilitarian evaluation with partial comparability was particularly investigated in that context. Similar uses of partial comparability can also be made in applying other welfare-economic criteria, such as the Rawlsian Maximin (or Lexicographic Maximin). And similar uses can be made in applying the capability perspective.

When precise information on well-being or freedoms are lacking, it is also possible to use stylized interpersonal comparisons with some explicit assumption about comparison of advantages of different persons. Consider the problem of the assessment – or measurement – of poverty. The most commonly used index of poverty is the head-count measure H, which identifies poverty with the proportion of people who have income levels below a chosen 'poverty line'. However, aside from the arbitrariness involved in identifying an appropriate 'poverty line' income, the head-count indicator pays no attention to the *extent* of the shortfall below the poverty line that people have. Nor does it take any interest in the distribution of the aggregate shortfall among those who are poor.

This has led to a search for distribution-sensitive measures of poverty. The literature on poverty measurement has tended to proceed by taking note of the income shortfalls of the different persons, giving greater weights to shortfall as we consider lower and lower income levels, and attaching more importance to each unit of shortfall of the relatively poorer person. The measure of poverty I initially proposed, partly moved by the need for economy of information, in 'Poverty: An Ordinal Approach to Measurement' (Sen (1976b)), is based only on income data. The measure increases the weight on income shortfalls along with the ranking of each poor person among the collectivity of the poor (using, in particular, rank-order weighting). Though based only on 'ordinal' information, this approach yields a surprisingly neat measure of poverty, built on the simultaneous use of the average extent of the income shortfall of the poor, I, and the Gini coefficient G of the income distribution among the poor, along with the head-count measure H. With axioms of some plausibility, the poverty measure P turns out to be given by:

$$P = H \, [I + (1 - I) \, G].$$

There has been a huge literature on distribution-sensitive poverty measures with axiomatic variations (the literature has been surveyed in Foster and Sen 1997). Many disagreements on valuational methods remain – as would be expected on a subject like this – but the need to bring in interpersonal comparisons in one way or another has been recognized in the entire literature.

The same can be said about distribution-sensitive measures of aggregate real income, and also of mobility.[iii] Rank-order weighting, which I used, valuing commodity j going to person i by the price of the commodity as well as the relative position of a person in the income distribution, yields a fairly easily useable measure (presented in my essay 'Real National Income', Sen (1976c)). But there are other ways of rising to the challenge of assessing aggregate income of a nation (or a community) while paying attention to the inequalities in distribution. It is easy to recognize that each method of doing interpersonal comparisons through some stylized assumption is open to criticism, and yet we have to bring in interpersonal comparisons in one way or another (and many economists and philosophers have made contributions to different ways of getting there).[iv] The escapist temptation to avoid addressing issues of inequality on grounds of the difficulties of making interpersonal comparisons can divert us very far away from the objects of welfare economics.

Happily, the rapidly expanding literature on multi-dimensional poverty evaluation has been making an important contribution in recent years towards linking welfare theory to empirical information. Among the new developments in the field are multi-dimensional measures of poverty and inequality, powerfully pursued in different forms by Atkinson and Bourguignon (1982), Maasoumi (1986), Alkire and Foster (2011a), (2011b), and others.[v] In understanding poverty and inequality, there is a strong case for looking at real deprivation and not merely at mental reactions to that deprivation.

The point has been brought out particularly clearly by recent investigations of gender inequality, focusing not just on happiness or unhappiness but on women's deprivation in terms of under-nutrition, clinically diagnosed morbidity, observed illiteracy, even unexpectedly high mortality (compared with physiologically justified expectations) and, in an anticipatory context, sex-specific abortion of female foetuses. Multi-dimensional interpersonal comparisons can be sensibly – and comfortably – accommodated within a broad framework of welfare economics and social choice theory, enhanced by the removal of informational constraints explicitly invoked or implicitly imposed in traditional welfare economics.

The broadening of the informational basis has become a major concern in modern social choice theory. This applies to tackling Arrow's impossibility result. It is central to being inequality-sensitive in welfare economics. It is relevant to being liberty-conscious in politics, law and the pursuit of human rights. And it is, of course, especially important for having better-informed normative measurement of the well-being of people. As the analyses presented in this book firmly bring out, reasoned use of appropriate information involve both epistemology and ethics. More engagement in each is crucially important for further progress in social choice and welfare economics.

REPRESENTATION AND INVARIANCE

Even as we celebrate the progress that is being made in the empirical work on normative measurement, we have to take note of the necessity of some further work on the analytical foundations of evaluative social choice, which too have been receiving attention in recent decades. There is certainly an important need for a theoretically sound framework for issues of measurement and interpersonal comparison of individual well-being – or 'utilities', which can, of course, be differently defined. I shall adopt – for the sake of brevity (and after due warning) – the well-established practice of using the term 'utility' for any indicator of individual advantage. It is, therefore, important to remember that the mathematical exercises presented here can have different interpretations, depending on how the term 'utility' is defined.

We have to expand the informational base of the traditional social choice approaches by enriching the content of the profiles of individual preference orderings $\{R_i\}$ to an n-tuple of individual utility functions $\{U_i(x)\}$. The intention here is not new, and indeed the classical utilitarian characterization of individual inputs took the form of utility n-tuples (in the works of Edgeworth, Marshall, Pigou, Ramsey and others). However, a difficulty arises from the fact that utilities are not defined over some natural units, and we can express the same utility function through different numerical representations: it may not make any difference if we choose (1, 2, 3) for three alternatives, or (2, 4, 6). This example can be thought of as a case of complete measurability, but we can also vary the measurability assumptions of individual utilities, and also the extents of comparability between different persons' utilities that are presumed to exist. These issues were quite extensively discussed in Chapter 7* of the old (1970) book.

Given the measurability and comparability assumptions of individual utilities, the utility functions have to be represented not by only one particular n-tuple of individual utilities, but by a set of n-tuples of individual utilities which are informationally identical (for the given assumptions of measurability and comparability). This problem is met in the approach of *social welfare functionals* (as used in Chapters 7* and 8* of the 1970 edition) through imposing a class of *invariance requirements* that make them informationally identical.

A social welfare functional (SWFL) specifies exactly one social ordering R over the set X of social states for any given n-tuple $\{U_i(\cdot)\}$ of personal utility functions, each defined over X, one for each person i: $R = F(\{U_i\})$. The invariance requirement takes the general form of specifying that for any two n-tuples in the same comparability set $\bar{L}$, reflecting the assumptions of measurability and interpersonal comparability of individual utilities, the social ordering generated must be the same:

$$R = F(\{U_i\}).$$

Invariance requirement

For any two n-tuples $\{U_i\}$ and $\{U_i^*\}$ belonging to the same comparability set $\bar{L}$:

$$F(\{U_i\}) = F(\{U_i^*\})$$

The specification of the measurability–comparability assumptions takes the form of characterizing $\bar{L}$. Depending on the assumption of measurability, each person i has a family L_i of (essentially equivalent) utility functions:

- each a positive, monotonic transformation of any other in the family in the case of ordinality;
- each a positive, affine transformation of any other in the family in the case of cardinality;
- each a positive, homogeneous linear transformation of any other in the family in the case of ratio-scale measure;
- and so on.

The Cartesian product of the n-tuple of families of utility functions $\{L_i\}$ is the measurability set $L = \prod_{i=1}^{n} L_i$, specifying all possible n-tuples of individual utility functions consistent with the measurability assumption for each individual utility. The assumption that we make about the nature and extent of interpersonal comparability will identify a subset $\bar{L}$ (the 'comparability set') of the measurability set L.

If there is no interpersonal comparability at all, then there is no further restriction, and $\bar{L} = L$. The entire measurability set (L) is also the comparability set ($\bar{L}$) in this case. If, however, interpersonal comparability of any type is permitted, then the freedom to vary an individual utility representation without varying those of others goes down, thereby restricting $\bar{L}$. So, in general, $\bar{L} \subseteq L$. For example, with full comparability, if a transformation $\psi(\cdot)$ permitted by the measurability assumption is applied to one person's utility function in moving from one n-tuple to $\{U_i\}$ another $\{U_i^*\}$, then the same transformation $\psi(\cdot)$ must be applied to everyone's utility function as a necessary and sufficient condition for $\{U_i\}$ and $\{U_i^*\}$ to belong to the same comparability set $\bar{L}$. Some distinguished cases of measurability–comparability assumptions are considered below, and discussed in the 1970 edition of this book (and also in Sen (1974), (1979)).[vi]

Alternative measurability–comparability frameworks

For any utility n-tuple $\{U^*_i\}$ belonging to $\overline{L}$, it is required that $\overline{L}$ must consist of exactly all n-tuples $\{U_i\}$ such that for some n-tuple of transformations $\{\psi_i\}$ satisfying the following alternative restrictions, for $U_i = \psi_i(U^*_i)$ all i:

- *ordinal non-comparability* (ONC): each ψ_i is a positive, monotonic transformation;
- *cardinal non-comparability* (CNC): for all i, each ψ_i is a positive affine transformation, $\psi_i(\cdot) = a_i + b_i \cdot (\cdot)$, with $b_i > 0$;
- *ratio-scale non-comparability* (RNC): for all i, each ψ_i is a positive, homogeneous linear transformation, $\psi_i(\cdot) = b_i \cdot (\cdot)$, with $b_i > 0$;
- *ordinal level comparability* (OLC): for all i, $\psi_i(\cdot) = \psi(\cdot)$, a positive, monotonic transformation;
- *cardinal full comparability* (CFC): for all i, $\psi_i(\cdot) = \psi(\cdot)$, a positive, affine transformation, $\psi(\cdot) = a + b \cdot (\cdot)$, with $b > 0$;
- *ratio-scale full comparability* (RFC): for all i, $\psi_i(\cdot) = \psi(\cdot)$, a positive, homogeneous, linear transformation, $\psi(\cdot) = b \cdot (\cdot)$, with $b > 0$;*
- *cardinal unit comparability* (CUC): each ψ_i is a positive, affine transformation, $\psi_i(\cdot) = a_i + b \cdot (\cdot)$, with $b > 0$, the same for all i;
- *cardinal level comparability* (CLC): each ψ_i is a positive, affine transformation, $\psi_i(\cdot) = a_i + b_i \cdot (\cdot)$, with $b_i > 0$, and there is a positive, monotonic transformation $\phi(\cdot)$ such that $U_i(x) = \phi(U^*_i(x))$, for all $x \in X$, for all i;
- *cardinal unit and level comparability* (CULC):[vii] each ψ_i is a positive, affine transformation, $\psi_i(\cdot) = a_i + b \cdot (\cdot)$, with $b > 0$, the same for all i, and there is a positive, monotonic transformation $\phi(\cdot)$ such that $U_i(x) = \phi(U^*_i(x))$, for all $x \in X$, for all i.[3]

---

[3] Utility values have to be confined to being non-negative in this case, to avoid perversity, but this is not an exacting requirement.

The invariance restriction applied to these respective cases will be denoted as ON, CN, RN, OL, CF, RF, CU, CL, and CUL, respectively (dropping the last C in each case). For example, ON is the invariance restriction for the case of ordinal non-comparability ONC. Note also that the less the precision of information, the wider the set $\bar{L}$, and the more demanding is the invariance restriction (because of its larger domain). With less information more signals are indistinguishable.

It will be convenient later to consider comparability cases that are not fully specified, e.g. levels being comparable whether or not anything else is.

Let $\bar{L}(L)$ and $\bar{L}(U)$ be comparability sets with ordinal level comparability and cardinal unit comparability respectively.

Level-plus comparability (L^+C) is defined as $\bar{L} \subseteq \bar{L}(L)$, and *unit-plus comparability* (U^+C) as $\bar{L} \subseteq \bar{L}(U)$, respectively, in each case. The invariance restriction applied to these measurability–comparability frameworks will be denoted as L^+ and U^+, respectively.

For an SWFL the Arrow conditions can be readily redefined.

Condition $\widetilde{U}$

The domain of $F(\cdot)$ includes all logically possible n-tuples of utility functions $\{U_i\}$, defined over X.

Condition $\widetilde{I}$

For any pair of social states $x, y \in X$, $R|^{(n, y)} = F^{(x, y)}(\{U_i(x), U_i(y)\})$, so that if $U_i(a) = U_i^4(a)$ for all i, for $a = x, y$, then $xF(\{U_i\})y$ if and only if $xF(\{U_i^*\})y$.

Condition $\widetilde{P}$

For any pair $x, y \in X$, $[\forall i: U_i(x) > U_i(y)] \Rightarrow xPy$.

Condition $\widetilde{D}$

There is no individual such that for all $x, y \in X$ and for all $\{U_i\}$ in the domain of $F(\cdot)$, $U_i(x) > U_i(y) \Rightarrow xPy$.

---

[4] Other cases of comparability and measurability combinations can be correspondingly specified.

Since Arrow's impossibility theorem concerns the case of ordinal non-comparability, the General Possibility Theorem translated to SWFLs yields the following:

(T.A3*.1) Arrow's impossibility theorem for SWFL
   For a finite H and $\#X \geq 3$, there is no SWFL satisfying Conditions $\tilde{U}, \tilde{I}, \tilde{P}, \tilde{D}$ and the invariance restriction ON.

This is established by noting that with ON, an SWFL is, in fact, an SWF, and observing that in this case Conditions $\tilde{U}, \tilde{I}, \tilde{P}$ and $\tilde{D}$ entail U, I, P and D, applied to the SWF to which the SWFL is reduced.

EXTENDING ARROW'S IMPOSSIBILITY TO CARDINAL UTILITY

There is a huge list of results that have been explored and established in the literature of social choice and welfare economics with interpersonal comparisons. There will be no hope here of achieving anything close to a comprehensive coverage, but a few specifically chosen results can give the reader some idea of what kind of use can be made of more information on interpersonal comparability of individual well-being and advantage.

   Arrow's impossibility result is easily extended to the case of *cardinal* non-comparability (see also Chapter 8* in the 1970 edition of this book – included here).

(T.A3*.2) Arrow's impossibility result extended to cardinal non-comparable utilities
   For a finite H and $\#X \geq 3$, there is no SWFL satisfying Conditions $\tilde{U}, \tilde{I}^2, \tilde{P}, \tilde{D}$ and the invariance restriction CN.

This, to recollect, is established by taking any two n-tuples of utility functions $\{U_i\}$ and $\{U_i^*\}$ such that each individual ranks the set X in the same way in the two cases. For every pair $x, y \in X$, by exploiting the two degrees of freedom in an affine transformation, an n-tuple of positive, affine transformations $\{\psi_i\}$ applied to $\{U_i^*\}$ yields $U_i'(z) = \psi_i(U_i^*(z)) = U_i(z)$, for $z = x, y$, for all i. By the independence condition $\widetilde{I}$, we get $xF(\{U_i\})y$ if and only if $xF(\{U_i'\})y$, and by CN, $xF(\{U_i'\})y$ if and only if $xF(\{U_i^*\})y$. Since this holds pair by pair, clearly $F(\{U_i\}) = F(\{U_i^*\})$, so the SWFL is, in fact, an SWF. The rest of the proof is the same as in T.A3*.1.

FURTHER POSSIBILITY RESULTS

While cardinality without interpersonal comparability does not change matters as far as the Arrow impossibility result is concerned,[viii] interpersonal comparability without cardinality does, however, make a real difference. There are a great many constructive possibility results that have emerged in the rapidly expanding literature, and only a few of them will be briefly discussed here.

With ordinal level comparability, Conditions $\widetilde{U}$, $\widetilde{I}$, $\widetilde{P}$ and $\widetilde{D}$ are perfectly consistent, and an example of these conditions being fulfilled along with the invariance restriction OL is provided by the so-called Rawlsian maximin criterion (interpreted in terms of individual utilities). But what about the *stronger* Pareto principle $\widetilde{P}*$?

Condition $\widetilde{P}*$

For any pair $x, y \in X$, if $[\forall i: U_i(x) \geq U_i(y)]$ and $\exists i: U_i(x) > U_i(y)$, then xPy.

The strong Pareto principle, which is violated by maximin, can also be satisfied, if we use the lexicographic version of the maximin rule (see Rawls 1971, p. 83), often called leximin.[5] Let $r(x)$ be the rth worst-off person in state x; in case of more than one person having the same utility level, rank them in any arbitrary strict order.

Leximin

For any $x, y \in X$, if there is k, $1 \leq k \leq n$, such that $U_{k(x)}(x) > U_{k(y)}(y)$, and for all $r < k$, $U_{r(x)}(x) = U_{r(y)}(y)$, then xPy. If on the other hand, for all r, $1 \leq r \leq n$, $U_{r(x)}(x) = U_{r(y)}(y)$ then xIy.

---

[5] *Strong Pareto principle* $(\widetilde{P}*)$: $\forall x, y \in X$, $[\forall i: xR_iy \ \& \ \exists i: xP_iy] \Rightarrow xPy$, and $[\forall i: xI_iy] \Rightarrow xIy$.

(T.A3*.3) Leximin in an SWFL satisfies Conditions $\widetilde{U}, \widetilde{I}, \widetilde{P}^*$, and $\widetilde{D}$ and OL.

This obviously also holds for 'level plus' invariance restrictions, and for all comparative information richer than OL, such as CL, CUL, CF, RF, etc.

It also satisfies several other conditions that have been proposed in the literature, such as Anonymity, Neutrality, Separability, Suppes' 'grading principle of justice' (Suppes (1966)), and several 'equity' criteria including Hammond's (1976) demanding Axiom E:

Condition $\widetilde{A}$ (anonymity)

If $\{U_i\}$ is a re-ordering (permutation) of $\{U_i^*\}$, then $F(\{U_i\}) = F(\{U_i^*\})$.

Condition $\widetilde{N}$ (neutrality)

If $\mu(\cdot)$ is a permutation function applied to X, and $\mu[R]$ is the ordering R modified by the same permutation $\mu(\cdot)$, and if for all i, $U_i(x) = U_i^*(\mu(x))$ for all $x \in X$, then $F(\{U_i^*\}) = \mu[F(\{U_i\})]$.

Condition SE (separability)

If the set H of individuals partitions into two proper subsets H_1 and H_2 such that for all i in H_1, $U_i(x) = U_i^*(x)$ for all x in X, and for all i in H_2, $U_i(x) = U_i(y)$ and $U_i^*(x) = U_i^*(y)$, for all x, y in X then $F(\{U_i\}) = F(\{U_i^*\})$.

Condition S (Suppes principle)

If $\rho(\cdot)$ is a permutation function applied to the set H of individuals, and if for any x, y in X, $U_i(x) \geq U_{\rho(i)}(y)$ for all i, then xRy. If additionally, for some i, $U_i(x) > U_{\rho(i)}(y)$, then xPy.

Condition HE (Hammond's equity axiom)

For any x, $y \in X$, if for some pair g, $h \in H$, $U_g(y) > U_g(x) > U_h(x) > U_h(y)$ and for all $i \neq g$, h, $U_i(x) = U_i(y)$, then xRy.

Anonymity states that permuting the utility functions among the people does not affect the social ordering. Neutrality asserts that permuting the social states in individual orderings permutes the social states in the social ordering in exactly the same way. Separability says that if the utility numbers for all states remain unchanged for all *non-indifferent* individuals, then the social ordering should not change either. The Suppes principle extends the Pareto principle by using dominance in an *anonymous* way. First, dealing with weak ranking, if each person in x is at least as well off as the corresponding person in y, then xRy. If, additionally, someone in x is strictly better off than the corresponding person in y then xPy. Hammond's equity principle demands that if person h is worse off than person g in both x and y and if h prefers x to y, while g prefers y to x, with all other persons indifferent between x and y, then xRy.

Both maximin and leximin can be seen as incorporating the dictatorship of a particular rank, viz. the rank of being worst-off. While ordinal level comparability provides an adequate informational base for escaping Arrow's impossibility theorem, it is interesting to enquire whether the escape must take the form of rules that incorporate dictatorship of *some* rank (e.g. of the worst-off, the best-off, the k-th worst-off). Certainly the Arrow conditions imposed on an SWFL satisfying invariance for ordinal level comparability push us in that direction, and all other possible rules – typically rather odd ones – can be weeded out by strengthening the condition of non-dictatorship to anonymity (see Gevers (1979) and Roberts (1980a)).

How and why does this work? With anonymity, in the presence of the other conditions, rank remains an invariant and usable signal (personal identity does not), and the absence of cardinality and of comparability of units makes rank effectively the only such invariant signal. This permits the translation of the Arrow-type reasoning about personal decisiveness to a corresponding reasoning about rank decisiveness, moving from the decisiveness of all ranks put together (guaranteed by the weak Pareto principle) to the decisiveness of some particular rank (as under the lemma on Contraction of Decisive Sets: T.A1*.5).

An important result on this came from the work of Kevin Roberts (1980a), (1980b) and Louis Gevers (1979).[ix]

(T.A3*.4) Rank dictatorship theorem

For a finite H and $\#X \geq 3$, an SWFL satisfying Conditions $\tilde{U}$, $\tilde{I}$, $\tilde{P}$, $\tilde{A}$ and the invariance restriction OL, must be rank-dictatorial, i.e. there will be a rank k such that for all x, y in X, $U_{k(x)}(x) > U_{k(y)}(y) \Rightarrow xPy$.

Leximin implies not only the dictatorship of the worst-off, but a whole hierarchy of dictatorial powers so that each rank has dictatorial power *when* the lower ranks are all indifferent. Leximax defines the opposite hierarchy, with the best-off being the unconditional dictatorial rank, and the other ranks enjoying dictatorial powers conditional on the higher ranks being indifferent. The definition of leximax is the same as that of leximin but for the change that the condition refers to $r > k$ in place of $r < k$. The rank dictatorship result can be modified to precipitate either leximin or leximax (see d'Aspremont and Gevers 1977), by demanding separability and replacing the weak Pareto principle by the strong Pareto principle $\widetilde{P}^*$ (corresponding to P^*, $\widetilde{P}$ as does to P).

(T.A3*.5) Leximin–leximax theorem
  For a finite H and $\#X \geq 3$, a SWFL satisfying Conditions $\widetilde{U}$, $\widetilde{I}^2$, $\widetilde{P}^*$, $\widetilde{A}$, SE and the invariance restriction OL, must be leximin or leximax.

AXIOMATIC DERIVATION OF LEXIMIN

It would be helpful to consider two variations (in fact, weakenings) of the demands of the Suppes principle, which, like the Pareto principle, builds on dominance of utilities (but does this in an anonymous way and is thus remarkably more extensive than the Pareto principle). One weakening confines the anonymous comparisons to permutations between exactly two persons only, and the other concentrates on indifference only (correspondingly to the Pareto indifference rule).

Condition S_2 (2-person Suppes principle)
  For any x, $y \in X$, if for any two persons g, $h \in H$, either $U_j(x) \geq U_j(y)$ for $j = g, h$, or $U_g(x) \geq U_h(y)$ and $U_h(x) \geq U_g(y)$, while

for all $i \neq g, h, U_i(x) \geq U_i(y)$, then xRy. If, furthermore, at least one of the two inequalities $\geq$ holds strictly $>$, then xPy.

Condition S^o (Suppes indifference rule)
For any $x, y \in X$, if for some permutation function $\rho(\cdot)$ applied to the set H of individuals $U_i(x) \geq U_{\rho(i)}(y)$ for all i, then xIy.

Condition S_2^o (2-person Suppes indifference rule)
For any $x, y \in X$, if for two persons $g, h \in H$, $U_g(x) = U_h(y)$ and $U_h(x) = U_g(y)$, while for all $i \neq g, h, U_i(x) = U_i(y)$ then xIy.

The Pareto indifference rule continues to hold.

Hammond's equity condition can also be weakened to what d'Aspremont and Gevers (1977) have called 'minimal equity', to derive leximin axiomatically.

Condition ME (minimal equity)
The SWFL is not the leximax principle.

Finally, consider the general relational independence:

Condition $\tilde{I}$ (relational independence):
For any subset $S \subseteq X$, if for all i, for all $x \in S$, $U_i(x) = U_i^*(x)$, then $F(\{U_i\})|^S = F(\{U_i^*\})|^S$.

Leximin has been differently axiomatized by Hammond (1976), (1979b), Strasnick (1976), (1978), d'Aspremont and Gevers (1977), (2002), Maskin (1979), Deschamps and Gevers (1978), (1979), Roberts (1977), (1980a), (1980b), Arrow (1977), Sen (1977c), Ulph (1978), Gevers (1979), Suzumura (1983), (2016), d'Aspremont (1985) and Blackorby, Bossert and Donaldson (2002), among others. The main results can be put in the form of a rather comprehensive theorem. In this theorem – and indeed in the discussion to follow – it is assumed that $\#X \geq 3$ and that H is finite (see Sen (1986b)).

(T.A3*.6) Leximin derivation theorem
An SWFL satisfying unrestricted domain $\tilde{U}$ and independence of irrelevant alternatives $\tilde{I}$ must be leximin if it satisfies invariance

for level-plus comparability L^+, and one of the following set of conditions:

(1) $\tilde{P}^*$, $\tilde{A}$, SE, ME and OL;
(2) S, SE, ME and OL;
(3) $\tilde{P}^*$, $\tilde{A}$ and HE;
(4) $\tilde{P}^*$, S^o and HE;
(5) $\tilde{P}$, S_2^o and HE;
(6) S and HE;
(7) S_2 and HE.

To point towards another result, define leximin-k as the leximin principle applied to ranking any pair of states over which there are exactly k non-indifferent persons. One of the unappealing features of leximin is that it permits the interest of one person (if relatively badly off) to override the interests of a great many others, possibly billions of them. This possibility can be eliminated by confining the application of leximin to cases of a small number of non-indifferent persons. It can, however, be shown that such a programme of constraining leximin would be hopeless for an SWFL satisfying unrestricted domain and independence because of the following result (for proof of this rather disturbing result, see Sen (1977c)):

(T.A3*.7) From Leximin-2 to Leximin in general
For any SWFL satisfying Conditions $\tilde{U}$ and $\tilde{I}$, leximin-2 implies leximin in general.

In view of this result, the leximin derivation can be simplified to first obtaining leximin-2 (giving priority to the interest of the worse-off position in a two-person conflict), and then getting from there to leximin in general.

STRONG NEUTRALITY AND STRONG ANONYMITY

As was mentioned earlier, leximin satisfies the conditions of neutrality and anonymity. In fact, it satisfies a stronger version of each condition. So do utilitarianism and many other procedures. Before proceeding any further it is useful to consider these stronger versions of neutrality and anonymity.

Condition SN (strong neutrality)

For any two pairs of social states $\{x, y\}$ and $\{a, b\}$, and any two n-tuples of utility functions $\{U_i\}$ and $\{U_i^*\}$, if for all i, $U_i(x) = U_i^*(a)$ and $U_i(y) = U_i^*(b)$, then $xF(\{U_i\})y$ if and only if $aF(\{U_i^*\})b$.

Condition SA (strong anonymity)

If for any pair of utility n-tuples $\{U_i\}$ and $\{U_i^*\}$, there is a permutation function $\rho(\cdot)$ over the set H of persons such that for some x, for all i, $U_i(x) = U_{\rho(i)}^*(x)$, and for all $y \neq x$, for all i, $U_i(y) = U_i^*(y)$, then $F(\{U_i\}) = F(\{U_i^*\})$.

Strong neutrality implies neutrality $\widetilde{N}$ and independence $\widetilde{I}$, and is indeed equivalent to the combination of the two. It permits neutrality to be applied pair by pair, and asserts that the utility information regarding any two social states is all that is needed for ranking that pair. Strong anonymity asks for invariance not merely when utility functions are permuted between the persons, but also when the utility *values* for any particular state x are permuted between the persons without doing anything to the utility values for other states. Clearly, such permutations can alter the list of preference orderings embedded in an n-tuple of utility functions, and ordering-based rules such as the Method of Majority Decision, while satisfying anonymity (and strong neutrality), do not in general fulfill strong anonymity.

Given strong neutrality, social welfare W can be seen as a function of the individual utility vectors u, bringing us back to a classic formulation of the Bergson–Samuelson social welfare function,[x]

$$W = W(\boldsymbol{u})$$

For SWFLs satisfying unrestricted domain and independence of irrelevant alternatives, the Pareto indifference rule $\widetilde{P}^{o}$ implies strong neutrality, and the Suppes indifference rule S^{o} implies both strong neutrality and strong anonymity.

Strong neutrality theorem
   For any SWFL fulfilling Conditions U and I, $P^{o} \Leftrightarrow SN$.

Strong anonymity theorem
   For any SWFL fulfilling Conditions U and I, $S^{o} \Leftrightarrow (SN \ \& \ SA)$.

For lines of proofs, see Sen (1977c).

HARSANYI'S THEOREMS ON UTILITARIANISM

Harsanyi's (1955) axiomatic treatment of utilitarianism provided an early – and classic – contrast to the ordering-based social welfare judgements in Arrow's social welfare function and related structures. A richer base of utility information permitted Harsanyi to consider the class of the weighted sum of individual utilities – a class that could not have been accommodated within Arrovian social welfare functions, or, for that matter, in SWFLs permitting only ordinal level comparability.

   Harsanyi (1955) established two – essentially independent – results about utilitarianism. One, which I shall call Harsanyi's Impersonal Choice Utilitarianism, requires any individual's social welfare function – reflecting his ethical judgements – to be based on what his preferences about the social states would have been if he had an equal chance of being in the position of anyone in the society.[6] With consistent choice the von Neumann–Morgenstern (1947)

[6] The approach of equity through equi-probability choice of being any one is discussed in Chapter 9 of the 1970 edition. On this way of characterizing social welfare, see also Vickrey (1945). For a critique of the moral acceptability of the approach, see Diamond (1967), and Harsanyi's (1977), (1979) views. For other types of critique,

postulates are assumed to be fulfilled. Then the social welfare from a state can be seen as the utility of an *as if* lottery, having a probability $1/n$ of being anyone in that state. If $W_i(x)$ is the utility of the prize i (i.e. of being person i), in state x in the von Neumann–Morgenstern scale, then clearly

$$W(x) = \frac{1}{n} \sum_{i=1}^{n} W_i(x) \text{ for all } x \in X \tag{H-1}$$

The other result, which I shall call Harsanyi's Utility Sum Theorem, has less of a moral basis, but is analytically more assertive. If, in a given situation, (1) the family of individual utility functions of each person i is cardinal, given by a class of positive affine transformations, (2) the social welfare function is also cardinal, given by a class of positive affine transformations, and (3) the Pareto indifference rule is assumed, i.e. $U_i(x) = U_i(y)$ for all i must imply $W(x) = W(y)$, then social welfare must be a linear weighted sum of individual utilities,

$$W(x) = \sum_{i=1}^{n} a_i U_i(x) \text{ for all } x \in X \tag{H-2}$$

In the discussions on utilitarianism that followed, it is Impersonal Choice Utilitarianism, as in (H-1), that has received much of the attention (see, for example, Arrow (1973)). This is a theorem about utilitarianism in a rather limited sense in that the von Neumann–Morgenstern cardinal scaling of utilities covers *both* W_i and W within *one* integrated system of numbering, and the individual utility numbers W_i do not have any independent meaning other than the value associated with each prize, in predicting choices over lotteries. There is no *independent* concept of individual utilities of which

---

see McClennen (1978) and Blackorby, Donaldson and Weymark (1980). The broader ethical issue of impersonal choice as the basis of moral judgements – going well beyond the utilitarian form – has been illuminatingly discussed by Harsanyi (1958) in his model of ethics in terms of hypothetical imperatives. See also Harsanyi (1977), (1979).

social welfare is shown to be the sum, and as such the result asserts a good deal less than classical utilitarianism does.

For example, consider the case in which a person's ethical judgements, and also his impersonal choices, are based on maximizing the sum of independently measured ratio-scale comparable (RF) individual utilities (uniformly non-negative) raised to the power t (a constant):[xi]

$$W(x) = \frac{1}{t}\sum_{i=1}^{n}(U_i(x))^t \text{ for all } x \tag{H-3}$$

With $t < 1$ social welfare is strictly concave on (and thus non-utilitarian in terms of) the independently measured utilities U_i. It would, however, appear to be utilitarian within the von Neumann–Morgenstern scaling system. Since the only role of W_i attributed to person i is to predict the person's choices under uncertainty, this is a rather superficial form of utilitarianism. As it happens (H-3) permits a whole class of non-utilitarian rules (for all cases other than $t = 1$),[7] and, by making t go to minus infinity, Rawlsian maximin or leximin can also be covered,[xii] for the independently scaled utilities.

Harsanyi's Utility Sum Theorem does not, however, suffer from this problem, and is in this sense a good deal more assertive. But it is primarily a representation theorem. It deals only with single-profile exercises and does not claim that the constants a_i in (H-2) will remain the same when the individual utility functions change (i.e. when the *family* L_i of positive affine transformations alters). Not only, therefore, does it not establish that all the a_i must equal each other as under the utilitarian formula (indeed for the axioms specified they can even be negative), but it does not even require that the set of a_i will be invariant with respect to changes in individual utility characteristics (as opposed to representational change *within* a given positive affine family).

The upshot of this discussion is that there is need for an

---

[7] Note that $U_i(\cdot)$ and $(U_i(\cdot))^t$ cannot belong to the same positive affine class unless, of course, $t = 1$.

axiomatic derivation of utilitarianism despite Harsanyi's theorems. What is needed is an axiomatization that (1) permits independent formulation of individual utilities, and (2) has the invariance property of being independent of the utility functions to be aggregated. Such axiomatic results have recently been presented, and will be taken up in the next subsection. But before closing the discussion on Harsanyi's framework, it is worth asserting unequivocally that the failure to provide a fully-fledged axiomatic derivation of utilitarianism does not render Harsanyi's results useless. Indeed, far from it. The representation theorem is of much interest in itself, and Harsanyi's framework of impersonal choice has proved to be a widely inspiring contribution in social ethics.

UTILITARIANISM: OTHER AXIOMATIC DERIVATIONS

Define a utilitarian SWFL as one which for any n-tuple of individual utility functions, for any x, $y \in X$, declares xRy if and only if $\sum_{i=1}^{n} U_i(x) \geq \sum_{i=1}^{n} U_i(y)$.[8] The following theorem, established by d'Aspremont and Gevers (1977, Theorem 3), uses the invariance requirement for cardinal *unit* comparability CU, in addition to other conditions, to eliminate rival rules to utilitarianism. Again, it is assumed that H is finite and $\#X \geq 3$.

(T.A3*.8) Utilitarianism derived with unit comparability
    An SWFL satisfying Conditions $\widetilde{U}$, $\widetilde{I}$, $\widetilde{P}^*$, $\widetilde{A}$ and CU must be utilitarian.

It is first checked that a utilitarian SWFL must indeed satisfy these conditions. This is immediate for $\widetilde{U}$, $\widetilde{I}$, $\widetilde{P}^*$ and $\widetilde{A}$. Regarding

---

[8] Yaari (1978) defines the utilitarian form less restrictively, using a weighted-sum *formula*, with the weights being endogenously determined. One set of assumptions is shown to lead to the equivalence of Rawlsian and utilitarian SWFLs. Yaari thus provides an axiomatic (and also intuitive) analysis of a much wider class of rules than utilitarianism as it is normally defined.

CU, it need only be noted that translating anyone's utility function by adding a constant (positive or negative) to it must leave all the differences $[U_i(x) - U_i(y)]$ unaffected. And multiplying each U_i by the same constant leaves the *relative* differences unchanged. So we need be concerned only with establishing that these conditions together do not permit any other kind of an SWFL.

It follows from the Strong Neutrality Theorem that the SWFL in question must be strongly neutral. Since given unrestricted domain, independence and anonymity, the Pareto indifference rule implies Suppes' indifference rule, the SWFL must also be strongly anonymous by the Strong Anonymity Theorem. So in ranking any pair x, y $\in Y$, we need be concerned only with the utility vectors for x and y, and we can permute the utility values among the individuals for any state without changing the social ranking.

Take, first, a case in which the individual utility sums for x and y are equal; we have to show xIy. Permute the utility numbers among the persons in each state separately in such a way that we have the utility order in line with the individual numbers: $U_n(a) \geq U_{n-1}(a) \geq \ldots \geq U_2(a) \geq U_1(a)$, for $a = x, y$. Now deduct from *each* $U_i(a)$ the minimal of the two values $\{U_i(x), U_i(y)\}$. (Note that this is a permitted transformation under CU, being a translation of individual origins, which can be freely done.) After the deductions permute the individual utilities again in each state to get them in line with individual numbers: $U_n^1(a) \geq U_{n-1}^1(a) \geq \ldots \geq U_2^1(a) \geq U_1^1(a)$. This yields $\{U_i^1\}$. By repeating this process, for some r, we shall get $U_i^r(a) = 0$, for all i and for $a = x, y$. By the Pareto principle, xIy for this utility n-tuple $\{U_i^r\}$, and by CU this must be the case for all $\{U_i\}$ in $\bar{L}$. Hence xIy.

If, instead, we started with the individual utility sum being larger for x than for y, then we would have reached $U_i^r(y) \geq 0$, for all i, with $U_i^r(x) > 0$ for some i. So by the strong Pareto principle, xPy. And this establishes that the SWFL is indeed utilitarian.

Various other axiomatizations of utilitarianism have also been presented.[xiii] Eric Maskin's (1978) elegant axiomatization uses a condition of separability (Condition *SE*) and a requirement of continuity.

(T.A3*.9) Utilitarianism derived with separability and continuity
An SWFL satisfying Conditions $\tilde{U}$, $\tilde{I}$, $\tilde{P}^*$, $\tilde{A}$, SE, continuity and the invariance requirement for cardinal full comparability CF, must be utilitarian.

It follows from the application of Debreu's (1960) theorem on additive separability, that due to $\tilde{U}$, $\tilde{I}$, $\tilde{P}^*$ and SE, it must be the case that there exist continuous functions $v_i(\cdot)$ such that xRy if and only if $\sum_{i=1}^{n} v_i(U_i(x)) \geq \sum_{i=1}^{n} v_i(U_i(y))$. By anonymity, for all i, $v_i(\cdot) = v(\cdot)$. Maskin completes the proof by demonstrating (with the help of the invariance requirement CF, and continuity, in addition to $\tilde{U}$, $\tilde{I}$, and $\tilde{P}^*$) that $v(\cdot)$ must be a positive affine transformation. That establishes that the SWFL is utilitarian.

(T.A3*.10) Joint characterization theorem
An SWFL satisfying Conditions $\tilde{U}$, $\tilde{I}$, $\tilde{P}$, $\tilde{A}$, SE, ME and the invariance condition CF, must be either leximin or of the utilitarian type.

We know from the Leximin Derivation Theorem that these conditions, with the additional requirement of invariance for ordinal level comparability OL, will lead to leximin. By broadening the utility informational framework to cardinal full comparability, the only additional rules that are admitted must be of the utilitarian type. If now leximin is excluded by some axiom, and there are many mild axioms that will do this, the class of utilitarian-type rules would have been axiomatized. The advantage of this route lies in the fact that it demands neither continuity, nor the informational limitation of CU, which renders an important parameter (*viz.* comparative utility levels) unavailable for use.[9] On the other hand, the Joint Characterization Theorem delivers quite a bit less, *viz.* it axiomatizes utilitarian-type rules rather than *the* utilitarian rule. Further, to get to utilitarianism in particular, rather than the joint characterization of utilitarian-type

[9] Myerson (1983) derives utilitarianism from Pareto optimality and a linearity condition, but – more importantly – shows that Pareto optimality, independence and a concavity condition together ensure that the social welfare rule must be *either* utilitarian *or* egalitarian.

rules and leximin, this route would require some additional exclusion, notably something to knock out leximin.

BORDA AND POSITIONAL RULES

I end this chapter with some brief observations on 'positional rules' first introduced by J. C. Borda – one of the pioneers of social choice theory (and a contemporary of Condorcet).[10] The so-called Borda rule of determining voting results is to take note of the position of an alternative vis-à-vis others in a ranking, weighting each alternative by its rank-order position. The Borda rule can be seen as based on attaching a valuational number to any alternative equal to the sum of its ranks in each person's preference ordering (e.g. in a 3-person, 3-state world, if x is first in one person's ordering and third in the other two people's rankings, then the Borda count for x is $1+3+3 = 7$). The Borda rule ranks the alternative states in the *inverse* order of these numbers, and the rule has been axiomatized in the social choice literature with different antecedent axioms.[xiv]

Gärdenfors (1973) and Fine and Fine (1974) have presented a thorough exploration of positional rules. These include finite ranking rules, which are based on attaching weightings according to the position occupied by an alternative in each person's ordering – the weights being a non-decreasing function of ranks, applied in the same way to everyone's ordering (that is, anonymously). The social ranking is made to reflect the ranking of the sum of weights on the different states. A special case of this is the Borda method. Another is a variant of utilitarianism with utilities taken to be reflected by positions. The *intersection* of all finite ranking rules yields a quasi-ordering exactly reflecting rank-dominance R^D, when xR^Dy if and only if for some interpersonal permutation, x occupies at least as high a position in each person's ordering as y does in the corresponding person's ordering.[xv] The axiomatic structure of various positional rules analysed in

---

[10] Prasanta Pattanaik (2011) has provided a highly illuminating account of positional rules, including an assessment of their advantages and limitations.

recent contributions have enriched our understanding of the nature and operation of these important classes of decision procedures (see Pattanaik (2002)).

Positional discrimination can also be combined with the use of ordinal level-comparable utilities, and the weights can be based on the rank of a station (x, i), i.e. that of being person i in state x, in an interpersonal order of the entire Cartesian product of X and H. While the general format will be that of ranking social states according to the sum of weights on all stations involving that state, the interpersonal rank-order rule (IROR) corresponds exactly to the Borda rule, in making the weight on each station equal its rank number.[xvi]

Consider an example with nine different stations, involving three states and three persons:

$(x, 1)$
$(y, 2)$
$(z, 3)$
$(x, 2)$
$(y, 3)$
$(z, 1)$
$(x, 3)$
$(y, 1)$
$(z, 2)$

The majority rule will yield here a preference cycle: yPx, zPy, and xPz. The Borda rule will yield universal indifference: xIy, yIz, zIx. In contrast, IROR will yield the strict ordering to xPy & xPz. So will the Rawlsian maximin (or leximin) rule, defined on utilities, in this case. But this coincidence does not always – in fact typically – hold. Indeed, a conflict between the two can be brought about by switching the positions of $(x, 3)$ and $(z, 2)$, which would leave the IROR ranking unchanged (with xPy & yPz) but reverse the Rawlsian ordering to zPy & yPx. These are all distinct rules, with their own respective rationale.

In the last case, i.e. with interpersonal positional rules, the positional information is used, as it were, to convert ordinal level comparability into some kind of a devised cardinal full comparability based on ranks in the extended ordering of $X \times H$. In the case of ordinary positional rules, including the Borda rule, the positional information is used to convert non-comparable ordinal utility information into assumed cardinal full comparability by building on the ranks in each person's ordering taken separately for each individual. It is the arbitrariness of translating rank values into numerical weights that is typically found to be the weakest aspect of both these classes of rules. Indeed Arrow's (1951a) defence of the condition of independence rested partly on the need to avoid such arbitrariness (as he discussed).

There are two ways of defining the Borda rule, depending on whether the Borda counts are based on the ranks in the total set X, or in the set S from which the choice $C(S)$ is to be made, with $S \subseteq X$. It can be easily checked that while the former, which may be called the 'broad Borda rule', violates independence but yields a transitive social ordering, the latter, which may be called the 'narrow Borda rule', satisfies the independence condition but can yield non-binary choice functions. The narrow version has the merit of providing a social choice function, possibly satisfying all of Arrow's conditions, viz. P, I and D, and much of universal domain U, except for collective rationality, which is part of Arrow's demand on U (it fails that demand, but does yield a non-binary but complete choice function). In this respect, the narrow Borda rule is a serious rival of social choice functions based on the transitive closures of the majority rule, investigated by Schwartz (1970), (1972), Bloomfield (1971), Campbell (1972), (1976), Bordes (1976) and Deb (1977), among others.

I shall not go more extensively into the approach of positional rules. The most famous of them – the Borda rule – does offer an easy quantification. This convenience is bought at some cost of arbitrariness in seeing the gaps between any two proximate alternatives to be exactly the same – for every person and every pair of alternatives. The popularity of the Borda rule has tended to rest on people's frustration about cycles generated by majority rule (or about there being no majority winner from some subsets). It has tended to appeal, despite its arbitrariness, as a kind of a second-best choice. That choice may have to be reassessed to the extent that Maskin's (1995),

(2014) demonstration of the versatility of majority rule tends to generate some reasons for more optimism about coherent majority outcomes.

Problems of neglecting inequality among people, because of ignoring interpersonal comparisons, do, of course, remain for both majority rule and the standard Borda rule (though the interpersonal version of the Borda rule, or IROR, addresses some of the worries). It is important to know what positive things we get from each of the rival social choice approaches, and also what they respectively fail to achieve. Once again, the case for informed public reasoning about the relative merits of the different routes to social choice is strong. Indeed, it is as important in welfare economics and social welfare assessment as it is for elections and political decisions.

Chapter A4
Democracy and Public Engagement

In the emergence of modern democracy, the post-Enlightenment experiences of Europe and America have clearly played a decisive role, so much so that it is tempting to think of democracy as a specifically Western idea. Indeed, that is precisely how it is often seen in contemporary political discussions. And yet, as the insightful commentator on American democracy Alexis de Tocqueville noted in the early nineteenth century, while the 'great democratic revolution' occurring then in Europe and America was 'a new thing', it was also an expression of 'the most continuous, ancient, and permanent tendency known in history'.[i] In understanding the idea behind democracy, we have to give adequate recognition to the attraction of participatory governance that has surfaced and resurfaced over a long period in different parts of the world.

THE DEMANDS OF DEMOCRACY

What exactly is democracy? There are at least two different ways of thinking about it, and the differences between the two interpretations have far-reaching implications for our understanding of the foundations of democracy (as I have discussed in *The Idea of Justice*, Sen (2009a)). There is, first, the institutional view of democracy, which characterizes it mainly in terms of elections and ballots. This view, which may be called the 'public ballot perspective', interprets democracy almost entirely in terms of voting, mainly as majority rule, and it has been forcefully presented as such by many organizational theorists, for example Samuel Huntington in his book, *The Third Wave: Democratization in the Late Twentieth Century*: 'Elections, open, free, and fair, are the essence of democracy, the inescapable sine qua non' (Huntington (1991), p. 9). Yet this can hardly be a definitive reading of what a representative democracy has to do, since the sovereignty in taking decisions of this kind must belong to the Parliament. But in the public-ballot perspective, the ballot-result is all that counts, no matter how incomplete and how marred by misleading ads and posters – sometimes even fanning racist sentiments – the public discussion preceding the voting might have been.

The second – much broader – interpretation sees democracy in terms of decisions based on public reasoning, combining participatory discussions with public decision-making. Voting and balloting are, in this broader understanding of democracy, just one part – though an important one – of a much larger story. There is need for supporting and cultivating open and informed discussion, and to help facilitate the responsiveness of public decisions to that interactive process. In this perspective, the democratic obligations must include the commitment to *protect* as well as to *utilize* public reasoning (including fact-checking and other facilities for helping public understanding and communication). This way of seeing democracy is certainly not new, but it has been particularly explored in recent years by political philosophers, led by John Rawls and Jürgen Habermas, and by public choice theorists, particularly James Buchanan. There is by now a fairly widespread understanding that – as Rawls puts it – 'the definitive idea for deliberative democracy is the idea of deliberation itself'.[ii] This way of understanding democracy, which John Stuart Mill did much to clarify, has been described in Millian lines as 'government by discussion' (a phrase attributed to Walter Bagehot).

Neither of these two perspectives on democracy has been an exclusively 'Western' preoccupation. Indeed, both have non-Western as well as Western antecedents, going back a long time. This is not to deny that the West has led the world in the practice of democracy in its present form. I am not referring here primarily to the role of ancient Greece, Athens in particular, in initiating the practice of voting for governmental decisions. Even though that was indeed a gigantic achievement for the world, it is hard to see ancient Greece as quintessentially a European country in the sixth century BC. Indeed, the partitioning of the world into discrete civilizations with geographical correlates, in which ancient Greece is seen as part and parcel of an identifiable 'Europe', is a cultural confusion. In this bemused perspective, no great difficulty is perceived in seeing the descendants of, say, Goths and Visigoths and Vikings as the inheritors of the Greek tradition ('they are all Europeans by race'), while there is resistance to taking note of the intellectual links of ancient Greeks with ancient Egyptians, Iranians and Indians, despite the much greater interest that the ancient Greeks themselves showed – as recorded in contemporary accounts – in talking to these non-Europeans, rather than clamouring to chat with the ancient Visigoths.

Following the early Greek innovation, voting procedures were used in other countries as well, but those were mainly in Asia (in Iran, Bactria and India), to the east of Greece. There is nothing to indicate that the Greek experience in electoral governance had much *immediate* impact on the countries to the west and the north of Greece and Rome, in say Britain or France or Germany. That would happen very much later. The ancient Asian experiments in democratic voting did not, alas, last very long. However, in Europe, more than a thousand years later, the art of governance made rapid progress through the second millennium AD, particularly in some of the flourishing Italian city-states.

However, democracy as we understand it today had to wait even longer. It was more than two thousand years after the ancient Athenian democratic elections that Europe started moving decisively towards democratic voting. This happened particularly in the eighteenth and nineteenth centuries. When it did, European theorists, such as Condorcet, Mill and Tocqueville, provided a basic – and plausible – case for democratic governance, and European countries, moving at different speeds, provided major examples of the growth of democratic practice.

A similar regional diversity can be found in the practice of democracy seen as 'government by discussion'. While Athens certainly had an excellent record in public discussion, open deliberation flourished also in several other ancient civilizations – sometimes spectacularly so. For example, some of the earliest open general meetings aimed specifically at settling disputes between different points of view, on social as well as religious matters, took place in India in the so-called Buddhist 'councils', where adherents of different points of view got together to argue out their differences, beginning in the fifth century BC. The first of these councils met in Rajagriha (modern Rajgir) shortly after Gautama Buddha's death, and the second was held, about a hundred years later, in Vaishali.

Ashoka, the Indian emperor, who hosted the third – and the largest – Buddhist Council in the third century BC in Patna (then called Pataliputra), the capital city of the Indian empire, also tried to codify and propagate what were among the earliest formulations of rules for public discussion (some kind of early version of the nineteenth-century *Robert's Rules of Order*). To consider another historical example, in early seventh-century Japan, the Buddhist Prince Shōtoku produced the so-called 'constitution of seventeen articles', in AD 604. The constitution insisted, much in the spirit of the Magna Carta (to be signed six centuries later in 1215), that: 'Decisions on important matters should not be made by one person alone. They should be discussed with many.'[iii] Indeed, the importance of public discussion was a recurrent theme in the history of many countries in the non-Western world, and the understanding of democracy went well beyond the perspective of ballots and elections.

From acknowledging the relevance of global history we must not, however, move to the presumption that we cannot break from the past to initiate a radical political departure. Indeed, new political initiatives have always been needed in different ways across the world. We do not have to be born into a tradition of democratic history to be able to choose that way today. The significance of history in this respect lies rather in the more general understanding that established traditions continue to exert some influence on people's ideas and imagination, that they can inspire or deter, and that they have to be taken into account, whether we are moved by them, or wish to resist or transcend them.

It is not, therefore, surprising – though it does deserve clearer recognition today – that in the fight for democracy led by visionary and fearless political leaders across the world (such as Sun Yat-sen, Jawaharlal Nehru, Nelson Mandela, Martin Luther King or Aung San Suu Kyi), an awareness of local as well as world history has played an important constructive part. In his autobiography, *Long Walk to Freedom*, Nelson Mandela describes how impressed and influenced he was, as a young boy, by seeing the democratic nature of the proceedings of the local meetings that were held in the regent's house in Mqhekezweni:

> Everyone who wanted to speak did so. It was democracy in its purest form. There may have been a hierarchy of importance among the speakers, but everyone was heard, chief and subject, warrior and medicine man, shopkeeper and farmer, landowner and laborer.[iv]

Mandela's understanding of democracy was hardly aided by the political practice that he saw around him in apartheid-based South Africa, run by people of European origin, who, it may be recalled, used to call themselves by the cultural term 'European' – rather than just 'white'. In fact, the 'European' culture of Pretoria had little to offer to Mandela's comprehension of democracy. His discernment of democracy came, as is abundantly clear from his autobiography, from his knowledge and understanding of global ideas as well as local African practice.

ON JUDGING DEMOCRACY

As was discussed earlier, social choice theory has been much influenced by a commitment to democratic participation. This is as clear in the early eighteenth-century ideas about social choice in revolutionary France (for example in the writings of Condorcet) as it is in the formulation that the modern theory of social choice received from the pioneering work of Kenneth Arrow. While both Condorcet and Arrow were influenced by the needs of what we called earlier the 'public ballot perspective', each also showed considerable interest in the demands of public reasoning as a background condition for the formal use of rules of elections and votes. Indeed, it is the possibility of inconsistent decisions of majority rule, and, in particular, the possibility of there being no majority winner in a public vote (the so-called Condorcet paradox), that was a principal challenge that early social choice theory faced. Arrow's impossibility theorem vastly strengthened the sense of inadequacy of voting procedures, originally generated by the Condorcet paradox: how to assess – and perhaps revise – the axiomatic demands that should be placed on social choice is itself a quintessential subject for public reasoning. A significant part of the discussion in the earlier chapters of this book has been directly associated with that task.

In the earlier (1970) edition of this book, the conditions that would ensure consistent majority decisions, and guarantee a clear majority winner, received considerable exploration (see Chapters 10 and 10*). This took the form mainly of what was called 'domain restriction', requiring that the configuration of individual preferences that are being aggregated should follow certain patterns. How to identify different ways of achieving consistent majority decisions has been extensively explored in the subsequent literature.[v]

If generating coherent and unambiguous social choices is one of the challenges that majority rule faces, examining whether majority decisions are sensible and normatively acceptable is surely another. It is easy to find situations in which a majority will benefit from a change that seems clearly unjust in terms of normal ethical assessment. For example, if half the hard-earned incomes of the poorest 20 per cent of the population is taken away from them and distributed among the richer 80 per cent, there would be a gain for a huge majority. If people always vote according to their narrowly defined self-interest, then an appalling redistribution like this – favouring the richer 80 per cent at the expense of the poorest fifth – will handsomely win in a majority vote. Considering cases like this, it is tempting to think that inconsistencies in majority rule, which muddy the water of social decisions, may well be ethically less unattractive than some consistent majority decisions, where a severely regressive change has clear-cut majority backing. Inconsistency may not be the worst that majority rule can produce.

Yet the idea that people must always vote according to their narrow self-interest – common enough in some parts of economics – reflects a very limited understanding of human behaviour, which ignores the role of values and commitments that influence people (as was discussed in Chapter A2). Indeed, if people must be assumed to be voting only according to their narrow self-interest, it would actually be difficult to explain why people bother to vote at all, and do so even at some cost or inconvenience, despite the fact that the probability of an individual vote making a difference to the outcome is often absolutely minute.[vi] The role of majority decision as a social choice mechanism has to be assessed in terms of people's actual priorities, taking note of all the values they have, and not just in terms of how they must vote if they were gripped completely by narrow self-interest.

This is where the understanding of democracy in broader terms becomes particularly relevant. Public reasoning can, of course, influence even voting decisions, as well as uphold the legitimacy of minority rights and personal liberties which a democratic structure may include and facilitate. The question then becomes not so much what would happen in a world of pure majority rule where people behave in narrowly self-interested ways, but what real people, with their variety of valuational concerns in diverse institutional settings, are likely to want. It is the legitimacy as well as the reach and likely performance of democratic systems that gives them plausibility as social choice mechanisms. As Habermas has argued, the role and influence of public reasoning encompasses 'moral questions of justice' as well as 'instrumental questions of power and coercion'.[1]

---

[1] A more comprehensive approach to democracy can embed majority decisions with votes and ballots drawing on a broad structure of institutions, values and social dialogues; see Joshua Cohen (1989) and Cohen and Rogers (1983). See also Bruce Ackerman (1980), Seyla Benhabib (1996), (2006), Jeremy Waldron (1999), Ronald Dworkin (2008) and the more recent contributions of Fabienne Peter (2011) and Hélène Landmore (2013).

EASY SUCCESSES AND HARDER BATTLES

I turn now to what may be regarded as a practical question. Does democracy, with majority rule and public reasoning, in fact work in the way its proponents, including John Rawls, Jürgen Habermas, Joshua Cohen and others tend to assume? I have argued for some decades (see Sen (1982c), (1983c), (1999)) that a functioning democracy can have easy success in preventing some types of disasters, such as famines, which are clearly preventable and for which blame can be readily assigned when they are not actually prevented. Consider India, which had widespread famines fairly regularly through the entire period of colonial rule by the British Raj, and which stopped with impressive speed as the country became independent with a democratic system of governance in 1947 (the last Indian famine was in 1943, the so-called 'Bengal famine', in which between 2 and 3 million people died). With a largely free press and periodic elections, no government can survive the political consequences of an unprevented famine. And this provides incentive enough for prompt governmental intervention to stop a threatening famine. Across the world, famines have continued to occur only in countries that do not have a functioning democratic system with a free press.

That is surely an important success. And yet the huge and hardened inequalities, related to class, caste and gender, that characterize the highly stratified society of India have remained largely unremedied. And while India has had no actual famines in its post-colonial history, there has been an astonishing tolerance of the nastiness of endemic undernourishment, which may not kill people through starvation but which can greatly elevate the incidence of illnesses, as well as leading to the underdevelopment of mental as well as physical faculties when children are the victims.

Why is there such a difference in the way a functioning democracy deals with famines and endemic, but non-extreme, undernourishment? One reason is the ease with which famines and massive death tolls from starvation and associated diseases can be politicized, in contrast with the difficulty of generating public understanding of less easily observed social failures, including persistent hunger. The endemic deprivations of all kinds in India have received extraordinarily little attention in public discussion (the recent reporting and discussion of rape is something of an exception here, mediated by public agitations following a high-profile case of rape in Delhi in December 2012). Inattention to widespread deprivation helps the tolerance – and continuation – of abject poverty and deprivation, despite the presence of extensive democratic institutions.

Where exactly does the epistemic role of public deliberation come into this story? We can begin with the question: why does famine prevention have such compelling force in pushing a ruling government to prompt action? The votes of famine victims in a system of majority decision cannot in itself explain the difference. The number of famine victims as a proportion of the total population is always quite small – usually no more than 5 per cent and hardly ever more than 10 per cent of the total population. If the affected or threatened people were the only persons who were moved by the importance and urgency of famine prevention, then electoral outcomes based on majority decision could not be particularly effective for this task. It is through public discussion and awareness that people in general – not just the minority threatened by famines – come to appreciate the suffering of the famine victims and understand the urgency of preventing such calamities. Public discussion also makes people better informed on the fact, which used to be denied, that famines can be easily stopped by prompt public intervention (on this see Sen (1981), and Drèze and Sen (1989)).[vii] That is how public reasoning, combined with regular and free elections, works as an antidote to famines in a functioning democracy.

In contrast with the observable calamity of famines, the continuation of endemic but non-extreme hunger, the persistence of illiteracy and the lack of good school education and basic health care, all of which take heavy tolls in the long run, do not easily generate the kind of excitement that the visible brutality of a famine tends to cause. In order to make the removal of on-going but undramatic deprivations an electorally powerful cause that can rally the bulk of the population and get them politically excited, we need information circulation and anger in the media, led by the commitment and skill of those who are involved in political debates and agitations. In the Indian general elections of 2014, when there was a decisive outcome (if only by a majority of Parliamentary seats being won by a party with minority support), issues such as illiteracy, absence of health care, and social and economic deprivation hardly figured in the campaign, and the media showed very little interest in relating the electoral options to these questions.

There is certainly a bias of coverage in the media which a distinguished editor, N. Ram (1989), delineated with clarity some decades ago. The problem certainly does not come from the paucity of newspapers in India. More than 96,000 different newspapers come out every day in India, which has, in fact, the largest circulation, by a substantial margin, of newspapers in the world. It also has one of the highest penetrations of audio and visual media. The difficulty lies rather in the nature and working of the Indian media, which tend to cater primarily to the concerns and interests of the comparatively privileged, combined with some additional features of general entertainment (such as films and popular music). As Jean Drèze and I have discussed in our book *An Uncertain Glory: India and Its Contradictions* (Drèze and Sen (2013)), investigation of the range of news coverage and of social analysis in the media bring out sharply the biases in the coverage of news and investigations in India, which influence the outcomes of elections and the choice of priorities in policy making. Basic issues about the lives of the poor – illiteracy, absence of health care, lack of immunization, terrible sanitary conditions and environmental hazards that particularly affect those who do not live in well-insulated homes – receive little space, let alone prominence, in the coverage of what is happening, and what, in particular, is *not* happening.

Successes such as in famine prevention illustrate what democracy can achieve – and that is certainly important. Yet it is not adequate to rely only on the public ballot features of democracy, nor can it be assumed that public reasoning would readily complete, given a free press and fair elections, the process of democratic engagement. The active development of public engagement to address the neglected questions is a non-trivial challenge. There is absolutely nothing automatic about the enjoyment of the potential fruits of democracy, which is an opportunity that has to be firmly seized, not a dispenser of benefactions that flow without human intervention.

EMPIRICAL EVIDENCE AND GENERAL ARGUMENTS

I am tempted to stop there – seeing democracy as an opportunity rather than as a cluster of forgone conclusions. But there have been interesting discussions on what we may expect from democracy in predictive terms, instead of being content to see it as a call for reasoned public action.[2] Some basic scepticism related to the working of democratic social choice theory has to be addressed.

It is certainly worth noting that the undermining of the case for democracy based on alleged failures of majority rule is often exaggerated. To take an often-repeated case, it has been argued, for example, that Hitler may have been a tyrant who suppressed democracy, but that he had come to office after winning a majority vote. This is supposed to show the contradiction that is ever-present in democratic governance. The historical reading that is presented to make this case is actually quite mistaken. Hitler became the leader of the Nazi party, the NSDAP (National Socialist German Workers Party) in 1921, and his first attempt to capture governing power was through a coup in 1923, which failed miserably (and after which Hitler was sent to prison for a while). In both the elections of 1932, in July and November, Hitler's Nazi party came second. Indeed, even after Hitler, acting as the head of a coalition government, managed to organize a propaganda war and generate mass hysteria against his opponents by playing up a strongly distorted interpretation of the Reichstag fire in February 1933, his party did not obtain a majority in the elections of March 1933 (its share of the popular vote was less than 44 per cent). What Hitler had won was a

---

[2] See Ian Shapiro's lucid discussion of what he aptly calls 'the real world of democratic theory' (Shapiro (2011)).

plurality (a higher vote share than any other party), which – as will be discussed in the next chapter – is a very different rule from majority decision. Of course, the edifice of democratic social choice theory, as investigated by Arrow or Inada or Suzumura or Pattanaik or Maskin, would not have radically altered had Hitler in fact got a majority vote rather than a plurality in a staged election. But the often-aired story that it was a majority vote that yielded Hitler's dominance, and ultimately his rule, is a historical fantasy.

There have, of course, been actual historical failures of majority rule that are easily diagnosed. It is, for instance, not difficult to find examples of an organized majority emerging against minorities, with the politics of racist propaganda. There does remain the empirical issue of what democracy can be expected to do, taking the rough with the smooth, and any generalization without exception would be hard to obtain. There is also the question what the alternatives to democracy and majority rule might be, and, in particular, whether an elite-run minority rule might end up being less unjust than a majoritarian democracy (as some have postulated). While an authoritarian system of one kind or other may be associated with the rich economic and social achievements of, say, Singapore or China (the merits of which must be recognized despite the presence of drawbacks), other authoritarian rules have generated gigantic human tragedies that we see in, say, North Korea today, or saw in military-run Argentina yesterday. There are surely reasons for pause here.

There have been in recent years some powerfully argued defences of democracy as a system, going well beyond the public ballot perspective. Particular emphasis has been placed, I believe rightly, on the epistemic contributions that a democratic system with freedom of speech and scrutiny, and informational inputs to participatory elections, can make. Fabienne Peter (2011) has argued in her extensive analysis of democratic legitimacy that, through a combination of procedural and epistemic facilities, a democratic system can plausibly be expected to do better – and, in particular, to have greater legitimacy – than the alternatives available. Similarly, Hélène Landemore (2013) has made 'a sustained epistemic case for democracy', in her book, *Democratic Reason: Politics, Collective Intelligence, and the Rule of the Many.*[viii] Information is central to intelligent social choice, and democracy has much to offer in this respect, provided – as was discussed earlier – the opportunities offered by democratic institutions are appropriately utilized.

In addition to egalitarian participation, the epistemic potentials of democratic systems need wider recognition than they tend to get. As I finish writing this extended edition sitting in Europe, viewing the vast economic and social damage done by the policies of austerity, autocratically chosen by the leaders of Europe's financial institutions (which wield so much power today), with extraordinarily little public discussion *before* the choices were made, it is not easy to escape the thought that more epistemic engagement with ordinary people (as well as a great many economists, whose dissents were often brushed away with impressive rapidity by financial leaders) could have helped. There could have been more clarity on the dangers of the policies about to be chosen, which were embraced by financial officialdom with extremely little open public discussion on economic reasoning or social consequences.[3]

If the neglect of the Millian idea of 'government by discussion' has taken its toll recently in generating confusion related to such events as the Brexit referendum, it has also exacted penalties through the rule of financial superpowers in Europe over the years by stifling economic growth and damaging the skills and futures of the young unemployed. To be sure, most of the governments across Europe that readily endorsed these authoritarian policies experienced defeat in the elections that followed, so that the democratic censure of disastrously authoritarian decisions was not escaped. But 'government by discussion' demands that discussions *precede* the decisions to be taken, rather than making heads roll *following* the implementation of inadequately discussed policies.

There was much more public discussion in the campaign which led to the 2016 victory of Donald Trump as the President-elect of the

---

[3] See the collection of essays, including a powerful introduction by Herman Van Rompuy, the former President of the European Council, *After the Storm: How to Save Democracy in Europe* (Middelaar and Van Parijs (2015)). My own views are contained in an essay in that volume, and also in Sen (2012). See also the illuminating analysis of Skidelsky (2012), (2014).

United States, and the debates were angry and long drawn out (even more than they usually are in American elections). And yet the epistemic quality of the exchanges was often extraordinarily low, with at least one of the candidates making vague promises of various drastic changes, such as building a solid wall separating Mexico from the United States, combined with thoroughly misleading statements about how such changes would be implemented. Much 'fake news' was hurled around. There were also official proclamations that took the form of innuendos, dressed as new factual discoveries, coming from the head of the Federal Bureau of Investigation (who did not appear to be particularly neutral in his approach). As it happens, the President-elect was victorious through the special American system of 'Electoral Colleges', without getting the support of a majority of voters. In fact, Hilary Clinton, the defeated candidate, got more votes than the victorious Trump. This is one of many respects in which the electoral system for US presidential elections seems defective (I shall return to this issue in the next chapter). But the inadequacy of informed and factually scrutinized public discussion was no less a prominent feature of the 2016 presidential election. This was certainly not a way of building the basis of a 'government by discussion'.

So I am inclined to close this chapter (before I get to some technical issues regarding majority rule and other voting schemes in Chapter A4*) with two basic submissions. First, democratic decision-making has enormous potentials which are often not fully realized, and which invite public engagement. Our formal understanding of the demands of majority rule in the public ballot perspective, important as it is (see Chapter A4*), has to be supplemented by improving the scope, reach and consequences of public reasoning.

Second, given the mixed bag of results that we can actually get from majoritarian democracy, its defence, important as it is, needs to be seriously supplemented by probing scrutiny of its limits and conditionalities. Democracy can promise, and indeed deliver, results if the opportunities offered by it are adequately seized. But it can also generate a false sense of security and smugness. The promotion of democracy has to go hand in hand with appreciation of what David Runciman (2013) has called, in his beautifully argued book, 'the confidence trap'.

Chapter A4*
Votes and Majorities

Majority rule has wide appeal, for reasons that are not far to seek.[i] However, what is called a 'majority vote outcome' in informal political discussion is quite often a result of a plurality decision, rather than the majority rule. Indeed, even though there is an aura of majority voting in, say, US elections, 'plurality rule' is probably the most widely used method in practice, with victory for the candidate that most voters rank first. But a plurality winner may well be defeated in a pairwise majority vote by several other candidates. The same is true of many other democratic countries, for example the United Kingdom, or India. At this time, the BJP (Bharatiya Janata Party) has a firm majority of seats in the Indian Parliament, won on the basis of minority support (only 31 per cent of the total vote cast went to the BJP) in the multi-party national elections.

The outcomes of plurality rule and majority vote can be quite different (on which see Maskin (2014), and also Maskin and Sen (2016), (2017)). Consider three alternative candidates, x, y and z, with the following distribution of preference rankings with three groups of voters.

Voter shares	40%	35%	25%
1st choice	x	y	z
2nd choice	z	z	y
3rd choice	y	x	x

Plurality rule will select x as the clear winner (with its commanding lead of 40 per cent support). And yet x will be defeated by y with a 60–40 margin in a majority vote. It will be defeated by z also by the same margin. In fact, with these preferences, there is a clear majority winner, namely z, which not only defeats x by a 60–40 margin, but also vanquishes y by a 65–35 margin. As Condorcet argued, the majority winner is one who prevails over each of the other candidates in pair-by-pair contests, and this brings out z as the real majority winner, despite its deficit in being the top-choice of the people (only 25%, as against 40% for x and 35% for y).

Despite the frequent invoking of the need for majority rule, it is some form or other of plurality rule that is, in effect, used in a variety of democratic countries, from the USA and UK to India and Japan. The appeal of the plurality winner is often enhanced by misdescribing it as a 'majority winner'. For example, as was just mentioned, the ruling BJP party in India got only 31 per cent of the votes, but a majority of parliamentary seats, and it has often been described as being 'the majority winner'.

The appeal of plurality rule arises partly from the fact that it yields ready-made answers in simple votes. The real majority winner can be determined through a set of pairwise comparisons, which can, of course, be easily done if the voters ranked all the candidates, as in the example above. If all the voters rank *all* the candidates, we can easily check whether there is going to be a majority winner or not, and which alternative will be that winner.

An electoral victory is more convincing if the winner has a majority of votes, rather than a mere plurality. That is an important distinction, but so is the fact that a plurality system, but not majority decision, can inhibit plausible candidates from contesting an election for fear of 'splitting' the votes for candidates with affinities. For example, Bernie Sanders or, for that matter, Michael Bloomberg, who could have entered the presidential race as independent candidates, refrained from doing so, perhaps for fear of splitting the anti-Trump vote (thereby helping Trump). But if the system were one of real majority decision, then Bloomberg or Sanders could have easily joined the race without forcing any vote-splitting, since each candidate would have been compared with the others in pair-by-pair comparison (a voter could rank both Clinton and Sanders above Trump, and each would have been compared *singly* with Trump). In that case, the presence of Sanders or Bloomberg in the list to be ranked would not have helped Trump, of whom all three were very critical. It would have, however, given the voters more choice, with some voters preferring Sanders (or Bloomberg) to both Clinton and Trump.

DOMAIN RESTRICTION
AND MAJORITY WINNER

Chapters 10 and 10* of the original edition of this book were much concerned with the existence of a clear majority winner, and also with the transitivity of majority decisions. Various domain restrictions were considered, which limit the patterns of voter profiles, or permissible configurations of individual rankings of all voters. The sufficiency conditions for the transitivity of majority rule (and for weaker requirements) were identified, including Value Restriction (VR), Extremal Restriction (ER) and Limited Agreement (LA).

It was shown in Sen and Pattanaik (1969), and in Chapter 10* here, that the necessary and sufficient conditions for a majority rule to yield a decisive result for every subset of alternatives is that the individual preference profiles should satisfy, for every triple of alternatives, either VR or ER or LA (Theorem 10*6). For full transitivity of majority decisions, only ER proves to be both necessary and sufficient (Theorem 10*7).[ii]

This complex picture can be simplified in an agreeable way if individual preferences are taken to be 'strict' (or anti-symmetric), that is, if there are no indifferences between distinct alternatives. *Then* ER entails VR, and so does LA. With that simplification, and taking the number of voters to be odd, we arrive at the result that Value Restriction is necessary and sufficient for full transitivity of the majority decision and for it to be an Arrovian social welfare function (see Theorem 10*9). In a remarkable theorem, Eric Maskin (1995) has shown how the power of majority decision to yield a transitive social welfare function from varying domains is unmatched by any other competitor satisfying elementary requirements of voting rules.

(TA4*.1) Maskin's Theorem:

If Ω is a domain of profiles of individual strict preference orderings over which some collective choice rule F satisfying anonymity, neutrality, the Pareto principle and the Independence of Irrelevant Alternatives (with the number of voters being odd) is a social welfare function (that is, it invariably generates transitive social orderings), then the method of majority decision MMD must also be a social welfare function (with transitive majority orderings) over that domain Ω. Furthermore, for any F that is not MMD, there is some domain Ω^* on which MMD is a social welfare function, and F is not.

For a proof of Maskin's theorem, see Maskin (1995), pp. 106–7. This result – and its extensions (see particularly Dasgupta and Maskin (2008a), (2008b) and Maskin (2014)) – show that the method of majority decision has a 'robustness' in terms of feasible domains that other voting rules do not possess.[iii]

NUMBER-SPECIFIC DOMAIN CONDITIONS

Note that the domain conditions considered so far (such as Value Restriction) do not impose any requirement of the numerical distribution of voters over different types of allowable preferences. However, it is possible to consider number-specific constraints on domains of preference profiles, which yields a different line of enquiry initiated by Michael Nicholson (1965) and Gordon Tullock (1967), and powerfully generalized by Jean-Michel Grandmont (1978).

The discussion that follows draws on my presentation in the *Handbook of Mathematical Economics* (Sen (1986b)), which also presents a much more detailed account of the results involved. Consider Tullock's sufficiency conditions for transitive majority rule (which have been subsequently generalized). Consider a real plane E^2. For any voter i, let a_i, a point in E^2, represent his or her best alternative; all alternatives are ranked by person i entirely on the basis of their distance from a_i. The indifference curves for everyone are, thus, circles with their centre at a_i, and not necessarily the same for different individuals. Tullock considers the requirement that the sets of a_i, that is, the sets of the centres (or best points for different individuals) are symmetrically distributed over a rectangle with centre a_i^*. It is shown that the majority relation must then be transitive.

The Tullock conditions are suitable for generalization in many different ways. First, the uniform distribution over a rectangle can be replaced by other distributions with similar effect, e.g. uniform distribution on the *boundary* of a rectangle with centre a^*, or on a disc (or on its boundary) with centre a^*. Second, instead of a plane, an m-dimensional characterization can be chosen, and the result correspondingly generalized (see Davis, DeGroot and Hinich (1972)). The important point about Tullock's example is that every line through a^* cuts the distribution of voters (i.e. of a_i) into two parts of equal measure, and every line that does such an equal division goes through a^*.

These properties have been generalized by Grandmont (1978). An expository discussion of the Grandmont conditions and how they work to generate transitive majority decisions can be found in Sen (1986b). These studies – and related investigations – have substantially enriched our understanding of the consistency problems of majority rule.

Two general comments on the number-specific approach to domain restriction may, however, be worth making here. First, even the domain conditions in the exclusion form of restricted preference can be given number-specific interpretations, so that the line between the two approaches may be less sharply drawn than it may at first appear.[iv] Second, in order to make the exercise worthwhile, the number-specific conditions must have some intuitive meaning that helps the interpretation of the nature of the preference configurations. Otherwise, there is the danger of merely translating the formal requirement of transitivity (or acyclicity) of the majority relation into a more elaborately stated – but equivalent – number-specific form. When $N(x, y)$ is the number of people who prefer x to y, clearly a condition that asserts that, for all $x, y, z, [N(x, y) \geq N(y, x) \ \& \ N(y, z) \geq N(z, y)] \Rightarrow [N(x, z) \geq N(z, x)]$ is a number-specific requirement for transitivity, which is irresistibly necessary *and* sufficient, and obviously no less general than any other condition. The merit of the conditions proposed and the characterizations provided rests in their ability to capture patterns that have *independent* interest and interpretative value.

WHAT IF THERE IS NO MAJORITY WINNER?

The domain conditions that yield a transitive majority relation, or at least a majority winner, from permissible combinations of alternatives allow us to think positively about majority decision. In commenting on Eric Maskin's (2014) article on the domain conditions for a social welfare function, including the comparative robustness of majority decision in terms of domain requirement, Kenneth Arrow (2014) has posed an apparently troublesome question:

> I do not yet quite understand how Eric's results can help us in the case where his conditions fail. Something has to happen if majority voting is intransitive or, in other words, where the restrictive set of preferences is insufficient to overcome the impossibility theorem. This is a pretty key issue.

And so it is. Actually, along with the optimistic reading of Maskin's theorem about the broader reach of majority rule, there is the pessimistic implication that, if Maskin's conditions fail and majority decision is intransitive, then all other voting rules would fail too. Maskin's theorem cannot really be seen as a dispenser of hope in these circumstances (nor was it so intended). In fact, quite the contrary, since it tells us that it would be futile to go looking for some other voting rule that might avoid the intransitivity. No such rule exists. Maskin identifies what our best hopes are, and if they are unfulfilled, then we are in deep trouble – at least as far as voting rules go.

What then? What if there is an inescapable intransitivity (or cyclicity) in majority decisions? We must then find some way of going beyond the indecision of the majority rule (the existence of this problem is a characteristic of the world – not a creation of the analyst). One method, which has had some support, is to have a contest between the two leading contenders in a situation with no majority winner. Fans of plurality winners tend to give strong support for the proposal that the two candidates with the 'highest votes' (that is, the candidates with most and second-most first preferences) should have a 'run off' between them (a provision used in the electoral practice of many countries in the world). On the logic of majority rule, there may, however, be a better case for having the run off between the two candidates with the most and second-most pairwise majority victories over the others (see Maskin and Sen (2016)).

It should be noted here that if we use majority rule to identify a winner through one particular sequence of pairwise voting and the eliminations through pairwise defeats that they might generate (without holding other pairwise voting that would bring out the intransitivity), then we may not *know* that the apparent majority winner would be defeated in a pairwise contest against an alternative which it has not – at least not yet – had to face. To accept what has emerged from one particular sequence of elimination votes would be to live in a fool's paradise. Going for a majority winner demands more.

I should address here a line of reasoning that is often presented by people responding to a majority cycle, when x defeats y, and y defeats z, while z in turn defeats x. It is frequently asked: when there is a majority cycle over, say, x, y and z, why not settle for taking all three of them as co-winners, from which any alternative could be chosen without embarrassment? But this approach of interpreting a preference cycle as an indifference class is not really satisfactory. For one thing, the ranking of any two alternatives can depend here on the presence or absence of a third (in the pairwise context, 'irrelevant') alternative. Furthermore, a serious embarrassment may well arise in this line of reasoning because the imagined indifference class can include a thoroughly unacceptable alternative. Being co-loser is not really like being co-winner, and, in fact, there is some essential discrimination that we have to bring in even with a majority cycle. This issue may be worth spelling out a bit.

Consider four alternatives x, y, z and w, and three voters with the following preference profiles:

Voter 1	Voter 2	Voter 3
x	y	z
y	z	w
z	w	x
w	x	y

In this case there is a full majority cycle, with x defeating y, and y defeating z, along with z defeating w, and w defeating x. It might look like that each may have a claim to win that is no less than that of any other.

But is that really the case? In fact, one of the four alternatives – in this case w – is Pareto inferior; everyone places it below an available alternative, z. It would be hard to think that there can be any case for selecting w, when z is available, just because w is a component of a majority cycle, even though absolutely everyone prefers z to w. There is a case for at least separating out w from the four alternatives caught in a majority cycle.[1]

So what can be done? We can look for some other social choice procedure that supplements – or supplants – the majority rule. One of the possibilities, supplementing majority-comparison procedures, is to hold a run off between the two alternatives that win the most (or most and second-most) majority victories over the other alternatives (this was mentioned earlier). This will separate out y and z, both of which win two pairwise contests (y wins against z and w; z wins against x and w), in contrast with x and w which win only one pairwise battle each. In the run-off between y and z, if everyone retains their original ranking of y and z, this will lead to the eventual victory for y. However, the purpose of run-offs includes giving the voters a

---

[1] Despite the Pareto inferiority of w, a sequence of majority votes may take us to w with majority approval in each round. Consider the sequence of one-by-one elimination that would result by putting y against z in a majority vote (y prevails), then the winner (y) against x (x prevails), and finally the winner (x) against w, with w winning that pairwise majority vote. So w – Pareto-inferior as it is (rejected by all in favour of z) – may apparently lead the pack in this particular sequence of majority voting.

chance to rethink on their ranking of the two final candidates, taking note of all considerations in a changed two-candidate final fight.

Another alternative approach is to abandon majority rule altogether, and to go for a rank-order voting system, such as the Borda rule, which is often used across the world. This rule, which was discussed in Chapter A3* and was originally proposed by Jean-Charles de Borda, can be plausibly used when a clear majority winner fails to emerge.

The Borda rule, as was explained in Chapter A3*, is based on attaching a number to each alternative that is equal to the sum of its ranks in each person's preference ordering. The procedure ranks the states socially in the inverse order of these aggregate numbers (the smaller the sum of the scores, the stronger the case for that particular candidate). In the four-alternative case discussed above in the context of majority-initiated run offs, the Borda score $B(.)$ for the four alternatives are: $B(x) = 8$, $B(y) = 7$, $B(z) = 6$, and $B(w) = 9$. This produces a strict ranking in the descending order of z, y, x, w, with the result that z wins the contest. This is a definite result, and can be very different from adjusted majority procedures, such as having a run-off vote between the two alternatives (or candidates) that win the most pairwise majority contests. But, as was discussed in Chapter A3*, the two versions of the Borda rule – the broad and the narrow – violate the demands of collective rationality and the condition of the independence of irrelevant alternatives, respectively.

The Borda rule is a special case of positional rules, which are rules based on attaching weights according to the position occupied by an alternative in each person's ordering: the weights are a non-decreasing function of ranks, counting upwards from the bottom, applied in the same way to everyone's ordering (i.e. anonymously). The Borda rule is the special case in which *each* of the distances between one alternative and the one next to it is normalized as one.[2] There is obviously some arbitrariness there.

---

[2] As a contrast, see also Brams and Fishburn's (1978), (1983) definitive exploration of 'approval voting', which is a flexible voting procedure *without* the use of positional data. It has some merit, particularly when the number to be elected is endogenously

DIFFERENT ROUTES
AND PUBLIC ENGAGEMENT

Positional rules (including the Borda method) are alternative ways of approaching the social choice problem that are different from the majority rule. But they share the characteristic of not bringing in interpersonal comparisons of individual well-being, or of individual advantage, judged in some particular scale (methods of different kinds of using interpersonal comparisons were discussed in Chapters A3 and A3*).

If the voters rank all the alternatives, then we have enough material to see whether there is a majority winner x, which can defeat all the other alternatives in pair-by-pair contests covering the entire field. Condorcet did argue for that. We can also see how the Borda rule will order the candidates, and even check whether there is a winner that stands above all the others for all positional rules (the dominance conditions can be usefully invoked to check this). So there are two different ways of proceeding here, without bringing in interpersonal comparisons.

Comparisons that take note of interpersonal differences in utility gains and levels (extensively discussed in Chapter A3*) provide different ways altogether of making social choice. But they are more demanding in information in a way that may make them unsuitable for general public ballots (as opposed to making welfare-economic evaluations). However, as Arrow (2014) has noted, interpersonal comparisons of well-being may well come into the formation of individual preferences, reflecting their respective social values that influence their ranking of candidates (or of alternative proposals). The use of public discussion and social engagement, emphasized throughout this book (which will be further discussed in Chapter A6), will be relevant here.

---

determined by a cut-off requirement of 'qualifying' support. However, the claim occasionally made that approval voting is consistent with all of Arrow's conditions is not, in fact, correct. For example, approval voting can violate Arrow's condition of independence of irrelevant alternatives.

Even when there is no initial agreement on social rankings, something close to an acceptable – and accepted – consensus may emerge on the basis of dedicated public discussions on what the facts really are, or what values should receive priority. There is, of course, no guarantee that such a consensus will emerge, but one of the aims of public engagement must be to seek such an accord, even if the accord is only partial. I shall return to this question in the last chapter of the book (Chapter A6).

Chapter A5
The Idea of Rights

The idea of rights is widely used in moral and political arguments. It is natural to expect that the concept and use of rights should find a place in social choice theory. However, even though Condorcet had considerable interest in the idea of rights, no room was given to the ethical idea of rights in his formal writings on social choice. Nor did it figure in the modern formulations of social choice theory, led by Kenneth Arrow. I made a small attempt at rectifying this omission and accommodating liberty and rights within the valuational structure of social choice in the original (1970) edition of this book. That discussion (in Chapter 6 and 6*) was, however, too brief and patchy, and the subject needed to be taken up more fully, linking the role of social choice evaluation with the idea of rights in moral and political philosophy.

As a part of my 1970 presentation, a theorem – on the 'Impossibility of the Paretian Liberal' (IPL) – figured prominently, which brought out a tension between 'rights-based' valuations and a 'utility-centred' evaluative framework. It showed that even the mildest demand of utility-based reasoning (in the form of utility-oriented Pareto principle, which makes a unanimous utility ranking socially decisive) tended to conflict with the minimal demands of personal liberty. The analytical result was also presented and discussed in a short article published in the same year in the *Journal of Political Economy* (Sen (1970c)).

Even though I had talked about this result at the Delhi School of Economics while teaching social choice theory there during 1966–8, and had presented it in a general critique of the Pareto principle in the Far Eastern Econometric Congress in Tokyo in the summer of 1968, I have to confess that I was somewhat doubtful about the significance of this impossibility theorem, analytically interesting though it was. For one thing, John Stuart Mill (1859) had discussed a hundred years earlier a basic conflict between aggregate utility maximization and the guaranteeing of individual liberty. Even though Mill had not noted that a modicum of insistence on the priority of personal liberty militates not only against aggregate utility maximization in general, but also against the minimally demanding Pareto principle (the existence of the conflict can be established through social choice reasoning, yielding the IPL), the IPL theorem can, in fact, be seen as an extension of Mill's basic insight.

The impossibility result seemed to generate interest among my colleagues at Harvard in 1968–9 when I came there as a Visiting Professor (as it had done in Tokyo the preceding summer), and I eventually decided to pursue it in the book. The theorem also fitted in well with analysing the inclusion of the idea of rights in social choice in general. In this chapter and the short – and more technical – one to follow (Chapter A5*) in this expanded edition, the IPL gets some attention in the context of understanding the role of rights and liberties in social choice. As it happens, the 1970 article in the *Journal of Political Economy*, presenting the IPL, generated an astonishingly large literature.[1]

Later on in this chapter, I shall come back to the impossibility of the Paretian liberal. I begin, however, with a broader discussion of the idea of rights in general in ethical contexts – going well beyond legal rights (which constitute, of course, a well-recognized category of legal analysis). I must also examine the much-discussed, if controversial, notion of human rights.[2] Social choice theory can contribute substantially to these older debates on rights and entitlements, by

---

[1] Commenting on my *JPE* article, presenting the IPL, Dennis Mueller (1996) noted in his critical essay on 'constitutional and liberal rights': 'neither Sen nor anyone else probably predicted the quantity of articles and books' this '6 page note' would generate (Mueller (1996), p. 114). It did indeed surprise me (though not unpleasantly).
[2] See Lynn Hunt (2007) for an illuminating historical analysis of the evolution of the idea of human rights.

clarifying the need for freedom-inclusive evaluation of adequately described states of affairs, which cannot but respond to the acknowledgement and exercise of minimally recognized rights.

ETHICAL AND LEGAL RIGHTS

There is a long history of invoking the idea of rights that are not – or at least not yet – legislated into the legal framework. The American Declaration of Independence took it to be 'self-evident' that everyone is 'endowed by their Creator with certain inalienable rights', and thirteen years later, in 1789, the French declaration of 'the rights of man' asserted that 'men are born and remain free and equal in rights'. However, Jeremy Bentham did not wait long, in his *Anarchical Fallacies*, written during 1791–2 (and aimed against the French 'rights of man'), to propose the total dismissal of all such claims. Bentham insisted that 'natural rights is simple nonsense: natural and imprescriptible rights (an American phrase), rhetorical nonsense, nonsense upon stilts' (Bentham (1792)). That dichotomy remains very alive today, and despite persistent use of the idea of human rights in momentous affairs in the world there are many who see the idea of human rights as no more than 'bawling upon paper' – to use another of Bentham's mocking phrases.

But should our ethics be so parasitic on law? Indeed, if we recognize articulation of human rights as non-legal (or pre-legal) ethical claims, social demands linked to the so-called 'rights of man' are no more nonsensical than are Bentham's own moral pronouncements based on utilitarian ethics. Indeed, the analogy between the status of utilitarian propositions and that of articulations of human rights has considerable force, even though Bentham managed to overlook the connection altogether in his classic hatchet job on natural rights in general and on the 'rights of man' in particular. Oddly enough, Bentham took the appropriate comparison to be, specifically, one between the *legal significance* respectively of declarations of human rights, on the one hand, and actually legislated rights, on the other. Not surprisingly, he found the former (that is, claims of human rights) to be lacking in legal status in the way that the latter (legislated rights) clearly had. Bentham's dismissal of human rights came, thus, with amazing simplicity of reasoning: '*Right*, the substantive *right*, is the child of law; from *real* laws come *real* rights; but from *imaginary* laws, from "laws of nature" [can come only] "*imaginary* rights".'[i]

Bentham's rejection of the idea of natural 'rights of man' depends on a privileged use of the term of 'rights', confining it to its specifically legal interpretation. However, insofar as human rights are taken to be significant ethical claims, Bentham's assertion that they do not necessarily have legal or institutional force – at least not yet – is as obvious as it is irrelevant. The right comparison is, surely, between, on the one hand, a utility-based ethics (championed by Bentham himself), which gives fundamental ethical importance to utilities but none to the idea of rights, and, on the other hand, an ethics that makes room for the normative significance of human rights (as the advocates of the 'rights of man' did), linked with the basic importance of human freedoms (and, related to that, of the corresponding social responsibilities).

Just as utilitarian ethical reasoning takes the form of insisting that the utilities of the relevant persons must be taken into account in deciding on what should be done, the human rights approach demands that the freedoms that are incorporated in the form of human rights must be given normative recognition. In fact, even as Bentham was busy writing down his dismissal of 'rights of man', in 1791–2, the reach and range of ethical interpretations of rights were being powerfully explored in Thomas Paine's *Rights of Man* (1791) and in Mary Wollstonecraft's *A Vindication of the Rights of Woman: with Strictures on Political and Moral Subjects* (1792). Neither appeared to have captured Bentham's interest.

LEGISLATION AND SOCIAL ACTION

In a rightly celebrated essay 'Are There Any Natural Rights?' Herbert Hart (1955), a leading expert on jurisprudence in our time, argued that people 'speak of their moral rights mainly when advocating their incorporation in a legal system'. Whereas Bentham saw rights as a 'child of law', Hart's view takes moral rights (within which human rights can be seen to be a category) as *parents* of law: they motivate and inspire specific legislations.

When Christabel Pankhurst asserted in a speech in London in 1911: 'we are here to claim our right as women, not only to be free, but to fight for freedom', adding that this is 'our right as well as our duty', she communicated a strong normative claim that had not yet been legislated into British law. Women did not have the right to vote in Britain in 1911, nor would that right be fully achieved, on a par with men, until 1928, seventeen years after Pankhurst's speech. Women would start exercising that general right only from the following year, 1929. The suffragist agitation, of which Christabel Pankhurst was a major leader, and the public discussion that went with it on women's normative 'right' to vote, would materially help the process that led to the legislation to give women the same voting rights as men in Britain already had.

Seen in this way, human rights relate closely to moral arguments, including arguments that are contingent on the particular circumstances involved (for example, in a country), such as women not having the voting rights that men had in Britain. As John Tasioulas (2007) has powerfully argued in an illuminating essay called 'The Moral Reality of Human Rights': 'human rights enjoy a temporally constrained form of universality, so that the question of which human rights exist can only be answered within some specified historical context' (p. 76). Thus the demand for the recognition of human rights need not have much to do with calls for legislation in some imagined 'state of nature', and in this sense there is an important difference between the ideas of 'natural rights' and 'human rights'. For example, if some residents are excluded from being covered by, say, social security (or from having a state-sponsored medical insurance) that others already have in the existing institutional structure, the moral and political demand in contention has to be seen in the specific context of the institutional arrangements that exist in that society. The demand then may be shaped by the need to eliminate arbitrary discrimination related, say, to gender, caste, class, community or sexual preference. This is shaped by normative critique of social states that allow such discrimination compared with those that do not.

The general territory of social choice provides a framework for systematic reasoning and assessment of putative claims to moral rights, including human rights. This can be readily seen in the invoking of inalienable rights in the American Declaration of Independence and reflected in the subsequent US legislation (including the Amendments to the Constitution). This is a route that has been well-trodden in the legislative history of many countries in the world. It has also been used to inspire legislative efforts, and to incite the making of new constitutions, perhaps most famously in the invitation to new legislation championed in the United Nations' Universal Declaration of Human Rights in 1948 (intellectually led by Eleanor Roosevelt). Providing inspiration for legislation is certainly *one* way in which the ethical force of human rights has been constructively deployed.

However, acknowledging that a strong connection exists between the ethics of human rights and legislative motivation is not the same thing as taking the relevance of human rights to lie *exclusively* in their playing an inspirational or justificatory role for actual legislation. It is important to see that the idea of human rights can be – and is – actually used in several other ways as well. It is easy to appreciate that if human rights are seen as powerful moral claims – indeed as 'moral rights' (to use Hart's phrase) – then surely there is reason for some catholicity in considering different avenues for promoting these claims. The ways and means of advancing the ethics of human rights need not, thus, be confined only to making new laws.

For example, monitoring gross violations of what people tend to take as human rights, and other activist support provided by such organizations as Human Rights Watch, or Amnesty International, or Oxfam, or Médecins Sans Frontières, Save the Children, the Red Cross or Action Aid (to consider many different types of non-governmental organizations or NGOs) can themselves help to advance the effective reach of acknowledged human rights. In many contexts, legislation may not, in fact, be at all involved. The point is not so much whether the legislative route can make the social ethics of human rights more effective; it certainly can do this in many cases. The point, rather, is that there are other routes which can also help to make the ethics of human rights more influential and effective. Public discussion, censure, exposure or condemnation can have a huge role in preventing violations of what are widely acknowledged to be moral rights of others. These examples of practical social choice have real bearing on the scope and applicability of social choice reasoning.[3]

ARE HUMAN RIGHTS IDEALLY LEGISLATED?

I have argued so far against seeing human rights only as consequences of appropriate legislation, or only as motivation for making such legislation. But what about the view, which has sometimes been aired, that human rights are best seen as *ideals* for legislation? This raises an interesting question about the appropriate reach of the legislative route. Would it be reasonable to claim that if a human right is regarded as important, then it must be ideal to legislate it into a precisely specified legal right?

This view too, while tempting, is hard to sustain. For some rights, the ideal route may well not be legislation, but something else, such as public discussion and education, and, of course, agitation, in the hope that the behaviour of those who contribute to the violation of human rights can be changed. For example, recognizing and defending a wife's moral right to be consulted in family decisions, even in a traditionally sexist society, may well be extremely important. And yet it seems entirely plausible to think that coercive legislation, with the imprisoning, or fining, of husbands for ignoring the views of their wives may be much too blunt a way of trying to make sure that

---

[3] In my book *The Idea of Justice* (Sen (2009a)), I have explored these connections, and also proposed a social-choice-based theory of justice that accommodates the idea of human rights.

husbands consult their wives in family decisions. Because of the importance of communication, advocacy, exposure and informed public discussion, human rights can have influence without necessarily depending on coercive legal rules. For example, Mary Wollstonecraft (1792) explored many different types of social change, including through public discussion, with the help of which 'the vindication of the rights of woman' could be advanced. That eighteenth-century insight about different ways and means of social change remains relevant today.

RIGHTS AND OBLIGATIONS

I should also comment briefly on the possible implications of recognizing some claims in the form of human rights, and, further, trying to understand their global relevance (I have discussed these issues more fully in my book *The Idea of Justice*: Sen (2009a)). A pronouncement of human rights is an assertion of the importance of the corresponding freedoms – the freedoms that are identified and privileged in the formulation of the rights in question.[4] For example, the human right not to be tortured springs from the importance of freedom from torture for all. This goes with the affirmation of the need for others to consider what they can reasonably do to secure the freedom from torture for all. For a would-be torturer, the demand is obviously quite straightforward, that is, to refrain and desist. The demand takes the clear form of what in his *Critique of Practical Reason* (1788), Immanuel Kant called a 'perfect obligation'.

However, for others too (that is, those other than the would-be torturers) there are responsibilities, even though they are less specific, and come in the general form of 'imperfect obligations' (to invoke another Kantian concept). Imperfect obligations are general

---

[4] See Joseph Raz's (1986) illuminating study of what he calls the 'morality of freedom'. For examples of different approaches to this large subject, see also O'Neill (1986), (1996), Scanlon (1988), (2003), Van Parijs (1995), (2000), Pettit (1997), (2001), Skinner (1998), Kamm (2007), Goodin, Pettit and Pogge (2007), Sen (2009a), Tasioulas (2012), (2013a) and Temkin (2012), among other contributions.

duties of anyone in a position to help to consider what he or she can reasonably do in the matter involved. The perfectly specified demand not to torture anyone is supplemented by the more general – and less exactly specified – requirement to consider the ways and means through which torture can be prevented and then to decide what, if anything, one should reasonably do to prevent torture in any particular case.

It is important to emphasize that the recognition of human rights is not an insistence that everyone everywhere must rise up to help prevent every violation of every human right, no matter where it occurs. It is, rather, an acknowledgement that if one is in a plausible position to do something effective in preventing the violation of such a right, then one does have an obligation to consider doing just *that*. It is still possible that other obligations, or non-obligational moral or practical concerns, may overwhelm – and outweigh – the case for undertaking that action. But the rights-based reasoning cannot be simply brushed away on the ground that it is 'none of my business'. Imperfect obligations must not be confused with no obligations at all.

A theory of human rights can leave room for further discussions, disputations and arguments. The approach of open public reasoning, which is central to the understanding of human rights (as characterized here), can definitively settle some disputes about coverage and content, but may have to leave other possibilities short of full resolution. The admissibility of a domain of continuing dispute is no embarrassment to a theory of human rights, for that is the nature of the subject matter we are dealing with.

In practical applications of human rights, such debates are, of course, quite common and entirely customary, particularly among human rights activists. What is being argued here is that the possibility of such debates – without losing the basic recognition of the importance and the global status of human rights – is not only a feature of what can be called 'human rights *practice*', they are an inherent part of the general *discipline* of human rights, rather than a limitation of that discipline. Variability of this kind within the normative discipline of human rights is not only not an embarrassment, it is much like other ambiguities that are standardly present in all general theories of substantive ethics.[5]

NORMATIVITY OF MORAL RIGHTS AND PUBLIC ENGAGEMENT

The question must, however, be asked: what would be the criterion of judging whether a putative claim for something to be a human right should be accepted or not? How do we assess the normative basis of human rights? How should we judge whether and why to take such claims seriously?

In line with what has already been discussed, it can be argued that any general plausibility that particular ethical claims – or their denials – have must be related to their survival and flourishing when they encounter unobstructed discussion and scrutiny, along with adequately wide informational availability. The connection between public reasoning and the formulation and use of human rights is extremely important to understand. The soundness of the normativity of a claim for a human right would be seriously undermined if it were possible to show that they are unlikely to survive open public scrutiny.

I should explain that, in making this connection, it is not necessarily being assumed that the normativity of human rights is actually a result of the survival of these claims in public reasoning. It could be a *result* (on one view), but it could also be (in another view) powerful *evidence* – perhaps even the most powerful evidence we can seek – that the claims in question have cognitive importance.[ii] In this book, I do not intend to go into the substantive philosophical difference between these two approaches to meta-ethics. My own understanding comes closer to the cognitivist position in many respects, but the

---

[5] Indeed, a similar diversity can be found within utility-centred ethics (see, for example, Chapters 7 and 7* in this book), even though typically this feature of that large ethical discipline tends to receive very little attention. It certainly received little discussion from Jeremy Bentham himself.

opportunity to take that philosophical argument forward will have to be taken up elsewhere. For the placing of rights and liberties in the social choice context this foundational difference need not be resolved. In either view, survivability in open general argument is critically important.

Within that approach of public reasoning, it is important to recognize that the case for human rights cannot be discarded simply by pointing to the fact that in politically and socially repressive regimes, which do not allow open public discussion, many of these human rights are not taken seriously at all. No claim can be undermined – as there is often a temptation to do – on the ground that it has not received local public support in a restricted or censored environment. Open critical scrutiny – actual or imagined – is as essential for a reasoned dismissal of a normative claim as it is for the defence of that claim.

John Rawls (1971), (1993) is among those who have argued powerfully that the objectivity of ethical and political claims must be ultimately judged by their survivability in unobstructed discussion. This fits in well with the position being advanced here. In assessing what would be just I would, however, like to resist Rawls's inclination, particularly in his later works (Rawls (1999b)), to limit such public confrontation within the boundaries of each particular nation (or each 'people', as Rawls calls such regional collectivity). Rawls presents a different approach for ethical treatment beyond the borders, relying on ideas of humanitarianism and other broader concerns in the treatment of people elsewhere, outside the domain of the theory of justice in particular. Rawls's confinement of public reasoning to the political space in within-nation encounters also fits broadly with Habermas's approach.

A contrasting perspective can be found in Adam Smith's *Theory of Moral Sentiments*, where it is argued that for normative viability a claim must also be examined from 'a certain distance'. The role of open public reasoning, allowing global use, in the understanding and recognition of human rights links closely with Adam Smith's approach to jurisprudence. There is also a similarity here with Hugo Grotius's invoking of the role of international law even when no formal legal agreement has been instituted. Beginning with *The Free Sea* (published in 1609), Grotius looked for reasoning that could, at least in its basic appeal, transcend the local boundaries of a state.[6]

Smith was very concerned about avoiding the biases of ethical myopia – within a nation and beyond its borders. Rather than trying to cater only to the dominant views of ruling groups in any country, Smith saw the need to bring in perspectives from other groups, and other classes, whose views were often ignored in national decision-making. This was, for him, a principal way for transcending, among other barriers, the limitations of class-based thinking (Smith was at least as firm on that subject as Marx would later be). Smith also used the need for broader evaluation to assert the necessity of seeking global argumentative encounters – actual or imagined – to check the plausibility of normative claims.

It is not that distant points of views would necessarily offer better reasoning than local – and possibly parochial – arguments (though sometimes that can actually be the case), but that different types of reasoning have to be examined to arrive at an informed and adequately scrutinized judgement, and bringing in distant perspectives allows that to happen in a way that examining locally popular arguments may not permit. One of Smith's illustrations of parochial values that could have been usefully confronted with views from elsewhere refers to the tendency of all political commentators in ancient Greece, including sophisticated Athenians, to regard infanticide as perfectly acceptable social behaviour. Smith pointed out that even Plato and Aristotle did not depart from expressing approval of this extraordinary practice, which 'uninterrupted custom had by this time . . . thoroughly authorized' in the local culture of ancient Greece.

Distant perspectives have clear relevance not only for critical assessment of what may be widely recognized to be repellent practices (such as the stoning of women accused of adultery under the

---

[6] I have discussed this issue in my Grotius Lecture: Sen (2011a), linking the literature of unlegislated human rights today to Grotius's old analysis of unlegislated 'laws' of the sea. See also Sen (1982b), (2009a), Raz (1986), Chatterjee (2008), Sengupta (2004), (2011), Kamm (2007) and Tasioulas (2012), (2013a).

Taliban rule in Afghanistan), but also to more debatable subjects, such as the acceptability of capital punishment. There is a kind of generic relevance of wanting to check whether some practice appears acceptable only in local and parochial assessment, or can be more broadly defended. This led to Smith's insistence, in his posthumously published *Lectures on Jurisprudence*, that 'the eyes of the rest of mankind' must be invoked to understand whether 'a punishment appears equitable'.[iii] The necessity of this arises, Smith argued, for the avoidance of bias related to either individual or sectional interest, or local parochialism:

> We can never survey our own sentiments and motives, we can never form any judgment concerning them; unless we remove ourselves, as it were, from our own natural station, and endeavour to view them as at a certain distance from us. But we can do this in no other way than by endeavouring to view them with the eyes of other people, or as other people are likely to view them.[7]

Global examination of each other's positions, Smith argued, is feasible enough if people go into it with genuine curiosity, rather than a sense of racial, or ethnic, or national superiority. The barriers to communication may come often from the arrogance of the more powerful rather than from the intellectual or educational limitations of the downtrodden. Bursting into something of a rage about the pretensions of the slave-owners in eighteenth-century Europe and America to their superiority over other human beings (allegedly fit to be enslaved), the indignant Smith remarked, in *The Theory of Moral Sentiments*: 'There is not a negro from the coast of Africa who does not, in this respect, possess a degree of magnanimity which the soul of his sordid master is too often scarce capable of conceiving'.[iv] Smith would have known that, literally taken, this generalized pronouncement was likely to be an exaggeration, but he clearly thought that the airing of a completely contrary perspective was a needed jolt in a

---

[7] I have discussed the Smithian perspective on moral reasoning in my paper 'Open and Closed Impartiality' (Sen (2002b)), and also in my 'Introduction' to the Penguin Classic edition of Smith's *The Theory of Moral Sentiments* (Sen (2009c)).

world full of racist arguments hugely influenced by the arrogance and conceit of the privileged.

SOCIAL CHOICE, CULMINATION AND COMPREHENSIVE OUTCOMES

Social choice theory is closely linked with the ranking of states of affairs, and with the choice of social states, based on the principles of evaluation or choice, identified by specific axioms. The framework allows some variation of specification. It is possible to define social states in terms of what can be called 'culmination outcomes' (e.g. 'Anne got the medical support to which she was socially entitled'), or more fully described as 'comprehensive outcomes' (e.g. 'Anne exercised her socially recognized right for medical support and obtained it, rather than being given it through charity'). An articulation of the comprehensive outcome can enrich bare-bone consequential descriptions by bringing into them the processes through which the final outcomes come about.[8] Since the terms 'consequences' and 'consequentialism' have most often been associated with concentrating only on culmination outcomes, there are good reasons to give some name other than 'consequences' to broadly defined comprehensive outcomes. I have used the expression 'social realization' for adequately described comprehensive outcomes, including the specification of the processes involved as well as the culmination states (on this see Sen (2009a)).

In social choice analysis, processes as well as culmination outcomes may have relevance, even though quite often rights are formally defined in terms of consequences only. One question that has frequently cropped up, particularly in scrutinizing the theorem on the Impossibility of the Paretian Liberal (IPL), is whether the culmination consequences have any relevance at all in specifying the demands

---

[8] On the far-reaching implications of the distinction between culmination outcomes and comprehensive outcomes, see *The Idea of Justice* (Sen (2009a)), particularly Chapters 10, 14, 17 and 18.

of liberty. The denial of the importance of culmination consequences has frequently come from libertarian theorists – quite often as a reprimand to social choice theorists for allegedly misunderstanding the idea of liberty. I shall have to take up that issue later on in this chapter.

THE IMPOSSIBILITY OF
THE PARETIAN LIBERAL

The IPL theorem presented in Chapter 6* in the 1970 edition invoked only one kind of right, that of personal liberty, in a very weak form. If people can have any preferences they like, then the formal demands of Pareto optimality, as defined on individual utilities, may conflict – it was shown – with some minimal demands of personal liberty. An illustration I used in 1970 may help us to understand what is going on. This involves a literary book that one person loves and another person hates.[9] The person called Prude hates the book, sees it as pornographic, and would not like to read it, but would suffer even more from its being read by the other person – called Lewd (there has been a renaming here, from the more unwieldy Lascivious) – who loves the book. Prude is particularly bothered that Lewd may be chuckling over the book. Lewd, on the other hand, would love to read the book, but would prefer even more that Prude reads it. For Lewd it is great fun to contemplate 'narrow-minded' Prude reading the book he detests.

There is here no liberty-supported case for no one reading the book, since Lewd clearly wants to read it, and his decision regarding whether to read or not read the book, it may be plausibly thought, is none of Prude's business. Nor is there a liberty-based case for Prude reading the book, since he clearly does not want to do so, and it is

[9] In the early days of the 1960s I fear I was naive enough to choose as an example D. H. Lawrence's *Lady Chatterley's Lover*, which would hardly be recognized as controversial today. I was influenced by the fact that Penguin Books had just before that time fought and won a case in the British courts to be allowed to publish this book as a work of literature, rather than it being seen as forbidden pornography.

none of Lewd's business to weigh into that choice, in which he is not directly involved. The only remaining alternative is for Lewd to read the book – which would, of course, be exactly what would happen if both the persons were left free to decide what to do (or not do). However, given their utilities as described, both Prude and Lewd receive more utility from Prude reading the book than Lewd reading it, so that the self-choice alternative seems to go against the Pareto principle. Indeed, insistence on Pareto optimality in terms of utilities, thus described, would rule out Lewd reading the book – but choosing either of the other two alternatives would violate the minimal demands of liberty. So nothing can be chosen satisfying the specified demands of reasoned social choice imposed here, since each available alternative is worse than some other alternative. Hence, there is no possibility of satisfying the Pareto principle and Minimal Liberty simultaneously.

This impossibility result, like other impossibility theorems in social choice theory (which we discussed earlier), is a useful *beginning* of a discussion of how the choice problem is to be tackled, not the *end* of possible arguments.[v] And it certainly has served that purpose.[vi] Some have used the impossibility theorem to argue that, for liberty to be effective, people should respect other people's liberty in their own preference, rather than trying to make others lead lives that, on their own, they would not themselves choose to lead. As Christian Seidl (1975) argued in an early contribution, the viability of liberal rights depends ultimately on the cultivation of liberal values.

Others have used the mathematical result to argue that even the Pareto principle, allegedly sacred in traditional welfare economics, may have to be violated sometimes. The case for this lies in the fact that the individual preferences here are obsessed with other people's lives, and their status is compromised by the recognition that, as John Stuart Mill (1859) put it in *On Liberty*, 'there is no parity between the feeling of a person for his own opinion, and the feeling of another who is offended at his holding it.' Still others have argued for making a person's right to liberty conditional on him or her respecting the liberty of others in their own personal preferences.

Other lines of proposed solutions have also been discussed. One that has evidently appealed to some enthusiasts can be called 'solution by collusion'. This is the suggestion that the problem is resolved if the parties involved have a Pareto-improving contract, whereby Prude reads the book to prevent Lewd from reading it. Is this really a solution?

There is, among other things, something of a methodological issue here. A Pareto-improving contract is always a theoretical possibility in any Pareto *inefficient* situation. To point to the possibility of a Pareto-improving contract does nothing to undermine the problem faced in a world in which individual choices take one to a Pareto-inefficient outcome. If we were really keen on getting to a Pareto-efficient outcome defined on utilities (I shall presently discuss why this may not be a reasoned outcome to seek), we shall have to discuss how that implementation problem can be addressed, rather than just point to the possibility of a Pareto-improving contract without a serious examination of incentive compatibility.[vii]

Note that there indeed is a big implementation problem (discussed by Breyer (1977), Basu (1984), and others) in going for this 'solution' (even if it were a solution).[viii] The Pareto-improving contract may not be viable, since the incentive to break it can be very strong. This may not be the principal argument against seeing a solution to the problem through collusion (the main argument relates to the reasoning behind the two parties offering and accepting such a contract), but it is one argument to be considered before the normative oddity involved in this proposed solution is taken up. We have to consider the credibility of such a contract, and the difficulty of ensuring its compliance (e.g. how to make sure that Prude actually reads the book and not just pretends to). This is no mean problem, but, perhaps more importantly, attempts at enforcing such contracts (e.g. a policeman checking that Prude is actually engaged in reading the book and not just turning the pages) in the name of liberty can powerfully – and chillingly – endanger liberty itself. Those who seek a liberal solution that would demand such intrusion into personal lives must have a rather odd idea of the demands of a liberal society.

Of course, such enforcement would not be necessary if people were to conform voluntarily to the agreement. If, however, individual utility rankings are taken to determine choice, this possibility is not open, since – given that choice – Prude will not read the book (at least, in the absence of intrusive policing). And if we see reason for people to act against their self-indulgent utility rankings and not seek to violate the contract, then we have to ask the prior question: should they have sought that contract, based merely on their self-indulgent utility rankings, in the first place?

The distinction between a self-indulgent utility ranking and the broader valuational ranking of the same person (taking note of all the values of that person) has some similarity with Arrow's (1951a) classic distinction between individual 'values' (taking everything into account) and their mere 'tastes'.[10] The utility rankings may reflect each person's taste – what they would love to see (forgetting concerns about their values regarding their desire to live in a liberal society). Taking the various concerns into account, it is not at all obvious why Prude and Lewd must inescapably go for a peculiarly 'other-regarding' social contract by which Prude agrees to read the book he hates in order to make the eager-to-read Lewd refrain from reading it, and Lewd in turn agrees to forgo reading a book he would love to read in order to make reluctant Prude read it instead. If people attach some importance to minding their own business rather than just following their immediate, self-indulgent desires, then that odd contract need not in fact materialize (cf. 'I wish Ann would not separate from Jack' does not carry the inescapable entailment, 'let me jump in and try to stop Ann').

For reasons I have never been able to comprehend, some authors seem to believe that the issue in question is whether rights are 'alienable' (in the sense of people being permitted to trade away their liberty-based rights) and whether the persons involved should be *allowed* to make such a contract. It has even been suggested (for example by Brian Barry (1986)) that I am against 'allowing' such a contract. In fact, I see no serious argument whatsoever why rights of this kind should not in general be taken to be open to contracting

---

[10] Arrow (1951a) relates a person's *'taste'* to 'the direct consumption of the individual', and *'values'* to include the person's 'general standards of equity' (p. 18).

and exchanging through mutual agreement. People do not (and I would venture to say, in general, should not) need anyone else's (or 'the society's') permission to have such a contract, or to trade their rights. But they do need a *reason* to have such a contract, and be driven not merely by their tastes, ignoring important values that they may themselves have. They also need an argument to *exercise* a right that they may actually have. Not having a reason to exercise a right is not the same as trading away that right. To offer as a reason, as some have done, for engaging in such an odd contract, the fact that it might be the only way of getting – and sustaining – a Pareto-efficient outcome is to beg the question, since one of the reasons for discussing the impossibility result is precisely to question and assess the priority of Pareto efficiency defined on utility rankings.

I would argue that the real issue here is the inadequacy of the reasons for having such a contract in the first place. Of course, if no-nonsense maximization of pleasure or desire-fulfilment (ignoring the principle of minding one's own business) were the only basis of reasoned action (as some versions of so-called 'rational choice theory' seem to presume), then people would have reason enough to seek or accept such a contract. But this would also give both Prude and Lewd good reasons for reneging on the contract even if signed, and both Lewd and Prude would have to take note of this fact. More importantly, even for desire-based choice, we must distinguish between a desire that someone should act in a particular way (e.g. Lewd's desire that Prude should read the book he hates), and a desire for a contract forcing this person to act in that way (e.g. Lewd's wanting Prude to sign a contract binding him to read the book which he would not otherwise read). If outcomes are seen in 'comprehensive' terms, the two objects of desire are not at all the same. It should not be hard to see that Lewd's general desire for Prude to read the book need not at all entail a choice – or even a desire – to have a contract that would force Prude to do so. The introduction of a contract also introduces ethical issues that cannot be escaped by just referring to simple desires regarding individual actions without any contracts in terms of culmination outcomes – ignoring comprehensive assessment of what altogether is happening.

To conclude, the impossibility of the Paretian liberal, like the more grand impossibility theorem of Arrow, is best seen as a contribution to public discussion, by bringing into focus questions that may not have been raised otherwise. The distinctions between values and tastes on the one hand, and between culmination outcomes and comprehensive outcomes on the other, are crucially involved in analysing the Impossibility of the Paretian Liberal.

SOCIAL CHOICE AND GAME FORMS

I end this chapter with an examination of the foundational issue of how rights in general – and rights to liberty in particular – should be formulated, and whether social choice theory provides an appropriate structure for an adequate formulation of rights. One question that has often been asked is whether social choice theory is capacious enough to accommodate a proper understanding of rights. Indeed, the argument that social choice theory is not adequate for this purpose has been repeatedly floated. Two rather different lines of criticism have been aired, which have to be clearly distinguished.

One criticism has taken the form of arguing that the kind of rights on which the Impossibility of the Paretian Liberal in social choice theory concentrates leaves out many other kinds of rights that are also important. This is indeed so, but the domain of rights in social choice theory should not be seen as being confined to a particular example that has been used to show an impossibility result. The very limited use of the idea of rights that is necessary to be invoked in establishing a particular theorem, for example in showing 'the impossibility of the Paretian Liberal', does not suggest any reason for neglecting the much wider range of rights that can be entertained and advanced in social choice theory in general.

There is, in fact, a motivational contrast here. In showing an impossibility result, the less we demand from the axioms, the more interesting (indeed, the more powerful) is the result – hence the concentration on showing that even 'minimal' demands can lead to an impossibility. But sticking only to a minimalist formulation can hardly be a good way of understanding the total reach of an idea in general. The invoking of 'minimal liberty' – adequate enough for getting it to IPL – cannot be a good way of assessing what social choice theory can, in general, do to accommodate ideas such as liberties and rights. A confounding of the two questions has to be avoided. I shall return to this larger issue presently.

The second line of critique is more substantial and important. It focuses on the fact that social choice theory is concerned with the valuation of social states, including what actually happens. This is taken to indicate that social choice formulation of rights must be connected with culmination outcomes, and not at all with processes (as it might, at least superficially, appear). In disputing the adequacy – and indeed the necessity – of social choice formulation of rights (thus diagnosed), it has been argued that a better way of formulating rights would not relate rights to outcomes at all, but only to what each person should be free to choose to do, no matter what consequences follow.

The pioneering move in this way of disputing the social choice formulation of rights came from Robert Nozick (1973), (1974). Even though Nozick developed his argument by taking up the impossibility of the Paretian liberal, the force of his criticism does not depend on any presumption that social choice theory cannot go beyond the kind of rights on which the IPL concentrates. Nozick was not arguing that social choice theory demands too little from rights, but far too much. A right, he argued, should not be seen as a guarantee of getting to any *outcome* at all, but only to actions and strategies that an individual should be free to choose. Social choice theory goes wrong, in Nozick's judgement, by characterizing rights as entitlements to particular outcomes. Nozick put the point in this way (commenting on the IPL theorem):

> The trouble stems from treating an individual's rights to choose among alternatives as the right to determine the relative ordering of these alternatives within a social ordering ... A more appropriate view of individual rights is as follows. Individual rights are co-possible; each person may exercise his rights as he chooses. The

exercise of these rights fixes some features of the world. Within the constraints of these fixed features, a choice may be made by a social choice mechanism based upon a social ordering; if there are any choices left to make! Rights do not determine a social ordering but instead set the constraints within which a social choice is to be made, by excluding certain alternatives, fixing others, and so on . . . If any patterning is legitimate, it falls *within* the domain of social choice, and hence is constrained by people's rights. How else can we cope with Sen's result?[ix]

This line of criticism – wanting rights to be defined in terms of people being free to do what they want, rather than having specific influences on the outcomes that emerge – deserves a substantial and elaborate discussion, as I have tried to present elsewhere (in Sen (1992b), (1996b)). But let me briefly note here two particular points of immediate relevance.

First, there are different kinds of rights and valuational concerns that influence our thinking. It is not hard to appreciate that rights and liberties may well be concerned both with *processes* (for example, our freedom to choose our actions freely) and *consequences* (including not just how we act but also what we end up getting). We have reason to be concerned with both.

The right to a process can be important in many contexts: for example, even if some authority can guess entirely accurately what I would most like to choose, my liberty may not be adequately respected if the authority bestows on me what I would have supposedly chosen, while denying me the right to choose for myself. The freedom to choose what to do cannot be jettisoned from an adequate understanding of personal liberty. On the other hand, a person's real freedom may actually link with outcomes as well. For example, in agitating for safe flights (and the freedom to survive air journeys), our focus may be on having competent (and non-suicidal) pilots who fly us safely, rather than obtaining for ourselves the freedom to choose to do whatever we would like to do in the cockpit. Similarly, if a person is keen to avoid some kind of meat – pork or beef or duck or whatever – to have the freedom to pick her own dish at a buffet, without being told which contains what, cannot be seen as vindication of her freedom to eat as she would like.

Second, the critique of social choice theory on the supposed ground that it must necessarily neglect the actual processes involved since it must concentrate attention only on what we end up with, assumes that outcomes in social choice theory (or states of affairs) must be seen only in the form of 'culmination outcomes' rather than as 'comprehensive outcomes'. Even though there may be some difficulty in particular cases in integrating processes within a broad view of outcome, there is, in general, no ban at all on looking beyond the final state and seeing what 'happened', including which processes and actions were involved. For example, the most immediate consequence of choosing to speak at a gathering is surely that such a speech act occurs, and we need not obliterate the fact of the speech act by concentrating exclusively on some further 'outcome' of the speech.

NOZICK'S CONCEPTION OF LIBERTY AND GAME FORMS

In his preferred characterization, Nozick sees rights to liberty in terms of giving the individual control over certain personal decisions, and 'each person may exercise his right as he chooses' (there is no guarantee of any outcome – it is only a right to the choice of action). There is a problem of formulation that needs to be sorted out, even if we want to follow Nozick's focus to choose actions rather than outcomes. A person's right to do certain things may be seen – even within Nozick's general motivation – as being dependent on what else is happening. Consider a person's freedom to sing his favourite hymn to others, which may be a right to which we can be, in general, favourably disposed. But that right would not, as normally interpreted, give the person the freedom to sing his hymn when others are singing some other song, like 'La Marseillaise', or 'The Star-Spangled Banner', or indeed another hymn.

The approach pioneered by Nozick has, as a result, been extended through a more complex formulation, in terms of what are called 'game forms' in standard game theory. When the demands of liberty are given a game-form formulation, each person has a set of permissible acts or strategies, from which each can choose one. The outcome depends on the choices of acts, or strategies, by all. The requirements of liberty are specified in terms of restrictions on permissible combinations of acts or strategies. The hymn-singer invoked earlier may not be free to sing his song when others are singing some other song, but may well be completely free to do so when others are silent and waiting for someone to make a move. This further specification is surely not in conflict with what Nozick wanted to put into the idea of liberty – and of rights.

In many cases, there are great advantages in thinking of liberty in terms of each person's agency (even though restricted by permissible combinations), rather than in terms of what emerges at the very end. Nozick's perspective is illuminating here. However, in many other cases and in different circumstances, liberty and freedom are not concerned only with the actions a person is allowed to undertake, but also with what emanates from those choices taken together. The importance of agency does not obliterate the relevance of the outcome.

Consider two problems in particular. First, the adequacy of a particular game form to achieve what liberty demands may depend on the presence of particular circumstances, and to ascertain this calls for some consequential analysis (a comprehensive outcome includes, *inter alia*, a culmination outcome too). A person's actual choices may be influenced by circumstances that could be appropriate to consider in judging whether a person really did have that liberty in a significant sense. Social influences may induce a person not to choose in the way he or she would really like, even when the game-form formality includes that option within the domain of permissible strategies. For example, in a deeply sexist society governed by rules about how women should dress, a woman may lack the courage to appear with her head uncovered, even though she would prefer not to conceal her hair. To note that the person was, in fact, free to undertake the necessary action (i.e. to go out with head uncovered) is not adequate for guaranteeing the realization of the appropriate rights in such cases. The phenomenon of 'choice inhibition' must not be assumed away if a theory of liberty is to be a useful guide to political philosophy, welfare economics and practical reason.

To consider another type of right, the right to poverty relief may be seen as being compromised, even when no actual application is refused, because of a decision of a would-be recipient not to apply for assistance despite wanting to have legitimate benefits. The failure to apply may be related to such factors as worry about social stigma in having to declare oneself as poor, or fear of unpleasant official investigation, or simply confusion or dejection. Even though the person could have got social support if he or she had chosen to apply for it, that in itself is an inadequate basis of being sure that the formal availability of a choice was a real availability that a person could actually take up, ignoring the circumstantial problems. Having, formally, the right to ask for poverty relief, but not doing so because of, say, the stigma of being seen as poor, cannot be seen as a realization of the right to poverty relief. When poverty relief in such forms as 'supplementary benefits' were introduced in Britain, a fair amount of governmental effort had to be spent to make sure that those who were entitled to get such support would not be inhibited from seeking – and getting – that support.

Second, another source of complexity relates to the problem of interdependence: a person's ability to do something may be seen as conditional on some other things happening or not happening. Interdependence in the realization of liberty is particularly important for taking note of what may be called 'invasive actions'. Sometimes the crucial agencies in one person's private sphere are not confined to those of the person herself. For example, your liberty not to have smoke blown in your face by a no-nonsense smoker, or your liberty to sleep peacefully at night without having to listen to ear-splitting music coming from next door, depends greatly on the actions of others. But these are indeed matters of *your* personal life and liberty. This type of 'invasive actions', in which other people's actions invade one's private sphere, has to be assessed through a consequential analysis of how people's private spheres are hugely influenced by the actions of others.

A non-smoker's right not to have smoke blown in her face is, of course, a right to an outcome, and no understanding of liberty can be adequate if it remains entirely detached from the outcome that emerges. The game-form formulations, if chosen, would have to be worked 'backwards' by moving from acceptable outcomes to the combinations of strategies that would yield one of those outcomes. Thus constructed game-form formulations will have to be effective and get at this problem *indirectly*. Indeed, historically, in order to achieve the socially chosen outcome of eliminating involuntary secondary smoking, policy pursuits have taken many different forms:

- prohibiting smoking if others object;
- banning smoking in the presence of others;
- forbidding smoking in public places no matter whether others are present or not (so that others do not have to stay away from places that should be useable by all).

Many societies have actually moved increasingly to more and more exacting demands on smokers when less restrictive constraints have been found to fail in bringing about the outcome needed for the realization of the liberty to avoid passive smoking.

The fact that convenience may well suggest that the specified procedure should take the form of choosing between different 'game forms' in some specific exercises cannot hide the fact that the choice of game forms has to be guided by the respective effectiveness in bringing about the social realizations that give people the right to have personal lives of the kind they want. When, in 1859, John Stuart Mill argued in *On Liberty* for a person's freedom to pursue effectively his or her religious practice (when it did not materially harm others), he was arguing not only against the prohibition of religious practices by the state, but also against disrupting activities by others in the society (for example, making divertingly loud noises when others are engaged in praying or meditating). It is not sufficient to allow people to choose their religious practices as they like without making sure that the chosen freedom can be actually realized without disruption.

There is no doubt that game forms can be characterized in a way that they can take note of interdependence and protect people from the invasive actions of others. Admissibility of strategies, that is, the characterization of permissible game forms, has to be worked out – directly or indirectly – in the light of the outcomes emerging from the combination of different people's strategies. If the driving force behind the choice of game forms is the judgement that involuntary secondary smoking is inadmissible, and that people should not have to stay away from public places to avoid 'passive smoking', then the game-form choices are indeed parasitic on the nature of the social realizations (or comprehensive outcomes) that emerge. We have to consider both the freedom of action and the nature of the consequences and outcomes to have an adequate understanding of liberty.

Without slighting in any way the instrumental convenience of thinking in terms of game forms, we can see that social choice theory, in broader formulation, can deal both with people's liberty to act and with their liberty to enjoy self-chosen – and uninvaded – personal lives. The game-form formulation is, in the last analysis, not an alternative that can stand independently of the social choices involved, but has to be seen together with the process of social choice.

Chapter A5*
Rights and Social Choice

The theorem of 'the Impossibility of the Paretian Liberal' (IPL) was established in the original (1970) edition of this book in relational terms (see Chapter 6*), including the requirement of acyclicity of the social preference relation R. But it was also explained that the theorem can be reformulated in a way that no social preference relation need be invoked (see the 1970 edition – page 133 here). A choice functional version of IPL is presented here first.

Let the functional collective choice rule (FCCR) determine a choice function $C(S)$ for social decisions for each n-tuple of individual orderings, for any set S in the domain of choice:

$$C(S) = F(\{R_i\}).$$

Next we define the Pareto relation and the condition of minimal liberty in choice functional terms. We define xP^*y as the choice functional statement that, if x is available in the menu for choice, then y must not be chosen.

xP^*y if and only if [for all T: $x \in T => y \notin C(T)$].

Condition P^C (Rejection of Pareto Inferior States):
   For any pair of social states $\{x, y\}$, if for all i: xP_iy, then xP^*y.

Condition ML^C (Rejection Based Minimal Liberty):
   There are at least two persons such that for each such person i there is a personal domain with at least one pair of social states $\{x, y\}$ satisfying: $xP_iy => xP^*y$, and $yP_ix => yP^*x$.

To elaborate, Condition P^C demands that a Pareto-inferior alternative must not be chosen in the presence of an alternative Pareto-superior to it. Condition ML^C requires that at least two persons must each have a non-empty personal domain: if an alternative x is strictly preferred by a person in his or her own personal domain to alternative y, then y must not be socially chosen if x is available for choice.

Condition U^C is the same as the unrestricted domain Condition U, except that it applies to the functional collective choice rule F.

(*Theorem A5*.1*):   There is no F satisfying U^C, P^C and ML^C.

Proof: Consider, first, the case in which the pairs of states in the two persons' 'personal domains' do not have any state in common. Let person i's domain include $\{a, b\}$ and person j's $\{c, d\}$. With the help of Condition U^C, consider the following preference orderings of i and j respectively: $dP_i a$, $aP_i b$, $bP_i c$, and $bP_j c$, $cP_j d$, $dP_j a$. Let everyone else k satisfy: $dP_k a$, and $bP_k c$. By the choice-functional Pareto principle P^C, neither a nor c can be chosen from the set $\{a, b, c, d\}$. But by the choice functional condition of minimal liberty ML^C, neither b nor d can be chosen from $\{a, b, c, d\}$. So *nothing* can be chosen from this set $\{a, b, c, d\}$, and thus $C(S)$ is not, in fact, a choice function over the relevant domain. Hence the result.

The proof can be formally completed by considering the cases in which one of the elements is common between $\{a, b\}$ and $\{c, d\}$, and the strategy of proof is much the same.

Note that the choice functional requirements P^C and ML^C are demands of 'external correspondence', not a condition of internal consistency (see Chapter A2*). They are statements on what must not be chosen given the individual preferences, and the motivation relates to the need to reject Pareto inferior alternatives and also to shun alternatives strictly dispreferred by an individual in his or her own personal domain. No internal consistency condition has been, on its own, imposed (even though the regularity of external correspondence will entail, by implication, some interrelation between the choices from different subsets). No concept of a social preference has been invoked, and this is an entirely choice functional impossibility theorem, with no imposition of so-called 'collective rationality' and no condition of internal consistency imposed on the choice function.

ISOMORPHISM BETWEEN IPL AND THE PRISONER'S DILEMMA

Mathematically the IPL and the Prisoner's Dilemma (PD) are exactly similar in form, or isomorphic. The main difference between the two lies in our attaching a value to the liberty of the two parties (e.g. Prude and Lewd) in the case of IPL, and no such intrinsic value in the case of PD. With IPL, the valuation of personal liberty may require that parties should be allowed to have what they prefer in their own respective personal spheres. This is a contrast with PD, where no such liberty-based valuation is involved, and the focus is on getting to Pareto efficiency, and, in particular, to the Pareto-superior outcome to the combination of isolated choices (which are given no liberty-related importance). So even though there is a mathematical isomorphism between the IPL and the PD, they involve different motivational interpretations and different priorities in social choice.

To check the isomorphism, first consider the PD, with C_i standing for confession respectively by the two persons 1 and 2, and N_i for non-confession by the respective individual i. The two persons have the following ordering respectively:

Person 1	Person 2
C_1, N_2	N_1, C_2
N_1, N_2	N_1, N_2
C_1, C_2	C_1, C_2
N_1, C_2	C_1, N_2

The dominant strategy for person 1 is C_1 and for person 2 is C_2. But (C_1, C_2) is strictly Pareto inferior to (N_1, N_2). That is where the PD bites in.

Now call person 1 Prude, and replace his confessing (C_1) and not confessing (N_1) respectively by his not reading the book he hates (F_1) and actually reading it (R_1). Similarly, call person 2 Lewd, and replace his confessing (C_2) and not confessing (N_2) respectively by his reading the book he loves (R_2) and forgoing that reading (F_2). Then we get the following set of orderings:

Prude	Lewd
F_1, F_2	R_1, R_2
R_1, F_2	R_1, F_2
F_1, R_2	F_1, R_2
R_1, R_2	F_1, F_2

It is readily seen that this is the preference profile that was attributed respectively to Prude and Lewd to generate the impossibility. Prude's dominant strategy is not to read the book (F_1) and Lewd's to read it (R_2). That produces a combination of (F_1, R_2), with Lewd reading the book he would love to read, and Prude avoiding the book that he would like to shun. There is no liberty-based tension there. But the nosiness of each makes them both get more joy out of Prude alone reading the book he hates rather than Lewd reading the book he would love to read. Hence the conflict between minimal liberty and the Pareto principle defined on utilities.

The question, as discussed in Chapter A5, is how seriously we should take the normative force of the Paretian judgement based on each person's nosey utilities, denying the Millian insight that there is 'no parity' between a person's feelings about his own personal life and his feelings about other people's personal lives. The mathematics of PD and IPL are exactly the same, and the difference lies only in the interpretations involved. The two cases involve very different takes on the personal liberty to choose, and quite disparate assessments of the ethical attraction of Pareto optimality in the space of utilities.

UTILITIES AND VALUES

As has been discussed in Chapter A5, people's valuational reasoning may find room both for feelings and pleasures, on one side, and their ethical concerns, including about the importance of liberty, on the other. There is no inconsistency in, say, Prude saying:, 'I would be even more pained by Lewd reading this awful book than the displeasure I would get from reading it myself, but that is not reason enough for me to read this stuff myself on condition that Lewd forgoes reading it – I value everyone's ability to do what they like in their personal lives, with Lewd reading what he likes, while I look after my own life.'

There are different orderings involved, including one of utilities (in the sense of pleasures or desires) and values (in the sense of what I think should happen, everything considered). To try to capture two dissimilar exercises under one ordering – that of 'preference' or even 'utility' (imprecisely defined) – may have a long tradition in parts of the social sciences, but that lack of distinction is one way of fogging up our analysis. It is not claimed that they 'must' differ, but only that they can differ, often with very good reason.

Recollect the *utility rankings* of Prude and Lewd (already discussed), in terms only of pleasures and pains. To reiterate:

Prude's utility ranking	Lewd's utility ranking
F_1, F_2	R_1, R_2
R_1, F_2	R_1, F_2
F_1, R_2	F_1, R_2
R_1, R_2	F_1, F_2

If they both have respect for liberty, and value the ability of each person to lead his or her own life that they respectively desire or value, this pair of utility rankings can easily co-exist with the following *valuational rankings* of liberty-respecting Prude and Lewd:

Prude's valuational ranking	Lewd's valuational ranking
F_1, R_2	F_1, R_2
F_1, F_2	R_1, R_2
R_1, R_2	F_1, F_2
R_1, F_2	R_1, F_2

The important departures here from the rankings only of pleasures is the liberty-valuing placement of F_1, R_2 (with Prude not having to read what he does not want to read, while Lewd reads what he wants to) at the top, though the not-best alternatives can be differently placed, depending on how the different imperfections are respectively evaluated. But no matter how these are rearranged, with the placing of F_1, R_2 (each being decisive on his own life) at the top, there is obviously no conflict between conditions of liberty and the demands of unanimity.

It is only when the unanimity condition is defined on the utility space (given by pleasures or desires) to get to the Pareto principle, defined in terms of utilities, and when people's pleasures and utilities remain obsessed with other people's lives, that the IPL has its bite. The usefulness of the IPL lies, among other things, on the need for us to recognize the importance of distinctions that are lost when just one ranking for each person is supposed to reflect many different things about him or her, losing the difference between the person's *pleasures* and *values* in particular (a distinction that was discussed fairly extensively in Chapter A2). The distinctions that are lost in seeing human beings as 'rational fools' who cannot distinguish between their pleasures and values (on the problems created by the loss of such motivational distinctions, see Sen (1976a)) need not take us to the allegedly rational – but actually bewildering – contract of Prude reading a book he really hates to read in order to prevent Lewd from reading what he would love to read. Social reasoning should be able to do better than that.

Chapter A6
Reasoning and Social Decisions

The role of reasoning in social choice is the principal subject of this book. Social choice theory can be seen as the pursuit of critical reasoning in dealing with group decisions, including aggregative assessment of the lives of people who constitute a group. Condorcet, the early social choice theorist in the eighteenth century, not only presented important mathematical results in voting theory and jury decisions, but also discussed extensively how the pursuit of reasoning – both on one's own and jointly with others – can influence social decisions. We need disciplined reasoning in the pursuit of social ethics and in the evaluation of claims about social justice, as with other problems of social choice.

As was discussed in the new Preface, there is scope for scrutinizing what systematic reasoning does, or does not, demand. There is a case for re-examining even well-established rules for reasoning in choice. Consider an allegedly basic requirement of rigorous reasoned choice. It is very common to assume that disciplined reasoning for decision-making must be based on the pursuit of optimality, that is, finding an alternative that is clearly the best among all the available ones. In this widely used interpretation, reasoning is taken to be unfinished until a conclusion emerges that is at least as satisfactory as every other conclusion.

Can this be correct? The insistence on 'optimality' (involving the identification of an 'ideal' – or 'best' – alternative) has to be distinguished from 'maximality', defined as a conclusion that is no less satisfactory than any other conclusion. To illustrate the contrast, when there are two alternatives x and y, neither of which is judged to be better than (or exactly as good as) the other, then in that pair of alternatives (x, y), both are maximal, but neither is optimal. We can reasonably choose either x or y, rather than go on dithering. The difference between optimality and maximality arises from the possibility of an incomplete ranking, but that is a very real possibility in reasoned assessment.

Buridan's famous ass, which made a brief appearance in the new Preface to this expanded edition, came to a sad end by seeking optimality when it could not figure out which of the two haystacks facing it was the better one to go for. As the tragic story runs, the ass died of starvation from dithering. It is possible that one of the haystacks was indeed larger – or more delicious – than the other, but if the ass could not figure out which one that was, it would surely have been better to go for either of the stacks rather than die from hunger. Given the stubborn incompleteness of the ordering of the two haystacks, both of them are maximal, and the choice of either – despite their lack of optimality – would have been a much better option than starvation. Even with unranked stacks and no identified best alternative, there is a reasoned approach to choice for Buridan's ass – which is to go for *either* haystack, rather than ending up starving to death.

If reasoning can identify the really inferior alternatives, it will have done a great job in allowing us to reject those alternatives. But there is neither any analytical, nor any practical, ground for thinking that reasoning should be able to rank every alternative against every other. Seeking maximality is part of the discipline of reasoning, which does not demand anything beyond what is feasible. Reasoned choice is not as forbiddingly difficult as it is sometimes made to look – often (as in the case of the philosophically famous donkey) with very sad consequences.

THE MAXIMAL AND THE OPTIMAL

The distinction between maximality and optimality is often overlooked in presentations on welfare economics and political philosophy. It is, however, a major contrast. We can diagnose a failure of reasoned decision-making if we choose to reject an identifiably better alternative, but that problem does not arise if there is no such option (as is the case in making a maximal choice in the absence of any optimal alternative). While optimality entails maximality, the converse does not hold, and the two demands need not coincide. As was mentioned in the new Preface, this crucial distinction was well identified by Bourbaki in their classic mathematical treatise, *Éléments de Mathématique* (Bourbaki (1939), (1966), (1968)). With special assumptions, in particular that there are no unranked pairs in a transitive ranking, the maximal will also be optimal, and the difference will, as was mentioned earlier, vanish. But there is no analytical reason, nor any practical necessity, why the ranking of alternative conclusions must take this highly restrictive form.

Let me discuss the distinction with an example. Consider a person, Ashraf, in contemporary West Asia, who has a strong commitment to try and prevent terrorism, and who is considering the possibility of two terrible events, both of which a terrorist group has threatened to carry out. One threatened event – let us call it x – is the total destruction of the historic city of Nineveh (with, however, no one being killed), and the other – called y – involves the killing of a hundred people at a different spot (without any destruction of Nineveh). Both are terrible things to happen, and Ashraf is considering what can be done to stop them. If it turns out that he and his fellow anti-terrorists can prevent one of the two ghastly events, but not both, then his decision would have to be about choosing between x and y.

It is a difficult choice, and there are very strong arguments on both sides. One involves the prevention of the murder of many people and the other the preservation of a great historical site which can be thought to be valuable in itself, but would also be enormously valued by a great many generations to come. We may decide that we have good reasons to give decisional priority in one direction, or alternatively in the other, but we cannot be sure that such an optimal alternative must emerge. We can continue to entertain a plurality of answers that need not be eliminated by what Rawls calls a 'reflective equilibrium'. It is of course acceptable (and nicely comforting) if such a clear answer emerges, but this need not actually happen. It is not a requirement of disciplined reasoning, nor a necessity of a 'reflective equilibrium', that Ashraf must (absolutely *must*) be able to rank the two alternatives x and y in one direction or the other – or judge them to be equally good (in fact, in this case, equally bad).

THE PROBLEM IS NOT NON-COMMENSURABILITY

Before I move on to the far-reaching implications of the distinction between maximality and optimality, let me make a quick clarificatory remark. The issue of unrankability must not be identified with the so-called problem – a much over-hyped issue – of 'non-commensurability' (i.e. that the different variables involved cannot be measured in the same units). Commensurability may make a choice perfectly obvious (like choosing two ounces of gold over one ounce of the same metal), but that is not the only kind of choice we can make – backed by reason. As a matter of fact, we very frequently make perfectly reasoned choices over non-commensurable alternatives. If I greatly like bananas and hate apples, I would not be deterred from choosing a banana by the extremely peculiar worry that bananas and apples cannot be measured in the same units, which is what commensurability is concerned with. If we definitely prefer a banana to an apple, they don't have to be measured in the same units for our reasoning our way into choosing the banana. Non-commensurability can be a bogus problem.

The real source of unrankability is not the absence of co-measurability, which is a very common and entirely mundane occurrence. In contrast, in the case of Ashraf's dilemma, the alternatives not only involve distinct components (as most alternatives do), but – and this is the crucial issue here – Ashraf's attempts at reasoned evaluation may not be able to put one of the alternatives above the other, despite his best effort at reasoning.

PARTIAL ORDERING AND
REASONED CHOICE

If Ashraf's thinking equilibriates in the position that he can neither say that saving Nineveh would be at least as good as saving a hundred people from being killed, nor that stopping a hundred murders would be at least as good as saving Nineveh from being destroyed, then he has what is technically called an incomplete ranking, on the basis of his *completed* – and possibly *complete* – reasoning. It is important to recognize that the presence of an incompletely ranked pair does not indicate that Ashraf is not making use of as much reasoning as he can invoke, or even as much as can possibly be invoked.

It is also important to note that, consistently with this, Ashraf may be able to rank many other pairs of alternatives in quite a definite way. For example, he may be able to find reason enough in favour of, say, allowing Nineveh to be destroyed rather than a whole country, such as Syria (not to mention Iraq, where Nineveh itself is situated). Reasoned rankings can co-exist with valuationally unranked pairs, even after taking reasoning as far as it will go. This is not an argument for slackening one's attempt at reasoning to rank every unranked pair, often with decisive results. There is no advocacy – or even tolerance – of valuational laziness in the claim being made here. There is, however, no analytical necessity, nor any practical reason, that guarantees that a complete ranking *must* emerge.

Note also that, even when Ashraf has an incomplete ordering, he need not be in a decisional impasse. If both x and y, while unranked vis-à-vis each other, are better than all the other alternatives in a set (including many even nastier ones such as the whole country being destroyed), he has reason enough to choose either x or y from that set of alternatives. Each of them is a 'maximal' alternative, in Bourbaki's sense. The fact that neither is 'optimal' need not leave Ashraf in a decisional impasse. He can sensibly choose either x or y, but not any of the other alternatives.

It may also be noted that a valuational incompleteness need not entail a valuational impasse. Let me try to bring out the problem

457

more clearly by elaborating on the logical structure of what is involved here. Take a partial ordering of three elements x, y, z in terms of their respective goodness: x is better than z, and y also is better than z, but neither is x better than (or as good as) y, nor is y better than (or as good as) x. There are a lot of comparative judgements here, for example that 'x is better than z', which is correct, while 'x is better than y' is incorrect. Note that in the example given, the correct–incorrect dichotomy can be applied to the comparison of every pair, *without exception*. In this particular case, the statement 'x is better than or as good as y' is incorrect, and so is the statement 'y is better than or as good as x'. The unrankability here does not show any valuational failure – merely the need to recognize that unrankability is the particular form that the outcome of the valuational exercise may take, in this case.

That the inclusion of unranked pairs of alternatives is an integral part of the mathematics of relations and sets is, of course, well-known. What I am arguing for here is the need to recognize that the existence of unranked pairs is an actual – and may even be a common – outcome of reasoned analysis of ethical and political evaluation. If it were claimed that there would be a mistake in a configuration that includes both the statements that 'x is not at least as good as y' and that 'y is not at least as good as x', that diagnosis would not arise from any analytical necessity, nor from the nature of practical reasoning. To reach that conclusion, we would have to impose some further restrictions to ensure that the correct–incorrect dichotomy 'must' – for some reason yet to be specified – take a particularly limited form. Such a special demand may take the form of insisting that, if x is not better than y, then y must be – *absolutely must be* – at least as good as x. However, if that particular restriction were to be proposed, we have every reason to ask: why?

In effect, this would be an assumption that there simply could not be a normative evaluation that yields any incompleteness of rankings – an unusually restrictive demand. This is not an analytical necessity, and if for some substantive reason it would be sensible to make such a demand, then we must be told what that reason is. To say this would be helpful for decision-making would, of course, be to beg the question, aside from reflecting a failure to recognize that maximality is adequate enough for reasoned choice.

Even though the contrast between the maximal and the optimal may seem like an esoteric mathematical issue, the distinction is of importance for practical decision-making (as the life and death of Buridan's ass bring out) as well as for moral and political philosophy in general. Indeed, this formal, or methodological, issue is absolutely central to many substantive ethical arguments, including the assessment of the respective claims of alternative theories of justice.[1]

Two and half centuries of work on 'social choice' has provided many practical examples of what can be called 'equilibriated incompleteness'. Even in terms of general principles there is no particularly compelling reason for insisting on the 'completeness' of all binary relations of normative judgement. There is no great analytical or practical difficulty in having systematic and reasoned choice with maximality, rather than optimality.[2]

ASSERTIVE AND TENTATIVE INCOMPLETENESS

Incompleteness of a ranking can arise not only from judgemental unresolvability (which I have tried to illustrate with the Nineveh case), but also from unbridgeable gaps in information (not just unbridged gaps, but those that are in practice unbridgeable). In fact, in any decisional choice the consequences of which would come in the future (and most decisional choices are of this type), we have to guess, not always confidently, what the consequences would in fact turn out to be. In many cases, the future effects may well be easy to guess, and, in some cases, we can deal with uncertainties through some acceptable

---

[1] I have discussed this contrast more fully in the Annual Lecture for 2015 of the Royal Institute of Philosophy: 'Reasoning and Justice: The Maximal and the Optimal', *Philosophy*, 92, January 2017 (Sen (2017)).

[2] For further discussion of reasoned decisions based on maximality, see Sen (1993a), (1997a). See also Bossert and Suzumura (2010) and Suzumura (2016), including the idea of 'Suzumura consistency'.

procedure of reasoning under uncertainty. (For example, someone many decide to rely on probability-weighted 'expected values', if there are reliable probability distributions *and* if she accepts the foundational axioms that make the discipline of expected valuation a sensible way to proceed.) But there is nothing extraordinarily odd if, in many cases, we cannot find reason to bridge the informational and judgemental gaps to arrive at a scrutinized complete ordering.

I turn now to 'tentative' incompleteness. In addition to equilibriated incompleteness that cannot be removed, we also have to deal with provisional incompleteness. Reasoning is a process rather than an instantaneous occurrence. At the moment when a decision has to be taken, we may quite possibly still be looking for more information, or for fuller resolution of contrary considerations. While a partial ranking (or a partial partition) can be of the 'assertive' type, it can also be 'tentative' – a reasoned contingent assertion at a particular stage of a possibly long-drawn-out exercise.[3]

Consider now the argumentative issues that relate particularly to tentative incompleteness. We may, for example, know that our inability to rank a pair is tentative because it could be resolved – in one direction or other – if and when more information of a particular type can be found, which we presently do not have. Even though this is not a case of assertive incompleteness, there is still a question of reasoned decision-making to be faced regarding what should be the right choice given where we inescapably are – at the point of decision-making. To say that we should rapidly find more information to eliminate the uncertainty is, of course, an evasion of the question being asked. So would be any advice to reflect more, if the tentative incompleteness arises not from an informational deficit, but from an actual failure to discern the truth because of the problem's complexity. We may, in fact, have good reason to abandon one of the more frequent assumptions in information theory which presumes

---

[3] Cases of unresolved conflicts and consequent incompleteness belong to the class of problems that Isaac Levi (1986) has called 'hard choice', and, as he has rightly argued, there is still a big normative question facing us (which Levi has illuminatingly analysed), to wit, what the right thing to do would be, given the incompleteness, even if it is tentative. See also Levi (2009).

that we 'know' everything that is analytically deducible from what is known (like knowing immediately the answer to any mathematical puzzle whenever we are given one).

INCOMPLETENESS AND REASONED SOCIAL CHOICE

Maximality is an adequate route to reason-based choice, and it can also serve as an acceptable basis for making social choice. Issues of this kind can arise frequently enough in group decisions, for example when there is considerable disagreement in the ranking of disparate alternatives, despite an agreement that each of them would avoid a much worse alternative – even a catastrophe. For example, two groups of environmentalists may agree that some carbon-reduction policy x (having high carbon-pricing through a functioning market) and another such policy y (regulatory intervention through banning certain carbon-generating activities) are each much better than doing nothing, as the globe warms up – that catastrophic outcome may be called alternative z. And yet one group may vastly prefer x to y, whereas the other group has the opposite preference. Their wrangling with each other may prevent any policy from being adopted, which would generate the worst possible result, namely z. There would clearly be a strong case here for choosing either x or y in order to avoid z, but that would not be a unanimous choice (and, in the case of altercations and prolonged disputes, it need not even be the likely outcome). However, if we take note only of unanimous agreements, we could note that in the Pareto ranking x and y would remain unranked, whereas x and y would both be placed socially higher than z. The discipline of maximal choice would then give us good reason to choose either x or y, but absolutely shun z. The analogy with the problem of Buridan's ass is easy to see.[4]

---

[4] Cass Sunstein (1995) has brought out the importance of 'incompletely theorized agreements' in generating a consensus even when people differ in their real beliefs and concerns. Maximality-based social choice can supplement that by pointing to

This may look like a rather special case (though it need not in fact be that), but wranglings of various kinds are common enough in social choice, even when the outcomes they lead to may be particularly inferior. Making reasoned use of incomplete rankings opens up many attractive possibilities in welfare economics and normative evaluation, as has been discussed in Chapters A3 and A3*. As was also examined there (and more fully in my book *The Idea of Justice*: Sen 2009a), the analysis of social justice can be greatly helped by the use of social choice theory in general, but even more so when social choice can proceed on the basis of partial orderings, relying on maximality as the criterion of reasoned choice.

COMPULSION VERSUS REASONING

Reason cannot but be central to social choice. This can involve individual reflection on one's own (seeking what John Rawls has called a 'reflective equilibrium'), but also public reasoning in the company of others. Ideas and scrutiny of different persons can interrelate and also interact with each other.[5] The conceptual underpinning of normative social choice theory as an approach is centrally dependent on reasoning in general, and public reasoning in particular. Indeed, the fundamental connection between public reasoning, on the one hand, and the demands of participatory social decisions, on the other, is central not just to the practical task of making democracy more effective (important as it is), but also for achieving an adequate understanding of the demands of social choice.

The historical background is quite important here in appreciating how social choice theory as a normative approach for social decisions has evolved, drawing on ideas that came into prominence

---

the possibility of reasoned agreement on action without complete agreement on *valuation*.

[5] Anthony Appiah (2009) has plausibly argued that I tend to assume implausibly high willingness of people to listen to each other's reasoning. He may well be right, but there is evidence of some willingness, and also of the possibility of enhancing that willingness through efforts to reach others.

during the European Enlightenment. The role of education and understanding in general was central to Condorcet's thinking about society and social choice. As an illustration, consider his nuanced views on the population problem, in contrast with Thomas Malthus's single-minded belief in the inescapable failure of human reasoning, ushering in a catastrophic tide of population growth that, in Malthus's view, could not but overwhelm humanity. As a matter of fact (though this is rarely recollected these days), Condorcet preceded Malthus in pointing to the possibility of the world getting seriously overpopulated if the population growth rate did not slow down – a pointer on which Malthus himself drew, as he acknowledged, as the first step in his alarmist theory on population disaster.

However, Condorcet did not stop there. He went on to argue in the *Esquisse* (Condorcet (1795)) that a more educated society, with social enlightenment and public discussion, including the expansion of women's education, would reduce the population growth rate dramatically and could even reverse it – a line of analysis that Malthus (1798) found completely implausible, and for which he chastised Condorcet's gullibility.[i]

Condorcet anticipated a voluntary reduction in fertility rates, and predicted the emergence of new norms of smaller family size based on 'the progress of reason'. He anticipated a time when people 'will know that, if they have a duty towards those who are not yet born, that duty is not to give them existence but to give them happiness'. This type of reasoning, buttressed by the expansion of education (especially female education, of which Condorcet was one of the earliest and most vocal advocates), would lead people, Condorcet reasoned, to lower fertility rates and smaller families, which people would choose voluntarily, 'rather than foolishly . . . encumber the world with useless and wretched beings' (Condorcet (1795); (1955), pp. 188–9).

Malthus thought the attribution of such power to reasoning was pure fantasy, and saw little chance of solving social problems through reasoned decisions by the families involved. As far as the effects of population growth were concerned, Malthus was convinced of the inevitability of population outrunning food supply, and took the limits of food production to be relatively inflexible. He was also completely sceptical of voluntary family planning. While he did refer to 'moral restraint' as an imagined alternative way of reducing the pressure of population (alternative, that is, to misery and elevated mortality), he saw no real prospect that such restraint would actually work.

Over the years, Malthus's views varied somewhat on what can be taken to be inevitable, and he was clearly less certain of his earlier prognosis as the years progressed. There is a tendency in modern Malthusian scholarship to emphasize the elements of 'shift' in his position, and there is indeed ground for distinguishing between the early Malthus and the late Malthus. But it is important to recognize that his basic distrust of the power of reason, as opposed to the force of economic compulsion, in making people choose smaller families, remained largely unmodified in his thinking. Indeed, in one of his last works (*A Summary View of the Principle of Population*), published in 1830 – he died in 1834 – he continued to insist on his conclusion that:

> there is no reason whatever to suppose that anything beside the difficulty of procuring in adequate plenty the necessaries of life should either indispose this greater number of persons to marry early, or disable them from rearing in health the largest families.[ii]

It was because of his disbelief in the voluntary route that Malthus focused on the need for a *forced* reduction in population growth rates, which he thought would come from the compulsion of nature. The fall in living standards resulting from population growth would not only increase mortality rates dramatically (what Malthus called 'positive checks'), but would also force people, through economic penury, to have smaller families. The basic link in the argument is Malthus's conviction that population growth rate cannot be effectively pulled down by 'anything beside the difficulty of procuring in adequate plenty the necessaries of life'. Malthus's opposition to poverty relief, such as the Poor Laws, and his loudly proclaimed arguments against public support for the poor and the indigent, were based on his belief in the causal connection of poverty with low population growth. While Condorcet, the initiator of social choice theory, focused on reasoning and education (particularly of women),

Malthus never abandoned his insistence that only draconian compulsion can help to stem the tide of high population growth. That debate continues in our time.

CHINA'S ONE-CHILD POLICY: A CASE HISTORY

The Chinese government has recently – in fact only in 2015 – relaxed the rigour of the severe compulsion institutionalized in its famous one-child policy, which has had many admirers across the world among intellectuals worried about high population growth. This is a good moment to examine what the one-child policy has done – or not done.[6] We have to question the potted history that China was stuck in the adversity of a high fertility rate until the one-child policy changed it all.

The one-child policy was introduced in 1978. However, China's fertility rate was already falling rapidly *before* the policy was introduced. In the ten years *preceding* the new policy, the fertility rate had already fallen from 5.87 in 1968 to 2.98 in 1978 (a gigantic drop in a decade). The fertility rate continued to fall even *after* the new compulsive policy came into force, but there was no dramatic jump, only a smooth continuation of the falling trend that preceded the restriction. Falling from 2.98 in 1978, the rate now is around 1.67, but the big decline (from 5.87) had occurred before the compulsion-based route was even introduced.

Clearly, something more than the one-child policy has been restraining population growth in China. Comparative statistics of different countries, as well as empirical analysis of data from hundreds of districts within India, bring out sharply that the two most potent factors leading to fertility reduction are: (1) women's schooling, and (2) women's remunerated employment.[iii] There is no mystery in this. The lives that are most battered by over-frequent bearing and

---

[6] On this, see my essay 'Women's Progress Outdid China's One-Child Policy', *New York Times*, 2 November 2015 (Sen (2015)).

rearing of children are those of young mothers, and both more schooling and more gainful employment give young women much more voice in family decisions, which tends to work in the direction of cutting down the frequency of births (on this see Drèze and Sen (2002) and the empirical literature cited there). Rapid expansion in China of school education, including female education, and the enhancement of job opportunities for young women occurred throughout the entire period, beginning well before the introduction of the one-child policy and continuing robustly after that. Fertility rate declines in China have been close to what we would expect on the basis of these social and economic influences.

China often gets too much credit from commentators on the alleged effectiveness of its harsher interventions, and far too little for the positive role of its supportive policies (including its massive focus on education and health care, from which many other countries can learn). While there are harrowing reports of hardship created in the lives of many people in China by the enforcement of the one-child policy, it is far from clear that this policy had a large impact on the fertility rate of the total population as a whole. The recent lifting of the removal of one-child policy may, in fact, have been an easy choice. There is little need for the harshness of this coercive policy, given the increasing role of reasoning about family decisions, and particularly the growing empowerment of Chinese women.

THE ROLE OF REASONING

The Condorcet–Malthus arguments are worth recollecting for an understanding of the importance of human reasoning that the original founder of social choice theory – Condorcet – strongly emphasized, which influenced the way he saw the demands of social choice based on people's reasoned valuations, in dialogue with each other. That belief in the reach of human reasoning unites the classical origins of social choice theory in the eighteenth century with the work in modern social choice theory initiated by Kenneth Arrow (1951a). Even when we depart from Arrow's own framework, as has occurred in this book in both the old (1970) and the new chapters, the connection with the role of human reasoning, including public reasoning, remains strong. It is an essential part of what we have been calling the social choice approach.

Along with that we have to see the relevance of Condorcet's focus on public reasoning, anticipating John Stuart Mill's championing of government by discussion. Reasoning in social contexts is much enriched by public discussion and interchange of ideas, concerns and beliefs, on which another Enlightenment theorist, Adam Smith, had much to say (Smith (1759), (1776)). The connections between individual values, public reasoning and open discussion with others cannot but be central to the art of social choice, broadly understood – an issue that has received illuminating exposition not only from Condorcet, Smith and Arrow, but also from the contemporary school of 'public choice', led by James Buchanan (1954a), (1954b), (1986).

Indeed, Frank Knight, the great economist who had a big role in inspiring the public choice theorists, commented on that necessary connection with much clarity: 'Values are established or validated or recognized through *discussion*, which is at once social, intellectual, and creative'.[iv] If the formal theorems and mathematical results of social choice theory have carved a space for the discipline in the systematic pursuit of public reasoning across the world, the analytical contributions of social choice theory cannot be dissociated from the reliance on reason on which human progress has depended over the centuries.

A CONCLUDING REMARK

Social choice theory has developed historically as a discipline of reasoned choice for a well-defined group (like the French Academy of Sciences, of particular interest to Condorcet and Borda in establishing the formal theory of voting and group decisions), or for a nation (the main focus of Arrow's attention). The arguments examined and developed in much of this book can also be immediately interpreted and used in the context of group decisions in general. That is important to recognize. However, no less importantly, some of the ideas presented in this work, including the legitimacy of incomplete rankings, the use of maximal (as opposed to optimal) choice, the recognition of rights (including human rights), the admission of interpersonal comparisons of well-being (including partial comparability), the importance of human freedom and capabilities, and the critical role of public reasoning and of fact-checking suggest the possibility and fruitfulness of applying the social choice framework to global problems as well.

In his powerfully reasoned book, *The Court and the World*, US Supreme Court Justice Stephen Breyer (2015) has argued for the need to take note of new global realities in the interpretation and enforcement of American law. The US Supreme Court has to deal increasingly with foreign activities, and there are new challenges arising from an increasingly interdependent world. Breyer argues for taking note of 'many voices', including 'representatives of foreign governments, who can explain relevant policies; foreign lawyers, who can describe relevant foreign laws and practices; and ordinary citizens, whom our decisions may well affect though they live and work abroad' (p. 7).

The implications of this conclusion can be supplemented by invoking another argument that pushes us in the same direction, in particular Adam Smith's advocacy of bringing in perspectives from a 'certain distance' in making reasoned social choice in any country in the world. As was discussed earlier, one of Smith's illustrations of parochial values that needed confrontation with views from elsewhere refers to the tendency of all political commentators in ancient Greece, including sophisticated Athenians (no less), to regard infanticide as perfectly acceptable social behaviour. Smith pointed out that even Plato and Aristotle did not depart from expressing approval of this 'barbaric' practice commonly accepted in the local culture. Smith's invoking of the idea of an Impartial Spectator – a collectivity of imagined observers who provide reasons that people may tend to overlook – served many purposes, including the challenge it offered to people being captivated by the mesmerizing effects of what Smith called 'self-love'. But, among other uses, it could serve, Smith argued, as a device to avoid being captured by the limitations of parochialism in locally confined reasoning.

For ethical claims to have normative viability, they have to be examined not just from close quarters, but also from a 'certain distance'. Smith made particular use of his thought-experiment of 'the Impartial Spectator' as a device for reasoned self-scrutiny, of which, he thought, reasoning human beings are perfectly capable. As Smith put it:

> We can never survey our own sentiments and motives, we can never form any judgment concerning them, unless we remove ourselves, as it were, from our own natural station, and endeavour to view them as at a certain distance from us. But we can do this in no other way than by endeavouring to view them with the eyes of other people, or as other people are likely to view them.[v]

Distant perspectives have clear relevance for the global diagnosis of nasty practices, such as the barbarities inflicted on women under the Taliban rule, and the massive use of capital punishment in some countries in the world, from China to the United States. There is a strong case for checking whether some practice appears acceptable only in local and parochial assessments. This led to Smith's insistence that 'the eyes of the rest of mankind' must be invoked to understand whether 'a punishment appears equitable'.[vi]

If this argument is correct, then the deliberations of the courts, including the US Supreme Court, have to take note of foreign arguments and foreign practices not only because of the new reality of interdependence, but also because of the old reality of possible parochialism of locally confined reasoning. Even though the case for taking note of what happens elsewhere and what is argued abroad may be much stronger today (as Justice Breyer has highlighted), there might never have been a time when the national shutters could be sensibly kept closed.

This departure makes reasoning on 'global justice' possible and momentous, and this is essential for addressing such international problems of social choice as world economic crises, or global warming, or the elimination of famines and persistent endemic undernourishment, or the prevention and management of global pandemics (such as the AIDS, or Ebola, or Zika epidemics). Our agreements may be only partial, even after as much public reasoning as we can have. This may, in fact, be so not only across the boundaries of states, but also within each country itself, since within each nation there tends to be a diversity of views (as any reader of serious newspapers can see), rather than disagreements being confined to clashes of what can be called national perspectives. Also, the ways and means of the implementation of the reasoned agreements can also involve considerable plurality of approaches (such as alternative strategies to address global warming, discussed earlier). Mary Wollstonecraft made a pioneering contribution on how the rights of women – and of men – can be pursued not just through the laws of a nation state, but also by many extra-legal means, including active public discussion and the exchange of news as well as views within *and* across the boundaries of a state (Wollstonecraft (1790), (1792)).[7]

While pursuing a different approach to justice from well-established theories that build on the idea of a national consensus (in what Rawls (1971) has called 'the original position'), we have to be reconciled to the likelihood that the extent of incompleteness would be inescapably larger than in an imagined world of total agreement and of perfectly compliant behaviour. This should not be seen as a fault, since – as I have discussed earlier – both tentative incompleteness and assertive incompleteness are very much part of the domain of reasoned choice. And if it is important to note that not all issues of decisional justice can be fully resolved by agreed reasoning on values, it is also crucial to recognize that a great many of these issues can be enormously helped by vigorous public discussion leading to an agreed partial ordering. That is the form that a reasoned approach to resolution may take – both within a nation and in our global existence.

Some of the most urgent problems in the world do not ask for the emergence of an agreed complete ordering – either of institutions, or of states of affairs. Nor need we wait for a world government to try to reduce global injustice, or enhance human security, or overcome miserable levels of well-being and freedom across the world. There is much to be done well before any grand institutional breakthrough

---

[7] On this see my note 'Mary, Mary, Quite Contrary' (Sen (2005b)).

emerges. The reach of social choice theory goes well beyond the hope of wonderful global governance – and even of perfect national administrations (nice as they are as ambitions and inspirations). Social choice reasoning addresses people in their diverse roles in the world, as dreamers as well as critics, and ultimately as agents of scrutiny and of change.

Notes

NEW PREFACE

i. Different aspects of these literatures have been surveyed by a number of distinguished social choice theorists in the *Handbook of Social Choice and Welfare*, edited by Arrow and Suzumura, along with me, vols. I and II (Arrow, Sen and Suzumura, eds., (2002), (2011)).

ii. Issues of great intellectual interest as well as practical relevance in voting theory have been raised in a number of distinguished contributions, including Caplin and Nalebuff (1988), (1991), Maskin (1995), Aleskerov (1997), (2002), Gaertner (2002), Brams and Fishburn (2002), Maskin and Sjöström (2002), Pattanaik (2002), Schofield (2002) and Dasgupta and Maskin (2008a), (2008b), among other contributions.

INTRODUCTION

i. 'Arthashastra', the Sanskrit word (the title of Kautilya's book), is best translated literally as 'Economics',' even though he devoted much space to political conflicts and the demands of statecraft. English translations of Aristotle's *Politics* and Kautilya's *Arthashastra* can be found respectively in E. Barker (1958) and L. N. Rangarajan (1987). Some interesting medieval European writings on voting issues are discussed in Ian McLean (1990).

ii. See Condorcet (1785). There are many commentaries on these analyses, including Arrow (1951a), Duncan Black (1958), William V. Gehrlein (1983), H. Peyton Young (1988) and McLean (1990). On the potential ubiquity of inconsistency in majority voting, see Richard D. McKelvey (1979) and Norman J. Schofield (1983).

iii. For a discussion of Condorcet's treatment of this case and others related to voting problems, see Emma Rothschild (2005).

iv. By varying the axiomatic structure, related impossibility results can also be obtained. Examples can be found in Arrow (1950), (1951a), (1952), (1963), Julian H. Blau (1957), (1972), (1979), Bengt Hansson (1969a,) (1969b), (1976), Tapas Majumdar (1969a), (1973), Sen (1969), (1970a), (1986b), (1993a), (1995a), Pattanaik (1971), (1973), (1978), Andreu Mas-Colell and Hugo Sonnenschein (1972), Thomas Schwartz (1972), (1986), Peter C. Fishburn (1973), (1974), Allan F. Gibbard (1973), Donald J. Brown (1974), (1975a), (1975b), Ken Binmore (1975), (1994), Maurice Salles (1975), Mark A. Satterthwaite (1975), Robert Wilson (1975), Rajat Deb (1976), (1977), Suzumura (1976a), (1976b), (1983), Blau and Deb (1977), Jerry S. Kelly (1978), (1987), Douglas H. Blair and Robert A. Pollak (1979), (1982), Jean-Jacques Laffont (1979), Bhaskar Dutta (1980), Graciela Chichilnisky (1982a), (1982b), David M. Grether and Charles R. Plott (1982), Chichilnisky and Geoffrey Heal (1983), Hervé Moulin (1983), Pattanaik and Salles (1983), David Kelsey (1984a), (1984b), Bezalel Peleg (1984), Hammond (1985), (1997a), Mark A. Aizerman and Fuad T. Aleskerov (1986), Campbell (1989a), (1995), Schofield (1996), Le Breton (1997), Le Breton and Weymark (1996), (2011), Aleskerov (1997), (2002) and Campbell and Kelly (1997a), (2002), among many other contributions.

v. See Chapters A1, A1*, A2 and A2*. The earlier (1970) edition has somewhat longer proofs (see Chapter 3*) closely following Arrow's (1950, 1952) own proof.

vi. Originally written in French for a talk at François Perroux's l'Institut des sciences économiques appliquées in Paris, and published as Arrow (1952). An English version was published later as 'The Principle of Rationality in Collective Decisions', Collected Papers of Kenneth J. Arrow, volume 1, chapter 3 (Arrow 1983), p. 51.

vii. See Hansson (1968), (1969a), (1969b), (1976), Sen (1969), (1970a), (1977a), (1993a), Schwartz (1970), (1972), (1986), Pattanaik (1971), (1973), Alan P. Kirman and Dieter Sondermann (1972), Mas-Colell and Sonnenschein (1972), Wilson (1972), (1975), Fishburn (1973), (1974), Plott (1973), (1976), Brown (1974), (1975), John A. Ferejohn and Grether (1974), Binmore (1975), (1994), Salles (1975), Blair et al. (1976), Georges A. Bordes (1976), (1979), Donald E. Campbell (1976), Deb (1976), (1977), Parks (1976a), (1976b), Suzumura (1976a), (1976b), (1983), Blau and Deb (1977), Kelly (1978), Peleg

(1978a), (1984), Blair and Pollak (1979), (1982), Blau (1979), Bernard Monjardet (1979), (1983), Salvador Barberà (1980), (1983), Chichilnisky (1982a), (1982b), Chichilnisky and Heal (1983), Moulin (1983), Kelsey (1984a), (1984b), (1985), Vincenzo Denicolò (1985), Yasumi Matsumoto (1985), Aizerman and Aleskerov (1986), Taradas Bandyopadhyay (1986), Isaac Levi (1986), and Campbell and Kelly (1997), among many other contributions.

viii. On the unequal consequences of this unifocal priority, see Sen (1970a), (1973a), John Rawls (1971), Peter J. Hammond (1976), (1977), Claude d'Aspremont and Louis Gevers (1977), and Blackorby, Donaldson and Weymark (1984).

ix. Since the presentation here is informal and permits some technical ambiguities, those concerned with exactness are referred to the formal statements in Chapter 3 and 3* in this book. See also Arrow (1951), (1963a), or Fishburn (1973), or Kelly (1978). See also Sen (1979b), (1986a), Blau (1972), Robert Wilson (1975), Barberà (1980), (1983), Binmore (1994) and John Geanakopolous (1996), among many other variants of the Arrow theorem.

x. For engaging accounts of the literature, see also Kelly (1978), Feldman (1980), Pattanaik and Salles (1983), Suzumura (1983), Hammond (1985), Walter P. Heller et al. (1986), Sen (1986a), (1986b), Mueller (1989), and Arrow et al. (1997), among other contributions.

xi. Baumol (1965), p. 2.

xii. There is an extensive literature on manipulation and on the challenges of implementation, on which see also Pattanaik (1973), (1978), Steven J. Brams (1975), Ted Groves and John Ledyard (1977), Barberà and Sonnenschein (1978), Dutta and Pattanaik (1978), Peleg (1978a), (1984), Schmeidler and Sonnenschein (1978), Dasgupta et al. (1979), Green and Laffont (1979), Laffont (1979), Dutta (1980), (1997), Pattanaik and Sengupta (1980), Sengupta (1980a), (1980b), Laffont and Maskin (1982), Moulin (1983), (1995), Leo Hurwicz et al. (1985), Maskin (1985), Maskin and Sjöström (2002) and Barberà (2011), among other contributions. There is also a nonstrategic impossibility in establishing an exact one-to-one correspondence between: (1) preferring, (2) not dispreferring, and (3) being indifferent, on the one hand, and (1*) voting for, (2*) voting against, and (3*) abstaining, on the other hand, no matter whether voting is costly, or enjoyable, or neither (see Sen 1964).

xiii. See Chapters A1 and A1*.

xiv. On this see Sen (1970c), (1977c), (1986a). See also Patrick Suppes (1966), Hammond (1976), (1977), (1985), Stephen Strasnick (1976), Arrow (1977), d'Aspremont and Gevers (1977), Maskin (1978), (1979), Gevers (1979), Kevin W. S. Roberts (1980a), (1980b), Suzumura (1983), (1997), Blackorby et al. (1984), d'Aspremont (1985) and d'Aspremont and Philippe Mongin (1998), among other contributions.

xv. On this, see Sen (1970a), (1970c), (1977c), Blackorby (1975), Ben J. Fine (1975), Kaushik Basu (1980), T. Bezembinder and P. van Acker (1980), and Levi (1986). The study of inexactness can also be extended to 'fuzzy' characterizations, on which see Salles (1986), (1990), (1992), (1998), M. Dasgupta and Deb (1991), (1996), (1999), (2001), Basu, Deb and Pattanaik (1992) and Barrett and Salles (2011), among others.

xvi. See Sen (1970a), (1977c), Rawls (1971), Edmund S. Phelps (1974), Hammond (1976), Strasnick (1976), Arrow (1977), d'Aspremont and Gevers (1977), Maskin (1978), (1979), Gevers (1979), Roberts (1980a), (1980b), Suzumura (1983), (1997), Blackorby et al. (1984) and d'Aspremont (1985), among other contributions.

xvii. The limitations of this type of distributional indifference for the assessment of equity are discussed in Sen (1973a) and Foster and Sen (1997).

xviii. On this and related issues, see Sen (1970a), (1977c), Hammond (1976), d'Aspremont and Gevers (1977), Robert Deschamps and Gevers (1978), Maskin (1978), (1979), Gevers (1979), Roberts (1980a), Basu (1980), Siddiqur R. Osmani (1982), Blackorby et al. (1984), d'Aspremont (1985), T. Coulhon and Mongin (1989), Nick Baigent (1994) and d'Aspremont and Mongin (1998), among many other contributions. See also Harsanyi (1955) and Suppes (1966) for pioneering analyses of the uses of interpersonal comparisons. Jon Elster and John Roemer (1991) have provided fine critical accounts of the vast literature on this subject.

xix. In my own work in welfare economics, I have drawn extensively on the broadened informational framework of recent social choice theory to explore the evaluation and measurement of *inequality* (Sen (1973a), (1992a), (1997b)), *poverty* (Sen (1976b), (1983b), (1985a), (1992a)), *distribution-adjusted national income* (Sen (1973b), (1976a), (1979a)) and *environmental evaluation* (Sen (1995a)). I should note here that the work I have tried to do on economic inequality (beginning with Sen (1973a)) has been particularly influenced by the pioneering contributions of Atkinson (1970), (1983), (1989). The literature on this subject has grown very fast in recent years; for a critical scrutiny as well as references to the contemporary literature, see Foster and Sen (1997).

xx. For contrasting perspectives on interpersonal comparisons of well-being, see Ian Little (1957), Sen (1970a), (1985b), Tibor Scitovsky (1976), Donald Davidson (1986), Gibbard (1986) and Elster and Roemer (1991); see also empirical studies of observed misery (for example, Drèze and Sen (1989), (1990), (1995), (1997), (2013); Erik Schokkaert and Luc Van Ootegem (1990); Robert M. Solow (1995)).

xxi. See Daniel Kahneman (1999), (2000); also Kahneman and Krueger (2006), Alan Krueger (2009) and Krueger and Arthur Stone (2014). For a proposal for using 'factual' utility comparisons for evaluation and policy making, see also Layard (2011a), (2011b).

xxii. An early contribution to a commodity-centred approach can be found in Franklin Fisher (1956); see also Fisher (1987).

xxiii. See Jorgenson, Lau and Stoker (1980), Jorgenson (1990) and Jorgenson, Landefeld and Schreyer (2014). The welfare relevance of real income comparisons can be dissociated from their mental-state correlates; see Sen (1979a). See also the related literature on 'fairness', seen in terms of non-envy; for example, Duncan Foley (1967), Serge-Christophe Kolm (1969), Elisha A. Pazner and David Schmeidler (1974), Hal R. Varian (1974), (1975), Lars-Gunnar Svensson (1977), (1980), Ronald Dworkin (1981a), (1981b), Suzumura (1983), Young (1985), Le Breton and Trannoy (1987), Campbell (1992), Moulin and William Thomson (1997), Marc Fleurbaey (2008), Fleurbaey and Maniquet (2011a), (2011b), (2012) and Fleurbaey and Blanchet (2013).

xxiv. See Sen (1980), (1985a), (1985b), (1992a), Martha Nussbaum (1988), (1992), (2011), Drèze and Sen (1989), (1995) and Nussbaum and Sen (1993). See also Roemer (1982), (1996), Basu (1987), Richard J. Arneson (1989), Atkinson (1989), (1995), G. A. Cohen (1989), (1990a), F. Bourguignon and G. Fields (1990), Keith Griffin and John Knight (1990), David Crocker (1992), Sudhir Anand and Martin Ravallion (1993), Meghnad Desai (1994), Arrow (1995) and Pattanaik (1997a), among other contributions. There have also been a number of important symposia on the capability perspective, beginning with *Giornale degli Economisti e Annali di Economia* (1994) and *Notizie di Politeia* (1996), Special Volume), including contributions by Alessandro Balestrino (1994), (1996), Giovanni Andrea Cornia (1994), Elena Granaglia (1994), (1996), Enrica Chiappero Martinetti (1994), (1996), Sebastiano Bavetta (1996), Ian Carter (1996), Leonardo Casini and Iacopo Bernetti (1996) and Shahrashoub Razavi (1996); see also Sen (1994), (1996a) with my responses to these contributions. Over the last couple of decades the literature on capability has expanded with such staggering speed that I have to forgo any attempt to bring the reading list anywhere near being up to date.

xxv. The approach of basic needs has been particularly explored by Paul Streeten (1984) and Frances Stewart (1985). See also Irma Adelman (1975), Dharam Ghai et al. (1977), James P. Grant (1978), Morris D. Morris (1979), Chichilnisky (1980), Nanak Kakwani (1981), (1984), Robert Goodin (1988) and Alan Hamlin and Phillip Pettit (1989), among other contributions. The origin of the approach of focusing on the fulfillment of 'minimum needs' can be traced to Pigou (1920).

xxvi. See Sen (1980), (1983b), (1985a), (1992a), (1993b), (1999), Kakwani (1984), Nussbaum (1988), Drèze and Sen (1989), (1995), Griffin and Knight (1990), Schokkaert and Van Ootegem (1990), Nussbaum and Sen (1993), Anand and Sen (1997) and Foster and Sen (1997), among other contributions.

xxvii. On these issues, see also Deaton and Muellbauer (1980b), (1986), Jorgenson (1990), Pollak (1991), Deaton (1995) and Slesnick (1998), among other contributions.

xxviii. See also Mohiuddin Alamgir (1980), Ravallion (1987), Drèze and Sen (1989), (1990), Jeffrey L. Coles (1995), Desai (1995), Osmani (1995), Peter Svedberg (1999) and Gráda (2009), on related matters.

xxix. As empirical studies of famines bring out, some actual famines have occurred with little or no decline in food production (such as the Bengal famine of 1943, the Ethiopian famine of 1973, or the Bangladesh famine of 1974), whereas others have been influenced substantially by declines in food production (on this see Sen 1981).

xxx. On these issues, see Bardhan (1974), Chen, Huq and D'Souza (1981), Sen (1983b), (1984), (1990a), (1990b), (2013), Jocelyn

Kynch and Sen (1983), Sen and Sunil Sengupta (1983), Megan Vaughan (1987), Drèze and Sen (1989), Barbara Harriss (1990), Nussbaum and Sen (1993), Bina Agarwal (1994), (2009), Nancy Folbre (1995), Kanbur (1995), Nussbaum and Jonathan Glover (1995) and Agarwal, Humphries and Robeyns (2004), among other contributions.

xxxi. The so-called 'Sen measure of poverty' can, in fact, be improved by an important but simple variation illuminatingly proposed by Anthony F. Shorrocks (1995). I have to confess favouring the 'Sen–Shorrocks measure' over the original 'Sen index'.

xxxii. For discussions of some of the major issues in the choice of an aggregative measure of poverty, see Anand (1977), (1983), Blackorby and Donaldson (1978), (1980), Foster (1984), (1985), (2011), Foster et al. (1984), Kanbur (1984), Atkinson (1987), (1989), Christian Seidl (1988), Foster and Shorrocks (1988), Satya R. Chakravarty (1990), Camilo Dagum and Michele Zenga (1990), Ravallion (1994), Frank A. Cowell (1995) and Shorrocks (1995), among many others (there is an extensive bibliography of this large literature in Foster and Sen (1997)). One of the important issues to be addressed is the need for – and limitations of –'decomposability' (and the weaker requirement of 'subgroup consistency', on which see also Shorrocks (1984)). Foster (1984) gives arguments in favour of decomposability (as did Anand (1977), (1983)), whereas Sen (1973a), (1977c) presents arguments against it. There is a serious attempt in Foster and Sen (1997) to assess both the pros and the cons of decomposability and subgroup consistency.

xxxiii. See Jocelyn Kynch and Sen (1983), Sen (1984), (1990), (2013), Bina Agarwal (1994), (2006), (2010), Nussbaum (1992), (2001), Ingrid Robeyns (2003), (2005), (2016), among others.

xxxiv. The literature on 'missing women' (missing in comparison with the expected number of women in the absence of the anti-female discrimination) is one example of such empirical analysis; on this see Sen (1984), (1990b), (1992c), (2003), (2013), Vaughan (1987), Drèze and Sen (1989), (1990), Ansley J. Coale (1991), Stephan Klasen (1994), (2009), Klasen and Wink (2002) and Klasen and Vollmer (2014). See also Kynch and Sen (1983), Harriss (1990), Ravi Kanbur and Lawrence Haddad (1990), Agarwal (1994), Folbre (1995) and Nussbaum and Glover (1995), among other works. Until recently the main cause of 'missing women' used to be the neglect of women – and of young girls in particular – in health care and diet, resulting in unnaturally higher female mortality rates (infanticide, despite its sporadic and horrific existence in some societies, has not been a demographically noticeable factor). In recent years, even as the relative neglect of girls (and women in general) has come down substantially, a new manifestation of anti-female bias has emerged in the form of sex-specific abortion of female foetuses (using the new technology of sex determination in the womb). One of the remarkable features of this new gender bias is that many families, for example in China or South Asia, that seem to treat girls and boys similarly still show strong 'boy preference' in aborting female foetuses (see Sen 2003, 2013).

xxxv. Different manifestations of gender bias have been analysed by Sen (1984), (1990a), Agarwal (1994), (2009), Strassman (1994), Benhabib et al. (1995), Folbre (1995), Anand and Sen (1996), Cornell (1998), (2002), Osmani and Sen (2003) and Klasen and Schüler (2011), among others.

xxxvi. See also Ken-Ichi Inada (1969), (1970), who has been a major contributor to this literature. See also William S. Vickrey (1960), Benjamin Ward (1965), Sen (1966a), (1969), Sen and Pattanaik (1969) and Pattanaik (1971). Other types of restrictions have also been considered to yield consistent majority decisions; see Michael B. Nicholson (1965), Plott (1967), Gordon Tullock (1967), Inada (1970), Pattanaik (1971), Otto A. Davis et al. (1972), Fishburn (1973), Kelly (1974a), (1974b), (1978), Pattanaik and Sengupta (1974), Eric S. Maskin (1976a), (1976b), (1995), Jean-Michel Grandmont (1978), Peleg (1978a), (1984), Wulf Gaertner (1979), Dutta (1980), Chichilnisky and Heal (1983) and Suzumura (1983), among other contributions. Domain restrictions for a wider class of voting rules have been investigated by Pattanaik (1970), Maskin (1976a), (1976b), (1995) and Ehud Kalai and E. Muller (1977). The literature has been helpfully surveyed by Gaertner (1998), (2002).

xxxvii. On different aspects of this general political issue, see Arrow (1951a), Buchanan (1954a), (1954b), Buchanan and Tullock (1962), Sen (1970a), (1973c), (1974), (1977d), (1984), Suzumura (1983), Hammond (1985), Pattanaik and Salles (1985), Andrew Caplin and Barry Nalebuff (1988), (1991), Young (1988) and Guinier (1991), among other writings, and also the 'Symposium' on voting procedures in the *Journal of Economic Perspectives*

(Winter 1995), with contributions by Jonathan Levin and Nale-buff (1995), Douglas W. Rae (1995), Nicolaus Tideman (1995) and Robert J. Weber (1995), as well as Michel Le Breton and John Weymark (1996) and Suzumura (1999), among others.

xxxviii. See Seidl (1975), (1997), Suzumura (1976b), (1983), (1999), Breyer (1977), Barnes (1980), Breyer and Gardner (1980), Gaert-ner and Lorenz Krüger (1981), (1983), Hammond (1982a), (1997a), Basu (1984), Kanger (1985), John L. Wriglesworth (1985), Rowley (1986), (1993), Levi (1986), Riley (1987), Muel-ler (1989), (1996), Deb (1994), Gaertner et al. (1992) and Pattanaik (1996), among other contributions. See also the sym-posium on the 'Liberal Paradox' in *Analyse & Kritik* (September 1996), including Binmore (1996), Breyer (1996), Buchanan (1996), Fleurbaey and Gaertner (1996), Anthony de Jasay and Hartmut Kliemt (1996), Kliemt (1996), Mueller (1996), Suzu-mura (1996) and van Hees (1996). Further, see the respective assessments of the issues involved by Hammond (1997), Pattan-aik (1997a) and Suzumura (1999).

xxxix. See particularly Peter Gärdenfors (1981), Robert Sugden (1981), (1985), (1993), Hillel Steiner (1990), Gaertner et al. (1992), Deb (1994) and Marc Fleurbaey and Gaertner (1996). See also Basu (1984), Pattanaik (1996), (1997), Suzumura (1996), (1999) and Hammond (1997a).

xl. A set of studies on this and related issues has been presented in a collection of essays edited by Jane Mansbridge (1990).

xli. Tocqueville (1840), book II, chapter VIII; in the 1945 edition, p. 122.

CHAPTER A1

i. Kenneth J. Arrow, 'The Origins of the Impossibility Theorem', in Maskin and Sen (2014), pp. 147–8.

ii. Arrow (1950); reprinted in his *Collected Papers*, vol. I, Arrow (1983), pp. 3–4.

iii. Buchanan (1954a), p. 116.

iv. Sugden (1993), p. 1948.

v. Buchanan (1960), pp. 88–9.

CHAPTER A1*

i. Properties of decisiveness with specified variations have received attention also from Fishburn (1970b), Hansson (1972), (1976), Brown (1974), Schmitz (1977) and Armstrong (1980), among others.

ii. On 'Suzumura consistency' see Bossert (2008), Bossert and Suzumura (2010) and Suzumura (2016).

iii. Gibbard's distinguished term paper (1969) remained unpublished for many decades, though his result was cited and discussed in Sen 1970a – the old edition of this book – see Chapters 4 and 4*. Happily, it has now been published (Gibbard (2014)), with editorial comments by John Weymark (Weymark (2014)). See also Schwartz (1972) and Deb (1977).

iv. Gibbard's theorem was extended in varying forms in important contributions by Schwartz (1972), Mas-Colell and Sonnenschein (1972), Guha (1972), Blair et al. (1976), Blau and Deb (1977), Blair and Pollak (1982), Kelsey (1983), (1984a), (1984b), Suzumura (1983), (2016) and Matsumoto (1985), among others.

v. See also Schwartz (1974), (1976), (1986). The cycle involved in the proof is that of the $(n-1)$-majority rule.

vi. On related matters, see Dummett and Farquharsen (1961), Murakami (1968), Craven (1971), Pattanaik (1971), Fishburn (1973), Ferejohn and Grether (1974), Deb (1976), Blau and Brown (1978), Nakamura (1978), Peleg (1978a), (1979) and Suzumura (1983).

vii. For discussions of the properties of semi-orders, see Luce (1956), Scott and Suppes (1958), Fishburn (1970a), (1975), Chipman et al. (1971), Jamison and Lau (1973), (1977), Sjoberg (1975) and Schwartz (1976).

viii. See Blau (1959), (1979), Schwartz (1974), Brown (1975b), Wilson (1975) and Blair and Pollak (1979).

ix. These relations can be seen as features of simple games; see von Neumann and Morgenstern (1947), Guilbaud (1952), Monjardet (1967), (1979), (1983), Bloomfield (1971), (1976), Wilson (1971), (1972), Nakamura (1975), (1978), (1979), Salles (1976) and Peleg (1978a), (1983), (1984).

x. Brown (1973), (1974), (1975a), Hansson (1972), (1976), Ferejohn (1977) and Blair and Pollak (1979) have made pioneering contributions to this area. Many other topological issues of interest in social choice theory have been illuminatingly pursued by Chichilnisky (1982a), (1982b), Chichilnisky and Heal (1983), Monjardet (1983) and others. See also Nicholas Baigent's (2011) helpful survey of the literature, and Priya Menon's (2016) comments on this topological pursuit.

CHAPTER A2

i. Hicks (1956), p. 6.
ii. Little (1949a), p. 90.

CHAPTER A2*

i. These issues and the related formal results (dealing with 'weak closure maximality' and 'strong closure maximality', and many other formal properties and their consequences) are critically surveyed in my chapter on social choice theory in the *Handbook of Mathematical Economics* (Sen (1986b)).

ii. See Schwartz (1970), (1972), Bloomfield (1971), Campbell (1972), (1976), (1980), Bordes (1976) and Deb (1977). It can be seen that the Schwartz rule amounts to the uniform use of strong closure maximality for all social choices. In contrast, Bloomfield (1971), Campbell (1972), (1976) and Bordes (1976) use weak closure maximality for social choice. Deb (1977) has helpfully analysed the relations between these two closure methods.

iii. See Fishburn (1973).

iv. Internal consistency conditions of choice have been used and analysed by Samuelson (1938), Houthakker (1950), Chernoff (1954), Arrow (1959), Hansson (1968), Sen (1971), Herzberger (1973), Suzumura (1976a), (1976b), (1983), (2016), Deb (1977), Aizerman (1985), Aizerman and Aleskerov (1986), Moulin and Thomson (1997) and many others.

v. In fact, the theorem can be slightly strengthened (as discussed in Sen 1986b) by weakening condition α to a somewhat less demanding condition, weak α, which requires only that a state x chosen from any set S and belonging to a subset T of S must be chosen from T if it is not rejected in the choice over any other subset of S, that is: $[x \in T \subseteq S$ & for all $Y \subseteq S$ such that $Y \neq T: x \in C(Y)] \Rightarrow x \in C(T)$. There is another more obvious weakening that is fine for retaining the result, in particular a weakening of the Independence condition of Arrow I^A into something that applies only to choices over pairs. These are fairly obvious extensions and not worth elaborate discussion here.

vi. On this see also Wulf Gaertner and Yongsheng Xu (1997), (1999).

vii. Buchanan went on to argue: 'Rationality or irrationality as an attribute of the social group implies the imputation to that group of an organic existence apart from that of its individual components' (1954, p. 116). See also Kemp (1953–4), Bergson (1954), Buchanan (1954b), Graaff (1957), Little (1957), Buchanan and Tullock (1962), Baumol (1965) and Elster and Hylland (1986), on related issues.

CHAPTER A3

i. James Meade (1976) has powerfully argued that we have excellent reasons to resist the summation formula of utilitarian theory (because of its neglect of distributional considerations), even though we may have good reasons to confine our attention to utilities only (thereby endorsing the basal space of utilitarianism while rejecting its aggregation formulation of sum-ranking). See also Kolm (1969), (1972), Atkinson (1970), (1983), Sen (1973a), (1992a), Hammond (1976), (1977), Foster (1985), Temkin (1986), (1993), Le Grand (1991), Tungodden (2003), (2009) and Cowell (2011), among other contributions.

ii. The literature on political philosophy includes several other ways of using the distinction between 'positive' and 'negative' freedoms, but I shall not go more into that issue in this work (I have had something to say on this question in Sen (2002a), (2009a).

iii. These issues have been discussed in Little (1957), Sen (1970a), (1973a), Davidson (1986) and Gibbard (1986), among others.

iv. Nozick (1973), pp. 60–61; and also Nozick (1974), pp. 165–6.

v. On related issues see also Buchanan (1954a), (1954b), Buchanan and Tullock (1962) and Sugden (1981), (1986).

vi. Rawls (1971), pp. 60–65, and Rawls (1988), pp. 256–7.

vii. Varian (1974), pp. 64–5.

viii. See Kolm (1969), (1972), Schmeidler and Yaari (1970), Schmeidler and Vind (1972), Pazner and Schmeidler (1972), (1974), (1978a), Feldman and Kirman (1974), Varian (1974), (1975), (1976a), (1976b), Daniel (1975), Gärdenfors (1975), Allingham (1977), Crawford (1977), (1979), Pazner (1977), Svensson (1977), (1980), Goldman and Sussangkam (1978), Archibald and Donaldson (1979), Crawford and Heller (1979), Feldman and Weiman (1979), Sobel (1979), Champsaur and Laroque (1981), Suzumura (1983)and Thomson (1995), (2011), among other – particularly more recent – works.

ix. See Svensson (1977) and Fleurbaey and Maniquet (2011a), (2011b).

x. John Roemer (1996) has provided a rich analysis of competing theories of justice with his evaluation of their respective merits and shortcomings, and has particularly explored the possibility of a structure more informed about the nature of human welfare and opportunities, and the role and limitations of the rewarding of talents (see also Roemer 1985). Richard Arneson (1989), (1990) and G. A. Cohen (1989), (1990a) have also enriched the theory of justice with another class of informational concerns. Their respective contributions can be examined and appreciated in terms of widening the informational basis of justice and the reasons they give for the direction in which they have chosen to proceed.

xi. See Smith (1776) – in the Penguin Classics edition, Smith (2009), pp. 351–2.

xii. The capability literature has expanded so rapidly that it is difficult to do anything like a proper bibliography on the subject. In getting some idea of the foundations of the approach, the following contributions, among others, can, however, be useful: Sen (1980), (1985a), (1985b), (2009a), Nussbaum (1988), (1992), (2006), (2011), Drèze and Sen (1989), (2013), Arneson (1989), Cohen (1989), Griffin and Knight (1990), Schokkaert and Van Ootegem (1990), Crocker (1992), (2008), Anand and Ravallion (1993), Sugden (1993), Atkinson (1995), Chiappero-Martinetti (1996), (2009), Gotoh (2001), Pogge (2001), Alkire (2002), (2005), Dutta (2002), Fleurbaey (2002), Chatterjee (2004), (2008), Ruger (2004), (2006), (2010), Kuklys (2005), Olsaretti (2005), Kaufman (2006), Heckman (2007), (2012), Qizilbash (2006), (2007),

(2009), Burchardt and Vizard (2009), Kakwani and Silber (2008), Crocker (2008), Bourguignon and Chakravarty (2009), Gotoh and Dumouchel (2009a), Schokkaert (2009), Robeyns (2009), (2016), Anderson (2010a), (2010b), Brighouse and Robeyns (2010), Schokkaert et al (2009), Alkire and Foster (2011a), (2011b), Basu and Lopez-Calva (2011), Venkatapuram (2011) and Suzumura (2016).

xiii. Examples of making social judgements in the assessment of distribution-sensitive real income evaluation and in the evaluation of income-based aggregate poverty with axioms of positional valuations can be found in Sen (1976b), (1976c).

xiv. On this subject see also Foster and Sen (1997), pp. 203–9.

xv. Samuelson (1947), p. 205.

CHAPTER A3[*]

i. See Kahneman (1999), (2000) and Krueger (2009), (2014).

ii. See Schokkaert (2009) and Basu and Lopez-Calva (2011).

iii. Measurement of social mobility has received intellectual attention reflecting quite divergent normative concerns; see, for example, Shorrocks (1978a), (1978b), Atkinson (1983), Chakravarty, Dutta and Weymark (1985), Fields and Ok (1996) and Mitra and Ok (1998), among others.

iv. For various interpretations of interpersonal comparisons, see Vickrey (1945), Little (1950), Harsanyi (1955), Arrow (1963), Suppes (1966), Sen (1970a), (1973a), (1979a), Jeffrey (1971), Rawls (1971), Waldner (1972), Hammond (1977), Borglin (1982) and Kahneman and Krueger (2006), among others.

v. See also Alkire et al. (2015) and Maasoumi and Racine (2016), among other contributions to the rich literature on multidimensional aggregation in the context of the measurement of inequality and poverty.

vi. See also Hammond (1976), (1977), Maskin (1978), (1979), Arrow (1977), d'Aspremont and Gevers (1977), (2002), Deschamps and Gevers (1978), Blackorby and Donaldson (1977), (1978), (1980), Blackorby, Donaldson and Weymark (1980), (1984), Roberts (1980a), (1980b), d'Aspremont (1985), d'Aspremont and Mongin (1997) and others.

vii. This is a somewhat wider class of $\bar{L}$ than under cardinal full comparability, thereby inducing a more demanding invariance restriction than under the latter, and represents less usable information than with cardinal full comparability. The difference will depend on X and the actual utility configurations. Gevers' (1979) case of almost co-cardinal (ACC*) corresponds to CULC except for requiring that the common monotonic $\phi(\cdot)$ function should apply not necessarily to the whole of X but to each pair of utility vectors separately. ACC* is in this sense still more demanding than CULC, requiring invariance over a wider class, and thus represents *less* informational availability.

viii. If, however, the independence condition is not imposed, then various possibilities exist, notably the Nash bargaining solution (see Chapter 8* of the 1970 edition). On Nash social welfare functions, see Nash (1950), Luce and Raiffa (1957), Sen (1970a), Kalai and Smordinsky (1975), Harsanyi (1977), Kaneko and Nakamura (1979), Kaneko (1980), Kim and Roush (1980), Coughlin and Nitzan (1981) and Binmore (1981), among other contributions.

ix. See also Deschamps and Gevers (1979), d'Aspremont (1985) and d'Aspremont and Gevers (2002).

x. See Samuelson (1947), pp. 228–9, 246, Bergson (1948), p. 418, and Graaff (1957), pp. 48–54.

xi. Mirrlees (1971) uses this formulation of social welfare (see also Mirrlees 1982). This formulation is axiomatically analysed and discussed by Roberts (1977), (1980b), and Blackorby and Donaldson (1977); see also Blackorby, Donaldson and Weymark (1984).

xii. On these derivations, see Atkinson (1970), Arrow (1973) and Hammond (1975).

xiii. See Deschamps and Gevers (1978), (1979), Maskin (1978), Blackorby and Donaldson (1977), (1979), Roberts (1980b), Myerson (1983) and Blackorby, Donaldson and Weymark (1984), without making the levels non-comparable, as in d'Aspremont and Gevers' (1977) method. For a very different route to the axiomatization of utilitarianism, see Ng (1975). See also Danielson (1973) and Mirrlees (1982).

xiv. On positional rules, see particularly Young (1974a), (1974b), (1975); see also Gärdenfors (1973), Smith (1973), Fine and Fine (1974), Fishburn and Gehrlein (1976), Hansson and Sahlquist (1976), Gardner (1977), Farkas and Nitzan (1979) and Nitzan and Rubinstein (1981).

xv. Fishburn (1973) has discussed such permuted dominance for strict orderings. Fine and Fine (1974) have provided extensive analysis – and axiomatic derivation – of rules of this type.

xvi. See Sen (1977c), section 5, Mizutani (1978) and Gaertner (1983).

CHAPTER A4

i. See Tocqueville (1840); in English translation, Tocqueville (1990), p. 1.

ii. Rawls (1999), pp. 579–80. See also Jürgen Habermas (1989).

iii. For a fuller discussion of these traditions, see *The Argumentative Indian* (Sen 2005) and *Identity and Violence* (Sen 2006).

iv. See Nelson Mandela, *Long Walk to Freedom* (Mandela (1994), p. 21).

v. See Gaertner (1979), (2011), (2012), for discussions of different ways of achieving consistent majority decisions.

vi. On this see Chamberlain and Rothschild (1981), and also Barzel and Silverberg (1973), Ferejohn and Fiorina (1974) and Beck (1975).

vii. See also Ravallion (1987), Osmani (1995) and Bose (2009).

viii. See also Katerina Linos's (2014) informative study of the role of democracy in spreading enlightened laws on health, family and employment across countries.

CHAPTER A4*

i. For a lucid axiomatization of the method of majority decision, see May (1952), (1953).

ii. See also Sen (1966a), Inada (1969), (1970), Majumdar (1969b), Sen and Pattanaik (1969), Pattanaik (1971), Fishburn (1973), Ferejohn and Grether (1974), Kelly (1974a), (1974b), Kaneko (1975), Salles (1975), Nakamura (1978) and Monjardet (1979), among many other contributions in this area.

iii. For related investigations, see also Maskin (1976a), (1979), Kalai and Muller (1977), Dasgupta, Hammond and Maskin (1979) and Kalai and Ritz (1980).

iv. See also Fishburn (1972), Denzau and Parks (1975), Saposnik (1975), Hinich (1977), Slutsky (1977) and Gaertner and Heinecke (1978).

CHAPTER A5

i. Jeremy Bentham, *The Works of Jeremy Bentham*, vol. II (1843), p. 523.

ii. Different arguments for the cognitivist position can be found in Railton (2003), Parfit (2011) and Scanlon (2014), among others.

iii. Adam Smith, *Lectures on Jurisprudence*, edited by R. L. Meek, D. D. Raphael and P. G. Stein (Oxford: Clarendon Press, 1978; repr. Indianapolis: Liberty Press, 1982), p. 104.

iv. For this reference and many similar ones, see Emma Rothschild and Amartya Sen, 'Adam Smith's Economics' (Rothschild and Sen (2006)).

v. The same can be said about the so-called 'Gibbard paradox', in which an interesting impossibility result is generated with demands only of liberty (without the need to invoke the Pareto principle), through making the requirements of liberty more exacting. On this see Gibbard (1974), Kelly (1976a), (1976b), Sen (1976a) and Breyer and Gardner (1980).

vi. The literature on this subject, as was noted earlier, is quite vast; on which see my critical surveys in Sen (1992b), and Wriglesworth (1985). For excellent analyses of the main issues involved, see Hammond (1982a), (1997a) and Suzumura (1996), (2011).

vii. On the question of incentive compatibility in these exercises and its implications, see Barnes (1980), Bernholz (1980), Gardner (1980), Suzumura (1980), Basu (1984) and Schwartz (1986).

viii. See Basu (1984), Mueller (1996), Pattanaik (1996), Suzumura (1996) and Breyer and Zweifel (1997), among other contributions.

ix. Nozick (1974), pp. 165–6.

CHAPTER A6

i. Condorcet (1785), (1795), and Malthus (1798).

ii. Malthus (1830), p. 243.

iii. See Drèze and Sen (2002), (2013), and the references cited there, particularly Drèze and Murthi (2001).

iv. See Knight (1947), and also Habermas (1989).

v. Adam Smith (1759) III, 1, 2; in the Penguin edition, Smith (2009), p. 133.

vi. Adam Smith, *Lectures on Jurisprudence*, posthumously published 1978; repr. 1982, p. 104.

Bibliography

Ackerman, Bruce A. (1980). *Social Justice in the Liberal State*. New Haven: Yale University Press.

Adelman, Irma. (1975). 'Development Economics – A Reassessment of Goals'. *The American Economic Review* 65 (2): 302–9.

Agarwal, Bina. (1994). *A Field of One's Own: Gender and Land Rights in South Asia*. Cambridge: Cambridge University Press.

———. (2009). 'Engaging with Sen on Gender Relations: Cooperative Conflicts, False Perceptions and Relative Capabilities'. In Basu and Kanbur (2009), vol. II: 157–77.

———. (2010). *Gender and Green Governance: The Political Economy of Women's Presence Within and Beyond Community Forestry*. Oxford: Oxford University Press.

Agarwal, Bina, Jane Humphries and Ingrid Robeyns, eds. (2006). *Capabilities, Freedom, and Equality: Amartya Sen's Work from a Gender Perspective*. Oxford: Oxford University Press.

Ahluwalia, Isher. (2009). 'Challenges of Economic Development in Punjab'. In Basu and Kanbur (2009), vol. II: 303–26.

Ahluwalia, Montek. (2009). 'Growth, Distribution and Inclusiveness: Reflections on India's Experience'. In Basu and Kanbur (2009), vol. II: 327–49.

Ahtisaari, Marko. (1991). 'Amartya Sen's Capability Approach to the Standard of Living'. Prize Essay, Columbia University.

Aizerman, Mark A. (1985). 'New Problems in the General Choice Theory: Review of a Research Trend'. *Social Choice and Welfare* 2 (4): 235–82.

Aizerman, Mark A. and Fuad T. Aleskerov. (1986). 'Voting Operators in the Space of Choice Functions'. *Mathematical Social Sciences* 11 (3): 201–42.

Akerlof, George. (1984). *An Economic Theorist's Book of Tales*. Cambridge: Cambridge University Press.

Alamgir, Mohiuddin. (1980). *Famine in South Asia: Political Economy of Mass Starvation*. Cambridge, Mass: Oelgeschlager, Gunn & Hain Inc.

Aleskerov, Fuad T. (1997). 'Voting Models in the Arrovian Framework'. In Arrow, Sen and Suzumura (1997).

———. (2002). 'Categories of Arrovian Voting Schemes'. In Arrow, Sen and Suzumura (2002): 95–129.

Alger, Ingela and Jörgen W. Weibull. (2009). 'Family Ties, Incentives and Development: A Model of Coerced Altruism'. In Basu and Kanbur (2009), vol. II: 178–201.

———. (2016a). 'Morality: Evolutionary Foundations and Economic Implications'. Paper prepared for conference 'The State of Economics, The State of the World'. World Bank, Washington, D. C., 8–9 June 2016.

———. (2016b). 'Evolution and Kantian Morality'. *Games and Economic Behavior* 98 (July): 56–67.

Alkire, Sabina. (2002). *Valuing Freedoms: Sen's Capability Approach and Poverty Reduction*. New York: Oxford University Press.

———. (2005). 'Why the Capability Approach?' *Journal of Human Development* 6 (1): 115–35.

———. (2008). 'Choosing Dimensions: The Capability Approach and Multidimensional Poverty'. In *The Many Dimensions of Poverty*, edited by Nanak Kakwani and Jacques Silber. London: Palgrave Macmillan.

———. (2009). 'Concepts and Measures of Agency'. In Basu and Kanbur (2009), vol. I: 455–74.

Alkire, Sabina and James E. Foster. (2011a). 'Counting and Multidimensional Poverty Measurement'. *Journal of Public Economics* 95 (7–8): 476–87.

———. (2011b). 'Understandings and Misunderstandings of Multidimensional Poverty Measurement'. *Journal of Economic Inequality* 9 (2): 289–314.

Alkire, Sabina, James E. Foster, Suman Seth, Maria Emma Santos, Jose Manuel Roche and Paola Ballon. (2015). *Multidimensional Poverty Measurement and Analysis*. Oxford: Oxford University Press.

Allen, R. G. D. (1959). *Mathematical Economics*. London: Macmillan.

Allingham, Michael G. (1977). 'Fairness and Utility'. *Economie Appliquée* 29 (2): 257–66.

Allingham, Michael G. and M. L. Burstein, eds. (1976). *Resource Allocation and Economic Policy*. London: Macmillan.

Anand, Paul, Prasanta Pattanaik and Clemens Puppe, eds. (2009). *The Handbook of Rational and Social Choice*. Oxford and New York: Oxford University Press.

Anand, Paul, Cristina Santos and Ron Smith. (2009). 'The Measurement of Capabilities'. In Basu and Kanbur (2009), vol. I: 283–310.

Anand, Sudhir. (1977). 'Aspects of Poverty in Malaysia'. *Review of Income and Wealth* 23 (1): 1–16.

———. (1983). *Inequality and Poverty in Malaysia: Measurement and Decomposition*. Oxford: Oxford University Press.

Anand, Sudhir and Martin Ravallion. (1993). 'Human Development in Poor Countries: On the Role of Private Incomes and Public Services'. *Journal of Economic Perspectives* 7 (1): 133–50.

Anand, Sudhir and Amartya K. Sen. (1995). 'Gender Inequality in Human Development: Theories and Measurement'. *Background Papers – Human Development Report 1995*. UNDP, New York: United Nations, 1996; reprinted in Fukuda-Parr and Shiva Kumar (2003).

———. (1997). 'Concepts of Human Development and Poverty: A Multidimensional Perspective'. In *Poverty and Human Development: Human Development Papers 1997*. UNDP, New York: United Nations.

Anand, Sudhir, Christopher Harris and Oliver Linton. (2009). 'On Ultrapoverty'. In Basu and Kanbur (2009), vol. I: 311–36.

Anderson, Elizabeth S. (1999). 'What Is the Point of Equality?' *Ethics* 109 (2): 287–337.

———. (2010a.) 'Equal Opportunity, Unequal Capability'. In Brighouse and Robeyns (2010): 61–80.

———. (2010b). 'Justifying the Capability Approach to Justice'. In Brighouse and Robeyns (2010): 81–100.

Appiah, Kwame Anthony. (2009). 'Sen's Identities'. In Basu and Kanbur (2009), vol. I: 475–88.

Appiah, Kwame Anthony and Amy Gutman. (1996). *The Political Economy of Race*. Princeton, N. J.: Princeton University Press.

Archibald, G. C. (1959). 'Welfare Economics, Ethics, and Essentialism'. *Economica* 26 (104): 316–27.

Aristotle. (1953). *The Nicomachean Ethics*. Translated by J. A. K. Thomson. London: Allen & Unwin.

———. (1998). *The Politics*. Translated by Ernest Barker. Oxford: Oxford University Press.

Armstrong, Thomas E. (1980). 'Arrow's Theorem with Restricted Coalition Algebras'. *Journal of Mathematical Economics* 7 (1): 55–75.

——. (1985). 'Precisely Dictatorial Social Welfare Functions'. *Journal of Mathematical Economics* 14 (1): 57–59.

Armstrong, W. E. (1950). 'A Note on the Theory of Consumer's Behaviour'. *Oxford Economic Papers* 2 (1): 119–22.

——. (1951). 'Utility and the Theory of Welfare'. *Oxford Economic Papers* 3 (3): 259–71.

Arneson, Richard J. (1989). 'Equality and Equal Opportunity for Welfare'. *Philosophical Studies* 56 (1): 77–93.

——. (1990). 'Liberalism, Distributive Subjectivism, and Equal Opportunity for Welfare'. *Philosophy and Public Affairs* 19 (2): 158–94.

——. (2010). 'Two Cheers for Capabilities'. In Brighouse and Robeyns (2010): 101–27.

Arrow, Kenneth J. (1950). 'A Difficulty in the Concept of Social Welfare'. *Journal of Political Economy* 58 (4): 328–46.

——. (1951a). *Social Choice and Individual Values*. New York: Wiley.

——. (1951b). 'An Extension of the Basic Theorems of Classical Welfare Economics'. In *Proceedings of the Second Berkeley Symposium on Mathematical Statistics and Probability*, edited by Jerzy Neyman. Oakland: The Regents of the University of California.

——. (1952). 'Le Principe de rationalité dans les décisions collectives: conférence'. *Economie Appliquée: Archives de l'Institut de Sciences Mathématiques et Economiques Appliquées; an International Journal of Economic Analysis* 5 (4): 469–84.

——. (1959). 'Rational Choice Functions and Orderings'. *Economica* 26 (102): 121–7.

——. (1963a). *Social Choice and Individual Values*. Republished 2nd edn. New Haven: Yale University Press.

——. (1963b). 'Uncertainty and the Welfare Economics of Medical Care'. *American Economic Review* 53 (3): 941–73.

——. (1965). *Aspects of the Theory of Risk-Bearing*. Helsinki: Yrjö Jahnssonin Säätiö.

——. (1967a). 'Public and Private Values'. In *Human Values and Economic Policy*, edited by Sidney Hook. New York: New York University Press.

——. (1967b). 'The Place of Moral Obligation in Preference Systems'. In *Human Values and Economic Policy*, edited by Sidney Hook. New York: New York University Press.

——. (1967c). 'Values and Collective Decision-Making'. In *Philosophy, Politics, and Society*, edited by Peter Laslett and W. G. Runciman, 3rd series. Oxford: Blackwell.

——. (1973). 'Some Ordinalist-Utilitarian Notes on Rawls' Theory of Justice', *Journal of Philosophy* 70 (9): 245–63.

——. (1977). 'Extended Sympathy and the Possibility of Social Choice'. *The American Economic Review* 67 (1): 219–25.

——. (1983). *Collected Papers of Kenneth J. Arrow: Social Choice and Justice*. Vol. 1. Cambridge, Mass.: Harvard University Press.

——. (1995). 'A Note on Freedom and Flexibility'. In Basu, Pattanaik and Suzumura (1995).

——. (2012). *Social Choice and Individual Values*. Republished, 3rd edn, with a Foreword by Eric Maskin. New Haven: Yale University Press.

——. (2014). 'Commentary'. In *The Arrow Impossibility Theorem*, by Eric Maskin and Amartya K. Sen. New York: Columbia University Press.

Arrow, Kenneth J., Samuel Karlin, and Patrick Suppes, eds. (1960a). *Mathematical Methods in the Social Sciences, 1959: Proceedings*. Stanford: Stanford University Press.

——. (1960b). 'Preference and Rational Choice in the Theory of Consumption'. In *Mathematical Methods in the Social Sciences, 1959: Proceedings*. Stanford: Stanford University Press.

Arrow, Kenneth J., Amartya K. Sen and Kotaro Suzumura. eds. (1997). *Social Choice Re-Examined*. International Economic Association Series. London and New York: Palgrave Macmillan.

——. (2002). *Handbook of Social Choice and Welfare*. Vol. 1. 2 vols. Amsterdam: Elsevier.

——. (2011a). *Handbook of Social Choice and Welfare*. Vol. 2. 2 vols. Amsterdam: Elsevier.

——. (2011b). 'Kenneth Arrow on Social Choice Theory'. In Arrow, Sen and Suzumura (2011a): 3–27.

Asali, Muhammad, Sanjay G. Reddy and Sujata Visaria. (2009). 'Inter-Country Comparisons of Income Poverty Based on a Capability Approach'. In Basu and Kanbur (2009), vol. II: 7–30.

Atkinson, Anthony B. (1970). 'On the Measurement of Inequality'. *Journal of Economic Theory* 2 (3): 244–63.

——. (1983). *Social Justice and Public Policy*. Cambridge, Mass.: MIT Press.

——. (1987). 'On the Measurement of Poverty'. *Econometrica* 55: 749–64.

——, ed. (1989). *Poverty and Social Security*. New York and London: Harvester Wheatsheaf.

———. (1995). 'Capabilities, Exclusion, and the Supply of Goods'. In Basu, Pattanaik and Suzumura (1995).

———. (2009). 'Welfare Economics and Giving for Development'. In Basu and Kanbur (2009), vol. I: 489–500.

———. (2015). *Inequality*. Cambridge, Mass.: Harvard University Press.

Atkinson, Anthony B. and François Bourguignon. (1982). 'The Comparison of Multi-Dimensioned Distributions of Economic Status'. *The Review of Economic Studies* 49 (2): 183–201.

Atkinson, Anthony B., Thomas Piketty and Emmanuel Saez. (2011). 'Top Incomes in the Long Run of History'. *Journal of Economic Literature* 49 (1): 3–71.

Aumann, Robert J. (1962). 'Utility Theory without the Completeness Axiom'. *Econometrica* 30 (3): 445–62.

———. (1964). 'Utility Theory without the Completeness Axiom: A Correction'. *Econometrica* 32 (1/2): 210–12.

Ayer, A. J. (1959). *Philosophical Essays*. London: Macmillan.

Bagchi, Amiya Kumar. (2009). 'The Capability Approach and Political Economy of Human Development'. In Basu and Kanbur (2009), vol. II: 31–47.

Baigent, Nicholas. (1990). 'Transitivity and Consistency'. *Economics Letters* 33 (4): 315–17.

———. (1991a). 'A Comment on One of Sen's Impossibility Theorems'. Mimeographed, Murphy Institute, Tulane University.

———. (1991b). 'Impossibility without Consistency'. Mimeographed, Murphy Institute, Tulane University

———. (1994). 'Norms, Choice, and Preferences'. Mimeographed, Institute of Public Economics, University of Graz, Austria, Research Memorandum No. 9306.

———. (2011). 'Topological Theories of Social Choice'. In Arrow, Sen and Suzumura (2011a): 301–34.

Baigent, Nicholas and Wulf Gaertner. (1996). 'Never Choose the Uniquely Largest: A Characterization'. *Economic Theory* 8 (2): 239–49.

Balestrino, Alessandro. (1994). 'Poverty and Functionings: Issues in Measurement and Public Action'. *Giornale degli Economisti e Annali di Economia* 53 (7/9): 389–406.

———. (1996). 'A Note on Functioning Poverty in Affluent Societies'. *Notizie di Politeia* 12: 97–105.

Balestrino, Alessandro and A. Petretto. (1995). 'Optimal Taxation Rules for "Functioning"-Inputs'. *Economic Notes* 23: 216–32.

Bandyopadhyay, Taradas. (1986). 'Rationality, Path Independence, and the Power Structure'. *Journal of Economic Theory* 40 (2): 338–48.

Banerjee, Abhijit V. (1992). 'A Simple Model of Herd Behavior'. *The Quarterly Journal of Economics* 107 (3): 797–817.

Banerjee, Dipak. (1964). 'Choice and Order: Or First Things First'. *Economica* 31 (122): 158–67.

Barberà, Salvador. (1980). 'Pivotal Voters : A New Proof of Arrow's Theorem'. *Economics Letters* 6 (1): 13–16.

———. (1983). 'Pivotal Voters: A Simple Proof of Arrow's Theorem'. In Pattanaik and Salles (1983): 31–5.

———. (2011). 'Strategy Proof Social Choice'. In Arrow, Sen and Suzumura (2011a): 731–831.

Barberà, Salvador and Hugo Sonnenschein. (1978). 'Preference Aggregation with Randomized Social Orderings'. *Journal of Economic Theory* 18 (2): 244–54.

Bardhan, Pranab K. (1974). 'On Life and Death Questions'. *Economic and Political Weekly* 9 (32/34): 1293–1304.

———. (2009). 'Economic Reforms, Poverty and Inequality in China and India'. In Basu and Kanbur (2009), vol. II: 350–64.

Barker, E. (1958). *The Politics of Aristotle*. London: Oxford University Press.

Barnes, Jonathan. (1980). 'Freedom, Rationality, and Paradox'. *Canadian Journal of Philosophy* 10 (4): 545–65.

Barone, Enrico. (1935). 'The Ministry of Production in the Collectivist State'. In *Collectivist Economic Planning; Critical Studies on the Possibilities of Socialism*, edited by Friedrich A. von Hayek, N. G. Pierson, Ludwig von Mises and George N. Halm. London: G. Routledge.

Barrett, C. R., Prasanta K. Pattanaik and Maurice Salles, (1986). 'On the Structure of Fuzzy Social Welfare Functions'. *Fuzzy Sets and Systems* 19: 1–10.

——— (1990). 'On Choosing Rationally When Preferences Are Fuzzy'. *Fuzzy Sets and Systems* 34 (2): 197–212.

——— (1992). 'Rationality and Aggregation of Preferences on Ordinally Fuzzy Framework'. *Fuzzy Sets and Systems* 49: 9–13.

Barrett, Richard and Maurice Salles. (1998). 'On Three Classes of Differentiable Inequality Measures'. *International Economic Review* 39 (3): 611–21.

———. (2011). 'Social Choice with Fuzzy Preferences'. In Arrow, Sen and Suzumura (2011a): 367–89.

Barry, Brian M. (1965). *Political Argument*. New York: Humanities Press.

———. (1986). 'Lady Chatterley's Lover and Doctor Fisher's Bomb Party: Liberalism, Pareto Optimality, and the Problem of Objectionable Preferences'. In *Foundations of Social Choice Theory*, edited by Jon Elster and Aanund Hylland: Cambridge: Cambridge University Press, 11–43.

Barzel, Yoram and Eugene Silberberg. (1973). 'Is the Act of Voting Rational?' *Public Choice* 16 (1): 51–8.

Basu, Kaushik. (1980). *Revealed Preference of Government*. Cambridge: Cambridge University Press.

———. (1984). 'The Right to Give up Rights'. *Economica* 51 (204): 413–22.

———. (1987). 'Achievements, Capabilities and the Concept of Well-Being'. *Social Choice and Welfare* 4 (1): 69–76.

Basu, Kaushik and Ravi Kanbur, eds. (2009). *Arguments for a Better World: Essays in Honor of Amartya Sen*. 2 vols. Oxford: Oxford University Press.

Basu, Kaushik and Luis Lopez-Calva. (2011). 'Functionings and Capabilities'. In Arrow, Sen and Suzumura (2011a): 153–87.

Basu, Kaushik, Rajat Deb and Prasanta K. Pattanaik. (1992). 'Soft Sets: An Ordinal Formulation of Vagueness with Some Applications to the Theory of Choice'. *Essays on Individual Decision-Making and Social Welfare*.

Basu, Kaushik, Prasanta K. Pattanaik and Kotaro Suzumura, eds. (1995). *Choice, Welfare, and Development: A Festschrift in Honour of Amartya K. Sen*. Oxford: Oxford University Press.

Bator, Francis M. (1958). 'The Anatomy of Market Failure'. *The Quarterly Journal of Economics* 72 (3): 351–79.

Baumol, William J. (1946). 'Community Indifference'. *Review of Economic Studies* 14 (1): 44–8.

———. (1965). *Welfare Economics and the Theory of the State*. 2nd edn. Cambridge, Mass.: Harvard University Press.

Bavetta, S. (1996). 'Individual Liberty, Control, and the "Freedom of Choice" Literature'. *Notizie di Politeia* 12 (43–44): 23–9.

Beck, N. (1975). 'A Note on the Probability of a Tied Election'. *Public Choice* 23: 75–9.

Begon, Jessica. (2016). 'Athletic Policy, Passive Well-Being: Defending Freedom in the Capability Approach'. *Economics and Philosophy* 32 (1): 51–73.

Beneria, Lourdes. (2009). 'From "Harmony" to "Cooperative Conflicts": Amartya Sen's Contribution to Household Theory'. In Basu and Kanbur (2009), vol. II: 202–18.

Benhabib, Seyla. (1996). *Democracy and Difference: Contesting the Boundaries of the Political*. Princeton: Princeton University Press.

———. (2006). *Another Cosmopolitanism*. Oxford: Oxford University Press.

Benhabib, Seyla, Judith Butler, Drucilla Cornell and N. Fraser, eds. (1995). *Feminist Contentions: A Philosophical Exchange*. New York: Routledge.

Bentham, Jeremy. (1789). *An Introduction to the Principles of Morals and Legislation*. London.

———. (1792). *Anarchical Fallacies; Being an Examination of the Declaration of Rights Issued during the French Revolution*. Republished 1843 in *The Works of Jeremy Bentham*, edited by John Bowring. Vol. 2. Edinburgh: William Tait.

———. (1907). *An Introduction to the Principles of Morals and Legislation*. Oxford: Oxford University Press.

Bergson, Abram. (1938). 'A Reformulation of Certain Aspects of Welfare Economics'. *The Quarterly Journal of Economics* 52 (2): 310–34.

———. (1948). 'Socialist Economics'. In *A Survey of Contemporary Economics*, edited by H. S. Ellis. Homewood, Ill.: Irwin.

———. (1954). 'On the Concept of Social Welfare'. *The Quarterly Journal of Economics* 68 (2): 233–52.

———. (1966). *Essays in Normative Economics*. Cambridge, Mass.: Harvard University Press; republished Cambridge, Mass.: Harvard University Press, 2013.

Bernholz, Peter. (1975). 'Is a Paretian Liberal Really Impossible: A Rejoinder'. *Public Choice* 23: 69–73.

———. (1980). 'A General Social Dilemma: Profitable Exchange and Intransitive Group Preferences'. *Zeitschrift für Nationalökonomie / Journal of Economics*, 40: 1–23.

Bernoulli, Daniel. (1954). '*Specimen Theoriae Novae de Mensura Sortis* (Exposition of a New Theory of the Measurement of Risk)'. Translated by L. Sommer. *Econometrica* 22: 23–36.

Bezembinder, Thom and Peter van Acker. (1980). 'Intransitivity in Individual and Group Choice'. In *Similarity and Choice: Essays in Honor of Clyde Coombs*, edited by Ernst Dieter Lantermann and Hubert Feger. New York: Wiley, 208–33.

Bhattacharyya, A, P. K. Pattanaik and Y. Xi. (2011). 'Choice, Internal Consistency and Rationality'. *Economics and Philosophy* 27: 123–49.

Binmore, Ken. (1975). 'An Example in Group Preference'. *Journal of Economic Theory* 10 (3): 377–85.

BIBLIOGRAPHY

———. (1981). *Nash Bargaining and Incomplete Information*. Cambridge: Department of Applied Economics, Cambridge University.

———. (1994). *Game Theory and the Social Contract, Vol. 1: Playing Fair*. Cambridge, Mass: MIT Press.

———. (1996). 'Right or Seemly?' *Analyse & Kritik* 18 (1): 67–80.

Birkhoff, Garrett. (1940). *Lattice Theory*. Providence, R. I.: American Mathematical Society.

Bishop, Robert L. (1964). 'A Zeuthen-Hicks Theory of Bargaining'. *Econometrica* 32 (3): 410–17.

Black, Duncan. (1948a). 'On the Rationale of Group Decision-Making'. *Journal of Political Economy* 56 (1): 23–34.

———. (1948b). 'The Decisions of a Committee Using a Special Majority'. *Econometrica* 16 (3): 245–61.

———. (1958). *The Theory of Committees and Elections*. Cambridge: Cambridge University Press.

Black, Max. (1964). 'The Gap Between "Is" and "Should".' *Philosophical Review* 73 (2): 165–81.

Blackorby, Charles. (1975). 'Degrees of Cardinality and Aggregate Partial Orderings'. *Econometrica* 43 (5/6): 845–52.

Blackorby, Charles and David Donaldson. (1977). 'Utility vs Equity: Some Plausible Quasi-Orderings'. *Journal of Public Economics* 7 (3): 365–81.

———. (1978). 'Measures of Relative Equality and Their Meaning in Terms of Social Welfare'. *Journal of Economic Theory* 18 (1): 59–80.

———. (1979). 'Interpersonal Comparability of Origin- or Scale-independent Utilities: Admissible Social Evaluation Functionals'. Discussion Paper No. 79-04. Department of Economics, University of British Columbia.

———. (1980). 'Ethical Indices for the Measurement of Poverty'. *Econometrica* 48 (4): 1053–60.

Blackorby, Charles, Walter Bossert and David Donaldson. (2002). 'Utilitarianism and the Theory of Justice'. In Arrow, Sen and Suzumura (2002): 543–96.

Blackorby, Charles, David Donaldson and John A. Weymark. (1980). 'On John Harsanyi's Defences of Utilitarianism'. Discussion Paper No. 80-04, Department of Economics, University of British Columbia.

———. (1984). 'Social Choice with Interpersonal Utility Comparisons: A Diagrammatic Introduction'. *International Economic Review* 25 (2): 327–56.

Blackwell, David and Meyer A. Girshick. (1954). *Theory of Games and Statistical Decisions*. New York: Wiley.

Blair, Douglas H. and Robert A. Pollak. (1979). 'Collective Rationality and Dictatorship: The Scope of the Arrow Theorem'. *Journal of Economic Theory* 21 (1): 186–94.

——. (1982). 'Acyclic Collective Choice Rules'. *Econometrica* 50 (4): 931–43.

——. (1983). 'Polychromatic Acyclic Tours in Colored Multigraphs'. *Mathematics of Operations Research* 8 (3): 471–6.

Blair, Douglas H, Georges Bordes, Jerry S. Kelly and Kotaro Suzumura. (1976). 'Impossibility Theorems without Collective Rationality'. *Journal of Economic Theory* 13 (3): 361–79.

Blanche, Robert. (1962). *Axiomatics*. Translated by G. B. Keene. New York: Free Press of Glencoe.

Blau, Julian H. (1957). 'The Existence of Social Welfare Functions'. *Econometrica* 25 (2): 302–13.

——. (1959). 'Aggregation of Preferences'. *Econometrica* 27 (January): 283.

——. (1972). 'A Direct Proof of Arrow's Theorem'. *Econometrica* 40 (1): 61–7.

——. (1975). 'Liberal Values and Independence'. *The Review of Economic Studies* 42 (3): 395–401.

——. (1979). 'Semiorders and Collective Choice'. *Journal of Economic Theory* 21 (1): 195–206.

Blau, Julian H. and D. J. Brown. (1978). 'The Structure of Neutral Monotonic Social Functions'. Cowles Foundation Discussion Paper No. 485.

——. (1989). 'The Structure of Neutral Monotonic Social Functions'. *Social Choice and Welfare* 6 (1): 51–61.

Blau, Julian H. and Rajat Deb. (1977). 'Social Decision Functions and the Veto'. *Econometrica* 45 (4): 871–9.

Bloomfield, Stefan D. (1971). 'An Axiomatic Formulation of Constitutional Games'. Technical Report No. 71-18, Operations Research House, Stanford University.

——. (1976). 'A Social Choice Interpretation of the von Neumann–Morgenstern Game'. *Econometrica* 44: 105–14.

Borda, J. C. (1781). '*Mémoire sur les élections au scrutin*'. *Memoires de l'Academie Royale des Sciences*, 1953. English translation by A. de Grazia, *Isis*, 44.

Bordes, Georges. (1976). 'Consistency, Rationality and Collective Choice'. *The Review of Economic Studies* 43 (3): 451–7.

——. (1979). 'Some More Results on Consistency, Rationality and Collective Choice'. In Laffont (1979).

Borglin, Anders. (1982). 'States and Persons – on the Interpretation of Some Fundamental Concepts in the Theory of Justice as Fairness'. *Journal of Public Economics* 18 (1): 85–104.

Bose, Sugata. (2009). 'Pondering Poverty, Fighting Famines: Towards a New History of Economic Ideas'. In Basu and Kanbur (2009), vol. II: 425–35.

Bossert, Walter. (2008). 'Suzumura Consistency'. In *Rational Choice and Social Welfare*, edited by Prasanta K. Pattanaik, Koichi Tadenuma, Yongsheng Xu and Naoki Yoshihara. Studies in Choice and Welfare. Berlin: Springer-Verlag, 159–79.

Bossert, Walter and Kotaro Suzumura. (2009). 'Rational Choice on General Domains'. In Basu and Kanbur (2009), vol. I: 103–35.

———. (2010). *Consistency, Choice, and Rationality*. Cambridge, Mass.: Harvard University Press.

Boulding, K. E. (1952). 'Welfare Economics'. In *Survey of Contemporary Economics*, edited by Howard Ellis. Philadelphia: Blakiston. Vol. 2: 412–48.

Bourbaki, Nicolas. (1939). *Éléments de mathématique: théorie des ensembles*. Éditions Hermann.

———. (1968). *Éléments de Mathématique*. Éditions Hermann.

Bourguignon, François. (2015). *The Globalization of Inequality*. Princeton: Princeton University Press.

Bourguignon, François and Satya R. Chakravarty. (2009). 'Multidimensional Poverty Orderings: Theory and Applications'. In Basu and Kanbur (2009), vol. I: 337–61.

Bourguignon, François and G. S. Fields. (1990). 'Poverty Measures and Anti-Poverty Policy'. DELTA Working Paper 90-04. DELTA (*Ecole normale supérieure*).

Bowen, Howard R. (1943). 'The Interpretation of Voting in the Allocation of Economic Resources'. *The Quarterly Journal of Economics* 58 (1): 27–48.

Braithwaite, R. B. (1955). *Theory of Games as a Tool for the Moral Philosopher. An Inaugural Lecture Delivered in Cambridge on 2 December 1954*. Cambridge: Cambridge University Press.

Brams, Steven J. (1975). *Game Theory and Politics*. New York: Free Press.

Brams, Steven J. and Peter C. Fishburn. (1978). 'Approval Voting'. *American Political Science Review* 72 (3): 831–47.

———. (1983). *Approval Voting*. Boston, Mass.: Birkhauser.

———. (2002). 'Voting Procedures'. In Arrow, Sen and Suzumura (2002): 173–236.

Brandt, Richard B. (1959). *Ethical Theory*. Englewood Cliffs, N. J.: Prentice Hall.

———. ed. (1961). *Social Justice*. Englewood Cliffs, N. J.: Prentice Hall.

———. (1964). 'R. M. Hare: "Freedom and Reason" (Book Review)'. *The Journal of Philosophy* 61 (4): 139.

Brennan, Geoffrey and Loren Lomasky. (1993). *Democracy and Decision: The Pure Theory of Electoral Preference*. Cambridge: Cambridge University Press.

Breyer, Friedrich. (1977). 'The Liberal Paradox, Decisiveness over Issues, and Domain Restrictions'. *Zeitschrift für Nationalökonomie / Journal of Economics* 37 (1/2): 45–60.

———. (1996). 'Comment on the Papers by J. M. Buchanan and by A. de Jasay and H. Kliemt'. *Analyse & Kritik* 18 (1): 148–52.

Breyer, Friedrich and Roy Gardner. (1980). 'Liberal Paradox, Game Equilibrium, and Gibbard Optimum'. *Public Choice* 35 (4): 469–81.

Breyer, Friedrich and P. Zweifel. (1997). *Health Economics*. Oxford: Oxford University Press.

Breyer, Stephen. (2015). *The Court and the World: American Law and the New Global Realities*. New York: Knopf.

Brighouse, Harry and Ingrid Robeyns, eds. (2010). *Measuring Justice: Primary Goods and Capabilities*. Cambridge: Cambridge University Press.

Broad, C. D. (1916). 'On the Function of False Hypotheses in Ethics'. *The International Journal of Ethics* 26 (3): 377–97.

Broome, John. (1991). *Weighing Goods: Equality, Uncertainty and Time*. Oxford: Blackwell.

———. (2009). 'Why Economics Needs Ethical Theory'. In Basu and Kanbur (2009), vol. I: 7–14.

Brown, Donald. (1973). 'Acyclic Choice'. Cowles Foundation Discussion Paper 360. Cowles Foundation for Research in Economics, Yale University.

———. (1974). 'An Approximate Solution to Arrow's Problem'. *Journal of Economic Theory* 9 (4): 375–83.

———. (1975a). 'Collective Rationality'. Cowles Foundation Discussion Paper 393. Cowles Foundation for Research in Economics, Yale University.

———. (1975b). 'Aggregation of Preferences'. *The Quarterly Journal of Economics* 89 (3): 456–69.

Buchanan, Allen. (1985). *Ethics, Efficiency, and the Market*. Totowa, N. J.: Rowman and Littlefield.

———. (2011). *Beyond Humanity*. Oxford: Oxford University Press.

Buchanan, Allen, Dan Brock, Norman Daniels and Daniel Wikler. (2000). *From Chance to Choice: Genetics and Justice*. Cambridge: Cambridge University Press.

Buchanan, James M. (1954a). 'Social Choice, Democracy, and Free Markets'. *Journal of Political Economy* 62 (2): 114–23.

———. (1954b). 'Individual Choice in Voting and the Market'. *Journal of Political Economy* 62 (4): 334–43.

———. (1960). *Fiscal Theory and Political Economy: Selected Essays*. Chapel Hill, N. C.: University of North Carolina Press.

———. (1961). 'Simple Majority Voting, Game Theory, and Resource Use'. *The Canadian Journal of Economics and Political Science / Revue Canadienne d'Economique et de Science Politique* 27 (3): 337–48.

———. (1986). *Liberty, Market and State: Political Economy and the 1980s*. New York: New York University Press.

———. (1996). 'An Ambiguity in Sen's Alleged Proof of the Impossibility of a Pareto Libertarian'. *Analyse & Kritik* 18 (1): 118–25.

Buchanan, James M. and Gordon Tullock. (1962). *The Calculus of Consent: Logical Foundations of Constitutional Democracy*. Ann Arbor: University of Michigan Press.

Burchardt, Tania and Polly Vizard. (2007). *Definition of Equality and Framework of Measurement*. CASE /120, STICERD. London School of Economics.

Campbell, Colin D. and Gordon Tullock. (1965). 'A Measure of the Importance of Cyclical Majorities'. *The Economic Journal* 75 (300): 853–7.

———. (1966). 'The Paradox of Voting – A Possible Method of Calculation'. *American Political Science Review* 60 (3): 684–5.

Campbell, Donald E. (1972). 'A Collective Choice Rule Satisfying Arrow's Five Conditions in Practice'. In *Theory and Application of Collective Choice Rule*, Institute for Quantitative Analysis of Social and Economic Policy, Working Paper No. 7206, University of Toronto.

———. (1973). 'Social Choice and Intensity of Preference'. *Journal of Political Economy* 81 (1): 211–18.

———. (1976). 'Democratic Preference Functions'. *Journal of Economic Theory* 12 (2): 259–72.

———. (1980). 'Algorithms for Social Choice Functions'. *The Review of Economic Studies* 47 (3): 617–27.

———. (1989). 'Equilibrium and Efficiency with Property Rights and Local Consumption Externalities'. *Social Choice and Welfare* 6: 189–203.

———. (1992). *Equity, Efficiency, and Social Choice*. Oxford: Oxford University Press.

———. (1995). 'Nonbinary Social Choice for Economic Environments'. *Social Choice and Welfare* 12: 245–54.

Campbell, Donald E. and Jerry S. Kelly. (1997a). 'Sen's Theorem and Externalities'. *Economica*. 64: 375–86.

———. (1997b). 'The Possibility-Impossibility Boundary in Social Choice'. In Arrow, Sen and Suzamura (1997).

———. (2002). 'Impossibility Theorems in the Arrovian Framework'. In Arrow, Sen and Suzumura (2002): 35–94.

Caplin, Andrew S. and Barry J. Nalebuff. (1988). 'On 64%-Majority Rule'. *Econometrica* 56 (4): 787–814.

———. (1991). 'Aggregation and Imperfect Competition: On the Existence of Equilibrium'. *Econometrica* 59 (1): 25–59.

Carnap, Rudolf. (1958). *Introduction to Symbolic Logic and Its Applications*. New York: Dover Publications.

Carter, Ian. (1995). 'Interpersonal Comparison of Freedom'. *Economics and Philosophy* 11 (1): 1–23; reprinted in Ian Carter, *A Measure of Freedom*. Oxford: Oxford University Press, 1999.

———. (1996). 'The Concept of Freedom in the Work of Amartya Sen: An Alternative Analysis Consistent with Freedom's Independent Value'. *Notizie di Politeia* 12 (43–44): 7–22.

———. (2014). 'Is the Capability Approach Paternalist?' *Economics and Philosophy* 30 (1): 75–98.

Casini, Leonardo and Iacapo Bernetti. (1996). 'Public Project Evaluations, Environment, and Sen's Theorem'. *Notizie di Politeia* 12 (43–44): 55–78.

Cassen, R. (1967). 'Alternative Approaches to the Theory of Social Choice'. Mimeographed.

Chakraborty, Achin. (1996). 'On the Possibility of a Weighting System for Functionings'. *Indian Economic Review* 31 (2): 241–50.

Chakravarty, Satya R. (1990). *Ethical Social Index Numbers*. Berlin and New York: Springer-Verlag.

Chakravarty, Satya R. and M. O. L. Bacharach. (1967). 'Alternative Preference Functions in Problems of Investment Planning on the National Level'. In *Activity Analysis in the Theory of Growth and Planning*, edited by Edmond Malinvaud. Proceedings of a Conference held by the

International Economic Association. London: Macmillan and New York: St. Martin's Press.

Chakravarty, S. R., B. Dutta and J. A. Weymark. (1985). 'Ethical Indices of Income Mobility'. *Social Choice and Welfare*, 2: 1–21.

Chamberlain, Gary and Michael Rothschild. (1981). 'A Note on the Probability of Casting a Decisive Vote'. *Journal of Economic Theory* 25 (1): 152–62.

Champsaur, Paul and Guy Laroque. (1981). 'Fair Allocations in Large Economies'. *Journal of Economic Theory* 25 (2): 269–82.

Chatterjee, Deen K., ed. (2004). *The Ethics of Assistance: Morality and the Distant Needy*. Cambridge: Cambridge University Press.

———. ed. (2008). *Democracy in a Global World: Human Rights and Political Participation in the 21st Century*. Lanham, Md.: Rowman & Littlefield.

Chen, Lincoln C. (2009). 'India-China: "The Art of Prolonging Life".' In Basu and Kanbur (2009), vol. II: 48–60.

Chen, Lincoln C., Emdadul Huq and Stan D'Souza. (1981). 'Sex Bias in the Family Allocation of Food and Health Care in Rural Bangladesh'. *Population and Development Review* 7 (1): 55–70.

Chen, Martha Alter. (2009). 'Famine, Widowhood, and Paid Work: Seeking Gender Justice in South Asia'. In Basu and Kanbur (2009), vol. II: 219–36.

Chernoff, Herman. (1954). 'Rational Selection of Decision Functions'. *Econometrica* 22 (4): 422–43.

Chiappero-Martinetti, Enrica. (1994). 'A New Approach to Evaluation of Well-Being and Poverty by Fuzzy Set Theory'. *Giornale degli Economisti e Annali di Economia* 53 (7/9): 367–88.

———. (1996). 'Standard of Living Evaluation Based on Sen's Approach: Some Methodological Suggestions'. *Notizie di Politeia* 12 (43–44): 37–53.

———. (2000). 'A Multidimensional Assessment of Well-Being Based on Sen's Functioning Theory'. *Rivista Internazionale di Scienze Sociali* 108 (2): 207–39.

———. (2009). 'Time and Income: Empirical Evidence on Gender Poverty and Inequalities from a Capability Perspective'. In Basu and Kanbur (2009), vol. II: 237–58.

Chiappero-Martinetti, Enrica and Stefano Moroni. (2007). 'An Analytical Framework for Conceptualizing Poverty and Re-Examining the Capability Approach'. *Journal of Behavioral and Experimental Economics (formerly The Journal of Socio-Economics)* 36 (3): 360–75.

Chichilnisky, Graciela. (1980). 'Basic Needs and Global Models: Resources, Trade and Distribution'. *Alternatives*, 6: 453–72.

———. (1982a). 'Social Aggregation Rules and Continuity'. *The Quarterly Journal of Economics* 97 (2): 337–52.

———. (1982b). 'The Topological Equivalence of the Pareto Condition and the Existence of a Dictator'. *Journal of Mathematical Economics* 9 (3): 223–33.

Chichilnisky, Graciela and Geoffrey Heal. (1983). 'Necessary and Sufficient Conditions for a Resolution of the Social Choice Paradox'. *Journal of Economic Theory* 31 (1): 68–87.

Chipman, John S. (1960). 'The Foundations of Utility'. *Econometrica* 28 (2): 193–224.

———. (1971). 'The Lexicographic Representation of Preference Orderings'. In *Preference, Utility, and Demand: A Minnesota Symposium*, edited by John S. Chipman, Leonid Hurwicz, Marcel K. Richter and Hugo S. Sonnenschein. New York: Harcourt, 276–88.

Chipman, John S., Leonid Hurwicz, Marcel K. Richter and Hugo S. Sonnenschein, eds. (1971). *Preference, Utility, and Demand: A Minnesota Symposium*. New York: Harcourt.

Chopra, Kanchan. (2009). 'Sustainable Human Well-Being: An Interpretation of Capability Enhancement from a "Stakeholders and Systems" Perspective'. In Basu and Kanbur (2009), vol. II: 61–75.

Church, Alonzo. (1956). *Introduction to Mathematical Logic*. Princeton, N. J.: Princeton University Press.

Cicero, Quintus Tullius. (AD 64). *How to Win an Election*. Translated by Philip Freeman. Princeton, N. J.: Princeton University Press, 2012.

Claassen, Rutger. (2014). 'Capability Paternalism'. *Economics and Philosophy* 30 (1): 57–73.

Coale, Ansley J. (1991). 'Excess Female Mortality and the Balance of the Sexes in the Population: An Estimate of the Number of "Missing Females".' *Population and Development Review* 17 (3): 517–23.

Cohen, G. A. (1989). 'On the Currency of Egalitarian Justice'. *Ethics* 99 (4): 906–44.

———. (1990a). 'Equality of What? On Welfare, Goods and Capabilities'. *Recherches Économiques de Louvain* 56 (3/4): 357–82; reprinted in eds. Martha Nussbaum and Amartya Sen, *The Quality of Life*. Oxford: Oxford University Press, 1993.

———. (1990b). 'Marxism and Contemporary Political Philosophy, Or Why Nozick Exercises Some Marxists More than He Does Any Egalitarian Liberals'. *Canadian Journal of Philosophy* 20 (Supplement): 363–87.

Cohen, Joshua. (1989). 'Deliberation and Democratic Legitimacy'. In *The Good Polity: Normative Analysis of the State*, edited by Philip Pettit and Alan Hamlin. Oxford: Blackwell.

Cohen, Joshua and Joel Rogers. (1983). *On Democracy: Toward a Transformation of American Society*. New York: Penguin.

Cohen, L. Jonathan. (1982). *Logic, Methodology, and Philosophy of Science VI: Proceedings of the Sixth International Congress of Logic, Methodology, and Philosophy of Science, Hanover 1979*. Amsterdam: Elsevier North-Holland.

Coleman, J. S. (1966a). 'Foundations for a Theory of Collective Choice'. *American Journal of Sociology* 71.

———. (1966b). 'The Possibility of a Social Welfare Function'. *The American Economic Review* 56 (5): 1105–22.

Coles, Jeffrey L. (1995). 'Walrasian Equilibrium without Survival: Existence, Efficiency, and Remedial Policy'. In Basu, Pattanaik and Suzumura (1995).

Comin, Flavio and Martha C. Nussbaum, eds. (2014). *Capabilities, Gender, Equality: Towards Fundamental Entitlements*. Cambridge: Cambridge University Press.

Comin, Flavio, Mozaffar Qizilbash and Sabina Alkire, eds. (2008). *The Capability Approach: Concepts, Measures and Applications*. Cambridge: Cambridge University Press.

Condorcet, Marquis de. (1785). *Essai sur l'application de l'analyse à la probabilité des décisions rendues à la pluralité des voix*. Paris: L'Imprimerie Royale.

———. (1795). *Esquisse d'un tableau historique des progrès de l'esprit humain*. Agasse; reprinted in *Oeuvres de Condorcet, Tome Sixième* (1847). Paris: Firmin Didot Frères; republished Stuttgart: Friedrich Frommann Verlag, 1968.

———. (1847). *Oeuvres de Condorcet, Tome Sixième*. Paris: Firmin Didot Frères; republished Stuttgart: Friedrich Frommann Verlag, 1968.

———. (1955). *Sketch for a Historical Picture of the Progress of the Human Mind*. Translated by June Barraclough. London: Weidenfeld and Nicolson.

Connor, Patrick E. and Stefan D. Bloomfield. (1977). 'A Goal Approach to Organizational Design'. In *Prescriptive Models of Organizations*, edited by Paul C. Nystrom and Starbuck. Amsterdam: North-Holland Publishing Company.

Contini, Bruno. (1966). 'A Note on Arrow's Postulates for a Social Welfare Function'. *Journal of Political Economy* 74 (3): 278–80.

Coombs, Clyde H. (1950). 'Psychological Scaling without a Unit of Measurement'. *Psychological Review* 57 (3): 145–58.

———. (1964). *A Theory of Data*. New York: Wiley.

Cornell, Drucilla L. (1998). *At the Heart of Freedom*. Princeton, N. J.: Princeton University Press.

———. (2004). *Between Women and Generations: Legacies of Dignity*. New York: Palgrave.

———. (2007). *Moral Images of Freedom: A Future for Critical Theory*. New York: Rowman and Littlefield.

Cornia, Giovanni Andrea. (1994). 'Poverty in Latin America in the Eighties: Extent, Causes, and Possible Remedies'. *Giornale degli Economisti e Annali di Economia* 53 (7/9): 407–34.

Coughlin, Peter. (2011). 'Probabilistic and Spatial Models of Voting'. In Arrow, Sen and Suzumura (2011a).

Coughlin, Peter and Shmuel Nitzan. (1981). 'Directional and Local Electoral Equilibria with Probabilistic Voting'. *Journal of Economic Theory* 24 (2): 226–39.

Coulhon, T. and P. Mongin. (1989). 'Social Choice Theory in the Case of von Neumann–Morgenstern Utilities'. *Social Choice and Welfare* 6 (3): 175–87.

Cowell, Frank A. (1980). 'On the Structure of Additive Inequality Measures'. *The Review of Economic Studies* 47 (3): 521–31.

———. (1995). *Measuring Inequality*. 2nd edn. New York: Prentice Hall.

———. (2011). *Measuring Inequality*. Revised edn. Oxford: Oxford University Press.

Craven, J. (1971). 'Majority Voting and Social Choice'. *The Review of Economic Studies* 38 (2): 265–7.

Crawford, Vincent P. (1977). 'A Game of Fair Division'. *The Review of Economic Studies* 44 (2): 235–47.

———. (1979). 'A Procedure for Generating Pareto-Efficient Egalitarian-Equivalent Allocations'. *Econometrica* 47 (1): 49–60.

Crawford, V. P. and W. P. Heller. (1979). 'Fair Division with Indivisible Commodities'. *Journal of Economic Theory* 21 (1): 10–27.

Criswell, Joan H., H. Solomon and Patrick Suppes, eds. (1962). *Mathematical Methods in Small Group Processes*. Stanford: Stanford University Press.

Crocker, David A. (1992). 'Functioning and Capability: The Foundations of Sen's and Nussbaum's Development Ethic'. *Political Theory* 20 (4): 584–612.

———. (1995). 'Functioning and Capability: The Foundation of Sen's and Nussbaum's Development Ethic, Part II'. In *Women, Culture, and*

Development: A Study of Human Capabilities, edited by Martha C. Nussbaum and Jonathan Glover. Oxford: Oxford University Press.

———. (2008). *Ethics of Global Development: Agency, Capability, and Deliberative Democracy*. Cambridge: Cambridge University Press.

Cunha, Flavio and James J. Heckman. (2009). 'The Economics and Psychology of Inequality and Human Development'. *Journal of the European Economic Association* 7 (2/3): 320–64.

Curry, Haskell B. and Robert Feys. (1958). *Combinatory Logic*. Amsterdam: North-Holland Publishing Company.

Dagum, Camilo, and Michele Zenga, eds. (1990). *Income and Wealth Distribution, Inequality and Poverty*. Studies in Contemporary Economics. Berlin: Springer Verlag.

Dahl, Robert A. (1956). *A Preface to Democratic Theory, Expanded Edition*. Chicago: University of Chicago Press.

Dahl, Robert Alan and Charles Lindblom. (1954). *Politics, Economics, and Welfare*. New York: Harper.

Daniel, T. E. (1975). 'A Revised Concept of Distributional Equity'. *Journal of Economic Theory* 11 (1): 94–109.

Daniels, Norman. (2008). *Just Health: Meeting Health Needs Fairly*. Cambridge: Cambridge University Press.

Danielson, Peter. (1973). 'Theories, Institutions and the Problem of World-Wide Distributive Justice'. *Philosophy of the Social Sciences* 3: 331–8.

Dasgupta, M. and R. Deb. (1991). 'Fuzzy Choice Functions'. *Social Choice and Welfare* 8 (2): 171–82.

———. (1996). 'Transitivity and Fuzzy Preferences'. *Social Choice and Welfare* 13 (3): 305–18.

———. (1999). 'An Impossibility Theorem with Fuzzy Preferences'. In *Logic, Game Theory and Social Choice*, edited by H. de Swart. Tilburg, Netherlands: Tilburg University Press, 482–90.

———. (2001). 'Factoring Fuzzy Transitivity'. *Fuzzy Sets Systems* 118 (3): 489–502.

Dasgupta, Partha and Eric Maskin. (2008a). 'On the Robustness of Majority Rule'. *Journal of the European Economic Association* 6 (5): 949–73.

———. (2008b). 'Ranking Candidates Is More Accurate Than Voting'. *Scientific American*, 6 October.

Dasgupta, Partha, Peter J. Hammond and Eric Maskin. (1979). 'The Implementation of Social Choice Rules: Some General Results on

Incentive Compatibility'. *Review of Economic Studies* 46 (2): 185–216.

d'Aspremont, Claude. (1985). 'Axioms for Social Welfare Orderings'. In *Social Goals and Social Organization: Essays in Memory of Elisha Pazner*, edited by Leonid Hurwicz, David Schmeidler and Hugo Sonnenschein. Cambridge: Cambridge University Press.

d'Aspremont, Claude and Louis Gevers. (1977). 'Equity and the Informational Basis of Collective Choice'. *The Review of Economic Studies* 44 (2): 199–209.

———. (2002). 'Social Welfare Functionals and Interpersonal Comparability'. In Arrow, Sen and Suzumura (2002):459–541.

d'Aspremont, Claude and Philippe Mongin. (1997). 'A Welfarist Version of Harsanyi's Aggregation Theorem'. CORE Discussion Paper 1997063. Université Catholique de Louvain, Center for Operations Research and Econometrics (CORE).

———. (1998). 'Utility Theory and Ethics'. In *Handbook of Utility Theory*, edited by S. Barberà, P. J. Hammond and C. Seidl. Dordrecht: Kluwer Academic, vol. 1: 371–481.

Davidson, Donald. (1980). *Essays on Actions and Events*. Oxford: Oxford University Press; 2nd edn, 2001.

———. (1986). 'Judging Interpersonal Interests'. In *Foundations of Social Choice Theory*, edited by Jon Elster and Aanund Hylland, Cambridge: Cambridge University Press, 195–211.

Davidson, Donald and Patrick Suppes. (1956). 'A Finitistic Axiomatization of Subjective Probability and Utility'. *Econometrica* 24 (3): 264–75.

Davis, Otto A., Morris H. DeGroot and Melvin Hinich. (1972). 'Social Preference Orderings and Majority Rule'. *Econometrica* 40 (1): 147–57.

Davis, R. G. (1958). 'Comment on Arrow and the "New Welfare Economics"'. *Economic Journal* 68: 834–5.

Deaton, Angus S. (1995). *Microeconomic Analysis for Development Policy: An Approach from Household Surveys*. Baltimore: Johns Hopkins Press (for the World Bank).

———. (2013). *The Great Escape: Health, Wealth, and the Origins of Inequality*. Princeton N. J.: Princeton University Press.

Deaton, Angus S. and John Muellbauer. (1980a.) 'An Almost Ideal Demand System'. *American Economic Review* 70 (3): 312–26.

———. (1980b). *Economics and Consumer Behaviour*. Cambridge: Cambridge University Press.

——. (1986). 'On Measuring Child Costs: With Applications to Poor Countries'. *Journal of Political Economy* 94 (4): 720–44.

Deb, Rajat. (1976). 'On Constructing Generalized Voting Paradoxes'. *The Review of Economic Studies* 43 (2): 347–51.

——. (1977). 'On Schwartz's Rule'. *Journal of Economic Theory* 16 (1): 103–10.

——. (1994). 'Waiver, Effectivity and Rights as Game Forms'. *Economica* 61 (242): 167–78.

Deb, Rajat. (2011). 'Nonbinary Social Choice'. In Arrow, Sen and Suzumura (2011a): 335–66.

Deb, Rajat, Indranil K. Ghosh and Tae Kun Seo. (2009). 'Justice, Equity and Sharing the Cost of a Public Project'. In Basu and Kanbur (2009), vol. I: 501–22.

Debreu, Gerard. (1954). 'Representation of a Preference Ordering by a Numerical Function'. In *Decision Processes*, edited by R. M. Thrall, Clyde H. Coombs and R. L. Davis. New York: Wiley, 159–65.

——. (1959). *Theory of Value: An Axiomatic Analysis of Economic Equilibrium*. New Haven: Yale University Press.

——. (1960). 'Topological Methods in Cardinal Utility Theory'. In Arrow, Karlin and Suppes (1960a)

De Grazia, A. (1953). 'Mathematical Derivation of an Election System'. *Isis*, 44: 42–51.

De Meyer, Frank and Charles R. Plott. (1970). 'The Probability of a Cyclical Majority'. *Econometrica* 38 (2): 345–54.

Denicolò, Vincenzo. (1985). 'Independent Social Choice Correspondences Are Dictatorial'. *Economics Letters* 19 (1): 9–12.

——. (1987). 'Some Further Results on Nonbinary Social Choice'. *Social Choice and Welfare* 4 (4): 277–85.

Denzau, A. T. and R. P. Parks. (1975). 'The Continuity of Majority Rule Equilibrium'. *Econometrica* 43 (5/6): 853–66.

Desai, Meghnad. (1994). *Poverty, Famine, and Economic Development*. London: Edward Elgar Publishing.

——. (1995). 'Measuring Political Freedom'. In *On Freedom: A Centenary Anthology*, edited by E. Barker. London: LSE Books.

Deschamps, Robert and Louis Gevers. (1977). 'Separability, Risk-bearing, and Social Welfare Judgments'. *European Economic Review* 10 (1): 77–94.

——. (1978). 'Leximin and Utilitarian Rules: A Joint Characterization'. *Journal of Economic Theory* 17 (2): 143–63.

——. (1979). 'Separability, Risk-bearing and Social Welfare Judgments'. In Laffont (1979).

Diamond, Peter A. (1967). 'Cardinal Welfare, Individualistic Ethics, and Interpersonal Comparison of Utility: Comment'. *Journal of Political Economy* 75 (5): 765.

Dietz, Simon, Cameron Hepburn and Nicholas Stern. (2009). 'Economics, Ethics and Climate Change'. In Basu and Kanbur (2009), vol. II: 365–86.

Dobb, Maurice H. (1955). *On Economic Theory & Socialism: Collected Papers*. New York: Routledge.

———. (1956). 'A Note on Index-Numbers and Compensation Criteria'. *Oxford Economic Papers* 8 (1): 78–9.

———. (1963). 'A Further Comment on the Discussion of Welfare Criteria'. *The Economic Journal* 73 (292): 765–71.

———. (1969). *Welfare Economics and the Economics of Socialism: Towards a Commonsense Critique*. Cambridge: Cambridge University Press.

Dodgson, Charles. (1876). *A Method of Taking Votes on More than Two Issues*. Oxford: Oxford University Press.

———. (1884). *The Principles of Parliamentary Representation*. London: Harrison and Sons.

Downs, Anthony. (1957). *An Economic Theory of Democracy*. New York: Harper.

———. (1961). 'Problems of Majority Voting: In Defense of Majority Voting'. *Journal of Political Economy* 69 (2): 192–9.

Drèze, Jean and Mamta Murthi. (2001). 'Fertility, Education and Development: Evidence from India'. *Population and Development Review* 27.

Drèze, Jean and Amartya K. Sen. (1989). *Hunger and Public Action*. Oxford: Oxford University Press.

———. eds. (1990). *The Political Economy of Hunger*. New York and Oxford: Oxford University Press.

———. (1995). *Economic Development and Social Opportunity*. Delhi: Oxford University Press.

———. (1997). *Indian Development: Selected Regional Perspectives*. Delhi and New York: Oxford University Press.

———. (2002). *India: Development and Participation*. Delhi: Oxford University Press.

———. (2013). *An Uncertain Glory: India and Its Contradictions*. Delhi: Penguin and Princeton, N. J.: Princeton University Press.

Dummett, Michael and Robin Farquharson. (1961). 'Stability in Voting'. *Econometrica* 29 (1): 33–43.

Dutta, Bhaskar. (1980). 'On the Possibility of Consistent Voting Procedures'. *Review of Economic Studies* 47 (3): 603–16.

———. (1987). 'Fuzzy Preferences and Social Choice'. *Mathematical Social Sciences*, 13: 215–29.

———. (1997). 'Reasonable Mechanisms and Nash Implementation'. In Arrow, Sen and Suzumura (1997).

———. (2002). 'Inequality, Poverty and Welfare'. In Arrow, Sen and Suzumura (2002).

———. (2009). 'Some Remarks on the Ranking of Infinite Utility Streams'. In Basu and Kanbur (2009), vol. I: 136–47.

Dutta, Bhaskar and Prasanta K. Pattanaik. (1978). 'On Nicely Consistent Voting Systems'. *Econometrica* 46 (1): 163–70.

Dworkin, Ronald. (1981a). 'What Is Equality? Part 1: Equality of Welfare'. *Philosophy and Public Affairs* 10 (3): 185–246.

———. (1981b). 'What Is Equality? Part 2: Equality of Resources'. *Philosophy and Public Affairs* 10 (4): 283–345.

———. (1995). 'Constitutionalism and Democracy'. *European Journal of Philosophy* 3 (1): 2–11.

———. (2008). *Is Democracy Possible Here? Principles for a New Political Debate*. Princeton, N. J.: Princeton University Press.

Edgeworth, Francis Ysidro. (1881). *Mathematical Psychics: An Essay on the Application of Mathematics to the Moral Sciences*. London: C. K. Paul.

Eilenberg, Samuel. (1941). 'Ordered Topological Spaces'. *American Journal of Mathematics* 63 (1): 39–45.

Ellman, Michael J. (1966). 'Individual Preferences and the Market'. *Economics of Planning* 6 (3): 241–50.

Ellsberg, Daniel. (1954). 'Classic and Current Notions of "Measurable Utility".' *The Economic Journal* 64: 528–56.

———. (1961). 'Risk, Ambiguity, and the Savage Axioms'. *The Quarterly Journal of Economics* 75 (4): 643–69.

———. (1963). 'Risk, Ambiguity, and the Savage Axioms: Reply'. *The Quarterly Journal of Economics* 77 (2): 336–42.

Elster, Jon and Aanund Hylland, eds. (1986). *Foundations of Social Choice Theory*. Cambridge: Cambridge University Press.

Elster, Jon and John E. Roemer, eds. (1991). *Interpersonal Comparisons of Well-Being*. Cambridge: Cambridge University Press.

Fagen, Richard R. (1961). 'Some Contributions of Mathematical Reasoning to the Study of Politics'. *The American Political Science Review* 55 (4): 888–900.

Farkas, Daniel and Shmuel Nitzan. (1979). 'The Borda Rule and Pareto Stability: A Comment'. *Econometrica* 47 (5): 1305–6.

Farquharson, Robin. (1957). 'An Approach to the Pure Theory of Voting Procedure'. Ph.D. Thesis, Oxford University.

Farrell, M. J. (1959). 'Mr. Lancaster on Welfare and Choice'. *The Economic Journal* 69 (275): 588.

———. (1976). 'Liberalism in the Theory of Social Choice'. *The Review of Economic Studies* 43 (1): 3–10.

Feldman, Allan M. (1980). *Welfare Economics and Social Choice Theory*. Boston, Mass.: Martinus Njihoff.

Feldman, Allan M. and Alan P. Kirman, (1974). 'Fairness and Envy'. *American Economic Review* 64 (6): 995–1005.

Feldman, Allan M. and David Weiman. (1979). 'Envy, Wealth, and Class Hierarchies'. *Journal of Public Economics* 11 (1): 81–91.

Fenchel, W. (1953). 'Convex Cones, Sets, and Functions'. Mimeographed. Department of Mathematics, Princeton University.

Ferejohn, John A. (1977). 'Decisive Coalitions in the Theory of Social Choice'. *Journal of Economic Theory* 15 (2): 301–6.

Ferejohn, John A. and Morris P. Fiorina. (1974). 'The Paradox of Not Voting: A Decision Theoretic Analysis'. *American Political Science Review* 68 (2): 525–36.

Ferejohn, John A. and David M. Grether. (1974). 'On a Class of Rational Social Decision Procedures'. *Journal of Economic Theory* 8 (4): 471–82.

Ferejohn, John A., David M. Grether, Steven A. Matthews and Edward W. Packel. (1980). 'Continuous-Valued Binary Decision Procedures'. *The Review of Economic Studies* 47 (4): 787–96.

Fields, G. S. and E. A. Ok. (1998). 'On the Evaluation of Economic Mobility'. Mimeographed, Boston College.

Fine, Ben. (1975). 'A Note on "Interpersonal Aggregation and Partial Comparability"'. *Econometrica* 43 (1): 169–72.

Fine, Ben and Kit Fine. (1974). 'Social Choice and Individual Rankings II'. *The Review of Economic Studies* 41 (4): 459–75.

Fishburn, Peter C. (1967). 'Interdependence and Additivity in Multivariate, Unidimensional Expected Utility Theory'. *International Economic Review* 8 (3): 335–42.

———. (1970a). 'Arrow's Impossibility Theorem: Concise Proof and Infinite Voters'. *Journal of Economic Theory* 2 (1): 103–6.

———. (1970b). 'Suborders on Commodity Spaces'. *Journal of Economic Theory* 2 (4): 321–8.

————. (1970c). 'Intransitive Individual Indifference and Transitive Majorities'. *Econometrica* 38: 482–9.

————. (1972). 'Lotteries and Social Choices'. *Journal of Economic Theory* 5 (2): 189–207.

————. (1973). *The Theory of Social Choice*. Princeton, N. J.: Princeton University Press.

————. (1974). 'On Collective Rationality and a Generalized Impossibility Theorem'. *The Review of Economic Studies* 41 (4): 445–57.

————. (1975). 'Semiorders and Choice Functions'. *Econometrica* 43 (5/6): 975–7.

Fishburn, Peter C. and William V. Gehrlein. (1976). 'Borda's Rule, Positional Voting, and Condorcet's Simple Majority Principle'. *Public Choice* 28 (1): 79–88.

Fisher, Franklin M. (1956). 'Income Distribution, Value Judgments, and Welfare'. *The Quarterly Journal of Economics* 70 (3): 380–424.

————. (1987). 'Household Equivalence Scales and Interpersonal Comparisons'. *The Review of Economic Studies* 54 (3): 519–24.

Fisher, Franklin M. and Jerome Rothenberg. (1961). 'How Income Ought to Be Distributed: Paradox Lost'. *Journal of Political Economy* 69 (2): 162–80.

————. (1962). 'How Income Ought to Be Distributed: Paradox Enow'. *Journal of Political Economy* 70 (1): 88–93.

Fleming, Marcus. (1952). 'A Cardinal Concept of Welfare'. *The Quarterly Journal of Economics* 66 (3): 366–84.

————. (1957). 'Cardinal Welfare and Individualistic Ethics: A Comment'. *Journal of Political Economy* 65 (4): 355–7.

Fleurbaey, Marc. (1995a). 'Equality and Responsibility'. *European Economic Review* 39 (3–4): 683–9.

————. (1995b). 'Equal Opportunity or Equal Social Outcome?' *Economics and Philosophy* 11 (1): 25–55.

————. (2002). 'Development, Capabilities, and Freedom'. *Studies in Comparative International Development* 37 (2): 71–7.

————. (2008). *Fairness, Responsibility, and Welfare*. Oxford: Oxford University Press.

Fleurbaey, Marc and Didier Blanchet. (2013). *Beyond GDP: Measuring Welfare and Assessing Sustainability*. Oxford: Oxford University Press.

Fleurbaey, Marc and Wulf Gaertner. (1996). 'Admissibility and Feasibility in Game Forms'. *Analyse & Kritik* 18 (1): 54–66.

Fleurbaey, Marc and François Maniquet. (2011a). 'Compensation and Responsibility'. In Arrow, Sen and Suzumura (2011a): 507–604.

——. (2011b). *A Theory of Fairness and Social Welfare*. Cambridge: Cambridge University Press.

——. (2012). *Equality of Opportunity: The Economics of Responsibility*. Hackensack, N. J.: World Scientific.

Fleurbaey, Marc and Vito Peragine. (2013). 'Ex Ante versus Ex Post Equality of Opportunity'. *Economica* 80 (317): 118–30.

Folbre, Nancy. (1995). *Who Pays for the Kids? Gender and the Structures of Constraint*. London and New York: Routledge.

Foley, Duncan K. (1967). 'Resource Allocation and the Public Sector'. *Yale Economic Essays* 7 (1): 73–6.

——. (1998). 'Resource Allocation and the Public Sector.' *Yale Economic Essays* 7 (1): 45–98.

Follesdal, Andreas and Thomas Pogge, eds. (2005). *Real World Justice*. Berlin: Springer-Verlag.

Foster, James E. (1984). 'On Economic Poverty: A Survey of Aggregate Measures'. *Advances in Econometrics* 3: 215–51.

——. (1985). 'Inequality Measurement'. In *Fair Allocation*, edited by H. P. Young, Providence, R. I.: American Mathematical Society, 31–68.

——. (2011). 'Freedom, Opportunity, and Well-Being'. In Arrow, Sen and Suzumura (2011a): 687–728.

Foster, James E. and Christopher Handy. (2009). 'External Capabilities'. In Basu and Kanbur (2009), vol. I: 362–74.

Foster, James E. and Amartya K. Sen. (1997). 'Addendum to Economic Inequality'. In *On Economic Inequality* by Amartya K. Sen. Oxford: Oxford University Press, 1973; enlarged edition 1997.

Foster, James E. and Anthony F. Shorrocks. (1988). 'Poverty Orderings'. *Econometrica* 56 (1): 173–7.

Foster, James E., Joel Greer and Erik Thorbecke. (1984). 'A Class of Decomposable Poverty Measures'. *Econometrica* 52 (3): 761–6.

Friedman, Milton. (1947). 'Lerner on the Economics of Control'. *Journal of Political Economy* 55 (5): 405–16.

——. (1953). *Essays in Positive Economics*. Chicago: University of Chicago Press.

Friedman, Milton and L. J. Savage. (1948). 'The Utility Analysis of Choices Involving Risk'. *Journal of Political Economy* 56 (4): 279–304.

——. (1952). 'The Expected-Utility Hypothesis and the Measurability of Utility'. *Journal of Political Economy* 60 (6): 463–74.

Frisch, R. (1932). *New Methods of Measuring Marginal Utility*. Tübingen: Mohr.

————. (1966). *Maxima and Minima: Theory and Economic Applications*. New York: Rand McNally.

Fukuda-Parr, Sakiko. (2009). 'Human Rights and Human Development'. In Basu and Kanbur (2009), vol. II: 76–99.

Fukuda-Parr, Sakiko and A. K. Shiva Kumar, eds. (2003). *Readings in Human Development*. New Delhi: Oxford University Press.

Gaertner, Wulf. (1979). 'An Analysis and Comparison of Several Necessary and Sufficient Conditions for Transitivity under the Majority Decision Rule'. In Laffont (1979).

————. (1983). 'Equity- and Inequity-type Borda Rules'. *Mathematical Social Sciences* 4 (2): 137–54.

————. (1993). 'Amartya Sen: Capability and Well-being'. In *The Quality of Life*, by Martha C. Nussbaum and Amartya K. Sen. Oxford: Oxford University Press.

————. (2001). *Domain Conditions in Social Choice Theory*. Cambridge: Cambridge University Press.

————. (2002). 'Domain Restrictions'. In Arrow, Sen and Suzumura (2002): 131–70.

————. (2013). 'Social Choice Theory.' In *Encyclopedia of Philosophy and the Social Sciences*, edited by Byron Kaldis. Thousand Oaks, Calif.: Sage Publications, Inc.

Gaertner, Wulf and Achim Heinecke. (1978). 'Cyclically Mixed Preferences – A Necessary and Sufficient Condition for Transitivity of the Social Preference Relation'. In *Decision Theory and Social Ethics*, edited by Hans W. Gottinger and Werner Leinfellner. Theory and Decision Library 17. Amsterdam: Springer Netherlands, 169–85.

Gaertner, Wulf and Lorenz Krüger. (1981). 'Self-Supporting Preferences and Individual Rights: The Possibility of Paretian Libertarianism'. *Economica* 48 (189): 17–28.

————. (1983). 'Alternative Libertarian Claims and Sen's Paradox [Rev. Vers.]'. *Theory and Decision* 15 (3): 211–29.

Gaertner, Wulf and Eric Schokkaert. (2012). *Empirical Social Choice: Questionnaire-Experimental Studies on Distributive Justice*. Cambridge: Cambridge University Press.

Gaertner, Wulf and Yongsheng Xu. (1997). 'Optimization and External Reference; a Comparison of Three Axiomatic Systems'. *Economics Letters* 57 (1): 57–62.

————. (1999a). 'On Rationalizability of Choice Functions: A Characterization of the Median'. *Social Choice and Welfare* 16 (4): 629–38.

———. (1999b). 'On the Structure of Choice under Different External References'. *Economic Theory* 14 (3): 609–20.

———. (2009). 'Individual Choices in a Non-Consequentialist Framework: A Procedural Approach'. In Basu and Kanbur (2009), vol. I: 148–66.

———. (2011). 'Reference-dependent Rankings of Sets in Characteristics Space'. *Social Choice and Welfare* 37: 717–28.

Gaertner, Wulf, Prasanta K. Pattanaik and Kotaro Suzumura. (1992). 'Individual Rights Revisited'. *Economica* 59 (234): 161–77.

Gärdenfors, Peter. (1973). 'Positionalist Voting Functions'. *Theory and Decision* 4 (1): 1–24.

———. (1975). 'Match Making: Assignments Based on Bilateral Preferences'. *Behavioral Science* 20 (3): 166–73.

———. (1981). 'Rights, Games and Social Choice'. *Noûs* 15 (3): 341–56.

Gardner, Roy. (1977). 'The Borda Game'. *Public Choice* 30 (1): 43–50.

———. (1980). 'The Strategic Inconsistency of Paretian Liberalism'. *Public Choice* 35 (2): 241–52.

Garman, Mark B. and Morton I. Kamien. (1968). 'The Paradox of Voting: Probability Calculations'. *Behavioral Science* 13 (4): 306–16.

Gauthier, David P. (1967). 'Morality and Advantage'. *Philosophical Review* 76 (4): 460–75.

———. (1968). 'Hare's Debtors'. *Mind* 77 (307): 400–405.

Geanakopolous, John. (1996). 'Three Brief Proofs of Arrow's Impossibility Theorem'. Cowles Foundation Discussion Paper No. 1128. Yale University.

Gehrlein, William. (1983). 'Condorcet's Paradox'. *Theory and Decision* 15 (2): 161–97.

Georgescu-Roegen, Nicolas. (1966). *Analytical Economics*. Cambridge, Mass.: Harvard University Press.

Gevers, Louis. (1979). 'On Interpersonal Comparability and Social Welfare Orderings'. *Econometrica* 47 (1): 75–89.

Ghai, Dharam P., Azizur R. Khan, E. Lee and T. A. Alfthan. (1977). *The Basic-Needs Approach to Development. Some Issues Regarding Concepts and Methodology*. Geneva: International Labour Organization.

Gibbard, Allan F. (1973). 'Manipulation of Voting Schemes: A General Result'. *Econometrica* 41 (4): 587–601.

———. (1974). 'A Pareto-Consistent Libertarian Claim'. *Journal of Economic Theory* 7 (4): 388–410.

———. (1986). 'Interpersonal Comparison: Preference, Good, and the Intrinsic Reward of Life'. In *Foundations of Social Choice Theory*, edited by Jon Elster and Aanund Hylland. Cambridge: Cambridge University Press.

———. (2014). 'Social Choice and the Arrow Conditions'. *Economics and Philosophy* 30 (3): 269–84.

Glover, Jonathan. (1977) *Causing Death and Saving Lives*. Harmondsworth: Penguin.

Glover, Jonathan. (2009). 'Identity, Violence and the Power of Illusion'. In Basu and Kanbur (2009), vol. II: 436–51.

Goldin, Ian. (2016). *The Pursuit of Development: Economic Growth, Social Change, and Ideas*. Oxford: Oxford University Press.

Goldman, Steven and Chal Sussangkarn. (1978). 'On the Concept of Fairness'. *Journal of Economic Theory* 19 (1): 210–16.

Goodin, Robert E. (1988). *Reasons for Welfare: The Political Theory of the Welfare State*. Princeton, N. J.: Princeton University Press.

Goodin, Robert, Philip Pettit and Thomas Pogge, eds. (2007). *A Companion to Contemporary Political Philosophy*. Oxford: Blackwell.

Goodman, Leo A. and Harry Markowitz. (1952). 'Social Welfare Functions Based on Individual Rankings'. *American Journal of Sociology* 58 (3): 257–62.

Gorman, W. M. (1953). 'Community Preference Fields'. *Econometrica* 21 (1): 63–80.

———. (1955). 'The Intransitivity of Certain Criteria Used in Welfare Economics'. *Oxford Economic Papers* VII (1): 25–34.

———. (1959). 'Are Social Indifference Curves Convex?' *The Quarterly Journal of Economics* 73 (3): 485–96.

———. (1968). 'The Structure of Utility Functions'. *The Review of Economic Studies* 35 (4): 367–90.

Gotoh, Reiko. (2001). 'The Capability Theory and Welfare Reform'. *Pacific Economic Review* 6 (2): 211–22.

———. (2009). 'Justice and Public Reciprocity'. In Gotoh and Dumouchel (2009a).

Gotoh, Reiko and Paul Dumouchel, eds. (2009a). *Against Injustice: The New Economics of Amartya Sen*. Cambridge: Cambridge University Press.

———. (2009b). 'Introduction'. In Gotoh and Dumouchel (2009a).

Graaff, Johannes de Villiers. (1949). 'On Optimum Tariff Structures'. *Review of Economic Studies* 17.

———. (1957). *Theoretical Welfare Economics*. Cambridge: Cambridge University Press.

———. (1962). 'On Making a Recommendation in a Democracy'. *The Economic Journal* 72 (286): 293–8.

Gráda, Cormac Ó. (2009). *Famine: A Short History*. Princeton, N. J.: Princeton University Press.

Gramsci, Antonio. (1967). *The Modern Prince and Other Writings*. Translated by L. Marks. London: Lawrence and Wishart.

———. (1971). *Selection from the Prison Notebooks*. London: Lawrence and Wishart.

Granaglia, Elena. (1994). 'Più o Meno Eguaglianza di Risorse? Un Falso Problema per Le Politiche Sociali'. *Giornale degli Economisti e Annali di Economia* 53 (7/9): 349–66.

———. (1996). 'Two Questions to Amartya Sen'. *Politeia* 43/44: 31–6.

Grandmont, Jean-Michel. (1978). 'Intermediate Preferences and the Majority Rule'. *Econometrica* 46 (2): 317–30.

Granger, G. G. (1956). *La Mathématique sociale du marquis de Condorcet*. Paris: Presses Universitaires de France.

Grant, James P. (1978). *Disparity Reduction Rates in Social Insurance*. Washington, D. C.: Overseas Development Council.

Green, Jerry R. and Jean-Jacques Laffont. (1979). *Incentives in Public Decision-Making*. Amsterdam: Elsevier Science Ltd.

Grether, David M. and Charles R. Plott. (1982). 'Nonbinary Social Choice: An Impossibility Theorem'. *Review of Economic Studies* 49 (1): 143–9.

Griffin, Keith B. and John B. Knight. (1990). *Human Development and the International Development Strategy for the 1990s*. London: Macmillan.

Grotius, Hugo. (1609). *Mare Liberum*. Lodewijk Elzevir.

Groves, Theodore and John O. Ledyard. (1977). 'Optimal Allocation of Public Goods: A Solution to the "Free Rider" Problem'. *Econometrica* 45 (4): 783–809.

Guha, A. S. (1972). 'Neutrality, Monotonicity, and the Right of Veto'. *Econometrica* 40 (5): 821–6.

Guilbaud, Georges-Théodule. (1952). 'Les théories de l'intérêt général et le probléme logique de l'agrégation'. *Economie Appliquée* 5 (4): 501–84.

———. (1966). 'Les théories de l'intérêt général et le probléme logique de l'agrégation (Engligh Translation)'. In *Readings in Mathematical Social Sciences*, edited by P. F. Lazarsfeld and N. W. Henry. Chicago: Science Research Associates.

Guinier, Lani. (1991). *The Tyranny of the Majority: Fundamental Fairness in Representative Democracy*. New York: Free Press.

Gutman, Amy and Dennis Thompson. (2004). *Why Deliberative Democracy?* Princeton, N. J.: Princeton University Press.

Habermas, Jürgen. (1989). *The Structural Transformation of the Public Sphere: An Inquiry Into a Category of Bourgeois Society.* Cambridge, Mass.: MIT Press.

———. (1990). *Moral Consciousness and Communicative Action.* Cambridge, Mass.: MIT Press.

Haddad, Lawrence and Ravi Kanbur. (1990). 'How Serious Is the Neglect of Intra-Household Inequality?' *The Economic Journal* 100 (402): 866–81.

Halmos, Paul Richard. (1962). *Algebraic Logic.* New York: Chelsea.

Hamlin, Alan P. and Philip Pettit. (1989). *The Good Polity: Normative Analysis of the State.* Oxford: Blackwell.

Hammond, Peter J. (1975). 'A Note on Extreme Inequality Aversion'. *Journal of Economic Theory* 11 (3): 465–7.

———. (1976). 'Equity, Arrow's Conditions, and Rawls' Difference Principle'. *Econometrica* 44 (4): 793–804.

———. (1977). 'Dual Interpersonal Comparisons of Utility and the Welfare Economics of Income Distribution'. *Journal of Public Economics* 7 (1): 51–71.

———. (1979a). 'Equity in Two Person Situations: Some Consequences'. *Econometrica* 47: 1127–36.

———. (1979b). 'Straightforward Individual Incentive Compatibility in Large Economies'. *Review of Economic Studies* 46: 263–82.

———. (1982a). 'Liberalism, Independent Rights and the Pareto Principle'. In *Logic, Methodology, and Philosophy of Science VI: Proceedings of the Sixth International Congress of Logic, Methodology, and Philosophy of Science, Hanover 1979*, edited by L. Jonathan Cohen. Amsterdam: Elsevier North-Holland.

———. (1982b). 'Utilitarianism, Uncertainty and Information'. In *Utilitarianism and Beyond*, edited by Amartya K. Sen and Bernard Williams. Cambridge: Cambridge University Press, 85–102.

———. (1985). 'Welfare Economics'. In *Issues in Contemporary Microeconomics and Welfare*, edited by G. Feiwel. Albany, N. Y.: SUNY Press, 405–34.

———. (1997a). 'Game Forms versus Social Choice Rules as Models of Rights'. In Arrow, Sen and Suzumura (1997): 82–95.

———. (1997b). 'Non-Archimedean Subjective Probabilities in Decision Theory and Games'. Working Paper 97038. Stanford University, Department of Economics.

———. (2009). 'Isolation, Assurance and Rules: Can Rational Folly Supplant Foolish Rationality?' In Basu and Kanbur (2009), vol. I: 523–34.

———. (2011). 'Competitive Market Mechanisms as Social Choice Procedures'. In Arrow, Sen and Suzumura (2011a), 47–151.

Hansson, Bengt. (1968). 'Choice Structures and Preference Relations'. *Synthese* 18 (4): 443–58.

———. (1969a). 'On Group Preferences'. *Econometrica* 37 (1): 50–54.

———. (1969b). 'Voting and Group Decision Functions'. *Synthese* 20 (4): 526–37.

———. (1972). 'The Existence of Group Preferences'. Working Paper No. 3. Lund, Sweden: The Mattias Fremling Society.

———. (1973). 'The Independence Condition in the Theory of Social Choice'. *Theory and Decision* 4 (1): 25–49.

———. (1976). 'The Existence of Group Preference Functions'. *Public Choice* 28 (1): 89–98.

Hansson, Bengt and Henrik Sahlquist. (1976). 'A Proof Technique for Social Choice with Variable Electorate'. *Journal of Economic Theory* 13 (2): 193–200.

Hare, R. M. (1963a). *Freedom and Reason*. Oxford: Oxford University Press.

———. (1963b). *The Language of Morals*. Oxford: Oxford University Press.

Harriss, Barbara. (1990). 'The Intrafamily Distribution of Hunger in South Asia'. In *The Political Economy of Hunger*, edited by Jean Drèze and Amartya K. Sen. New York and Oxford: Oxford University Press.

Harsanyi, John C. (1953). 'Cardinal Utility in Welfare Economics and in the Theory of Risk-Taking'. *Journal of Political Economy* 61: 434–5.

———. (1955). 'Cardinal Welfare, Individualistic Ethics, and Interpersonal Comparisons of Utility'. *Journal of Political Economy* 63 (4): 309–21.

———. (1956). 'Approaches to the Bargaining Problem Before and After the Theory of Games: A Critical Discussion of Zeuthen's, Hicks', and Nash's Theories'. *Econometrica* 24 (2): 144–57.

———. (1958). 'Ethics in Terms of Hypothetical Imperatives'. *Mind* 67 (267): 305–16.

———. (1966). 'A General Theory of Rational Behavior in Game Situations'. *Econometrica* 34 (3): 613–34.

———. (1977). *Rational Behaviour and Bargaining Equilibrium in Games and Social Situations*. Cambridge: Cambridge University Press.

———. (1979). 'Bayesian Decision Theory, Rule Utilitarianism, and Arrow's Impossibility Theorem'. *Theory and Decision* 11 (3): 289–317.

Hart, H. L. A. (1955). 'Are There Any Natural Rights?' *The Philosophical Review* 64 (2): 175–91.

———. (1973). 'Rawls on Liberty and Its Priority'. *The University of Chicago Law Review* 40 (3): 534–55.

Hayek, Friedrich August. (1960). *The Constitution of Liberty*. Chicago: University of Chicago Press.

Heckman, James J. (2007). 'The Economics, Technology, and Neuroscience of Human Capability Formation'. *Proceedings of the National Academy of Sciences* 104 (33): 13250–55.

———. (2012). *Giving Kids a Fair Chance*. Cambridge, Mass.: MIT Press.

Heckman, James, Robert Nelson and Lee Cabatingan, eds. (2009). *Global Perspectives on the Rule of Law*. New York: Routledge.

Hees, Martin van. (1996). 'Individual Rights and Legal Validity'. *Analyse & Kritik* 18 (1): 81–95.

———. (1998). 'On the Analysis of Negative Freedom'. *Theory and Decision* 45 (2): 175–97.

Heller, Walter P., Ross M. Starr and David A. Starrett, eds. (1986). *Social Choice and Public Decision Making: Essays in Honor of Kenneth J. Arrow*. Vol. 1. Cambridge: Cambridge University Press.

Herrero, Carmen. (1996). 'Capabilities and Utilities'. *Review of Economic Design* 2 (1): 69–88.

Herstein, I. N. and John Milnor. (1953). 'An Axiomatic Approach to Measurable Utility'. *Econometrica* 21 (2): 291–7.

Herzberger, Hans G. (1973). 'Ordinal Preference and Rational Choice'. *Econometrica* 41 (2): 187–237.

Hicks, John R. (1939a). 'The Foundations of Welfare Economics'. *The Economic Journal* 49 (196): 696–712.

———. (1939b). *Value and Capital: An Inquiry Into Some Fundamental Principles of Economic Theory*. Oxford: Oxford University Press.

———. (1940). 'The Valuation of the Social Income'. *Economica* 7 (26): 105–24.

———. (1941). 'The Rehabilitation of Consumers' Surplus'. *The Review of Economic Studies* 8 (2): 108–16.

———. (1942). 'Consumers' Surplus and Index-Numbers'. *The Review of Economic Studies* 9 (2): 126–37.

———. (1948). 'The Valuation of the Social Income – A Comment on Professor Kuznets' Reflections'. *Economica* 15 (59): 163–72.

———. (1956). *A Revision of Demand Theory*. Oxford: Oxford University Press.

Hilbert, David and Wilhelm Ackermann. (1960). *Principles of Mathematical Logic*. New York: Chelsea.

Hildreth, Clifford. (1953). 'Alternative Conditions for Social Orderings'. *Econometrica* 21 (1): 81–94.

Hinich, Melvin J. (1977). 'Equilibrium in Spatial Voting: The Median Voter Result Is an Artifact'. *Journal of Economic Theory* 16 (2): 208–19.

Hobsbawm, E. J. (1955). 'Where Are British Historians Going?' *The Marxist Quarterly* 2: 14–26.

Holland, Breena. (2014). *Allocating the Earth: A Distributional Framework for Protecting Capabilities in Environmental Law and Policy.* Oxford: Oxford University Press.

Hook, Sidney, ed. (1967). *Human Values and Economic Policy.* New York: New York University Press.

Hook, Sidney and Paul A. Samuelson, eds. (1967). 'Arrow's Mathematical Politics'. In *Human Values and Economic Policy.* New York: New York University Press.

Hooker, C. A., J. J. Leach and E. F. McClennen, eds. (1978). *Foundations and Applications of Decision Theory.* Vol.1: *Theoretical Foundations.* Dordrecht and Boston: D. Reidel Publishing Company.

Hossain, Iftekhar. (1990). *Poverty as Capability Failure.* Helsinki: Swedish School of Economics and Business Administration.

Houthakker, H. S. (1950). 'Revealed Preference and the Utility Function'. *Economica* 17 (66): 159–74.

———. (1965). 'On the Logic of Preference and Choice'. In *Contributions to Logic and Methodology in Honor of J. M. Bocheński*, edited by A.-T. Tymieniecka. Amsterdam: North-Holland.

Humphries, Jane and Kirsty McNay. (2009). 'Death and Gender in Victorian England'. In Basu and Kanbur (2009), vol. II: 259–79.

Hunt, Lynn. (2007). *Inventing Human Rights: A History.* New York: W. W. Norton & Company.

Huntington, Samuel P. (1991). *The Third Wave: Democratization in the Late Twentieth Century.* Norman: University of Oklahoma Press.

Hurwicz, L. (1951). 'Optimality Criteria for Decision Making under Ignorance'. Cowles Commission Discussion Paper, Statistics 370.

———. (1960). 'Optimality and Informational Efficiency in Resource Allocation Processes'. In *Mathematical Methods in the Social Sciences, 1959: Proceedings*, edited by Kenneth J. Arrow, Samuel Karlin and Patrick Suppes. Stanford: Stanford University Press.

Hurwicz, Leonid, David Schmeidler and Hugo Sonnenschein, eds. (1985). *Social Goals and Social Organization: Essays in Memory of Elisha Pazner.* Cambridge: Cambridge University Press.

Inada, Ken-ichi. (1955). 'Alternative Incompatible Conditions for a Social Welfare Function'. *Econometrica* 23 (4): 396–9.

———. (1964a). 'A Note on the Simple Majority Decision Rule'. *Econometrica* 32 (4): 525–31.

———. (1964b). 'On the Economic Welfare Function'. *Econometrica* 32 (3): 316–38.

———. (1969). 'On the Simple Majority Decision Rule'. *Econometrica* 37 (3): 490–506.

———. (1970). 'Majority Rule and Rationality'. *Journal of Economic Theory* 2 (1): 27–40.

Islam, Rizwanul. (2009). 'Has Development and Employment through Labour Intensive Industrialization Become History?' In Basu and Kanbur (2009), vol. II: 387–410.

Jain, Satish K. (2009). 'The Method of Majority Decision and Rationality Conditions'. In Basu and Kanbur (2009), vol. I: 167–92.

Jalal, Ayesha. (2009). 'Freedom and Equality: From Iqbal's Philosophy to Sen's Ethical Concerns'. In Basu and Kanbur (2009), vol. II: 452–69.

Jamison, Dean T. and Lawrence J. Lau. (1973). 'Semiorders and the Theory of Choice'. *Econometrica* 41 (5): 901–12.

———. (1977). 'The Nature of Equilibrium with Semiordered Preferences'. *Econometrica* 45 (7): 1595–1605.

Jasay, Anthony de and Hartmut Kliemt. (1996). 'The Paretian Liberal, His Liberties and His Contracts'. *Analyse & Kritik* 18 (1): 126–47.

Jeffrey, Richard C. (1971). 'On Interpersonal Utility Theory'. *The Journal of Philosophy* 68 (20): 647–56.

Jensen, Niels Erik. (1967). 'An Introduction to Bernoullian Utility Theory: I. Utility Functions'. *The Swedish Journal of Economics* 69 (3): 163–83.

Johansen, Leif. (1965). *Public Economics*. Amsterdam: North-Holland Publishing Company.

Jorgenson, Dale W. (1990). 'Aggregate Consumer Behavior and the Measurement of Social Welfare'. *Econometrica* 58 (5): 1007–40.

Jorgenson, Dale W., J. Steven Landefeld and Paul Schreyer, eds. (2014). *Measuring Economic Sustainability and Progress*. Chicago: University of Chicago Press.

Jorgenson, Dale W., Lawrence J. Lau and Thomas M. Stoker. (1980). 'Welfare Comparison under Exact Aggregation'. *American Economic Review* 70 (2): 268–72.

Kahn, R. F. (1935). 'Some Notes on Ideal Output'. *The Economic Journal* 45 (177): 1–35.

Kahneman, Daniel. (1999). 'Objective Happiness'. In *Well-Being: Foundations of Hedonic Psychology*, edited by Daniel Kahneman, Edward Diener and Norbert Schwarz. New York: Russell Sage Foundation.

———. (2000). 'Evaluation by Moments: Past and Future'. In *Choices, Values, and Frames*, edited by Daniel Kahneman and Amos Tversky. Cambridge: Cambridge University Press.

Kahneman, Daniel and Alan B. Krueger. (2006). 'Developments in the Measurement of Subjective Well-Being'. *The Journal of Economic Perspectives* 20 (1): 3–24.

Kahneman, Daniel and Amos Tversky, eds. (2000). *Choices, Values, and Frames*. Cambridge: Cambridge University Press.

Kahneman, Daniel, Jack L. Knetsch and Richard H. Thaler. (1990). 'Experimental Tests of the Endowment Effect and the Coase Theorem'. *Journal of Political Economy* 98 (6): 1325–48.

Kakwani, Nanak. (1981). 'Welfare Measures: An International Comparison'. *Journal of Development Economics* 8 (1): 21–45.

———. (1984). 'Issues in Measuring Poverty'. *Advances in Econometrics* 3: 253–82.

———. (1986). *Analysing Redistribution Policies*. Cambridge: Cambridge University Press.

Kakwani, Nanak and Jacques Silber, eds. (2008). *The Many Dimensions of Poverty*. London: Palgrave Macmillan.

Kalai, Ehud and Eitan Muller. (1977). 'Characterization of Domains Admitting Nondictatorial Social Welfare Functions and No manipulable Voting Procedures'. Discussion Paper 234. Northwestern University, Center for Mathematical Studies in Economics and Management Science.

Kalai, Ehud and Zvi Ritz. (1980). 'Characterization of the Private Alternatives Domains Admitting Arrow Social Welfare Functions'. *Journal of Economic Theory* 22 (1): 23–36.

Kalai, Ehud and Meir Smorodinsky. (1975). 'Other Solutions to Nash's Bargaining Problem'. *Econometrica* 43 (3): 513–18.

Kalai, Gil. (2002). 'Social Choice without Rationality'. Levine's Working Paper Archive. David K. Levine.

Kaldor, Mary. (2009). 'Protective Security or Protection Rackets? War and Sovereignty'. In Basu and Kanbur (2009), vol. II: 470–87.

Kaldor, Nicholas. (1939). 'Welfare Propositions in Economics'. *The Economic Journal* 49.

———. (1946). 'A Comment [on Baumol]'. *Review of Economic Studies* 14: 49.

Kamm, Frances M. (2007). *Intricate Ethics: Rights, Responsibilities, and Permissive Harm*. New York: Oxford University Press.

Kanbur, Ravi. (1984). 'The Measurement and Decomposition of Inequality and Poverty'. In *Mathematical Methods in Economics*, edited by Frederick van der Ploeg. New York: Wiley.

———. (1995). 'Children and Intra-Household Inequality: A Theoretical Analysis'. In Basu, Pattanaik and Suzumura (1995).

Kaneko, Mamoru. (1975). 'Necessary and Sufficient Conditions for Transitivity in Voting Theory'. *Journal of Economic Theory* 11 (3): 385–93.

———. (1980). 'An Extension of the Nash Bargaining Problem and the Nash Social Welfare Function'. *Theory and Decision* 12 (2): 135–48.

Kaneko, Mamoru and Kenjiro Nakamura. (1979). 'The Nash Social Welfare Function'. *Econometrica* 47 (2): 423–35.

Kanger, Stig. (1975). 'Choice Based on Preference'. Mimeographed. University of Uppsala.

———. (1985). 'On Realization of Human Rights'. *Acta Philosophica Fennica* 38: 71–8.

———. (2001). 'Choice Based on Preference'. In *Collected Papers of Stig Kanger with Essays on His Life and Work*, edited by Ghita Holmström-Hintikka, Sten Lindström and Rysiek Sliwinski. Synthese Library 303. Amsterdam: Springer Netherlands, 214–30.

Kant, Immanuel. (1785). *Grundlegung zur Metaphysik der Sitten*. English translation by T. K. Abbott, *Fundamental Principles of the Metaphysics of Ethics*, 3rd edn. London: Longmans, 1907.

———. (1788). *Kritik der Praktischen Vernunft*. English translation by L. W. Beck, *Critique of Practical Reason*. New York: Liberal Arts Press, 1956.

Kaufman, Alexander. (2006). 'Capabilities and Freedom'. *Journal of Political Philosophy* 14 (3): 289–300.

Kelly, Jerry S. (1974a). 'Necessity Conditions in Voting Theory'. *Journal of Economic Theory* 8 (2): 149–60.

———. (1974b). 'Voting Anomalies, the Number of Voters and the Number of Alternatives'. *Econometrica* 42: 239–52.

———. (1976a). 'Rights Exercising and a Pareto-Consistent Libertarian Claim'. *Journal of Economic Theory* 13 (1): 138–53.

———. (1976b). 'The Impossibility of a Just Liberal'. *Economica* 43 (169): 67–75.

———. (1978). *Arrow Impossibility Theorems*. Cambridge, Mass.: Academic Press.

———. (1987). *Social Choice Theory: An Introduction*. Berlin and Heidelberg: Springer-Verlag.

Kelsey, David. (1983). 'Topics in Social Choice'. D. Phil. Thesis, Oxford.

———. (1984a). 'Acyclic Choice without the Pareto Principle'. *The Review of Economic Studies* 51 (4): 693–9.

———. (1984b). 'The Structure of Social Decision Functions'. *Mathematical Social Sciences* 8 (3): 241–52.

———. (1985). 'The Liberal Paradox: A Generalization'. *Social Choice and Welfare* 1: 245–50.

Kemp, Murray C. (1953–54). 'Arrow's General Possibility Theorem'. *The Review of Economic Studies* 21 (3): 240–43.

Kemp, Murray C. and A. Asimakopulos. (1952). 'A Note on "Social Welfare Functions" and Cardinal Utility'. *Canadian Journal of Economics and Political Science* 18 (2): 195–200.

Kenen, Peter B. and Franklin M. Fisher. (1957). 'Income Distribution, Value Judgements, and Welfare: A Correction'. *The Quarterly Journal of Economics* 71 (2): 322–4.

Kennedy, Charles. (1950). 'The Common Sense of Indifference Curves'. *Oxford Economic Papers* 2 (1): 123–31.

———. (1952–53). 'The Economic Welfare Function and Dr. Little's Criterion'. *The Review of Economic Studies* 20 (2): 137–42.

———. (1963). 'Comments [on Little and Sen]'. *The Economic Journal* 73 (292): 778–81.

Khilnani, Sunil. (2009). 'Democracy and Its Indian Past'. In Basu and Kanbur (2009), vol. II: 488–502.

Kim, Ki Hang and Fred W. Roush. (1980). 'Special Domains and Nonmanipulability'. *Mathematical Social Sciences* 1 (1): 85–92.

Kirman, Alan P. and Dieter Sondermann. (1972). 'Arrow's Theorem, Many Agents, and Invisible Dictators'. *Journal of Economic Theory* 5 (2): 267–77.

Klahr, David. (1966). 'A Computer Simulation of the Paradox of Voting'. *The American Political Science Review* 60 (2): 384–90.

Klasen, Stephan. (1994). ' "Missing Women" Reconsidered'. *World Development* 22 (7): 1061–71.

———. (2008). 'Missing Women: Some Recent Controversies on Levels and Trends in Gender Bias in Mortality'. Ibero-America Institute for Economic Research (IAI) Discussion Paper 168.

———. (2009). 'Missing Women: Some Recent Controversies on Levels and Trends in Gender Bias in Mortality'. In Basu and Kanbur (2009), vol. II: 280–98.

Klasen, Stephan and Francesca Lamanna. (2009). 'The Impact of Gender Inequality in Education and Employment on Economic Growth: New Evidence for a Panel of Countries'. *Feminist Economics* 15 (3): 91–132.

Klasen, Stephan and Janneke Pieters. (2015). 'What Explains the Stagnation of Female Labor Force Participation in Urban India?' *World Bank Economic Review* 53 (1): 44–62.

Klasen, Stephan and Dana Schüler. (2011). 'Reforming the Gender-Related Development Index and the Gender Empowerment Measure: Implementing Some Specific Proposals'. *Feminist Economics* 17 (1): 1–30.

Klasen, Stephan and Sebastian Vollmer. (2014). 'A Flow Measure of Missing Women by Age and Disease', Working Paper 113, Program on the Global Demography of Aging, Harvard University.

Klasen, Stephan and Claudia Wink. (2002). 'A Turning Point in Gender Bias in Mortality? An Update on the Number of Missing Women'. *Population and Development Review* 28 (2): 285–312.

Kliemt, Hartmut. (1996). 'Das Paradox des Liberalismus – Eine Einführung'. *Analyse & Kritik* 18 (1): 1–19.

Knight, Frank H. (1935). *The Ethics of Competition*. London: Allen & Unwin.

———. (1947). *Freedom and Reform: Essays in Economic and Social Philosophy*. New York: Harper; republished Indianapolis: Liberty, 1982.

Knight, John and Sai Ding. (2002). *China's Remarkable Economic Growth*. Oxford: Oxford University Press.

Kolm, Serge-Christophe. (1969). 'The Optimum Production of Social Justice'. In *Public Economics: An Analysis of Public Production and Consumption and Their Relations to the Private Sectors*, edited by J. Margolis and H. Guitton. Proceedings of a Conference Held by the International Economic Association. London: Macmillan, 145–200.

———. (1972). *Justice et équité*. 2nd edn. Paris: Editions du Centre National de la Recherche Scientifique.

Koopmans, T. C. (1951). 'Efficient Allocation of Resources'. *Econometrica* 19 (4): 455–65.

———. (1957). *Three Essays on the State of Economic Science*. New York: McGraw-Hill.

———. (1960). 'Stationary Ordinal Utility and Impatience'. *Econometrica* 28 (2): 287–309.

———. (1964). 'On Flexibility of Future Preference'. In *Human Judgments and Optimality*, edited by Maynard Wolfe Shelly and Glenn L. Bryan. New York: Wiley.

———. (1966). 'Structure of Preferences over Time'. Cowles Foundation Discussion Paper, 206.

Koopmans, T. C., P. A. Diamond and R. E. Williams. (1964). 'Stationary Utility and Time Perspective'. *Econometrica* 32: 82–100.

Krantz, D. H., R. D. Luce, Patrick Suppes and A. Tversky. (1971) *Foundations of Measurement*. Vol. 1. New York: Academic Press.

Kreps, David. (1988). *Notes on The Theory of Choice*. Boulder, Colo.: Westview Press.

Kreps, David M. (1979). 'A Representation Theorem for "Preference for Flexibility"'. *Econometrica* 47 (3): 565–77.

Kreps, David M, Paul Milgrom, John Roberts and Robert Wilson. (1982). 'Rational Cooperation in the Finitely Repeated Prisoners' Dilemma'. *Journal of Economic Theory* 27 (2): 245–52.

Krueger, Alan B., ed. (2009). *Measuring the Subjective Well-Being of Nations: National Accounts of Time Use and Well-Being*. Chicago: University of Chicago Press.

Krueger, Alan B. and Arthur A. Stone. (2014). 'Progress in Measuring Subjective Well-Being'. *Science* 346 (6205): 42–3.

Kuhn, H. W. and A. W. Tucker. (1953). *Contributions to the Theory of Games*. Vol. 3. Princeton, N. J.: Princeton University Press.

Kuklys, Wiebke. (2005). *Amartya Sen's Capability Approach: Theoretical Insights and Empirical Applications*. Berlin: Springer-Verlag.

Kuznets, Simon. (1948a). 'On the Valuation of Social Income – Reflections on Professor Hicks' Article: Part I'. *Economica* 15 (57): 1–16.

———. (1948b). 'On the Valuation of Social Income – Reflections on Professor Hicks' Article: Part II'. *Economica* 15 (58): 116–31.

Kynch, Jocelyn. (2009). 'Entitlements and Capabilities: Young People in Post-Industrial Wales'. In Basu and Kanbur (2009), vol. II: 100–118.

Kynch, Jocelyn and Amartya K. Sen. (1983). 'Indian Women: Well-Being and Survival'. *Cambridge Journal of Economics* 7 (3–4): 363–80.

Laden, Anthony. (2012). *Reasoning: A Social Analysis*. New York: Oxford University Press.

Laffont, Jean-Jacques. (1979). *Aggregation and Revelation of Preferences*. Amsterdam: North-Holland Publishing Company.

Laffont, Jean-Jacques and Eric Maskin. (1982). 'Nash and Dominant Strategy Implementation in Economic Environments'. *Journal of Mathematical Economics* 10 (1): 17–47.

Lancaster, Kelvin. (1958). 'Welfare Propositions in Terms of Consistency and Extended Choice'. *The Economic Journal* 68 (271): 464–70.

———. (1959). 'Welfare and Expanded Choice – Proof of the General Case'. *The Economic Journal* 69 (276): 805–7.

Lancaster, Kelvin and R. G. Lipsey. (1956). 'The General Theory of Second Best'. *The Review of Economic Studies* 24 (1): 11–32.

Landemore, Hélène. (2013). *Democratic Reason: Politics, Collective Intelligence, and the Rule of the Many*. Princeton, N. J. and Oxford: Princeton University Press.

Lange, Oscar. (1942). 'The Foundations of Welfare Economics'. *Econometrica* 10 (3–4): 215–28.

———. (1945). 'The Scope and Method of Economics'. *The Review of Economic Studies* 13 (1): 19–32.

Lange, Oscar and Fred Taylor. (1952). *On the Economic Theory of Socialism*. Minneapolis: University of Minnesota Press.

Laplace, P. S. (1814). *Théorie analytique des probabilités*. 2nd edn. Paris: Courcier.

Laslett, Peter and W. G. Runciman, eds. (1958). *Philosophy, Politics and Society: First Series*. Oxford: Blackwell.

———. eds. (1962). *Philosophy, Politics and Society: Second Series*. Oxford: Blackwell.

———. eds. (1967). *Philosophy, Politics and Society: Third Series*. Oxford: Blackwell.

Layard, Richard. (2011a). *Happiness: Lessons from a New Science?* 2nd edn. London and New York: Penguin.

———. (2011b). 'Measuring Subjective Wellbeing for Public Policy: Recommendations on Measures' (with Paul Dolan and Robert Metcalfe). CEP Special Report, 23, March 2011.

Le Breton, Michel. (1997). 'Arrovian Social Choice on Economic Domains'. In Arrow, Sen and Suzumura (1997): 72–96.

Le Breton, Michel and Alain Trannoy. (1987). 'Measures of Inequality as an Aggregation of Individual Preferences about Income Distribution: The Arrovian Case'. *Journal of Economic Theory* 41 (2): 248–69.

Le Breton, Michel and John A. Weymark. (1996). 'An Introduction to Arrovian Social Welfare Functions on Economic and Political Domains'. In *Collective Decision-Making: Social Choice and Political Economy*, edited by Norman Schofield. Boston: Kluwer Academic Publishers, 25–61.

———. (2011). 'Arrovian Social Choice Theory on Economic Domains'. In Arrow, Sen and Suzumura (2011a): 191–299.

Le Grand, Julian. (1991). *Equity and Choice: An Essay in Economics and Applied Philosophy*. London: HarperCollins Academic.

Leibenstein, Harvey. (1962). 'Notes on Welfare Economics and the Theory of Democracy'. *The Economic Journal* 72.

———. (1965). 'Long-Run Welfare Criteria'. In *The Public Economy of Urban Communities*, edited by J. Margolis. Baltimore: Johns Hopkins Press.

Lenin, V. I. (1966). *The State and Revolution*. Moscow: Foreign Languages Publishing House.

Lenti, Targetti R. (1994). 'Sul Contributo Alla Cultura dei Grandi Economisti: Liberta Diseguaglianza e Poverta nel Pensiero di Amartya Sen'. *Rivista Milanese di Economica* 50: 5–12.

Leontief, Wassily. (1947a). 'Introduction to a Theory of the Internal Structure of Functional Relationships'. *Econometrica* 15 (4): 361–73.

———. (1947b). 'A Note on the Interrelation of Subsets of Independent Variables of a Continuous Function with Continuous First Derivatives'. *Bulletin of the American Mathematical Society* 53 (4): 343–50.

Lerner, A. P. (1944). *Economics of Control*. New York: Macmillan.

Levi, Isaac. (1986). *Hard Choices: Decision Making Under Unresolved Conflict*. Cambridge: Cambridge University Press.

———. (2009). 'Convexity and Separability in Representing Consensus'. In Basu and Kanbur (2009), vol. I: 193–212.

Levin, Jonathan and Barry Nalebuff. (1995). 'An Introduction to Vote-Counting Schemes'. *Journal of Economic Perspectives* 9 (1): 3–26.

Lieberman, B. (1967). 'Combining Individual Preferences into Social Choice'. In Research Memorandum SP-111.3. Pittsburgh: Department of Sociology, University of Pittsburgh.

Linos, Katerina. (2013). *The Democratic Foundations of Policy Diffusion: How Health, Family and Employment Laws Spread Across Countries*. Oxford: Oxford University Press.

List, Christian and Philip Pettit. (2005). 'On the Many as One'. *Philosophy and Public Affairs* 33 (4): 377–90.

———. (2011). *Group Agency*. Oxford: Oxford University Press.

Little, I. M. D. (1949a.) 'A Reformulation of the Theory of Consumer's Behaviour'. *Oxford Economic Papers* 1 (1): 90–99.

———. (1949b). 'The Foundations of Welfare Economics'. *Oxford Economic Papers* 1 (2): 227–46.

———. (1950). *A Critique of Welfare Economics*. Oxford: Oxford University Press; republished 1957.

———. (1952). 'Social Choice and Individual Values'. *Journal of Political Economy* 60 (5): 422–32.

———. (1962). 'Welfare Criteria: An Exchange of Notes'. *The Economic Journal* 72.

———. (1963). 'Comment [on Dobb and Sen]'. *The Economic Journal* 73 (292): 778–81.

Littlewood, John Edensor. (1967). 'The Mathematician's Art of Work'. Republished in *Littlewood's Miscellany*, edited by Bela Bollobas. Cambridge: Cambridge University Press, 1986.

Lorimer, Peter. (1967). 'A Note on Orderings'. *Econometrica* 35 (3–4): 537–39.

Lucas, J. R. (1959). 'Moralists and Gamesmen'. *Philosophy* 34 (128): 1–11.

Luce, R. D. (1956). 'Semiorders and a Theory of Utility Discrimination'. *Econometrica* 24 (2): 178.

———. (1966). 'Two Extensions of Conjoint Measurement'. *Journal of Mathematical Psychology* 3 (2): 348–70.

Luce, R. D. and Howard Raiffa. (1957). *Games and Decisions*. New York: Wiley.

Luce, R. D. and J. W. Tukey. (1964). 'Simultaneous Conjoint Measurement: A New Type of Fundamental Measurement'. *Journal of Mathematical Psychology* 1: 1–27.

Maasoumi, Esfandiar. (1986). 'The Measurement and Decomposition of Multi-Dimensional Inequality'. *Econometrica* 54 (4): 991–7.

Maasoumi, Esfandiar and J. S. Racine. (2016). 'A Solution to Aggregation and an Application to Multidimensional "Well-Being" Frontiers'. *Journal of Econometrics* 191 (2): 374–83.

Machina, Mark J. (1981). ' "Rational" Decision Making versus "Rational" Decision Modelling?' *Journal of Mathematical Psychology* 24 (2): 163–75.

Madell, Geoffrey. (1965). 'Hare's Prescriptivism'. *Analysis* 26 (2): 37–41.

Majumdar, Mukul and Amartya K. Sen. (1976). 'A Note on Representing Partial Orderings'. *The Review of Economic Studies* 43 (3): 543–45.

Majumdar, Tapas. (1956). 'Choice and Revealed Preference'. *Econometrica* 24 (1): 71–3.

———. (1957). 'Armstrong and the Utility Measurement Controversy'. *Oxford Economic Papers* 9 (1): 30–40.

——. (1962) *The Measurement of Utility*. 2nd edn. New York: Macmillan.

——. (1969a). 'A Note on Arrow's Postulates for a Social Welfare Function – A Comment'. *Journal of Political Economy* 77 (4): 528–31.

——. (1969b). 'Sen's General Theorem on Transitivity of Majority Decisions: An Alternative Approach'. In *Growth and Choice: Essays in Honour of U. N. Ghosal*, edited by Tapas Majumdar. Oxford: Oxford University Press.

——. (1973). 'Amartya Sen's Algebra of Collective Choice'. *Sankhyā* 35 (4): 533–42.

Malinvaud, E. (1952). 'Note on von Neumann–Morgenstern Strong Independence Axiom'. *Econometrica* 20 (4): 679.

——. (1953). 'Capital Accumulation and Efficient Allocation of Resources'. *Econometrica* 21 (2): 233–68.

Malthus, Thomas Robert. (1798). *An Essay on the Principle of Population, As It Affects the Future Improvement of Society with Remarks on the Speculation of Mr. Godwin, M. Condorcet, and Other Writers*. London: J. Johnson; republished, edited by Anthony Flew, Harmondsworth: Penguin, 1982.

——. (1830). *A Summary View on the Principle of Population*.

——. (1982). *An Essay on the Principle of Population*. Edited by Anthony Flew. Harmondsworth: Penguin.

Mandela, Nelson. (1994). *Long Walk to Freedom: The Autobiography of Nelson Mandela*. New York: Little, Brown and Co.

Manne, Alan S. and A. Charnes. (1952). 'The Strong Independence Assumption – Gasoline Blends and Probability Mixtures'. *Econometrica* 20 (4): 665–9.

Mansbridge, Jane, ed. (1990). *Beyond Self-Interest*. Chicago: University of Chicago Press.

Marglin, Stephen A. (1963). 'The Social Rate of Discount and the Optimal Rate of Investment'. *The Quarterly Journal of Economics* 77 (1): 95–111.

Margolis, Julius, ed. (1965). *The Public Economy of Urban Communities*. Baltimore: Johns Hopkins Press.

Margolis, Julius and H. Guitton. (1969a.) 'Planner's Preferences: Optimality, Distribution, and Social Welfare'. In *Public Economics: An Analysis of Public Production and Consumption and Their Relations to the Private Sectors*, edited by Julius Margolis and H. Guitton. Proceedings of a Conference Held by the International Economic Association. London: Macmillan.

———. eds. (1969b). *Public Economics: An Analysis of Public Production and Consumption and Their Relations to the Private Sectors.* Proceedings of a Conference Held by the International Economic Association. London: Macmillan.

Marquand, David. (2014). *Mammon's Kingdom: An Essay on Britain, Now.* London: Penguin.

Marschak, Jacob. (1950). 'Rational Behavior, Uncertain Prospects, and Measurable Utility'. *Econometrica* 18 (2): 111–41.

Marshall, Alfred. (1890). *Principles of Economics.* London: Macmillan.

Marx, Karl. (1959). *Economic and Philosophic Manuscript of 1844.* Moscow: Foreign Languages Publishing House.

———. (1967). *Critique of the Gotha Programme.* Moscow: Foreign Languages Publishing House.

Marx, Karl and Friedrich Engels. (1948). *Critique of the Gotha Programme.* Moscow: Foreign Languages Publishing House.

Mas-Colell, Andreu and Hugo Sonnenschein. (1972). 'General Possibility Theorems for Group Decisions'. *The Review of Economic Studies* 39 (2): 185–92.

Maskin, Eric. (1976a). 'Social Welfare Functions on Restricted Domains'. Mimeographed. Harvard University.

———. (1976b). 'On Strategyproofness and Social Welfare Functions when Preferences are Restricted'. Mimeographed. Darwin College and Harvard University.

———. (1978). 'A Theorem on Utilitarianism'. *Review of Economic Studies* 46 (4): 93–6.

———. (1979). 'Decision-Making under Ignorance with Implications for Social Choice'. *Theory and Decision* 11 (3): 319–37.

———. (1985). 'The Theory of Implementation in Nash Equilibrium: A Survey'. In *Social Goals and Social Organization: Essays in Memory of Elisha Pazner,* edited by Leonid Hurwicz, David Schmeidler and Hugo Sonnenschein. Cambridge: Cambridge University Press.

———. (1995). 'Majority Rule, Social Welfare Functions, and Games Forms'. In Basu, Pattanaik and Suzumura (1995).

———. (2014). 'The Arrow Impossibility Theorem: Where Do We Go From Here?' In Maskin and Sen (2014).

Maskin, Eric and Jean-Jacques Laffont. (1982). 'The Theory of Incentives: An Overview'. In *Advances in Economic Theory (Invited Lectures from the 4th World Congress of the Econometric Society),* edited by W. Hildenbrand. Cambridge: Cambridge University Press, 31–94.

Maskin, Eric and Amartya K. Sen. (2014). *The Arrow Impossibility Theorem*. New York: Columbia University Press.

———. (2016). 'How to Let Majority Rule'. *New York Times*, 1 May 2016.

———. (2017). 'The Rules of the Game: A New Electoral System'. *New York Review of Books*, 19 January 2017.

Maskin, Eric and Tomas Sjöström. (2002). 'Implementation Theory.' In Arrow, Sen and Suzumura (2002): 237–88.

Matsumoto, Yasumi. (1982). 'Choice Functions: Preference, Consistency, and Neutrality'. D. Phil. Thesis, Oxford.

———. (1985). 'Non-Binary Social Choice: Revealed Preferential Interpretation'. *Economica* 52 (206): 185–94.

May, Kenneth O. (1952). 'A Set of Independent Necessary and Sufficient Conditions for Simple Majority Decision'. *Econometrica* 20 (4).

———. (1953). 'A Note on the Complete Independence of the Conditions for Simple Majority Decision'. *Econometrica* 21 (1): 172–3.

McClennen, Edward F. (1978). 'The Minimax Theory and Expected-Utility Reasoning'. In *Foundations and Applications of Decision Theory*, edited by C. A. Hooker, J. J. Leach and E. F. McClennen. Dordrecht: D. Reidl, 337–67.

McGarvey, David C. (1953). 'A Theorem on the Construction of Voting Paradoxes'. *Econometrica* 21 (4): 608–10.

McKelvey, Richard D. (1979). 'General Conditions for Global Intransitivities in Formal Voting Models'. *Econometrica* 47 (5): 1085–112.

McLean, Ian. (1990). 'The Borda and Condorcet Principles: Three Medieval Applications'. *Social Choice and Welfare* 7 (2): 99–108.

Meade, James Edward. (1962). 'Welfare Criteria: An Exchange of Notes'. *The Economic Journal* 72.

———. (1976). *The Just Economy*. London: Allen & Unwin.

Middelaar, Luuk van and Philippe Van Parijs, eds. (2015). *After the Storm: How to Save Democracy in Europe*. Tielt, Belgium: Lannoo.

Mill, John Stuart. (1859). *On Liberty*. New York: Gateway, 1959.

———. (1861). 'Utilitarianism'. *Fraser's Magazine*. London: Dent, 1929.

Mills, C. W. (1953). *The Power Elite*. New York: Oxford University Press.

Minnesota Symposium. (1969). 'Consumption Theory without Transitive Indifference'. Unpublished.

Mirrlees, J. A. (1971). 'An Exploration in the Theory of Optimum Income Taxation'. *Review of Economic Studies* 38 (2): 175–208.

———. (1982). 'Migration and Optimal Income Taxes'. *Journal of Public Economics* 18 (3): 319–41.

Mishan, Ezra J. (1957). 'An Investigation into Some Alleged Contradictions in Welfare Economics'. *The Economic Journal* 67 (267): 445–54.

———. (1958). 'Arrow and the "New Economics": A Restatement'. *The Economic Journal* 68 (271): 595–7.

———. (1960). 'A Survey of Welfare Economics, 1939–59'. *The Economic Journal* 70 (278): 197–265.

———. (1962). 'Welfare Criteria: An Exchange of Notes: A Comment'. *The Economic Journal* 72 (285): 234–44.

———. (1964). 'The Welfare Criteria That Aren't'. *The Economic Journal* 74 (296): 1014–17.

Mizutani. S. (1978). 'Collective Choice and Extended Orderings'. M.Phil. Dissertation. London University.

Monjardet, Bernard. (1967). 'Remarques sur une classe de procédures de vote et les "Théorèmes de Possibilité" '. *La Décision: actes du colloque international sur la décision* 2 (2): 177–84.

———. (1978). 'Une autre preuve du théorème d'Arrow'. *RAIRO – Operations Research – Recherche Opérationnelle* 12 (3): 291–6.

———. (1979). 'Duality in the Theory of Social Choice'. In Laffont (1979): 131–43.

———. (1983). 'On the Use of Ultrafilters in Social Choice Theory'. In Pattanaik and Salles (1983): 73–8.

Montague, Roger. (1965). 'Universalizability'. *Analysis* 25: 189–202.

Morris, Christopher W., ed. (2009). *Amartya Sen*. Cambridge: Cambridge University Press.

Morris, M. D. (1979). *Measuring the Condition of the World's Poor: The Physical Quality of Life Index*. Oxford: Pergamon Press.

Morris, W. E. (1966). 'Professor Sen and Hare's Rule'. *Philosophy* 41 (158): 357–8.

Moulin, Hervé. (1983). *The Strategy of Social Choice*. Amsterdam: North-Holland Publishing Company.

———. (1995). *Cooperative Microeconomics: A Game-Theoretic Introduction*. Princeton, N. J.: Princeton University Press.

———. (2002). 'Axiomatic Cost and Surplus Sharing'. In Arrow, Sen and Suzumura (2002): 289–357.

Moulin, Hervé and William Thomson. (1997). 'Axiomatic Analysis of Resource Allocation Problems'. In Arrow, Sen and Suzumura (1997): 15–37.

Mueller, Dennis C. (1989). *Public Choice II: A Revised Edition of Public Choice*. 2nd edn. Cambridge: Cambridge University Press.

———. (1996). 'Constitutional and Liberal Rights'. *Analyse & Kritik* 18 (1): 96–117.

Murakami, Yasusuke. (1961). 'A Note on the General Possibility Theorem of the Social Welfare Function'. *Econometrica* 29 (2): 244–6.

———. (1966). 'Formal Structure of Majority Decision'. *Econometrica* 34 (3): 709–18.

———. (1968). *Logic and Social Choice*. London: Macmillan and New York: Dover.

Myerson, Roger B. (1981). 'Utilitarianism, Egalitarianism, and the Timing Effect in Social Choice Problems'. *Econometrica* 49 (4): 883–97.

———. (1983). 'Mechanism Design by an Informed Principal'. *Econometrica* 51 (6): 1767–97.

Myint, U. Hla. (1948). *Theories of Welfare Economics*. Cambridge, Mass.: Harvard University Press.

Myrdal, Gunnar. (1954). *The Political Element in the Development of Economic Theory: A Collection of Essays on Methodology*. Cambridge, Mass.: Harvard University Press.

Myrdal, Gunnar and Paul Streeten, eds. (1958). *Value in Social Theory: A Selection of Essays on Methodology*. Abingdon: Routledge & Kegan Paul.

Nagel, Thomas. (1970). *The Possibility of Altruism*. New York: Oxford University Press.

———. (1986). *The View from Nowhere*. New York: Oxford University Press.

———. (1998). *The Last Word*. Chicago: University of Chicago Press.

Nakamura, Kenjiro. (1975). 'The Core of a Simple Game without Ordinal Preferences'. *International Journal of Game Theory* 4 (1): 95–104.

———. (1978). 'Necessary and Sufficient Conditions on the Existence of a Class of Social Choice Functions'. *The Economic Studies Quarterly* 29 (3): 259–67.

———. (1979). 'The Vetoers in a Simple Game with Ordinal Preferences'. *International Journal of Game Theory* 8 (10): 55–61.

Nanson, E. J. (1882). 'Methods of Elections'. *Transactions and Proceedings of the Royal Society of Victoria* 18.

Nash, John. (1950). 'The Bargaining Problem'. *Econometrica* 18 (2): 155–62.

———. (1953). 'Two-Person Cooperative Games'. *Econometrica* 21 (1): 128–40.

Neumann, John von and Oskar Morgenstern. (1947). *Theory of Games and Economic Behavior*. Princeton, N. J.: Princeton University Press.

Newman, Peter. (1959). 'Mr. Lancaster on Welfare and Choice'. *The Economic Journal* 69 (275): 588–90.

Neyman, Jerzy, ed. (1951). *Proceedings of the Second Berkeley Symposium on Mathematical Statistics and Probability*. Berkeley: The Regents of the University of California.

———. ed. (1956). *Proceedings of the Third Berkeley Symposium on Mathematical Statistics and Probability*. Berkeley: The Regents of the University of California. http://projecteuclid.org/euclid.bsmsp/1200500251.

Ng, Y.-K. (1975). 'Bentham or Bergson? Finite Sensibility, Utility Functions and Social Welfare Functions'. *The Review of Economic Studies* 42 (4): 545–69.

Nicholson, Michael. (1965). 'Conditions for the "Voting Paradox" in Committee Decisions'. *Metroeconomica* 17 (1–2): 29–44.

Niemi, Richard G. (1969). 'Majority Decision-Making with Partial Unidimensionality'. *The American Political Science Review* 63 (2): 488–97.

Niemi, Richard G. and Herbert F. Weisberg. (1968). 'A Mathematical Solution for the Probability of the Paradox of Voting'. *Behavioral Science* 13 (4): 317–23.

Nitzan, Shmuel and Ariel Rubinstein. (1981). 'A Further Characterization of Borda Ranking Method'. *Public Choice* 36 (1): 153–8.

Nowell-Smith, P. H. (1954). *Ethics*. Harmondsworth: Penguin.

Nozick, Robert. (1973). 'Distributive Justice'. *Philosophy & Public Affairs* 3 (1): 45–126.

———. (1974). *Anarchy, State, and Utopia*. New York: Basic Books.

———. (1989). *The Examined Life: Philosophical Meditations*. New York: Simon & Schuster.

Nussbaum, Martha C. (1988). 'Nature, Function, and Capability: Aristotle on Political Distribution'. *Oxford Studies in Ancient Philosophy*, Supplementary Volume: 145–84.

———. (1992). 'Human Functioning and Social Justice: In Defense of Aristotelian Essentialism'. *Political Theory* 20 (2): 202–46.

———. (2001). 'Disabled Lives: Who Cares?' *The New York Review of Books*, 11 January.

———. (2006). *Frontiers of Justice: Disability, Nationality, Species Membership*. Cambridge, Mass.: Harvard University Press.

———. (2009). 'The Clash Within: Democracy and the Hindu Right'. In Basu and Kanbur (2009), vol. II: 503–21.

———. (2011). *Creating Capabilities*. Cambridge, Mass.: Harvard University Press.

Nussbaum, Martha C. and Jonathan Glover, eds. (1995). *Women, Culture, and Development: A Study of Human Capabilities*. Oxford: Oxford University Press.

Nussbaum, Martha C. and Amartya K. Sen, eds. (1993). *The Quality of Life*. Oxford: Oxford University Press.

Olafson, Frederick A., ed. (1961). *Justice and Social Policy*. Englewood Cliffs, N. J.: Prentice Hall.

Olsaretti, Serena. (2005). 'Endorsement and Freedom in Amartya Sen's Capability Approach'. *Economics and Philosophy* 21 (1): 89–108.

Olson, Mancur. (1964). *The Logic of Collective Action*. Cambridge, Mass.: Harvard University Press.

O'Neill, Onora. (1986), *Faces of Hunger: An Essay on Poverty, Justice, and Development*. London: Allen & Unwin.

———. (1996). *Towards Justice and Virtue*. Cambridge: Cambridge University Press.

———. (2000). *Bounds of Justice*. Cambridge: Cambridge University Press.

Osmani, S. R. (1982). *Economic Inequality and Group Welfare: A Theory of Comparison with Application to Bangladesh*. Oxford: Oxford University Press.

———. (1995). 'The Entitlement Approach to Famine: An Assessment'. In Basu, Pattanaik and Suzumura (1995): 253–94.

———. (2009). 'The Sen System of Social Evaluation'. In Basu and Kanbur (2009), vol. I: 15–34.

Osmani, Siddiqur and Amartya Sen. (2003). 'The Hidden Penalties of Gender Inequality: Fetal Origins of Ill-Health'. *Economics & Human Biology* 1 (1): 105–21.

Ostrom, Elinor. (2009). 'Engaging Impossibilities and Possibilities'. In Basu and Kanbur (2009), vol. II: 522–40.

Paine, Thomas. (1776). *Common Sense; Addressed to the Inhabitants of America, on the Following Interesting Subjects*. Philadelphia: W. and T. Bradford; republished New York: Penguin, 1982.

———. (1791). *Rights of Man: Being an Answer to Mr. Burkes' Attack on the French Revolution*; republished London: Dent, 1930.

Pareto, V. (1897). *Cours d'économie politique*. Lausanne: Rouge.

———. (1906). *Manuale di Economia Politica*. Milano: Societa Editrice Libraria.

———. (1909). *Manuale di Economia Politica* (French Translation, Revised). Paris: Giard.

Parfit, Derek. (1984). *Reasons and Persons*. Oxford: Oxford University Press.

———. (2011). *On What Matters*. 2 vols. Oxford: Oxford University Press.

Park, R. E. (1967). 'A Comment [on Coleman]'. *American Economic Review* 57 (5): 1300–1304.

Parks, Robert P. (1976a). 'Further Results on Path Independence, Quasitransivity, and Social Choice'. *Public Choice* 26 (26): 75–87.

———. (1976b). 'An Impossibility Theorem for Fixed Preferences: A Dictatorial Bergson–Samuelson Welfare Function'. *Review of Economic Studies* 43 (3): 447–50.

Parsons, T. and E. Shils. (1951). *Toward a General Theory of Value*. Cambridge, Mass.: Harvard University Press.

Pattanaik, Prasanta K. (1967a). 'A Note on Leibenstein's "Notes on Welfare Economics and the Theory of Democracy"'. *The Economic Journal* 77 (308): 953–6.

———. (1967b). 'Aspects of Welfare Economics'. Ph.D. Thesis, Delhi University.

———. (1968a). 'A Note on Democratic Decision and the Existence of Choice Sets'. *The Review of Economic Studies* 35 (1): 1–9.

———. (1968b). 'Risk, Impersonality, and the Social Welfare Function'. *Journal of Political Economy* 76 (6): 1152–69.

———. (1968c). 'Transitivity and Choice under Multi-State Majority Decisions'. Discussion Paper 52. Harvard Institute of Economic Research.

———. (1969). 'A Generalization of Some Theorems on the Transitivity of Social Decisions with Restricted Individual Preferences'. Mimeographed.

———. (1970). 'Sufficient Conditions for the Existence of a Choice Set under Majority Voting'. *Econometrica* 38 (1): 165–70.

———. (1971). *Voting and Collective Choice*. Cambridge: Cambridge University Press.

———. (1973). 'On the Stability of Sincere Voting Situations'. *Journal of Economic Theory* 6 (6): 558–74.

———. (1978). *Strategy and Group Choice*. Amsterdam: North-Holland Publishing Company.

———. (1996). 'The Liberal Paradox: Some Interpretations When Rights Are Represented as Game Forms'. *Analyse & Kritik* 18 (1): 38–53.

———. (1997a). 'On Modelling Individual Rights: Some Conceptual Issues'. In Arrow, Sen and Suzumura (1997): 100–128.

———. (1997b). 'Some Paradoxes of Preference Aggregation'. In *Perspectives on Public Choice*, edited by Dennis Mueller. Cambridge: Cambridge University Press, 201–26.

———. (2002). 'Positional Rules of Collective Decision-Making'. In Arrow, Sen and Suzumura (2002): 361–94.

———. (2009). 'Rights, Individual Preferences, and Collective Rationality'. In Basu and Kanbur (2009), vol. I: 213–30.

Pattanaik, Prasanta K. and Maurice Salles, eds. (1983). *Social Choice and Welfare*. Amsterdam: North-Holland Publishing Company.

Pattanaik, Prasanta K. and Manimay Sengupta. (1974). 'Conditions for Transitive and Quasi-Transitive Majority Decisions'. *Economica* 41 (164): 414–23.

———. (1980). 'Restricted Preferences and Strategy-Proofness of a Class of Group Decision Functions'. *Review of Economic Studies* 47 (5): 965–73.

Pattanaik, Prasanta K. and Yongsheng Xu. (1990). 'On Ranking Opportunity Sets in Terms of Freedom of Choice'. *Recherches Économiques de Louvain* 56 (3/4): 383–90.

Pazner, Elisha A. (1977). 'Pitfalls in the Theory of Fairness'. *Journal of Economic Theory* 14 (2): 458–66.

Pazner, Elisha A. and David Schmeidler. (1972). 'Decentralization, Income Distribution and the Role of Money in Socialist Economies'. Technical Report No. 8. Foerder Institute of Economic Research, Tel-Aviv University.

———. (1974). 'A Difficulty in the Concept of Fairness'. *The Review of Economic Studies* 41 (3): 441–3.

———. (1978a). 'Egalitarian Equivalent Allocations: A New Concept of Economic Equity'. *Quarterly Journal of Economics* 92 (4): 671–87.

———. (1978b). 'Decentralization and Income Distribution in Socialist Economies'. *Economic Inquiry* 16 (2): 257–64.

Peleg, Bezalel. (1978a). 'Consistent Voting Systems'. *Econometrica* 46 (1): 153–61.

———. (1978b). 'Representations of Simple Games by Social Choice Functions'. *International Journal of Game Theory* 7 (2): 81–94.

———. (1983). 'On Simple Games and Social Choice Correspondences'. In Pattanaik and Salles (1983).

———. (1984). *Game Theoretic Analysis of Voting in Committees*. Cambridge: Cambridge University Press.

———. (2002). 'Game-Theoretic Analysis of Voting in Committees'. In Arrow, Sen and Suzumura (2002): 395–423.

Peleg, Bezalel, O. Moeschlin and D. Pallaschke. (1979). 'Game Theoretic Analysis of Voting Schemes'. In *Game Theory and Related Topics*. Amsterdam: North-Holland Publishing Company.

Peter, Fabienne. (2011). *Democratic Legitimacy*. London: Routledge.

Pettit, Philip. (1997). *Republicanism: A Theory of Freedom and Government*. Oxford: Oxford University Press.

———. (2001a). *A Theory of Freedom: From Psychology to the Politics of Agency*. Oxford: Oxford University Press.

———. (2001b). 'Deliberative Democracy and the Discursive Dilemma'. *Philosophical Issues* 11 (1): 268–99.

Phelps, Edmund S., ed. (1973a). *Economic Justice: Selected Readings*. Harmondsworth: Penguin.

———. (1973b). 'Taxation of Wage Income for Economic Justice'. *The Quarterly Journal of Economics* 87 (3): 331–54.

———. (2009). 'The Good Life and the Good Economy: The Humanist Perspective of Aristotle, the Pragmatists and Vitalists, and the Economic Justice of John Rawls'. In Basu and Kanbur (2009), vol. I: 35–49.

Piacentino, D. (1996). 'Functioning and Social Equity'. Mimeographed. University of Urbino. Presented at the *Politeia* meeting on 'Environment and Society in a Changing World: A Perspective from the Functioning Theory'.

Pigou, Arthur Cecil. (1913). *Unemployment*. London: William and Norgate.

———. (1920). *The Economics of Welfare*. London: Macmillan.

Piketty, Thomas. (2014). *Capital in the Twenty-First Century*. Cambridge, Mass.: Harvard University Press.

Plott, Charles R. (1967). 'A Notion of Equilibrium and Its Possibility under Majority Rule'. *American Economic Review* 57 (4).

———. (1973). 'Path Independence, Rationality, and Social Choice'. *Econometrica* 41 (6): 1075–91.

———. (1976). 'Transcript of a Five-Member Committee Experiment'. Working Paper 110. California Institute of Technology, Division of the Humanities and Social Sciences.

Pogge, Thomas. (2001a). *Global Justice*. Oxford: Oxford University Press.

———. (2001b). 'What We Can Reasonably Reject'. *Philosophical Issues* 1: 118–47.

Pollak, Robert A. (1979). 'Bergson–Samuelson Social Welfare Functions and the Theory of Social Choice'. *The Quarterly Journal of Economics* 93 (1): 73–90.

———. (1991). 'Welfare Comparisons and Situation Comparisons'. *Journal of Econometrics* 50 (1): 31–48.

Pratt, John Winsor, Howard Raiffa and Robert Schlaifer. (1965). *Introduction to Statistical Decision Theory*. New York: McGraw-Hill.

Puppe, Clemens. (1996). 'An Axiomatic Approach to "Preference for Freedom of Choice"'. *Journal of Economic Theory* 68 (1): 174–99.

Putnam, Hilary. (2002). *The Collapse of the Fact/Value Dichotomy and Other Essays*. Cambridge, Mass.: Harvard University Press.

———. (2004). *Ethics without Ontology*. Cambridge, Mass.: Harvard University Press.

Qizilbash, Mozaffar. (1996). 'Capabilities, Well-Being and Human Development: A Survey'. *Journal of Development Studies* 33 (2): 143–62.

———. (2006). 'Capability, Happiness and Adaptation in Sen and J. S. Mill'. *Utilitas* 18 (1): 20–32.

———. (2007). 'Social Choice and Individual Capabilities'. *Politics, Philosophy & Economics* 6 (2): 169–92.

———. (2009). 'The Adaptation Problem, Evolution and Normative Economics'. In Basu and Kanbur (2009), vol. I: 68–79.

Quine, Willard V. O. (1940). *Mathematical Logic*. Cambridge, Mass.: Harvard University Press and New York: Harper.

Rader, T. (1963). 'The Existence of a Utility Function to Represent Preferences'. *Review of Economic Studies* 31 (3): 229–32.

Radner, R. and J. Marschak. (1954). 'Note on Some Proposed Decision Criteria'. In *Decision Processes*, edited by R. M. Thrall, Clyde H. Coombs, and R. L. Davis. New York: Wiley, 61–8.

Rae, Douglas W. (1995). 'Using District Magnitude to Regulate Political Party Competition'. *Journal of Economic Perspectives* 9 (1): 65–75.

Raiffa, Howard. (1953). 'Arbitration Schemes for Generalized 2-Person Games'. In *Contributions to the Theory of Games*, edited by H. W. Kuhn and A. W. Tucker. Vol. 3. Princeton, N. J.: Princeton University Press.

———. (1968). *Decision Analysis: Introductory Lectures on Choices under Uncertainty*. Reading, Mass. and London: Addison-Wesley.

Railton, Peter. (2003). *Facts, Values and Norms: Essays towards a Morality of Consequences*. Cambridge: Cambridge University Press.

Ramsey, Frank P. (1931). *The Foundations of Mathematics and Other Logical Essays*. London: Paul, Trench, Trubner.

Rangarajan, L. N., trans. (1987). *The Arthasastra of Kautilya*. Harmondsworth: Penguin.

Ranis, Gustav, Emma Samman and Frances Stewart. (2009). 'Country Patterns of Behavior on Broader Dimensions of Human Development'. In Basu and Kanbur (2009), vol. II: 119–38.

Rapoport, Anatol. (1960). *Fights, Games, and Debates*. Minnesota: University of Michigan Press.

Ravallion, Martin. (1987). *Markets and Famines*. Oxford and New York: Oxford University Press.

———. (1994a). *Poverty Comparisons*. Chur, Switzerland: Harwood Academic Press.

———. (1994b). 'Measuring Social Welfare With and Without Poverty Lines'. *The American Economic Review* 84: 359–64.

———. (1994c). 'Poverty Rankings using Noisy Data on Living Standards'. *Economic Letters* 45: 481–5.

———. (2009). 'On the Welfarist Rationale for Relative Poverty Lines'. In Basu and Kanbur (2009), vol. I: 375–96.

Rawls, John. (1951). 'Outline of a Decision Procedure for Ethics'. *The Philosophical Review* 60 (2): 177–97.

———. (1955). 'Two Concepts of Rules'. *Philosophical Review* 64 (1): 3–32.

———. (1958). 'Justice as Fairness'. *Philosophical Review* 67 (2): 164–94. Republished in *Justice and Social Policy*, edited by Frederick A. Olafson. Englewood Cliffs, N. J.: Prentice Hall, 1961, and also in *Philosophy, Politics and Society: Second Series*, edited by Peter Laslett and W. G. Runciman. Oxford: Blackwell, 1962.

———. (1963a). 'Constitutional Liberty and the Concept of Justice'. In *Justice: Nomos 8*, edited by C. J. Friedrich and J. Chapman. New York: Atherton Press.

———. (1963b). 'The Sense of Justice'. *The Philosophical Review* 72 (3): 281–305.

———. (1967). 'Distributive Justice'. In *Philosophy, Politics and Society: Third Series*, edited by Peter Laslett and W. G. Runciman. Oxford: Blackwell.

———. (1968). 'Chapters on Justice'. Materials for Philosophy 171 at Harvard University, unpublished.

———. (1971). *A Theory of Justice*. Cambridge, Mass.: Harvard University Press.

———. (1988). 'The Priority of Right and Ideas of the Good'. *Philosophy & Public Affairs* 17 (4): 251–76.

———. (1993). *Political Liberalism*. New York: Columbia University Press.

———. (1999a). *Collected Papers*. Edited by Samuel Richard Freeman. Cambridge, Mass.: Harvard University Press.

———. (1999b). *The Law of Peoples: With 'The Idea of Public Reason Revisited'*. Cambridge, Mass.: Harvard University Press.

Raz, Joseph. (1986). *The Morality of Freedom*. Oxford: Oxford University Press.

Razavi, Shahrashoub. (1996). 'Excess Female Mortality: An Indicator of Female Subordination? A Note Drawing on Village-Level Evidence from Southeastern Iran'. *Notizie di Politeia* 12 (43–44): 79–95.

Reder, Melvin Warren. (1947). *Studies in the Theory of Welfare Economics*. New York: Columbia University Press.

———. (1950). 'Theories of Welfare Economics'. *Journal of Political Economy* 58 (2): 158–61.

Rescher, Nicholas. (1967). *The Logic of Decision and Action*. Pittsburgh: University of Pittsburgh Press.

Richardson, Henry S. (2006). 'Rawlsian Social-Contract Theory and the Severely Disabled'. *The Journal of Ethics* 10 (4): 419–62.

Richter, Marcel K. (1966). 'Revealed Preference Theory'. *Econometrica* 34 (3): 635–45.

Riker, William H. (1961). 'Voting and the Summation of Preferences: An Interpretive Bibliographical Review of Selected Developments during the Last Decade'. *American Political Science Review* 55 (4): 900–911.

———. (1965). 'Arrow's Theorem and Some Examples of the Paradox of Voting'. In *Mathematical Applications in Political Science*, edited by S. Ulmer. Carbondale: Southern Illinois University Press.

Riley, Jonathan. (1987). *Liberal Utilitarianism: Social Choice Theory and J. S. Mill's Philosophy*. Cambridge: Cambridge University Press.

Robbins, Lionel. (1932). *An Essay on the Nature and Significance of Economic Science*. London: Macmillan.

———. (1938). 'Interpersonal Comparisons of Utility: A Comment'. *The Economic Journal* 48 (192): 635–41.

Roberts, Kevin W. S. (1977). 'Voting over Income Tax Schedules'. *Journal of Public Economics* 8 (3): 329–40.

——— (1980a). 'Interpersonal Comparability and Social Choice Theory'. *The Review of Economic Studies* 47 (2): 421–39.

——— (1980b). 'Possibility Theorems with Interpersonally Comparable Welfare Levels'. *The Review of Economic Studies* 47 (2): 409–20.

——— (1995). 'Valued Opinions or Opinionated Values: The Double Aggregation Problem'. In Basu, Pattanaik and Suzumura (1995).

—— (2009). 'Irrelevant Alternatives'. In Basu and Kanbur (2009), vol. I: 231–49.

Robertson, D. H. (1952). *Utility and All That: And Other Essays*. London: Macmillan.

——. (1954). 'Utility and All What?' *The Economic Journal* 64 (256): 665–785.

Robeyns, Ingrid. (2003). 'Sen's Capability Approach and Gender Inequality: Selecting Relevant Capabilities'. *Feminist Economics* 9 (2–3): 61–92.

——. (2005). 'The Capability Approach: A Theoretical Survey'. *Journal of Human Development* 6 (1): 93–117.

——. (2006). 'The Capability Approach in Practice'. *Journal of Political Philosophy* 14 (3): 351–76.

——. (2009). 'Justice as Fairness and the Capability Approach'. In Basu and Kanbur (2009), vol. I: 397–413.

——. (2016). 'Capabilitarianism'. *Journal of Human Development and Capabilities* 17 (3): 397–414.

Robinson, Joan. (1962). *Economic Philosophy*. Chicago: Aldine.

Roemer, John E. (1982). *A General Theory of Exploitation and Class*. Cambridge, Mass.: Harvard University Press.

——. (1985). 'Equality of Talent'. *Economics and Philosophy* 1 (2): 151–88.

——. (1996). 'Equality versus Progress'. *Nordic Journal of Political Economy* 23: 47–54.

——. (1998). *Theories of Distributive Justice*. Cambridge, Mass.: Harvard University Press.

Ross, William David. (1930). *The Right and the Good*. Oxford: Oxford University Press.

Rosser, John Barkley and Atwell Rufus Turquette. (1952). *Many-Valued Logics*. Amsterdam: North-Holland Publishing Company.

Rothenberg, Jerome. (1953a). 'Marginal Preference and the Theory of Welfare'. *Oxford Economic Papers* 5 (3): 248–63.

——. (1953b). 'Conditions for a Social Welfare Function'. *Journal of Political Economy* 61 (5): 389–405.

——. (1960). 'Non-Convexity, Aggregation, and Pareto Optimality'. *Journal of Political Economy* 68 (5): 435–68.

——. (1961). *The Measurement of Social Welfare*. Englewood Cliffs, N. J.: Prentice Hall.

Rothschild, Emma. (2001). *Economic Sentiments*. Cambridge, Mass.: Harvard University Press.

———. (2005). ' "Axiom, Theorem, Corollary &c.": Condorcet and Mathematical Economics'. *Social Choice and Welfare* 25 (2/3): 287–302.

Rothschild, Emma and Amartya K. Sen. (2006). 'Adam Smith's Economics'. In *The Cambridge Companion to Adam Smith*, edited by Knud Haakonssen. Cambridge: Cambridge University Press.

Rousseau, J. J. and M. Cranston. (1763). *Du contract social.* English translation *The Social Contract.* Harmondsworth: Penguin, 1974.

Rowley, Charles K. (1986). Review Article. *Public Choice* 48 (1): 93–99.

———. (1993). *Liberty and the State.* London: Edward Elgar Publishing.

Rubinstein, Ariel. (2012). *Economic Fables.* Cambridge: Open Book Publishers.

Ruger, Jennifer Prah. (2004). 'Health and Social Justice'. *The Lancet* 364 (9439): 1075–80.

———. (2006). 'Health, Capability, and Justice: Toward a New Paradigm of Health Ethics, Policy and Law'. *Cornell Journal of Law and Public Policy* 15 (2): 403–82.

———. (2010). *Health and Social Justice.* Oxford: Oxford University Press.

Ruggles, Nancy. (1949). 'The Welfare Basis of the Marginal Cost Pricing Principle'. *Review of Economic Studies* 17 (1): 29–46.

Runciman, David. (2013). *The Confidence Trap: A History of Democracy in Crisis from World War I to the Present.* Princeton, N. J.: Princeton University Press.

Runciman, W. G. (1965). *Social Justice.* Cambridge: Cambridge University Press.

Runciman, W. G. and Amartya K. Sen. (1965). 'Games, Justice and the General Will'. *Mind* 74 (296): 554–62.

Russell, Bertrand. (1910). *Philosophical Essays.* London: Longmans; republished London: Allen and Unwin, 1966 and New York: Simon and Schuster, 1967.

———. (1938). *The Principles of Mathematics.* 2nd edn. Cambridge: Cambridge University Press.

Saari, Donald G. (2011). 'Geometry of Voting'. In Arrow, Sen and Suzumura (2011a): 897–945.

Salles, Maurice. (1975). 'A General Possibility Theorem for Group Decision Rules with Pareto-Transitivity'. *Journal of Economic Theory* 11 (1): 110–18.

———. (1976). 'Characterization of Transitive Individual Preferences for Quasi-Transitive Collective Preference under Simple Games'. *International Economic Review* 17: 308–18.

————. (1992). 'On Two Classes of Differential Inequality Measures'. Discussion Paper 92-16. Department of Economics, University of Birmingham.

————. (1998). 'Fuzzy Utility'. In *Handbook of Utility Theory*, vol. 1, edited by S. Barberà, P. J. Hammond and C. Seidl. Dordrecht: Kluwer, 321–44.

————. (2009). 'Limited Rights and Social Choice Rules'. In Basu and Kanbur (2009), vol. I: 250–61.

Samuelson, Paul A. (1938). 'A Note on the Pure Theory of Consumer's Behaviour'. *Economica* 5 (17): 61–71.

————. (1947). *Foundations of Economic Analysis*. Cambridge, Mass.: Harvard University Press.

————. (1948). 'Consumption Theory in Terms of Revealed Preference'. *Economica* 15 (60): 243–53.

————. (1950a). 'The Problem of Integrability in Utility Theory'. *Economica* 17 (68): 355–85.

————. (1950b). 'Evaluation of Real National Income'. *Oxford Economic Papers* 2 (1): 1–29.

————. (1952). 'Probability, Utility, and the Independence Axiom'. *Econometrica* 20 (4): 670–78.

————. (1956). 'Social Indifference Curves'. *The Quarterly Journal of Economics* 70 (1): 1–22.

————. (1957). 'Foreword'. In *Theoretical Welfare Economics*, by J. de Graaff. Cambridge: Cambridge University Press, vii–viii.

————. (1964). 'A. P. Lerner at Sixty'. *Review of Economic Studies* 31: 169–78.

————. (1966). *The Collected Scientific Papers of Paul Samuelson*. Edited by Joseph E. Stiglitz. 2 vols. Cambridge, Mass.: MIT Press.

Saposnik, Rubin. (1975). 'Social Choice with Continuous Expression of Individual Preferences'. *Econometrica* 43 (4): 683–90.

Satterthwaite, Mark Allen. (1975). 'Strategy-Proofness and Arrow's Conditions: Existence and Correspondence Theorems for Voting Procedures and Social Welfare Functions'. *Journal of Economic Theory* 10 (2): 187–217.

Savage, L. J. (1950). 'Note on the Strong Independence Assumption'. *Econometrica* 20.

————. (1954). *The Foundations of Statistics*. New York: Wiley.

Scanlon, Thomas M. (1988). 'The Significance of Choice'. In *The Tanner Lectures on Human Values*, edited by Sterling M. McMurrin. Cambridge: Cambridge University Press and Salt Lake City: University of Utah Press, 149–216.

——. (1998). *What We Owe to Each Other*. Cambridge Mass.: Harvard University Press.

——. (2003). *The Difficulty of Tolerance: Essays in Political Philosophy*. Cambridge: Cambridge University Press.

——. (2009). 'Rights and Interests'. In Basu and Kanbur (2009), vol. I: 68–79.

——. (2014). *Being Realistic about Reasons*. Oxford: Oxford University Press.

Schelling, Thomas. (1984). *Choice and Consequence*. Cambridge, Mass.: Harvard University Press.

Schmeidler, David and Hugo Sonnenschein. (1978). 'Two Proofs of the Gibbard–Satterthwaite Theorem on the Possibility of a Strategy-Proof Social Choice Function'. In *Decision Theory and Social Ethics*, edited by Hans W. Gottinger and Werner Leinfellner. Theory and Decision Library 17. Amsterdam: Springer Netherlands, 227–34.

Schmeidler, David and Karl Vind. (1972). 'Fair Net Trades'. *Econometrica* 40 (4): 637–42.

Schmeidler, David and Menahem E. Yaari. (1970). 'Fair Allocation'. Oral Presentation C. O.R. E. 1969, Stanford.

Schmitz, Norbert. (1977). 'A Further Note on Arrow's Impossibility Theorem'. *Journal of Mathematical Economics* 4 (2): 189–96.

Schofield, Norman. (1983). 'Generic Instability of Majority Rule'. *The Review of Economic Studies* 50 (4): 695–705.

——. ed. (1996). *Collective Decision-Making: Social Choice and Political Economy*. Berlin and New York: Springer.

——. (2002). 'Representative Democracy as Social Choice'. In Arrow, Sen and Suzumura (2002): 425–55.

Schokkaert, Erik. (2009). 'The Capabilities Approach'. In *The Handbook of Rational and Social Choice*, edited by Paul Anand, Prasanta Pattanaik and Clemens Puppe. New York and Oxford: Oxford University Press, 542–66.

Schokkaert, Erik and Luc Van Ootegm. (1990). 'Sen's Concept of the Living Standard Applied to the Belgian Unemployed'. *Recherches Économiques de Louvain / Louvain Economic Review* 56 (3/4): 429–50.

Schwartz, Thomas. (1970). 'On the Possibility of Rational Policy Evaluation'. *Theory and Decision* 1 (1): 89–106.

——. (1972). 'Rationality and the Myth of the Maximum'. *Noûs* 6 (2): 97–117.

——. (1974). 'Notes on the Abstract Theory of Collective Choice'. Mimeographed. Carnegie Mellon University.

———. (1976). 'Choice Functions, "Rationality" Conditions, and Variations on the Weak Axiom of Revealed Preference'. *Journal of Economic Theory* 13 (3): 414–27.

———. (1981). 'The Universal-Instability Theorem'. *Public Choice* 37 (3): 487–501.

———. (1986). *The Logic of Collective Choice*. New York: Columbia University Press.

Scitovsky, Tibor. (1941). 'A Note on Welfare Propositions in Economics'. *Review of Economic Studies* 9 (1): 77–88.

———. (1942). 'A Reconsideration of the Theory of Tariffs'. *The Review of Economic Studies* 9 (2): 89–110.

———. (1951). 'The State of Welfare Economics'. *The American Economic Review* 41 (3): 303–15.

———. (1964). *Papers on Welfare and Growth*. Stanford: Stanford University Press.

———. (1976). *The Joyless Economy*. Oxford: Oxford University Press.

Scott, Dana and Patrick Suppes. (1958). 'Foundational Aspects of Theories of Measurement'. *The Journal of Symbolic Logic* 23 (2): 113–28.

Searle, John R. (1964). 'How to Derive "Ought" From "Is"'. *Philosophical Review* 73 (1): 43–58.

———. (1969). *Speech Acts: An Essay in the Philosophy of Language*. Cambridge: Cambridge University Press.

Seidl, Christian. (1975). 'On Liberal Values'. *Zeitschrift für Nationalökonomie / Journal of Economics* 35 (3/4): 257–92.

———. (1988). 'Poverty Measurement: A Survey'. In *Welfare and Efficiency in Public Economics*, edited by D. Bos, M. Rose and C. Seidl. New York: Springer.

———. (1997). 'Foundations and Implications of Rights'. In Arrow, Sen and Suzumura (1997).

Sen, Amartya K. (1960). *Choice of Techniques*. Oxford: Basil Blackwell.

———. (1963). 'Distribution, Transitivity and Little's Welfare Criteria'. *The Economic Journal* 73 (292): 771–8.

———. (1964). 'Preferences, Votes and the Transitivity of Majority Decisions'. *The Review of Economic Studies* 31 (2): 163–5.

———. (1965). 'Mishan, Little and Welfare: A Reply'. *The Economic Journal* 75 (298): 442.

———. (1966a). 'A Possibility Theorem on Majority Decisions'. *Econometrica* 34 (2): 491–9.

———. (1966b). 'Hume's Law and Hare's Rule'. *Philosophy* 41 (155): 75–9.

———. (1966c). 'Planners' Preferences: Optimality, Distribution, and Social Welfare'. In International Economic Association, *Economics of the Public Sector*, papers presented at the Round-Table Conference at Biarritz, 1966; republished in *Public Economics*, edited by J. Margolis and H. Guitton. London: Macmillan, 1969.

———. (1967a). 'Isolation, Assurance and the Social Rate of Discount'. *Quarterly Journal of Economics* 81 (February): 112–24.

———. (1967b). 'The Nature and Classes of Prescriptive Judgements'. *The Philosophical Quarterly* 17 (66): 46–62.

———. (1969). 'Quasi-Transitivity, Rational Choice and Collective Decisions'. *The Review of Economic Studies* 36 (3): 381–93.

———. (1970a). *Collective Choice and Social Welfare*. San Francisco: Holden Day; republished Amsterdam: Elsevier North-Holland, 1979.

———. (1970b). 'Interpersonal Aggregation and Partial Comparability'. *Econometrica* 38 (3): 393–409.

———. (1970c). 'The Impossibility of a Paretian Liberal'. *Journal of Political Economy* 78 (1): 152–7.

———. (1971). 'Choice Functions and Revealed Preference'. *The Review of Economic Studies* 38 (3): 307–17 (reprinted in Sen 1982a).

———. (1973a). *On Economic Inequality*. Oxford: Oxford University Press; republished with Addendum by James Foster and Amartya Sen (Oxford: Oxford University Press, 1997).

———. (1973b). 'Behaviour and the Concept of Preference'. *Economica* 40 (159): 241–59.

———. (1973c). 'On the Development of Basic Income Indicators to Supplement GNP Measures'. *Economic Bulletin for Asia and the Far East* 24 (2): 1–11.

———. (1974). 'Choice, Orderings, and Morality'. In *Practical Reason: Papers and Discussions*, edited by Stephan Körner. New Haven: Yale University Press.

———. (1976a). 'Liberty, Unanimity and Rights'. *Economica* 43 (171): 217–45.

———. (1976b). 'Poverty: An Ordinal Approach to Measurement'. *Econometrica* 44 (2): 219–31.

———. (1976c). 'Real National Income'. *The Review of Economic Studies* 43 (1): 19–39.

———. (1977a). 'Rational Fools: A Critique of the Behavioral Foundations of Economic Theory'. *Philosophy & Public Affairs* 6 (4): 317–44.

———. (1977b). 'On Weights and Measures: Informational Constraints in Social Welfare Analysis'. *Econometrica* 45 (7): 1539–72.

———. (1977c). 'Social Choice Theory: A Re-Examination'. *Econometrica* 45 (1): 53–89.

———. (1977d). 'Starvation and Exchange Entitlements: A General Approach and Its Application to the Great Bengal Famine'. *Cambridge Journal of Economics* 1 (1): 33–59.

———. (1979a). 'Personal Utilities and Public Judgments: Or What's Wrong with Welfare Economics'. *The Economic Journal* 89 (355): 537–58.

———. (1979b). 'The Welfare Basis of Real Income Comparisons: A Survey'. *Journal of Economic Literature* 17 (1): 1–45.

———. (1980). 'Equality of What?' In *The Tanner Lecture on Human Values*, I: 197–220. Cambridge: Cambridge University Press.

———. (1981). *Poverty and Famines: An Essay on Entitlement and Deprivation*. Oxford: Oxford University Press.

———. (1982a). *Choice, Welfare and Measurement*. Oxford: Blackwell; republished Cambridge, Mass.: Harvard University Press, 1997.

———. (1982b). 'Rights and Agency'. *Philosophy & Public Affairs* 11 (1): 3–39.

———. (1982c). 'How Is India Doing?' *The New York Review of Books* 21 (Christmas Number).

———. (1983a). 'Liberty and Social Choice'. *Journal of Philosophy* 80 (1): 5–28.

———. (1983b). 'Poor, Relatively Speaking'. *Oxford Economic Papers* 35 (2): 153–69.

———. (1983c). 'Development: Which Way Now?' *The Economic Journal* 93 (372): 745–62.

———. (1984). *Resources, Values, and Development*. Cambridge, Mass.: Harvard University Press.

———. (1985a). *Commodities and Capabilities*. Amsterdam: North-Holland Publishing; republished Delhi: Oxford University Press, 1999.

———. (1985b). 'Well-Being, Agency and Freedom: The Dewey Lectures 1984'. *Journal of Philosophy* 82 (4): 169–221.

———. (1986a). 'Information and Invariance in Normative Choice'. In *Essays in Honor of Kenneth J. Arrow*, edited by Walter Heller, Ross Starr and David Starrett. Vol. 1. Cambridge: Cambridge University Press.

———. (1986b). 'Social Choice Theory'. In *Handbook of Mathematical Economics*, edited by Kenneth J. Arrow and Michael D. Intriligator. Vol. 3. Amsterdam: Elsevier, 1073–181.

———. (1987a). *On Ethics and Economics*. Oxford: Blackwell.

———. (1987b). *The Standard of Living: Tanner Lectures by Amartya Sen, with Comments from Keith Hart, Ravi Kanbur, John Muellbauer, and Bernard Williams*. Edited by Geoffrey Hawthorn. Cambridge: Cambridge University Press.

———. (1990a). 'Gender and Cooperative Conflicts'. In *Persistent Inequalities*, edited by Irene Tinker. New York: Oxford University Press, 123–49.

———. (1990b). 'More Than 100 Million Women Are Missing'. *The New York Review of Books*, 20 December.

———. (1992a). *Inequality Reexamined*. Cambridge, Mass.: Harvard University Press.

———. (1992b). 'Minimal Liberty'. *Economica* 59 (234): 139–59.

———. (1992c). 'Missing Women'. *British Medical Journal* 304 (6827): 587–8.

———. (1993a). 'Internal Consistency of Choice'. *Econometrica* 61 (3): 495–521.

———. (1993b). 'Positional Objectivity'. *Philosophy & Public Affairs* 22 (2): 126–45.

———. (1994). 'Well-Being, Capability, and Public Policy'. *Giornale degli Economisti e Annali di Economia* 53 (7/9): 333–47.

———. (1995a). 'Environmental Evaluation and Social Choice: Contingent Valuation and the Market Analogy'. *The Japanese Economic Review* 46 (1): 23–37.

———. (1995b). 'How to Judge Voting Schemes'. *Journal of Economic Perspectives* 9 (1): 91–8.

———. (1995c). 'Rationality and Social Choice'. *The American Economic Review* 85 (1): 1–24.

———. (1996a). 'Freedom, Capabilities and Public Action: A Response'. *Notizie di Politeia* 12.

———. (1996b). 'Rights: Formulation and Consequences'. *Analyse & Kritik* 18 (1): 153–70.

———. (1997a). 'Maximization and the Act of Choice'. *Econometrica* 65 (4): 745–80.

———. (1997b). 'From Income Inequality to Economic Inequality'. *Southern Economic Journal* 64 (2): 384–401.

———. (1997c). 'Individual Preference as the Basis of Social Choice'. In Arrow, Sen and Suzumura (1997): 15–37.

———. (1999). *Development as Freedom*. Oxford: Oxford University Press.

———. (2002a). *Rationality and Freedom*. Cambridge, Mass.: Harvard University Press.

———. (2002b). 'Open and Closed Impartiality'. *Journal of Philosophy* 99 (9): 445–69.

———. (2002c). 'Processes, Liberty and Rights'. In Sen (2002a).

———. (2003). 'Missing Women – Revisited'. *British Medical Journal* 327 (7427): 1297–8.

———. (2005a). *The Argumentative Indian: Writings on Indian History, Culture and Identity*. London: Allen Lane.

———. (2005b). 'Mary, Mary, Quite Contrary!' *Feminist Economics* 11 (1): 1–9.

———. (2006). *Identity and Violence: The Illusion of Destiny (Issues of Our Time)*. New York: W. W. Norton & Company.

———. (2009a). *The Idea of Justice*. Cambridge, Mass.: Harvard University Press.

———. (2009b). 'Capability: Reach and Limit'. In *Debating Global Society: Reach and Limits of the Capability Approach*, edited by Enrica Chiappero-Martinetti. Rome: Fondazione Giangiacomo Feltrinelli, 15–28.

———. (2009c). 'Introduction'. In *The Theory of Moral Sentiments*, by Adam Smith. London: Penguin.

———. (2011a). 'The Global Status of Human Rights (Thirteenth Annual Grotius Lecture Series)'. *American University International Law Review* 27 (1).

———. (2011b). 'The Informational Basis of Social Choice'. In Arrow, Sen and Suzumura (2011a): 29–46.

———. (2012). 'What Happened to Europe? Democracy and the Decisions of Bankers'. *The New Republic*, 23 August.

———. (2013). 'India's Women: The Mixed Truth'. *The New York Review of Books*, 10 October.

———. (2015). 'Women's Progress Outdid China's One-Child Policy'. *New York Times*, 2 November.

———. (2017). 'Reasoning and Justice: The Maximal and the Optimal'. *Philosophy* 92.

Sen, Amartya K. and Prasanta K. Pattanaik. (1969). 'Necessary and Sufficient Conditions for Rational Choice under Majority Decision'. *Journal of Economic Theory* 1 (2): 178–202.

Sen, Amartya K. and Sunil Sengupta. (1983). 'Malnutrition of Rural Children and the Sex Bias'. *Economic and Political Weekly* 18 (19/21): 855–64.

Sen, Amartya K. and Bernard Williams. (1982). *Utilitarianism and Beyond*. Cambridge: Cambridge University Press.

Sengupta, Arjun. (2004). 'The Human Right to Development'. *Oxford Development Studies* 34.

———. (2009). 'Elements of a Theory of the Right to Development'. In Basu and Kanbur (2009), vol. I: 80–100.

Sengupta, Manimay. (1980a). 'Monotonicity, Independence of Irrelevant Alternatives and Strategy-Proofness of Social Decision Functions'. *The Review of Economic Studies* 47 (2): 393–407.

———. (1980b). 'The Knowledge Assumption in the Theory of Strategic Voting'. *Econometrica* 48 (5): 1301–4.

Shapiro, Ian. (2011). *The Real World of Democratic Theory*. Princeton, N. J.: Princeton University Press.

Shelah, Saharon. (2005). 'On the Arrow Property'. *Advances in Applied Mathematics* 34 (2): 217–51.

Shorrocks, Anthony F. (1978a). 'The Measurement of Mobility'. *Econometrica* 46: 1013–24.

———. (1978b). 'Income Inequality and Income Mobility'. *Journal of Economic Theory* 19: 376–93.

———. (1984). 'Inequality Decomposition by Population Subgroups'. *Econometrica* 52: 1369–85.

———. (1995). 'Revisiting the Sen Poverty Index'. *Econometrica* 63 (5): 1225–30.

Shorrocks, Anthony F. and Guanghua Wan. (2009). 'Ungrouping Income Distributions: Synthesising Samples for Inequality and Poverty Analysis'. In Basu and Kanbur (2009), vol. I: 414–35.

Shubik, Martin, ed. (1967). *Essays in Mathematical Economics, in Honor of Oskar Morgenstern*. Princeton, N. J.: Princeton University Press.

Sidgwick, Henry. (1874). *The Methods of Ethics*. London: Macmillan & Co.

———. (1966). *The Methods of Ethics*. New York: Dover.

Siegel, Sidney and Lawrence E. Fouraker. (1960). *Bargaining and Group Decision Making: Experiments in Bilateral Monopoly*. New York: McGraw-Hill.

Singer, Marcus G. (1961). *Generalizations in Ethics: An Essay in the Logic of Ethics, with the Rudiments of a System of Moral Philosophy*. New York: Knopf.

Sjoberg, Lennart. (1975). 'Models of Similarity and Intensity'. *Psychological Bulletin* 82: 191-206.

Skidelsky, Robert. (2014). *Five Years of Economic Crisis*. London: Centre for Global Studies.

Skidelsky, Robert and Edward Skidelsky. (2012). *How Much Is Enough? Money and the Good Life*. New York: Other Press.

Skinner, Quentin. (1998). *Liberty before Liberalism*. Cambridge: Cambridge University Press.

Slesnick, Daniel T. (1998). 'Empirical Approaches to the Measurement of Welfare'. *Journal of Economic Literature* 36 (4): 2108–65.

Slutsky, Steven. (1977). 'A Voting Model for the Allocation of Public Goods: Existence of an Equilibrium'. *Journal of Economic Theory* 14 (2): 299–325.

Smith, Adam. (1759). *The Theory of Moral Sentiments*. Printed for A. Millar, in the Strand and A. Kincaid and J. Bell, in Edinburgh; republished London: A. Millar in 1790; and London: Penguin in 2009, with an introduction by Amartya K. Sen.

———. (1776). *An Inquiry into the Nature and Causes of the Wealth of Nations*. London: W. Strahan and T. Cadell; republished, eds. R. H. Campbell and A. S. Skinner, Oxford: Oxford University Press, 1976; and Penguin Classics edition, 1982.

Smith, Adam. (1978). *Lectures on Jurisprudence*. Edited by R. L. Meek, D. D. Raphael and P. G. Stein. Oxford: Oxford University Press; reprinted Indianapolis: Liberty Press, 1982.

Smith, John H. (1973). 'Aggregation of Preferences with Variable Electorate'. *Econometrica* 41 (6): 1027–41.

Snow, C. P. (1951). *The Masters*. Strangers and Brothers. London: Macmillan.

Sobel, Joel. (1979). 'Fair Allocations of a Renewable Resource'. *Journal of Economic Theory* 21 (2): 235–48.

Sobhan, Rehman. (2009). 'Agents into Principals: Democratizing Development in South Asia'. In Basu and Kanbur (2009), vol. II: 542–62.

Solow, Robert M. (1995). 'Mass Unemployment as a Social Problem'. In Basu, Pattanaik and Suzumura (1995).

———. (2009). 'Imposed Environmental Standards and International Trade'. In Basu and Kanbur (2009), vol. II: 411–21.

Sonnenschein, Hugo. (1965). 'The Relationship between Transitive Preference and the Structure of the Choice Space'. *Econometrica* 33 (3): 624–34.

———. (1967). 'Reply to "A Note on Orderings"'. *Econometrica* 35 (3–4): 540–42.

Steiner, Hillel. (1990). 'Putting Rights in Their Place'. *Recherches Économiques de Louvain / Louvain Economic Review* 56 (3/4): 391–408.

Stern, Nicholas. (2006). *The Stern Review on the Economics of Climate Change*. Cambridge: Cambridge University Press.

———. (2009). *A Blueprint for a Safer Planet*. London: Bodley Head.

———. (2015). *Why Are We Waiting? The Logic, Urgency, and Promise of Tackling Climate Change*. Cambridge, Mass.: MIT Press.

Stevens, Stanley S. (1951a). 'Mathematics, Measurement, and Psychophysics'. In *Handbook of Experimental Psychology*, edited by Stanley S. Stevens. New York: Wiley.

———. ed. (1951b). *Handbook of Experimental Psychology*. New York: Wiley.

———. (1960). 'The Psychophysics of Sensory Function'. *American Scientist* 48 (2): 226–53.

Stevenson, Charles. (1944). *Ethics and Language*. New Haven: Yale University Press.

———. (1963). *Facts and Values: Studies in Ethical Analysis*. New Haven: Yale University Press.

Stewart, Frances. (1985). *Planning to Meet Basic Needs*. London: Macmillan.

Stigler, G. J. (1943). 'A Note on the New Welfare Economics'. *American Economic Review* 33 (2): 355–9.

Stiglitz, Joseph E. (2009). 'Simple Formulae for Optimal Income Taxation and the Measurement of Inequality: An Essay in Honor of Amartya Sen'. In Basu and Kanbur (2009), vol. I: 535–66.

Strasnick, Steven. (1976). 'Social Choice and the Derivation of Rawls's Difference Principle'. *The Journal of Philosophy* 73 (4): 85–90.

Strassman, Diana L. (1994). 'Feminist Thought and Economics; Or, What Do the Visigoths Know?' *American Economic Review* 84: 153–8.

Streeten, Paul. (1950). 'Economics and Value Judgment'. *Quarterly Journal of Economics* 64 (4): 583–95.

———. (1958). 'Introduction'. In *Value in Social Theory: A Selection of Essays on Methodology*, edited by Gunnar Myrdal and Paul Streeten. Abingdon: Routledge & Kegan Paul.

———. (1981). *Development Perspectives*. London: Macmillan.

———. (1984). 'Basic Needs: Some Unsettled Questions'. *World Development* 12 (9): 85–99.

Strotz, Robert H. (1958). 'How Income Ought to Be Distributed: A Paradox in Distributive Ethics'. *Journal of Political Economy* 66: 189–205.

———. (1961). 'How Income Ought to Be Distributed: Paradox Regained'. *Journal of Political Economy* 69: 271–8.

Subramanian, S. (2009). 'A Practical Proposal for Simplifying the Measurement of Income Poverty'. In Basu and Kanbur (2009), vol. I: 435–52.

Sugden, Robert. (1981). *The Political Economy of Public Choice: An Introduction to Welfare Economics*. New York: Wiley.

———. (1985). 'Liberty, Preference and Choice'. *Economics and Philosophy* 1: 213–29.

———. (1986). *The Economics of Rights, Co-Operation, and Welfare*. Oxford: Blackwell.

———. (1993). 'Welfare, Resources, and Capabilities: A Review of Inequality Reexamined by Amartya Sen'. *Journal of Economic Literature* 31 (4): 1947–62.

———. (1998). 'The Metric of Opportunity'. *Economics and Philosophy* 14: 307–37.

Sunstein, Cass R. (1990). *After the Rights Revolution: Reconsidering the Regulatory State*. Cambridge, Mass.: Harvard University Press.

———. (1995). 'Incompletely Theorized Agreements'. *Harvard Law Review*, 108.

Suppes, Patrick. (1951). 'The Role of Subjective Probability and Utility in Decision-Making'. In *Proceedings of the Second Berkeley Symposium on Mathematical Statistics and Probability*, edited by Jerzy Neyman. The Regents of the University of California. http://projecteuclid.org/euclid.bsmsp/1200500251.

———. (1958). *Introduction to Logic*. Princeton, N. J.: Van Nostrand.

———. (1966). 'Some Formal Models of Grading Principles'. *Synthese* 16 (3–4): 284–306.

———. (1987). 'Maximizing Freedom of Decision: An Axiomatic Approach'. In *Arrow and the Foundations of the Theory of Economic Policy*, edited by George R. Feiwel. London: Macmillan.

Suppes, Patrick and Muriel Winet. (1955). 'An Axiomatization of Utility Based on the Notion of Utility Differences'. *Management Science* 1 (3–4): 259–70.

Suzumura, Kotaro. (1976a). 'Rational Choice and Revealed Preference'. *The Review of Economic Studies* 43 (1): 149–58.

———. (1976b). 'Remarks on the Theory of Collective Choice'. *Economica* 43 (172): 381–90.

———. (1980). 'Liberal Paradox and the Voluntary Exchange of Rights-Exercising'. *Journal of Economic Theory* 22 (3): 407–22.

———. (1983). *Rational Choice, Collective Decisions, and Social Welfare*. Cambridge: Cambridge University Press.

———. (1995). *Competition, Commitment, and Welfare*. Oxford: Oxford University Press.

———. (1996). 'Welfare, Rights, and Social Choice Procedure: A Perspective'. *Analyse & Kritik* 18 (1): 20–37.

———. (1997). 'Interpersonal Comparisons of the Extended Sympathy Type and the Possibility of Social Choice'. In Arrow, Sen and Suzumura (1997): 202–29.

———. (1999). 'Consequences, Opportunities, and Procedures'. *Social Choice and Welfare* 16 (1): 17–40.

———. (2011). 'Welfarism, Individual Rights, and Procedural Fairness'. In Arrow, Sen and Suzumura (2011a): 605–85.

———. (2014). *Between Welfare and Rights*. Kyoto: Minerva.

———. (2016). *Choice, Preferences, and Procedures: A Rational Choice Theoretic Approach*. Cambridge, Mass.: Harvard University Press.

Suzumura, Kotaro, Amartya K. Sen, and Kenneth J. Arrow, eds. 1997. *Social Choice Re-Examined*. International Economic Association Series. London; New York: Palgrave Macmillan.

Svedberg, Peter. (1999). *Poverty and Undernutrition: Theory, Measurement, and Policy*. Oxford: Oxford University Press.

Svensson, Lars-Gunnar. (1977). *Social Justice and Fair Distributions*. Lund: Lund University.

———. (1980). 'Equity among Generations'. *Econometrica* 48 (5): 1251–6.

Swift, Adam. (1999). 'Public Opinion and Political Philosophy: The Relation between Social-Scientific and Philosophical Analysis of Distributive Justice'. *Ethical Theory and Moral Practice* 2: 337–63.

Szpilrajn, Edward. (1930). 'Sur l'extension de l'ordre partiel'. *Fundamenta Mathematicae* 16 (1): 386–9.

Tarski, Alfred. (1941). *Introduction to Logic: And to the Methodology of Deductive Sciences*. New York: Oxford University Press; revised 1946 and 1965.

Tasioulas, John. (2007). 'The Moral Reality of Human Rights'. In *Freedom From Poverty as a Human Right: Who Owes What to the Very Poor?* Edited by Thomas Pogge. Oxford: Oxford University Press and New York: UNESCO.

———. (2012). 'Towards a Philosophy of Human Rights'. *Current Legal Problems* 65.

———. (2013a). 'Justice, Equality and Rights'. In *The Oxford Handbook of the History of Ethics*, edited by Roger Crisp. Oxford: Oxford University Press.

———. (2013b). 'Rights, Legitimacy, and International Law'. *American Journal of Jurisprudence* 58.

Temkin, Larry S. (1986). 'Inequality'. *Philosophy & Public Affairs* 15 (2): 99–121.

———. (1993). *Inequality*. Oxford: Oxford University Press.

———. (2012). *Rethinking the Good: Moral Ideals and the Nature of Practical Reasoning*. Oxford: Oxford University Press.

Theil, H. (1963). 'On the Symmetry Approach to the Committee Decision Problem'. *Management Science* 9 (3): 380–93.

Thirlwall, Anthony. (2011). *Economics of Development: Theory and Evidence*, 9th edn. New York: Russell Sage Foundation.

Thomson, William. (1995). *The Theory of Fair Allocation*. Princeton, N. J.: Princeton University Press.

———. (2011). 'Fair Allocation Rules'. In Arrow, Sen and Suzumura (2011a): 393–506.

Thrall, R. M., Clyde H. Coombs and R. L. Davis, eds. (1954). *Decision Processes*. New York: Wiley.

Thrustone, L. L. (1927). 'A Law of Comparative Judgment'. *Psychological Review* 34: 273–86.

Tideman, Nicolaus. (1995). 'The Single Transferable Vote'. *Journal of Economic Perspectives* 9 (1): 27–38.

Tintner, Gerhard. (1946). 'A Note on Welfare Economics'. *Econometrica* 14 (1): 69–78.

Tocqueville, Alexis de. (1840). *De la démocratie en Amérique*. London: Saunders and Otley.

———. (1945). *Democracy in America*. New York: A. A. Knopf.

———. (1990). *Democracy in America*. Edited by George Lawrence. Chicago: Encyclopaedia Britannica.

Trannoy, Alain and John A. Weymark. (2009). 'Dominance Criteria for Critical-Level Generalized Utilitarianism'. In Basu and Kanbur (2009), vol. I: 262–79.

Traub, S., C. Seidl and U. Schmidt. (2009). 'An Empirical Study of Individual Choice, Social Welfare, and Social Preference'. *European Economic Review* 53: 385–400.

Tuck, Richard. (2008). *Free Riding*. Cambridge, Mass.: Harvard University Press.

Tullock, Gordon. (1959). 'Problems of Majority Voting'. *Journal of Political Economy* 67 (6): 571–9.

———. (1961). 'Problems of Majority Voting: Reply to a Traditionalist'. *Journal of Political Economy* 69 (2): 200–203.

———. (1964). 'The Irrationality of Intransitivity'. *Oxford Economic Papers* 16 (3): 401–6.

———. (1967). 'The General Irrelevance of the General Impossibility Theorem'. *The Quarterly Journal of Economics* 81 (2): 256–70.

———. (1968). *Toward a Mathematics of Politics*. Ann Arbor: The University of Michigan Press.

Tungodden, Bertil. (2003). 'The Value of Equality'. *Economics and Philosophy* 19 (1): 1–44.

———. (2009). 'Equality and Priority'. In *The Handbook of Rational and Social Choice*, edited by Paul Anand, Prasanta Pattanaik and Clemens Puppe. Oxford: Oxford University Press.

Tymieniecka, Anna-Teresa, ed. (1965). *Contributions to Logic and Methodology in Honor of J. M. Bocheński*. Amsterdam: North-Holland Publishing Company.

Ulmer, S., ed. (1965). *Mathematical Applications in Political Science*. Carbondale: Southern Illinois University Press.

Ulph, Alistair M. (1978). 'A Model of Resource Depletion with Multiple Grades'. *Economic Record* 54 (3): 334–45.

United Nations Development Programme (UNDP). (1990). *The Human Development Report 1990*. New York: Oxford University Press.

Uzawa, H. (1960). 'Preference and Rational Choice in the Theory of Consumption'. In *Mathematical Methods in the Social Sciences, 1959: Proceedings*, edited by Kenneth J. Arrow, Samuel Karlin and Patrick Suppes. Stanford: Stanford University Press.

Van Parijs, Philippe. (1995). *Real Freedom for All: What (if Anything) Can Justify Capitalism?* Oxford: Oxford University Press.

———. (2000). 'A Basic Income for All'. *Boston Review*, October–November.

Varian, Hal R. (1974). 'Equity, Envy, and Efficiency'. *Journal of Economic Theory* 9 (1): 63–91.

———. (1975). 'Distributive Justice, Welfare Economics, and the Theory of Fairness'. *Philosophy & Public Affairs* 4 (3): 223–47.

———. (1976a). 'On the History of Concepts of Fairness'. *Journal of Economic Theory* 13 (3): 486–7.

———. (1976b). 'Two Problems in the Theory of Fairness'. *Journal of Public Economics* 5 (3–4): 249–60.

Varshney, Ashutosh. (2009). 'Poverty and Famines: An Extension'. In Basu and Kanbur (2009), vol. II: 139–54.

Vaughan, Megan. (1987). *The Story of an African Famine: Gender and Famine in Twentieth-Century Malawi*. Cambridge: Cambridge University Press.

Veblen, Thorstein. (1899). *The Theory of the Leisure Class: An Economic Study of Institutions*. London: Macmillan.

Venkatapuram, Sridhar. (2011). *Health Justice: An Argument from the Capabilities Approach*. Cambridge: Polity Press.

Vickrey, William. (1945). 'Measuring Marginal Utility by Reactions to Risk'. *Econometrica* 13 (4): 319–33.

———. (1960). 'Utility, Strategy, and Social Decision Rules'. *The Quarterly Journal of Economics* 74 (4): 507–35.

Waldner, Ilmar. (1972). 'The Empirical Meaningfulness of Interpersonal Utility Comparisons'. *The Journal of Philosophy* 69 (4): 87–103.

Waldron, Jeremy, ed. (1984). *Theories of Rights*. Oxford and New York: Oxford University Press.

———. (1999). *Law and Disagreement*. Oxford: Oxford University Press.

Walsh, Vivian. (1996). *Rationality, Allocation, and Reproduction*. Oxford: Oxford University Press.

———. (2003). 'Sen after Putnam'. *Review of Political Economy* 15 (3): 315–94.

Ward, Benjamin. (1965). 'Majority Voting and Alternative Forms of Public Enterprise'. In *The Public Economy of Urban Communities*, edited by Julius Margolis. Baltimore: Johns Hopkins Press.

Weber, Robert J. (1995). 'Approval Voting'. *Journal of Economic Perspectives* 9 (1): 39–49.

Weibull, Jörgen W. (1995). *Evolutionary Game Theory*. Cambridge, Mass.: MIT Press.

Weldon, J. C. (1962). 'On the Problem of Social Welfare Functions'. *Canadian Journal of Economics and Political Science* 18 (4): 452–63.

Werhane, Patricia Hogue. (1991). *Adam Smith and His Legacy for Modern Capitalism*. Oxford: Oxford University Press.

Weymark, John A. (2014). 'An Introduction to Allan Gibbard's Harvard Seminar Paper'. *Economics and Philosophy* 30 (3): 263–8.

Whitehead, Alfred North, and Bertrand Russell. (1913). *Principia Mathematica*. Cambridge: Cambridge University Press.

Wicksell, Knut. (1935). *Lectures on Political Economy: Money*. London: Routledge.

Williams, Bernard. (1981). *Moral Luck*. Cambridge: Cambridge University Press.

———. (1985). *Ethics and the Limits of Philosophy*. Cambridge, Mass.: Harvard University Press.

Williamson, Oliver E. and Thomas J. Sargent. (1967). 'Social Choice: A Probabilistic Approach'. *The Economic Journal* 77 (308): 797–813.

Wilson, James Q. and Edward C. Banfield. (1958). 'Public-Regardingness as a Value Premise in Voting Behavior'. *The American Political Science Review* 58 (4): 876–87.

Wilson, Robert B. (1968a). 'A Class of Solutions for Voting Games'. Working Paper No. 3. Graduate School of Business, Stanford University.

———. (1968b). 'A Game Theoretic Analysis of Social Choice'. Discussion Paper No. 2. Institute of Public Policy Analysis, Stanford University.

———. (1968c). 'An Axiomatic Model of Logrolling'. Working Paper No. 3, Graduate School of Business, Stanford University.

———. (1971). 'A Game-Theoretic Analysis of Social Choice'. In *Social Choice*, edited by B. Leiberman. New York: Gordon and Breach.

———. (1972). 'The Game-Theoretic Structure of Arrow's General Possibility Theorem'. *Journal of Economic Theory* 5 (1): 14–20.

———. (1975). 'On the Theory of Aggregation'. *Journal of Economic Theory* 10 (1): 89–99.

Wolff, Jonathan and Avner de-Shalit. (2007). *Disadvantage*. Oxford Political Theory. Oxford: Oxford University Press.

Wollstonecraft, Mary. (1790). *A Vindication of the Rights of Men, in a Letter to the Right Honourable Edmund Burke; Occasioned by His Reflections on the Revolution in France*.

———. (1792). *A Vindication of the Rights of Woman: With Strictures on Political and Moral Subjects*.

———. (1929). *The Rights of Woman*. London: Dent and New York: Dutton.

———. (1996). *A Vindication of the Rights of Men*. Amherst: Prometheus Books.

———. (2010). *A Vindication of the Rights of Woman: With Strictures on Political and Moral Subjects*. Cambridge: Cambridge University Press.

Wood, John Cunningham and Robert D. Wood, eds. (2007). *Amartya Sen: Critical Assessments of Contemporary Economists*. London: Routledge.

Wright, G. H. von. (1963). *Logic of Preference*. Edinburgh: Edinburgh University Press.

Wriglesworth, John L. (1985). *Libertarian Conflicts in Social Choice*. Cambridge: Cambridge University Press.

Yaari, Menahem E. (1978). 'Separably Concave Utilities or the Principle of Diminishing Eagerness to Trade'. *Journal of Economic Theory* 18 (1): 102–18.

Yaari, Menahem E. and M. Bar-Hillel. (1984). 'On Dividing Justly'. *Social Choice and Welfare* 2.

Young, H. P. (1974a). 'An Axiomatization of Borda's Rule'. *Journal of Economic Theory* 9 (1): 43–52.

———. (1974b). 'A Note on Preference Aggregation'. *Econometrica* 42: 1129–31.

———. (1975). 'Social Choice Scoring Functions'. *SIAM Journal on Applied Mathematics* 28 (4): 824–38.

———. (1977). 'Extending Condorcet's Rule'. *Journal of Economic Theory* 16 (2): 335–53.

———. ed. (1986). *Fair Allocation*. Providence, R. I.: American Mathematical Society.

———. (1988). 'Condorcet's Theory of Voting'. *The American Political Science Review* 82 (4): 1231–44.

Zeckhauser, Richard. (1968). 'Group Decision and Allocation'. Discussion Paper No. 51. Cambridge, Mass.: Harvard Institute of Economic Research.

———. (1969). 'Majority Rule with Lotteries on Alternatives'. *The Quarterly Journal of Economics* 83 (4): 696–703.

Zeuthen, Frederik. (1930). *Problems of Monopoly and Economic Warfare*. Abingdon: Routledge & Kegan Paul.

Subject Index

Name Index